Textiles for Residential and Commercial Interiors

2nd Edition

Jan I. Yeager
Associate Professor
Textiles, Apparel and Merchandising
West Virginia University

Lura K. Teter-Justice
Allied member ASID

Fairchild Publications
New York

Executive Editor: **Olga Kontzias**
Production Editor: **Joann Muscolo**
Editorial Assistant: **Beth Applebome**
Art Director: **Nataliya Gurshman**
Cover Photography: Supplied by **Artville LLC**
Photographer: **Lynne Reynolds**
Production Manager: **Priscilla Tauger**
Production Services: **UG / GGS Information Services, Inc.**
Sixth Printing, © 2005
Fifth Printing, © 2004
Fourth Printing ©2003
Third Printing ©2002
Second Printing ©2001
Second Edition ©2000
Fairchild Publications, Inc

First Edition ©1988
Harper & Row, Publishers, Inc.

Library of Congress Catalog Card Number: 99-85789

ISBN: 1-56367-178-6

GST R 133004424

Printed in the United States of America

Contents

Extended Contents		v
Preface		xi
Acknowledgments		xii

Unit One:	**The Fundamentals of Textiles for Interiors**	**1**
1.	The Interior Textile Industry	2
2.	Selecting and Evaluating Textiles for Interiors	13
3.	Textile Fibers	23
4.	Fundamental Fiber Properties	44
5.	Textile Yarns and Yarn-like Structures	65
6.	Fabricating Textiles for Interiors: Weaving	79
7.	Fabricating Textiles for Interiors: Other Techniques	96
8.	Textile Colorants, Color Perception, and Color Application	107
9.	Converting Interior Textile Greige Goods	132
10.	Interior Textile Product Labeling	149
11.	Interior Textile Products and Fire	163

Unit Two:	**Upholstered Furniture Coverings and Fillings**	**190**
12.	Construction Features of Upholstered Furniture	192
13.	Upholstery Coverings	204
14.	Evaluation and Maintenance of Finished Upholstery Fabric	227

Unit Three: Window and Wall Coverings   246

15.   Selection Criteria for Window Treatments   248

16.   Window Treatment Styles   260

17.   Window Coverings and Linings   277

18.   Evaluation and Maintenance of Finished Window
        Covering Fabrics   299

19.   Textile and Nontextile Coverings for Walls and Panels   312

Unit Four: Soft Floor Coverings and Cushions   322

20.   Selection Criteria for Soft Floor Coverings   324

21.   Fibers, Yarns and Constructions Used in Textile Floor
        Coverings   340

22.   Construction of Floor Coverings: Tufting   346

23.   Construction of Floor Coverings: Weaving and Other
        Machine Techniques   358

24.   Construction of Floor Coverings: Hand Techniques   370

25.   Carpet and Rug Cushions   378

26.   Evaluations and Specifications for Soft Floor Coverings 386

27.   Installation and Maintenance of Floor Covering
        Assemblies   397

Unit Five: Household and Institutional Textiles   418

28.   Textile Products for the Bath   420

29.   Textile Bedding Products   431

30.   Textile Accessories for Tabletops   449

        Glossary   457
        Bibliography   500
        Appendix A   505
        Appendix B   506
        Index   509

Extended Table of Contents

Preface   xi

Acknowledgments   xii

Unit One: The Fundamentals of Textiles for Interiors   1

1.   The Interior Textile Industry   2
          Major Segments of the Industry   3
          Associate Members of the Industry   7
          Economic Factors Affecting the Industry   8
          Environmental Factors Affecting the Industry   9

2.   Selecting and Evaluating Textiles for Interiors   13
          Selecting Interior Textiles   14
          Evaluating Interior Textiles   17
          Agencies Regulating Product Selections   19
          Organizations Establishing Model Building Codes   20

3.   Textile Fibers   23
          Fiber Classification and Identification   24
          Fiber Composition and Structure   27
          Natural Fibers   29
          Manufactured Fibers   33

4.   Fundamental Fiber Properties   44
          Aesthetic Features   45
          Mechanical Properties   47
          Chemical Properties   54

5.   Textile Yarns and Yarn-like Structures   65
          Yarn Production   66
          Yarn Classification and Nomenclature   70
          Designation of Yarn Construction   73
          Formation of Yarn-like Structures   75

6.   **Fabricating Textiles for Interiors: Weaving**   **79**

Weaving   80

Basic Interlacing Patterns   85

Decorative Interlacing Patterns   87

Pile Weaving   89

Triaxial Weaving   93

7.   **Fabricating Textiles for Interiors: Other Techniques**   **96**

Knitting   97

Tufting and Fusion Bonding   101

Knotting and Twisting Yarns   102

Braiding Yarns   103

Combining Fibers   103

Extruding Polymer Solutions   105

8.   **Textile Colorants, Color Perception, and Color Application**   **107**

Colorants and Color Perception   108

Dyeing Fabrics and Fabric Components   110

Printing Greige Goods   116

Combining Dyeing and Printing   127

Factors Affecting Apparent Color   127

9.   **Converting Interior Textile Greige Goods**   **132**

Transforming Surface appearance   133

Improving the Quality and Serviceability of Structural Features   139

Engineering Functional Performance   142

10.   **Interior Textile Product Labeling**   **149**

The Federal Trade Commission   150

Regulatory and Advisory Labeling   151

Voluntary Labeling Programs   156

11.   **Interior Textile Products and Fire**   **163**

The Consumer Product Safety Commission   164

The Flammable Fabrics Act   164

Combustion Processes and By-products   166

Stages of an Interior Fire   167

Flammability Testing   168

Unit Two:	**Upholstered Furniture Coverings and Fillings**	**190**
12.	**Construction Features of Upholstered Furniture**	**192**
	Exterior Construction Features	193
	Interior Textile Components	197
	Fillings Used in Upholstered Furniture	198
13.	**Upholstery Coverings**	**204**
	Fiber and Yarn Usage	205
	Flat Upholstery Fabrics	207
	Pile Upholstery Fabrics	218
	Leather Upholstery	221
	Vinyl and Simulated Leather and Suede Fabrics	222
14.	**Evaluation and Maintenance of Finished Upholstery Fabric**	**227**
	Standards for Structural Qualities	228
	Evaluations of Physical Performance Properties	229
	Examination of Color Consistency and Retention	235
	Maintenance of Upholstery Fabrics	240
Unit Three:	**Window and Wall Coverings**	**246**
15.	**Selection Criteria for Window Treatments**	**248**
	Appearance Factors	249
	Functional Values	251
	Cost Factors	256
	Performance Standards	257
16.	**Window Treatment Styles**	**260**
	Curtain and Drapery Treatments	261
	Blinds and Shades	272
	Awnings and Shutters	275
17.	**Window Coverings and Linings**	**277**
	Components Used in Curtains and Draperies	278
	Woven Curtain and Drapery Fabrics	280
	Knitted Window Covering Fabrics	292
	Knotted and Twisted Window Coverings	293
	Coverings Formed from Fibrous Webs	293
	Drapery Lining Materials	294

18.   Evaluation and Maintenance of Finished Window Covering Fabrics   **299**

Standards for Physical Performance Properties   300

Evaluations of Colorfastness   304

Evaluations of Flame Resistance   308

Maintenance of Window Covering Structures   309

19.   Textile and Nontextile Coverings for Walls and Panels   **312**

Selection and Serviceability   313

Components and Constructions   314

Installation Techniques   317

Unit Four: Soft Floor Coverings and Cushions   **322**

20.   Selection Criteria for Soft Floor Coverings   **324**

Appearance Features   325

Serviceability Expectations   333

Design and Performance Regulations   337

Cost Factors   337

21.   Fibers, Yarns and Constructions Used in Textile Floor Coverings   **340**

Fibers used in Carpet and Rugs   341

Yarn Features Affecting Serviceability   342

Constructions Used in Soft Floor Coverings   343

22.   Construction of Floor Coverings: Tufting   **346**

Basic Components of Tufted Floor Coverings   347

Tufting Operations   349

Structural Qualities of Tufted Constructions   352

23.   Construction of Floor Coverings: Weaving and Other Machine Techniques   **358**

Weaving Pile Floor Coverings   359

Other Machine Operations   366

24.   Construction of Floor Coverings: Hand Techniques   **370**

Hand-woven Pile Rugs   371

Hand-constructed Flat Rugs   373

25.   **Carpet and Rug Cushions**   **378**
Fibrous Cushion Structures   379
Cellular Rubber Cushions   380
Urethane Foam Cushions   382
Listing Specification Data for Carpet Cushions   382
Evaluating the Performance of Cushions   383

26.   **Evaluations and Specifications for Soft Floor Coverings**   **386**
Listing Specification Data for Carpet   387
Evaluating Functional Features   387
Evaluating Performance Properties   391

27.   **Installation and Maintenance of Floor Covering Assemblies**   **397**
Installing Soft Floor Coverings and Cushions   398
Maintaining Textile Floor Coverings   407

Unit Five: **Household and Institutional Textiles**   **418**

28.   **Textile Products for the Bath**   **420**
Towels and Toweling   421
Bath Rugs and Mats   427
Shower Curtains   428

29.   **Textile Bedding Products**   **431**
Fiber and Yarn Usage in Beddings   432
Mattresses, Mattress Foundations, and Mattress Protectors   433
Fillings Used in Bedding Products   436
Pillows   438
Sheets and Pillowcases   439
Blankets   441
Bedspreads, Quilts, and Comforters   443

30.   **Textile Accessories for Tabletops**   **449**
Producing Tabletop Coverings   450
Labeling Textile table Accessories   454

Glossary   **457**
Bibliography   **500**
Appendix A   **505**
Appendix B   **506**
Index   **509**

Preface

The second edition of Textiles for Residential and Commercial Interiors reflects the suggestions of several professors who used the first edition. Many of these professors also willingly shared comments offered by their students. Together, their input led to changes in the organization, pedagogy, and scope of the work. The book continues to be, however, written for use by students, educators, extension personnel, practicing interior designers and architects, retailers, and consumers with a professional or personal interest in textile furnishings.

The major objectives for the second edition are the same as for the first edition:

- To present a consolidated and comprehensive coverage of the textile products available for use in residential and commercial interiors.

- To explain product components, manufacturing processes, installation procedures, and maintenance practices affecting textile furnishing serviceability.

- To review consumer product selection criteria influencing the design of interior textile end products.

- To identify labeling practices used to inform and protect professionals and consumers.

- To review government regulations applying to interior textile product marketing and selection.

- To examine end-use variables that affect product selection.

- To cover test methods, performance standards, and quality control work used in the industry.

- To present codes that are important to professionals and members of the industry.

- To review the fire-related behavior of interior textiles and the work already undertaken to widen the margin of safety in the event of fire.

- To increase awareness of product features and installation practices that can help rather than hinder the mobility of those with physical limitations.

- To enhance understanding by including extensive sketches and photographs.

Because readers will have different levels of knowledge about textiles, the text begins with a focus on textile fundamentals. As requested by users of the earlier edition, all structural, aesthetic, mechanical, and chemical fiber properties are examined in greater depth, and all information concerning fibers has been consolidated. Similarly, all information of fire safety and interior textiles is combined into one chapter.

The scope of the book has been expanded to include in-depth coverage of institutional textiles, as well as household textile goods. Critically important material has been added on codes, standards, environmental concerns, and green products.

For the benefit of the instructor and the student, there are key terms and review questions for each chapter. Case studies provide a means for student to analyze a problem. The appendices include a listing of generic class definitions and selected manufactured fiber trade names, formulas for metric conversions, a bibliography, and an extensive glossary. The text is richly illustrated, with line drawings and photographs of fibers, yarns, fabrics, equipment used in manufacturing, coloring, and finishing, as well as end products and end-use settings.

The text is presented in five units, with Unit One having a focus on textile fundamentals. Readers having previous formal study of textiles and professionals with knowledge from experience may use this unit for review; others may study the material more thoroughly, to master information built on in later units. Units Two through Five are divided by end product category. Unit Two includes discussion of upholstered furniture coverings and fillings; Unit Three has a focus on window coverings, drapery linings, and textile wall coverings; Unit Four covers soft floor coverings and cushions; and Unit Five presents material on both functional and decorative textile bath, bedding, and tabletop products used in household and institutional settings.

In larger institutions with extensive offerings, Textiles for Residential and Commercial Interiors is appropriate for a course to follow completion of introductory textiles and interior design courses. It can be used in either textiles or interior design departments. In smaller institutions where course offerings may be more limited, the text would be useful in an introductory course with an expansive scope (e.g., apparel textiles and interior textiles, or housing and interior textiles). The book's organization permits the selection of units or chapters dealing with topics in the order preferred by the instructor.

Acknowledgments

We are grateful to the many colleagues who provided ideas and helpful comments as we developed this edition. We are equally appreciative of our support staff who were always ready to photocopy, package, and ship yet one more chapter or fax yet one more revision. Special thanks goes again to a friend, Peter Lessing, who took most of the photographs in the work. As with the first edition, he was always patient and willing to use his time and expertise to provide the many prints.

Other readers selected by the publisher were also very helpful. They included: Wendy Beckwith, La Roche College; Jan Cummings, Johnson County Community College; Rita Christoffersen, University of Wisconsin-Stout; Elizabeth P. Easter, University of Kentucky; Karen LaBat, University of Minnesota; Ann Beth Presley, Auburn University; Leanne C. Stone, University of Nevada-Reno; Katherine Wiggins, Madison Area Technical College; Patricia Williams, University of Wisconsin-Stevens Point; and Robyne Williams, North Dakota State University.

Textiles for Residential and Commercial Interiors

The Fundamentals
of Textile for Interiors

Unit One focuses on the fundamentals of textiles, with an eye to interiors. Chapter 1 reviews the nature of the industry, including the sequential flow of product manufacturing and distributing. Also discussed is the economic health of the industry made by contributions from auxiliary enterprises such as trade associations and contract design firms. Chapter 2 identifies criteria influencing interior textile product selection. Some criteria, such as flammability codes, are set forth by regulatory agencies; other criteria, such as aesthetic considerations and environmental concerns, are the prerogatives of the consumer. Scientific and technical associations serving the industry and organizations establishing model building codes are identified. The chapter emphasizes that industry members need to work cooperatively to ensure that the products they offer are acceptable to the contemporary consumer.

Following the normal sequence of fabric production, Chapters 3 and 4 focus on textile fibers and their properties, Chapter 5 focuses on yarns and yarn substitutes, Chapters 6 and 7 identify methods of fabrication, and Chapter 8 discusses color-related variables and methods of color application. Conver-sion operations, the final processes in fabric manufacturing, are discussed in Chapter 9.

Chapter 10 covers mandatory, advisory, and voluntary labeling practices relating to textile furnishing products. Their value to informed consumers, designers, and architects in selecting or specifying is noted. The chapter stresses the need for members of the industry to avoid engaging in unfair or deceptive labeling practices, that the Federal Trade Commission is empowered to prevent.

Because concern for personal safety and reduced property loss in the event of fire has grown significantly in recent years, the final chapter in the unit examines the involvement of textiles in interior fires. The chapter discusses the responsibilities and powers of the Consumer Product Safety Commission in carrying out the purposes and provisions of the Flammable Fabrics Act, including the establishment of new flammability standards.

1

The Interior Textile Industry

Major Segments of the Industry
    Fiber Suppliers and Producers
    Yarn Producers
    Fabric Manufacturers
    Textile Colorists, Designers, and Stylists
    Converters
    End-Product Producers
    Distributors
    Design Professionals
    Consumers

Associate Members of the Industry
    Trade Associations
    Publishers
    Advertising Firms
    Service Organizations for Maintenance

Economic Factors Affecting the Industry
    Inflation
    Income-related Variables
    Energy Costs and Concerns
    Mortgage Interest Rates and Building
      Costs
    Mergers and Acquisitions
    Other Factors

Environmental Factors Affecting the Industry
    Developments in the Textile Industry
    Design Considerations
    Environmental Agencies

The interior textile industry, like the apparel and industrial textile industries, encompasses several segments, each of which is an important link in the chain of production and distribution. Although these segments are composed of many independent firms, there is mutual dependence among firms in different segments: firms in **downstream segments** need suppliers, and firms in **upstream segments** need purchasers. Furniture producers, for example, must have a supply of fillings, linings, and finished fabrics. In turn, they must also have interior designers and architects who are willing to recommend their upholstered products to clients and retailers who are willing to offer them to their customers.

Sharing a common goal—operating profitably—all members of the industry work cooperatively to ensure that the end products offered are widely accepted by contemporary consumers. To secure this acceptance and realize their goal, suppliers, producers, and distributors often support and seek assistance from such auxiliary enterprises as trade associations and advertising firms. While such groups are not directly involved in the manufacturing sequence, they can have a major influence on quality, awareness, and selection of the industry's goods.

Although consumer acceptance or rejection of the products available primarily determines the economic health of the industry and its members, it is also directly affected by such variables as environmental issues, mergers and acquisitions, and mortgage interest rates. Industry executives must be aware of and respond to these variables if their firms are to be financially viable.

Major Segments of the Industry

The major segments of the interior textile industry and their positions in the flow of production and distribution are shown in Figure 1.1. Natural fiber suppliers and manufactured fiber producers initiate the work of the industry; it culminates with the residential and commercial consumer.

Figure 1.1 The interior textile industry.

Fiber Suppliers and Producers

Natural fiber suppliers recover already-formed or "readymade" fibers, principally from sheep, silk caterpillars, cotton bolls, and flax plants. The responsibility of the supplier is to assist nature and ensure the production of high yields of quality fibers. To be successful, suppliers must cope with the challenges of today's rising costs of labor, feed, pest-control agents, fertilizers, and transportation. They must also contend with growing competition from foreign suppliers and from manufactured fiber producers who are constantly seeking to capture a larger share of the fiber market. Increasingly, natural fiber suppliers must respond to concerns for the environment (e.g., limit runoff of pesticides and fertilizers into water supplies), and they must seek to protect the health and safety of their employees (e.g., reduce pesticide residue on workers' clothing). Also, they must alleviate the apprehension of animal rights activists (e.g., use humane treatment for the fiber-producing animals in their care).

Beginning with such natural materials as wood chips, **manufactured fiber producers** make rayon and acetate, and beginning with such natural substances as petroleum and coal, they manufacture acrylic, nylon, polyester, olefin, and several other types of synthesized fibers. Manufactured fiber producers are challenged by the rising costs of petroleum and labor, changing trade balances, and persistent competition from natural fiber suppliers. Like natural fiber suppliers, manufactured fiber producers must be concerned for any negative effects the byproducts of production have on the environment, as well as ensuring the health and safety of their employees.

Fiber suppliers and producers forward staple fibers, filament fibers, and tow to yarn producers. **Staple fibers**, such as wool, cotton, and linen, are relatively short fibers, measured in inches or centimeters. **Filament fibers**—silk and manufactured fibers—are relatively long fibers measured in yards or meters. **Tow** is a bundle of manufactured filaments that has been given a two- or three-dimensional crimp or coil but no twist.

Yarn Producers

Yarn producers are responsible for combining fibers into usable yarn structures. **Spinners** align, spin, and twist staple-length fibers into spun yarns, and **throwsters** combine filament-length fibers into untwisted or twisted multifilament yarns. Tow may be directly combined into yarns or it may be reduced to staple-length fibers (Figure 5.3), which are then spun. Yarn producers frequently employ multiple twisting or plying operations to expand the assortment of yarns available to fabric manufacturers.

Fabric Manufacturers

Fabric manufacturers use a variety of **fabrication techniques**, including weaving, knitting, knotting and twisting, braiding, and tufting, to combine yarns into fabric structures. They use such techniques as felting, spunbonding, and needlepunching to produce fabrics directly from fibers, bypassing the yarn stage, and they use extruding to produce polymer film sheeting directly from solutions, bypassing both the fiber and yarn stages. With extrusion operations, the manufactured fiber/film producer is functioning as the fabric manufacturer.

Fabric producers and textile machinery engineers work cooperatively to develop new equipment and devise more efficient fabrication techniques, continually striving to fulfill two major goals. First, they seek to reduce production time and energy consumption and thus to reduce their manufacturing costs. Second, they work to engineer textile structures that will be accepted by and perform satisfactorily for the ultimate consumer.

After fabrication is completed, the results are still unfinished and often bear little resemblance to fabrics selected by professionals and consumers. These unfinished fabrics, known as **greige goods**, are forwarded to converters for finishing, or they may first be sent to dyers and printers.

Textile Colorists, Designers, and Stylists

Textile colorists and fabric stylists may be involved at any stage in the production sequence. Manufactured fiber producers may incorporate dye pigments within filaments as they are extruded; dyers may immerse fibers, yarns, or fabrics in a solution of dyestuff. Printers generally apply colorful patterns to greige goods, although they can produce some unique color styles by printing sheets of yarns and tubes of knitted fabric.

Textile chemists and colorists constantly strive to reduce their utilization of water: the copious amounts of water used in dyeing operations must be purified to minimize pollution. And, drying hundreds of pounds of fiber or yarn or thousands of yards of fabric requires sizable amounts of often-costly utilities.

Well in advance of production, **textile designers** and **fabric stylists** must identify the aesthetic features preferred by contemporary consumers. They must be alert for slight shifts in the selection of such fashion-related qualities as fabric weight, textural characteristics, and drapability. They must tally the selections of woven-in patterns and printed patterns, noting preferences for simple and elaborate design motifs, for small-scale and large-scale repeats, and for fiber, yarn, and fabric color styling. Stylists must also accurately interpret and forecast trends and anticipate variations, making certain they are suitable for large-scale production operations. To protect their creative work, textile designers can copyright their work.

Stylists face another challenge: they must ensure that the fabric's service-related properties meet requirements and expectations. This means that stylists must work closely with converters who can change aesthetic and performance qualities during fabric finishing.

Converters

Converters are fabric finishers; they convert greige goods into finished fabrics. Using mechanical treatments and chemical agents, they can alter such appearance features as pile yarn orientation and luster and such performance characteristics as water- and soil-repellency, wrinkle recovery, and shape retention. By applying coatings and fabrics to the backs of carpet rollgoods and textile wall coverings, converters can improve the functional characteristics and stability of these structures and facilitate their efficient installation.

End-Product Producers

Using fibers, yarns, and finished fabrics, as well as some nonfibrous materials, **end-product producers** construct items that are ready for immediate use or for installation in an interior setting. Some are specifically produced for use in private or **residential interiors**—mobile homes, apartments, and other private residences. Other products are specifically designed and constructed to withstand the higher levels of use in public or **commercial interiors**—stores and shopping centers, offices, schools, hospitals, hotels and motels, libraries and public buildings, religious buildings, restaurants and clubs, dormitories, airport terminals, nursing homes, and theaters.

The many interior textile products may be divided into four broad categories, namely upholstered furniture, window and wall coverings, soft floor coverings and cushions, and household and institutional textiles. The upholstered furniture market includes chairs, sofas, ottomans, and the like, each covered by a textile fabric or such non-textile coverings as vinyl or leather; most items, however, have a textile or cellular foam filling or stuffing. Window coverings range from sheer curtains to blinds and shades containing grasses or metal slats. Wall coverings may be an elegant moiré taffeta or a rough burlap cloth made of jute. Soft floor coverings range from scatter rugs to wall-to-wall carpet to exquisite Oriental rugs. Carpet and rug cushions or padding may be cattle hair, jute, or polyurethane. **Household textiles** used in residential interiors include beddings, towelings, and such tabletop accessories as napkins, tablecloths, and runners. When such products are designed and selected for use in hospitality or care-type facilities, they are referred to as **institutional textiles** and the items are required to conform with performance criteria and life safety codes. Among the assortment of products included in each of these categories, there are differences in fiber content, yarn features, fabric structure, color styling, finishes, and product design. In most cases, fabric stylists and **end-product designers** work cooperatively with producers and marketing specialists to plan the combinations needed to meet a variety of consumer needs and desires or to conform with specific requirements set by the design professional or an agency having jurisdiction over an installation.

Domestic producers must compete with one another and with foreign producers; this competition forces them continually to refine their existing products and to develop new and unique items. They must analyze the design, composition, and performance characteristics of their products to confirm that the characteristics offered are those sought by contemporary interior designers, architects, and consumers. At the same time they must contend with the rising costs of materials, labor, and equipment, and seek ways to reduce their consumption, and thus their cost, of energy. Whatever the number and magnitude of the challenges facing them, producers must succeed in meeting them to operate profitably.

It should be noted that some textile firms are organized vertically. These large firms use their own facilities and labor force to complete several sequential production operations. They may, for example, spin yarns, weave fabrics, apply color, convert greige goods, and construct end products. Such corporations normally have the resources needed to support extensive research and development activities and to create and fund effective marketing programs.

Distributors

Several types of retail operations present interior textile products to consumers. Department stores offer home furnishings and household linens, as well as apparel and accessories for all members of the family. Specialty stores offer a limited line of merchandise, such as upholstered furniture or carpet and rugs. Discount stores and factory outlets sell less expensive goods, and mail-order operations offer an ever-expanding assortment of products in a range of prices. Increasingly, consumers have the option of shopping for interior textile products via television or the Internet.

The retailer is sometimes bypassed in the distribution of interior furnishings. An upholstered furniture manufacturer, a wall coverings designer, or a carpet and area rug producer, for example, may elect to maintain a **product showroom** where merchandise is shown to professional interior designers, architects, and other **members of the trade**. These professionals select products that conform to their clients' aesthetic preferences, serviceability requirements, and interior furnishings budgets.

Design Professionals

Design professionals, primarily licensed or certified interior designers and architects, select textiles for such hospitality sites as hotels, motels, and restaurants; for such retail establishments as department stores and boutiques; for offices; and for such residences as apartments and homes. Depending upon state legislation, interior designers may become licensed or certified by passing, for example, the National Council for Interior Design Qualification (NCIDQ) examination. Architects are licensed by individual states. Design professionals may operate their own firms, partnerships, or corporations, or be employed by independent firms of any size. In any case, they normally provide services in accordance with the terms of a contractual agreement made with their residential and commercial clients. The frequent use of such a legal document has given rise to the term **contract design** to describe the work of these professionally trained persons. These legal documents can be an oral agreement between the client and professional or a lengthy written document. Most importantly, contracts establish legal responsibility between a client and design professional.

Interior designers and architects serve as critical links between the industry and the consumer. They have a positive economic effect on the industry when they select new products and when they recommend or specify products that are consistent with their clients' selection criteria. To do their jobs well, they must be familiar with the industry's array of products and be prepared to assess the ability of different products to perform satisfactorily under a particular set of end-use conditions. Designers and architects must be aware of codes governing the selection and installation of products in a facility or in a particular location within a facility. In this work, manufacturers' representatives play an important role in providing information to the designer and architect who are specifying products, especially in commercial projects. Ultimately, the accuracy with which interior designers and architects recommend or specify products helps to determine their professional reputations. It can also have a major influence on the willingness of their clients to be repeat customers of particular interior textile products.

Consumers

The **consumer** is whoever pays for the end product: thus, the consumer may be a person, a group, a corporation, an agency, or an institution. Residential and commercial consumers may prefer to use their own talents and judgment when selecting products, or they may elect to contract for the services of an interior designer or architect. In the latter case, the professionals select, recommend, or specify products, functioning as consultants; their clients, who pay for the merchandise, are consumers.

At this point the work of the industry and the wants and needs of the consumer must coincide. Unless the assortment of products offered by the industry is acceptable to the consumer, the volume of sales will not be high enough for end-product producers to pay their suppliers, cover their operating expenses, and realize an adequate profit. Because a reduction in end-product sales results in a reduction in the amount of fibers, yarns, and finished fabrics needed, it threatens the financial stability of upstream firms as well. Moreover, low profit margins limit the ability of firms to expand. Therefore, all members of the industry strive to ensure that the assortment of products offered conforms to the selection criteria of the contemporary consumer; these criteria are examined in Chapter 2.

Associate Members of the Industry

Various enterprises provide valuable assistance to the textile furnishings industry. While their work is primarily intended to generate profit for themselves and for members of the industry, many of their activities are also useful to students, educators, retailers, and consumers. Among the groups serving the industry are trade associations, publishers, advertising firms, and service organizations. Several of these groups are listed in Appendix C.

Trade Associations

Trade associations are organized to represent, protect, and promote the interests of their members, who provide financial support for the operation and activities of the association. Trade association personnel establish liaisons between their members and various federal and state agencies and legislative bodies. They prepare and distribute educational material and technical literature. They devise marketing programs to increase the recognition and acceptance of their members' products. Some associations also maintain testing laboratories to evaluate and certify the quality of these products.

Some trade associations are composed of firms that compete with one another in the marketplace but also share a common goal. The American Fiber Manufacturers Association, for example, is supported by several independent firms, each of which is competing for sales orders from downstream firms. At the same time, however, these producers recognize the value of cooperating to provide information about manufactured fibers and to extend their use. Other trade associations are made up of firms belonging to different segments of the industry but having a vested interest in the marketing and widespread use of a particular category of products. The Carpet and Rug Institute, for example, works to increase the use of soft floor coverings; Cotton Incorporated works to increase the use of products containing cotton; and The Wool Bureau, Inc. works to increase the use of products

containing wool. The Association for Contract Textiles was established to effectively market contract upholstery fabric manufactured by its members. The organization developed performance standards and promotes the use of symbols to identify fabrics conforming to the standards. (These symbols are shown in Figure 10.4.) The Upholstered Furniture Action Council has member firms from throughout the upholstered furniture industry who have a vested interest in fire safety. They joined together to demonstrate that the majority of their member firms would voluntarily participate in improving the ability of upholstered furniture to resist catching fire from a burning cigarette.

Publishers

Writers and publishers provide members of the industry, students, educators, practicing professionals, retailers, and consumers with a wide assortment of articles, books, marketing magazines, technical journals, and trade newspapers focusing on products available for use in interiors. Some of these publications are for the professional preparation of students; some apprise personnel in the industry of new techniques, new products, research findings, marketing plans, and consumer preferences; and some exist to inform the consumer.

Advertising Firms

Industry members use advertising firms and advertisements to introduce and promote new equipment, new components, and new products. Upstream firms direct their advertisements to downstream firms; end-product producers direct their advertisements to members of the trade, to retailers, and to consumers; retailers direct their advertisements to retail consumers. In some cases, the cost of an advertising campaign is shared: for instance, a fiber producer shoulders a portion of the charges assessed for promotions run by an end-product manufacturer.

Service Organizations for Maintenance

In contrast to promoting the sales or improving the safety of a textile product, some organizations have a focus on the efficient, proper, and economical maintenance of the goods. The **National Association of Institutional**

Linen Management (NAILM), for example, has members in textile care and environmental services (e.g., hospitals, nursing homes, educational institutions, hotels, motels, etc.). It also has member businesses such as chemical manufacturers and textile manufacturers. The **International Fabricare Institute (IFI)** provides education, research, legislative representation, and industry-specific information to its members.

Economic Factors Affecting the Industry

Several of the factors affecting the work and economic health of the textile industry originate elsewhere, in other industries and in government. They nevertheless have a direct impact by favoring or restricting production and expansion in the industry.

Inflation

Inflation (when demand exceeds supply and prices rise) makes it necessary for many consumers to alter their spending and savings patterns. Together with high interest rates on personal loans, inflation forces many consumers to postpone purchases of more expensive durable and semidurable goods, including carpet, upholstered furniture, and automobiles.

Income-related Variables

The demand for textile furnishings is directly affected by the level of income realized by consumers. Their **disposable or real income** is affected by federal and state income taxes and Social Security taxes. A reduction in personal income taxes may result in increased savings, reduced interest rates, and an increased demand for durable goods. On the other hand, a reduction in taxes when interest rates are high may result in increased spending for nondurable goods; consequently, spending for durable and semidurable goods may continue to be delayed.

Fluctuations in the costs of such basic necessities as food, clothing, and shelter, together with the costs of such other things as education and transportation, also influence the demand for interior textile products. These costs alter the **discretionary income** of consumers, increasing or decreasing the amount of income left to spend on the basis of want rather than need.

Energy Costs and Concerns

Concern for energy conservation and the pressure of rising energy costs encourage many residential and commercial consumers to increase their use of soft floor coverings and textile window coverings as insulation materials. In the industry, such energy-related factors have fostered the development of more efficient and economical production techniques and equipment.

Mortgage Interest Rates and Building Costs

Mortgage interest rates and the costs of building materials directly affect the number and size of new constructions. Of course, high rates and costs have a negative effect, slowing construction and reducing the need for such products as carpet, rugs, upholstered furniture, textile wall coverings, and curtains and draperies. At the same time, the negative impact of such slowdowns may be somewhat tempered by increases in the replacement or refurbishment of these items in existing residential and commercial structures.

Mergers and Acquisitions

Within the industry, mergers and acquisitions can result in companies with greater financial resources, more efficient operations, and a greater number of proficient and skilled personnel. Such large firms are better able to support valuable and necessary research activities, mount effective marketing campaigns, and respond quickly and accurately to changes in consumer needs and wants. They are also more likely to undertake lobbying efforts, the results of which may benefit all members of the industry.

Other Factors

Other factors influencing the economic stability and expansion of the industry include fluctuations in the cost of raw materials, labor, and equipment, and international trade agreements that foster or restrict the import or export of components and end products. In addition, the cost of compliance with mandatory performance and safety specifications generally necessitates an increase in the price of certain products, which can slow their sales, at least temporarily.

An increase in the prices of new automobiles or the cost of gasoline encourages many consumers to select smaller passenger cars. At times, a reduction in car size may have a negative effect on firms producing automotive carpet, as well as on those firms supplying upholstery, tire cord, and interior roof and trunk linings.

Environmental Factors Affecting the Industry

Consumers and professionals in many industries are becoming more conscious of environmental concerns, particularly as they relate to textiles. In developing an environmental awareness, consumers and manufacturers are voluntarily reducing the consumption of components and finished goods, reusing materials, and recycling resources. Consumers are separating their garbage and recycling such common materials as glass, plastic, and paper. Members of the industry are seeking to reduce the use of chemicals in processing in order to minimize the subsequent negative effects on **indoor air quality (IAQ)**. Products may carry a reference to a **green standard** to attract environmentally conscious consumers. Since there are no regulations concerning labeling for environmentally friendly products or what constitutes "green," consumers must evaluate two competing products to decide the validity of manufacturers' claims. Concurrently, organizations such as the Environmental Protection Agency and the Occupational Safety and Health Administration are working to identify or regulate what qualifies as environmentally responsible.

Developments in the Textile Industry

The protection of our environment has become increasingly important. In order to assist in this monumental task, consumers and professional members of the textile industry are seeking new ways to reduce the consumption of raw materials and processing agents, to recycle existing products in a second product, and to reuse existing products in alternative ways. More manufacturers have, for example, increased their use of recycled materials for product packaging. In the industry, every aspect of production and processing is being redefined, from the growing of natural fibers to the recycling of plastic "pop" bottles for fiber conversion. Some practices are industry-wide and some are "quality" practices developed by individual companies.

Reduction of Raw Material Consumption and Processing Agent Usage

In an attempt to reduce chemicals used to grow natural fibers, researchers are experimenting with **organically grown** cotton. In this work, the cotton is cultivated on land that has been chemical-free for a minimum of three years and is nurtured without the use of chemical fertilizers or pest-control agents. Other advances include the development of genetically colored cotton that allows subsequent dyeing processes to be eliminated and reduces the chemicals that exist on the fibers. Design Tex has developed fabrics that are reported to be virtually nontoxic, yet durable, attractive, and in compliance with the Association for Contract Textiles (ACT) standards (see Chapter 14). Developments like these have led to a significant reduction in chemical usage in the industry, making it more environmentally safe.

Reuse of Existing Textile Products

Reusing a product is a second way to eliminate materials that must be sent to a landfill. Many carpet producers, for example, are seeking new ways to use byproducts from carpet manufacturing. They cut surplus carpet into mats for sales to consumers for use as track-off mats to protect floor surfaces or to repair damaged areas. For safety, it is important to use an adhesive tape to properly secure loose mats. Shredded carpet fibers can be used in a concrete mixture for reinforcement. The Georgia Institute of Technology reports that the fibers increase durability.[1] Any reused material preserves available raw materials and eliminates the waste going to a landfill.

Recycling of Existing Textile Products

Recycling is the reconditioning of one product to produce another. Recycling reduces trash that would otherwise go to a landfill and results in a new, environmentally friendly product. A few specific examples of recycling in the textile industry are discussed here.

One of the most successful recycling efforts involves recycling plastics into "green" products. In 1996,

Fortrel® Ecospun® fibers were first introduced in the residential furniture industry by Malden Mills at their Glenn Street Studio.[2] These fibers are produced from recycled plastic bottles that are converted into fibers. In order for the process to be successful, the plastic containers must first be sorted by color and type. In preparation for the conversion process, the bottles are cleaned, crushed, and chopped into fine flakes. The flakes are changed to liquid, then used to produce fibers that are combined into yarns ready for weaving. Standard methods of weaving are used to produce EcoSpun® velvet. It takes some 200 two-liter bottles to produce the 15 to 20 yards of fabric required for upholstering an average sofa.[3] While the fibers are cost prohibitive for the residential market, Malden Mills is successfully producing the fiber for the contract market. Recycled PET (polyethylene terephthalate, better known as polyester) is particularly appealing to the hospitality market because it is extremely durable. Quality fabrics containing the recycled fiber can meet all ACT standards.

Recycling carpet is significant to the industry because "over 6 billion pounds of carpet are produced each year and an estimated 3.4 billion pounds of old carpet are removed."[4] Successful recycling programs include the BASF 6ix Again program, DuPont's "Partnership in Carpet Reclamation," and United Recycling. The challenge of recycling carpet begins with collecting the bulky, heavy floor covering and delivering it to a central collection site. In order to be successful, carpet must be sorted by fiber content. Because fibers are nearly impossible to visually identify, the content is determined by melting point, or, more recently, by near-infrared technology.[5] Once the fibers are identified, the carpet is sorted, shredded, crushed, and converted to pellets. The pellets are most often used in industrial, automotive, or building materials. The process is successful in keeping carpet out of landfills, but more research is necessary to develop a cost-effective process for generating new carpet from recycled components.

Design Considerations

In order to be more environmentally aware, consumers and interior designers need to know that textiles are often treated with flame retardant agents, stain resistant agents, and other compounds for a wide variety of aesthetic and functional purposes. Even natural products have chemicals applied during cleaning and for such things as mothproofing and stain resistance. Any residue remaining on the textile may emit toxic fumes, reducing indoor air quality. In regard to cleaning agents, there are water-based products that offer less toxicity than petroleum-based products.

The reduction of chemicals used in the growth of fibers or in textile production also assists the interior designer with reducing the problem of indoor air quality. IAQ is a serious issue and is consistently ranked in the top five concerns by the Environmental Protection Agency.[6] IAQ is significant because the average American spends 90 percent of his or her time indoors, thus requiring that sufficient fresh air is circulated throughout the space and potential pollutants are controlled. Pollution may be generated from new furnishings and finishes and the chemicals with which they are treated. For this reason, most manufacturers recommend a **gassing-off** period, which allows the gases to permeate the air and be dissipated while the space is still vacant.

Environmental Agencies

In addition to voluntary acts of consumers and manufacturers, several agencies exist in the United States to promote or to regulate issues concerning human well-being in the environment. Some of these agencies are described in this section.

U.S. Environmental Protection Agency (EPA)

The **Environmental Protection Agency (EPA)** was established to "protect human health and safeguard the natural environment—air, water, and land—upon which life depends." This protection includes maintaining the quality of air, water, and land.

One of the voluntary programs created by the EPA is EnviroSense: Partners for the Environment. It is the mission of this group to solve environmental problems with common sense. The group facilitates voluntary participation and widespread environmental awareness with corporate partners. It is proving that voluntary guidelines can be successful by committing to programs such as Indoor Air, Indoor Radon, Design for the Environment, and WasteWi$e. Cooperative efforts of consumers and industry members are necessary to continue to achieve improvements in environmental protection and accomplish greater success.

Centers for Disease Control and Prevention (CDC)

The **Centers for Disease Control and Prevention (CDC)** was organized "to promote health and quality of life by preventing and controlling disease, injury and disability." In addition to its mission, the CDC is committed to providing a healthy environment in which individuals can achieve personal growth. The organization uses the highest-quality data to make all public health decisions.

Occupational Safety and Health Administration (OSHA)

The goal of the **Occupational Safety and Health Administration (OSHA)** is to save lives, prevent injuries, and protect the health of workers. One of OSHA's primary activities is inspecting the workplace. There are over 2,000 inspectors who investigate complaints. This organization also enforces standards and provides technical support and consultation to employers and employees to ensure safer work environments.

Summary

The primary goal of all firms in the interior textile industry is to operate profitably. All members of the industry recognize that this goal depends on consumer acceptance of the end products offered. They strive to secure the initial and repeated selection of their assorted products. In this effort, they often enlist the support of such auxiliary enterprises as trade associations, advertising and publishing agencies, and contract design firms.

To succeed, industry members must cope with competition from other firms and with various external factors. Among the external factors are mortgage interest rates that may encourage or retard new construction, pressure from foreign producers, imposed product performance mandates, and growing concern about environmentally safe practices. Whatever challenges are posed by these variables, all industry firms must focus their attention on the wants and needs of contemporary residential and commercial consumers.

Key Terms

Centers for Disease Control and Prevention (CDC)

commercial interiors

consumer

contract design

converters

discretionary income

disposable or real income

downstream segments

end-product designers

end-product producers

Environmental Protection Agency (EPA)

fabric stylists

fabrication techniques

filament fibers

gassing-off

green standard

greige goods

household textiles

indoor air quality (IAQ)

inflation

institutional textiles

International Fabricare Institute (IFI)

manufactured fiber producers

members of the trade

National Association of Institutional Linen Management (NAILM)

natural fiber suppliers

Occupational Safety and Health Administration (OSHA)

organically grown

product showroom

residential interiors

spinners

staple fibers

textile colorists

textile designers

throwsters

tow

trade associations

upstream segments

Review Questions

1. Identify the major segments of the interior textile industry and discuss their interconnectedness.

2. The following is a skeletal profit and loss statement. Discuss what a firm can do with each variable to increase its net profit (e.g., increase sales).

$$\begin{aligned} &\$ \text{ retail sales} \\ &- \text{ wholesale costs} \\ &= \text{ operating profit} \\ &- \text{ expenses} \\ &= \text{ net profit} \end{aligned}$$

3. Discuss the environmental challenges that face natural fiber suppliers and manufactured fiber producers.

4. Why is it critically important that members of the industry monitor slight shifts in both the aesthetic features and the functional expectations of interior textile products?

5. Identify several interior textile products, including those used in residential and commercial interiors. What interior textile products are used in hospitality settings?

6. Differentiate between household textiles and institutional textiles.

7. What challenges face domestic producers, and why must they meet these challenges?

8. Discuss the consequences of offering interior textile products that do not coincide with the wants and needs of the consumer.

9. Discuss the role of interior designers and architects in choosing textiles. What legal ramifications are associated with their decisions?

10. Why would competing firms work cooperatively in a trade association?

11. Explain the critical importance of IAQ. How can the negative effects of interior textiles on the IAQ be reduced?

12. Identify ways the professional designer can strive to protect the environment when selecting textiles.

13. Cite three ways soft floor coverings are being reused or recycled.

14. Discuss the recycling of plastic bottles into textile applications.

15. What advantages are offered by Fortrel® Ecospun® fiber?

16. Discuss the external factors that affect the economic health of the industry.

Notes

1. Kathryn Wise, "The Carpet Industry—Covering the Future," *American Dyestuff Reporter*, 1999.

2. Katherine D. Stutton, "Green Market," *Interiors*, CLVII, 6, 1998.

3. Ibid.

4. Wise, "The Carpet Industry."

5. Ibid.

6. Ibid.

2

Selecting and Evaluating Textiles for Interiors

Selecting Interior Textiles
  Challenges to Members of the Industry
  Challenges to Design Professionals and
    Consumers
  Aesthetic Considerations
  Performance and Safety Factors
  Maintenance Considerations
  Environmental Concerns
  Cost and Installation Factors

Evaluating Interior Textiles
  Standard Methods of Testing
  Performance Specifications
  Codes
  Scientific and Technical Associations

Agencies Regulating Product Selections
  Federal Housing Administration (FHA)
  Social Security Administration (SSA)

General Services Administration (GSA)
Federal Aviation Administration (FFA) and
    National Highway Traffic Safety
    Administration (NHTSA)

Organizations Establishing Model Building Codes
  International Codes Council (ICC)
  Council of American Building Officials
    (CABO)
  Building Officials and Code Administrators
    (BOCA)
  International Conference of Building
    Officials (ICBO)
  Southern Building Code Council
    International (SBCCI)

Each residential and commercial consumer has a unique set of criteria governing the selection of **textile end products**. Some of these variables relate to appearance and tactile characteristics; some focus on service-related performance; some are concerned with maintenance and installation; and some are necessarily determined by cost factors. Consumers and design professionals must work together to determine the relative importance of each criterion and to accommodate those considered most important. Industry firms must be aware of these variables in order to offer products that meet the current selection criteria.

As part of their effort to secure the initial and repeated selection of their products, many firms measure specific properties of the products' components and assess the potential serviceability of the finished items prior to marketing. Initially, this work enables them to make statements about their products' performance on labels and in promotional materials in order to capture the attention of professionals and prospective purchasers. Subsequently, these evaluations help to ensure that their goods will continue to exhibit an acceptable level of **in-use performance**, satisfying consumers and encouraging them to go on selecting the company's products. In many cases, this **quality-control work** involves the use of standard methods of testing and performance specifications published by scientific and technical associations.

Many producers also evaluate their products in accordance with standards established by various regulatory agencies. Products complying with the design or performance specifications set forth in these codes can be used in interiors that come within the scope of legally binding requirements. Design professionals are liable for selecting textiles that meet or exceed the governing codes pertinent to the installation.

Selecting Interior Textiles

Several characteristics considered in the selection of textile furnishings are listed in Tables 2.1 through 2.5. In most cases, the residential or commercial consumer determines the relative importance of these variables, personally deciding whether any compromises can be made.

For certain commercial products, however, various regulatory agencies have the authority to require compliance with specific product standards and building codes.

Challenges to Members of the Industry

To remain profitable, firms in the industry must constantly monitor consumer selections, noting and quickly responding to changes in consumer preferences. The aesthetic features currently preferred must be mirrored in the products offered, the service-related characteristics expected must be available, and any mandated design and performance properties must be exhibited. Additionally, required maintenance and installation procedures must coincide with those preferred by consumers, and the price of the product, along with any charges for assembly, delivery, and installation, must not exceed the ability or willingness of the consumer to pay.

Challenges to Design Professionals and Consumers

In order to provide the best solution for the function and aesthetics of the interior, consumers, and such design professionals as interior designers and architects, should be informed when making their interior textile product selections. They must, for example, consider the factors affecting the apparent color of textiles to ensure that the color characteristics chosen will look the same when seen in the interior setting. They must understand how the components and structural features of a product influence its functional properties and use-life. Consumers and professionals should therefore be aware of inherent and engineered fiber properties, yarn and fabric features, factors affecting color retention, and the effects of finishing treatments and agents. They should be prepared to identify the activities, conditions, and substances to which the item will be subjected in use, and be able to make reliable judgments regarding the ability of the item to perform satisfactorily when exposed to the anticipated stresses and agents. These several product and end-use variables will be discussed in detail throughout this book.

The task in design is especially challenging because residential and commercial consumers have widely varying and constantly changing aesthetic preferences and performance needs. Designers and architects must be knowledgeable of market trends within the industry. They must be aware of the resources available for reliable information, including trade publications, professional journals, and the Internet.

When contract designers and architects are selecting interior textile products for commercial use, they must ascertain which, if any, agency has jurisdiction over the project, and they must identify all applicable codes affecting their selections. In turn, they must confirm that their planned product selections conform to all mandated selection criteria. Interior designers and architects are, in fact, legally and ethically responsible for choosing textiles that meet all applicable industry and government standards and codes, particularly performance standards and life safety codes. It may be necessary for the design professional to educate the consumer, explaining that codes and safety requirements may preclude the choice of certain aesthetic or structural features with a textile product.

Aesthetic Considerations

Several aesthetic or sensory characteristics are considered in the selection of interior textile products (see Table 2.1). These include such **design elements** as color, line, texture, and form, and such **design principles** as emphasis, rhythm, contrast, and harmony. While the initial visual impact of these features is a primary concern, consideration must also be given to such variables as the effects of end-use lighting on the apparent color, the availability of matching items, and the life expectancy of the fashion features.

Performance and Safety Factors

Among the selection criteria held by consumers are several variables pertaining to performance (see Table 2.2). For some consumers, such functional attributes as glare reduction and acoustic control may be critical; for others, texture retention may be of paramount importance; and for still others, durability and wear-life may be high on the list. At the same time, many consumers are increasingly aware of the desirability of having flame-resistant textiles that can widen the margin of safety in the event of fire. For some commercial interiors, flame resistance may not only be desirable, it may be mandatory.

Table 2.1 Aesthetic Product Selection Criteria

	Variable Characteristics
Design Elements	form: 3-D form of upholstered furniture, pillows color characteristics: hue, value, and intensity texture: smooth or rough resulting from the fiber, yarn, or fabric structure or from an applied finish pattern: detail, size, and repetition of motifs light: level of reflectance; level of transmittance
Design Principles	scale: size of motifs; fullness of window coverings emphasis: dominant visual characteristic rhythm: repetition of elements contrast: differentiates items in the visual field harmony: pleasing arrangement of parts
Styling Features	color styling: heather, multicolored, solid-colored texture styling: nonpile, cut pile, uncut pile, level, multilevel hand: warm, cool, smooth, rough, soft, harsh drapability: fluid, stiff end-product styling: trimmed, plain, traditional, contemporary availability of matching and/or coordinated items coordination with existing interior and current furnishings life expectancy of fashion features

Maintenance Considerations

Products are selected for their appropriateness for an interior, as well as for the enjoyment they will provide during their expected use-life. Part of this enjoyment centers on the type and level of maintenance required and its effectiveness. Proper maintenance of textiles affects their serviceability, in terms of appearance retention, wear, durability, and safety. Dirt that is not removed from carpet, for example, will facilitate an abrasive action between traffic and the carpet fibers, as well as affect the apparent color. Concomitantly, the aesthetic value of the floor covering would be diminished. Both the consumer and design professional should become aware of proper maintenance, including the cleaning agents and equipment needed. These and other maintenance factors are listed in Table 2.3.

Table 2.2 Performance and Safety Product Selection Criteria

	Variable Characteristics
Functional Properties	insulation, glare reduction, static reduction, fatigue reduction, acoustic control, mobility improvements, safety enhancement
Appearance Retention	color retention, texture retention, resistance to pilling and snagging, soil hiding, soil repellency, soil shedding, soil release
Durability and Wear-life	abrasion resistance, tear resistance, dimensional stability, fuzzing, fiber loss, repairability, warranty availability
Structural Stability	tuft bind strength, delamination strength, stability of yarn twist
Flame Resistance	inherent or applied
Design and Performance Mandates	flame resistance, indoor air quality, structural stability, colorfastness, wear resistance functional properties: acoustical value, static reduction

Table 2.3 Maintenance Product Selection Criteria

	Variable Characteristics
Cleanability	washable, dry cleanable, ease of stain removal, appearance after cleaning
Cleaning Location	on-site versus off-site cleaning
Level of Ironing Required	none, touch-up, extensive
Frequency of Cleaning	daily, weekly, monthly
Cleaning Products Required	toxic, biodegradable, readily available

Table 2.4 Environmental Product Selection Criteria

	Variable Characteristics
Manufacturing Issues	effluents produced during manufacturing products made of recycled materials
Product Issues	potential for product recycling potential impact of required cleaning agents

Table 2.5 Cost and Installation Product Selection Criteria

	Variable Characteristics
Initial Cost	product price, accessories prices fees for design professional delivery charges installation charges
Long-Term Costs	maintenance costs, including equipment, cleaning agents, and labor warranty costs, insurance costs energy costs interest charges
Installation Factors	site preparation labor, tools, and level of skill needed permanence: movable, removable, permanent

Environmental Concerns

Increasingly, manufacturers and consumers of today's textile products are showing greater interest in recycling goods. In addition, they are showing greater concern for the environmental effects of effluents and other waste materials that are produced during manufacturing. These and other environmental concerns are listed in Table 2.4.

Cost and Installation Factors

Textile product costs may be categorized by **initial cost** and **life-cycle cost**. Initial cost starts with the cost of the product, as well as the cost incurred for installation, including site preparation, labor, and any accessories that are needed (see Table 2.5). A detailed **project bid** provides prices for each of the products chosen, together with the installation charges, thus enabling the client and designer to ascertain the affordability of the project. If necessary, the project may be completed in phases.

Life-cycle cost is comprehensive and is listed in a formal **project specification**. Consideration is given to several factors, including the initial cost, installation expenses, ongoing maintenance costs, and the anticipated life-span of the product. With life-span in mind, the initial costs may be amortized: for example, an expensive textile product that is expected to be serviceable for ten years could, in fact, be less costly than one whose initial cost was less but whose life expectancy was shorter.

Maintenance procedures should be examined prior to installation to determine that the practices are both doable and affordable. With commercial installations, interviews with the maintenance personnel would be helpful in determining any deficiencies in equipment, as well as the feasibility of the necessary maintenance procedures. Insufficient or incorrect maintenance may lead to premature replacement of a product and greatly add to the long-term cost. Together with the cost of utilities, the energy efficiency of a product will result in long-term savings or long-term expense.

Evaluating Interior Textiles

Together with other informed and interested persons, many members of the textile industry participate in the work of several scientific and technical associations. Participants in most of these groups voluntarily share their expertise and opinions to help develop standards pertaining to such things as definitions, recommended practices, methods of testing, classifications, design specifications, or performance specifications. Producers throughout the industry may elect to use these standards when they evaluate their components and end products.

Unless adopted by a regulatory agency, standards are not legally binding. A design professional, however, is responsible for using the information to best meet the needs of the client. The Association for Contract Interiors (ACT), for example, suggests that general contract upholstery should withstand 15,000 double rubs with the Wyzenbeek method (see Chapter 14) if it is to give satisfactory abrasion resistance in use; heavy-duty upholstery should withstand 30,000 double rubs. Thus, the ACT standard is a recommendation for satisfactory end-use performance; it is not, however, mandatory.

In the event that an agency having regulatory power adopts a design or performance specification as a requirement, the standard is often then known as a code. Codes are legally binding requirements.

Standard Methods of Testing

A **standard test method** prescribes specific procedures to be followed when making a given measurement, for instance, the measurement of yarn distortion after surface friction. A test method details the selection, size, number, and preparation of the test specimens; describes the test apparatus; specifies test conditions; sets forth test procedures; and lists the observations and calculations to be made in analyzing and reporting the test results. Unless specifically stated otherwise, testing is carried out in a controlled atmosphere of 70 ± 2 °F and 65 ± 2 percent RH (relative humidity). In order to produce accurate and reproducible results, textile researchers and quality-control personnel must strictly adhere to all details included in a standard test method. Performance comparisons can be made only among specimens tested in a like manner. (While the summaries of test methods provided in later chapters are adequate for discussion, they are not sufficient for carrying out testing. Interested persons can read the full text of standard test methods in such publications as the *AATCC Technical Manual* and the *Annual Book of ASTM Standards*. These publications are listed in the bibliography.) Test methods simulate the conditions to which textile items may be subjected in actual use. Such small-scale laboratory techniques minimize the need for large-scale, long-term, and more expensive evaluation procedures. Standard test methods enable producers efficiently and economically to measure their products' quality and performance.

Many manufacturers use test results as the basis for claims that their products exhibit specific functional and use-life characteristics. They may also analyze test results to determine the advisability of putting their name or other identifying mark on the product label.

Performance Specifications

While analysis of the results of a standard test method may require numerical calculations, it may or may not specify numerical limitations or boundaries pertaining to performance. By contrast, such performance-related requirements are always included in a **standard performance specification**. These requirements represent the minimum or maximum levels—the limits—of performance that the specimens should exhibit when tested in accordance with the designated method.

Design professionals develop performance specifications to establish criteria for project contracts and bidding. This allows the designer to define the product requirements. When textiles are submitted for project approval, evidence of compliance with the specifications is required. Results of the product tests may be requested from the manufacturer or a sample can be tested.

Manufacturers use performance specifications to compare the level of performance recorded for their products with the level recommended in the standard, and, if necessary, to alter the composition or processing of their items accordingly. Compliance with such recommendations ensures that the component or product will exhibit an acceptable level of in-use performance, which in turn will help to secure consumer goodwill and repeat business for the complying company.

Codes

Codes are mandatory practices or mandated performance specifications concerned with the safety and well-being of the general population. Codes are laws enacted by federal, state, and local governments. Individual jurisdictions may write their own laws or rely on the work of government agencies or model building code organizations. Frequently, a regulatory agency will adopt a standard performance specification as a code, in effect turning a recommendation into a requirement. Several state-level fire marshal's offices, for example, have adopted as codes selected standards set forth in the NFPA Life Safety Code®. Some organizations responsible for developing model building codes are discussed later in this chapter.

Because codes are mandatory, the design professional is legally responsible for selecting products that comply with all applicable codes. California Technical Bulletin 133, for example, is a flammability standard that has been adopted as a code by several states. When a designer incorporates a customer's own material (COM) in an occupancy in a state where Cal 133 is the code, the designer must have the fabric tested in accordance with the procedures set forth in Cal 133. The challenge for the designer is to adequately research and accurately specify textile products that meet or exceed all code requirements applicable to the project.

Scientific and Technical Associations

Among the many scientific associations involved in establishing standards, six are of particular interest to producers and consumers of textile furnishing. Participants serve voluntarily in five of the six groups.

American Association of Textile Chemists and Colorists (AATCC)

Founded in 1921, **AATCC** is a technical and scientific society that is internationally recognized for its standard methods of testing dyed and chemically treated fibers and fabrics. The test methods are designed to measure and evaluate such performance characteristics as colorfastness to light and washing, shrinkage, water resistance, flammability, and many other conditions to which textiles may be subjected. While it is beyond the scope of AATCC to set standard performance specifications, the test methods help producers and retailers to ensure the marketability and satisfactory performance of textile fabrics.

AATCC maintains a technical center that serves as a test demonstration center. Its laboratory is equipped with all of the testing apparatus used in AATCC test methods; personnel at the center provide technical support to members engaged in the work of the Association. Members receive the Association's monthly journal, *Textile Chemist and Colorist*, which presents information concerning recent developments in dyes, finishes, and equipment used in the wet processing of textiles, and also includes reports of current research activities in the field of textiles.

American Society for Testing and Materials (ASTM)

The term "materials" in this organization's name indicates that materials other than textiles—such as metals, concrete, and acoustical board—also receive attention from the society's members. The Society publishes the *Annual Book of ASTM Standards;* this consists of 72 volumes, divided among 16 sections, each focusing on a limited variety of materials, products, or processes. Included in each volume are all proposed, tentative, and formally adopted standards, guidelines, and performance specifications developed for use with the specific materials or processes covered.

The work of **ASTM** is carried out by 132 committees. Each major committee is given a letter and number, followed by a general product designation, for instance, D-13 Committee on Textiles. Further numerical designations are used for subcommittees, for example, D-13.21 Subcommittee on Pile Floor Coverings, or D-13.56 Subcommittee on Performance Standards for Textile Fabrics. Standards developed by ASTM committees are described as "full-consensus" standards. ASTM members and nonmembers who have an interest in a standard or who would be affected by its application are encouraged to participate in the development of the standard. Each committee and subcommittee has the participation of both producers and users of the products in question, to ensure a balanced representation of all biases and opinions.

National Fire Protection Association (NFPA)

Organized in 1896, the **NFPA** invites the membership of persons concerned with fire safety. NFPA committees establish standards designed to reduce extent of injury, loss of life, and destruction of property from fire. This work is not limited to the development of test methods and performance specifications for textile products. NFPA standards have also been issued for items ranging from household warning equipment to fire fighters' helmets, as well as for the design of egress facilities permitting the prompt escape of occupants from burning buildings or into safe areas within the buildings.

American National Standards Institute (ANSI)

Unlike the other groups discussed here, **ANSI** is a private corporation, not a voluntary association. ANSI undertakes the development of standards only when so commissioned by an industry group or a government agency. The Institute seeks to reduce the duplication of effort among the many organizations developing voluntary standards and identifies nationally accepted standards. ANSI is the official U.S. representative to the International Organization for Standardization.

International Organization for Standardization (ISO)

ISO engages in the development of standards to help foster international textile trade. ISO 1139 Designation of Yarns, for example, describes the tex direct yarn numbering system, and is intended to encourage firms throughout the world to identify yarns with their tex number, rather than with their denier or indirect yarn number. (Yarn numbering systems are discussed in Chapter 5.)

Designation and Cross-listing of Standards

Standards developed by the above-mentioned organizations as well as by other associations are issued with fixed designations. For example, ASTM designates standards by the letter assigned to the committee and an identifying number. Immediately following the designation is a number indicating the year of original adoption or of the last revision; a number in parentheses indicates the year of the last reapproval. However it is designated, the latest edition of a standard should always be used in quality-control and research activities.

Standards developed by one scientific association are often shared with and cross-listed by other associations. ASTM E-84 The Standard Method of Test of Surface Burning Characteristics of Building Materials, for example, is also identified as NFPA 255 and as ANSI A2.5. Cross-listing may indicate widespread acceptance of a standard, but it does not change its voluntary status. Standards developed by these scientific and technical associations are recommendations, not mandates. The associations have no power or authority to enforce the use of standard test methods or compliance with standard performance specifications. Local, state, or federal regulatory agencies, however, often adopt voluntary standards established by these groups; the standard then becomes mandatory.

Agencies Regulating Product Selections

Regulatory agencies are outside of the textile industry but have the power to oversee the selection of many of its products. Some of the federal agencies involved in these activities are identified here. The reader must be cautioned that the jurisdiction, responsibilities, and mandates of all regulatory agencies change frequently. Contract designers and architects must contact the various agencies to confirm their current jurisdictions and requirements.

Federal Housing Administration (FHA)

The **FHA**, a division of the Department of Housing and Urban Development has jurisdiction over the materials used in the interiors of such places as elderly and care-type housing, low-rent public housing projects, and structures insured by FHA. The minimum standards established for materials used in these facilities are set forth in the Use of Materials Bulletin 44d, which is available from the FHA.

Social Security Administration (SSA)

The **SSA**, a division of the Department of Health and Human Services, administers the Medicare and Medicaid programs. In order to participate in these programs, hospitals and extended care facilities must comply with SSA regulations dealing with such things as fire safety and acoustics. Some of these regulations apply to the textile products selected for these facilities.

General Services Administration (GSA)

The **GSA** oversees the selection of materials for federal facilities. Federal Test Method Standard No. 191A, issued July 20, 1978, describes the general physical, chemical, and biological methods used to test textile fibers, yarn, thread, rope, other cordage, cloth, and fabricated textile products for conformity with mandated and performance specifications. Revised and new test methods are issued as needed.

Federal Aviation Administration (FAA) and National Highway Traffic Safety Administration (NHTSA)

The **FAA** and the **NHTSA** are divisions of the Department of Transportation (DOT). The FAA regulates the selection and installation of textile items in the crew and passenger compartments of airliners, and the NHTSA oversees the selection and installation of textile products in automobiles and certain other vehicles. Flammability standards established by these agencies are discussed in Chapter 11.

There are several other agencies regulating the selection of textile products. Some cities, notably Boston and New York, have stringent flammability mandates, and virtually all states have established criteria related to the flammability of products used in commercial interiors. The reader must again be cautioned that the jurisdiction,

responsibilities, and codes of all regulatory agencies are frequently changed.

The **Consumer Product Safety Commission (CPSC)** is a federal agency concerned with the safety of most consumer products, including the flammability of textile products. The Commission does not, however, set standards pertaining to product selection. Rather, it prohibits the initial introduction of highly flammable products into commerce and thus prevents them from being available for selection. The Commission and its work are discussed in Chapter 11.

Organizations Establishing Model Building Codes

Several organizations establish model codes. The focus of these model codes ranges from plumbing to mechanical features to fire safety. Design professionals should be familiar with the nature of these codes as they plan the interior spaces. Note that once a model code is adopted as law, it becomes a code, that is, a mandate.

International Codes Council (ICC)

In 1994, the Building Officials and Code Administrators (BOCA), the International Conference of Building Officials (ICBO), and the Southern Building Code Council International (SBCCI) established the International Codes Council. The goal of the **ICC** is to develop a single coordinated set of national codes. ICC is also responsible for publishing the International Building Code (IBC) and the International Residential Code (IRC).

Council of American Building Officials (CABO)

CABO was developed to unify the three nationally recognized model code organizations, BOCA, ICBO, and SBCCI. In the past CABO was dedicated to maintaining the standard for Accessible and Usable Buildings and Facilities. CABO responsibilities will be integrated into the ICC organization.

Building Officials and Code Administrators (BOCA)

BOCA International was established in 1915. It is the oldest professional code association and is used with other codes to protect human safety and well-being in Canada. BOCA also publishes the National Building Code (NBC) and monitors its enforcement.

International Conference of Building Officials (ICBO)

The **ICBO** is a nonprofit service organization. The organization was founded in 1922 and is used in the midwestern and western regions of the United States.

Participating cities, counties, and states have control and ownership of the group. ICBO publishes the Uniform Building Code (UBC).

Southern Building Code Council International (SBCCI)

The **SBCCI** supplies government agencies engaged in building codes administration and enforcement with extensive technical, educational, and administrative support. The SBCCI also dispenses information to designers and builders, and publishes the Standard Building Code (SBC), which is used in the southeastern part of the United States.

Summary

Residential and commercial consumers consider many variables when they select textile products. The nature and relative importance of these variables is constantly changing. Members of the industry are challenged to identify the current criteria and to offer products that coincide with them.

To ensure that their products will exhibit an acceptable level of in-use performance and satisfy the consumer, most producers of textile components and end products evaluate their goods prior to shipment. This quality-control work generally involves the use of standard test methods and performance specifications, many of which are developed by members of scientific associations. The use of such standards is voluntary unless they have been adopted by a regulatory agency, in which case products must comply with the criteria set out by the agency before they can be selected for a specific interior.

Key Terms

AATCC Technical Manual
American Association of Textile Chemists and Colorists (AATCC)
American National Standards Institute (ANSI)
American Society for Testing and Materials (ASTM)
Annual Book of ASTM Standards
Building Officials and Code Administrators (BOCA)
codes
Consumer Product Safety Commission (CPSC)
Council of American Building Officials (CABO)
design elements
design principles
Federal Aviation Administration (FAA)
Federal Housing Administration (FHA)

General Services Administration (GSA)
initial cost
International Codes Council (ICC)
International Conference of Building Officials (ICBO)
International Organization for Standardization (ISO)
in-use performance
life-cycle cost
National Fire Protection Association (NFPA)
National Highway Traffic Safety Administration (NHTSA)
project bid
project specification
quality-control work
regulatory agencies

Social Security Administration (SSA)

Southern Building Code Council International (SBCCI)

standard performance specification

standard test method

textile end products

Review Questions

1. Explain the nature of quality-control work and the reasons members of the interior textile industry engage in this activity.

2. Why is it important that interior textile products exhibit an acceptable level of performance in-use?

3. Explain what is meant by consumer product selection criteria and the importance of these criteria to interior textile product manufacturers.

4. Discuss the challenges faced by the design professional in selecting and specifying interior textile products.

5. Discuss the impact of design elements and principles on textile product selection.

6. What purposes do standard performance specifications have for manufacturers?

7. Distinguish between standard methods of testing and standard performance specifications, and between standards and codes.

8. Characterize the work of such regulatory agencies as the FHA, the FAA, and the CPSC. Then, compare and contrast the focus of the work of these agencies.

9. Explain how organizations that develop test methods for evaluating textiles function.

10. Explain the meaning of "full consensus" standards.

3

Textile Fibers

Fiber Classification and Identification
    Classification
    Identification

Fiber Composition and Structure
    Molecular Units
    Molecular Arrangements
    External Features

Natural Fibers
    Production
    Protein Fibers

Cellulosic Fibers
Mineral Fiber
Natural Fiber Engineering

Manufactured Fibers
    Production
    Cellulosic Fibers
    Noncellulosic Fibers
    Manufactured Fiber Engineering

Fibers used in contemporary textile furnishings are chemically the same as those used in apparel and industrial textile products. Wool fibers, for example, are used in fine crepe apparel fabrics, durable upholstery coverings, and thick insulation felt for industrial applications; nylon fibers are used in lingerie, carpet, automobile seat belts, and tires; and polyester fibers are used in ready-to-wear apparel, upholstery, draperies, bedding, and tent fabrics. The characteristics that make a given fiber suitable for a particular end-use application are inherent and/or are engineered by production and processing techniques.

Natural fiber suppliers and manufactured fiber producers allocate millions of dollars annually toward extensive research and development projects. They support these activities in order to remain competitive and to capture a larger share of the fiber market. The results of this work are fibers with improved appearance and performance characteristics, many of which are specifically engineered for use in interior textile applications.

Whether a fiber is natural or manufactured, it is distinguished by its chemical composition and characterized by specific internal and external physical features. Such characteristics are inherent features of natural fibers; they are engineered features of manufactured fibers. In either case, these variables make for the appearance, chemical reactions, and performance properties of fibers.

Because their chemical composition distinguishes textile fibers, they are classified and named on the basis of this composition. A review of the nomenclature will serve to introduce the basic vocabulary used to discuss fibers and to label and promote textile products.

Fiber Classification and Identification

Specific textile fibers are identified by their common or generic name for purposes of discussion or disclosure on a sample or product label. Fibers grouped under the same name are chemically related and tend to exhibit similar properties. Consumers and professionals who are familiar with these names, and with the properties that typically characterize each group, are better equipped to make reliable fiber selections and to identify unnamed fibers.

Classification

A fiber classification system is presented in Table 3.1. Textile fibers are first classified on the basis of how they are produced, whether natural or manufactured. Although all manufactured fibers are produced from natural substances, some of which are inherently fibrous, none can be classified as a natural fiber because the **usable fiber form** is a product of industrial processing.

Within the two broad fiber groupings, further classification may be made on the basis of general chemical composition, for instance, protein, cellulosic, noncellulosic, or mineral. Finally, fibers are classified by their **common or generic names**. For purposes of fiber identification and product labeling, the centuries-old common or family names used for natural fibers are considered their generic names.

Generic names or classes for manufactured fibers were established by the Federal Trade Commission in accordance with a congressional directive. Each class is defined in terms of specific chemical composition. The generic class *acrylic*, for example, describes "a manufactured fiber in which the fiber-forming substance is any long chain synthetic polymer composed of at least 85% by weight of acrylonitrile units." By contrast, the generic class *nylon* specifies "a manufactured fiber in which the fiber-forming substance is a long chain synthetic polyamide in which less than 85% of the amide . . . linkages are attached directly to two aromatic rings." A complete listing of the generic class names and definitions set forth by the Commission, as well as those promulgated by the International Organization for Standardization, is presented in Appendix A.

The mandatory use of generic names in textile fiber product labeling and promotion is discussed in Chapter 10. Also discussed in that chapter are the powers and responsibilities of the Federal Trade Commission with respect to the commercial activities of the industry.

Identification

In some instances, a professional or a consumer may encounter a fabric of unknown fiber content. The fabric may be, for example, a customer's own material (known as **COM**) and carry no labeling. Or it may be commercial

Table 3.1 Textile Fiber Classification

Natural Fibers

Protein (animals)	Cellulosic (plants)	Mineral (rock)
Alpaca (alpaca)	Leaf	Asbestos
Angora (angora rabbit)	abaca (manila fiber)	
	banana	
Camel (Bactrian camel)	henequen	
Cashmere (Cashmere goat)	pina (pineapple)	
Cattle hair (cattle)	sisal	
Fur fibers (beaver, fox, mink, sable, etc.)		
Horse hair (horse)	Seed	
Llama (llama)	coir (coconut)	
	cotton	
	kapok	
Mohair (angora goat)		
Qiviut (musk ox)		
Silk (silkworm)	Stem (bast)	
Vicuna (vicuna)	hemp	
Wool (sheep)	jute	
	kenaf	
	linen	
	ramie (China grass)	

Manufactured Fibers

Cellulosic	Protein	Rubber
Acetate	Azlons[b]	Rubber (natural liquid rubber)
Lyocell[a]		
Rayon		
Triacetate[b]		

	Noncellulosic			Mineral
Acrylic	Novoloid[c]	Rubber (Synthetic)	PBI[d]	Glass
Anidex[b]	Nylon	Saran	Sulfar[d]	Metallic
Aramid[c]	Nytril[b]	Spandex		
Lastrile[b]	Olefin	Vinal[b]		
Modacrylic	Polyester	Vinyon		

[a]Name established in 1996.

[b]These groups are not currently produced in the United States; some may be imported, however.

[c]Name established in 1974.

[d]Name established in 1986.

yardage that has become separated from its labels. In any case, various testing and examination procedures can help expedite the identification of unknown fibers. Among these techniques are solubility and staining tests, measurement of fiber density, microscopic examination, burning tests, and visual examination. Because some of these procedures require special reagents, microscopes, infrared spectrometers, exhaust hoods, and the like, they can only be conducted in an adequately equipped laboratory. On the other hand, the burning test can readily be conducted by designers, architects, retailers, and consumers, all of whom have access to matches.

To conduct a burning test, the following procedure can be used, with caution:

1. Hold several fibers or a yarn from a fabric with metal tweezers over an ashtray to catch ashes and drips.
2. Strike a match away from the body for safety and to avoid inhaling the smoke and fumes.
3. Observe the reaction of the specimen as it approaches the flame, when it is in the flame, and after the ignition source is removed. Note the odor and examine the cooled residue.

Table 3.2 Reaction of Textile Fibers to Heat and Flame

Fiber	When Approaching Flame	When in Flame	After Removal of Flame	Residue	Odor
Natural					
Protein					
Wool	Curls away from flame	Burns slowly	Self-extinguishing[a]	Brittle, small black bead	Similar to burning hair or feathers
Silk	Curls away from flame	Burns slowly and sputters	Usually self-extinguishing[a]	Beadlike, crushable black	Similar to burning hair or feathers
Cellulosic					
Cotton	Does not shrink away, ignites upon contact	Burns quickly without melting	Continues to burn; afterglow	Light, feathery ash, light gray to charcoal in color	Similar to burning paper
Linen	Does not shrink away, ignites upon contact	Burns quickly without melting	Continues to burn; afterglow	Light feathery ash, light charcoal in color	Similar to burning paper
Manufactured					
Cellulosic					
Acetate	Melts and fuses away from flame	Burns quickly with melting	Continues to burn rapidly with melting	Brittle, irregular-shaped bead, black	Acrid (hot vinegar)
Rayon	Does not shrink away, ignites upon contact	Burns quickly without melting	Continues to burn; afterglow	Light, fluffy ash, small amount	Similar to burning paper
Mineral					
Glass	Shrinks away from flame	Melts and glows red to orange	Glowing ceases, does not burn	Hard bead, white in color	None
Metallic pure	May shrink away from flame or have no reaction	Glows red	Glowing ceases, does not burn, hardens	Skeleton outline of fiber	None
Coated	Fuses and shrinks away from flame	Burns according to behavior of coating	Reacts according to behavior of coating	Hard bead, black in color	Characteristic of coating
Noncellulosic					
Acrylic	Fuses and shrinks away from flame	Burns with melting	Continues to burn with melting	Brittle, irregular-shaped bead, black	Acrid
Modacrylic	Fuses away from flame	Burns slowly and irregularly with melting	Self-extinguishing[a]	Hard, irregular-shaped bead, black	Acid chemical
Nylon	Fuses and shrinks away from flame	Burns slowly with melting	Usually self-extinguishing[a]	Hard, tough, round bead, gray in color	Celery
Olefin	Fuses, shrinks, and curls away from flame	Burns with melting	Continues to burn with melting, black sooty smoke	Hard, tough tan bead	Chemical or candle wax
Polyester	Fuses and shrinks away from flame	Burns slowly with melting	Usually self-extingushing[a]	Hard, tough, round bead, black in color	Chemical
Saran	Fuses and shrinks away from flame	Burns very slowly with melting, yellow flame	Self-extinguishing[a]	Hard, irregular-shaped bead, black	Chemical
Spandex	Fuses but does not shrink away from flame	Burns with melting	Continues to burn with melting	Soft, crushable, fluffy, black ash	Chemical
Vinyon	Fuses and shrinks away from flame	Burns slowly with melting	Self-extinguishing[a]	Hard, irregular-shaped bead, black	Acrid

[a]Self-extinguishing fibers stop burning when the source of ignition is removed.

Observations from a completed burning test can be compared with the reactions listed in Table 3.2. (Other heat-related fiber properties are identified in Table 4.8 and the pyrolytic characteristics of selected fibers are detailed in Table 4.6, pages 55 and 56.) If a mixture of reactions is noted when a yarn is burned, a blend may be suspected. Visual characteristics may help the observer to separate different fibers in the yarn and repeat the test.

In some cases, the results obtained in a burning test may not permit identification of the generic class of the unknown fiber; the results will, however, always enable the observer to classify the specimen in a meaningful category, such as protein or cellulosic. Visual examination may help to support further identification.

Fiber Composition and Structure

All textile fibers, natural and manufactured, are relatively fine: that is, they are long and thin and have comparatively high ratios of length to width. This structural feature ensures the flexibility required for manufacturing and end-use serviceability. Differences among textile fibers result not only from their different chemical compositions, but also from variations in the arrangement of their interior units and the nature of their external features.

Molecular Units

With the exception of the inorganic glass and metal fibers, virtually all fibers have carbon (C) and hydrogen (H) atoms. Some fibers, such as cotton, linen, rayon, acetate, and polyester, also have oxygen (O); others, such as wool, silk, acrylic, and nylon, also have nitrogen (N); and wool also has sulfur (S). The various atoms present in each fiber are combined into distinctive molecular fiber-forming units known as **monomers** (from the Greek *mono*, "one," and *mer*, "part"). Through a process known as polymerization, thousands of monomers are linked by strong chemical bonds into extremely long, chain-like units known as **polymers** (from the Greek *poly*, "many," and *mer*, "part"). (A rough analogy would be the linking of thousands of paper-clips into one long chain.) The monomeric units used to form several fibers are identified later in this chapter.

Molecular Arrangements

Within textile fibers, the polymer chains assume or are made to assume, different types of arrangements. Four of these arrangements are schematically illustrated in Figure 3.1.

When the polymer chains are not aligned parallel to each other, a disordered, **amorphous** arrangement exists. When the chains are aligned parallel to the long axis of the fiber, the arrangement is **oriented**. When the chains are laterally or longitudinally parallel to each other and closely packed, a high number of chemical bonds or attractions, weaker than the main chain bonds, may form between adjacent chains. Such ordered regions are **crystalline**.

The schematic illustration of an amorphous arrangement shown in Figure 3.1a may remind the reader of cooked spaghetti. This analogy can help us appreciate that fibers, such as wool, that have these highly disordered interiors are characterized by relatively high flexibility and low strength: the stronger chemical bonds linking the monomer units are not aligned lengthwise, the direction of stress in textile fibers. By contrast, fibers with an oriented chain arrangement (Figure 3.1b) have their strongest bonds longitudinally aligned, enabling them to bear heavier loads. In any tug-of-war, the winning participants are aligned to offer a collective resistance to the opposing force.

Figure 3.1 Molecular arrangements in fibers.

a) amorphous

b) oriented

c) nonoriented crystalline

d) oriented crystalline

Textile fibers cannot have a totally oriented, crystallized interior arrangement because such fibers would be brittle and inflexible and would snap under stress. Fibers that tend to be highly ordered, such as linen, have relatively low extensibility (ability to extend or be elongated) and flex abrasion resistance (wear resistance). Fabrics composed of such stiff fibers are also less drapable.

External Features

The external features of textile fibers include their cross-sectional shape, their longitudinal configuration, their surface texture, and their length. These features, like molecular composition and arrangement, directly influence the properties of fibers.

Cross-sectional Shape

The cross-sectional shape of a fiber may be basically round, square, flat, or triangular, or it may be multilobal, having from three to five or more lobes with either slightly concave or deeply indented sides. The effects of cross-sectional shape on the look, stiffness, and tactile characteristics of fibers are explained in Chapter 4. The effects of various shapes on the ability of fibers to hide accumulated soil, an important service-related characteristic for fibers used in soft floor coverings, are also discussed in the following chapter.

Surface Texture

The surface of textile fibers may be smooth or wrinkled, somewhat rough, or otherwise irregular. Some typical textures are schematized in Figure 3.2. Together with other external features, texture affects the luster and tactile properties of fabric, aesthetic variables that are relatively important selection criteria for many consumers.

Longitudinal Configuration

Lengthwise, fibers may be fairly straight or twisted, or they may have a two- or three-dimensional crimp or coil. While the form of natural fibers is determined by nature, the form of manufactured fibers is often engineered during fiber or yarn processing. The longitudinal configurations of wool, cotton, rayon, and a conventional manufactured fiber are illustrated in Figure 3.2.

a) overlapping surface scales of wool

Unmercerized Fiber

Mercerized Fiber

b) twisted configuration and wrinkled surface of cotton

c) straight configuration and irregular surface of viscose rayon

d) straight configuration and smooth surface of conventional manufactured fiber

Figure 3.2 Longitudinal forms and surface textures of selected fibers.

The longitudinal configuration of fibers affects such aesthetic features as luster and hand. It also affects such performance properties as elasticity, resiliency, and abrasion resistance.

Length

Textile fibers range in length from a fraction of an inch or millimeter to several miles or meters. Most cotton is $^{13}/_{16}$ inch in length; most wool fibers are between one and eight inches in length; silk filaments approach two miles; and manufactured fibers can be produced to any continuous length desired.

If other features are equal, longer staples are stronger than shorter staples, and filaments are stronger than staples. In turn, the strength of a fiber helps to determine its abrasion resistance. In addition, yarns made from filaments and longer staple fibers generally appear smoother, and have a cooler hand than do yarns made from shorter staples.

Natural Fibers

The production of all fibers, natural and manufactured, follows this highly simplified sequence:

atoms → monomers → polymer chains → usable fibers

For most natural fibers, this entire sequence is carried out by animals or plants; an exception is asbestos, which is a mineral.

Production

The production of natural fibers is accomplished by nature with human assistance but without direct human involvement. Sheep, silk caterpillars, cotton and flax plants, and other organisms synthesize the monomers, form the polymer chains, and produce the usable fibers. The contribution of suppliers is important but limited. They must nurture and protect their animals and plants, keeping their sheep and caterpillars healthy and fed and their cotton and flax plants fertilized, weed-free, and protected from harmful insects. Wool fleeces must be shorn from the sheep, silk filaments must be unwound from the cocoons, linen fibers must be removed from the flax stalks, and cotton fibers must be separated from the seeds in the bolls. Once the fibers are recovered, they must be cleaned, sorted, and graded prior to yarn production.

Protein Fibers

Table 3.1 shows several protein fibers and the animals on which each grows as the natural coat. Although each animal and its fiber makes interesting study, such extensive treatment of fibers is beyond the scope of this book. Interested readers may review more expansive discussions in one or more of the introductory textiles textbooks listed in the bibliography, Appendix D. Here, discussions will focus on the more frequently used protein fibers, wool and silk.

Wool

Some textile authorities distinguish between *wool* and *sheep's wool* because the Wool Products Labeling Act of 1939 does, in fact, permit the use of term *wool* to be used for the fiber grown naturally as the fleece of the sheep or lamb or hair of the Angora or Cashmere goat, camel, alpaca, llama, and vicuna (see Chapter 10). These labeling rules also permit the use of the specialty fiber name, which is the more common practice. In these discussions, *wool* is understood to be fiber retrieved from sheep.

In protein fibers, the atoms combine into monomeric units known as **alpha amino acids**. These monomers can be represented by the generalized formula:

$$HO - \overset{\displaystyle \overset{O}{\|}}{C} - \overset{\displaystyle \overset{H}{|}}{\underset{\displaystyle \underset{R}{|}}{C}} - NH_2$$

By replacing the letter R with specific groupings of atoms, the 18 or 19 alpha amino acids that make up the wool protein, known as **keratin**, can be identified. Wool fibers are characterized by an amorphous molecular arrangement. The polymer chains have a coiled or helical configuration that is replicated by the three-dimensional crimp of the fiber (not unlike naturally curly hair.) The overlapping surface scales on the fiber (Figure 3.2a) enable the fibers to adhere to one another readily in yarn spinning, as well as to intermesh and entangle in felting shrinkage. Felting shrinkage may be used to advantage in the production of fibrous batts (see Chapter 7) but it presents cleaning problems (see Chapter 29) with consumer products.

The wool fleece is removed from the sheep once per year. While most sheep are shorn (Figure 3.3), some fleece are removed with chemicals. Potassium salts in the form of "sheep sweat" or *suient* must be washed away, and a weak acid solution may be used in **carbonizing** to destroy such vegetable matter as twigs and cockle burrs. As a byproduct, the natural lanolin held by the fibers is retrieved for eventual processing into cosmetic products.

Wool fibers are black (actually, an extremely dark brown), gray, tan, yellow, or off-white. Frequently, the fabric stylist will specify the retention of the rich, darker natural colors as they are often sought after in such items as wall coverings and floor coverings. When fashion colors are planned, **tinting** may be used to neutralize the inherent color. Here, violet tints are added to the fibers to neutralize the yellow hues typically characterizing the fibers. (Readers may be familiar with the use of violet or violet-blue tints to neutralize the yellow cast often seen in

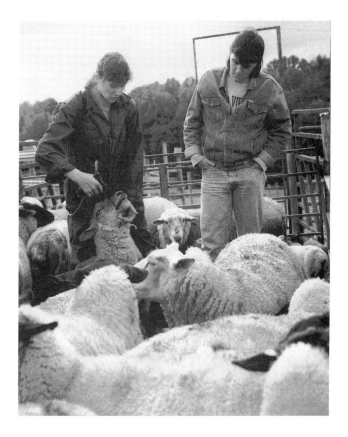

Figure 3.3 An animal science technician (Sarah Beamer) at West Virginia University skillfully shearing a sheep, removing the fleece in one piece.

gray or white hair.) Subsequently, the fibers may be dyed in the fiber stage (see Chapter 8) or processed into yarn.

Although wool fibers and products are relatively expensive, the fibers offer some exceptional properties: excellent resiliency (wrinkle or crush recovery), relatively high elasticity (stretchability), inherent flame resistance, and inherent stain repellency. As noted earlier, the tendency to exhibit felting shrinkage may be an advantage or a disadvantage.

Silk

Silk fibers are highly prized for high-end interior applications, including custom-made draperies and upholstery applications and **document fabrics**, those fabrics that replicate historic textiles in fiber content, fabrication, weight, pattern, and color. More widespread usage of the fiber is primarily precluded by the relatively high cost of the fiber, as well as its low resistance to sunlight and moderate resistance to rubbing (abrasion).

The protein in silk, **fibroin**, is composed of 11 to 12 alpha amino acids. The absence of the sulfur-containing amino acid **cystine** accounts for the lack of vulnerability of silk to moths. Unlike wool polymer chains, which are coiled and amorphous, silk has polymer chains in a pleated configuration and they are somewhat extended. The increased orientation and crystallinity contribute strength to the fiber. And, unlike other natural fibers which are in staple lengths, silk fibers are in filament form ranging from 300 to 700 yards long.

Silk is produced by the silk caterpillar (often referred to as a silkworm) in the following life cycle sequence:

female silk moth lays eggs → eggs develop into silkworms → silkworms devour huge quantities of mulberry leaves and convert them into fibroin → silkworm extrudes two strands of silk filament and **sericin** (a gummy compound that holds the filaments together) in a figure-eight fashion to **form** a cocoon → silkworm matures into a moth and breaks through the cocoon (rupturing the filaments) to start the life cycle again

When the cocoons are to be harvested for the silk filaments, they are exposed to heat that will end the life of the silkworm and preserve the filament length intact. In **reeling** the sericin is softened in warm water, and skilled technicians collect the filament ends and unwind the cocoons. **Throwing** is used to skillfully combine several filaments into multifilament silk yarns. Any staple-length silk, known as **noil**, which is recovered is combined into spun silk yarns (see Chapter 5).

Silk may be sufficiently whitened by boiling the filaments in a detergent solution. This operation, **boiling off**, removes the sericin, the off-white or yellow gummy compound covering the fine fibers. If the sericin is left in place, the silk is marketed as **raw silk**.

Silk is one of the strongest natural fibers and has medium elongation and moderate abrasion resistance. While the lower abrasion resistance does not support the selection of upholstery fabrics of silk, they nonetheless are used when luxury and luster are sought. Although silk is **tendered** or weakened by sunlight, it is used when historic restoration calls for authenticity in document fabrics. Dry cleaning or hand washing is generally recommended for cleaning fabrics of silk, not only to avoid damaging the fiber with strong alkaline solutions, but also to prevent fastness problems with unstable dyestuffs.

Cellulosic Fibers

Among the several cellulosic fibers listed in Table 3.1, only cotton, linen, jute, and coir fibers are relatively important to the interior textile industry. Each of these fibers comes from a different portion of the plants, but all share the same chemical composition.

In the natural cellulosic fibers, lyocell, and rayon, the monomeric unit is **anhydrous glucose** (shown below). The basic repeating unit, however, is the **cellubiose unit** formed by rotating alternate anhydrous glucose units.

$$CH_2OH$$

(chemical structure of anhydrous glucose)

Coir

Coir (*co-yer*) fibers are **seed fibers** retrieved from the husk or hull of the coconut. The fibers are extremely stiff, resistant to moisture and the elements, and resistant to abrasion. In combination, these features support the use of coir fibers in walk-off or entrance mats (see Figure 23.11, p. 367).

Cotton

Cotton fibers are extremely important for both the interior textile industry and the apparel industry. Some 57 percent of interior products, including toweling, curtains, draperies and linings, upholstery fabric, beddings, and tabletop accessories, are composed of cotton.[1]

The polymer chains within cotton fibers are grouped into tightly knit bundles called **fibrils**. The fibrils spiral at an angle of 30 degrees to the long axis of the fiber, causing the twisted configuration shown in Figure 3.2b. The twists deflect incident light rays, giving the fiber a matte luster. The fiber has a hollow core, known as the **lumen**, that becomes smaller as the fiber grows and matures.

Cotton fibers are seed fibers that grow from the surface of seeds held in the bolls or tops of the cotton plant. The fibers emerge from the seed and fill the boll, which opens to reveal thousands of fine fibers. As the fiber dries, it collapses into a "kidney bean" form (Figure 3.2b). **Ginning** separates the fibers from the seeds, and the fibers are sorted prior to dyeing or yarn production.

Among the variables used in sorting cotton are staple length, color, and fiber fineness. **Sea Island cotton**, originally grown off the coast of Georgia, is up to 2½ inches in length. **Egyptian cotton**, which originated in the Nile Valley, is up to 1½ inches in length. **Pima cotton**, grown in the American southwest, is fine and up to 1⅝ inches long. **Upland cotton** (so-named because it is grown inland in contrast to on an island) has relatively short staples, most of which is ¹³⁄₁₆ inch long. Cotton fibers range from white to light cream to tan in color.

Extremely short fiber ends are removed from the seed surface and shipped for processing into manufactured cellulosic fibers, although this use is decreasing. The seeds yield cottonseed oil, and, subsequently, the seeds are ground into livestock feed.

Cotton is relatively strong, has a soft **hand or handle**, and a pleasing appearance. Unlike wool, cotton lacks strong cross-linking bonds to stabilize the fiber and contribute resilient behavior. To compensate for this, chemical cross-linking resins are used to impart resiliency and wrinkle recovery (see Figure 9.17, p. 145). Cotton has good moisture absorption, is stronger wet than dry, and dries quickly, good features for household and institutional textiles. The fibers have **wickability**, the inherent ability to move moisture by capillary action, as, for example, moving a fluid fuel up a wick to the flame. (This property helps to keep people wearing cotton cool in the summer as the fiber wicks perspiration away from their skin.). Because the twists in the fiber deflect light rays (see Figure 4.1d, p. 45), the fiber has a matte luster. The luster, strength, and moisture absorption of the fiber can be increased with mercerization (see Chapter 9). Because cotton is flammable, it may be desirable or necessary to use a flame-retardant finish.

Jute

Jute is a **bast fiber**, that is, the fibers lay within the stem of the plant. **Retting** is used to separate the fiber bundles in the bark-like covering from the woody core. In the process, moisture (dew or water) and bacteria or chemicals are used to dissolve the binding agents, known as *pectins*. Jute has relatively high moisture absorption and is resistant to microorganisms. It has low elasticity and is stiff. Fabric composed of jute, **burlap**, is used in the construction of upholstered furniture (see Chapter 12), as backings for soft floor coverings (see Figure 22.2a, p. 348), and as components of carpet and rug cushions (see Figure 25.1b,

p. 379). In recent years, supply and delivery problems with jute have encouraged a shift to olefin (polypropylene) fibers in these applications.

Linen

Linen fiber is retrieved from the flax plant, which leads some textile authorities and consumers to use the term *flax fiber* in lieu of *linen fiber*; either is acceptable. Earlier, *linens* described sheets, towels, tablecloths, napkins, and related products composed entirely or primarily of linen fiber. The use of linen fiber in these goods has declined significantly, but many merchandisers and consumers continue to refer to them as linens. Today, linen fiber is used in interior applications that range from upholstery and drapery fabrics to toweling, bedding, and tabletop accessories.

The polymer chains within linen fibers are highly oriented, with the fibrils spiraling at a low angle of five degrees to the long axis of the fiber. Linen has longer polymer chains and a higher level of crystallinity than does cotton, making the fiber stronger but more brittle and less flexible than cotton. The cross-section and surface appearance are said to resemble bamboo. **Line** fibers are extremely long, ranging from 12 inches to more than 24 inches, while **tow** fibers are less than 12 inches long.

Like cotton, flax plants yield more than just fiber. After the flax stalks are harvested by pulling to preserve the full length of the fibers, which extend below ground level, the stalks are bundled and dried. **Rippling**, pulling the tips of the stalks through a coarse metal comb, is used to remove the seeds, which will be processed to retrieve linseed oil. As with jute and such other bast fibers as hemp and ramie, **retting** is used to separate the fiber bundles from the woody core. **Breaking** is used to crumble the rotted core, and **scutching** is used to scrape away the clinging core material. Finally, in **hackling**, the fiber bundles are pulled through rows of metal tines that align the long fibers prior to spinning.

While the relatively high degree of orientation and level of crystallinity contribute high fiber strength, they also make the fiber somewhat brittle. Linen has extremely low elongation, low flexibility, and low abrasion resistance; the last-named property is a problem, especially when fabrics of linen fibers are rubbed while bent or folded as is the case with tablecloths and napkins that are repeatedly folded on the same crease line

Figure 3.4 Linen fiber napkin showing splits as a result of edge abrasion.

for storage (Figure 3.4). The extremely low resiliency of fabrics composed of linen can be improved with cross-linking resins which give the fibers "memory" for the flat, nonwrinkled state and make ironing an option (see Figure 9.17, p. 145). Linen has relatively high moisture absorption, is quick drying, and produces no lint, all properties that support its use in dish towels. At the same time, the rough hand of the fiber precludes its use in bath towels.

Mineral Fiber

Formerly, one mineral fiber, **asbestos**, was used in such interior applications as insulation around pipes and in walls and ceilings. Although asbestos is fireproof and offers a wide margin of safety in the event of fire, its use has been dropped because the fiber is a known carcinogen.

Natural Fiber Engineering

With natural fibers, appearance and performance engineering must be accomplished by working with already-formed fibers having a given set of inherent properties. Thus, converters, not fiber suppliers, are generally responsible for altering the inherent characteristics of these fibers. While some treatments, such as the application of moth-repellent agents and cross-linking resins, produce chemical changes within the fibers, they are nonetheless introduced during conversion of the greige goods. This work is discussed in Chapter 9.

Manufactured Fibers

Currently, three major groups of manufactured fibers are produced. These include the cellulosic fibers, the noncellulosic fibers, and the mineral fibers. As shown in Table 3.1, not all fibers that have been invented continue to be available. Among those no longer produced in the United States are triacetate, azlons, anidex, lastrile, nytril, and vinal. Some of these fibers may be manufactured overseas and imported into the domestic market.

Production

Virtually all manufactured fibers are produced in this sequence:

obtain fiber-forming substances → form polymer solutions → incorporate polymer additives → extrude and solidify filaments → draw → heat set

For manufactured fibers, the chemist becomes responsible for production at the monomer stage, even when nature provides the monomers and polymers.

Obtaining Fiber-forming Substances

Most fiber-forming substances are obtained by one of three techniques: extract them from fibrous materials, synthesize them from nonfibrous natural materials, and combine inorganic compounds.

Extracting Cellulosic Polymers To produce rayon, acetate, and lyocell fibers, the chemist extracts cellulosic material from such things as wood chips and cotton linters. Although both materials are fibrous, wood fibers lack the flexibility needed for textile processing and end-use applications and linters are too short to spin into quality yarns. As noted earlier, the use of linters has declined in recent years.

Synthesizing Monomers To produce polyester, nylon, acrylic, olefin, and other noncellulosic fibers, the chemist must first synthesize the monomers from such nonfibrous natural materials as natural gas, oil, and coal. Subsequently, the monomers are polymerized in vessels resembling pressure cookers. During this step of the process, the chemist can often control the **degree of polymerization**, that is, the extent to which the monomers link to form polymer chains. When high strength and abrasion resistance are needed, for example, the chemist will form longer chains.

Combining Inorganic Compounds Manufactured mineral fibers, including glass and metal fibers, are inorganic fibers. Glass fibers are formed by heating silica sand, limestone, and other compounds until they fuse and liquefy; distinctive fiber-forming units are not produced. The resulting solution is normally converted into marbles that can be inspected for clarity. Today, glass fibers have diminished use because of the weight and relatively low flexibility.

True metal fibers are made from such substances as gold, silver, copper, and stainless steel. The expense of gold and silver, of course, precludes their widespread use; other structures have been developed to simulate their appearance.

Forming Polymer Solutions

The second step in the production of manufactured fibers is the formation of a solution of the fiber-forming substance. In some cases, a solvent is used to dissolve the polymer compound; in other cases, heat is used to melt the substance.

Incorporating Additives

After the polymer solution is formed, the producer may incorporate **additives** to engineer specific properties. Such additives include dye pigments for superior colorfastness, optical brighteners to improve apparent whiteness and brightness, ultraviolet absorbers to minimize light degradation, flame-retardant agents to reduce flammability, delusterants to reduce light reflectance and hide accumulated soil, and antistatic agents to increase electrical conductivity.

Extruding and Solidifying Filaments

Filaments are formed in a mechanical spinning operation. This type of spinning should not be confused with yarn spinning, the combining of staple-length fibers into textile yarn structures.

The spinning operation involves the extrusion of the polymer solution through a device called a **spinneret**. As schematized in Figure 3.5, a spinneret is similar to a shower head. In the same manner as pressure forces water through a shower head, pressure forces the polymer solution through the minute openings in the spinneret.

Figure 3.5 Spinneret device for spinning manufactured fibers. *Courtesy of Kosa.*

The openings in spinnerets are often no more than a few ten-thousandths of an inch in diameter, but their size can be varied to produce finer or coarser filaments. This enables the producer to regulate the flexibility of the filaments, to increase or decrease the area that the filaments will cover, and to control the amount of surface area per unit of volume the filaments present for soil adhesion. In some spinning operations, the shape of the apertures is designed to produce filaments with specific cross-sectional shapes.

Four basic spinning techniques are used to extrude and solidify filaments: wet spinning, solvent spinning, dry spinning, and melt spinning.

Wet Spinning   In **wet spinning,** a solvent is used to dissolve the polymer. The solution is extruded through the spinneret into an acidic, aqueous bath where the solvent is extracted and the extruded strands coagulate or harden. Wet spinning is used in the production of rayon and some acrylic and spandex fibers.

Solvent Spinning   **Solvent spinning** is similar to wet spinning in that a solvent is used to dissolve the polymer and the solution is extruded through a spinneret into a fluid bath. The bath, however, is not water based; it is a solvent that is recovered for continued use. Solvent spinning is used in the production of lyocell, a relatively new cellulosic fiber.

Dry Spinning   In **dry spinning**, a highly volatile solvent is used to dissolve the polymer compound, producing the spinning solution. The solution is extruded through a spinneret into a warm air chamber where the solvent evaporates, solidifying the fine filaments. Dry spinning is used in the production of acetate, triacetate, and some acrylic, modacrylic, spandex, and vinyon fibers.

Melt Spinning   In **melt spinning**, heat is used to melt the polymer, producing the liquid spinning *dope*. The liquid is extruded through the spinneret into a cool air chamber where the filaments harden as they cool. Variations in aperture shapes are often used in melt spinning as the filaments retain the shape of the openings. Melt spinning is used for the production of polyester, nylon, olefin, and glass fibers.

Drawing

Because most extruded filaments are disordered, they must be drawn or stretched to increase the orientation of their polymer chains and their degree of interior order. The drawing operation may be carried out by the fiber producer or by the throwster.

Drawing lengthens the filaments and reduces their diameters, aligning the chains and causing them to pack more closely. These changes increase the likelihood that crystalline regions will result from extensive lateral bonding. As the degree of interior order increases, there are parallel increases in strength and stiffness and decreases in extensibility and the rate at which such substances as water, dye, and finishing agents will be absorbed. Producers develop an appropriate balance among these properties by controlling the extent of drawing, always limiting the operation to avoid producing a totally oriented and crystallized arrangement.

Drawing or stretching an extruded filament introduces strain within the fiber, like that created within an elastic band when it is stretched. If an unstabilized drawn filament were exposed to conditions such as water and heat that encourage the release of this imposed strain, the polymer chains would relax, reverting back to the undrawn, amorphous arrangement. This would be accompanied by a shortening of the fiber, a reaction like that of an elastic band returning to its original length after the stretching force releases it. In order to prevent this interior relaxation and loss of length, manufacturers generally stabilize drawn filaments by exposing them to controlled amounts of heat.

Heat Setting

Heat can be used to stabilize or set **thermoplastic or heat-sensitive fibers**—fibers that soften and shrink when exposed to a controlled amount of heat, and melt when exposed to an excessive amount of heat. With the exception of rayon, lyocell, and the high-temperature resistant aramid and novoloid fibers, most manufactured fibers are thermoplastic.

In the **heat setting** operation, the fiber is heated to its **glass transition temperature**. At this temperature, lateral bonds within the fiber are disturbed and the polymer chains can shift their positions. In order to prevent excessive shrinkage, the heated fiber is held under some tension. As the fiber cools, new bonds form to "lock" the polymer chains into their new position, stabilizing the length of the filament.

Heat setting will be postponed until the yarn stage when the filaments are to be given a two- or three-dimensional crimped or curled configuration. It will be postponed until the greige good stage when a three-dimensional, embossed design is planned, or when the converter intends to improve the alignment of the yarns and stabilize the dimensions of the fabric. Whenever heat setting is performed, it must be carried out at approximately 50 °F higher than the temperatures that may be encountered later in processing, laundering, or ironing. Exposure to temperatures higher than those used for heat setting will overcome the initial set and stability of the textile item.

Cellulosic Fibers

In the 1800s and early 1900s, chemists eagerly sought to invent a fiber to substitute for the luxurious but costly silk. Early tries included a fibrous but explosive combination of cellulose and nitrogen. Subsequently, chemists created an **artificial silk** in the late 1800s, and the fibers were commercially produced in the United States in 1910. Because of negative connotations associated with the term "artificial," fiber producers wanted to discontinue its use, and the name *rayon* was coined and used in the mid-1920s. Further work resulted in two additional cellulose-based fibers, **acetate** and **triacetate**, being introduced to consumers in 1924. The production of triacetate fibers in the United States, however, was discontinued in the mid-1980s. More recently, in the early 1990s, a fourth cellulosic fiber, **lyocell**, was created.

Acetate

The Federal Trade Commission defines acetate as "a manufactured fiber in which the fiber-forming substance is cellulose acetate. Where not less than 92 percent of the hydroxyl groups are acetylated, the term *triacetate* may be used."

Production of acetate begins with cellulose, generally from wood, reacting with acetic acid and acetic anhydride. These compounds replace hydroxyl units in the cellubiose units, resulting in secondary, or cellulose, acetate. Because these acid compounds alter or modify the composition of the extracted anhydrous glucose chains, these fibers are often referred to as cellulose-based, derivative cellulosic, or modified cellulosic fibers. The fibers are dry spun.

Fabrics of acetate have high drapability and the look and feel of silk, but are more reasonably priced. A major problem is **gasfastness**. With exposure to such gaseous pollutants or air contaminants as oxides of nitrogen or sulfur, acetate dyed with disperse dyestuffs permanently changes color: blue turns pink, brown becomes yellowish, and green converts to a reddish hue. This unsightly problem, known as **fume or gas fading**, can be prevented with solution dyeing (see Chapter 8). Fume fading is an especially important consideration for such interior textile products as drapery and upholstery fabrics. Should the original color of such items be lost, the harmony of the interior would be destroyed, necessitating an unplanned, costly, and disruptive replacement.

Acetate was the first manufactured fiber that was thermoplastic or heat sensitive. Although heat setting can be used, its use is restricted to preserve high flexibility and drapability. Consumers must be cautious with ironing temperatures to avoid melting the fibers.

Lyocell

When fabrics of lyocell fiber were first introduced, they were marketed as a rayon fiber. In 1996, however, the Federal Trade Commission defined lyocell as "a manufactured fiber composed of solvent-spun cellulose." Lyocell fibers are derived from the wood of the eucalyptus tree. The fibers are pure cellulose, like cotton, and have a degree of polymerization that is higher than that of rayon but lower than that of cotton. The fibers are strong, absorbent, and have a pleasing hand. Consumers may be familiar with the tradename used with the first domestically marketed lyocell fiber, Tencel®, which is owned by Acordis Cellulosic Fibers (formerly Courtalds Fibers, Inc.).

Rayon

According to the Federal Trade Commission, rayon is "a manufactured fiber composed of regenerated cellulose, as well as manufactured fibers composed of regenerated cellulose in which substituents have replaced not more than 15 percent of the hydroxyl groups." Rayon fibers may be a conventional type (e.g., viscose or cuprammonium), or an improved type (e.g., medium or high strength or high wet modulus [HWM]). The conventional cuprammonium rayons are no longer produced in the United States.

The basic wet spinning process has been continuously used for the production of conventional viscose rayon fibers since the 1940s. The term *viscose* comes from the viscous, syrup-like polymer solution formed. In order to compete more effectively in the fiber market, rayon fiber producers have altered the viscose process, including the spinning operation, to produce improved fibers with higher strength and/or a higher wet elastic modulus. Fabrics made of the HWM fibers resist deformation under humid or wet conditions, exhibiting better dimensional stability than the conventional types, and can be laundered.

Conventional viscose rayon fibers have relatively low strength and poor dimensional stability, properties requiring that dry cleaning be used. The fibers are soft, absorbent, and drapable, and, because they have the luster and sheen so prized with silk, they are often used in lieu of the more expensive fiber. Rayon is used in curtain and drapery fabrics, upholstery fabrics, table linens, and blankets. It also is used in such window treatment trimmings as cords and galloons.

Noncellulosic Fibers

Noncellulosic fibers are derived from such materials as natural gas, oil, and coal. Because of the initial synthesis of the monomers, the term *synthetic* was formerly applied to these fibers. Negative connotations are sometimes associated with this term, however, and its use has diminished. Today, the term *noncellulosic* is widely used in reference to this group of manufactured fibers. Use of this term is limited to this group of manufactured fibers; it does not include such noncellulosic fibers as wool, silk, glass, and metal fibers.

Acrylic

Acrylic fibers are defined by the Federal Trade Commission as "a manufactured fiber in which the fiber-forming substance is any long-chain synthetic polymer composed of at least 85% by weight of acrylonitrile units,"

$$(-CH_2-CH-)$$
$$|$$
$$CH$$

The fibers are derived from elements taken from natural gas, air, water, and petroleum. After synthesis of the monomers, the polymer solution is formed, additives are included, and the filaments are dry or wet spun.

Acrylic fibers are prized for their ability to be engineered to resemble wool. Here, the more economical manufactured fiber offers the convenience and cost-savings of laundering rather than dry cleaning; an inherent resistance to moths, carpet beetles, and the outdoor elements; and superior resistance to the damaging rays in sunlight. These various properties support the use of acrylic in warm, lightweight blankets that can be laundered. They also support the use of acrylic in carpet and rugs, curtains and draperies, and as awnings and coverings for outdoor furniture (Figure 3.6). Foamed acrylic is also applied as a coating to the back of drapery fabric (see Figure 17.30, p. 294).

Aramid

The Federal Trade Commission defines aramid as "a manufactured fiber in which the fiber-forming substance is a long-chain synthetic aromatic polyamide in which at least 85% of the amide linkages are attached directly to two aromatic rings." Because these fibers have high temperature and flame resistance, they are increasingly used

Figure 3.6 Area rug and upholstery fabric composed of acrylic fiber. *Courtesy of Drexel Heritage Furnishings, Inc.*

in aircraft upholstery and carpet. The relatively high stiffness, however, precludes their widespread use in interior furnishings.

Modacrylic

The Federal Trade Commission definition of modacrylic is "a manufactured fiber in which the fiber-forming substance is any long-chain synthetic polymer composed of

less than 85% but at least 35% by weight of acrylonitrile units." Thus, a significant portion of the fiber, from 15 percent to 65 percent, is a second monomer or **copolymer**. Such compounds as vinyl chloride, vinylidene chloride, or vinyl bromide are used.

Modacrylic fibers are resilient, abrasion resistant, quick drying, flame resistant, and heat sensitive. Their relatively high flame resistance supports their use in scatter rugs and in window covering fabrics for such commercial interiors as theaters, hospitals, schools, and restaurants. Their thermoplasticity allows them to be shaped and heat set, as in the case of wigs. It also allows them to be used effectively in simulated fur for apparel and upholstery applications.

Nylon

Nylon fibers were the first truly synthesized manufactured fibers. They were unceremoniously introduced into the consumer market in 1938 as a replacement for boar's bristles in toothbrushes. Thereafter, they were introduced in sheer hosiery, as a replacement for silk and rayon. With the outbreak of World War II, however, nylon was quickly withdrawn for use in war material.

Nylon may be produced with a single monomer or with two monomers. Nylon 6, for example, is manufactured from a single monomer, caprolactam: the "6" indicates that the compound has six carbon atoms. Nylon 6,6, the more common copolymer type manufactured in the United States, is made from adipic acid and hexamethylene diamine, each having six carbon atoms. After the monomers are synthesized from petroleum or natural gas, air, and water, they are polymerized and melt spun, drawn, and heat set.

Because nylon is melt spun, the fibers retain the shape of the spinneret holes, making it possible to engineer selected features into the fibers. These features range from a change in hand to a change in luster and soil-hiding ability.

Drawing and heat setting are controlled to engineer the desired amount of strength, elongation, abrasion resistance, and resiliency. The strength and abrasion resistance of nylon fibers support their use in carpet and rugs and upholstery fabrics (Figure 3.7). Curtains, bedspreads, and scatter rugs made of nylon are easily laundered and retain their dimensional stability and resiliency. The low moisture absorbency of the fibers gives quick drying items but encourages static buildup.

Figure 3.7 Upholstery fabric composed of nylon fiber. *Courtesy of Hickory Hill Furniture Corp.*

Olefin

At this point, it may be useful to highlight the definition of olefin fibers. The name *olefin* is assigned to "a manufactured fiber in which the fiber-forming substance is any long-chain synthetic polymer composed of at least 85% by weight of ethylene, propylene, or other olefin units."

It should be noted that the frequently used terms *ethylene* and *propylene* identify specific olefin units; they are not generic names. Producers often pair ethylene or propylene with olefin, or even incorrectly use the terms alone, to indicate the presence or absence of ethylene units. Ethylene compounds melt at relatively low temperatures, too low to permit their use in virtually any textile furnishings.

Olefin fibers are generally melt spun and solution dyed. Like cotton, the fibers have wickability. They are chosen for both indoor and outdoor carpet and upholstery fabric because of their abrasion resistance, and their resistance to rot and weather adds to their success as a fiber in outdoor carpet (Figure 3.8). Their heat sensitivity requires careful temperature control in drying and ironing, while their extremely low moisture absorption makes olefin products quick drying.

Polyester

Although polyester has been available in the domestic market only since 1953, its importance has grown dramatically for both the apparel and interior textile industries, excluding the soft floor coverings market where nylon is dominant. The Federal Trade Commission defines polyester as "a manufactured fiber in which the fiber-forming substance is any long-chain synthetic polymer composed of at least 85% by weight of an ester of a substituted aromatic carboxylic acid, including but not restricted to substituted terephthalic units,"

$$p(-R-O-\underset{\underset{O}{\|}}{C}-C_6H_4-\underset{\underset{O}{\|}}{C}-O-)$$

Figure 3.8 Sofa upholstery fabrics composed of olefin fiber. *Courtesy of Hickory Hill Furniture Corp.*

"and parasubstituted hydroxy-benzoate units,"

$$p(-R-O-C_6H_4-\underset{\underset{O}{\|}}{C}-O-)$$

Thus, polyester fibers are copolymers, and like nylon and olefin, are melt spun, giving the producer the ability to engineer fiber properties by controlling the shape and form of the fibers. With drawing and heat setting, the strength, elongation, abrasion resistance, resiliency, and dimensional stability of the fiber can also be controlled.

Polyester is used in soft floor coverings, curtain and drapery fabrics and linings, bedding, wall coverings, and table linens. The fibers are frequently blended with cotton or rayon for use in household and institutional textiles, including toweling.

Saran

Saran was first introduced into the commercial market in 1941. The Federal Trade Commission defines saran as "a manufactured fiber in which the fiber-forming substance is any long-chain synthetic polymer composed of at least 80% by weight of vinylidene chloride units,"

$$(-CH_2-CCl_2-)$$

As shown in Table 4.2, saran is a relatively heavy fiber. The fiber also has a relatively low softening point (Table 4.8). With its resistance to chemicals, water, mildew, and sunlight, the fiber is frequently and successfully used for the webbing and coverings on patio chairs. It also is used for fabrics installed in public transportation vehicles.

Spandex

Spandex is defined by the Federal Trade Commission as "a manufactured fiber in which the fiber-forming substance is a long-chain synthetic polymer comprised of at least 85% of a segmented polyurethane." These elastomeric fibers are widely appreciated for their high elongation, high elastic recovery, and high holding power in such apparel items as swimwear, girdles, and sock tops. In recent years, their superior elasticity supports their use in upholstery fabric that is applied to curved furniture forms.

Manufactured Fiber Engineering

For more than two decades, the primary focus of manufactured fiber research has been on fiber engineering, not on fiber invention. This work has resulted in the refinement of production procedures and the development or identification of polymer additives that can produce fiber variants. Technological advances are often described as belonging to a particular "generation" of manufactured fiber development.

Fiber Variants

A **fiber variant** is chemically related to other fibers in its generic class, but it is distinguished by one or more features. Among several polyester fibers, for example, one variant may have a round cross-sectional shape, a relatively large diameter, and a comparatively high degree of orientation; another may have a pentalobal cross-sectional shape, be inherently flame resistant, and dull; and yet another may be inherently antistatic, have a relatively small diameter, and be bright.

The availability of hundreds of fiber variants enables end-product manufacturers to be highly selective when they choose fibers. In turn, this helps them to offer products that conform closely to the selection criteria of contemporary consumers.

Generations of Manufactured Fiber Development

Members of the industry recognize generations or levels of manufactured fiber development. Each new designation has been used to distinguish major scientific breakthroughs from earlier achievements. Such distinctions were used extensively in the promotion of noncellulosic fiber variants, especially those intended for use in soft floor coverings.

First Generation The first level of manufactured fiber development is considered to be the level of invention. Following the invention and commercial production of the cellulosic fibers, research chemist Wallace Carothers developed the foundations of high polymer chemistry. His pioneering work led directly to the development of nylon. As knowledge of polymer science grew, fiber chemists manufactured such other fibers as acrylics, modacrylics, olefins, polyesters, spandexes, and vinyons.

Second Generation The second phase of manufactured fiber development saw the refinement of the several general groups of fibers. Their aesthetic features were enhanced and their performance properties improved. Some of the technologies used included modification of fiber cross sections for soil hiding, alteration of fiber diameters for controlled stiffness, and inclusion of such polymer additives as delusterants, dye pigments, antistatic agents, and flame-retardant compounds. Experimentation and evaluation provided greater understanding of the effects of varied amounts of drawing on fiber performance. Heat-setting procedures were perfected and used to improve resiliency and dimensional stability. Texturing methods were developed to introduce multidimensional configurations to smooth, straight filaments, enabling producers to control such things as covering power, resiliency, pill formation, and fiber cohesiveness.

Third Generation   The third generation included such developments as the production of bicomponent fibers, biconstituent fibers, and blended filaments. **Bicomponent fibers** are made by combining two generically similar compounds into one filament; **biconstituent fibers** are made by combining two generically dissimilar compounds into one filament; and **blended filaments** are made by combining two generically dissimilar filaments into a single yarn structure immediately after extrusion. Other developments of this generation included the processing techniques that enable producers to offer manufactured fibers having the aesthetic features of natural fibers.

Fourth and Advanced Generations   In the fourth and advanced generations, fiber technology became increasingly sophisticated. Fibers were engineered to exhibit specific service-related characteristics, many of which were appropriate for a limited assortment of products. Fiber cross-sectional shapes, for example, underwent further modification to provide soil shedding as well as better soil hiding and controlled levels of luster in soft floor coverings. Innovative filament compositions and designs very nearly overcame static problems. Newer polymer additives provided inherent stain and soil repellency. Fibers having hollow or tubular shapes provided higher insulation without added weight. The inventions of the high-temperature and flame-resistant aramid and novoloid fibers were other developments of the fourth or advanced generation.

Developments in fiber engineering continue today. Numbered generations, however, are not widely used in marketing. On the other hand, such other marketing tools as trade names and logos are extensively used for purposes of promotion and marketing (see Chapter 10).

Summary

All textile fibers have a similar physical form; they are relatively long and thin. But there are numerous differences among fibers—their molecular arrangements, cross-sectional shapes, longitudinal configurations, and chemical compositions. Differences in chemical composition serve as the basis for classifying fibers into useful generic groups or classes.

The synthesis and production of all fibers includes the combining of atoms into monomers, the linking of monomers into polymers, and the forming of a fine, usable strand. With natural fibers this sequence is carried out without direct human involvement, but subsequently inherent characteristics may be altered during fabric conversion. With manufactured fibers the sequence of synthesis and production is controlled by the fiber chemist and producer, who can introduce specific characteristics during production. Such fiber engineering has become increasingly sophisticated, enabling the producer to offer fibers that exhibit the aesthetic and performance features preferred or required by residential and commercial consumers.

Key Terms

acetate
additives
alpha amino acids
amorphous

anhydrous glucose
artificial silk
asbestos
bast fiber

bicomponent fibers

biconstituent fibers

blended filaments

boiling off

breaking

burlap

carbonizing

cellubiose unit

COM

common or generic names

copolymer

crystalline

cystine

degree of polymerization

document fabrics

drawing

dry spinning

Egyptian cotton

fiber variant

fibrils

fibroin

fume or gas fading

gasfastness

ginning

glass transition temperature

hackling

hand or handle

heat setting

keratin

line

lumen

lyocell

melt spinning

monomers

noil

oriented

Pima cotton

polymer additives

polymers

raw silk

reeling

retting

rippling

scutching

sea island cotton

seed fibers

sericin

solvent spinning

spinneret

tendered

thermoplastic or heat sensitive fibers

throwing

tinting

tow

triacetate

upland cotton

usable fiber form

wet spinning

wickability

Review Questions

1. Explain how generic classes are defined. Are there similarities among fibers within the same class? Are there differences, as well?

2. When will the burning test for fiber identification be useful? What is one distinctive reaction that will support the identification of protein fibers?

3. What is one distinctive reaction that will support the identification of a cellulosic fiber? To visually distinguish between cotton and rayon or lyocell, what features should be considered?

4. What is one distinctive reaction that will support the identification of a thermoplastic fiber? Name a thermoplastic fiber that smells like celery when undergoing the burning test. Name a thermoplastic fiber that smells like hot vinegar.

5. Explain the meaning of *self-extinguishing fiber*. How could a self-extinguishing fiber provide a margin of safety in the event it was ignited?

6. Explain the influence of polymer chain orientation on fiber strength. How can the level of orientation be increased?

7. Identify some textural features of textile fibers that affect their hand, their luster, and their ability to adhere to one another.

8. Which fibers occur naturally in staple length? in filament length? Are manufactured fibers produced in staple or filament length?

9. Arrange the following in the sequence of production: polymer chains, atoms, usable fibers, and monomer. What is the responsibility of the natural fiber supplier in this production? the role of the manufactured fiber producer?

10. Cite both positive and negative properties of wool.

11. Why is silk not vulnerable to moth attack (as long as the fiber is clean)?

12. What is responsible for the twisted configuration of cotton fibers? Does the twist affect any features of the fiber?

13. Identify properties of cotton that support its use in household and institutional textiles.

14. Distinguish among the following terms: *flax plant, flax fiber, linen fiber,* and *linens.*

15. Why has the use of asbestos been discontinued?

16. Explain how properties are engineered in fabrics made of natural fibers.

17. Trace the production sequence of manufactured fibers. Explain how fiber engineering is accomplished during the production.

18. Are there similarities between wet spinning and solvent spinning?

19. Explain the drawing operation and why the fiber producer carefully controls the process.

20. How does heat setting benefit the consumer? Are there concomitant challenges?

21. Cotton, rayon, and lyocell are cellulosic fibers, each having the same anhydrous glucose monomer. Why aren't rayon and lyocell called natural cellulosic fibers?

22. What advantages do acrylic fibers offer over wool fibers?

23. What fiber features can be engineered by using a particular shape for the spinneret openings? Which fibers retain the shape of the openings?

24. What properties support the use of olefin and saran fibers in outdoor textile applications?

25. Summarize the achievements in each "generation" of manufactured fiber development.

Note

1. Textile Economics Bureau, Inc., *Textile Organon*, Vol. 69, No. 10, October 1998, 176.

4

Fiber Properties

Aesthetic Features
- *Optical Properties*
- *Tactile Characteristics*

Mechanical Properties
- *Abrasion Resistance*
- *Covering Power*
- *Elasticity*
- *Resiliency*
- *Stiffness*
- *Soil Reduction*
- *Soil Shedding*
- *Strength*

Chemical Properties
- *Chemical Resistance*
- *Fire-related Fiber Properties*
- *Heat-related Properties*
- *Microbe Resistance*
- *Moisture-related Properties*
- *Moth Resistance*
- *Soil Repellency*
- *Static Propensity*
- *Sunlight Resistance*

This chapter covers the aesthetic, mechanical, and chemical properties of fibers that influence the selection and serviceability of all interior textile products. It should be noted that all fiber properties may be altered in yarn production, fabric manufacturing, color application, and finishing. Some changes are negative and unavoidable; others are positive and intentional. In any event, the properties exhibited by a fiber in finished fabrics and end products may differ from those that characterize the fiber prior to yarn production.

Aesthetic Features

The aesthetic features of textile fibers—their appearance and tactile characteristics—are products of their external structural features. Their appearance also depends on the influence of natural colorants and selected polymer additives.

Optical Properties

Fabric and end-producers recognize that color, whether it is natural or added, is a critically important consumer selection criterion. They also recognize that consumers generally prefer brightness to dullness and sheen over shine. To engineer the preferred **optical properties**, producers have developed various cross-sectional shapes and selectively add colorants, delusterants, and optical brighteners to the polymer solution.

Color

Virtually all natural fibers have some **inherent color**. As noted in Chapter 3, wool fibers are black, gray, tan, yellow, or off-white. Silk filaments vary from yellow to off-white, linen fibers range from brown to tan to cream, and cotton fibers are markedly to slightly off-white. When fibers are to be dyed or printed, natural colors are usually removed or neutralized to prevent their interaction with applied colors.

When fiber producers incorporate **dye pigments** into polymer solutions, the **colorants** become an integral part of the extruded and solidified filaments. Solution-dyed fibers ordinarily exhibit a relatively high degree of color-fastness.

Luster

The **luster** of textile fibers depends on the quantity of light waves reflected from their surfaces and the direction in which these waves are traveling. Luster is determined by such features as **cross-sectional shape**, **longitudinal configuration**, **surface texture**, and the presence of **delusterants**. Figure 4.1 shows that fiber surfaces reflect some

Figure 4.1 Effects of external features and delusterant particles on fiber luster.

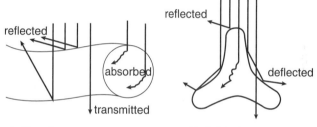

a) Manufactured fiber having a round shape and smooth surface

b) Trilobal with marked indentations

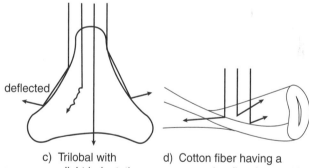

c) Trilobal with slight indentations

d) Cotton fiber having a somewhat flat shape with twisted configuration

e) Wool fiber having overlapping scales and a three-dimensional crimp

f) Manufactured fiber having a round shape, a smooth surface, and delusterant particles

a) cross-sectional view

b) longitudinal view

Figure 4.2 Photomicrograph of Ultron® nylon with a slightly concave trilobal cross section. *Courtesy of Solutia Inc., Fibers Division.*

portions of incident light waves, transmit other portions, and absorb still other portions. Fibers with round cross sections and smooth surfaces typically reflect large quantities of rays in one direction (Figure 4.1a); they produce shiny brightness like that produced by glass tree ornaments. To reduce the shine while preserving luster and brightness, fiber engineers created concave shapes, some with marked indentations (Figure 4.1b) and some with slight ones (Figure 4.1c). Light waves striking the indented surfaces are scattered or reflected in several directions, producing sheen, not shine. Deep indentations and prominent lobes create the same unidirectional reflection that characterizes smooth, round shapes. Fibers with irregularly shaped cross sections and rough surfaces typically reflect light rays in several directions; less surface luster appears.

Fibers having crimped or twisted configurations will show reduced levels of reflected light. Although the flat shape of cotton should produce high reflectance, the natural twist interrupts the reflection of rays (Figure 4.1d), giving fabrics composed of cotton low luster. The surface scales and three-dimensional crimp of wool fibers scatter incident light rays (Figure 4.1e) to develop a subdued, matte luster. Manufactured fiber producers often strive to create such a soft luster. In this effort, producers may add **titanium dioxide** (TiO_2) particles to the polymer solution. Light rays striking the minute, white particles are scattered or deflected, dulling the fiber (Figure 4.1f).

Incorporating too much delusterant, however, results in a muddy or chalky luster.

Some producers have combined a slightly concave, trilobal cross section with a small quantity of delusterant to simulate the natural luster of wool. A photomicrograph of such a fiber is shown in Figure 4.2.

Apparent Whiteness and Brightness

Optical brighteners are used to overcome the dulling effects produced by the accumulation of soil and soil-detergent mixtures that normally result from improper laundering. Brighteners are **fluorescent compounds**; whether they are incorporated as an integral part of manufactured fibers or adsorbed onto exterior fiber surfaces, they increase reflectance by the same mechanism. Incident ultraviolet rays excite brightener molecules, causing them to reflect more light waves or fluoresce. In effect, brighteners convert invisible wavelengths to visible wavelengths, increasing the **apparent**, not the actual, **whiteness or brightness** of fibers and fabrics. The effectiveness of most brighteners depends on the quantity of ultraviolet rays incident on the textile surface.

Soil Hiding

Residential and commercial consumers are extremely critical of textile floor coverings that rapidly accumulate high levels of soil. To overcome such problems and satisfy consumers, fiber chemists and engineers have manipulated fiber cross-sectional shapes and experimented with different polymer additives. Their efforts have been directed to the development of three properties: soil hiding, soil shedding, and soil repellency. Soil shedding and soil repellency are discussed later in this chapter.

Soil hiding is the ability of a fiber or coloration to hide or camouflage dirt. The carpet will look cleaner than it is, in contrast to **soil magnification,** in which fibers magnify accumulated soil and the surface looks dirtier than it is. The peculiar problem of soil magnification occurs when soil particles reflect incident waves through round, nondelustered fibers (Figure 4.3a). Industry researchers first sought to overcome this problem by adding delusterant compounds (Figure 4.3b). As the amount of delusterant was increased, the soil-hiding power also increased, but an undesirable muddiness would at some point become apparent in the luster. Researchers then created various non-round cross-sectional shapes that produce an acceptable level of soil hiding as well as the preferred luster and sheen.

Light waves are diffused from a multilobal design (see Figures 4.1b and c). Although deeply indented or "leggy" shapes effectively hide soil, their highly concave sides provide crevices or spaces where dirt particles can become entrapped, making their removal more difficult. The modified trilobal design illustrated in Figure 4.1c avoids this problem.

An innovative approach to soil hiding is the introduction of **microscopic voids**, also referred to as conduits or tunnels, lengthwise within fibers. The interior voids deflect incident waves, obscuring the appearance of soil. Carpet nylon produced with a rounded-square shape and interior voids is illustrated in Figure 4.3c and that produced with a pentalobal shape and microscopic voids is shown Figure 4.3d.

Tactile Characteristics

The term **hand** or **handle** refers to the tactile characteristics of a textile structure. These characteristics include such things as the perceived temperature and the level of surface smoothness or roughness.

Whether a fabric has pleasant hand or "feel" is a subjective evaluation that often governs consumer selection. This important variable is strongly influenced by the external structural features of the constituent fibers. Fibers with irregularly shaped cross sections, textured surfaces, and three-dimensional forms may feel warm and perhaps harsh or rough. By contrast, fibers with round cross sections, smooth surfaces, and straight, nontextured forms may feel cool and slick when touched.

Mechanical Properties

The mechanical or physical properties of textile fibers are measured in accordance with standard test methods. The test results provide the means for assessing the relative performance of fibers on a number of variables. Several of these performance variables help to determine the use-life characteristics of end products.

Abrasion Resistance

Abrasion resistance is the ability of a textile structure to resist damage and fiber loss by friction. Abrasion may not only diminish the wear-life, it can also cause changes in the textural features and apparent luster of the surface. Abrasion of a soft floor covering can come from the movement of shoe soles, pets, furniture, and equipment across the structure. Abrasive rubbing, especially when coupled with accumulated grit, can cause carpet and rug fibers to rupture, as though they had been sawn by a serrated knife blade. As split fibers are gradually removed, worn and tattered areas develop and expose the backing. This unsightly problem is more likely to develop first in areas where rubbing actions are concentrated, such as on the nosing of stairs and at pivotal points in traffic paths. Because nylon has excellent abrasion resistance, several manufacturers using the fiber are able to offer long-term warranties against significant fiber loss and wear.

Abrasion of bedding and upholstery comes with use as people slide over the surfaces. Similarly, toweling is abraded as it is moved over glassware or skin. Repeated laundering removes the weakened fibers and the fabrics get thinner.

Abrasive forces can cause **pilling** to occur. Here, free fibers and fiber ends are rolled up into minute balls that are unsightly and a nuisance to remove. While pills composed of some staple fibers may be removed by subsequent surface abrasion, those composed of filaments or of strong nylon or polyester staple fibers tend to cling tenaciously.

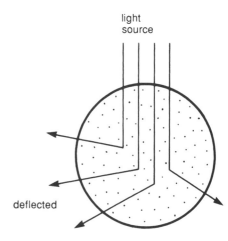

a) soil magnification by transparent, round cross section

b) delustering and soil hiding by delusterant particles

c) soil hiding by voids and a rounded square cross section.
4.3c is Courtesy of E. I. duPont de Nemours & Co.

d) soil hiding by voids and a pentalobal cross section.
4.3d is Courtesy of BASF Corporation Fibers Division.

Figure 4.3 Effects of cross-sectional shape, delusterants, and microscopic voids on soil magnification and soil hiding.

The ability of a fiber to resist abrasion depends largely on its **toughness**, which is determined by the strength and elongation of the fiber. To a large extent, producers can engineer the necessary toughness by controlling the drawing and heat-setting operations used with thermo-plastic fibers. Table 4.1 presents the relative abrasion resistance of selected fibers. The relative abrasion resistance of fibers depends on whether the textile is being abraded while flat, flexed (bent), or folded (edge). Abrasion resistance is markedly affected by yarn and fabric structure.

Table 4.1 Abrasion Resistance of Selected Textile Fibers	
Fiber	**Level of Resistance**
Nylon	Excellent
Olefin	
Polyester	
Acrylic	
Cotton	
Linen	
Rayon	
Wool	
Silk	Poor

Table 4.2 Specific Gravities of Selected Textile Fibers	
Glass	2.50–2.70
Saran	1.68–1.75
Cotton	1.52
Linen	1.52
Rayon	1.50–1.52
Polyester	1.22–1.38
Modacrylic	1.30–1.37
Vinyon	1.37
Wool	1.34
Acetate	1.32
Silk	1.25
Acrylic	1.14–1.19
Nylon	1.14
Olefin (polypropylene)	0.91

Covering Power

Covering power is the ability of a textile structure to cover or conceal an area without undue weight. The effectiveness with which fibers cover a surface depends on structural features—across-sectional shape and longitudinal configuration—and specific gravity.

Fibers having round shapes cover less surface area than do fibers of equal volume with flat configurations. This difference is schematically illustrated in Figure 4.4. Fibers with a natural or engineered crimped or coiled configuration cover more surface area than do straight fibers. The effect is more evident when the multidimensional fibers are grouped into yarn structures (see Figure 5.1, p. 66).

Specific Gravity

In order to obtain maximum cover with minimum weight, a fiber with a low specific gravity should be selected. **Specific gravity** is the **density** (mass or amount of matter per unit of volume) of a fiber relative to that of water at 4 °C, which is 1. Fibers having a specific gravity greater than 1 are heavier than an equal volume of water; those with a specific gravity less than 1 are lighter and would

float on water. Table 4.2 presents the specific gravities of fibers used extensively in interior textile products.

If the diameters of two fibers are equal, the fiber with the lower specific gravity will cover more area with less weight than will the fiber with the higher specific gravity. Covering power is an especially critical variable when sizable amounts of fiber are used in structures designed to cover large areas, like window, wall, and floor coverings.

As shown in Table 4.2, the specific gravity of glass, 2.50–2.70, is higher than that of all other fibers commonly used for interior applications. Thus, window coverings of glass would weigh more than identical fabrics composed of other fibers. For this reason, glass fiber generally has been used in open casements (see Figure 15.3, p. 252).

The weight and cost of textile floor coverings relate to the specific gravity of the fiber used. An analogy can demonstrate how this is so. Drinking straws represent olefin fibers, wooden chopsticks represent nylon fibers, and glass stirring rods represent polyester fibers; these items, with their obvious differences in density, were chosen to reflect the specific gravities of the fibers (see Table 4.2). If equal weights of the three are given, as Figure 4.5 shows, the lowest amount of cover will be provided by the polyester "rods" and the highest amount by the olefin "straws." To develop coverage equal to that of olefin, more or larger nylon and still more or larger polyester fibers would have to be used. Needless to say, the weight of the floor covering would increase in either case, as probably would also its cost; the actual cost difference would depend on the difference in the costs of the fibers at the time of production. As fiber engineers have im-

| **Figure 4.4** Effects of cross-sectional shape on covering power.

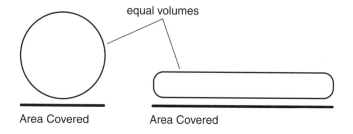

equal volumes

Area Covered   Area Covered

area to be covered

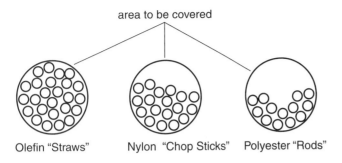

Olefin "Straws"   Nylon "Chop Sticks"   Polyester "Rods"

Figure 4.5 Schematic representation of the effect of specific gravity on covering power.

Nylon
Denier 30

Polyester
Denier 30

Figure 4.6 Effect of fiber density on denier and fiber diameter.

proved the absorption and dyeability and reduced the heat sensitivity of olefin fibers, their use in interior floor coverings has increased.

The relationship between fiber density and denier is partly responsible for the success of nylon over polyester in the face yarn market. Figure 4.6 shows a nylon fiber and a polyester fiber of equal deniers. Manufacturers could produce more carpet—cover more surface area with fewer filaments and less weight—with nylon than with polyester. Increasing the diameter of the polyester to equal that of the nylon would also increase the polyester's weight and cost. Because stiffness increases and resiliency improves as diameters grow larger, it follows that a polyester carpet must be heavier and thus more costly than a nylon carpet to provide the necessary texture retention.

Elasticity

Fiber elasticity includes three performance variables, elastic modulus, elongation, and elastic recovery. Elastic modulus is a fiber's initial resistance to being deformed. Elongation is a fiber's ability to be extended or elongated; elastic recovery is its ability to recover from the extension.

Elastic Modulus

The initial resistance to deformation stress exhibited by a fiber is known as its **elastic modulus**. A fiber may have high initial resistance and then yield readily as the stress load increases. Such a response is typical of spandex fibers and partly accounts for their success in foundation garments and swimwear. The superior elastic modulus of spandex provides the necessary holding power, but the fiber can be extended five to seven times its relaxed length by higher stress loads before rupturing.

Unlike spandex fibers, conventional rayon fibers have a low elastic modulus, especially when they are wet or when the level of humidity is relatively high. Under these conditions, the fibers may readily yield to the stress of their own weight and that of the absorbed moisture and lengthen. This lack of fiber stability would cause the panels in curtains and draperies to sag; when the humidity decreases, the fibers and the fabric would shorten again. This phenomenon, variously termed the *elevator effect*, the *yo-yo effect*, and *hiking*, may be quite pronounced with loosely constructed fabrics. As noted in Chapter 3, rayon fiber producers have engineered high wet modulus (HWM) fibers that resist deformation under humid conditions. Fabrics composed of these fibers will not exhibit the elevator effect, and can be laundered as well.

Elongation

Elongation depends on the internal arrangement and external structural features of fibers. Fibers that are highly oriented and crystallized will display minimal elongation (Figure 4.7a). By contrast, fibers having highly amorphous interiors will tend to exhibit high elongation, with the polymer chains straightening and extending under stress (Figure 4.7b). This molecular arrangement, and high elongation, are characteristic of wool fibers. The molecular arrangement and thus extensibility of most manufactured fibers can be engineered to a great degree by controlling the amount of drawing used in fiber production.

Fibers with a natural or engineered crimp have greater extensibility than do fibers with an essentially straight, nontextured configuration (compare Figures 4.7c and d). For example, the natural waviness of wool augments the extensibility of the amorphous interior. The elongation of cotton derives largely from the unwinding of the natural twist. Linen not only has high orientation and crystallinity but also lacks a twist, and so exhibits extremely low elongation.

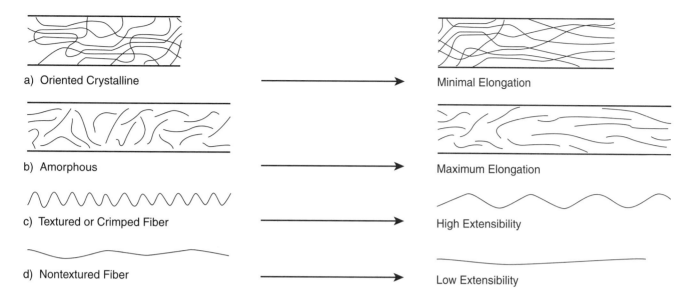

a) Oriented Crystalline → Minimal Elongation

b) Amorphous → Maximum Elongation

c) Textured or Crimped Fiber → High Extensibility

d) Nontextured Fiber → Low Extensibility

Figure 4.7 Effects of molecular arrangement and longitudinal configuration on elongation.

The extensibility of textile fibers is generally measured at the breaking point. In the laboratory, a fiber specimen is held straight, but not stretched, between clamps on a test apparatus. Some equipment used for this work is engineered to exert force and extend the specimen at a constant rate until it ruptures; such machines are known as constant-rate-of-extension (CRE) machines. Other machines apply the load or force at a constant rate; these are called constant-rate-of-load (CRL) machines. Still other machines are designed to move the clamps at a constant rate; these are known as constant-rate-of-traverse (CRT) machines. All these machines may be equipped to record the breaking load or force in grams and the length of the specimen at the point of rupture.

After completion of the test, the elongation of the specimen is calculated and expressed as a percentage of the original relaxed length, using the following formula:

$$\% \text{ elongation at break} = \frac{\text{length stretched} \times 100}{\text{original length}}$$

If, for example, a 3-inch length of fiber ruptured when it was 4 inches long, the percent elongation at break is 33.3. (Note that the length stretched is 1 inch, not 4 inches.) Table 4.3 includes elongation measurements for selected textile fibers.

Table 4.3 Elastic Behavior of Selected Textile Fibers

Fiber	% Elongation at Break	% Elastic Recovery from (X%) Strain
Natural		
Protein		
Wool	25–35	99–100 (2), 63 (20)
Silk	13–31	92 (2), 33 (20)
Cellulose		
Cotton	3–7	74 (2), 45 (5)
Linen	3	65 (2)
Manufactured		
Cellulose-based		
Acetate	23–45	48–65 (4)
Rayon		
(conventional	15–30	82 (2)
Rayon		
(improved)	9–26	95 (2)
Mineral		
Glass	3.1–5.3	100 (2)
Noncellulosic		
Acrylic	34–50	99 (2)
Modacrylic	25–60	100 (1), 55 (10)
Nylon	16–65	100 (5), 99–100 (10)
Olefin		
(polypropylene)	14–8	97–100 (2), 95 (10)
Polyester	12–67	67–92 (2), 33 (10)
Saran	15–25	100 (1), 95 (10)
Spandex	500–700	100 (2), 98 (200)
Vinyon	18	

Elastic Recovery

Elastic recovery measurements indicate how completely a fiber returns to its original length after being strained or elongated. In standard methods of testing, fibers are generally extended 2 percent of their relaxed length, held in the deformed position for 30 seconds, and allowed 1 minute for recovery. In actual use, fibers are normally subjected to greater deformations for longer periods of time.

Fibers having highly disordered interiors typically exhibit an inherent desire to return to their relaxed state. Those having an inherent or heat-stabilized crimp or coil also tend to display better recovery than that shown by noncrimped fibers. Table 4.3 presents the immediate elastic recovery values for several fibers; measurements taken after longer periods would normally show higher recovery.

Resiliency

Resiliency is the ability of a textile structure to recover from deformations other than stretch or elongation. Resilient behavior includes recovery from such deformations as folding, bending, and crumpling, which helps prevent undesirable mussiness and surface wrinkles. Resilient behavior also includes recovery from compression and crushing; a resilient product returns to its original depth after such deformation.

The resiliency of finished fabrics and fillings depends on the behavior of their constituent fibers. If the polymer chains pack closely when the fiber is deformed, new lateral bonds may form and restrict recovery. Such chain packing and bonding is minimized when the polymer chains have large laterally bonded groups, such as those seen in wool. Fibers with relatively strong lateral bonds, such as those present in spandex and wool, and fibers with a natural or heat-set crimp or coil display better recovery. Stiff fibers, with relatively large diameters and multilobal cross sections, offer greater resistance to deformation and exhibit better recovery than do highly flexible fibers.

The resiliency of textile fibers is generally rated in relative terms: excellent, good, fair, and poor. Table 4.4 lists the relative performance of fibers frequently used in interior textile products.

Table 4.4 Resiliency of Selected Textile Fibers

Wool	Excellent
Polyester	Excellent
Nylon	Good
Acrylic	Good
Olefin (polypropylene)	Good
Acetate	Fair
Rayon	Poor
Cotton	Poor
Linen	Poor

In order to overcome the inherently poor resiliency of cellulosic fibers, converters employ chemical cross-linking resins. The use of these finishing compounds is reviewed in Chapter 9.

Stiffness

The degree of **stiffness** or **flexibility** exhibited by fibers directly affects fabric draping quality, which is especially important in curtains and draperies. Consumers and designers generally handle and shake sample fabrics and readymade panels and make subjective evaluations about their drapability or fluidity. Pleats and folds in panels composed of stiff fibers like linen and higher denier glass may not hang freely and evenly, causing the panels to have bows or bulges.

Fiber stiffness also affects the flex abrasion resistance of curtain and drapery fabrics. This is an important property for fabrics that will rub against furniture, walls, window frames, or companion panels as they are repeatedly opened and closed. Because fibers displaying low flexibility and elasticity may split and break when subjected to such stress, it may be advisable to use them in stationary panels or in infrequently opened casements.

Earlier, the high stiffness and low flex abrasion resistance of conventional, high denier glass fibers resulted in a problem known as **fibrillation**, the breaking off of minute slivers of glass from the filaments when they were handled or laundered in an automatic washer. The minute particles were similar to the "angel hair" used in holiday decorations, and caused skin irritation. To minimize the problem, extremely low denier glass fibers are now being manufactured.

Soil Reduction

A physical approach for reducing the quantity of soil accumulated involves the extrusion of fibers with an extra large **denier per filament (dpf)**. The larger diameter covers more carpet surface area so fewer of the filaments are required for carpet production.

Soil Shedding

Continuing the research toward achieving control of soiling problems, a **soil-shedding** carpet fiber was developed. The trilobal fiber has a microrough surface that reduces soil adhesion; the producer has stated that the microridges effectively "tee up" soil for easy shedding or removal. The behavior of soil on this fiber is roughly similar to that of a decal that fails to adhere to a rough surface.

Strength

As explained in Chapter 3, fibers with highly ordered interior arrangements, high degrees of polymerization, and/or longer lengths are generally stronger than shorter fibers with disordered interiors and/or low degrees of polymerization. These variables are givens in natural fibers, but in manufactured fibers, these qualities can be engineered during polymerizing, spinning, drawing, and heat setting.

The relative terms "weak" and "strong" are often used to describe the strength of textile fibers. These assessments are based on measurements obtained through laboratory testing. Machines equipped to record the length of test specimens at the break point are also equipped to record the grams of force or load that caused the rupture. This information is used to calculate a specimen's strength or **breaking tenacity** as the force per unit of **linear density** required to rupture the fine strand. The value is reported as **grams per denier** (g.p.d. or g/den) or **grams per tex** (g.p.t. or g/tex). (Denier and tex indicate weight or mass per unit of length, i.e., linear density. The terms are explained further in Chapter 5.)

The breaking tenacities of several fibers are listed in Table 4.5. Although it is nearly identical to cotton and

Table 4.5 Breaking Tenacities of Selected Textile Fibers

Fiber	Grams/Denier Dry	Wet
Natural		
Protein		
Wool	1.5	1.0
Silk	4.5	3.9
Cellulose		
Cotton	4.0	5.0
Linen	5.5	6.5
Manufactured		
Cellulose-based		
Acetate	1.2–1.5	0.8–1.2
Rayon (conventional)	0.73–2.6	0.7–1.8
Rayon (improved)	2.5–6.0	1.8–4.6
Mineral		
Glass	7.0	7.0
Petroleum-based		
Acrylic	2.0–3.5	1.8–3.3
Modacrylic	2.0–3.5	2.0–3.5
Nylon	2.5–9.5	2.0–8.0
Olefin (polypropylene)	4.8–7.0	4.8–7.0
Polyester	2.5–9.5	2.5–9.4
Saran	1.5	1.5
Spandex	0.7	
Vinyon	0.7–1.0	0.7–1.0

rayon in chemical composition, linen is stronger than either because of its longer length, higher orientation, and greater crystallinity. The greater tenacity of natural cellulosic fibers when wet is one performance variable supporting their widespread use in toweling.

The noncellulosic fibers exhibit little or no change in tenacity when they are tested wet. This behavior helps make some of these manufactured fibers suitable for end products manufactured for outdoor use, such as awnings, lawn furniture, and patio carpet.

Fiber strength is an important variable in textile product performance, but elongation must be considered as well in any judgment of potential serviceability. Elongation is especially crucial to abrasion resistance. A strong fiber with low extensibility may not have good resistance to rubbing, especially when folded or curved. Furthermore, the strength exhibited by a fiber may not be the principal determinant of the strength of the fabric. Weak fibers may be found in strong fabrics, and vice versa.

Chemical Properties

The chemical properties of textile fibers help to determine the end-use serviceability of interior textiles. An inherent chemical property may limit the suitability of a fiber for some end-use applications, and it may dictate the use of finishing agents. The chemical properties of fibers, like their physical properties, can be measured in the laboratory, following the procedures set forth in standard test methods.

Chemical Resistance

Various **pollutant gases** can destroy colorants (see Chapter 14) and, after combining with moisture, they also can destroy textile fibers. When vapor-phase moisture within fibers, yarns, or folds in panels reacts with such gases as sulfur oxide and nitrogen oxide, weak sulfuric acid (H_2SO_4) and weak nitric acid (HNO_3) will be formed. Indoors, droplets of these compounds may be described as **interior acid rain**. Gradually, the acids attack the chemical bonds within the fibers, interrupting the polymer chains and weakening the fibers. The effects of this degradation may not become evident until laundering or dry cleaning, and they may be more pronounced with cellulosic fibers.

Fire-related Fiber Properties

As noted earlier, textile fibers must be long and thin for flexibility. This physical form results in high ratios of surface area to volume. Thus, for their volume, all fibers expose a disproportionately large amount of surface area to the atmospheric oxygen needed for combustion reactions. At the same time, their various chemical compositions result in differences in their pyrolytic characteristics and relative flammability.

Pyrolytic Characteristics

In the cyclic combustion process (see Chapter 11), the supply of available oxygen continually decreases. Without sufficient oxygen in the burning area, and with the source of ignition removed, some fibers **self-extinguish**. The amount of oxygen required to support the combustion of a fiber is measured and reported as the **limiting oxygen index (LOI)**. Fibers with an LOI above 21 self-extinguish

after combustion reduces the level of oxygen below the normal 21 percent concentration and the source of ignition is removed; under the same conditions, fibers having an LOI below 21 continue to burn until they are consumed.

Textile fibers burn at different temperatures and have different **heat of combustion values**. These values specify the amount of heat energy generated that could cause burn injuries as well as maintain the temperature required for further decomposition and combustion. The heats of combustion, ignition temperatures, and other pyrolytic characteristics of selected fiber groups are listed in Table 4.6.

Relative Flammability

Relative terms indicate the flammability of textile fibers: Fibers are described as flammable, flame resistant, noncombustible, or fireproof. A **flammable fiber** is relatively easy to ignite and sustains combustion until it is consumed. A **flame-resistant fiber** may have, for example, relatively high decomposition and ignition temperatures, a slow rate of burning, or a high LOI value. **Noncombustible fibers** do not burn or contribute significant amounts of smoke; they are not fireproof, however, since they can melt and decompose at high temperatures. A **fireproof fiber** is unaffected by fire. Asbestos is considered fireproof, although it may glow if heated to a sufficiently high temperature. The use of asbestos in consumer products and interior environments is limited, however, because it has been found to be a carcinogen. Table 4.7 includes a listing of the relative flammability of several fibers.

Heat-related Properties

A discussion of the effects of heat on textile fibers can easily become a tangle of confusing terms. This discussion will limit itself to three heat-related properties: thermoplasticity, susceptibility to heat, and heat conductivity. Flammability or combustibility is also a reaction to heat. Because the involvement of textile structures in interior fires has become a significant issue in recent decades, the pyrolytic characteristics of textile fibers were separately discussed above.

Thermoplasticity

Chapter 3 explained that thermoplastic fibers soften when heated to their glass transition temperatures, per-

Table 4.6 Pyrolytic Characteristics of Selected Textile Fibers

	Temperatures					
	Decomposition °		Ignition		Heats of Combustion (BTUs/lb)	Limiting Oxygen Index
	°F	°C	°F	°C		
Fiber						
Natural						
Protein						
Wool	446	230	1,094	590	9,450	25.2
Cellulose			Self-extinguishing			
Cotton	581	305	752	400	7,400	17–20
Mineral						
Asbestos			Fireproof			
Manufactured						
Cellulose-based						
Acetate	572	300	842	450	7,700	18.4
Rayon	350–464	177–240	788	420	7,400	18.6
Mineral						
Glass	1,500	815	Noncombustible			
Noncellulosic						
Acrylic	549	287	986	530	1,300	18.2
Aramid	Decomposes above 800 °F (427 °C)					
Modacrylic	455	235	Will not support combustion; self-extinguishing			
Novoloid	Decomposes (converts to carbon) and resists over 5,000 °F (2,760 °C); does not burn					
Nylon	653	345	989	532	12,950	20.1
Olefin (propylene)						18.6
Polyester	734	390	1,040	560	9,300	20.6
Saran	168	76	Will not support combustion; self-extinguishing			
Vinyon			Will not support combustion; self-extinguishing			

Table 4.7 Relative Flammability of Selected Textile Fibers

Fireproof	Noncombustible	Flame-Resistant	Flammable
Asbestos	Glass	Aramid	Cotton
		Novoloid	Linen
		Wool	Rayon
		Modacrylic	Acetate
		Vinyon	Triacetate
		Saran	Acrylic
		Silk	Nylon
			Polyester
			Olefin

mitting manufactured fiber producers to use heat setting as an engineering tool. In this application, **thermoplasticity** is a positive fiber characteristic; but thermoplasticity is a negative characteristic when a fiber is heated to its melting point by such items as lit cigarettes, glowing embers, candle flames, and overly hot irons. When such an unfortunate event occurs, the fiber shrinks and melts.

Subsequently, the molten polymer cools into an unsightly, hardened mass, producing a permanently damaged area in the fabric that generally must be replaced or repaired by a skilled person.

The softening and melting points of selected thermoplastic fibers are listed in Table 4.8. The table also lists temperatures recommended for ironing fabrics composed of these and other fibers.

The frequent use of **heat sensitivity** as a synonym for thermoplasticity, while not incorrect, often causes confusion. Not all fibers are heat sensitive in this sense of the term; that is, not all fibers soften and melt when heated. However, all fibers are sensitive (or susceptible) to heat—they all decompose, scorch, melt, or otherwise react to elevated temperatures.

Susceptibility to Heat

Although the natural fibers, rayon, and lyocell are not heat sensitive, and thus cannot be permanently set with

Table 4.8 Effects of Heat on Textile Fibers

	Softening Point		Melting Point		Safe Ironing Temperature[a]	
	°F	°C	°F	°C	°F	°C
Natural						
Protein						
Wool	Does not soften		Does not melt		300	149
Silk	Does not soften		Does not melt		300	149
Cellulose						
Cotton	Does not soften		Does not melt		425	218
Linen	Does not soften		Does not melt		450	232
Manufactured						
Cellulose-based						
Acetate	400–455	205–230	500	260	350	177
	Sticks, 350–375	177–191				
Triacetate	482	250	575	302	464	240
Rayon	Does not soften		Does not melt		375	191
Mineral						
Glass	1350+	732+				
Noncellulosic						
Acrylic	450–497	232–258	Degrades before true melt		320	160
Aramid	Does not melt		Carbonizes above 800 °F			
Modacrylic	300	149	Degrades before true melt			
	Shrinks, 250	121				
Novoloid	Does not melt		Carbonizes above 5000 °F			
Nylon	445	229	500	260	350	177
Olefin	230–239	110–115	260	127	Do not iron	
Polyethylene	Sticks, shrinks, 140–212	60–100				
Polypropylene	311	155	325–335	163–168	150 (Heat cannot be maintained this low on some irons)	66
Polyester	460–490	238–254	480–550	249–288	325	163
Saran	240–280	116–138	260	127	Do not iron	
Vinyon	170	77	260	127	Do not iron	
	Shrinks, 150	66				

[a] Reproduced by permission of Burlington Industries, Inc.
Sources: Man-Made Fiber Association, *Guide to Man-Made Fibers; Modern Textile Business*, March 1983.

heat, they are nonetheless **susceptible to heat**. Exposing natural fibers to elevated temperatures, especially for prolonged periods, may cause degradation and discoloration. For example, excessively high ironing temperatures weaken and scorch cotton and linen.

Heat Conductivity

Heat conductivity and **heat transmittance** are synonymous terms used to refer to the rate at which a material conducts heat. Most textile fibers have low rates of conduction and contribute to the insulative value of textile structures. While the transfer of heat is influenced by the conductivity rate of the fibers used, it primarily depends on the thickness of the textile structure. This interrelationship is discussed in detail in Chapter 26.

Microbe Resistance

Protecting soft floor coverings from the deterioration, discoloration, and odor development caused by microorganisms is an area of ongoing research in the floor coverings industry. For floor coverings installed in damp areas, the growth of odor-causing mildew and bacteria should be inhibited; for carpet and rugs exposed to pets, the retention of odors in the structure should be prevented. Carpet installed in hospitals, nursing homes, and similar facilities should be resistant to a variety of bacteria and fungi, so that the structures will remain odor-free and will not harbor microbes that could spread disease and slow patient recovery.

Biological resistance has been engineered into nylon carpet fibers by incorporating **antimicrobial agents** into the polymer solution or by adding them early in the production sequence. Examples of trade names indicating that microbe resistance has been introduced include Microfresh®, owned by DuPont; HaloFresh®, owned by Allied Fibers; Zeftron® 500™ ZX, owned by BASF Corporation; BioFresh®, owned by Burlington Industries, Inc.; and Slygard™, owned by Dow Corning.

Moisture-related Properties

Two moisture-related properties, absorbency and wickability, affect the serviceability of textile fibers, as well as their suitability for various end-use applications. Absorbency also affects the dyeability, cleanability, and soiling of fibers.

Absorbency

Comparisons of the abilities of fibers to absorb moisture are based on their **moisture regain values**, which indicate their abilities to absorb **vapor-phase moisture** These values are calculated by the following formula:

$$\% \text{ moisture regain} = \frac{\text{conditioned weight} - \text{dry weight}}{\text{dry weight}} \times 100$$

Dry weight is the weight of the oven-dry specimen. Conditioned weight is determined after the dry specimen has been kept in an atmosphere of 70 ± 2 °F and 65 ± 2 percent relative humidity for a period of 24 hours or until the specimen reaches equilibrium.

The increase in conditioned weight over dry weight shows the amount of vapor-phase moisture absorbed by the fiber. The difference is expressed as a percentage of the dry weight. Typical moisture regain values are listed in Table 4.9.

Fibers with high regain values, including wool and the natural and manufactured cellulosic fibers, are referred to as **hydrophilic** ("water-loving") fibers. These fibers are

Table 4.9 Percentage Moisture Regain of Selected Textile Fibers

Wool	16.0
Rayon	13.0
Linen	10.0–12.0
Cotton	8.5
Acetate	6.0
Nylon	4.0–4.5
Acrylic	1.3–2.5
Polyester	0.4–0.8
Vinyon	0.5
Olefin (polypropylene)	0.0
Saran	0.0
Glass	0.0

easily colored with aqueous dyestuffs, but they require protective finishes for use in exterior textile products. Fibers with low regain values are called **hydrophobic** ("water-hating") fibers. These are suitable for use in some outdoor textile applications, but some have virtually no capacity for moisture absorption and are difficult and expensive to dye, limiting their color-styling possibilities.

The moisture absorbency of fibers has a direct effect on their cleanability. Hydrophilic fibers are more easily cleaned as they readily absorb the detergent solution. By contrast, hydrophobic fibers and cellulosic fibers treated with chemical cross-linking resins may require the application of finishing agents or the use of special laundry aids to improve their cleanability.

Hydrophilic fibers will have a limited buildup of electrical charges on their surfaces when the level of humidity is relatively high. This lessens their attraction for such airborne soil particles as pet hairs, dust, and lint. On the other hand, these fibers, with the exception of wool, may be more easily stained by waterborne substances, such as the staining agents in grape juice, orange soda, and red wine. In wool, an invisible film, known as the epicuticle, covers the scales and provides temporary protection; staining can be avoided by quickly sponging up spilled fluids.

Some hydrophobic fibers, including nylon, polyester, and olefin, are quite resistant to waterborne staining but are subject to oilborne staining. Converters often apply fluorocarbon compounds to greige goods composed of these fibers to minimize this problem.

Several carpet fibers, including acrylic, polyester, and polypropylene olefin, have comparatively low moisture regain values (see Table 4.9). If other characteristics are appropriate, these fibers may be used in carpet to be installed outdoors. Drawing and heat setting are used to increase the crystallinity and reduce the absorbency of nylon, making the fiber suitable for use in such products as synthetic turf for sports stadiums. Fibers with comparatively high regain values, such as wool, may have reduced static problems when the level of relative humidity is high, but they absorb more moisture and require longer drying times when exposed to wet cleaning agents.

Fibers used in the backing layers of structures to be installed below-grade (below ground level) should have low absorbency to resist microbe damage and odor. The lack of absorbency of olefin fibers supports their selection for such installations; the moisture-induced degradation exhibited by jute makes it inappropriate for such a use.

Wickability

Wickability is the ability of a fiber to transport moisture along its surface by capillary action, as a lamp wick transports flammable fluid upward to the site of the flame. Cotton has inherent wickability, which supports its extensive use in beddings and towelings. Currently, fiber chemists are working to improve the wickability and absorbency of several noncellulosic fibers.

Moth Resistance

Unless wool carpet and rug fibers are treated to be **moth resistant**, they may be attacked by moth larvae and carpet beetles (see Chapter 9). All domestic wool floor coverings are treated to repel these insects, but residential and commercial consumers must examine the labels of imported products to confirm the use of such treatments.

Soil Repellency

Recently, carpet fibers have been engineered for built-in **soil repellency**, the ability to reduce initial attraction for soil and to retard the rate of soil accumulation. This is accomplished by chemically modifying the fiber. Generally, a **fluorocarbon compound** is incorporated in the polymer solution. Because this compound lowers the critical surface energy of fibers, dirt, dust, and grime do not readily adhere to their surfaces, and spilled liquids bead up rather than pass into the fibers. Examples of soil-repellent carpet fibers include Anso® IV nylon, produced by Allied Fibers, Trevira® Pentron™ polyester, produced by Hoechst Fibers Industries, and Zeftron® 500™ ZX nylon, produced by BASF Corporation.

Soil repellency can also be introduced by coating the surfaces of the fibers with fluorocarbon compounds. The agents may be applied to the filaments at the point of extrusion or sprayed over the fibers during conversion of the greige goods. In the latter case, converters must see that placement of the compound is not limited to the upper portion of the pile yarns. Examples of trade names indicating the application of soil-repellent compounds include Milliguard® Carpet Protector, owned by Milliken and Company, R9000 Soil Shield®, owned by Armstrong World Industries, and Scotchgard® and 3M Brand Carpet Protector, supplied by the 3M Company.

Static Propensity

The electrical properties (**static propensity**) and **moisture absorbency** of fibers, rather than the way they are incorporated into a covering, determine the level of static generated by a soft floor covering. For this reason, the principal approach to static control is through fiber engineering. Conductive elements sometimes play a part in backings and backcoatings as well. The mechanism of static development should be reviewed for a good understanding of the techniques devised to control static.

Static Development and Voltage Levels

Static development is initiated by the **frictional heat energy** created by the rubbing of shoe soles on carpet and rug fibers. The heat energy causes negatively charged electrons to transfer from the fiber surfaces to the body, where they accumulate. When the person touches a good electrical conductor, such as a metal doorknob, the accumulated electrons rapidly flow from the body to the conductor. It is the sudden discharge of this high energy potential that results in an electrical shock.

The buildup of electrical energy on the body can be plotted graphically as shown in Figure 4.8. As a person walks, increments of electrical charge build up, reaching equilibrium or the steady state after a period of 10 to 20 seconds, or after twenty to thirty steps. Fortunately, the voltage level does not keep increasing over time: some electrons are released into the surrounding air and some are transferred back into the carpet. If the person stops walking, the charge rapidly dissipates.

The level of voltage on the body when contact is made with a conductor determines the severity of the shock. Almost no one is sensitive to the discharge of

Figure 4.8 Static voltage buildup versus time. *Courtesy of Solutia Inc., Fibers Division.*

Table 4.10 Tribolelectric Series for Selected Textile Fibers

Positive end of series	Low
Wool	↑
Nylon	
Cotton	Level of heat
Polyester	energy required
Vinyon	for electron release
Acrylic	↓
Polypropylene olefin	
Negative end of series	High

Sources: Adapted from D. J. Montgomery, *Solid State Physics*, 1959, 9, 139, quoted in W. R. Harper, *Contact and Frictional Electrification*, Oxford University Press, 1967, 352. Position of vinyon provided by Avtex Fibers.

2,500 or fewer static volts. When the charge level is between 2,500 and 3,500 static volts, almost everyone will feel a shock, and the lower end of this range is known as the **threshold of human sensitivity**. As the charge level increases above 3,500 static volts, people are likely to experience an increasingly severe shock.

Fiber Properties Affecting Voltage Buildup

Fibers are not inherently static or antistatic. Static is generated only when the separation of dissimilar materials, here shoes and fibers, results in the transfer of electrons. Certain fiber properties do, however, influence the availability of electrons and the ease with which they are removed.

Electrical Properties **Electrical conductivity** and **resistivity** are terms of opposite meaning that describe the relative ease with which a fiber conducts or resists the flow of electrons. The continual movement and rapid dissipation of electrons over large areas are critical influences on static development. All fibers allow for some degree of flow and some degree of resistance. Specific resistivity values can be used to rank textile fibers; however, these numerical values range widely, and because conductivity and resistivity are relative, the use of such terms as "good" and "poor" is more meaningful.

Fibers that keep electrons flowing, minimizing their accumulation, are classified as **conductors**, in contrast to insulators. Olefins, acrylics, and modacrylics are conductors. Metal fibers are especially good conductors. Fibers that offer higher resistance to the flow of electrons are **insulators**. These fibers, which include nylon, wool, and polyester, allow "pools" of electrons to form on their surfaces, readily available for transfer.

Fibers have other electrical properties that help to determine their static propensity. They vary in their tendencies to develop their own electrical charges. The

triboelectric series for fibers presented in Table 4.10 helps make this clear. *Tribo* is Greek for "rubbing"; the series shows the relative ease with which fibers allow electrons to be rubbed from their surface atoms, leaving a positive balance. Fibers listed at the positive end of the series release electrons relatively easily, that is, release occurs with low levels of frictional heat energy. The reverse is true of fibers listed at the negative end of the series.

The amount of heat energy available to cause electron release is determined in great part by the manner of walking. Slow, light-footed walking generates less heat energy than a rapid, heavy gait. Great amounts of heat energy and high levels of electron release accompany scuffing and shuffling since these movements involve vigorous rubbing of the fiber surfaces.

Like fibers, shoe sole materials vary in the ease with which they release electrons. When a fiber and sole material are paired, the potential for electron transfer is greater the more widely separated the materials are on the triboelectric scale. Neolite, for example, is fairly close to polyester and olefin on the scale. When neolite soles are paired with these fibers, neither fiber nor sole releases electrons readily, and voltage buildup is minimal. Pairing neolite soles with wool or nylon, however, would result in high electron transfer. Of course, if everyone everywhere wore the proper sole materials for the carpet fibers present, the need for static control measures might be overcome—an interesting concept, but an unreasonable expectation.

Absorbency Fibers displaying high moisture regain values will show fewer static problems when the level of humidity is relatively high. Moisture encourages the flow of electrons and limits their pooling on fiber surfaces. It must not be assumed, however, that fibers having little or no capacity to absorb water vapor will automatically have the most marked static problem when relative humidity is low. Olefins, for example, have a moisture regain value of 0.0 percent, but they require higher levels of heat energy for electron release than many fibers do and they are conductors, not insulators.

Controlling levels of **relative humidity** is a year-round, routine practice in such interiors as computer rooms and medical facilities. This control helps ensure that sensitive equipment does not malfunction as a result of extra electrical signals picked up from the floor covering. The ability to increase relative humidity is particularly helpful in the winter months, when interiors may have levels as low as 5 to 10 percent. Some consumers find, however, that higher humidity levels result in condensation forming on windows, and some would rather not pay for a humidity-producing unit or its energy consumption.

To summarize, the following sequence leads to static shock:

Pooling of electrons on fiber surfaces → release and transfer of electrons to the body → accumulation of more than 2,500 static volts of energy on the body → sudden discharge of the built-up energy from the body to a conductor → shock.

It is apparent from this sequence that static problems could be lessened at the outset if the pooling of electrons were minimized. As well as by regulating the relative humidity, static control in textile floor coverings is accomplished, in fact, by incorporating conductive elements, several of which are conductive fibers, to minimize pooling.

Fibers Used to Control Static Generation

Electrical conductivity can be increased by periodically incorporating fine metal filaments in floor coverings. It may also be increased by periodically incorporating a textile fiber engineered for improved conductivity. The aim is to prevent the level of voltage buildup from exceeding the threshold of human sensitivity.

Fibers with Additives One of the first techniques devised to improve fiber conductivity was to add a compound, such as polyethylene glycol, to the polymer solution prior to extrusion. Such additives can contribute soil-hiding as well as static reduction properties.

Coated Filaments By enclosing a nylon filament in a sheath of a conductive material, such as silver, and plying these coated filaments with other fibers, some companies have developed an effective way to prevent electron pooling. X-Static®, marketed by Sauquoit Industries, Inc., is produced in this manner.

A similar technique is used to make Zefstat® products, produced by BASF Corporation. In these structures, however, the positions of the components are reversed. The conductive material, aluminum, forms the core and a colored polymer compound is used as the coating.

A third variation, no longer much used, involved coating a nylon filament with carbon black paste, a highly conductive compound. The use of this technique has diminished because heavy traffic gradually removed the antistatic coating. The coating was also visible in lighter-colored pile layers.

Metal Fibers Metal fibers placed at regular intervals in textile floor coverings effectively drain away electrons. These extremely fine fibers, in staple or filament form, can be added by themselves, spun with staple carpet fibers, or thrown with multifilament yarns. The fibers' fineness ensures their flexibility. Examples of fine stainless steel fibers are Brunsmet®, produced by Brunswick Corporation, and Bekinox®, produced by the Bekaert Steelwire Corporation. When spun yarns of Bekinox® are plied with wool, nylon, or polyester yarns, the blended yarns are distinguished by the name Bekitex®.

Figure 4.9 Antron® Legacy soil-hiding four-void hollow fibers containing a monofilament of anistat manufactured with a conductive carbon core.
Courtesy of E. I. duPont de Nemours & Co., Inc.

a) cross-sectional view

b) longitudinal view

Figure 4.10 Photomicrograph of conductive fiber used with Ultron® nylon. *Courtesy of Solutia Inc., Fibers Division.*

Conductive Filaments Some fiber producers have capitalized on the conductivity of carbon black by incorporating the compound into nonuniform filament structures. These filaments are categorized as biconstituent or conjugate fibers, fibers composed of dissimilar compounds.

DuPont has developed a conductive filament whose core of carbon black is surrounded by a round sheath of nylon. This fiber is combined with several soil-hiding nylon fibers (Figure 4.9).

Solutia Inc., Fibers Division has engineered a conductive fiber that incorporates carbon black as a "lightning rod" down the side. This conjugate fiber is 5 percent carbon black and 95 percent nylon. The round cross-section fiber is plied with soil-hiding trilobal Ultron® nylon to form the yarn bundle used in carpet production. Photomicrographs of this fiber are shown in Figure 4.10.

Sunlight Resistance

Because fabrics and other textile components used in interior and exterior window treatments are exposed to the sun's rays for prolonged periods of time, the sunlight resistance of the fibers used is a crucial service-related property. Consumers and professionals may be more familiar with the negative effects of sunlight on the color component of textile products than with the concurrent loss in fiber tenacity. All fibers are weakened or **tendered** by sunlight, but some are degraded more rapidly. Over time, the radiant energy of natural light alters the interior structure of fibers, breaking their chemical bonds and reducing the length of their polymer chains. The damage caused to fibers is somewhat analogous to that caused by sunburning the skin, and in both cases prolonged exposure increases the extent of the damage.

The rate and extent of fiber damage by sunlight is influenced by several factors, including fiber composition, length of exposure, intensity of the light, atmospheric conditions, the presence of colorants, and the use of polymer solution additives. Delusterants can act as catalysts and speed fiber deterioration; ultraviolet absorbers, on the other hand, can effectively protect the fiber from harmful rays. Usually colorants accelerate the rate of fiber degradation by light while at the same time their own structure and characteristics are negatively affected by the radiant energy. This is vividly shown in Figure 4.11, where fabric damage is greatest in the checks having colored warp yarns and colored filling yarns.

Table 4.11 compares the sunlight resistance of selected textile fibers. An "excellent" rating indicates slower,

Figure 4.11 Accelerated fiber degradation by textile colorants. The degradation is greatest in the gingham checks which are made up of both colored warp yarns and colored fillings yarns.

Table 4.11 Sunlight Resistance of Selected Textile Fibers

Glass	Excellent
Acrylic	
Modacrylic	
Polyester	
Linen	
Cotton	
Rayon	
Triacete	
Acetate	
Olefin	
Nylon	
Wool	
Silk	Poor

Source: Norma Hollen, Jane Saddler, and Anna L. Langford, *Textiles*, 5th ed., New York: Macmillan, 1979.

and a "poor" rating more rapid, deterioration. Glass fiber is rated as having excellent resistance; it has nevertheless been found to lose approximately 50 percent of its wet tenacity after three years of exposure to natural light.[1]

The loss in tenacity suffered by fibers exposed to light may not become evident until the fabric is cleaned.

Consumers may wish to hold the owner of the cleaning establishment responsible for what actually is the result of already-weakened fibers rupturing under cleaning procedures. For this reason, cleaners may ask customers to sign a statement releasing the firm from responsibility in the event the fabric deteriorates.

Summary

The aesthetic, chemical, and mechanical properties of textile fibers depend greatly on their chemical compositions, the arrangement of their internal units, and the nature of their external features. Residential consumers, contract designers, and architects should consider fiber properties when selecting or specifying interior textile products, to ensure that the constituent fibers exhibit properties suitable for the end-use application.

Key Terms

abrasion resistance

antimicrobial agents

apparent whiteness or brightness

breaking tenacity

colorants

conductors

covering power

cross-sectional shape

delusterants

denier per filament (dpf)

density

dye pigments

elastic modulus

elastic recovery

electrical conductivity

electrical resistivity

elevator effect

elongation

fiber toughness
fibrillation
fireproof fiber
flame-resistant fiber
flammable fiber
flexibility
fluorescent compound
fluorocarbon compound
frictional heat energy
grams per denier
grams per tex
hand or handle
heat conductivity
heat of combustion values
heat sensitivity
heat transmittance
hiking
hydrophilic fiber
hydrophobic fiber
inherent color
insulators
interior acid rain
limiting oxygen index (LOI)
linear density
longitudinal configuration
luster
microscopic voids
moisture absorbency

moisture regain values
moth resistance
noncombustible fiber
optical brighteners
optical properties
pilling
pollutant gases
relative humidity
resiliency
self-extinguishing fiber
soil hiding
soil magnification
soil repellency
soil shedding
specific gravity
static propensity
stiffness
surface texture
susceptibility to heat
tendered
thermoplasticity
threshold of human sensitivity
titanium dioxide
triboelectric series
vapor-phase moisture
wickability
yo-yo effect

Review Questions

1. Discuss the importance of color as a consumer product selection criterion.

2. What is "inherent color" and when is it preserved? When and why is it removed or neutralized?

3. How does the cross-sectional shape of a fiber influence its soil-hiding ability? Are there limitations to multi-lobal shapes having deep indentations?

4. Given the relatively flat cross-sectional shape of cotton, why doesn't the fiber have a high level of luster?

5. Explain the influence of the surface texture and longitudinal form of wool on the luster of the fiber.

6. What is meant by the term "apparent" when used with whiteness and brightness? Distinguish between "apparent" and "actual" whiteness and brightness.

7. Distinguish between "soil hiding" and "soil magnification."

8. Explain the effectiveness of delusterants in hiding soil.

9. How do interior fiber voids obscure the appearance of soil?

10. How important is the "hand" or "handle" of a textile product to consumers? Is hand largely subjective? What fiber features influence the hand of a textile?

11. How do the effects of abrasive forces on textile products show up to the consumer? How are abrasion and pilling related? How do fiber producers engineer fiber toughness? Why is it critical to select a fiber having relatively high abrasion resistance for use in soft floor coverings?

12. Distinguish between specific gravity and density.

13. What influence does specific gravity have on the covering power of a textile? Why is covering power an important consideration for textile structures used to cover large surface areas?

14. How do the weight and cost of textile floor coverings relate to the specific gravity of the fiber used?

15. Explain the relationship between fiber density and fiber denier.

16. How does the elastic modulus of a fiber contribute to the dimensional stability of a fiber and fabric?

17. Why can fabrics of high wet modulus rayon fibers be laundered instead of dry cleaned?

18. Explain the influence of the internal arrangement and external structural features of fibers on their extensibility and their recovery.

19. Identify interior textile products whose serviceability is improved by having fibers exhibiting a high level of resiliency.

20. Discuss the influence of fiber stiffness on the resiliency and abrasion resistance of textile fabrics.

21. How does the dpf of a fiber affect its soil accumulation?

22. How does a microrough fiber surface reduce its level of soil accumulation?

23. The breaking tenacities of cotton and linen are higher when the fibers are wet. Does this have an influence on their end-use performance?

24. What constitutes "interior acid rain" and how does it affect interior textile products?

25. Why do fibers having an LOI greater than 21 offer greater safety in the event of ignition than do fibers having LOI values less than 21?

26. Differentiate among these terms: flammable, flame resistant, noncombustible, and fireproof.

27. When is thermoplasticity of a fiber an advantage? When is it a disadvantage?

28. Can products composed of cotton be heat set?

29. Cite end-use applications where textile products should be resistant to microbes.

30. Distinguish between hydrophilic and hydrophobic fibers, and cite benefits and limitations of each fiber type.

31. How is soil repellency introduced to manufactured fibers?

32. What is the role of fluorocarbon compounds in soil reduction?

33. What is frictional heat energy and how does it contribute to static development?

34. Explain the buildup of electrical energy on the body as a person walks.

35. Explain "pooling" of electrons as it relates to static development.

36. What is shown by the triboelectric series for textile fibers? Why is it a consideration in the static propensity of fibers?

37. Summarize the sequence leading to electrical shock.

38. Explain the role of vapor-phase moisture in static development.

39. Discuss static control techniques that use fibers.

40. What effects does the presence of colorants, delusterants, and ultraviolet absorbers have on the rate and extent of sunlight degradation of textiles?

Note

1.   Esther M. Cormany, "Service Qualities of Sheer Curtain Fabrics," *Journal of Home Economics*, Vol. 51, No. 10, December 1959, 873.

5

Textile Yarns and Yarn-like Structures

Yarn Production
  Throwing
  Texturing
  Spinning
  Yarn Twisting

Yarn Classification and Nomenclature
  Simple Yarns
  Complex Yarns

Designation of Yarn Construction
  Yarn Number
  Describing Single Yarns

Describing Ply Yarns
Describing Cord Yarns

Formation of Yarn-like Structures
  Chenille Yarns
  Felted Wool Yarns
  Metallic Yarns
  Polymer Tapes
  Twisted Paper
  Other Structures

All textile yarns, like textile fibers, must be relatively long and thin to provide the flexibility required in manufacturing and use. However, yarns can have marked differences in their degrees of twist, textural characteristics, complexity, and relative fineness. The fineness of yarns can be measured and reported in numerical terms. These numbers, along with other notations, are used in designations of yarn construction.

Simple yarns, structures having minimal design value, are typically used in carpet, rugs, towels, sheets, and tabletop accessories. By contrast, decorative, complex yarns are often used in textile wall coverings and in upholstery, curtain, and drapery fabrics. Complex yarns have slubs, loops, curls, and other irregular textural effects that add tactile and visual interest. This chapter describes the production and qualities of the widely used simple and complex yarns.

Although most interior textile products are composed entirely of textile yarns or fibers, some are composed in whole or in part of yarn-like structures. Although these components are handled like textile yarns, they are not formed by conventional yarn production processes, and several contain no fibers.

Yarn Production

One type of yarn, known as a **monofilament yarn**, is actually manufactured by the fiber producer. In this process, a single filament is treated as a yarn structure. For strength and stability, the filament has a relatively large diameter and is drawn and heat set. Monofilament yarns are often used in the production of lightweight, transparent window coverings. They are also used as strong sewing thread in the construction of many interior textile products. In this application, the filaments may be clear or smoke-colored so that they will assume the color of the textile structure being sewn and produce an inconspicuous seam.

While fiber producers manufacture monofilament yarns, **throwsters** produce multifilament yarns and **spinners** produce spun yarns. Throwsters may use a texturing process to introduce such characteristics as bulk and cohesiveness to groups of filaments, some of which are then reduced to staple lengths and spun.

Throwing

The great length of silk and manufactured filaments allows them to be directly combined or "thrown" together into multifilament yarn structures; no textile yarn spinning process is required. If drawn manufactured filaments are supplied, the throwster needs only to gather and twist several of the fine strands. If undrawn filaments are supplied, the throwster must combine drawing and twisting. For a limited number of applications, throwsters will produce untwisted multifilament yarns.

Texturing

Texturing processes introduce multidimensional configurations to otherwise parallel and smooth filaments. Such physical changes may decrease strength, but they can impart elasticity, create a softer, warmer hand, help to simulate a natural appearance, and increase fiber cohesiveness. They also increase the **bulk or apparent volume** of the grouped filaments to provide greater covering power, as showing in Figure 5.1. In use, fabrics composed of textured yarns have reduced levels of pilling and better di-

Figure 5.1 Identical skeins of nylon filaments showing increase in apparent bulk or volume produced by texturing. *Courtesy of Solutia Inc., Fibers Division.*

a) false-twist coiling

b) stuffer box crimping

c) knit-de-knit crinkling

d) gear crimping

Figure 5.2 Yarn texturing processes.

From "Yarns," by Stanley Backer. Copyright © 1972 by Scientific American, Inc. All rights reserved.

mensional stability and resiliency, and retain their original appearance for a longer period of time than do fabrics made of staple fibers.

Among the texturing processes used with interior textile product components are false-twist coiling, stuffer-box crimping, knit-de-knit crinkling, and gear crimping. These processes are schematized in Figure 5.2. Yarns textured by these and other techniques are known as **bulked continuous filament (BCF) yarns**.

False-Twist Coiling

In **false-twist coiling**, the yarn bundle is twisted, heated, and untwisted in one continuous operation. A heat-set coil within each filament results; the yarn itself has no twist (hence the name "false-twist").

Stuffer-Box Crimping

The **stuffer-box crimping** technique is so called because the yarns are rapidly stuffed into a heated, box-like chamber. Because the yarns are withdrawn slowly, they buckle and back up on themselves. The three-dimensional crimp is permanently set by the heat.

Knit-De-knit Crinkling

Knit-d... ...rinkling produces a crinkled or wavy configurati... ...ian ...nt yarns are first knitted into a fabric. The ...s then heat set and subsequently unraveled ("de-knit"). The knitting gauge (the number of loops per inch) determines the size of the yarn waves. This technique is frequently combined with the application of dyestuffs to produce uniquely colored and textured yarns for soft floor coverings (see Figure 8.6, p. 113).

Gear Crimping

In **gear crimping**, intermeshing gears introduce a planar or two-dimensional crimp to filaments. Heat can be used to permanently set the crimped configuration.

When filaments are to be reduced to staple lengths and spun into yarns, they are first grouped into a rope-like bundle known as **tow**. This untwisted bundle is then textured, generally by gear or stuffer-box crimping, to impart the **fiber cohesiveness** required for the production of spun yarns. The textured tow is stretched or cut into staple fibers of the desired length, generally from 1 to 6 inches. The staple fibers in Figure 5.3 were cut from gear-crimped tow.

Figure 5.3 Staple-length fibers cut from gear-crimped tow.

Spinning

Staple-length fibers are converted into usable yarn strands by processing them through various spinning systems, including the cotton, woolen, worsted, and linen systems. Formerly, the system used depended upon the type of fiber being spun; today, as manufactured fibers are increasingly used to simulate natural fibers, the choice of spinning systems is largely based on the length of the staples being processed. In any case, the basic procedures used in the several systems are similar, with each successive operation producing a structure that is more yarn-like.

Cotton System

The following highly simplified summary identifies the basic procedures used in the **cotton spinning system** and describes the changes produced in each step:

1. **Opening and cleaning:** loosening, cleaning, and blending the cotton fibers.
2. **Picking:** fluffing the compacted fibers into a loose, disoriented mass.
3. **Carding:** initially aligning the fibers in a somewhat parallel fashion and forming a card sliver, a long, loose strand that is approximately 1 inch in diameter.

4. Combing: further aligning the fibers and separating the shorter staples before forming a comb sliver.

5. Drawing out: reducing the diameter of the sliver to produce a roving, a long, fine strand that is approximately ¼ inch in diameter.

6. Spinning and twisting: reducing the diameter of the roving and twisting the resulting fine strand into a usable spun yarn.

The cotton system is used for spinning fibers that are approximately ½ inch to 1½ inches in length. Yarns with relatively long and highly aligned fibers are known as **combed yarns**; those having both long and short staples and relatively little fiber alignment are called **carded yarns**. Today, polyester and rayon staples, alone or blended with cotton, are frequently spun on the cotton system.

Woolen and Worsted Systems

The basic equipment in the woolen spinning system is designed to handle fibers from 2 to 3 inches in length; that in the worsted system is designed to handle fibers from 3 to 5 inches in length. Spinners can adjust the equipment, however, to spin the longer staples frequently used in interior textile yarns. **Woolen yarns**, like carded yarns, have varied lengths of staples and less fiber alignment; **worsted yarns**, like combed yarns, contain only long staples that are highly aligned.

Because spun yarns have many fiber ends protruding from their surfaces, their level of light reflectance is less than that of multifilament yarns. Spinners use this characteristic to advantage when they process staple-length acrylic, nylon, and olefin fibers on the woolen system to produce yarns with a subdued, mellow luster, imitating the much-admired natural luster of wool.

Linen System

The linen spinning system is designed to align and twist linen tow fibers, which are approximately 12 inches in length, and linen line fibers, which are approximately 24 inches in length. Tow fibers are spun into relatively heavy yarns for use in such interior textile products as wall coverings, upholstery, and drapery fabrics, while line fibers are spun into fine yarns for use in such items as woven table linens, bed sheets, and lace doilies. Groups of aligned linen fibers in Figure 5.4 resemble switches of human hair prior to yarn twisting.

Figure 5.4 Aligned linen fibers prior to drawing out and twisting.
Courtesy of MASTERS OF LINEN, International Linen Promotion Commission.

Yarn Twisting

Twisting must be used for all spun yarns, and while it is optional for multifilament yarns, it is generally used to stabilize the fine, parallel filaments. Whatever the type of yarn, twist can be specified by its direction and level.

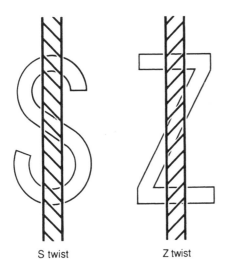

S twist   Z twist

Figure 5.5 Direction of twist in textile yarns.

Direction of Twist

The letters *S* and *Z* are used to describe the direction of twist in all textile yarns (Figure 5.5). A left-handed or counterclockwise twist is called an **S twist**; the fibers ascend from right to left and align with the central portion of the letter. A right-handed or clockwise twist is termed a **Z** twist; the fibers ascend from left to right and again align with the central portion of the letter. Neither direction confers an advantage over the other.

Level of Twist

The level or amount of twist used in yarn formation is denoted by the number of **turns per inch** (turns/inch or tpi). Multifilament yarns may have as few as 2 or 3 tpi, while spun yarns often have as many as 30 or 40 tpi. Optimum levels have evolved from years of experience and yarn testing by spinners and throwsters.

Spun yarns with a relatively low level of twist are comparatively soft, large, weak, and dull. Up to a point, increasing the twist will produce a concomitant increase in yarn firmness, fineness, strength, and luster. When more than about 40 tpi are used, kinks and ridges may form, reducing the elasticity and strength of the yarns. Such surface irregularities may deflect incident light waves, dulling the yarns in much the same way as coils dull fibers.

Throwsters and spinners use a variety of techniques to control the aesthetic features and service-related quali-

ties of yarns and expand the assortment of yarns available to producers and consumers. They may vary the level of twist used, introduce decorative effects, or combine various numbers and types of yarn strands. The resulting yarns are then classified and named on the basis of their structural characteristics.

Yarn Classification and Nomenclature

Yarns produced by throwing or spinning textile fibers are classified and described by the number of their parts and their design features. A brief outline will serve to introduce the classification system used with textile yarns and the extensive number of names used for decorative yarns.

   I. Simple Yarns
      A. Single
      B. Ply
      C. Cord
      D. Cable
      E. Rope
      F. Hawser
  II. Complex Yarns
      A. Singles
         1. Slub
         2. Thick-and-thin
         3. Speck
      B. Plies and cords
         1. Plied slub
         2. Flame
         3. Flock or flake
         4. Spiral
         5. Corkscrew
         6. Nub
         7. Knot
         8. Seed
         9. Splash
       10. Spike or snarl
       11. Ratiné
       12. Bouclé
       13. Loop or curl
       14. Gimp

Simple Yarns

Yarns having a smooth appearance and a uniform diameter along their length are classified as **simple yarns**. Simple yarns may be composed of a single yarn or a number of single yarns twisted or plied together in various ways.

Single, Ply, and Cord Yarns

Simple single yarns are produced in a single spinning or throwing operation, or, in the case of monofilament yarns, in a single extruding operation. Although simple multifilament yarns are composed of multiple filaments, they are classified as single yarns. Twisting or plying two or more single yarns together forms **simple ply yarns**. Twisting two or more ply yarns together forms **simple cord yarns**. These yarns are illustrated in Figure 5.6.

As long as the fineness or size of the components is not reduced, plying increases yarn strength. So that ply and cord yarns will be balanced and smooth, each successive twisting or plying procedure uses about half the amount of twist as the previous one and S and Z twists are alternated. The standard practice followed in designating the construction of these yarns is discussed later in this chapter.

Cable, Rope, and Hawser Yarns

When simple cord yarns are plied, the resulting structure is called a **cable yarn**; when cable yarns are plied, the new structure is called **rope**; and when rope strands are com-

bined, the structure becomes a **hawser**, a structure that is strong enough to anchor a ship. Rope structures composed of sisal or hemp fibers frequently appear in handwoven chair seats.

In comparison with complex yarns, simple yarns have minimal design value. Spinners and throwsters can, however, combine various hues and shades of fibers and yarns to enhance the visual interest of simple yarns. Such distinctive yarn color styles as heather, marled, and ombré, and the methods used to produce them, are described in Chapter 8.

Complex Yarns

Yarns with variations in the level of twist used along their length, three-dimensional decorative features, or components with different fiber contents are called **complex yarns**. The unique combination of features characterizing each of these decorative yarns determines its yarn name.

Complex Single Yarns

Complex single yarns may be spun or extruded. A **slub yarn** (Figure 5.7a) is composed of staple-length fibers and has both fine and coarse segments along its length. These differences in diameter are produced by varying the level of twist used in the final spinning operation. Because fewer tpi are used for the coarse areas, they are softer and weaker than the fine areas. As the name suggests, a **thick-and-thin yarn** also has variations in diameter, but these are less pronounced than those in slub yarns (Figure 5.7b). Varying the extrusion pressure used during the formation of manufactured filaments produces the slight variations. Duppioni silk filaments have a similar appearance as a result of the irregularities created when two cocoons are spun in contact with one another. A **speck yarn** (Figure 5.7c) is produced by periodically incorporating small tufts of contrastingly colored fibers during spinning. The colorful tufts interrupt the smoothness of the yarn, creating greater visual interest.

Complex Plies and Cords

Complex plies and cords are formed by twisting together two or more single yarns that may themselves be simple or complex structures. Frequently, distinctive forms of twisting are used to produce complex structures

Figure 5.6 Simple single, ply, and cord yarns.

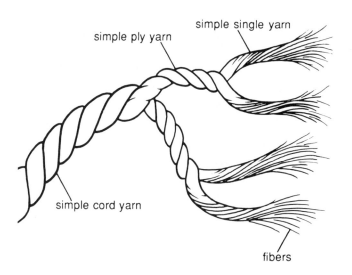

simple single yarn

simple ply yarn

simple cord yarn

fibers

a) slub yarn

b) thick-and-thin yarn

c) speck yarn

Figure 5.7 Complex single yarns.
Photomicrograph of the thick-and-thin yarn is courtesy of Solutia Inc., Fibers Division.

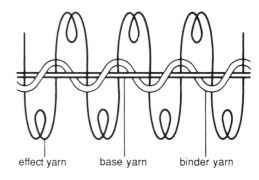

effect yarn   base yarn   binder yarn

Figure 5.8 Basic components of complex ply and cord yarns.

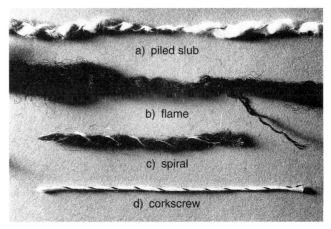

a) piled slub

b) flame

c) spiral

d) corkscrew

Figure 5.9 Complex two-ply yarns.

from simple components. Because the basic textural and design features of a complex yarn can be produced by using single or plied components, many textile authorities make no distinction between complex ply yarns and complex cord yarns.

Basic Components   As shown in Figure 5.8, complex plies and cords may have three distinct components. The **base yarn**, which is also known as the core, foundation, or ground yarn, provides stability and determines the yarn length. The **effect yarn**, which is also known as the fancy yarn, contributes the novelty or decorative appearance. The **binder or tie yarn** secures the effect yarn to the base yarn. Some complex yarns have only two of these components.

Complex Yarn Names and Descriptions   Complex plies and cords are distinguished by their appearance and structural features. These features determine the name assigned to the yarn.

Plied slub yarns, pictured in Figure 5.9a, are formed by twisting two slub yarns together. As shown in Figure 5.9b, twisting a simple yarn around a single slub yarn that has large and elongated areas of low twist produces a **flame yarn**. **Flock or flake yarns** have an appearance similar to that of single slub yarns; but in these multicomponent structures, the enlarged segments are created by periodically binding thin bits of roving between plied single yarns. While the removal of the fibers from a slub yarn would destroy its stability, removal of the fibers inserted in flock yarns would destroy only their appearance: the plied singles would maintain the stability of the yarns.

The components of **spiral and corkscrew yarns** differ in their construction, fiber content, level of twist, degree of luster, or size. Together they create a visual spiral. (While plying simple yarns that differ only in color would produce a spiral appearance, such yarns do not come within the definition of spiral and corkscrew yarns. They would be classified as simple, two-ply yarns.) For greater emphasis on the visual spiral, a spun yarn may be combined with a filament yarn, or a yarn-like metallic strand may be combined with a spun yarn. Although many textile authorities use "spiral" and "corkscrew" as synonyms, a distinction may be made when yarns of different sizes are plied. As shown in Figure 5.9c and d, "spiral" applies when the heavier yarn twists around the finer yarn, and "corkscrew" when the finer yarn twists around the heavier yarn.

Imaginative forms of plying can produce complex yarns from simple components. **Nub yarns**, which are also called **spot or knap yarns**, have tightly compacted projections at irregular intervals along their lengths. These three-dimensional nubs are created by wrapping a simple yarn several times around a base yarn. When bits of tightly compacted and contrastingly colored fibers are incorporated into the nubs, the plied yarn may be called a **knot or knop yarn**. **Seed yarns** have tiny nubs and **splash yarns** have elongated nubs. Examples of yarns with nub effects are shown in Figure 5.10.

Several complex yarns have loop-type textural effects. These include spike, ratiné, bouclé, and loop yarns. **Spike or snarl yarns** are composed of yarns having different levels of twist. During the plying operation, the more highly twisted yarn is introduced at a faster rate, causing the extra length to form well-defined kinks or loops. **Ratiné yarns** (Figure 5.11a and b) have uniformly spaced loops of equal size. In their production, a fuzzy effect yarn is fed faster than the base during the plying sequence, producing small, tightly spaced loops that are almost perpendicular to the base. Some ratiné yarns are produced with a smooth effect yarn, causing the projec-

Figure 5.11 Complex yarns with loop effects.

tions to assume a diamond shape similar to that in rickrack trim. **Bouclé yarns** (Figure 5.11c) have pronounced, closed loops that vary in size and spacing. **Loop or curl yarns** (Figure 5.11d) have open, airy loops. Frequently, the effect yarns are loosely spun of mohair fibers.

Gimp yarns are formed by spirally wrapping one yarn around another, or by braiding three or more strands around one central yarn; in either case, the core yarn is completely covered. Gimp yarns frequently have yarn-like metallic strands on the exterior; such decorative yarns are occasionally used to embellish towels and such other interior textile items as tablecloths and wall hangings.

Core-spun and covered-core yarns are special types of gimp yarns having a rubber or spandex filament as the core component. When staple-length fibers are spun around the elastomeric filament, the structure is called a **core-spun yarn**; when filaments are wrapped or braided around the filament, the structure is called a **covered-core yarn**.

Designation of Yarn Construction

ASTM D 1244 Standard Practice for Designation of Yarn Construction includes recommendations for describing the structural features of simple yarns (the standard does not cover the description of complex yarns). Three basic notations are used to designate the construction: yarn number, direction of twist, and number of components.

Figure 5.10 Complex yarns with nub effects.

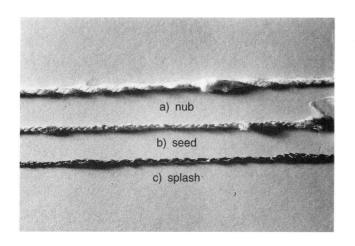

Yarn Number

Yarn numbers designate the fineness or size of yarns. They are determined according to various yarn numbering systems, but the number or count of one system can be converted to its equivalent number in other systems.

Indirect Yarn Numbering Systems

In **indirect yarn numbering systems**, the yarn number or size is based on length per unit of mass (weight), and the yarn diameter decreases as the yarn number increases. These systems are traditionally used for spun yarns.

Cotton Count (cc) System

The **cc system** is used to determine the yarn number of yarns spun on the cotton spinning system. The cc yarn number is equal to the number of 840-yard lengths or hanks of yarn produced from one pound of fiber. For example, a cc of 1 means that one 840-yard hank of yarn was produced from one pound of fiber, while a cc of 50 means that 50 hanks or 42,000 yards of yarn were produced from one pound of fiber.

Linen Lea (ll) System

The **ll system** is used to determine the yarn number of yarns produced on the linen spinning system. In this system, the ll number is equal to the number of 300-yard hanks of yarn produced from one pound of fiber.

Woolen Run (wr) System

The **wr system** is used to determine the yarn number of yarns produced on the woolen spinning system. The wr number is equal to the number of 1,600-yard hanks of yarn produced from one pound of fiber. Some spinners may choose to use the woolen cut (w/c) system instead of the wr system. In the w/c system, the yarn number is equal to the number of 300-yard hanks of yarn produced from one pound of fiber.

Worsted Count (wc) System

The **wc system** is used to determine the yarn number of yarns on the worsted spinning system. The wc number is equal to the number of 560-yard hanks of yarn produced from one pound of fiber.

Direct Yarn Numbering Systems

In **direct yarn numbering systems**, the yarn number or size is based on mass (weight) per unit of length, and the yarn diameter increases as the yarn number increases. These systems are generally used with silk and manufactured filaments.

Denier (den) System

In this system, the **den number** is equal to the weight in grams of 9,000 meters of a monofilament or multifilament yarn. A den number of 200, for example, means that 9,000 meters of yarn weighed 200 grams.

Tex System

In this system, the **tex number** is equal to the weight in grams of 1,000 meters of a monofilament or multifilament yarn. This system is recommended by the International Organization for Standardization. While the system is finding some acceptance for international trade purposes, many experienced technicians are resisting its universal adoption because they are more familiar with the denier and indirect yarn numbering systems.

Because converting yarn numbers or counts determined in one system to equivalent numbers in other systems is laborious and time consuming, selected conversions are presented in Table 5.1. For conversion of yarn counts or numbers not included in the table, readers may consult ASTM D 2260 Standard Tables of Conversion Factors and of Equivalent Yarn Numbers Measured in Various Numbering Systems.

Describing Single Yarns

Information pertaining to the construction of single spun yarns is stated in this order: the yarn number and the numbering system used, the direction of twist, and the amount of twist (e.g., 50cc S 15 tpi). For single multifilament yarns, the letter *f* followed by the number of component filaments is inserted after the yarn number (e.g., 10 den f40 S 3 tpi). Monofilaments are designated as f/1.

Describing Ply Yarns

Two groups of data are used to describe ply yarns. The first group describes the single yarn components, listing the information as directed in the previous paragraph.

Table 5.1 Yarn Number Conversions

Cotton Count (840 yd per lb)	Linen Lea (300 yd per lb)	Woolen Run (1,600 yd per lb)	Worsted Count (560 yd per lb)	Denier (g per 9,000 m)	Tex (g per 1,000 m)
Coarsest					
0.357	1.000	0.188	0.536	14,890.0	1,654.0
0.667	1.867	0.350	1.000	7,972.0	885.2
1.000	2.800	0.525	1.500	5,315.0	590.5
1.905	5.333	1.000	2.857	2,790.0	310.0
3.333	9.333	1.750	5.000	1,595.0	177.2
3.810	10.67	2.000	5.714	1,395.0	155.0
40.00	112.00	21.00	60.00	132.9	14.80
50.00	140.0	26.25	75.00	106.3	11.80
60.00	168.0	31.50	90.00	88.58	9.84
531.5	1,488.0	279.1	797.3	10.00	1.11
Finest					

Courtesy of Celanese Corporaton.

The second group describes the ply yarn, stating the number of single yarn components in the plied yarn and the direction and the amount of plying twist. The two groups are separated by a small "x": An example is 50cc S 15 tpi x 2 Z 7 tpi.

Describing Cord Yarns

A third group of notations is used to describe cord yarns. This group follows the groups used to describe the single and ply components and states the number of ply yarns and the direction and amount of twist used to form the cord.

Some downstream producers prefer designations of yarn construction to be stated in an order opposite that described (i.e., cord-ply-single or ply-single). Interested readers may refer to ASTM D 1244 for a review of these and other notations.

Formation of Yarn-like Structures

Several components incorporated in interior textile products are yarn-like structures. While some of these strands are composed of textile fibers, and are generally referred to as yarns, they are produced with techniques other than throwing and spinning.

Figure 5.12 Chenille yarn cut from leno-woven fabric.

Chenille Yarns

Chenille yarns are actually narrow strips cut from a leno-woven fabric. In leno-weave interlacing, illustrated in Figure 6.13 (p. 88), pairs of warp (lengthwise) yarns are crossed in a figure-eight fashion around the filling or weft (crosswise) yarns. The warp yarns are simple and highly twisted, and the filling yarns are simple, low-twist strands. After weaving, the fabric is carefully cut lengthwise between the leno-entwined warp yarns, producing fuzzy, caterpillar-like structures (Figure 5.12). Locking precut lengths of fibers between plied base yarns can also produce chenille yarns; this avoids the initial weaving operation and cutting procedure.

Felted Wool Yarns

Research projects sponsored by the Wool Bureau, Inc., have led to the development of unique wool yarns for use in soft floor coverings. One technique exposes loosely knitted strands of wool rovings to heat, agitation, and moisture, causing felting shrinkage and converting the strands into yarn-like structures. In this way—by capitalizing on the inherent tendency of wool fibers to shrink and matt together—manufacturers produce wool carpet yarns while avoiding the expense and time involved in conventional spinning, twisting, and plying. This helps to offset the relatively high cost of the fibers in the finished product.

Metallic Yarns

Metallic yarns, in contrast to metal filaments, are formed in various ways. Frequently, silver-colored foil is encased between clear polyester film sheeting. The layered structure is then slit into thin, yarn-like strands. The highly reflective strands may be used alone or in combination with conventional textile yarns.

Polymer Tapes

Polymer ribbons or tapes are produced by extruding a polymer solution as a wide sheet of film, much like sandwich wrap but thicker. The film sheeting is then slit into long strands of the desired width (Figure 5.13). These structures, often referred to as fibrillated ribbons or fibrillated tapes, are usually composed of polypropylene olefin or saran. Fibrillated polypropylene olefin tapes predominate in backing fabrics produced for use with pile floor coverings (see Figure 22.2b, p. 348), and they are colored and used extensively as the face yarns in carpet designed to be installed outdoors and in laundry rooms, locker rooms, basements, and barns.

Figure 5.13 Fibrillated polymer tapes.

Twisted Paper

Two yarn-like structures are formed by tightly twisting tough sheets of paper. Fiber rush is intended to simulate natural rush, which is described below. **Kraftcord** is traditionally made of paper produced from cellulose recovered from titiaceous plants, which are related to lime plants. The heavy, cord-like strands have been used in the back layers of woven floor coverings (see Unit Four).

Other Structures

Various natural substances are converted into yarn-like structures and used for such products as hand-woven chair seats and backs. **Natural rush** strands are produced by twisting two or three flat cattail leaves into a long unit. **Sea grass,** also known as *Chinese grass* and *Hong Kong grass,* is produced by twisting plied strands of grass into a cord; the natural color suggests a resemblance to rope. **Cane** is retrieved from the rattan, a climbing palm. The outer bark is shaved and cut into various widths, ranging from ⅛ inch or less to ⁵⁄₁₆ inch.

Summary

Spinners use various systems to align and twist staple-length fibers into spun yarns, and throwsters use simple twisting operations to combine filament-length fibers into multifilament yarns. Throwsters may also use a texturing procedure to impose a multidimensional configuration on filaments, increasing their elasticity, cohesiveness, or apparent volume. Spinners and throwsters can vary the level of twist and employ several plying operations to produce an extensive assortment of yarn styles, many with decorative and distinctive effects.

The construction of simple textile yarns is described in accordance with practices outlined in standards established by such voluntary scientific associations as the American Society for Testing and Materials and the International Organization for Standardization. These designations typically include the yarn number, direction of twist, and number of components. Informed persons can interpret a yarn's designation and learn several important facts about its features without actually examining the yarn itself.

Various yarn-like structures supplement the supply of spun and thrown yarns available to fabric producers. Some of these structures, including felted wool rovings and chenille yarns, are composed of fibers; others are composed of such materials as paper, grass, and film-coated foil.

Key Terms

base yarn

binder or tie yarn

bouclé yarns

bulked continuous filament (BCF) yarns

bulk or apparent volume

cable yarns

cane

carded yarns

carding

cc system

chenille yarns

combed yarns

combing

complex plies and cords

complex single yarns

complex yarns

core-spun yarn

cotton spinning system

covered-core yarn

den number

direct yarn numbering systems

drawing out

effect yarn

false-twist coiling

fiber cohesiveness

flame yarn

flock or flake yarns

gear crimping

gimp yarns

hawser

indirect yarn numbering systems

knit-de-knit crinkling

knot or knop yarn

kraftcord

ll system

loop or curl yarns

metallic yarns

monofilament yarn

natural rush

nub yarns

opening and cleaning

picking

plied slub yarns

polymer ribbons or tapes

ratiné yarns

rope

sea grass

seed yarns

simple cord yarns

simple ply yarns

simple single yarns

simple yarns

slub yarns

speck yarn

spike or snarl yarns

spinners

spinning and twisting

spiral and corkscrew yarns

splash yarns

spot or knap yarns

stuffer-box crimping

S twist

tex number

texturing

thick-and-thin yarns

throwsters

tow

turns per inch

twisting

wc system

woolen yarns

worsted yarns

wr system

yarn numbers

Z twist

Review Questions

1.   Identify the advantages textured yarns bring to textile end-products.

2.   Describe the techniques used to texture filaments.

3.   Does one direction of yarn twist, S or Z, offer an advantage over the other?

4.   Why is the level of twist decreased and the direction of twist alternated in successive twisting or plying procedures?

5.   Explain the importance of twisting spun yarns.

6.   Distinguish between slub yarns and thick-and-thin yarns, between drawing filaments and drawing out in the cotton spinning system.

7.   What yarn features are changed as the level of twist is increased?

8.   Differentiate between indirect and direct yarn numbering systems.

9.   Here is an example of notation used to describe a yarn: 50cc Z 30 tpi x 3 S 15 tpi x 2 Z 7 tpi. Is the yarn a ply, cord, or cable? How many single yarns are used? What yarn numbering system is used? How many ply yarns are used?

10.   Describe the production of chenille yarns. Would this process make these yarns more or less expensive than conventional yarns, and why?

11.   Distinguish between metallic yarns and metal fibers.

6

Fabricating Textiles for Interiors: Weaving

Weaving
   Yarn Components and Positions
   Loom and Weaving Fundamentals

Basic Interlacing Patterns
   Plain Weave and its Variations
   Twill and Herringbone Weaves
   Satin and Sateen Weaves

Decorative Interlacing Patterns
   Dobby Weave
   Surface-Figure Weaves

Leno Weave
Jacquard Weave

Pile Weaving
   Incorporating Extra Filling Yarns
   Incorporating Extra Warp Yarns

Triaxial Weaving

Fabrications are ways to produce fabrics, and each of the several fabrication techniques used to produce textile fabrics creates a structure with distinctive aesthetic and structural features. Because these features affect the serviceability of the fabric, as well as its installation and maintenance requirements, they influence the suitability of the fabric for various end-use applications. The method of fabrication also has a direct effect on the cost of the end product, an important criterion in the selection of most residential and commercial interior textile products.

With the exception of soft floor coverings, most textile fabrics are produced by interlacing yarns in one of several fabrication operations. Among these operations are basic or biaxial weaving, pile weaving, and triaxial weaving. In basic weaving, a set of warp yarns and a set of filling yarns are interlaced at 90-degree angles to each other, to produce an essentially flat, two-dimensional fabric. In pile weaving, one or more sets of additional yarns are interlaced with the base warp and filling to create a pile or depth layer. Three sets of yarns are used in triaxial weaving; the yarns are interlaced at 60-degree angles to produce a flat fabric.

Weaving

Basic or **biaxial weaving** operations involve the crosswise interlacing of one set of yarns with a second set of yarns that is held parallel and tensioned on a loom. Each successive crosswise yarn is passed over and under selected lengthwise yarns in a predetermined interlacing pattern. To a large extent, the complexity of an interlacing pattern reflects the loom used to produce it. Simple interlacing patterns are executed on simple looms, and complex interlacing patterns are executed on complex looms. In any case, all looms have some common features, and all woven fabrics have some common components.

Yarn Components and Positions

Most woven fabrics have one set of lengthwise yarns, known as the **warp yarns**, and one set of crosswise yarns, known as the **filling yarns**, the **weft yarns**, or the **woof**

yarns. (Multiple sets of yarns are used in some decorative interlacing patterns.) One warp yarn is often referred to as an **end**, and one filling yarn as a **pick**. The **true bias**, which is at a 45-degree angle to the warp and filling yarns, exhibits higher elasticity than other directions in fabric. A quality woven fabric is **grain-straight**: all the warp yarns are perpendicular to all the filling yarns (Figure 6.1). Conversion operations used to correct the yarn alignment in off-grain fabrics are discussed in Chapter 9.

Selvages are the narrow (¼ to ¾ inch) lengthwise edges of woven fabric. They are designed to prevent or minimize raveling. Fabrics produced on conventional looms have **conventional selvages**, whereas those produced on newer types of looms may have **tucked-in**, **compacted**, or **leno-reinforced selvages** (see Figure 6.2). When composed of thermoplastic fibers, fabrics woven on newer looms often have a **fused selvage** produced by heat-sealing the edges.

The closeness or compactness of the yarns in woven fabrics is numerically reported as the **fabric count**. Specifically, fabric count is equal to the number of warp

Figure 6.1 Components and features of a grain-straight bi-axially woven fabric.

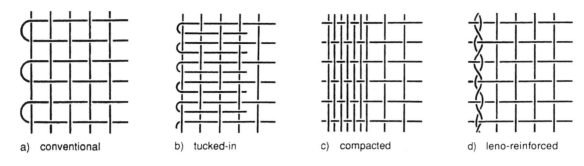

a) conventional   b) tucked-in   c) compacted   d) leno-reinforced

Figure 6.2 Selvages found on biaxially woven fabrics.

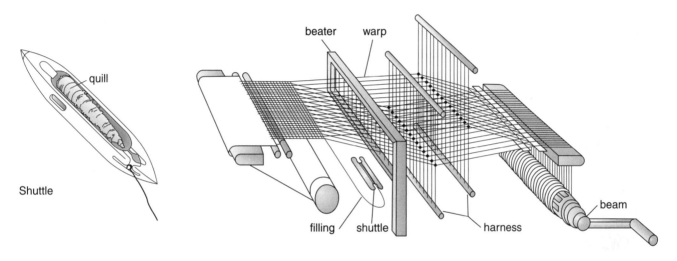

Figure 6.3 Basic parts of a simple loom.
Shuttle is reproduced by permission of Kosa. Loom is reproduced by permission of Brickel Associates Inc.

and filling yarns in one square inch of greige goods. The number of warp yarns is listed first (e.g., 90 × 84). When one number is given—a frequent practice with bed sheets—a **balanced construction**, that is, an equal number of warp and filling yarns, can be assumed. (Fabric count should not be confused with yarn count.)

The **compactness of construction** used in weaving helps to determine the appearance and serviceability of fabrics, as well as their cost. The compactness of curtain and drapery fabrics, for example, influences their decorative characteristics, their ability to reduce glare, their ability to minimize heat gain and loss, and their cost.

Loom and Weaving Fundamentals

Looms used in weaving operations vary in width and efficiency, as well as in complexity. Some looms are constructed to weave fabrics in widths of 36, 45, or 60 inches;

others to weave narrow trimmings efficiently; still others to weave such wide structures as sheeting, blanketing, and carpet. Today, some looms are capable of weaving multiple widths of fabric simultaneously (see Figure 28.2, p. 423).

To execute even a simple interlacing pattern, a loom must have components and control mechanisms to systematically raise and lower specific warp yarns, insert the filling yarns, align each successive filling yarn, and advance the warp yarns and woven fabric as the operation progresses. A complex interlacing pattern requires a loom with additional components and sophisticated control mechanisms.

Parts of a Simple Loom

The component parts of a simple loom are shown in Figure 6.3. **Loom beams** hold the supply of warp yarns. The warp yarns are threaded through **heddles**, thin metal, nylon, or string strips with eye-like openings. The number of heddles required depends on the complexity of the interlacing pattern, the compactness of construction, and the fabric width. **Harnesses** hold the heddles and move up and down, shifting the position of selected warp yarns. The **reed**, a comb-like device with openings called **dents**, helps to keep the warp yarns aligned and ensure grain straightness. The number of **dents per inch** in the reed determines the compactness of the warp yarns. The reed is locked into the **beater bar** or **lay**, which moves forward and backward to beat or lay each new pick into position. A **cloth beam** hold the woven fabric.

On industrial looms, before each warp end is threaded through a heddle, it is threaded through a **drop wire**, a small, curved metal device. If a strained warp yarn breaks during weaving, its drop wire drops, immediately stopping the operation and preventing an unsightly flaw in the fabric.

On conventional looms, the filling yarn is wound on a **bobbin** or **quill** that is carried by a canoe-shaped **shuttle**, shown in detail in Figure 6.3. The devices used on newer looms to carry the filling picks are described later in this chapter.

Threading the Loom

In preparation for drawing-in or threading the warp yarns on the loom, large packages of yarn, known as **cheeses**, are mounted on a **creel frame** (Figure 6.4). Hundreds of yarns are taken from the cheeses and wound evenly on a beam. The yarns are then treated with a hot

Figure 6.4 Warping: winding hundreds of yarns from "cheeses" mounted on a creel frame onto warp beams. *Courtesy of Burlington Industries, Inc.*

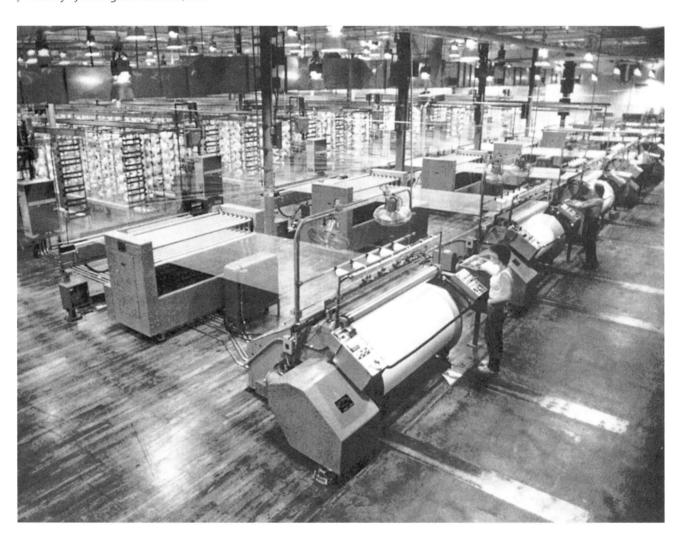

starch or sizing compound in an operation known as **slashing**. This treatment makes the yarns smoother and stronger, enabling them better to withstand the weaving stresses. It should be noted that warp yarns are usually simple yarns. Complex yarns generally lack the strength needed to withstand the weaving tension, and their decorative effects could be abraded by the drop wires, heddles, and the reed.

The loom beam full of slashed and dried warp yarns is placed on the loom. Each end is then unwound, threaded through a drop wire, an eye in a heddle, and a dent in the reed, and tied onto the cloth beam. A pattern draft or point design serves as a guide for drawing the warp yarns through the heddles.

Pattern Drafts **Pattern drafts** or **point designs** are graphic representations of an interlacing pattern only; they do not indicate yarn size or fabric count. Blocked paper is used to record the planned interlacings. Each lengthwise division of the draft paper represents one warp end and each crosswise division represents one filling pick; each block thus represents the perpendicular crossing of the yarns. When an end passes over a pick, the intersection is darkened; when an end passes behind a pick, the intersection is left blank.

The draft of a plain-weave interlacing pattern is shown in Figure 6.5. Because each end passes over and under successive picks in this weave, the draft resembles a checkerboard. It is apparent that more involved interlacing patterns have more elaborate drafts (see Figures 23.3, p. 361, and 27.16, p. 406).

Figure 6.5 Draft of pattern draft of plain-weave interlacing.

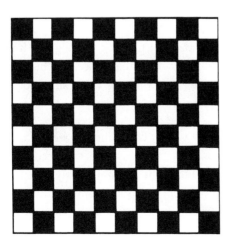

Following the draft of the plain weave, for example, the technician would draw-in or thread all even-numbered warp yarns through the heddles on one harness and all odd-numbered warp yarns through the heddles on a second harness. The need for more heddles and harnesses with more complicated interlacing patterns will be understood after the basic weaving operation is reviewed.

Basic Weaving Operation

Whether a simple or a complex interlacing pattern is being woven, the weaving sequence includes four steps: **shedding**, **picking**, **battening**, and **taking up and letting off**.

Shedding   In shedding, some harnesses are raised, lifting the warp yarns threaded through heddles held by these harnesses, and some harnesses are lowered, lowering the remaining warp yarns. This creates a V-shaped opening called the **shed**. Mechanized attachments automatically position the harnesses on industrial looms, whereas artisans selectively depress foot-controlled treadles and hand-controlled levers to regulate shedding on hand looms.

Picking   In this step, one or more picks are propelled or carried through the shed. Conventional looms, often called **flying shuttle looms**, have stick-like attachments that hammer the shuttle and send it "flying" through the shed. Because these looms are comparatively slow and create a great deal of noise, they are being replaced with quieter, more efficient looms.

Newer, so-called **shuttleless looms** have ingenious devices for inserting the picks. Some use a **rapier** (from the French for "sword"), a flexible or rigid metal tape, to "thrust" the picks. As shown in Figure 6.6, one rapier carries the pick to the center of the shed. Here, it is grasped by a second rapier and carried through the remaining width of the shed. The rapiers illustrated are flexible, coiling and recoiling during picking.

Other shuttleless looms use a jet of air or a jet of water to "shoot" the picks, and still others use small projectiles to "grip and pull" the picks. As shown in Figure 6.7, a projectile grips a cut end of a pick and is propelled through the shed, pulling the trailing pick into position. When the projectile reaches the far side of the shed, the grip is released, the pick is cut, and the two ends are turned and tucked into the next shed. Because a jet

Figure 6.6 Action of flexible metal tapes on a rapier loom.
Courtesy of Sulzer-Ruti, Inc.

Figure 6.7 Metal projectile used for picking on a shuttleless loom.
Courtesy of Sulzer-Ruti, Inc.

stream of air disperses rapidly, early air jet looms were relatively narrow. Today, however, air jet looms are capable of weaving wide bed sheeting as they have auxiliary jets to support the picks through the sheds.

Battening In this step, the beater bar or lay moves forward, pushing the inserted pick and aligning it parallel to the other filling yarns. This procedure helps to ensure uniform spacing of the filling yarns and good crosswise grain in the fabric.

Taking Up and Letting Off The last step in the weaving sequence includes two concurrent procedures. Woven fabric is taken up on the cloth beam, and more warp yarn length is let off from the loom beam.

This four-step sequence is repeated until the supply of warp yarns is exhausted. In each successive shedding operation, however, the positions of the harnesses are changed prior to picking.

Because the number of harnesses limits the complexity of the draft that can be followed in drawing-in the warp yarns, it also limits the variety of sheds that can be formed. More than two harnesses are required for interlacing yarns in patterns other than the plain weave and its variations.

Basic Interlacing Patterns

The basic interlacing patterns include the plain, twill, and satin weaves. Each of these weaves has one or more variations. The variations can be produced by slightly altering the shed patterns used, by varying the number of picks inserted in each shed, and by using warp and filling yarns that have different yarn counts.

Plain Weave and its Variations

The **plain weave** is also known as the **tabby** or **homespun weave**. The notation used to describe the interlacing pattern is 1 × 1. This indicates that one warp yarn and one filling yarn alternately pass over one another (see Figure 6.5).

Variations of the basic plain weave include the basket, warp-rib, and filling-rib weaves. The basket variation involves slightly altering the pattern of drawing the warp yarns through the heddles and changing the number of picks inserted in each shed. The rib weaves use an unbalanced fabric count or a combination of yarns with different yarn counts.

Basket Weave

In the **basket weave**, two or more warp yarns, side by side, interlace with one or more filling yarns. When two warp yarns alternately pass over and under one filling yarn, the pattern is described as a 2 × 1 basket weave (Figure 6.8a). Interlacing two warp yarns with two filling yarns is a 2 × 2 basket weave (Figure 6.8b). When the loom is threaded for this pattern, the first two warp yarns are drawn through heddles on one harness, the next two warp yarns are drawn through heddles on the second harness, and so on. Each shed has alternating groups of two warp yarns raised and two warp yarns lowered. The 2 × 2 interlacing is then executed by inserting two picks in each shed.

a) 2x1 interlacing

b) 2x2 interlacing

Figure 6.8 Pattern drafts of selected basket-weave interlacings.

Warp-Rib Weave

The **warp-rib weave** creates a rib effect lengthwise in the fabric. The ribs may be produced by combining warp yarns having different counts or by using a combination of interlacing patterns. **Dimity**, a warp-rib woven fabric, is pictured in Figure 6.9, together with a draft of the interlacing pattern. This photograph is a close-up of the dimity shown in Figure 17.6, p. 282.

Filling-Rib Weave

Filling-rib weave fabrics generally have a 1 × 1 interlacing, but they are distinguished by crosswise three-dimensional ribs or ridges (see Figure 13.3, p. 210). The ribs are produced by cramming (using a higher number of ends than picks per inch) or by incorporating larger yarns in the crosswise direction. These larger yarns may result from extruding filaments or spinning yarns with oversized diameters, plying several single yarns, or grouping several single yarns together without twist.

a) dimity

b) draft of interlacing pattern

Figure 6.9 Dimity, a warp-rib woven fabric.

a) 2/1 interlacing
regular
right-hand
warp-faced

b) 2/4 interlacing
steep
left-handed
filling-faced

c) 2/2 interlacing
regular
herringbone
even

Figure 6.10 Drafts and characteristics of selected twill interlacings.

Twill and Herringbone Weaves

The interlacing patterns used in **twill weaves** are more involved than the patterns used in the plain weave and its variations. Looms must have three or more harnesses to execute twill interlacing patterns.

Notations used with twill weaves describe the interlacing pattern of each warp yarn. The 2/1 notation describing Figure 6.10a, for example, indicates that each warp yarn passes or floats over two filling yarns, under one filling yarn, over two filling yarns, and so on. (Students should note the difference between the notation used for the basket and the twill weave, e.g., a 2 × 1 basket and a 2/1 twill.) In a 2/4 interlacing depicted in the draft shown in Figure 6.10b, each warp yarn passes over two filling yarns and under four filling yarns.

Angle and Direction of the Visual Diagonal

To create the **visual diagonal** characteristic of twill-woven fabrics, each warp yarn must be interlaced one filling yarn above or below the filling yarn interlaced by the adjacent warp yarn. The angle of the visual diagonal de-

pends on the pattern of interlacing and the compactness of construction. Increasing the length of the warp float and increasing the number of warp yarns per inch, for example, increases the angle. The diagonal can be **regular** (at a 45-degree angle), **reclined** (at a less than 45-degree angle), or **steep** (at a greater than 45-degree angle). This diagonal is an appearance feature only; the warp and filling yarns always interlace at a 90-degree angle in basic weaving.

As noted in Figures 6.10a and b, the direction of the visual diagonal is described as either right-hand or left-hand. **Left-hand twills** have a diagonal pattern that descends from left to right; **right-hand twills** have a diagonal that descends from right to left.

Even and Uneven Twill Interlacings

In twill interlacings, each warp or filling yarn must float or pass over a minimum of two yarns before interlacing. When the warp yarns float over a greater number of filling yarns than they pass behind, they cover a greater portion of the fabric surface, and the fabric is described as an **uneven warp-faced twill**. When the filling yarns float over a greater number of warp yarns than they pass behind, the fabric is described as an **uneven filling-faced twill**. The difference between a warp-faced twill and a filling-faced twill can be seen by comparing Figures 6.10a and b. When an interlacing pattern has equal amounts of warp and filling yarns covering the fabric surface, as illustrated in Figure 6.10c, the fabric is described as an **even twill**.

Herringbone Weave

In **herringbone weaves**, the direction of the visual diagonal is continually reversed across the width of the fabric, as shown by the draft in Figure 6.10c. Lengthwise, successive diagonals repeat in the same direction.

Satin and Sateen Weaves

Like warp-faced twill fabrics, **satin** fabrics have floating warp yarns. In satin interlacings, however, a visual diagonal does not appear because adjacent warp yarns do not interlace with adjacent filling yarns.

Satin interlacing patterns require more shed variations than do basic twill patterns. To produce the satin weave depicted in Figure 6.11a, five harnesses would need to be threaded. This pattern is described as five-shaft construction, indicating that each warp yarn is floating over four picks and under the fifth.

Satin-woven fabrics are characterized by high luster and sheen, primarily produced by the reflection of large amounts of light from the smooth, uninterrupted surface areas of the floats, but also frequently augmented by the use of bright fibers. The level of luster will be reduced if abrasion ruptures the floating yarns during use.

Figure 6.11 Drafts of selected satin and sateen (filling-faced satin) interlacings.

a) 5-shaft satin   b) sateen

Sateen Weave

In **sateen** interlacing, the filling yarns float over the warp yarns (Figure 6.11b). This weave, which is also known as the **filling-faced satin weave**, is frequently used to produce drapery lining fabrics (see Chapter 17).

Decorative Interlacing Patterns

The relative simplicity of the basic weaves and their variations can readily be appreciated when they are compared to the decorative weaves, in which several simple weaves and multiple sets of yarns are often used. The decorative weaves include the dobby, the surface-figure, the leno, and the Jacquard weaves. Because decorative appearance features are often important selection criteria, these complex interlacing patterns are used extensively in the production of interior textile fabrics.

Dobby Weave

Dobby weaving is used to interlace yarns into fabrics having small, geometric motifs. Although the motifs are comparatively simple, dobby looms must have as many as twenty or thirty harnesses to produce the variety of sheds required.

In order to ensure accurate weaving of the motifs, the technician must carefully follow the pattern draft when drawing the warp yarns through the many heddles held by the several harnesses. During weaving, the positions of the harnesses for each shed are mechanically controlled by a unit attached to the side of the loom. This unit has a pattern roll similar to the paper music roll used with player pianos. The holes punched in the pattern roll determine which harnesses will be raised and which will be lowered, as the holes punched in the music roll determine which keys will be played.

Surface-Figure Weaves

Surface-figure weaves are executed on a dobby loom, using extra yarns to produce raised figures while the base fabric is being woven. These interlacing patterns, including dot or spot weaving, swivel weaving, and lappet weav-

a) Dot or Spot Weave   b) Swivel Weave   c) Lappet Weave

Figure 6.12 Surface figure weaves.

ing, are used to produce several curtain fabrics (see Chapter 17), and the dot or spot technique is used to produce assorted upholstery fabrics (see Figure 13.9, p. 212).

Dot or Spot Weave

In **dot or spot weaving**, extra yarns are periodically interlaced with the base yarns to create a small dot or figured spot (Figure 6.12a). Between the decorative figures or dots, the extra yarns are floated on the back of the fabric. When the floating yarns are left in place, the fabric is known as an **unclipped dot or spot fabric**; when the floating yarns are cut away, the fabric is known as a **clipped dot or spot fabric**. When the base fabric is sheer, the floats should be clipped to avoid linear shadows, especially when the fabric is intended for use as a window covering. Either side of a clipped dot or spot fabric can be used as the face side (Figure 17.11, p. 285). The floating yarns should be left unclipped in opaque fabrics to minimize the possibility that the dots or spots will be removed by in-use abrasion and cleaning.

Swivel Weave

In **swivel weaving**, extra yarns periodically swivel around or encircle the base yarns to create small, secure dots (Figure 6.12b). Some imported **dotted swiss** is produced with this interlacing technique, but the relatively slow rate of production precludes its widespread use.

Lappet Weave

In **lappet weaving**, hundreds of needles are used to interlace extra warp yarns. The needles are shifted laterally to create a zigzag surface pattern that resembles hand embroidery (Figure 6.12c). Lappet fabrics, like swivel

Figure 6.13 Leno-weave interlacing.

fabrics, are woven at comparatively slow rates, and their availability has greatly diminished.

Leno Weave

Looms with special attachments are used for the **leno weave**, in which paired warp yarns cross as they encircle and secure the filling yarns. As sketched in Figure 6.13, the warp yarns do not twist around one another; one yarn in each pair always passes in front of the second yarn. Although the individual warp yarns are not parallel, the paired groups are, and the structure is essentially biaxial.

Marquisette, a transparent, leno-weave window covering is pictured in Figures 15.2a (p. 250), and 17.13

(p. 286). **Casements** with leno interlacings are pictured in Figures 15.3 (p. 252) and 17.14 (p. 281).

Jacquard Weave

Jacquard-woven fabrics often have extremely complex interlacing patterns combining two or more simple weaves, multiple sets of yarns, and strategically placed colors. Typically, the pattern repeats are large and composed of various motifs, each having finely detailed curved and swirled shapes. It is apparent that the Jacquard loom must have the capacity to form an almost unlimited variety of intricate sheds and to facilitate the selection of specific colors of picks.

As explained earlier, the variety of possible shed patterns can be explained by increasing the number of harnesses. For intricate Jacquard patterns, however, the number of sheds required to complete one repeat may be so large that hundreds of harnesses would be needed. Not only would a loom so equipped be massive in size, but drawing-in the warp yarns would be difficult. To avoid these problems, Jacquard looms have a system of cords and hooks in lieu of harness frames. These cords are visible in the central portion of the loom pictured in Figure 6.14.

Each warp yarn is threaded through a cord heddle that is linked to a needle by a rod and hook apparatus. In effect, each cord heddle functions as a miniature harness that can be raised and lowered independently of all the other heddles. The position of each cord, and thus of each warp yarn, in a shed is controlled by a programmed card resembling that formerly used with computers or, increasingly, by computer tape. One programmed card is key-punched for each shed in the pattern repeat. Figure 6.14 shows the several cards suspended above the loom.

In the Jacquard weaving operation, a programmed card is brought into position and the needles shift forward. When a needle encounters a hole in the card, the hook is permitted to rise, carrying the warp yarn upward; when a needle encounters a solid portion of the card, the hook is not permitted to rise and the warp yarn remains down. The picking, battening, and taking up and letting off weaving procedures follow. The second card is then brought into position, and the four-step weaving operation is repeated. This sequence is continued until the pattern repeat is completed. A second repeat is then woven, again using the programmed cards to control the interlacings.

Today, computer software is increasingly used to design the intricate motifs and to control the complex shedding used in Jacquard weaving. Jacquard woven upholstery fabrics are pictured in Chapter 13, and Jacquard woven drapery fabrics are pictured in Chapter 17. The use of Jacquard mechanisms in the weaving of Wilton carpet is explained in Chapter 23.

Pile Weaving

Woven pile fabrics are constructed by interlacing three sets of yarns: one set of warp yarns and one set of filling yarns for the base fabric and one set of warp or filling yarns for the pile layer. In the finished fabrics, the pile yarns are more or less perpendicular to the base yarns, introducing a dimension of height to otherwise two-dimensional fabrics.

Incorporating Extra Filling Yarns

Filling pile fabrics, including corduroy and velveteen, are produced by incorporating an extra set of filling yarns. Corduroy has lengthwise ridges of pile yarns, called wales, whereas velveteen has uniformly spaced pile yarns; the manner of interlacing the pile yarns differs for each fabric.

Producing Corduroy

To produce **corduroy**, the filling pile yarns are floated over a number of base warp yarns and then interlaced with others. For wider **wales**, which are often preferred for interior applications, the pile yarns may be floated over five or six base yarns before they are interlaced. Each successive pile yarn must cross over and under the same base warp yarns to ensure that the floats are aligned in lengthwise rows. For high pile density, two, three, four, or more pile yarns may be interlaced before a base filling is interlaced.

After the weaving operation has been completed, thin metal guides are used to lift the floats as circular knives cut them. When wide and narrow wales are planned, the floats are cut off-center. The surface is then brushed to raise the cut ends, forming the lengthwise wales and exposing the fabric areas that had been covered by the

Figure 6.14 Jacquard loom.
Courtesy of the American Textile Manufacturers Institute.

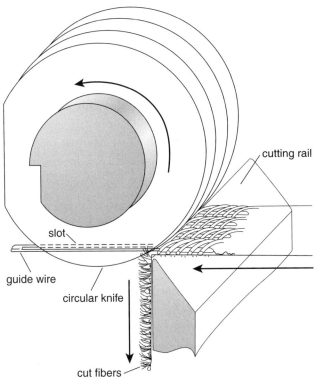

Figure 6.15 Production of corduroy, a filling pile fabric. *Courtesy of Crompton & Knowles Corporation.*

floats. These weaving, cutting, and brushing procedures are illustrated in Figure 6.15.

During fabric conversion, the pile yarns are laid in one direction, introducing a surface feature known as pile lay, pile sweep, or fabric nap. This reorientation of the pile yarns (illustrated in Figure 9.4, p. 135) alters the reflective characteristics of the surface, as well as the tactile features. The marked sweep of the pile yarns in the fabric pictured in Figure 6.16 is evident; this novelty corduroy has a patterned pile with some of the floats left uncut for added visual interest.

Producing Velveteen

Velveteen construction differs from that of corduroy in three major ways. First, the filling pile yarns used are usually much finer than those used in corduroy. Second, each successive pile yarn crosses over and under different base warp yarns to avoid having the floats aligned in lengthwise rows. Third, the pile yarns are floated over no more than two base warp yarns, and more floats are used per inch. Collectively, these construction features produce a

Figure 6.16 Novelty corduroy having a patterned pile with some filling pile floats left uncut.

short, dense pile layer without wales. As with corduroy, the floats are cut, raised, and laid in one direction after the weaving operation has been completed.

Incorporating Extra Warp Yarns

Warp pile fabrics are made by incorporating an extra set of warp yarns during weaving. Three kinds of weaving operations are used to produce these fabrics.

Doublecloth Construction Technique

The **doublecloth construction technique** produces two lengths of velvet in one weaving operation. As shown in Figure 6.17, the pile layers are formed by alternately interlacing the extra set of warp yarns with the base yarns forming the upper fabric and with those forming the lower fabric. The interlacing pattern is controlled to avoid the formation of crosswise wales. As the weaving progresses, the pile yarns joining the two fabrics are cut, and the two fabrics are taken up on separate cloth beams.

The pile yarns may be interlaced in such a manner that the pile tufts have a V-shaped configuration or a W-shaped configuration. In the **V pattern** (Figure 6.18a), each pile yarn is anchored by one base filling, while in the **W pattern** (Figure 6.18b), each pile yarn is anchored by three base yarns. The W form is inherently more stable, but the V form can be stabilized by weaving the base compactly and applying an adhesive coating to the fabric back. Using a high pile density with either pattern will improve texture retention and abrasion resistance during the product's use.

Over-the-Wire Construction Technique

The **over-the-wire construction technique** is used for weaving some pile upholstery fabrics and some carpet. In this procedure, illustrated in Figure 6.19, wires are used to support the pile yarns during weaving. The height of the pile layer can be controlled by the height of the wires used. The wires are withdrawn after several successive rows of pile loops have been woven. When a cut pile sur-

Figure 6.17 The doublecloth construction technique. *Courtesy of Crompton & Knowles Corporation.*

Cross Section

a) V interlacing

Cross Section

b) W interlacing

Figure 6.18 V and W forms of pile interlacing patterns. *Courtesy of Brickel Associates, Inc.*

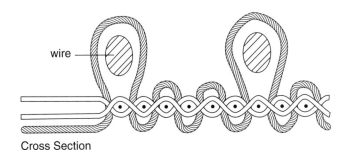

wire

Cross Section

Figure 6.19 The over-the-wire construction technique. *Reproduced with adaptations courtesy of Brickel Associates, Inc.*

face texture is planned, the wires have a knife blade on one end; the wires have rounded ends when an uncut pile surface is planned.

The over-the-wire construction technique is used for **frieze** and **grospoint** upholstery fabrics (see Figures 13.24, p. 219, and 13.25, p. 220, respectively). It also is used for weaving **velvet carpet** (see Chapter 23).

Slack Tension Technique

The warp pile weaving operation used to produce terry toweling (Figure 28.1, p. 422) is known as the **slack tension technique**. During weaving, the base warp yarns are held under regular (high) tension, and the pile warp yarns are held under slackened tension. As the reed moves forward in the battening operation, it compacts the filling picks and pushes the slackened yarns into pile loops on the fabric surface. For greater durability, the number of picks per crosswise row of loops may be increased from three to four or five, but the number of picks must be limited to preserve the number of pile loops available for absorption. A Jacquard mechanism may be used to produce elaborate, multicolored patterns in the pile layer (Figure 28.2. p. 423).

Triaxial Weaving

Triaxial weaving is a relatively new fabrication technique. In this operation, two sets of warp yarns and one set of filling yarns are interlaced at 60-degree angles rather than 90-degree angles. Whereas selected warp yarns are raised and lowered in basic shedding operations, in triaxial shedding operations all yarns in each set of warp yarns are alternately raised and lowered. This results in one set of warp yarns always passing over the filling yarns and the other set always passing behind the filling yarns, as illustrated in Figure 6.20.

Triaxially woven fabrics are strong, yet lightweight. This feature, along with stretchability and high resistance to tearing, supports the increased use of these fabrics for upholstered furniture and automobile seat coverings.

Figure 6.20 Triaxial interlacing pattern.

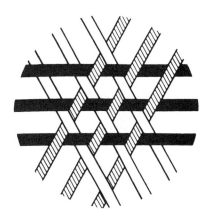

Summary

Among the fabrication techniques used to interlace textile yarns or yarn-like structures are basic weaving, pile weaving, and triaxial weaving. Relatively simple interlacing patterns, like the plain, twill, and satin weaves and their respective variations, can be executed on comparatively simple looms. By contrast, complicated interlacing patterns, like those followed in the dobby, surface-figure, leno, and Jacquard weaves, must be produced on complex looms with sophisticated control mechanisms.

Pile weaving operations use a minimum of three sets of yarns. Two sets are interlaced to form the base fabric, while the third set is simultaneously incorporated to form a pile or depth layer. Such woven pile fabrics as corduroy, velvet, terry, and carpet are used for a wide variety of interior applications.

Three sets of yarns are also used in triaxial weaving operations. In this technique, the yarns are interlaced at 60-degree rather than 90-degree angles. Triaxial weaving is increasingly used by fabric producers to expand the assortment of greige goods available to downstream firms.

Key Terms

balanced construction

basket weave

battening

beater bar

biaxial weaving

bobbin

casements

cheeses

clipped dot or spot fabric

cloth beam

compacted selvage

compactness of construction

conventional selvage

corduroy

creel frame

dents

dents per inch

dimity

dobby weave

dot or spot weave

dotted swiss

doublecloth construction technique

drop wire

end

even twill

fabric count

filling pile fabric

filling-faced satin weave

filling-rib weave

filling yarns

flying shuttle loom

friezé

fused selvage

grain-straight

grospoint

harnesses

heddles

herringbone weave

homespun weave

Jacquard weave

lappet weaving

lay

left-hand twill

leno weave

leno-reinforced selvage

loom beam

marquisette

over-the-wire construction technique

pattern drafts

pick

picking

plain weave

point designs

quill

rapier

reclined diagonal

reed

regular diagonal

right-hand twill

sateen

satin

selvages

shed

shedding

shuttle

shuttleless looms

slack tension technique

slashing

steep diagonal

swivel weave

tabby weave

taking up and letting off

triaxial weave

true bias

tucked-in selvage

twill weave

unclipped dot or spot fabric

uneven filling-faced twill

uneven warp-faced twill

V pattern interlacing

velvet carpet

velveteen

visual diagonal

W pattern interlacing

wales

warp pile fabric

warp-rib weave

warp yarns

weft yarns

woof yarns

Review Questions

1. Differentiate between biaxial and triaxial weaving.

2. Identify the features of a grain-straight fabric.

3. Explain the function of each part of the loom in the basic weaving process.

4. Why are complex yarns rarely, if ever, used as warp yarns?

5. Why are shuttleless looms replacing flying shuttle looms?

6. Would hydrophilic fibers be used in fabric being woven on water jet looms?

7. Name some specific advantages offered by air jet looms.

8. Explain the following notations: 2×1, 2×2, 4×4, $2/1$, and $2/2$.

9. Examine the close-up photograph and pattern draft of dimity shown in Figure 6.9 and explain why some textile authorities say that dimity is a basket-weave fabric.

10. How is the visual diagonal created in twill weaving?

11. Why is the sateen weave sometimes referred to as the filling-faced satin weave?

12. When should the floats be clipped in dot or spot weaving? When should they be left unclipped?

13. Why are harnesses not used on Jacquard looms?

7

Fabricating Textiles for Interiors: Other Techniques

Knitting
> *Warp Knitting*
> *Weft or Filling Knitting*
> *Crocheting*
> *Chain Stitching*

Tufting and Fusion Bonding
> *Tufting*
> *Fusion Bonding*

Knotting and Twisting Yarns
> *Producing Macramé*
> *Lace Making*

Braiding Yarns

Combining Fibers
> *Bonding Fibrous Batts*
> *Felting Fibrous Batts*
> *Needlepunching Fibrous Batts*
> *Spunbonding Webs of Filaments*
> *Spunlacing Fibers*

Extruding Polymer Solutions

Besides the techniques used to weave or interlace yarns, several other methods can be used to combine yarns into textile structures suitable for interior applications. Yarns can be interlooped, inserted or embedded, braided, or knotted and twisted. Techniques are also available that use no yarns, enabling producers to combine fibers directly into fabrics, and one technique uses neither yarns nor fibers, allowing producers to convert polymer solutions directly into film fabrics.

In recent years, existing fabrication techniques have been revised and combined, and entirely new processes have been invented, expanding the variety of fabric production methods available to the industry. While the primary goal of this expansion was to control or reduce production time and material costs, textile engineers also sought to enable manufacturers to control the aesthetic, functional, and structural features of their fabrics efficiently. The resulting operations have helped producers respond more quickly and accurately to changing product selection criteria among consumers.

Knitting

Three major interior textile fabrications use yarn interlooping operations to produce fabrics: the age-old techniques of knitting and crocheting, and the relatively new technique of chain-stitching.

Knitting operations are separated into two major categories, warp knitting and weft or filling knitting, according to the manner in which the yarns are interlooped. Although different stitches are used in these operations, all knitted fabrics have some common features.

Rows of yarn loops running lengthwise in a knitted fabric are known as **wales**, and those running crosswise are known as **courses**. The wales and courses should be at right angles to one another, in much the same way as warp and filling yarns should be perpendicular to one another in woven fabrics. Unlike woven fabric, in which the true bias offers the greatest elasticity, knitted fabrics are generally most stretchable in the crosswise direction, since the rounded loops expand and contract laterally.

The compactness of construction of knitted fabrics is determined by the gauge used. The **gauge** is the number of loops per inch or per bar inch (1½ inches) and is controlled by the size of the knitting needles. Along with the size of the yarns used, gauge helps to determine the transparency, porosity, and weight of the fabric.

Warp Knitting

In **warp knitting**, fabrics are produced by the simultaneous interlooping of adjacent warp yarns. As shown in Figure 7.1, a portion of each yarn has a diagonal orientation but the wales are essentially parallel. Although courses can be identified, no filling yarns are used.

Warp knitting is an extremely fast operation, with large machines producing more than four million loops per minute. Warp knitting machines can construct fabrics up to 168 inches in width, but only in flat, rectangular shapes.

Stitches

Two warp knitting stitches, the tricot stitch and the raschel stitch, are commonly used for interior fabrics.

Figure 7.1 Interlooping of adjacent yarns in warp knitting.

Head of Spring Needle

Figure 7.2 Head of spring needle used in tricot stitching. *Courtesy of Kosa.*

Head of Latch Needle

Figure 7.3 Head of latch needle used in raschel stitching. *Courtesy of Kosa.*

The **tricot stitch** is produced using spring needles, illustrated in Figure 7.2, and one or two **guide bars**, attachments that guide or shift yarns around the hooked or curved portion of the needles prior to interlooping.

Tricot fabrics are distinguished by the presence of herringbone-like wales on the face of the fabric and by a crosswise rib-like effect on the back of the fabric. Tricot-stitched fabrics have comparatively low stretchability. When these fabrics are made of thermoplastic fibers, heat setting can be used to improve their dimensional stability. Tricot fabrics are used for automobile interiors, upholstered furniture coverings, and wall coverings.

The **raschel stitch** is executed on a machine that may be equipped with up to thirty guide bars, which select and position the various yarns in preparation for interlooping. Increasing the number of guide bars is equivalent to increasing the number of harnesses on looms; thus, raschel machines are extremely versatile. As shown in Figure 7.3, the needles used have a latch that opens and closes to secure the yarn, enabling the manufacturer to use virtually any fiber and any style of yarn.

Raschel-stitched fabrics often have a lace-like appearance and are used as window coverings (see Figure 17.25, p. 292). They are also often produced for use as tabletop accessories.

Weft Insertion

Warp knitting and weaving are combined in a relatively new fabrication technique known as **weft insertion**. In this operation, weft or filling yarns are inserted or "woven" through the loops being formed in a tricot-stitching operation. One of the distinct advantages weft-inserted fabrics offer is readily apparent in Figure 7.4. Virtually all of the fabric weight and cover is provided by the weft yarns; thus, the need for larger and more expensive warp yarns is reduced. Because the transparency and covering power of the fabric can be controlled by the size and character of the weft yarns used, manufacturers are increasingly using weft insertion to produce window coverings (see Figure 17.26, p. 292).

Figure 7.4 Fabric produced by weft insertion. *Courtesy of Celanese Corporation.*

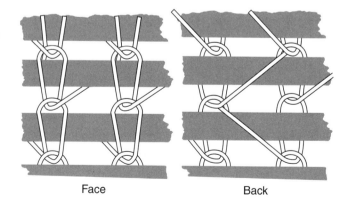

Face   Back

Weft or Filling Knitting

In **weft** or **filling knitting** (Figure 7.5), fabrics are produced by continuously interlooping one or more yarns from side to side, creating one course after another. No warp yarns are used.

Filling knitting is slower than warp knitting. Approximately three million loops are formed per minute. While warp knitting machines can produce only flat, straight-sided fabrics, filling knitting machines can produce rectangular fabrics, fabrics with a circular or tubular form, and fabrics with a preplanned, angular shape. Knitting flat-to-shape, a procedure used extensively in the production of apparel items, is rarely if ever used in the production of interior textile items. Circular knitting, shown in Figure 7.6, produces the fabric used in the knit-de-knit yarn texturing method explained in Chapter 5.

Stitches

Among the filling knitting stitches used to manufacture interior fabrics are the jersey stitch and the interlock stitch. The **jersey stitch**, used in some bedsheets, creates herringbone-like wales on the face of the fabric and crescent-shaped loops on the back of the fabric. Knitted pile fabrics, used to make simulated fur bedspreads, are formed by incorporating additional yarns or fibers into a jersey-stitched base fabric.

Figure 7.5 Continuous interlooping of one yarn in filling knitting.

The **interlock stitch** is formed by continuously interlooping two yarns. The completed fabric appears to be two interknitted fabrics, as shown schematically in Figure 7.7. Interlock-stitched fabrics are resistant to running and snagging and have high dimensional stability when heat set. These characteristics support the selection of **doubleknit fabrics**—interlock-stitched fabrics with relatively large loops—for use as furniture and wall coverings.

Crocheting

Crocheting can be described as knitting with one needle. The needle is continually manipulated to interloop one yarn into previously formed loops. Artisans use crocheting to make decorative borders for pillowcases and to create such accessories as afghans, doilies, and potholders.

Chain-Stitching

Over the past several years, advances in technology have enabled manufacturers to produce fabrics more rapidly than they could with conventional techniques. In two fast new techniques, stitch-knitting and stitch-bonding, knitting stitches are used as stabilizing chain-stitches.

Stitch-Knitting

Stitch-knitting, which is also known as knit-sewing and by the patented name of Malimo, is an innovative fabrication technique. In this operation, webs of yarns are layered and chain-stitched together to produce a usable fabric structure. The chain-stitching is, in effect, "sewing" with knitting stitches, and the rate of fabric production is high. As no abrasive mechanisms (such as drop wires, heddles, or reeds) are used, highly decorative, complex yarns can be incorporated in either fabric direction. This yarn placement flexibility permits manufacturers to control the level of fabric transparency easily and produce fabrics that vary widely in their visual and textural features. Fabrics produced by this technique are shown in Figure 17.27, (p. 293).

Figure 7.6 Circular knitting machine.
Courtesy of the American Textile Manufacturers Institute.

Stitch-Bonding

Stitch-bonding operations involve chain-stitching across a fibrous batt, converting the layered webs of fibers into a usable textile structure. A stitch-bonded window covering is shown in Figure 17.29 (p. 294).

Figure 7.7 An interlock-stitched fabric.

Tufting and Fusion Bonding

Tufting and fusion bonding operations are used to introduce pile yarns to already-formed fabrics. Both techniques are fast and efficient.

Tufting

In **tufting** operations, pile yarns are threaded through needles that are mounted across the tufting machine and suspended vertically above the base fabric. As shown in Figure 7.8, the needles punch through the back of the fabric and loopers engage the yarns. As each needle is withdrawn, a pile loop is formed. If a cut-pile texture is desired, the loopers are equipped with oscillating knives.

At this stage, the tufted pile yarns could easily be pulled out as they are only held in the base fabric mechanically. To provide better stability, a thin coating of an adhesive compound is applied to the fabric back.

Tufting has captured a modest portion of the upholstery fabrics market, but it has taken over the soft floor coverings market, accounting for more than 96 percent of

Figure 7.8 Tufting operations.
Courtesy of Kosa.

Formation of Loop Pile

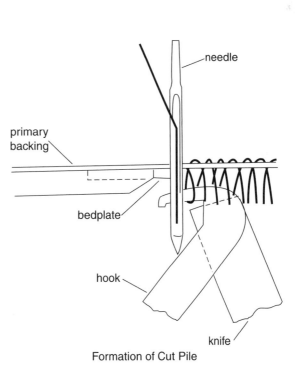

Formation of Cut Pile

all carpet and rugs produced. Readers may refer to Chapter 22 for an extensive discussion of tufting processes.

Fusion Bonding

In **fusion bonding** operations, pile yarns are inserted, or, more precisely, embedded, into an adhesive coating that has been applied to a base fabric. This technique, increasingly used in the production of soft floor coverings, is discussed and illustrated in Chapter 23.

Knotting and Twisting Yarns

Highly decorative lace and macramé fabrics are produced by knotting or twisting intersecting yarns. A major difference between these two kinds of fabric is the size of the yarns used, with macramé items made up of heavier strands.

Producing Macramé

Macramé is usually a relatively heavy fabric constructed by knotting and twisting textile cords. Machine-made macramé is used in vertical blinds, and hand-made macramé panels are used as decorative hangings.

Lace Making

In the manufacture of lace fabrics, complex machinery is used to twist relatively fine yarns around one another. The yarns in lace fabrics are not parallel and perpendicular; they are instead oriented in various directions. Machine-made lace is used in window coverings, bed coverings, and tabletop accents. Hand-made lace, produced using small bobbins, is used as trimming for bedding products and is constructed into such items as dresser scarves and **doilies**.

Creating Bobbin Lace

Multiple pairs of bobbins are used to twist and cross yarns in the production of **bobbin lace**. The small wooden bobbins are wound with a length of yarn and hung below the work area to keep the yarns under slight tension. With practice, skill, and patience, artisans manipulate the several bobbins in twisting and crossing motions (Figures 7.9a and b). These motions are combined to execute various stitches, two of which are illustrated in Figures 7.9c and d.

Bobbin lace may be designed and constructed for such interior uses as open casements in window treatments. It may also be produced for use as coverings for decorative pillows.

Figure 7.9 Basic motions and stitches used in the production of bobbin lace.

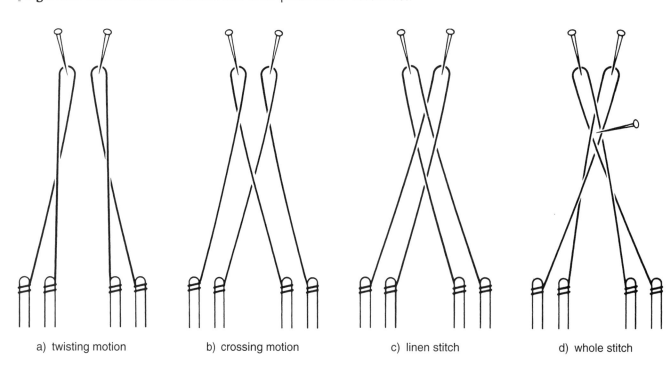

a) twisting motion   b) crossing motion   c) linen stitch   d) whole stitch

Creating Tatted Lace

In **tatting**, the artisan deftly moves one small bobbin to twist fine yarns into open fabric structures. Tatting often produces such small items as doilies and other tabletop accessories.

Braiding Yarns

Braiding techniques are similar in some ways to basic weaving, triaxial weaving, and twisting operations. As in basic weaving, the yarn strands are interlaced; as in triaxial weaving, the yarns are interlaced at a less than a 90-degree angle; and as in twisting, the direction or orientation of the yarns is continually reversed as production progresses.

To produce **flat braids**, which are frequently used as trims or converted into rugs, three yarns or yarn-like structures are interlaced (see Figure 23.12, p. 367). To produce the **circular braids** often used as accent tiebacks for draperies, several strands are interlaced around a textile cord or other round structure.

Combining Fibers

Textile machinery engineers and producers have devised new ways to produce fabric structures while bypassing the yarn stage. Techniques such as spunbonding and spunlacing have joined the age-old technique of felting and the efficient method of needlepunching as ways to combine fibers directly into fabrics.

Bonding Fibrous Batts

In one fabrication, **fibrous batts** are bonded into essentially flat structures with a paper-like quality. (These nonwoven structures must not be confused with the three-dimensional fibrous batts produced for use as fillings and paddings; see Chapter 12). Webs of fibers are first layered to form a relatively thin batt. The webs may be layered parallel to each other, as shown in Figure 7.10, at right angles, or randomly. An adhesive must be sprayed over the batt to cause nonthermoplastic fibers to adhere to one another. Heat can be used to soften thermoplastic fibers and cause them to stick together.

Bonded-web or **nonwoven fabrics** are used as interfacing in upholstery skirts, adding body and weight. They are also used to interface the heading in curtains and draperies, providing support for such treatments as pleats and scallops (see Chapter 16).

Felting Fibrous Batts

In the production of **felt**, wool fibers are cleaned and carded into thin webs, which are then layered at right angles to form a batt. The batt is exposed to controlled heat, agitation, moisture, and pressure. These conditions cause the overlapping scales of the fibers to intermesh and entangle, compacting and shrinking the batt into felt.

Felt is widely used to prevent artifacts from scratching hard-surfaced tabletops. Thick felt is an effective insulation material. To reduce its cost, felt can be produced from a blend of wool and rayon fibers.

Figure 7.10 Bonding fibrous batts.

Webs of Fibers   Batt of Layered Webs of Fibers   + adhesive or heat   Bonded-Web Fabric

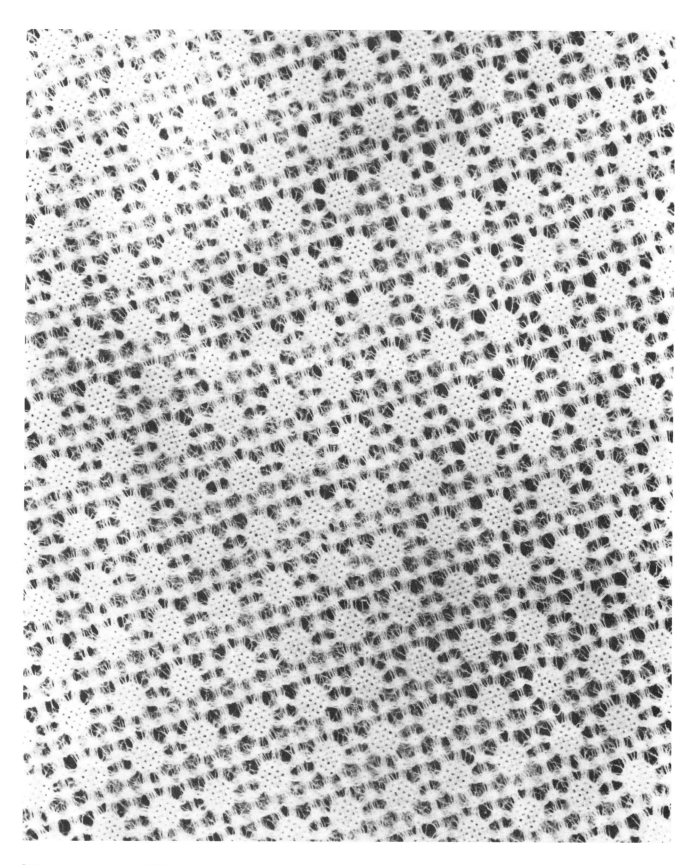

Figure 7.11 Spunlaced fabric.
Courtesy of Burlington Industries, Inc.

Needlepunching Fibrous Batts

The technique of using barbed needles to create a mechanical chain-stitch within a fibrous batt has long been employed in the production of some carpet cushions and saddle blankets. More recently, the method has been refined and used in the production of some carpet, wall coverings, and blankets. For added stability, a loosely woven fabric, called a **scrim**, or an adhesive may be enclosed within the batt prior to **needlepunching**. This fabrication technique is shown in Figure 23.13 (p. 368).

Spunbonding Webs of Filaments

Spunbonding converts thermoplastic filaments directly into fabric structures. After the filaments are arranged into a thin web, they are stabilized with heat or chemical binders. For added strength, stability, weight, or reduced transparency, additional compounds can be sprayed over the fine web. Spunbonded fabrics are increasingly used as tablecloths, as coverings for bedding products, and as backings for wall coverings and carpet.

Spunlacing Fibers

Textile fabrics produced by mechanically entangling fibers are referred to as **spunlaced** fabrics. While an adhesive or other type of binder is generally used with spunbonded and bonded-web fabrics, the fibers in spunlaced fabrics are stabilized solely by fiber-to-fiber friction (Figure 7.11). Today, spunlaced fabrics are used to back textile wall coverings, simulated leather upholstery fabrics, mattress pads, and comforters, and they are also made into pillow coverings.

Extruding Polymer Solutions

Polymer solutions can be converted directly into **film sheeting** fabrics. This is accomplished by extruding the solution through a spinneret that has a narrow slit rather than minute holes. As the polymer ribbon emerges, it is stretched into a thin film or sheet. The thickness of the film can be controlled by varying the extrusion pressure and the amount of stretching. Film sheetings are used for such interior products as simulated leather upholstery coverings, drapery linings, and shower curtains.

Summary

To manufacture the wide variety of interior textile components and fabrics required by end-product producers, a wide range of fabrication techniques is necessarily employed. Several of these techniques enable the fabric producer to interloop, insert, or otherwise combine yarns into greige goods, supplementing the methods used to interlace yarns. Other techniques enable the producer to combine fibers and convert solutions directly into usable structures, avoiding spinning, throwing, and fiber extruding operations. Many of the fabrications reviewed in this chapter are more efficient and less costly than weaving.

Following the sequence of production outlined in Chapter 1, the greige goods produced by weaving, knitting, tufting, spunbonding, and so on are forwarded to colorists or converters. These members of the industry work to make the goods more attractive and functional, helping to ensure their selection by consumers, contract designers, and architects.

Key Terms

bobbin lace

bonded-web fabric

circular braids

courses

crocheting

doilies

doubleknit fabric

felt

fibrous batts

filling knitting

film sheeting

flat braids

fusion bonding

gauge

guide bars

interlock stitch

jersey stitch

knitting

macramé

needlepunching

nonwoven fabric

raschel stitch

scrim

spunbonding

spunlacing

stitch-bonding

stitch-knitting

tatting

tricot stitch

tufting

wales

warp knitting

weft insertion

weft knitting

Review Questions

1. Why is the most stretchable position in knitted fabric generally the crosswise direction?

2. What is the function of the guide bars?

3. How can one distinguish between tricot and jersey fabrics?

4. Both warp knitting and filling knitting are extremely fast production techniques. Does this translate into savings for the ultimate consumer?

5. Why is stitch-knitting sometimes referred to as knit-sewing?

6. Differentiate between tufting and fusion bonding.

7. Why are bonded-web fabrics known as nonwoven fabrics?

8. Distinguish between spunbonded and spunlaced fabrics.

8

Textile Colorants, Color Perception, and Color Application

Colorants and Color Perception
  Nature of Light
  Color Characteristics
  Colorants

Dyeing Fabrics and Fabric Components
  Dyeing in the Fiber Stage
  Coloring in the Yarn Stage
  Dyeing Greige Goods

Printing Greige Goods
  Hand Printing
  Roller Printing
  TAK Printing
  Jet Printing
  Screen Printing

Warp Printing
Transfer Printing
Pigment Printing
Acid Printing

Combining Dyeing and Printing
  Discharge Printing
  Resist Printing

Factors Affecting Apparent Color
  Light Source
  Quantity of Light
  Changes in Texture
  Soil Accumulation
  Composition and Structural Variables

Interior environments are enhanced when the addition of colored textiles is carefully planned. The planning effort entails an examination of factors that alter the apparent characteristics of the textile colorants. Whatever characteristics are chosen, they will appear different when viewed under different conditions; an obvious example of such a condition is the lighting of a particular environment.

The importance of color-related variables to the selection of interior textile products is reflected in the availability of several methods for applying colorants. These methods may be divided into three major categories: dyeing, printing, and dyeing and printing combinations. Colorists select the method of application that can introduce the color styling features preferred by the contemporary consumer or specified by the contract designer or architect.

Carpet and rug fibers, yarns, and greige goods can be colored by the same basic techniques used with other textiles. However, different equipment and procedures are often required for handling these heavier, wider, and bulkier structures, and larger amounts of dyestuff and water are needed to produce an acceptable level of color intensity. In recent years, increased energy costs and heightened concern for water conservation have led to the development of new and innovative techniques for dye application.

Although most natural fibers have some color-producing substances, which may or may not be retained, and most textiles have color-producing substances added, no fibers or other textile structures have intrinsic color. Not until incident light waves are reflected, and interpreted by an observer, will color be perceived.

Colorants and Color Perception

For color to be perceived, incident light waves must first be reflected to the eye. In turn, these rays must stimulate the eye to transmit optical sensations to the brain for interpretation. Only then will the viewer see a particular "color." What the viewer is responding to, in fact, is a concentration of light waves of certain lengths. Because light waves play a critical role in color stimulus and sensation, a brief review of the nature of light will augment our discussion of textile colorants and color perceptions.

Nature of Light

Light is visible electromagnetic energy, which accounts for a relatively small portion of the **electromagnetic spectrum**. This spectrum, schematized in Figure 8.1, includes waves of vastly different lengths, but all are very short. At one end are cosmic and gamma rays, which are quite short; at the opposite end are radio and electrical power waves, which are relatively long in comparison with cosmic waves. The actual length of most waves—the distance from the crest of one wave to the crest of the next—is measured and reported in minuscule units called **nanometers** (nm). One nanometer is equal to one billionth of a meter or to 0.000000039 inch.

In the central portion of the electromagnetic spectrum is an area known as the **visible spectrum**. The lengths of waves in this region range from some 400 nm to about 700 nm. When reflected to the eye, these radia-

| **Figure 8.1** The electromagnetic spectrum.

tions stimulate the eye to send messages to the brain, allowing us to interpret the sensation and see color. While the human eye is not sensitive to wavelengths outside of the visible spectrum, we are aware that some of the so-called invisible rays, for instance, ultraviolet and infrared rays, can have negative effects on colored textiles, altering the reflective characteristics of colorants and degrading the fibers.

Natural and artificial light sources emit all wavelengths within the boundaries of the visible spectrum. They do not, however, have equal mixtures of the various lengths: some have predominantly longer waves, others predominantly shorter waves. Colorants differ in their capacities to reflect the various wavelengths. The length of the waves emitted by the light source together with the length of the waves reflected by the colorant determine the particular color or hue perceived and affect other color characteristics as well.

Color Characteristics

Three color characteristics are determined by the emission, reflection, and interpretation of light waves. These are hue, value, and intensity.

Hue

Depending on the light source, larger quantities of certain wavelengths will be emitted, and, depending on the colorant, larger quantities of certain lengths will be reflected. The length of the waves that predominate in both emission and reflection will determine the particular **hue** or color perceived. When blue is perceived, for example, the illuminant is emitting a high concentration of waves around 465 nm in length and the colorant is reflecting a high concentration of these waves and absorbing other lengths. When green is perceived, a high concentration of waves around 520 nm is being emitted and reflected; when red is perceived, waves around 650 nm are being emitted and reflected; and so on.

Value

Value and **luminosity** are synonyms referring to the effect of the quantity of light being reflected from a textile or other surface. Higher levels of incident light and higher levels of reflected light produce lighter hues. Conversely, lower levels of incident and reflected light produce darker hues. When a compound known to re-

flect all wavelengths, creating white, is used with colorants, a **tint** is produced and value is increased. When a compound known to absorb all wavelengths, creating black, is used with colorants, a **shade** is produced and value is decreased.

Intensity

Intensity and **chroma** are terms used to describe the purity or strength of a color. A blue hue, for example, may appear strong, bright, and clear, or weak, grayed, and dull. Changes in intensity generally produce concomitant changes in value.

The effects of various fiber- and fabric-related variables—such as the presence of delusterants, fiber cross-sectional shapes, and the use of floating yarns—on the luster and brightness of colored textiles were discussed in earlier chapters. The effects of certain finishing agents and processes on color dimensions are described in Chapter 9.

The challenge to the dye chemist is to select a colorant or a mixture of colorants and additives that can create the planned hue, value, and intensity. To accomplish this, the chemist must work cooperatively with fiber, yarn, and fabric producers, as well as with converters.

Colorants

Textile colorants may be dyes or pigments. **Dyes or dyestuffs** are color-producing compounds that are normally soluble in water. **Pigments** are also color-producing agents, but they are insoluble in water. The chemical structure of either type of colorant enables it selectively to absorb and reflect certain wavelengths.

Colorants contain groups called auxochromes and groups called chromophores. **Auxochromes** are responsible for the selective absorption and reflection of light waves: these groups determine the hue. **Chromophores** control the quantity of waves reflected, influencing the value of the hue. The intensity is controlled by the mixture of colorants and the amount of dyestuff accepted by the fibers. Some highly amorphous fibers, such as wool, readily accept high amounts of dye; other fibers, especially those with highly crystallized interiors, do not readily accept dyestuffs, and high pressure and temperature or dye-carriers may be required during the dyeing operation. In some cases, the affinity between the fiber and the dyestuff can be improved by the use of special agents known as **mordants**.

Extensive formal study in the fields of dye chemistry and textile chemistry is necessary for a thorough understanding of colorants and their reaction with or attraction for different fibers. This high level of knowledge is mandatory for the dye chemist, but not for the interior designer, architect, and consumer. Textile chemists and colorists recognize that consumers will prefer fashionable colors to out-of-date ones, and they direct their work accordingly.

Whereas the dye chemist is responsible for the correct match of fiber and colorant, the precise application of the dyestuff or pigment is the responsibility of the dyers and printers. Dyers and printers recognize that adequate penetration of the colorant is needed to produce the planned intensity and to ensure an acceptable level of color retention. They also recognize that accurate placement or registration of all colors will make for better clarity and definition of printed designs.

Dyeing Fabrics and Fabric Components

Dye operations can be carried out at the fiber, yarn, or fabric stage. Most dyeing operations require immersion of the textile into **dye liquor**, an aqueous solution of dyestuff.

Dyeing in the Fiber Stage

Color-producing agents can be added in the fiber stage by one of two methods, solution dyeing and fiber or stock dyeing. Solution dyeing can be used only with manufactured fibers, but fiber dyeing may be used with both natural and manufactured fibers.

Solution Dyeing

Solution dyeing and **dope dyeing** are synonyms for an operation in which dye pigments are added to the polymer solution prior to extrusion. This produces manufactured filaments with coloring agents locked inside the fiber. The term **color-sealed** identifies solution-dyed fibers; because the manufactured fiber producer adds the color, the term **producer-colored** may also be used.

With the color-producing pigment incorporated as an integral part of the fiber, solution-dyed fibers have comparatively high color retention and stability. This supports the use of solution dyeing to color fibers that will be used in carpet produced for installation outdoors. Because such fibers must have little or no capacity to absorb moisture, they cannot absorb sufficient quantities of aqueous dye liquor. The relatively high cost of the pigments, however, precludes the routine use of this technique.

Fiber or Stock Dyeing

Immersing natural or manufactured fibers into dye liquor is known as **fiber or stock dyeing**. Because loose masses of the fibers are submerged, the dyestuff can be absorbed more readily and thoroughly than it can when yarns or fabrics are immersed. In yarn structures, fiber packing and twisting may physically restrict the level of dyeing; in fabrics, yarn crossings and structural compactness may present physical barriers. The old phrase **dyed-in-the-wool** meaning through and through, deeply ingrained, or staunchly dedicated, arose from the observation that wool fibers dyed prior to spinning had richer and deeper colors than those produced by dyeing yarns or fabrics.

Fiber dyeing is frequently used with manufactured staple fibers to produce carpet yarns that simulate the soft, mellow patina of wool. The wool-like appearance is further enhanced when the colored fibers are spun on the woolen system.

Fiber dyeing can be used in combination with yarn production to produce yarns having distinctive color styling. When two or more colors of fibers are uniformly distributed throughout a spun yarn, the term **heather** identifies the coloration. A heather appearance can also be produced by throwing different colors of filaments.

The term **marled** identifies the coloration produced by combining two differently colored rovings together in spinning. Although the resulting structure is a single yarn, its visual spiral resembles that produced by plying two differently colored yarns. A marled yarn is pictured in Figure 8.2.

Ombré, French for **shade**, describes color styling in which there is a gradual change in the value of a single hue, for instance, from pink to red to maroon. In yarns, this delicate color style is produced by carefully controlling the introduction of fibers of the appropriate shade or tint during yarn spinning. If the process is well executed, the location of a change is barely perceptible.

Figure 8.2 A marled yarn.

Figure 8.3 Dyeing packages of yarn in a dye beck.
Courtesy of Solutia Inc., Fibers Division.

Coloring in the Yarn Stage

Adding colorants to yarn structures before fabric formation is known as **yarn dyeing**. Certain techniques, collectively known as space dyeing, can be used to produce multicolored yarns; these techniques are described later in this chapter. Most yarn-dyeing operations, however, produce single-colored yarns, and these yarns cannot be distinguished from those constructed of one color of fiber.

Package Dyeing

The equipment used in **package dyeing** is shown in Figure 8.3. Yarns are first wound on perforated cylinders to form packages of yarn. Because carpet and rug yarns have relatively large diameters, smaller amounts of the strands are wound on the packages. Several packages are then mounted on posts and lowered into a pressure cooker-like vessel known as a **dye beck**. Dye liquor is then forcibly circulated throughout each package of yarn. To ensure adequate penetration of the dye, high levels of pressure and temperatures may be used in the operation; this may be necessary when manufactured fibers with low moisture regain values, such as polyester, nylon, and acrylic, are being dyed.

Beam Dyeing

Beam dyeing is a second way of dyeing yarns a single color. In preparation for the operation, warp yarns are wound on a perforated beam barrel. The beam is then loaded into a beam dyeing machine (Figure 8.4), and the dye liquor is circulated through the yarns, from the outside to the inside and from the inside to the outside, via the perforations. The beams of dyed warp yarns, when rinsed and dried, are ready to be placed on a loom, by-

fabric roll   perforated beam

dye flow

Beam Dyeing Machine

Figure 8.4 Beam dyeing.
Courtesy of Kosa.

passing the unwinding and rewinding operations required after package dyeing. Beam dyeing may also be used for greige goods. (A machine used to beam dye carpet roll-goods is shown in Figure 8.9).

Skein Dyeing

Immersing long skeins of yarn into troughs filled with dye liquor is known as **skein dyeing** (Figure 8.5). This procedure may be employed when the winding and compacting of yarns on cylinders or beam barrels could alter their textural features, or when a relatively small quantity of custom-colored yarn is required. The procedure is rarely used for dyeing large quantities of yarns, however, because it is a relatively slow and therefore costly operation.

Single-colored yarns, each dyed a different shade of the same hue or a different hue, are often plied. Such combinations produce a color style described as **moresque**.

Space Dyeing

Space-dyeing operations produce multicolored yarns. Unlike heather yarns in which the colors are uniformly distributed throughout the yarns, and unlike ombré yarns in which various values of one color are repeated, space-dyed yarns have differently colored segments along their lengths. The various hues may be related or contrasting; the segments may be equal or unequal in length; and the junctures between colors may be sharp or muted.

Although space-dyed yarns, also known as **variegated yarns**, have long been used in the hand and machine knitting of apparel items, their use in interior textiles, es-

Figure 8.5 Skein dyeing carpet pile yarns. *Courtesy of Solutia Inc., Fibers Division.*

pecially in upholstery fabrics and pile carpet, is recent. The styling not only provides visual interest, but the mixture of colors also effectively camouflages the soil that accumulates in use.

Various techniques can produce this color styling. Although some of these techniques are printing rather than dyeing operations, they fall in the category of space dyeing because they create the characteristic coloration. When well-defined, sharp color junctures are planned, sheets of yarns will be printed. When muted junctures of the selected colors are desired, segments of the yarns will be dipped into dye liquor or **jet spraying** may be used. In the latter technique, pressurized dye jets spray dye liquor onto skeins of yarns. Another method uses dye-loaded needles, called **astrojets**, to give packages of yarn repeated, programmed "injections." This **package-injection technique** requires minimal handling of the yarns.

Knit-De-knit Space Dyeing   Yarn texturing and color application are combined in **knit-de-knit space dyeing**. Pile yarns, undyed or precolored, are rapidly knitted into a long, jersey-stitched tube (Figure 5.2c, p. 67). One or more colors are then printed onto the tubing with dye jets before heat setting. Finally, the tube is de-knit or unraveled, producing variegated, crinkled pile yarns (Figure 8.6a). A carpet with a pile layer of these randomly colored yarns is pictured in Figure 8.6b.

Figure 8.6 Knit-de-knit space-dyed yarns and carpet. *Courtesy of Fred Whitaker Company.*

a) knit-de-knit space-dyed yarns

b) level loop space-dyed carpet

Dyeing Greige Goods

Unless colored fibers or yarns were used in fabrication, greige goods bear little resemblance to those offered to residential and commercial consumers. Except for any textural and visual interest contributed by complex yarns or decorative interlacings, such fabrics have virtually no aesthetic appeal. Lacking the critical fashion element of color, such coverings would be summarily rejected by most consumers. For greater consumer appeal, greige goods are virtually always colored.

Dyeing operations once could produce only solid-colored surfaces, and printing techniques only patterned surfaces. Advances in dye chemistry and technology now enable colorists to use immersion processes for the production of multicolored designs and printing techniques for the production of solid-colored surfaces.

Piece Dyeing

Piece dyeing is carried out after fabrication by immersing the piece goods or greige goods into dye liquor. It produces single-colored fabrics with identical color characteristics on both sides.

In dyeing operations involving the immersion or circulation of tufted greige goods in dye liquor, the primary backing may be thinly coated with an adhesive to stabilize the pile tufts. A secondary backing is not applied. Any secondary backing would add bulk and weight, making handling of the long lengths more difficult. A secondary backing of jute would absorb a large amount of dye liquor, increasing the cost of the dyestuffs, as well as the time and expense of drying the floor covering. However, prior to printing greige goods, a secondary backing is normally applied to add dimensional stability and ensure good registration of the colors in the motifs.

Greige rollgoods and rugs may be dyed in a discontinuous or a continuous dyeing operation. Discontinuous operations are so named because the coloring process is interrupted when the wet carpet must be removed from the dyeing machine and dried elsewhere.

Discontinuous Dyeing   Because relatively small quantities or batches of carpet can be dyed in **discontinuous-dyeing** operations, they are often known as **batch-dyeing** operations. They are carried out in various vessels or becks, including a carpet winch, a jet beck, and a horizontal beam-dyeing machine.

SUPRAFLOR with Loading Plaiter

Figure 8.7 The interior of the Supraflor® carpet winch. *Courtesy of Bruckner Machinery Corporation.*

Figure 8.8 The interior of the MCS high temperature jet beck. *Courtesy of Keiltex Corporation.*

In preparation for dyeing in a **carpet winch** (Figure 8.7), the ends of a batch of greige goods weighing approximately 2,000 pounds are sewn together and loaded into the beck. This weight roughly corresponds to 327 linear yards of goods. The full width of carpet is plaited or folded as it is fed into the dye liquor. If the plaiting operation is controlled so that it will produce folds from 8 to 16 inches deep and never creases the carpet in the same place twice, the development of crosswise surface markings will be minimized; avoiding these markings is especially important for velour and plush textures. The carpet is cycled through the dye liquor, which is continually filtered, for an average of two to four hours, and it is then rinsed, unloaded, and dried.

In preparation for dyeing in a **jet beck**, a batch of carpet in rope form is loaded into a long vessel (Figure 8.8).

The unit is nearly 40 feet long, and can accommodate some 2,800 pounds of goods. Jets introduce the dye, and the carpet is cycled through the liquor. For effective dyeing of polyester, temperature and pressure can be elevated.

Beam-dyeing operations begin with the winding of an open width of greige goods on a perforated beam. The beam can accommodate approximately 218 linear feet of carpet that has a total thickness of 0.32 inch and a maximum width of 17.5 feet. The batch is loaded into a horizontal dyeing machine (Figure 8.9) and the dye liquor is forcibly circulated through the rolled goods. Because the carpet is rolled in beam dyeing, soft, deep pile textures would be severely deformed. This technique is therefore generally restricted to the dyeing of low pile, loop textures. A distinct advantage of the operation is that no crossmarks can develop because no folding is involved. When required, higher temperatures can also be used.

Two factors support the increased use of batch-dyeing operations. First, an increase in consumer demand for specialized colorations requires the use of equipment that can economically dye smaller amounts of greige goods. Second, the challenge of reducing the consumption of water and energy can be more effectively met with batch-dyeing operations than with continuous-dyeing methods. Specifically, the becks are designed to use comparatively low **liquor ratios** (pounds of liquor to pounds of carpet). Since water is the principal component in most dye liquors, this results in substantial savings in water cost and drying expenses.

Continuous Dyeing Continuous-dyeing operations are used when large quantities of greige goods are to be dyed one color. Because several lengths of greige goods or undyed carpet are generally sewn together, their construc-

Figure 8.9 Supraflex® carpet beam-dyeing machine. *Courtesy of Bruckner Machinery Corporation.*

tion and composition must be identical or quite similar if uniform color characteristics are to be reproduced. The dyeing systems, known as **ranges**, comprise units for wetting the carpet pile, applying the dyestuff, steaming, washing, drying, and rolling up the dyed and dried goods. These units are aligned so the carpet goes directly from one step to the next. Such operations do not require unloading of the greige goods and transporting them to other units for final processing, so they are said to be continuous.

When carpet is introduced into a continuous-dyeing range, it is wetted to increase dye absorption. In some systems, a squeegee-like blade transfers the dye liquor from a roller to the wet carpet surface. Steaming helps increase the movement or **migration** of the liquor through the pile layer, promoting uniform application of the dye and avoiding the problem of **tippiness**, the concentration of color on the tips of the pile yarns. As the carpet continues through the system, it is washed, dried, and rolled.

Formerly, continuous-dyeing operations required comparatively high liquor ratios. In recent years, these ratios have been reduced by applying the dye in forms that are not highly aqueous solutions. In some cases, the dye is applied as a spray, that is, a mixture of air and dye; in other cases, the dye is carried on the surface of bubbles. One method involves depositing dye on the carpet as foamed dye liquor. The foam is an unstable froth that collapses on the fiber and dyes it.

The spray, bubbles, or foam can be delivered through tubes, jets, or spray nozzles oriented toward the pile layer. They may also be delivered by blades and rollers, blowers, and rotary screens. In any case, the tremendous reduction in water usage in these new dye application methods has resulted in marked savings in processing costs.

Cross Dyeing

Cross dyeing, also called **differential dyeing**, is a color application process based on chemical variables. The process produces a multicolored fabric from a single immersion in one dyebath formulation. Two or more fibers that are chemically different—classified in different generic groups or variants of the same fiber—are strategically placed in yarns or in greige goods. Carpet and rug producers generally use a blend of nylon variants, rather than generically dissimilar fibers, in this coloring operation. For a heather appearance, different fibers are uniformly distributed in the yarns; for plaids or stripes, warp or filling yarns with different fiber contents are used in

bands; and for multicolored design motifs, yarns of different fibers are selectively incorporated during fabrication.

A single dyebath is formulated. The dye chemist, often with the aid of a computer, may select specific dyestuffs, each of which will be accepted by one fiber and rejected by all other fibers, or use one dyestuff that will be absorbed in different amounts by related fiber variants. In the former case, each type of fiber or variant has a different hue, and, in the latter case, each variant has a different level of intensity of the same hue. The economic advantage of cross dyeing is readily apparent: "you only dye once."

A second major advantage of cross dyeing is that orders for specific colors can be filled accurately and quickly. Whatever the color mixture ordered, the stored greige goods are ready for immediate dyeing, finishing, and shipping. Without cross-dyeing technology, fibers or yarns would have to be dyed the necessary number of colors in separate dyebaths; the fibers would then have to be spun or thrown; and, finally, the colored yarns packaged or wound on beams and sent to the mill for preparation of the loom and for winding of the bobbins or cones used for the filling yarns. Shipment would be further delayed by the time required for fabrication and subsequent finishing. Producers who attempt to save time another way—by second guessing the fashion colors of the distant future and coloring fabrics in advance of orders—may find themselves with a sizable inventory of unpopular colors.

Union Dyeing

Like cross dyeing, **union dyeing** is based on chemical variables. Unlike cross dyeing, however, union dyeing is chosen when two or more different fibers are used in a fabric that is to become a single, uniform color. Again, a single dyebath is formulated but each fiber becomes the same color. The use of this method of color application has paralleled the increased use of fiber blends, especially cotton and polyester.

Printing Greige Goods

High-speed mechanized operations are generally used to print greige goods when stylists or contract designers specify printed fabrics. Printing requires thicker dyestuffs than those used in dyeing operations. Whereas migration or movement of the dye is required to achieve a uniform

Figure 8.10 Carved block used in block printing.

level of color in dyed textile structures, such migration in printed goods would result in poor definition of the shapes and details of the motifs. Therefore, the dyestuff used in most printing operations is a **dye paste** rather than a highly aqueous dye liquor. After application of the dye paste, the textile is exposed to steam, heat, or chemicals to fix the dye in or on the fibers.

Hand Printing

Using hand-carved blocks or resist-printing operations, artisans create distinctive block prints, batik prints, tie-dye prints, and ikat prints. Because such hand-printing procedures are time- and labor-intensive, the prints would be expected to be comparatively expensive. They are generally made, however, by artisans in developing countries where labor costs are relatively low.

Block Printing

In preparation for **block printing**, all shapes of the planned design that will be the same color are carved to stand in relief on the face of a block of wood. A separate block is prepared for each color to be printed. The block pictured in Figure 8.10 is unusual in that it is curved instead of square or rectangular; it can be used to print medallion-like motifs.

Figure 8.11 Authentic block print.

During printing, the artisan dips the face of the carved design into the dyestuff and then presses it onto the fabric surface. Since the printer may pick up different amounts of dye paste each time and exert different amounts of pressure with each printing action, various levels of intensity may be seen for the same hue, as in Figure 8.11.

Batik Printing

Beeswax is the resist agent in traditional **batik printing**. It is melted and applied with a tjanting tool to all areas of the fabric that are to resist penetration of the dye liquor. The tjanting has a small copper cup and a tiny spout. In use, the tool functions somewhat like a fountain pen, and skilled artisans can apply fine lines of wax to create intricate details within the motifs.

After the wax hardens, the fabric is immersed into a dye bath; only the nonwaxed areas absorb the dye. The wax is then removed from the fabric by boiling. The artisan again applies melted wax, this time to all areas—including those that are to remain the first color—that are to resist the second dye liquor. If a **crackle effect** characterized by linear striations is planned, the artist randomly cracks the hardened wax at this time. Piece dyeing then results in absorption of the second color in all unwaxed areas, as well as in those areas below any cracks (Figure 8.12). This sequence of wax removal, wax application, and immersion is repeated until all planned colors have been applied.

Tie-Dye Printing

In **tie-dyeing**, folds, gathers, and knots, which are introduced in the fabric and secured with waxed thread, function as the resist medium. These are selected and positioned according to the motifs and pattern scale planned. When the fabric is immersed into the dye bath, the tied-off areas resist penetration of the dye liquor. The fabric is then opened flat and again tied off and immersed in a second dye bath. The processes will be repeated in sequence until all planned colors and designs have been introduced. The tie-dye fabric pictured in Figure 8.13 was produced through two folding and immersing operations.

Figure 8.12 Authentic batik print with crackle effects.

Figure 8.13 Authentic tie-dye print.

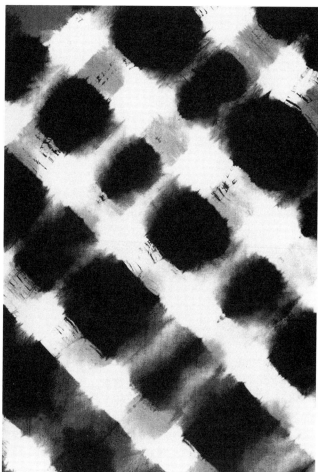

Ikat Printing

In **ikat** (e-cot) **printing**, specific portions of bundles of warp and filling yarns, not fabric, are wrapped to resist dye penetration. The wrapping is carefully positioned to create the planned motifs. Subsequent dyeing results in absorption of the dye liquor by the unwrapped yarn portions only. Portions of the wrapping may be removed and additional colors applied. Because the aqueous dye liquor migrates through the yarns and varied levels of relaxation shrinkage may occur after weaving, ikat motifs have a striated appearance (Figure 8.14).

Although consumers may prefer an authentic block, batik, tie-dye, or ikat printed fabric, many are unable to find the yardage or they conclude that the costs of the imported goods exceed their interior furnishings budget. Recognizing this dilemma, manufacturers often simulate the hand-printed patterns with high-speed, commercial printing techniques. Professionals and consumers can readily distinguish authentic prints from most simulated ones by examining the back of the fabric. Except for block prints, all authentic hand prints have the same depth of color on both sides of the fabric.

Roller Printing

Lighter weight, flat fabrics can be printed with engraved metal rollers. The shapes of those portions of the repeat

Figure 8.14 Authentic ikat print.

that are to be the same color are etched into the surface of one roller. The number of colors planned thus dictates the number of rollers prepared. As schematized in Figure 8.15, small cylinders revolve through the dye paste and transfer the paste to the engraved rollers. A metal squeegee-like blade, called a **doctor blade**, then removes the excess dye paste from the smooth, nonengraved surface areas. As the rollers revolve against the fabric surface, the dye paste is transferred and the pattern repeat is completed. Here, the rollers and the fabric must be properly aligned to ensure that patterns, especially those having linear motifs, are printed on grain.

Large areas, whether in the ground or in the design, cannot be roller printed because the revolving motion of the rollers would create waves in the dye, causing poor registration and definition of the design. Coloring large areas of the ground is more readily accomplished by discharge printing, a technique discussed later in this chapter, and coloring large-scale motifs is more effectively accomplished by screen printing. Screen printing must also be used to print pattern repeats whose lengths exceed the circumference of the rollers.

Although **roller printing** is an extremely fast operation, its use has diminished because the cost of copper, the metal normally used to cover the rollers, and the cost of the labor needed to prepare the rollers have increased. Growing competition from screen printing has also had an effect.

Stalwart Roller Printing

Because carpet and rugs are comparatively heavy textile structures and their printed pattern repeats are typically large, they cannot be printed with engraved metal-covered rollers. They can, however, be roller printed with large cylinders covered with three-dimensional sponge forms (Figure 8.16). The sponges are cut accord-

Figure 8.15 Roller printing.

Figure 8.16 Preparation of the sponge-covered cylinders used in Stalwart printing.
Courtesy of Solutia Inc., Fibers Division.

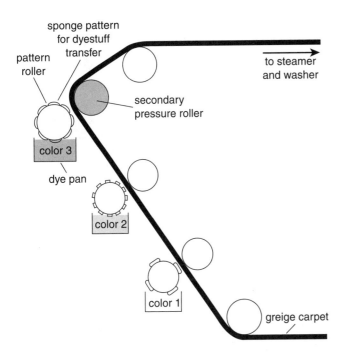

Figure 8.17 The Stalwart roller printing process. *Courtesy of Solutia Inc., Fibers Division.*

ing to the shapes planned for the designs. All the shapes that are to be one color are positioned on the surface of one cylinder; the shapes to be a second color are placed on a second cylinder, and so on.

Stalwart roller printing is illustrated schematically in Figure 8.17. As the sponge-covered rollers rotate against the moving greige goods, the dye paste is transferred to the pile yarns. The printed designs have muted, rather than sharply defined, edges. Use of this printing operation has decreased as more efficient units, especially jet-printing systems, are put into service.

TAK Printing

TAK (from Textile Austustungs, a German carpet firm, and Kusters, the machinery supplier) printing units have been employed to add intense colors to precolored carpet surfaces. Because dye liquor, not dye paste, is used, some authorities refer to this operation as TAK dyeing. But because the application of the dye liquor is mechanically controlled, most colorists prefer to label the operation as **TAK printing**.

In TAK printing, dye is doctored from a revolving roller as a sheet of liquor. As the sheet flows downward, it is cut or interrupted by laterally oscillating chains. The liquor is thus sprinkled or deposited as randomly placed droplets on the moving carpet.

Use of TAK printing units has diminished as consumer preferences for color styling have changed and new equipment has been engineered. The Multi-TAK® unit developed by Kusters, for example, is somewhat more versatile than the conventional TAK apparatus. This unit can deposit liquor in simple geometric and wave-like patterns. The doctor blade has a notched or carved edge. During the printing operation, the blade oscillates laterally, and the liquor is removed from the roller only by the extended blade edges. Thus, the liquor flows in waves to the moving carpet. Attachments can be added to interrupt the descending streams and effect planned patterns.

Jet Printing

Jet-printing technologies are among the more recent and innovative developments for coloring soft floor coverings. In most cases, the same dye applicator units used to produce solid-colored surfaces in continuous-dyeing operations, including tubes, nozzles, blowers, and jets, are used in these operations. In jet printing, however, the delivery of the dye is precisely controlled to create detailed designs and pattern repeats.

The engineering is so sophisticated in some jet printing systems that the intricate color placement and elaborate patterns of authentic Oriental rugs can be replicated. The Foamcolor® unit developed by Kusters uses a computer to control jets that shoot air at streams of dye foam, deflecting them from their vertical path of descent. The Jet Foam Printer®, marketed by Otting, and the Colorburst® unit, manufactured by Greenwood, use photoelectric cells and solenoid systems to regulate the opening and closing of the valves controlling the flow of spray to print nozzles. In still another system, the Millitron® system, owned by Milliken Carpets, has hundreds of dye jets directed toward the moving carpet surface. Printing is electronically controlled by a computer that triggers the jets to "shoot" the surface with dye liquor in a programmed sequence.

Some jet-printing systems have applicator components placed only 0.10 inch apart. This helps to ensure full coverage of the surface. To ensure the production of sharp, well-defined designs, greige goods are generally sheared and vacuumed prior to printing. Because no equipment is in contact with the floor covering during printing, the potential problem of pile distortion is avoided.

Along with a high rate of production, the utilization of relatively little water, dye, and energy makes jet printing a comparatively inexpensive operation. The cost advantages of the operation, however, may be offset by the high capital investment initially required to purchase and install the various units.

Screen Printing

Two methods of **screen printing**, flat-bed screen printing and rotary screen printing, are available for use with textile greige goods. Both methods can deliver large amounts of dyestuff, and both can facilitate the printing of large-scale motifs and pattern repeats. Since most upholstery fabrics are relatively heavy and require large amounts of dye, and since sheetings and curtain and drapery fabrics are often designed with large-scale motifs and pattern repeats, these interior fabrics are very frequently screen printed.

The apparatus and procedures used in flat-bed and rotary screen printing operations differ. Both techniques, however, are based on the principle of a stencil: portions of the printing equipment are blocked to resist the flow of dye.

Flat-bed Screen Printing

In preparation for **flat-bed screen printing**, large rectangular frames are covered with a fine, strong fabric. The compactness of the fabric determines the amount of dye paste allowed to flow through the fabric interstices. Today, nylon and polyester filaments have replaced silk filaments in these fabrics, mostly as a result of the higher cost of the natural fiber. The frames are as wide as the greige goods, generally 45 or 60 inches, and up to 80 inches in length.

Each screen will be used to print one color, so the number of planned colors determines the number of screens that must be prepared. Some areas of each screen are treated with a compound that can prevent or block the flow of the dye paste; other areas are left untreated to allow the paste to pass through the fabric. The untreated areas on each screen are in the shapes of the designs in the repeat that are to be the same color.

For printing, the screens are aligned and mounted horizontally above the fabric, as shown in Figure 8.18.

Figure 8.18 The Zimmer flat-bed screen printing machine. *Courtesy of Solutia Inc., Fibers Division.*

The dye paste is spread over the screen surface from one side to the other, flowing through the untreated areas and printing the fabric below. The fabric is then advanced and the procedure is repeated. Because each screen adds one color, the fabric must advance under all the screens for the coloration of the repeat to be completed. It is evident that the width of the pattern repeat and the width of the fabric govern the number of repeats that can be printed side by side; the length of the repeat and the height of the screen limit the number of repeats that can be simultaneously printed end to end.

Because large amounts of dyestuff can be passed through the screens, a good level of saturation can be obtained in screen printing heavier flat fabrics and pile structures. When working with pile structures, printers must carefully position the screens to avoid distortion of the pile yarns, and the dye paste must be drawn into the pile layer or the colored design will be carried only by the yarn tips.

Zimmer Flat-bed Screen Printing   The **Zimmer flat-bed screen printing** operation is shown in Figure 8.18. The dye paste is drawn into the pile by an electromagnetic field. A needle belt advances the carpet one pattern repeat at a time. Other flat-bed printing units use a vacuum system to pull the print paste into the pile yarns.

Rotary Screen Printing

Developed in the early 1960s, **rotary screen printing** (Figure 8.19) has become the predominant method of printing textile structures. The technique is used to print

Figure 8.19 Rotary screen printing.
Courtesy of Stork Brabant B. V., Boxmeer, Holland.

Figure 8.20 Photomicrographs of the surface openings in nickel-plated rotary screens. *Courtesy of Stork Screens B. V., Boxmeer, Holland.*

flat fabrics as well as such three-dimensional structures as velveteen and velvet. It is also used to print sheets of warp yarns with motifs and with randomized, space-dyed effects. In addition, it is frequently used to print the paper used in transfer-printing operations, which are discussed in the following section.

Rotary screen printing is so widely used because several of its features make it economical. It is generally faster and more accurate than other printing techniques, and it produces a more uniform level of coloration when large quantities of goods are being run.

The cylindrical rollers used in rotary screen printing have microscopic openings in their nickel-coated surfaces. While earlier screens had some 120 holes per inch, newer screens have up to 215 holes per inch. As shown in Figure 8.20, the holes in the newer screens are more regular and well defined, and the surface is smoother. These improvements have facilitated more precise control of shaded effects and better definition of design details.

The planned pattern motifs are transferred to the surfaces of the cylinders. The holes in the areas to be printed are left open and those in the adjacent areas are blocked with water-insoluble lacquer. During printing, the dye paste is continually forced from the interior of the cylindrical screen through the minute openings. A diagram of the flow mechanism is given in Figure 8.21.

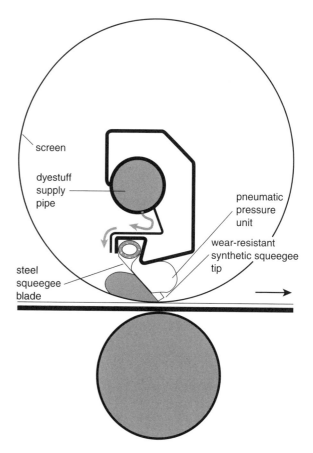

Figure 8.21 The flow mechanism of a rotary screen. *Courtesy of Stork Brabant B. V., Boxmeer, Holland.*

Figure 8.22 Close-up photograph of rotary screen printing. *Courtesy of Stork Brabant B. V., Boxmeer, Holland.*

As shown in Figure 8.22, one color of the repeat is applied by each rotating screen. After the fabric has passed under all screens, all colors and designs will have been added. Some rotary screen printing machines can accept up to 20 screens, so they can print up to 20 colors.

Rotary-screen printing is used infrequently to print soft floor coverings. In most cases, rotary screens have not been designed to supply the large amount of paste required for dyeing heavier pile layers. The recent introduction of a system that uses foam instead of paste, however, may increase the popularity of this high-speed printing technique.

Warp Printing

In **warp printing**, engraved rollers, flat-bed screens, or rotary screens are used to apply color to a sheet of yarns.

The segments will have sharp color divisions, and the length of each color is easily controlled. A drapery fabric having a warp-printed motif is shown in Figure 17.21 (p. 290).

Transfer Printing

Transfer printing, also known as **heat transfer printing** and **sublistatic printing**, involves the use of heat to transfer dyestuff from paper to fabric. The technique has long been used to print the outlines of motifs in preparation for hand embroidering, and, more recently, colored motifs have been available as tear-out pages in popular magazines. The technique was adapted for the industrial-scale printing of textile fabric in the early 1970s.

In preparation for this operation, transfer paper is

Gravure   Flexo   Rotary Screen

Figure 8.23 Techniques used for printing transfer paper. *Courtesy of Fred Salaff and the American Association of Textile Chemists and Colorists.*

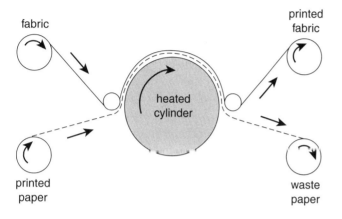

Figure 8.24 Heat transfer printing. *Courtesy of Kosa.*

printed by one of three techniques, gravure, flexo, or rotary screen printing (Figure 8.23). "Gravure" identifies roller printing with engraved copper-covered rollers, and "flexo" identifies roller printing with engraved rubber-covered rollers.

For printing, the colored paper is placed face down on the face of the greige goods (Figure 8.24). The dyestuffs used have a higher affinity for the fibers than for the paper; when they are exposed to heat, they **sublime**, changing from a solid on the paper, to a gas, to a solid on the fabric. The procedure is fast and energy-efficient, and the fabric requires no afterwash because no excess dyestuff remains.

The use of transfer printing as an industrial technique was initially encouraged by widespread consumer acceptance of polyester knits in the 1970s. The inherent elasticity of the fiber and the knitted structure resulted in relatively high relaxation shrinkage following release of the tension used in roller and screen printing operations. The shrinkage caused distortion of the printed patterns. In order to avoid this problem, manufacturers used transfer printing, which requires minimal fabric tensioning.

As long as polyester fiber, especially in knits, continues to increase its share of the window and wall coverings markets and other interior textile markets, the use of transfer printing will no doubt increase as well. However, problems remain: print machinery engineers continue searching for ways to overcome pile distortion, and dye chemists continue working to correct the dyestuff's inadequate penetration of heavier structures.

Pigment Printing

In **pigment printing**, water-insoluble pigments are mixed with an adhesive compound or resin binders and applied to textile surfaces. As the pigments are not absorbed by the fibers, the printed designs stand in slight relief. Frequently, white or metallic-colored pigments are printed on a previously dyed surface, and may then be referred to as **overprinting**.

Fusion Printing

Fusion printing is a type of pigment printing used to secure colorants to the surface of fabrics composed of glass fiber. Colored acrylic resins are first printed on the surface of the fabric. Heat is then used to soften the thermoplastic compound and fuse it to the nonabsorbent glass. Like other pigment-printed designs, fusion-printed designs stand in slight relief.

Acid Printing

Acid printing produces a color style known as a **burnt-out or etched-out print**. In this styling, the motifs and the ground have different levels of transparency. Because this technique is a chemically dependent process and one in which no colorants are added, some textile authorities prefer to classify the procedure as a finishing operation. On the other hand, because the technique produces a patterned effect, other authorities classify the procedure as a printing operation.

Fabrics used in an acid-printing operation must be composed of an acid-resistant fiber and an acid-degradable fiber; a blend of nylon and rayon is typically used. During printing, weak sulfuric acid (H_2SO_4) is printed on selected areas of the fabric, destroying or burning away the acid-degradable rayon. This chemical reaction changes the composition of these areas to 100 percent nylon, creating a higher level of transparency than is seen in the untreated areas. An burnt-out print produced for use as curtain fabric is shown in Figure 17.24 (p. 291).

Combining Dyeing and Printing

Fabric immersion can be used in combination with a printing procedure to produce interior fabrics having colored backgrounds and noncolored design motifs. Industrial methods involving such combinations include discharge printing and resist printing.

Discharge Printing

Discharge printing is an efficient way to color large areas of the ground and create a pattern. The fabric is first piece dyed, producing the same depth of color on both sides. It is then printed with a reducing agent wherever the design motifs are planned. The agent reduces or discharges the dyestuff. Recent developments in discharge-printing equipment turn discharging and immediate color printing into one sequential operation. A discharge print is shown in Figure 17.20 (p. 290).

Resist Printing

In industrial **resist-printing** operations, a water-insoluble compound that will not allow absorption of the dyestuff is first printed on the fabric in the shapes of the planned motifs. When the fabric is subsequently piece dyed, the dye liquor is absorbed only in the areas that are free of the resist compound. Artisans use several hand resist-printing operations to create distinctive interior fabrics. These techniques, including batik, tie-dye, and ikat operations, were discussed and illustrated earlier in this chapter.

Gum Printing

In **gum printing**, a gum compound known to resist dye absorption is applied to the tips of the pile yarns prior to dyeing. The gum will prevent dye absorption and migration, causing the upper portion of the pile layer to have a frosted appearance. **Frostiness** describes the absence of dye on the yarn tips. It is a planned color style, unlike tippiness, the unplanned and unwanted concentration of dye on the yarn tips that occurs when dye migration is not sufficient to produce uniform intensity. Gum printing for frostiness has the drawback of consuming additional utilities in removing the gum.

Following virtually every method of color application, the textile structures must be washed, rinsed, and dried. Dyed goods may be tentered, and some may be heat set. A secondary backing will be applied to tufted structures that were dyed. To restore distorted pile yarns to their upright position, the carpet will be passed against an angled blade that lifts the yarns. Cut pile textures may be sheared to create a uniform pile height and vacuumed to remove lint. A final inspection is made prior to shipment.

A colorant may be scientifically selected and precisely applied, but the immediate and long-term appearance of the color may nonetheless be affected by various environmental conditions and end-use activities. Some substances and conditions, such as cleaning agents and atmospheric contaminants, can produce changes in actual color characteristics. These variables, and test methods to measure their effects, are described in later units. The potential effects of various factors on apparent color characteristics are discussed here.

Factors Affecting Apparent Color

Several factors have no direct effect on colorants but may alter perception of the original color of a product. Some of these factors, including changes in texture and soiling, relate to end-use activities; others, such as the source and quantity of light, are aspects of the interior environment. These variables alter the **apparent color** characteristics of interior textiles; the **actual color** characteristics are unchanged.

Light Source

Color may be the most important aesthetic variable in the selection of an interior textile product. Unfortunately, color choices are often made in a setting other than the one in which the product will be used. Inevitably, the lighting in the showroom or retail display area differs from that in the residential or commercial interior. Viewing a colored item in the separate locations, an observer may perceive marked differences in hue and value. If the product is installed in an interior, the harmony and color coordination planned for the space may not be realized.

As mentioned earlier in this chapter, artificial light sources differ from each other and from natural light in the mixture of visible wavelengths they emit. While natural light emits almost equal quantities of all wavelengths, artificial sources emit unequal quantities. Cool fluorescent illuminants, for example, emit large amounts of shorter wavelengths, those resulting in violet, blue, and green hues, and small amounts of red-producing wavelengths. By contrast, incandescent illuminants create predominantly longer wavelengths, those producing yellow, orange, and red hues, and they are deficient in blue-producing rays. The source of light thus limits the mixture of wavelengths having the potential to be reflected.

A textile colorant known to reflect a concentration of wavelengths in the red area (around 650 nm) nevertheless appears as a weakened red when viewed under cool fluorescent light and as a strong red when viewed under incandescent light. Similarly, the hue of a colorant known to reflect blue rays is perceived as a strong blue under cool fluorescent light and as a weakened or grayish blue under incandescent sources.

Quantity of Light

The quantity of light incident on a textile directly affects its color characteristics, especially its value or luminosity: increases in the level of light produce apparent increases in the lightness of the surface. The amount of light emitted from artificial illuminants can be controlled by rheostats and the wattages of lamps. The amount of natural light can be regulated by the compactness of the window coverings and the use of exterior awnings. Of course, the size of windows and skylights and their orientation to the seasonal angles of the sun are also very important.

In interior settings, the quantity of light is not limited to that radiating through the windows and emanating from artificial sources. A significant amount can be **reused or indirect light**, that being reflected from light-colored walls, ceilings, doors, and furnishings.

Because natural light and artificial light sources differ in their distribution of wavelengths, it is readily apparent that an increase or decrease in the level of light emitted by any source would affect both the value and intensity of the hue perceived. The apparent changes can be as different as night and day, especially so when strong sunlight in the daytime alternates with dim interior lighting in the evening. Browns, for example, may darken and appear almost black as sunlight diminishes and evening falls.

Changes in Texture

The abrasive and crushing forces that textile structures may encounter during use produce changes in their original textural features. Such changes affect the apparent lightness and darkness of colored surfaces.

As people shift their seated positions and move their arms over upholstery fabrics, they can rupture the yarns and destroy prominent decorative effects. Such physical changes have no effect on the colorants, but the abraded areas appear darker because the pattern of light reflection is altered.

When fibers and yarns used in soft floor coverings are abraded by shoe soles, furniture casters, and the like, their surfaces may be roughened as dirt and sharp-edged grit particles grind severely against the fibers. Deterioration of the smoothness of the fibers and yarns results in deflection of incident light waves and a decrease in apparent value. A decrease in lightness is also apparent when abrasive forces rupture the loops of pile floor coverings and other pile fabrics, because the quantity of light reflected from the fiber ends is less than that reflected from the sides of the yarns in the intact loops.

Textural changes caused by crushing, especially of pile surfaces, may be less readily noticed or less objectionable if the compression is spread uniformly over the surface. But people tend to sit in the central portion of upholstered cushions, to repeatedly lean against the same region of back cushions, and to walk in established traffic patterns. These practices result in localized compression, which may gradually result in a nonuniform pile depth across the textile surface. This creates variations in the apparent value of the surface, with flattened areas appearing lighter and distorted areas appearing darker than undisturbed pile areas. Consumers and professionals can minimize the development of this unsightly effect by selecting pile fabrics made of resilient fibers and having high pile construction densities when a high level of use is expected.

Soil Accumulation

Residential and commercial consumers may be convinced that the original color of their textile product has changed when in fact it is merely masked by soil. As soil accumulates, especially on bright, solid-colored surfaces, the coloration appears duller. As is true for changes in texture, soiling is often localized, with heavier buildup occurring on the arms and seat cushions of furniture and in traffic lanes and entrance areas.

If soil accumulation is expected to be rapid, a multicolored surface that can mask the appearance of soil should be considered. Protective items, such as removable arm covers and walk-off mats, are also available.

Composition and Structural Variables

Different fibers have different color characteristics even when dyed the same color. This difference is the result of the chemical structures of the fibers and dyes used and the affinity the fibers have for the colorants. Increasing or decreasing yarn size causes accompanying changes in the intensity of the chosen hue. Similar effects appear with changes in pile construction density. Contract designers and architects must consider the potential impact on apparent color of specifying composition or construction features that differ from those characterizing the color samples.

Consumers and professionals must be aware that even yarns and fabrics intended to look identical generally have differences in color intensity when dyed or printed in different operations. To avoid this problem, the initial order should include sufficient yardage for the planned project.

Summary

For a particular hue to be perceived, the source of incident light must include a high concentration of wavelengths known to produce the hue, and the colorant used must reflect, not absorb, these waves. Although the dye chemist is responsible for selecting the correct colorant, consumers and professionals are responsible for examining the effects of the lighting conditions on the hue, value, and intensity of the colorant. Whenever possible, a swatch of fabric, a cushion, an arm cover, or a carpet sample should be examined in the end-use setting under a variety of lighting conditions. Consumers and professionals are also responsible for assessing the potential effects that such in-use variables as soil accumulation, abrasion, and crushing may have.

Dyers and printers are responsible for selecting and executing the appropriate method of color application. This method is largely determined by the features that the fabric stylist or contract designer specifies. Fiber dyeing is used when multicolored yarns are needed; yarn dyeing when plaid patterns or other types of woven-in motifs are to be produced; and screen printing when large-scale motifs and pattern repeats are specified. Ultimately, dye chemists, fabric stylists, and textile colorists must be guided by the color and styling preferences of the contemporary consumer.

Textile chemists, colorists, and engineers constantly strive to refine and improve methods of applying color to textile structures. The urgent need to conserve energy and reduce production costs encourages this effort. Moreover, the rapid shifting of consumer style preferences requires that colorists be capable of an equally speedy response to remain competitive.

Key Terms

acid printing

actual color

apparent color

astrojets

auxochromes

batch dyeing

batik printing

beam dyeing

block printing

burnt-out or etched-out print

carpet winch

chroma

chromophores

color-sealed

continuous dyeing

crackle effect

cross dyeing

differential dyeing

discharge printing

discontinuous dyeing

doctor blade

dope dyeing

dye beck

dye liquor

dye migration

dye paste

dyed-in-the-wool

dyeing ranges

dyes or dyestuffs

electromagnetic spectrum

fiber or stock dyeing

flat-bed screen printing

frostiness

fusion printing

gum printing

heather

heat transfer printing

hue

ikat printing

intensity

jet beck

jet printing

jet spraying

knit-de-knit space dyeing

liquor ratio

luminosity

marled

mordants

moresque

nanometers

ombré

overprinting

package dyeing

package-injection technique

piece dyeing

pigment printing

pigments

producer-colored

resist printing

reused or indirect light

roller printing

rotary screen printing

screen printing

shade

skein dyeing

solution dyeing

space dyeing

Stalwart roller printing

sublime

sublistatic printing

TAK printing

tie-dyeing

tint

tippiness

transfer printing

union dyeing

value

variegated yarns

visible spectrum

warp printing

yarn dyeing

Zimmer flat-bed screen printing

Review Questions

1. Discuss the impact that increased energy costs and heightened concern for water conservation have had on the dyeing and printing industries.

2. Explain the difference between the electromagnetic spectrum and the visible spectrum.

3. What is meant by "wavelength?"

4. Explain how the combination of incident light waves and colorant present determine the hue we see.

5. Distinguish between tints and shades.

6. What is the role of a mordant?

7. Why are the terms color-sealed and producer-colored used as synonyms for solution dyed fibers?

8. What is a distinct advantage of solution dyeing? Why isn't it routinely used?

9. Explain how fiber or stock dyeing gave rise to the old adage "dyed-in-the-wool."

10. Differentiate among the following color styling terms: heather, marled, ombré, and moresque.

11. Why is the use of skein dyeing generally limited to smaller quantities of yarn?

12. Which operation is more efficient, discontinuous dyeing or continuous dyeing?

13. Why do dyers avoid creasing or sharply folding pile fabrics in dyeing operations?

14. Distinguish between tippiness and frostiness.

15. Explain the advantages of cross dyeing. What has led to the growth of both cross dyeing and union dying?

16. What are the resist media used in batik, tie-dye, and ikat printing?

17. Why can't large motifs and large pattern repeats be printed with rollers?

18. Discuss the advantages of rotary screen printing.

19. Why has the growth of heat transfer printing paralleled the growth of knitted fabric?

20. What do dyestuffs do when they sublime?

21. Could a blue fabric with white polka dots be made with either discharge printing or resist printing?

22. Explain the critical need to examine colored textiles in the setting in which they will be used or installed.

23. Cite examples where changes in texture occur and have concomitant changes in the apparent luster of a colored textile surface.

24. If different fibers and various sizes of yarns are dyed the same color, will they all look the same?

9

Converting Interior Textile Greige Goods

Transforming Surface Appearance
   Removing Inherent Color
   Controlling Surface Luster
   Introducing Three-dimensional Designs
   Changing the Orientation of Pile Yarns
   Embellishing Fabric Surfaces

Improving the Quality and Serviceability of Structural Features
   Correcting Fabric Grain
   Minimizing Yarn Slippage
   Stabilizing Fabric Shape
   Improving Texture Retention
   Reducing Pilling

Engineering Functional Performance
   Increasing Apparent Brightness
   Reducing Fiber Flammability
   Increasing Insulative Value
   Reducing Microbial Action
   Increasing Moisture Absorption
   Repelling Moths
   Increasing Water Repellency
   Imparting Soil and Stain Resistance
   Introducing Soil Release
   Improving Smoothness Retention

Colored greige goods are more appealing than noncolored goods. However, until the goods are converted into finished fabrics, they may lack the aesthetic characteristics preferred by consumers of interior textile products. The fabrics may also lack structural stability, and they may not exhibit the service-related performance features sought by consumers or required by an agency with jurisdiction over their selection and installation.

In many cases, the finishing agents and processes to be used are specified by the fabric stylist, who has monitored consumer preferences for various aesthetic features, functional attributes, and care requirements. Sometimes they are dictated by the contract designer or architect, who may require an interior fabric with a unique appearance characteristic or a specific level of performance in end use. The appropriate selection and proper application of finishes greatly expands the variety of fabrics available to end-product producers and consumers.

Transforming Surface Appearance

With appropriate agents and processes, converters can transform the surface appearance of greige goods. When necessary they can remove or neutralize inherent color, and when specified they can control the level of surface luster, alter the fabric form, and embellish the fabric face.

Removing Inherent Color

The **inherent colors** of natural fibers were discussed in Chapter 4. Unless the stylist specifies their retention, converters remove or neutralize them. When fashion colors are planned, the removal or neutralization precedes the addition of colorants, preventing the subsequent reflection of a mixture of light waves from two sources. When no colorants are to be added, the process precedes other conversion operations to prevent the natural colorants from interfering with the appearance of the finished fabrics.

Bleaching

Bleaching agents remove unwanted color from cellulosic fibers by oxidation. Hydrogen peroxide (H_2O_2) and sodium hypochlorite (NaCLO) are generally used.

Grassing

In **grassing**, sunlight removes inherent color from linen fibers spread over a grass field. Because grassing is slower than other bleaching methods, its use to prepare linen fibers for manufacture into fine tabletop products is quite rare today.

Controlling Surface Luster

Whereas manufactured fiber producers are responsible for controlling the **luster** of fabrics composed of their fibers—decreasing it by incorporating delusterant particles in the polymer solution—converters are generally charged with controlling the luster of fabrics composed of natural fibers. The conversion processes involved virtually always increase, rather than decrease, the quantity of light reflected from the fabric surface.

Friction Calendering

With the help of high levels of pressure and heat and a fast rate of revolution, highly polished metal cylinders, known as **calendering rollers** can be used to flatten the cross section of the yarns, thus increasing the amount of surface area available to reflect light. This change in the physical configuration of the yarns is illustrated in Figure 9.1. Friction calendering is frequently used to increase the reflection of sateen-woven drapery linings.

Beetling

Converters may use a process known as **beetling** to increase the surface luster of fabrics composed of linen. In the operation, heavy wooden planks hammer the fabric and flatten the cross section of the yarns, similar to the change shown in Figure 9.1. This process is often used on elaborately woven **damask** fabrics. Although damask table linens are normally white or a solid pastel color, the yarns in the varied interlacings reflect incident light in different directions and in different quantities; beetling

a) noncalendered fabric

b) calendered fabric

Figure 9.1 Effect of friction calendering on the cross section of yarns.

augments the reflections and enables the viewer to see the distinctive patterns (Figure 9.2). The increased amount of light reflected from the floating yarns increases the visual distinction between the motifs and the ground.

Glazing

In **glazing** operations, the surface of greige goods is impregnated with resin, shellac, or wax, and high-speed calendering rollers then buff and polish the surface. Glazing produces a smooth surface texture and a high level of surface luster. **Chintz** fabrics produced for use as upholstered furniture coverings and curtain fabrics are frequently glazed (see Figure 17.2, p. 281).

Schreinering

The **schreinering** process creates fine hills and valleys on the surface of the fabric. In preparation for this mechanical treatment, calendering rollers are etched with fine, parallel lines that approximate the angle of yarn twist. The number of etched lines may range from 250 to 350 per inch. After schreinering, the modified surface develops a soft luster as light is reflected in different directions from the fine peaks and flattened valleys. The effect is not permanent unless heat or resin treatments are also performed. The use of these treatments is discussed below with embossing operations.

Moiréing

Moiréing is a special type of calendering used on filling-rib woven fabrics; frequently the fabric chosen is **taffeta**. Two fabrics are laid face to face and passed between paired calendering rollers. The pressure causes the mirrored ribs to impact on one another, slightly altering

Figure 9.2 Close-up of motifs in damask tablecloth.

their form and changing the pattern of light reflection. Moiré fabrics are described as having a wood-grain appearance or a **water-marked effect** (Figure 9.3).

Introducing Three-dimensional Designs

Embossing, like schreinering and moiréing, involves the use of calendering rollers and alters the form of the greige goods. The changes produced by embossing are, however, greater than those produced by schreinering and moiréing. Embossing creates highly visible three-dimensional surface designs. Whether the changes are slight or marked, their preservation depends on the application of heat or resins.

Embossing

Embossing treatments convert flat, essentially two-dimensional fabrics into three-dimensional structures with convex and concave design forms. The planned designs are first etched into the surface of one calendering roller, which is then paired with a soft-surfaced roller. As the fabric passes between the two intermeshing rollers, it conforms to the etched forms. Greige goods are often embossed for use as decorative curtain fabrics.

Calendering rollers can be heated to emboss, schreiner, or moiré fabrics composed of thermoplastic fibers. In this way, the converter can introduce three-dimensional designs and heat set them in one operation. The heat loosens the strained lateral bonds of the distorted fibers, and the new lateral bonds that form as the fibers cool preserve the imposed configuration.

When fabrics composed of nonthermoplastic fibers, such as cotton and rayon, are processed, chemical cross-linking resins must be applied to preserve the imposed changes. The resins form lateral bonds, linking adjacent polymer chains and stabilizing the distorted configurations of the fibers. (This treatment, also used to improve resiliency, is schematized in Figure 9.17).

Changing the Orientation of Pile Yarns

Mechanical treatments are used to alter the upright positions of the pile yarns in virtually all pile fabrics. The re-alignment affects the reflective characteristics and tactile features of the pile layer.

Brushing, Smoothing, and Shearing

Brushing, smoothing, and shearing operations are used to align, smooth, and level the pile yarns in such fabrics as corduroy, velveteen, and velvet. In **brushing**, cylinders covered with straight wires revolve against the matted cut-pile surface, raising the pile yarns and aligning them parallel to one another. Brushing is followed by **smoothing**, laying the pile yarns in one direction. The results of these processes are essentially the same as those produced by combing and brushing hair. Because the angle at which the pile yarns are oriented to the base fabric is reduced, a surface feature known as **pile sweep**, **directional pile lay**, or **fabric nap** is introduced (Figure 9.4).

After the pile yarns have been brushed and smoothed, they undergo **shearing** to produce an even pile height. This is accomplished by passing the fabric against a rotating cylinder with a spiral blade. The shearing cylinder is similar to that in rotary lawn mowers.

Obviously, the tactile characteristics of a pile surface will be altered by these operations. The fabric will feel smooth when stroked in the direction of lay and rough when stroked in the opposite direction. And because the quantity of light waves reflected by the sides of the yarns will be significantly greater than that reflected by the cut

Figure 9.3 Moiré taffeta.

Figure 9.4 Directional pile lay, pile sweep, or fabric nap.

tips, the level of luster observed will depend on the position of the viewer. The tactile and visual qualities of nap make it imperative that all fabric pieces cut for an item and all adjoining carpet lengths have the same direction of pile lay. Usually, for such items as upholstered furniture, pile yarns are oriented downward to help maintain the original appearance. The positioning of pile lay in carpet is discussed in Chapter 27.

Crushing

A mechanical finishing operation known as **crushing** is used on some velvet fabrics. In this operation, the pile yarns in some areas are crushed or flattened, while the pile yarns in the adjacent areas are oriented in various directions. Because each area reflects incident light waves in different quantities and in different directions, the surface has various levels of luster. A crushed velvet upholstery fabric is pictured in Figure 13.23 (p. 219).

Embellishing Fabric Surfaces

The appearance of greige goods, especially those to be used as curtain fabrics and tabletop accessories, is often embellished by the addition of fibers or yarns to their surfaces. Yarns are added in an embroidering operation, and fibers are added in a flocking operation.

Skilled artisans use textile yarns or fabrics to create such items as needlepoint pictures, crewel pillow coverings, quilts, doilies, throws, laces, and soft sculptures. They may hold onto completed projects for personal use or sell them in wholesale or retail markets. In some cases, an artist is commissioned to design and produce a needlework item for use as an accent in a specific interior, such as a corporate office, an airport lounge, or a bank.

Hand Needleworking

Fiber artists use various techniques to embellish fabric surfaces for use as accents in interiors. Among these are needlepoint stitching, embroidering, and appliquéing.

Needlepoint Stitching

In **needlepoint stitching**, also referred to as **canvas embroidering**, yarns are used to cover all or part of the surface of a canvas fabric. Typically, the surface has a solid-colored ground surrounding a multicolored, detailed pattern (Figure 9.5), or the design repeats identical or mirror-image geometric motifs.

Needlepoint projects may be done with either **single-mesh canvas**, which is plain woven, or **double-mesh (penelope) canvas**, which has closely spaced pairs of warp and filling yarns. The term *mesh* refers to one intersection of the yarns used in the canvas; the compactness of construction of the fabric is designated by the number of **meshes per inch**. **Fine canvas**, with 18 or more meshes per inch, is used for petitpoint work. These projects usually have small motifs and are framed and hung as wall accents or placed on tabletops. **Medium canvas**, with 10 or 12 meshes per inch, is used in such needlepoint items as dining chair seat coverings, a rendition of a company logo, and backgammon and other game boards. **Coarse canvas**, with 3 to 7 meshes per inch, is used to construct rugs.

Needlepoint work uses Persian yarns and tapestry yarns. **Persian yarns** are loosely twisted three-ply strands composed of wool. Frequently, the plied yarns are untwisted and a single strand is used in stitching. **Tapestry yarns** are highly twisted, four-ply yarns, which are used without being separated. Examples of frequently used needlepoint stitches are shown in Figure 9.6.

Hand Embroidering

Embroidering is the stitching of colored yarns in decorative patterns on a portion of a base fabric, leaving the other portion unadorned to serve as the ground and accentuate the slightly raised motifs. Embroidered fabrics are used as the outer coverings of decorative pillows and as cases for bed pillows. They are also framed and hung as wall accents, and cut and finished for use as tabletop accessories.

Crewel, floss, pearl, and candlewick yarns are used for embroidery work. **Crewel yarns** are fine, two-ply strands composed of wool; **floss yarns** are loosely twisted, six-ply strands composed of mercerized cotton; **pearl yarns** are fine cords formed by plying three two-ply yarns composed of mercerized cotton; and **candlewick yarns** are four-ply yarns composed of unmercerized cotton. Since these yarns vary in texture, size, and luster, they produce distinct appearances when used in any of the many embroidery stitches, examples of which are illustrated in Figure 9.7.

Embroidery techniques are primarily distinguished by the type of yarn used, not by differences in the stitches used. One exception is **candlewicking** in which the design motifs are created by the extensive use of French knots. The knots are used singly, but collectively they create a recognizable pattern (Figure 9.8).

a) chain stitch   b) satin stitch   c) French knot

Figure 9.7 Common embroidery stitches.

Figure 9.5 Needlepoint wallhanging, 5 feet by 3.5 feet, features a stylized dragon and Oriental motifs. The detail shows the 3-inch long dragonfly done in petitpoint (20 stitches per inch.)
Courtesy of Kathy Lessing.

Figure 9.8 Candlewicking embroidery used to embellish the outer covering of a decorative pillow.
Courtesy of Norma Long Mayfield.

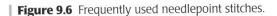

Figure 9.6 Frequently used needlepoint stitches.

a) Continental   b) Bargello or Florentine

Appliquéing   In most **appliqué work**, shaped pieces of coordinating or contrasting fabric are placed over the face of a second fabric. The raw edges are turned under and blind stitches or embroidery stitches are used to secure the applique. Appliquéd fabrics are constructed into decorative pillow coverings, bedspreads, and tablecloths, and are used as the face fabric in quilts.

An intricate appliqué technique is employed by needlework artisans in South America to produce molas. **Molas** have multiple layers of fabric and are typically characterized by highly stylized animal motifs (Figure 9.9). Various colors of fabrics are layered and a large, shaped area is cut from the top fabric. The raw edges are turned under, and the folded edge is stitched to the second fabric. A slightly smaller shape is then cut from the second fabric and the raw edges are turned and stitched to the third fabric; this **reverse appliqué** sequence is repeated until the base fabric is reached. Molas are prized as framed wall accents and decorative pillow coverings.

Machine Embroidering

Because hand embroidering, like hand printing, is labor- and time-intensive, **machine embroidering** is employed to embellish fabric surfaces with motifs resembling those created by artisans. Many machine-embroidered curtain and drapery fabrics are stitched on Schiffli machines. Each of these machines is equipped with more than a thousand needles that operate at right angles to the base fabric. For multicolored motifs, each needle is threaded with a specific color of yarn; control mechanisms similar to those used on the dobby loom are programmed with the planned design shapes and shift the position of the fabric during the embroidering operation. A Schiffli-embroidered curtain fabric is pictured in Figure 17.19b (p. 290).

Flocking

In **flocking** operations, extremely short fibers, known as **flock**, are embedded in an adhesive or resin compound. In curtain and drapery fabrics, the flock is generally used to create raised motifs and pattern repeats. In simulated suede upholstery fabrics and some blankets and floor mats, the flock is applied to the entire fabric surface. Both types of flock placement are used in textile wall coverings.

In preparation for flocking, an adhesive or resin is printed on all areas of the greige goods to be flocked. In **mechanical flocking** processes, the flock is then sifted through a screen to the coated surface (Figure 9.10). Beater bars encourage the short fibers to orient themselves perpendicularly to the base fabric. In **electrostatic flocking** operations, an electrostatic field induces the flock to embed itself into the coating (see Figure 13.28, p. 223).

Quilting

Commercial quilting may be done by sewing or by melding. The quilting operation serves to join the sep-

Figure 9.9 Mola, a textile accent produced by a reverse appliqué technique.

arate layers and sometimes to impart a surface pattern as well.

Machine stitching and pinsonic melding are used in commercial quilting operations. The equipment used in **machine stitching** operates in the same manner as a conventional sewing machine, except that many needles stitch at the same time. In **pinsonic melding**, a wide cylinder with raised designs is rolled over the multilayer structure while heat and sound waves meld the layers at the contact points. The meld points simulate the appearance of sewn quilting stitches (Figure 9.11).

Three patterns are typical of commercial quilting. In **channel quilting**, the stitches or meld points are aligned in parallel rows (Figure 9.12a). In **pattern quilting** (Figures 9.12b and c), the quilting lines develop a surface pattern with slightly three-dimensional motifs. Such

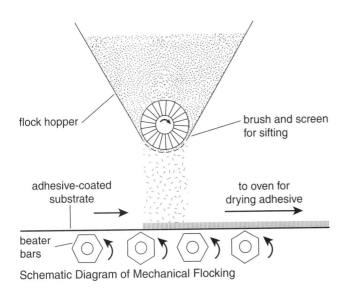

flock hopper

brush and screen
for sifting

adhesive-coated
substrate

to oven for
drying adhesive

beater
bars

Schematic Diagram of Mechanical Flocking

Figure 9.10 Mechanical flocking.
(Courtesy of Solutia Inc., Fibers Division.)

Figure 9.11 Fabric quilted by pinsonic melding.

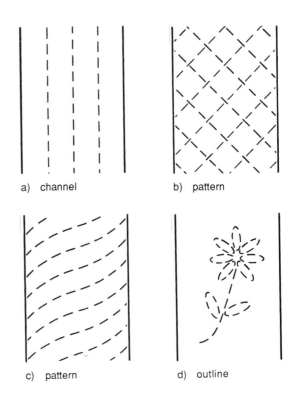

a) channel

b) pattern

c) pattern

d) outline

Figure 9.12 Quilting patterns.

quilting is frequently used on solid-covered fabrics. In **outline quilting** (Figure 9.12d), the stitches follow the outline of pattern motifs, making them stand in slight relief.

Hand Quilting With quilting stitches, artisans join three layers: a face fabric, a fibrous batting, and a backing or lining fabric. The face fabric may be an appliquéd fabric, a solid-colored or printed fabric, or constructed of small pieces of coordinated fabrics. Both commercial and hand-stitched quilts are discussed in Chapter 29.

Improving the Quality and Serviceability of Structural Features

Converters use finishing procedures to improve the quality and potential serviceability of the structural features of greige goods. They can, for example, use a mechanical process to improve the alignment of yarns in woven fabrics; a heat setting operation to stabilize the shape and form of fabrics composed of thermoplastic fibers; and small flames to minimize the formation of pills on fabrics composed of cellulosic fibers.

Correcting Fabric Grain

When all the warp yarns are not perpendicular to all the filling yarns in a biaxially woven fabric, the fabric is said to be **off-grain**. Off-grain fabrics have a negative effect on appearance when used in the construction of such end products as upholstered furniture, curtains, draperies, and tabletop accessories. For example, a drapery fabric with a **bowed yarn alignment** produces treatments that appear to sag, and, as illustrated in Figure 9.13a, an undulating or waving effect could develop if several widths are used. Fabrics with a **skewed yarn alignment** produce a lop-sided appearance, as shown in Figure 9.13b, and attempts to align crosswise pattern repeats when seaming fabric widths only compound the problem. The negative effects of off-grain upholstery fabrics are illustrated in Figure 14.1 (p. 229).

Tentering

To minimize distortions resulting from bow and skew, converters use a mechanical finishing process known as **tentering**. In this operation, the fabric is mounted full-width on a tenter frame. Tension is applied to properly align the warp and filling yarns, and the fabric is then steamed and passed through a heated oven and dried. Today, computer-assisted mechanisms often monitor and control the alignment of the yarns during the operation. Small holes are visible in the selvage areas of tentered fabrics, indicating where the fabric was secured by pins or metal clips.

When greige goods are to be printed, tentering should precede the printing operation. Correcting the grain of printed fabrics would distort the shapes of the motifs and the positions of the pattern repeats.

Minimizing Yarn Slippage

If plain weave and other simple fabrics are produced from smooth, multifilament yarns in loose constructions, converters may apply an adhesive compound, such as polyurethane, polyacrylonitrile, or latex, to the fabric back. The coating helps to prevent yarn slippage and yarn raveling. **Yarn slippage** is the sliding or "traveling" of warp or filling yarns, shown schematically in Figure 9.14. In patterned coverings, slippage distorts the shapes and details of the design motifs. Yarn slippage may also occur at seamlines, with the yarns moving away from the stitching and leaving a gap or opening; a testing procedure for evaluating slippage at seamlines is described in Chapter 14.

Yarn raveling occurs when yarns fall from cut edges of fabrics. This becomes a problem in upholstery when seam allowances have been closely trimmed to reduce bulk and the fabric has been pulled to fit smoothly over the frame and filling. The stress exerted on the seams with use may force the yarns in the narrow seam allowances to slide off the cut edge, weakening the seam and causing the stitching to rupture.

Figure 9.13 Effects of bowed and skewed yarn alignments on the appearance of window treatments.

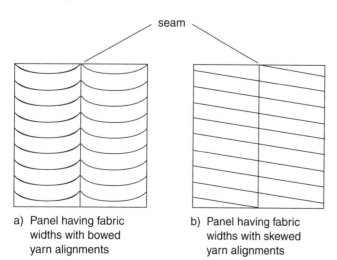

a) Panel having fabric widths with bowed yarn alignments

b) Panel having fabric widths with skewed yarn alignments

Figure 9.14 Yarn slippage.

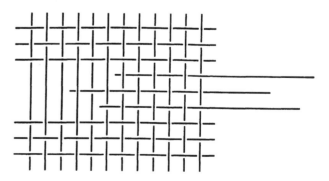

Stabilizing Fabric Shape

A textile structure that maintains its original size and shape after use and care is said to have **dimensional stability**. Dimensionally stable fabrics do not exhibit "growth"—bagging and sagging from unrecovered stretch—nor do they exhibit shrinkage.

With most interior textile fabrics, there is great concern for the potential problems caused by relaxation shrinkage, and to a lesser extent for those caused by residual shrinkage. **Residual shrinkage** is shrinkage of the fibers; it generally occurs over time in such frequently laundered items as towels and table linens. **Relaxation shrinkage** occurs when strained components relax after the stress forces involved in various manufacturing processes are released.

Several processes subject fibers and yarns to stress, deforming and straining them. Extruding and drawing strain the polymer chains in manufactured filaments, while drawing out and spinning can strain spun yarns. During weaving, tension introduces strain to the warp yarns, and bobbin tensioning devices may impart strain to the filling yarns. The pulling and forcing of yarns and fabrics through dyeing or printing and finishing operations can add various amounts of strain.

The behavior of strained fabric components is similar to that of elastic bands that have been stretched, but there is a marked difference between the rates at which the two materials recover from imposed deformations. When the stretching force is released from an elastic band, it will generally exhibit immediate and complete relaxation shrinkage, returning to its original length. By contrast, when manufacturing stress forces are released, textile components relax only gradually and incompletely. Unless the imposed strain has been released or the fabric components have been intentionally stabilized prior to shipment to the end product producer or fabric retailer, full recovery may not occur until sometime during end use, destroying the appearance or fit of the fabric.

Converters encourage relaxation of strained components with heat setting, fulling, and compressive shrinkage operations. The technique used is determined by the fiber composition of the greige goods.

Heat Setting

Fabrics composed of thermoplastic fibers can be stabilized by **heat setting**. Unless textured yarns have been used, this procedure is normally carried out during tentering of the greige goods to ensure that the strains introduced during fabrication are released.

When heat setting is combined with tentering, converters must correctly align the warp and filling yarns in woven structures. Fabrics that have been heat set off-grain cannot be straightened.

Fulling

Fabrics composed of wool fibers are encouraged to relax by a finishing process known as **fulling**. The goods are exposed to controlled conditions of moisture, heat, and pressure, which cause the yarns to relax and shrink, resulting in a fuller, more compact fabric. Although this procedure reduces the potential for relaxation shrinkage of the fabrics in end use, it does not reduce the possibility of felting shrinkage.

Compressive Shrinkage Treatments

The dimensional stability of fabrics composed of cotton can be improved during tentering or with a **compressive shrinkage treatment**. In compressive shrinkage procedures, the greige goods are laid over a supporting fabric, moistened, and mechanically shifted to encourage relaxation of the yarns. Labeling practices that distinguish fabrics stabilized by such treatments are discussed in Chapter 10.

During tentering, cotton yard goods can be compressed lengthwise by feeding them onto the metal pins at a faster rate than the pins are moving forward. This technique encourages the warp yarns to relax; in some cases, a 10-yard length of fabric can shrink to 8 yards.[1] Crosswise relaxation can be encouraged by reducing the distance between the parallel rows of tenter pins.

Heat-setting operations help to minimize bagging and sagging of fabrics composed of thermoplastic fibers; fulling and compressive shrinkage treatments have little or no effect on this performance feature. Wool fibers are highly elastic and fabrics composed of them recover well after being stressed. However, cellulosic fibers, including cotton, linen, and rayon, have comparatively low elasticity and may exhibit excessive growth.

Improving Texture Retention

As explained earlier in this chapter, smoothing and crushing operations are used to alter the positions of pile yarns, producing the depth, directional lay, and reflective features specified by the stylist and preferred by the consumer. The serviceability of pile fabrics depends on the extent to which these features are retained. For long-term retention, the pile yarns must be resilient. In fabrics composed of thermoplastic fibers, heat setting can be used to engineer this performance property. In fabrics composed of cotton, such as corduroy and velveteen, this feature can be improved by using a high pile construction density, a structural characteristic that of course is controlled by the fabric manufacturer, not by the converter. Texture retention can also be improved by blending a resilient fiber such as nylon or polyester with the cellulosic fiber.

Reducing Pilling

Pilling occurs when abrasive forces cause free fibers and fiber ends to roll up into minute balls that are unsightly and a nuisance to remove. While pills composed of some staple-length fibers may be removed by subsequent surface abrasion, those composed of filaments or of strong nylon or polyester staple-length fibers tend to cling tenaciously. In either case, the initial formation of pills can be reduced by singeing the greige goods.

Singeing

Small gas flames are used to burn away loose fibers, bits of lint, and fiber ends from fabrics composed of cotton, linen, rayon, and lyocell (Figure 9.15). Fabrics made of thermoplastic fibers cannot be singed with flames because the intense heat would melt the base fabric; instead, hot, smooth metal plates are used carefully to soften and shrink the protruding fibers so they can be sheared from the surface. Fabrics composed of wool or silk are not singed because these fibers decompose and form a crusty residue when exposed to flame.

Figure 9.15 Mercerized cotton.
Courtesy of Brickel Associates, Inc.

Mercerized Fiber

Engineering Functional Performance

Converters use numerous finishing agents and treatments to develop specific functional properties—performance features that are not characteristic of the components and cannot be introduced by improving the structural features of the greige goods. These functional properties improve the service-related performance of textile fabrics; they include, for example, retarding the rate and level of soil accumulation, minimizing ironing, and so on. Such properties are primarily service-related, but are frequently important to consumer selection, and may lead to a preference for one firm's product over that of another.

Increasing Apparent Brightness

The use of **optical brighteners** to increase the **apparent whiteness and brightness** of manufactured fibers was discussed in Chapter 4. Brighteners also can be added by the converter as a surface application, or by the consumer who chooses a detergent containing brighteners. In any case, the effectiveness of the brighteners is dependent upon the nature of the light waves incident on the textile surface.

Reducing Fiber Flammability

Flame resistance is engineered in natural cellulosic fibers by adding **flame retardants** to the greige goods. These agents are normally based on phosphorous or nitrogen and include various amounts of such compounds as diammonium phosphate $((NH_4)_2HPO_4)$, ammonium sulfate $((NH_4)_2SO_4)$, and boric acid (H_3BO_3). These compounds inhibit or halt the combustion process at some stage in the cycle. Flame resistance is engineered in manufactured fibers by incorporating a compound based on chlorine or bromine in the polymer solution prior to extrusion.

Increasing Insulative Value

The insulative value of textile structures can be increased by a mechanical process known as napping. It can also be increased by applying a cellular coating to the face or back of a fabric.

Napping

In **napping** operations, the ends of many fibers are raised to the surface; fabrics napped on both sides are called **flannel**, those napped on one side are called **flannelette**. In use, the raised fibers entrap air and provide thermal insulation, while also providing a soft hand and pleasing appearance.

Applying Coatings

Converters frequently apply foamed acrylic compounds to the back of drapery fabrics to increase their insulative value (see Figure 17.30, p. 294). There is, however, a concomitant decrease in drapability of the fabric. The effectiveness of this treatment is discussed in Chapter 17.

Reducing Microbial Action

Mattress covers and pads, especially those produced for use in hospitals and nursing facilities, may be treated with agents that effectively reduce the action of such **microbes** as bacteria and fungi. **Bacteria** and **fungi** are extremely simple vegetative plant forms that lack chlorophyll. Bacteria can react with perspiration to cause odor and can cause infection and slow the healing process. Fungi, such as molds and mildew, feed on cellulosic fibers and sizings. These microbes are often described as "saprophytic" (from the Greek for "rotten growth"); they produce stains and odors, and weaken and rot fibers.

Antimicrobial chemicals can resist a microbe either by killing the pest or retarding its normal activities. Agents such as quaternary ammonium compounds (four organic groups bonded to nitrogen), metallic salts, and other organic compounds can help protect fibers. Converters are now able to apply these agents with others in a single operation, reducing production time and expense while affording fibers greater protection.

Protecting soft floor coverings from the deterioration, discoloration, and odor development caused by microorganisms is an area of ongoing research in the floor coverings industry. For floor coverings installed in damp areas, the growth of odor-causing mildew and bacteria should be inhibited; for carpet and rugs exposed to pets, the retention of odors in the structure should be prevented. Carpet installed in hospitals, nursing homes, and similar facilities should be resistant to a variety of bacteria and fungi so that the structures will remain odor-free and will not harbor microbes that could spread disease and slow patient recovery.

Biological resistance has been engineered into nylon carpet fibers by incorporating antimicrobial agents into the polymer solution or by adding them early in the production sequence. Examples of trade names indicating that microbe resistance has been introduced include Microfresh®, owned by DuPont; HaloFresh®, owned by Allied Fibers; Zeftron® 500™ZX, owned by BASF Corporation; BioFresh®, owned by Burlington Industries, Inc.; and Slygard®, owned by Dow Corning.

Increasing Moisture Absorption

To improve the ability of cellulosic fibers, especially cotton, to absorb moisture, converters use a process known as mercerization. This chemical treatment also affects the luster of the fibers and their ability to withstand stress loads and abrasive forces.

Mercerizing

In **mercerization**, threads, yarns, or fabrics are exposed to sodium hydroxide ($NaOH$) or liquid ammonia while they are held under tension to prevent excessive shrinkage. This treatment alters various internal and external structural features of the fibers, producing changes in their properties. The degree of orientation is increased, increasing the strength or tenacity of the fibers, and the level of crystallinity is reduced, increasing the moisture absorption. As shown in Figure 9.15, mercerized cotton has a rounded cross-sectional shape and virtually no longitudinal twist. These external features may be compared with the flat shape and highly twisted configuration characterizing unmercerized cotton (see Figure 3.2b, p. 28). Although flat cross sections typically reflect higher amounts of incident light than do round cross sections, removal of the twist results in increased luster.

Because mercerization improves the absorption, as well as the luster and strength, of cotton, the finish is routinely used on greige towelings and sheetings. Colorants are generally applied after mercerization, using the increased absorbency to develop deep, rich color characteristics.

Repelling Moths

Insects, most notably moth and carpet beetle larvae, thrive on wool fibers after they break the **disulfide cross links** (-S-S-) contained in the cystine monomer. Moths and beetles prefer to live and breed in dark places, where the larvae will be undisturbed and can sustain themselves on the nutrients obtained from the wool fibers. In unprotected wool carpet the damage is more likely to be seen under rarely moved furniture, and in wool blankets and wool upholstery the attack generally occurs during storage. Today, all domestic wool floor coverings are treated to repel these insects, but residential and commercial consumers must examine the labels of imported products to confirm the use of such treatments.

Converters render wool fiber durably moth resistant by chemically modifying the disulfide linkage, making the fiber indigestible. Several compounds can be used, including **permethrin**. Because mothproofing treatments are generally combined with dyeing or finishing operations to control processing costs, the protective agents become integral parts of the fibers.

Naphthalene compounds, available in such familiar forms as moth balls, crystals, blocks, and sprays, can be used in storage areas to protect wool products from attack by moth larvae. Naphthalene fumes do not kill moth adults or larvae; rather they repel them by giving the wool fibers and the immediate area a noxious odor, so unattractive to moths that they will seek other places for laying their eggs. A note should be added about safety: if internalized, naphthalene compounds are potentially hazardous to humans. To prevent their being ingested by young children or companion animals, moth balls and crystals may be knotted inside sheer hosiery; the porous construction of the hosiery will not hinder the effectiveness of the fumes.

Increasing Water Repellency

Converters can apply **silicone compounds** to reduce the rate at which textile structures absorb water. Because these compounds offer little or no protection from oily soiling and staining, their use is diminishing in favor of fluorocarbon compounds, which provide both water and soil resistance.

Imparting Soil and Stain Resistance

Many textile authorities differentiate "soil" and "stain" on the basis of how tenaciously the soil or dirt clings to the textile structure. When dirt or other foreign matter is mechanically held and comparatively easy to remove, it is known as **soil**; when the dirt becomes chemically bonded to the fiber surfaces and is comparatively difficult to remove, it is called a **stain**. Converters seek to prevent staining by using compounds that enable the fibers to repel or resist soil by increasing surface tension or by blocking sites where selected foreign matter could chemically bond.

Fluorocarbon compounds are used extensively to help textile fibers and fabrics repel or resist soil accumulation. These agents make the textile component more **oleophobic** or oil-hating, as well as more **hydrophobic**. Rather than spreading over the fabric surface, wetting it, and penetrating into the fibers and yarns, spilled water and oily compounds bead up, maintaining their surface tension. As schematized in Figure 9.16a, **high surface tension** means that the molecules in the foreign matter have a higher affinity for one another than for the fibers. Similar action can be observed when raindrops bead up on a waxed car surface.

Spilled liquids should be absorbed immediately from the surface because the protection is temporary; the rate of absorption is slowed, not halted. As the surface tension gradually lowers, the droplets will spread, as shown in Figure 9.16b, wetting and potentially staining the fabric.

Trade names identifying fluorocarbon finishing compounds include Scotch-gard®, produced by the 3M Company, and Teflon® and ZePel®, produced by DuPont.

Colorless acid dyes are used to help carpet fibers resist staining. Here, the carpet is saturated with a dyestuff that attaches itself to acid-receptive sites on the fibers. As these compounds occupy sites to which foreign matter, especially such foods as acid-colored fruit drinks, could attach, stain-

Figure 9.16 Surface tension and fabric wetting.

a) high surface tension   b) low surface tension

ing is prevented. Trade names identifying carpet protected in this manner include StainMaster®, owned by DuPont; and Anso V Worry Free®, owned by Allied Fibers.

Introducing Soil Release

Soil release compounds may be used to help fibers release food stains. These compounds are designed to function in unison with detergent molecules in the laundry solution. The detergent molecules will reduce the surface tension of the water; in effect, this makes the water "wetter" by causing it to spread rather than bead. At the same time, the fluorocarbon-based finishing agent will increase the surface energy of the fibers, making them more hydrophilic, so the water can more readily carry the detergent molecules into the fiber crevices and emulsify and remove the soil and stain material.

Improving Smoothness Retention

The extent to which textile fabrics retain their original smoothness in use and after care depends on their ability to recover from the strains and deformations imposed by such stress forces as bending, folding, twisting, and crushing. Fabrics exhibiting a high level of recovery are resilient; in effect, they "remember" their original configuration. **Resiliency** and "memory" can be engineered by applying heat or by incorporating resins in a durable press finishing operation.

Heat Setting

The application of heat to stabilize the dimensions of fabrics composed of thermoplastic fibers was discussed earlier in this chapter. Heat setting also can be used to help flat fabrics remain smooth and wrinkle-free, minimizing the need for ironing.

Durable Press Finishing

Smooth fabrics composed of cotton, linen, or rayon exhibit extremely poor recovery when crushed, folded, or wrinkled, and remain crumpled and mussed. To compensate for this poor resiliency, converters use **durable press finishing** treatments with the greige goods.

In these chemical finishing processes, the fabrics are impregnated with a **resin or reactant compound**, which has generally been a formaldehyde-based substance. Heat is

Figure 9.17 Resin cross links introduced into cellulosic fibers to improve their resiliency.

then used to cure the compound, causing it to form strong cross links between the polymer chains within the cellulosic fibers. These bonds, schematized in Figure 9.17, function in the same manner as those found in wool and thermoplastic fibers. They stabilize the positions of the chains and introduce to the fibers the so-called "memory" for whatever shape and form they were in when heat-cured.

Relatively high amounts of resin must be applied to ensure no-iron performance. While the resin significantly improves the resiliency, it also decreases absorption and increases soil retention. There may be a temporary "fishy" odor that remains until any unreacted resin is washed away. The resin weakens the fibers, lowering their abrasion resistance and shortening their use-life. The loss in abrasion resistance also can result in a **frosted** appearance. This unsightly problem occurs when abrasive forces remove some of the resin-weakened cellulosic fibers: as the color carried by the fibers is also removed, the abraded area appears faded and lighter than the adjacent areas. Although frosting is a color-related problem, it is the result of fiber failure, not of colorant failure.

To compensate for the decreased strength and abrasion resistance suffered by the cellulosic fibers, manufacturers often blend them with polyester fiber. The polyester extends the wear-life of the fabric. It does not strengthen the cellulosic components. Together with the potential for loss of the cellulosic fiber, development of a frosted appearance remains a possibility in blends.

Currently, various federal agencies, scientific associations, chemical suppliers, and product manufacturers are investigating the possibility that health hazards may be associated with the use of formaldehyde compounds and their subsequent release from durable press fabrics. Some consumers have, in fact, reported an allergic reaction to such resins. Members of the textile industry are now supporting research activities focused on the development and perfection of new durable press finishing agents and procedures.

Summary

Finishing operations are important to the commercial success of all segments of the interior textile industry. They convert greige goods into finished fabrics exhibiting the appearance features, structural qualities, and functional performance properties preferred by contemporary consumers or mandated by regulatory agencies.

The final conversion process is inspection: trained personnel carefully examine the finished fabrics for flaws and defects, rejecting those that contain an unacceptable number of irreparable defects. Together, quality-control tests and visual examinations help to ensure acceptance of the fabrics by end product producers and residential and commercial consumers. These evaluations also help suppliers and producers to determine the advisability of labeling the product with their company name or a name owned by their company. If the qualities of the finished fabrics are unacceptable, their suppliers and producers may be denied the use of voluntary labeling, an effective marketing tool discussed in the following chapter.

Key Terms

antimicrobial chemicals
apparent whiteness and brightness
appliqué work
appliqué, reverse
bacteria
beetling
bleaching agents
bowed yarn alignment
brushing
calendering rollers
candlewicking
candlewick yarns
canvas embroidering
channel quilting
chintz
coarse canvas
commercial quilting
compressive shrinkage treatment
crewel yarns
crushing
damask
dimensional stability
directional pile lay
disulfide cross links
double-mesh (penelope) canvas
durable press finishing
electrostatic flocking
embossing

embroidering
fabric nap
fine canvas
flame resistance
flame retardant
flannel
flannelette
flock
flocking
floss yarns
fluorocarbon compounds
frosting
fulling
fungi
glazing
grassing
hand embroidering
heat setting
high surface tension
hydrophobic
inherent color
luster
machine embroidering
machine stitching
mechanical flocking
medium canvas
mercerization
meshes per inch

microbes

moiréing

molas

naphthalene

napping

needlepoint stitching

off-grain

oleophobic

optical brighteners

outline quilting

pattern quilting

pearl yarns

permethrin

Persian yarns

pile sweep

pilling

pinsonic melding

relaxation shrinkage

residual shrinkage

resiliency

resin or reactant compounds

schreinering

shearing

silicone compounds

single-mesh canvas

skewed yarn alignment

smoothing

soil

soil release

stain

taffeta

tapestry yarns

tentering

water-marked effect

yarn raveling

yarn slippage

Review Questions

1. Explain the physical changes to fibers and yarns imposed by friction calendering, beetling, schreinering, and moiréing. Are these changes permanent?

2. Virtually all moiré fabric is one color. How is it possible, then, to see a water-marked or wood-grain pattern on the fabric surface?

3. Discuss the effect of pile sweep, pile lay, or fabric nap on the luster of a fabric. Why is it critical to carefully position adjoining fabric pieces or carpet lengths having directional pile lay?

4. Cite examples or commercial locations of textile works created by artisans that you have seen.

5. Explain what is meant by "reverse" appliqué.

6. Differentiate between mechanical flocking processes and electrostatic flocking operations.

7. Sketch some applications of interior textile products, such as a window treatment or a piece of upholstered furniture. Then, add a bowed and a skewed fabric to each and note the appearance. Does this help you to appreciate the critical need for grain-straight fabrics, especially those having strong motifs, stripes, or plaids?

8. Why are production costs lowered when converters combine tentering and heat setting?

9. Sketch a simple motif, one representing part of a pattern repeat. Now, introduce yarn traveling. Does the design take on a stained appearance?

10. Why is it critically important to release imposed strain in textile fibers, yarns, and fabrics?

11. Identify ways to improve texture retention.

12. Why is singeing useful in reducing pilling? Does it reduce the number of pills or does it simply make them easier to remove?

13. Are the approaches for reducing the flammability of natural and manufactured fibers different?

14. In what end-use applications is it highly advisable to reduce microbial action?

15. How does mercerization increase the absorption and dyeability of cellulosic fibers? How does it extend the wear-life of the fibers? What effect does it have on the luster of cotton fibers?

16. How do naphthalene compounds protect wool fiber from moth damage? How do converters render wool fibers permanently mothproof?

17. Explain the type of protection offered by silicone compounds and by fluorocarbon compounds.

18. What role does surface tension play in water and soil repellency?

19. How do colorless acid dyes reduce staining? How would a consumer know whether this stain resistant method had been used?

20. Explain how "memory" is introduced to fabrics composed of thermoplastic fibers and to fabrics composed of cellulosic fibers.

21. Differentiate among tippiness, frostiness, and frosting.

22. Why is frosting said to be caused by failure of the fiber not the colorant?

Note

1. Morris Evans, "Mechanical Finishing," *American Dyestuff Reporter*, Vol. 71, No. 5, May 1982, 36.

10

Interior Textile Product Labeling

Federal Trade Commission
    Responsibilities and Powers
    Investigative and Rulemaking Procedures

Regulatory and Advisory Labeling Practices
    Fiber Product Labeling Acts
    Trade Regulation Rules Regarding
      Labeling
    Trade Practice Rules and Guides
      Regarding Labeling

Voluntary Labeling Programs
    Use of "TM" and ®
    Fiber Trademarks
    Certification Marks
    Licensing Programs
    Warranty Programs
    Sample Labeling

Textile markets are highly competitive: companies must utilize effective marketing techniques to succeed at capturing an adequate share of the consumer market. Several corporations have concentrated their competitive efforts on developing distinctive methods of product labeling. Trade associations have also undertaken similar efforts on behalf of their member firms. Often, a name or symbol is added to the label to increase product recognition; sometimes information about such things as quality, care, reliability, and special performance features is put on the label. Such information assists the consumer and design professional in successfully choosing textile products which meet their private needs or which conform with specification requirements. The immediate goal of this voluntary, optional labeling is to secure the initial purchase of a firm's products; the long-term goal is to encourage repeated selection of products bearing the firm's label.

Use of voluntary product labeling is optional, but compliance with certain prescribed commercial practices is not. Textile companies must avoid unfair and deceptive marketing practices and activities that would weaken the competitive position of an industry member and restrain trade illegally. To ensure that consumers and members of the industry are protected from abusive practices, the United States Congress and the Federal Trade Commission have established labeling rules and guidelines, as well as antitrust regulations.

Federal Trade Commission

The **Federal Trade Commission (FTC)** was created by an act of Congress in 1914.[1] Initially, the Commission was empowered and directed to prevent "unfair methods of competition in commerce." The scope of the Commission's work was expanded by the Wheeler-Lea Act of 1938 also to include "unfair or deceptive acts or practices." An example of such a practice is the failure to disclose that a product or material is not what it appears to be; for instance, disclosure is necessary for a non-leather fabric resembling leather.

Responsibilities and Powers

Improvements in the Commission's operations and revisions of its jurisdiction, responsibilities, and powers have continued over the years. Today, the FTC has the responsibility to investigate commercial trade practices, to encourage voluntary corrective action and compliance, and to commence legal proceedings when necessary. The Commission also has the power to "prescribe interpretative rules and general statements of policy with respect to unfair or deceptive acts or practices in or affecting commerce." This provision has led the FTC to issue various rules and guidelines to be followed in labeling textile products.

The FTC has enforcement and administrative responsibilities for several practices pertaining to the marketing of interior textiles. Within the FTC, the Bureau of Consumer Protection has several major program divisions that gather and provide information, investigate practices reported to be deceptive, monitor marketplace activities, and enforce federal statutes assigned to them. The Energy and Product Information Division, for example, focuses its work principally on energy policy and conservation, enforcing such rules as the one governing the disclosure of the insulative value (R-value) of home insulation, much of which is glass fiber batting.

Of particular interest to interior textile consumers and producers is the work of the Product Reliability Division. This division is responsible for enforcement of the **Magnuson-Moss Warranty Act**, which sets forth the procedures to be followed when written warranties are offered. This act and the growing use of warranties for interior textiles are described later in this chapter. Also of critical interest is the work of the Regional Offices Division. The offices in this unit are located in major cities nationwide and have exclusive responsibility for enforcing the mandatory fiber product labeling acts passed by Congress, as well as the trade regulation rules prescribed and promulgated by the FTC.

Investigative and Rulemaking Procedures

As noted earlier, the FTC is empowered to investigate marketplace activities and to develop rules affecting the commercial practices of an entire industry. A review of the investigative and rulemaking procedures followed by the Commission will provide greater understanding of the role it assumes in halting unfair and deceptive marketing practices.

The FTC is not authorized to handle individual consumer complaints, but acts when it sees a pattern of marketplace abuse. Complaints from individual consumers may serve to provide the pattern plus the evidence necessary to begin an investigation.

Investigations can begin in many different ways. Complaint letters, scholarly articles on consumer or economic subjects, or congressional requests may trigger an investigation. Investigations are either "public" or "nonpublic." Generally, public announcements will be made of investigations of the practices of an entire industry. An investigation of an individual company will probably be "nonpublic" in order to protect that company's privacy until the agency is ready formally to make an allegation.

After an investigation, the staff may find reason to believe that a business has violated the law. If the case is not settled voluntarily by some official corrective action by the company (a "consent order"), the Commission could issue a "complaint." After that, and if no settlement is reached, a formal hearing is held before an administrative law judge. Members of the public can participate at this point if they have evidence relating to the case. The administrative law judge issues a decision. There may be an appeal to the FTC commissioners. The commissioners' decision may be appealed to the United States Court of Appeals and ultimately to the United States Supreme Court.

After an investigation, the FTC staff may find what it believes to be unfair or deceptive practices in an entire industry. The staff then could make a recommendation to the commissioners to begin rulemaking. If the recommendation is accepted, a presiding officer is appointed, and a notice is published in the *Federal Register*, setting out the proposed rule and what the commissioners believe are the central issues to be discussed. Members of the public can, at this point, comment or testify on the rule or suggest issues to be examined.

The presiding officer conducts public hearings, which include cross-examination on certain issues. After the hearings, the staff prepares a report on the issues. This is followed by the presiding officer's report. Then members of the public have another opportunity to comment on the entire rulemaking record.

The matter then goes before the commissioners who deliberate on the record (which includes the presiding officer's report, the FTC staff report, and the public comments) to decide whether to issue the rule. They can make changes in the provisions of the rule and issue a revised version as they judge appropriate. This procedure has been followed to establish labeling and marketing rules that apply to various segments of the interior textile industry. Some of these rules are mandatory; others are advisory.

Regulatory and Advisory Labeling Practices

Labeling rules and guidelines are intended to afford consumers protection, not from any hazardous product, but from such things as misrepresentation of the composition of textile products. There are regulations, such as flammability standards, that focus on safety concerns, but product labeling is not generally required with these laws. Mandatory labeling rules also serve to protect industry members by specifying acceptable and legal practices for them to follow when engaged in commercial activities.

Fiber Product Labeling Acts

The United States Congress has passed three acts specifically designed to protect consumers and producers from the unrevealed presence of substitutes and mixtures in fibrous products and from misrepresentation and false advertising of the fiber content of textile fiber products. The provisions of these acts are especially important today as fibers can be engineered successfully to simulate the appearance of other fibers: acrylic can resemble wool; rayon can imitate linen; and acetate, nylon, and polyester can look like silk.

Failure accurately to disclose fiber content is an unfair and deceptive act or practice in commerce. Such illegal misbranding can be avoided by strict adherence to the provisions set forth in each act and its accompanying set of rules and regulations. The latter are established and issued by the FTC to help producers, distributors, and consumers interpret the mandates of each act.[2]

Wool Products Labeling Act of 1939 (WPLA)

The **WPLA of 1939**, effective July 15, 1941, focuses on the labeling requirements for products containing any percentage of wool fiber. (The meaning of "wool" in this act is given below.) Interior textile products subject to the provisions of the WPLA include, for example, conventional blankets and underblankets that are composed in whole or in part of wool. Interior textile products that have been specifically exempted include carpets, rugs, mats, and upholsteries.

Products included within the scope of the WPLA must conspicuously display a label or hangtag disclosing the following information:

1. The percentages of all fibers present in amounts of 5 percent or more of the total fiber weight of the product. Those fibers present to the extent of less than 5 percent should be disclosed as "other fiber" or "other fibers." Constituent fibers are identified by the following terms:

    Wool means the fiber from the fleece of the sheep or lamb or hair of the Angora or Cashmere goat (and may include the so-called specialty fibers from the hair of the camel, alpaca, llama, and vicuna) that has never been reclaimed from any woven or felted wool product. In lieu of the word "wool," the specialty fiber name may be used; "mohair" may be used for naming the fibers from the Angora goat; and "cashmere" may be used for naming the fibers from the Cashmere goat.

    Recycled wool means the constituent fibers were obtained by reducing (shredding) a previously manufactured product to its original fibrous state and then again subjecting the fibers to the product manufacturing sequence. Legal use of this term was provided by an amendment to the WPLA, effective July 4, 1980. "Recycled wool" replaces the terms **reprocessed wool** and **reused wool**. The term "reprocessed wool" was used to identify the resulting fiber when wool had been woven or felted into a wool product that, without ever having been used in any way by a consumer, subsequently had been returned to a fibrous state. The term "reused wool" was used to identify the resulting fiber when wool or reprocessed wool had been spun, woven, knitted, or felted into a wool product that, after having been used by a consumer, subsequently had been returned to a fibrous state. Labels no longer indicate whether or not remanufactured fibers were previously used by consumers.

    Virgin wool, **new wool**, and "wool" are synonymous terms. The use of these terms means the constituent fibers have undergone manufacturing only once; they have not been reclaimed from any spun, woven, knitted, felted, braided, bonded, or otherwise manufactured or used product. These terms could not be used, for example, if fibers were recovered from yarns or excess fabric pieces. No quality specifications are included in the definition of these terms.

    When natural fibers other than wool or manufactured fibers are contained in wool products, they are identified by their generic names. These names were discussed in Chapter 3.

2. The identifying name or registered number of the manufacturer of the product. Registered numbers are assigned upon application to the FTC, and the assigned number may be used in complying with the provisions of other labeling acts."[3]

3. The country of origin. The FTC and the United States Customs Service have issued country-of-origin regulations. Under the FTC rules, all products entirely manufactured and made of materials manufactured in the United States must bear the label "Made in the U.S.A." For products substantially manufactured in the United States using materials from another country, the label must read "Sewn in the U.S.A. of Imported Components" or words of equivalent meaning.

On October 31, 1984, new country-of-origin regulations established by the United States Customs Service, a unit of the Department of Treasury, went into effect and are used in determining the country of origin of imported goods for the purpose of product labeling. These rules apply to products fully processed in one or more foreign countries and subsequently imported into the United States under trade quotas. For quota purposes, the Customs Service designates the country in which there has been a substantial transformation (generally cutting and sewing) of the product as the country of origin; the product is then counted in that country's import quota. (The Customs Service believes these regulations also will curb the practice of exporting products to the United States via countries having an unfilled quota or no quota limitation.)

These country-of-origin rules apply to products manufactured on or after December 24, 1984. Mail-order catalogs printed after this date also must provide country-of-origin information. It should be noted that the importing firm is responsible for the accurate and complete labeling of imported textile goods.

Fur Products Labeling Act (FPLA)

The **FPLA**, effective August 9, 1952, governs the labeling and advertising of furs and fur products. The term "fur product" means any article of apparel made in whole or in part of fur or used fur. The FPLA's provisions do not apply to products other than apparel products.

Textile Fiber Products Identification Act (TFPIA)

Before World War II, consumers, distributors, and producers had few types of fibers from which to choose in comparison to the number available today. There were the widely used natural fibers, including wool, silk, linen, and cotton, and the less widely used natural fibers, such as jute, hemp, sisal, and camel. Rayon and acetate, initially known as "artificial silk" fibers, were also available. While consumers were familiar with the appearance, general performance properties, and care requirements of most of these fibers, they were not familiar with the characteristics of the several types of synthesized fibers subsequently introduced.

The first fully synthesized manufactured fiber, nylon, was unceremoniously adopted for use in toothbrush bristles in 1938, and enthusiastically welcomed in sheer hosiery in 1939. It was available to consumers for only a brief time before World War II required its use to be redirected to the production of war matériel such as parachute fabric and tents. The chemical knowledge gained in the development of nylon, together with advances in production technology, led to the postwar production of an expanding number of manufactured fibers.

As each new fiber was developed and manufactured by various companies, each of which assigned a different name to the fiber, the market became filled with what appeared to be many distinct and unrelated fibers. Consumers, distributors, and producers had no way of knowing the composition of the new fibers, what performance to expect, and what care might be appropriate. Ultimately, growing concern to minimize this confusion, as well as to prevent unfair and deceptive marketing practices (intentional or not), led to the passage of the **TFPIA** in 1958. The act became effective on March 3, 1960.

Provisions of the TFPIA apply to many textile fiber products, including articles of wearing apparel, bedding, curtains, casements, draperies, tablecloths, floor coverings, towels, furniture slipcovers, afghans and throws, and all fibers, yarns, and fabrics. Specifically exempted are such products as upholstery stuffing (unless it was previously used); outer coverings of furniture, mattresses, and boxsprings; and backings of, and paddings or cushions to be used under, floor coverings. Thus, although carpets, rugs, and mats are specifically exempted from the WPLA, the face or pile layers of these floor products are subject to the provisions of the TFPIA. Also, while upholsteries are exempted from the WPLA, they come under the TFPIA when they are marketed in fabric form, that is, when not permanently attached to the furniture frame.

Products included within the scope of the TFPIA must bear a conspicuous label or hangtag displaying the following information:

1. The constituent fiber or combination of fibers in the textile fiber product, designating with equal prominence each natural or manufactured fiber in the textile fiber product by its generic name and percentage in the order of predominance by weight, if the weight of such fiber is 5 percent or more of the total fiber weight of the product. Fibers present to the extent of less than 5 percent of the total fiber weight of the product are designated as "other fiber" or "other fibers," except when a definite functional significance has clearly been established. In the latter case, the percentage by weight, the generic name, and the functional significance of the fiber should be set out, for example, 3 percent spandex for elasticity.

2. The identifying name or registered number of the manufacturer of the product.

3. The country of origin, according to the rules established by the FTC and the United States Customs Service. These regulations were described in the discussion of the WPLA.

Nondeceptive and truthfully descriptive terms are permitted with the generic name, for example, combed cotton, solution-dyed acetate, and antistatic nylon. The information voluntarily provided by this and other forms of permissive labeling is particularly helpful to consumers and design professionals selecting interior textile products.

If any reference is made in advertising to one fiber used in a blend, then the generic names of all fibers present in amounts greater than 5 percent must be listed. Again, the names must be in descending order according to weight.

When products are labeled in accordance with these acts, consumers are not challenged to recognize fibers by their appearance or to know the performance properties and care requirements of many individual fibers. Instead, they need only become familiar with the features generally characteristic of each generic class of chemically related fibers. We should note that care instructions are not required under the WPLA, the FPLA, or the TFPIA. The disclosure of safe care procedures for finished fabrics and apparel items is governed by a trade regulation rule.

Trade Regulation Rules Regarding Labeling

Trade regulation rules set out provisions for mandatory and acceptable practices considered to be in the public interest. Producers following the rules will avoid illegal and unacceptable marketing practices as defined in the FTC Act.

In the marketing of interior textile products, some of the rules apply to a specific market segment. There is, for example, the Trade Regulations Rule Relating to the Deceptive Advertising and Labeling as to Size of Tablecloths and Related Products (see Chapter 30). A second example illustrating specific orientation to one market sector is the Trade Regulation Rule Relating to Failure to Disclose that Skin Irritation May Result from Washing or Handling Glass Fiber Curtains and Draperies and Glass Fiber Curtain and Drapery Fabrics (see Chapter 17).

In April 1974, the FTC gathered comments concerning the advisability of expanding the scope of the Trade Regulation Rule Related to the Care Labeling of Textile Wearing Apparel, 16 CFR Part 423, which had gone into effect on July 3, 1972. After analyzing the comments, the Commission published, in June 1976, a proposed amended rule recommending the extension of the current rule's coverage to draperies, curtains, slipcovers, linens, piece goods sold for covering furniture or making slipcovers, leather and suede apparel, yarn,

carpets and rugs, and upholstered furniture. Oral testimony and written comments were continuously received and analyzed until June 1982; based on these, the Commission did not approve the proposed extensions. The new title of the amended rule, Care Labeling of Textile Wearing Apparel and Certain Piece Goods, reflects this decision. The amended rule became effective on January 2, 1984. The amended rule also included a glossary of standard terms based on ASTM D 3136 Standard Terminology Relating to Care Labels for Textile and Leather Products Other Than Textile Floor Coverings and Upholstery.[4] With passage of the North American Free Trade Agreement that promotes free trade among Mexico, Canada, and the United States, it became necessary to provide care instructions that were not language dependent. Working through ASTM, members of the industry developed a guide that provides a uniform system of care symbols: a washtub represents the washing process; a triangle represents the bleaching process; a square represents the drying process; the iron represents the ironing or pressing process; and the circle represents the drycleaning process (Figure 10.1).

Although textile floor coverings and textile upholstered furniture were not included in the 1984 Care Labeling amendment, there remained an interest by consumers for care instructions for carpet, rugs, and upholstery. In response, ASTM continued its work on care instructions for these products and published ASTM D 5253 Standard Terminology of Writing Care Instructions and General Refurbishing Procedures for Textile Floor Coverings and Textile Upholstered Furniture. This ASTM standard provides a uniform language for the writing of care instructions to be supplied with carpets, rugs, and upholstered furniture, excluding leather. The terminology is recommended for use by sellers who voluntarily choose to provide care information to their consumers.

The role of the FTC should not be construed as strictly adversarial in nature. Although it has been assigned exclusive responsibility for enforcing specific congressional acts and for monitoring commerce in general, the Commission also continually strives to inform and educate both the consuming public and industry members concerning fair market practices. Trade practice rules and labeling guides have been helpful to this endeavor.

CONSUMER GUIDE TO CARE SYMBOLS

Figure 10.1 Commercial and home laundering and dry cleaning symbols.
Reprinted, with permission, from the 1996 Annual Book of ASTM Standards.

Trade Practice Rules and Guides Regarding Labeling

As generally set forth in the introduction of each **trade practice rule and guide**, the provisions are "interpretive of laws administered by the Commission, and thus are advisory in nature." These rules "are designed to foster and promote the maintenance of fair competitive conditions in the interest of protecting industry, trade, and the public." By complying with the stated provisions, industry members can avoid engaging in unfair and deceptive marketing practices that can lead to litigation.

The major difference between trade practice rules and guides lies in who initiated the proceedings. In the case of trade practice rules, a single industry segment has requested assistance from the FTC in an effort to clarify what trade practices are acceptable. Conferences are then held to provide a forum for all industry members; thereafter, proposed rules are published, responses considered, and final advisory rules published. Guides are the result of proceedings initiated by the Commission, and they supersede several trade practice rules.

Trade practice rules and guides, like trade regulation rules, have a specific and limited scope. There are, for example, guides for the household furniture industry and guides for the feather and down products industry. These guides are explained in Chapters 12 and 29, respectively.

To ensure that they are using fair and nondeceptive marketing practices, textile firms must label their products in accordance with all applicable acts, rules, and guides. In order to gain a competitive edge in the marketplace, they may also choose to label their products with a distinctive name or logo or to offer a warranty pertaining to in-use performance. The use of such labeling is permissible and strictly voluntary.

Voluntary Labeling Programs

Voluntary labeling programs are used extensively in the marketing of interior textile products. These programs are primarily intended to increase sales, assisting in the commercial success of all suppliers, producers, and distributors of the labeled product. At the same time, such labeling is helpful to contract designers, architects, and consumers who understand the intention or implication of the various kinds of labeling, such as those relating to

nondescriptive fiber names, certification marks, licensing programs, and warranty programs. In virtually all programs, a trademark is a valuable promotional aid.

Use of "TM" and ®

Trademarks are distinctive names, words, phrases, and stylized logos (letters or symbols) that aim at capturing the attention of professionals and consumers. The ownership and use of trademarks is carefully guarded.

Producers and trade associations allocate significant amounts of money, time, and talent to coining names, designing graphic symbols, and writing eye-catching phrases that will be effective trademarks. Once this effort is completed, the chosen name, phrase, or logo appears on product labels and in promotional materials accompanied by the letters *TM*. This labeling constitutes basic ownership of the trademark, assuming the person or firm was the first to use the trademark in commerce. Frequently, the user elects to apply for registered ownership of the trademark with the United States Patent and Trademark Office. Following approval of the application, the symbol ® is used in lieu of TM to indicate registered ownership.

Trademarks are widely promoted to ensure recognition of the mark by the consumer. At the same time, the use of the mark is carefully controlled. Every effort is taken to protect the reputation of the trademark, as well as to ensure that the legal owner is the only one benefiting from the increased recognition and selection of products labeled with the mark. Unauthorized adoption of a trademark is illegal: in recent years, such piracy has resulted in several multimillion-dollar lawsuits and confiscation of illegally branded goods.

Fiber Trademarks

Fiber suppliers and producers use trade names and logos to distinguish their products from those of their competitors. Manufactured fiber producers use trade names extensively, and apparently their promotional efforts have been successful. Many consumers are more familiar with fiber trade names than with their generic names. A trademarked fiber may be considered unique when in fact several other chemically related fibers produced by other companies are also available. Appendix A lists fiber trade names with their generic classes and the characteristics they designate.

Informed consumers and trained professionals can make valuable use of fiber trade names, especially those that designate a special property. They may, for example, know that solution dyeing has been used or that a fiber is self-extinguishing (i.e., stops burning when the source of ignition is removed) when special trade names are used.

Cotton Incorporated grants permission to qualifying retailers, manufacturers, and mills to use its registered trademark on packaging, hangtags, or in advertisements. The trademark is a stylized design, the Cotton Seal, illustrated in Figure 10.2.

Some companies license or certify the use of their fiber trade names on end products. In this marketing, the fiber company tests fabrics or end products for quality and performance. Fiber trademark licensing and certifying should not be confused with other licensing and certification programs applying to textile products.

Certification Marks

Certification marks are coined names and stylized logos that may be used alone or in conjunction with other types of voluntary labeling. They may be used on the labels of end products that conform with fiber content specifications or performance specifications established by the owner of the mark.

Some fiber trade associations control or certify the use of their registered trademark logos. The Wool Bureau, Inc., for example, owns and controls the use of the Woolmark and the Woolblend Mark (Figure 10.3). End products carrying these symbols have been quality tested by The Wool Bureau, Inc. for compliance with performance and fiber content specifications.

For contract or commercial upholstery fabrics, members of the industry created the Association for Contract Textiles (ACT) in 1985. The objective for this organization was to address issues concerning contract fabrics, including performance standards and industry education. Members of the association established performance guidelines for colorfastness to wet and dry crocking, colorfastness to light, resistance to pilling, strength, seam slippage, and abrasion resistance. (Standard methods of testing these performance variables are discussed in Chapter 14.) Recommendations were delineated for both general contract use and heavy duty contract use.

Figure 10.2 The Cotton Seal.
Registered trademark of Cotton Inc.

Figure 10.3 Registered trademark logos used by The Wool Bureau, Inc. in certification labeling.
Courtesy of The Wool Bureau, Inc.

PURE WOOL

The sewn-in Woolmark label is your assurance of quality-tested fabrics made of the world's best...Pure Wool.

PURE WOOL PILE

The Woolmark label is your assurance of quality-tested products made of the world's best...Pure Wool Pile.

WOOL BLEND

The sewn-in Woolblend Mark label is your assurance of quality-tested fabrics made predominantly of wool.

Futura ACT

Symbol	Function
❡	flammability
☙	colorfastness to wet & dry crocking
✳	colorfastness to light
☆	physical properties
▣	abrasion
◮	abrasion

Figure 10.4 Symbols used with contract fabric to denote compliance with ACT performance standards *Courtesy of the Association for Contract Textiles.*

Compliance with the recommended standards is denoted by corresponding symbols, each of which is shown in Figure 10.4.

Licensing Programs

Licensing companies sell the right to use their company-owned processes to producers and converters; they do not process any components or manufacture any end products. Licensing companies do, however, certify the use of their coined names in the labeling and marketing of products. The Sanforized Company, for example, licenses the use of its compressive shrinkage and durable press processes. Producers using these fabric conversion techniques may label and promote their end products with such names as Sanforized®, Sanfor-Knit®, and Sanfor-Set®, trade names owned by the Sanforized Company.

Consumers, contract designers, and architects must recognize that certification and **licensing programs** provide assurances, not guarantees. The presence of a certified or licensed name or logo on a label may confirm a specific fiber content, the use of a particular process, or that the product has met standard performance specifications, but it does not guarantee any features.

Warranty Programs

Today, **warranty or guarantee programs** are used more frequently in textile marketing than they were in earlier, less economically challenging times. Budgetary pressures have increasingly encouraged designers, architects, and consumers to seek or even demand a legally binding agreement guaranteeing the long-term satisfactory performance of some interior textile products. They are, of course, seeking protection from defective or faulty merchandise and the expense of premature replacement.

In order to meet the demands of professionals and consumers, and thus to remain competitive, several producers of textile components and end products offer written warranties. Fiber companies may, for example, try to enhance their competitive position by voluntarily offering to stand behind products composed of their fiber but manufactured by a downstream firm. This is an especially frequent practice with soft floor coverings.

There are important differences among the various types of warranties. A review of the major types of warranties—spoken, implied, and written—can help to identify and clarify these differences.

Spoken Warranties

Spoken warranties are merely verbal promises, virtually impossible to enforce. Consumers and professionals should have spoken warranties put into writing.

Implied Warranties

Implied warranties are not written, and they are not voluntary; they are rights provided to consumers by state law. These rights include such things as the "warranty of merchantability," for instance, that an electric blanket will heat, and the "warranty of fitness for a particular purpose," for instance, that a carpet produced for installation around a swimming pool will not dissolve in water. In states having such laws, implied warranties are not voluntary; they come automatically with every sale unless the product is sold "as is."

Written Warranties

A **written warranty** constitutes a legally binding promise that the warrantor is insuring quality and performance and is willing to stand behind the warranted product, assuming it is neither misused nor abused by the warrantee. While written warranties are strictly voluntary, when they are offered they are subject to the provisions of the Magnuson-Moss Warranty Act, passed by the U.S. Congress in 1975. This act is under the jurisdiction of the FTC.

Like the textile labeling mandates discussed earlier, the Magnuson-Moss Warranty Act serves and protects both producers and consumers. By strictly adhering to the provisions of the act, producers can avoid unfair and deceptive marketing practices. By examining the features included in any warranty offered, and by exercising their rights under the act, consumers can protect themselves from defective products.

The act requires that written warranties offered on consumer products costing more than fifteen dollars must be made available to prospective consumers prior to the sale of the product. The warranty shall "fully and conspicuously disclose in simple and readily understood language the terms and conditions of such warranty." This provision prohibits the use of "legalese" and fine print. Specific information that must be set forth in written warranties includes, but is not limited to, the following items:

1. The clear identification of the names and addresses of the warrantors.
2. The identity of the party or parties to whom the warranty is extended; this is often stated as "original purchasers only."
3. The products or parts covered.
4. What the warrantor will do in the event of a defect, malfunction, or failure to conform with such written warranty, at whose expense, and for what period of time.
5. What the consumer must do and what expenses the consumer must bear.
6. The step-by-step procedure the consumer should take in order to obtain performance of any obligation under the warranty, including the identification of any person or class of persons authorized to perform the obligations set forth in the warranty.
7. The characteristics, properties, or parts of the product that are not covered by the warranty.

Written warranties are required also to carry the designation "full" or "limited." These designations indicate what the warrantor agrees to do for the purchaser, as well as what is expected of the purchaser. An examination of the meanings and implications of these designations will provide greater understanding of warranty labeling.

FULL WARRANTY: The title FULL on a warranty tells you that:

- A defective product will be repaired or replaced for free, including removal and reinstallation when necessary.
- The product will be repaired within a reasonable time period after you have told the company about the problem.
- You will not have to do anything unreasonable to get warranty service (such as return a heavy product to the store).
- The warranty is good for anyone who owns the product during the warranty period.

- If the product has not been repaired after a reasonable number of tries, you can get a replacement or a refund. (This is commonly known as the "lemon" provision.)
- You do not have to return a warranty card for a product with a FULL warranty. But, a company may give a registration card and suggest that it be returned, so long as it is clear that the return of the card is voluntary.
- Implied warranties cannot be disclaimed or denied or limited to any specific length of time.

Warning: The title FULL does NOT mean:

- That the entire product is covered by the warranty.
- That the warranty has to last for one year or any other particular length of time.
- That the company must pay for "consequential or incidental damages" (such as towing, car rental, food spoilage, etc.).
- That the product is warranted in all geographic areas.

LIMITED WARRANTY: The title LIMITED on a warranty tells you that the warranty gives you less than what the FULL warranty gives you. You have to read your warranty to see what protection is missing. For example:

- You may have to pay for labor, reinstallation, or other charges.
- You may be required to bring a heavy product back to the store for service or do something else you may find difficult.
- Your warranty may be good only for the first purchaser (that is, a second owner would not be entitled to any warranty service).
- You may be promised a pro-rata refund or credit which means you will have to pay for the time you owned the product before the defect appeared.
- You may have to return your warranty registration card to get warranty coverage.
- Your implied warranties may expire when your written warranty expires. (For example, a one-year limited warranty can say that the implied warranties only last for one year.)
- The "lemon" provision does not apply to limited warranties, but even under a limited warranty you are enti-

tled to what the warranty promises. If the company cannot do what it has promised to do, the company has to do something else comparable for you.

Warning: The title LIMITED does NOT mean:

- That your product is inferior or will not work as promised.
- That only part of the product is covered. For example, you may have a LIMITED warranty that covers the entire product.
- That the warranty only covers the cost of repair parts. A LIMITED warranty can include labor, too.
- That the warranty will last for any particular length of time.
- That you can only have warranty service done in a few locations.

A product can carry more than one written warranty. For example, an automatic washer can have a FULL warranty on the entire product for one year and a LIMITED four-year warranty on the gear assembly.[5]

Sample Labeling

Another form of voluntary labeling used by interior textile product producers that should be highlighted is the use of style, color, and design names on product samples displayed in product showrooms and retail outlets. In most cases, these names are nondescriptive and provide no useful information, but they may have the effect of attracting and holding prospective purchasers' attention. For example, "blue-green" may identify a color accurately, but "sea foam" may sound more enticing; the terms "level, cutpile" may describe a carpet texture informatively, but "plateau" may seem more interesting; "polka dot" may be readily understandable, but "micro dot" may add contemporary flair; and so on.

It is apparent that the marketing strategy behind this type of sample labeling is the same as that behind the use of a well-known designer's name on product labels. Producers purchase the right to use the name, after confirming that it will be a persuasive and effective marketing aid.

Summary

Members of the interior textile industry must disclose the fiber composition and country of origin of most of their products, using the practices prescribed in the congressional fiber product labeling acts. Members of certain industry segments also must adhere to trade regulation rules, and some are advised also to comply with recommendations set forth in a trade practice rule or in guides. Compliance with these acts and guidelines helps to ensure that producers are not engaged in unfair or deceptive commercial activities related to product disclosures. It also helps to ensure that consumers and professionals have useful and accurate information, enabling them to make reliable decisions when they select textile products for interior applications.

To enhance the marketability of their products, many producers use voluntary labeling programs. They may distinguish their products with trade names or certification marks, or they may elect to guarantee their quality or performance. The use of such labeling offers reciprocal advantages for producers and consumers. Producers gain a competitive edge in the marketplace, and consumers are provided more information or protection than is legally required.

Key Terms

certification marks
Federal Trade Commission (FTC)
FPLA
full warranty
guides
implied warranties
licensing programs
limited warranty
Magnuson-Moss Warranty Act
new wool
recycled wool
reprocessed wool

reused wool
spoken warranties
TFPIA
trademarks
trade practice rules
trade regulation rules
virgin wool
warranty or guarantee programs
wool
WPLA of 1939
written warranties

Review Questions

1. Explain what is meant by "unfair or deceptive acts or practices" in commerce.

2. Describe the investigative and rulemaking procedures followed by the FTC.

3. What are the purposes of the fiber product labeling acts?

4. Differentiate among "reprocessed," "reused," and "recycled" as they apply to wool product labeling.

5. When a product is labeled "virgin wool," are there connotations of quality?

6. How is the country of origin determined for imported textile products? How are these regulations used in controlling textile imports to the United States?

7. Distinguish between the provisions of trade regulation rules and labeling acts and between the provisions of trade regulation rules and trade practice rules. Differentiate between trade practice rules and guidelines.

8. Are care instructions required for textile upholstered furniture, carpet, and rugs?

9. How have members of the industry responded to the desire and need for care instructions for these products?

10. Explain the use of "TM" and ®.

11. Discuss the importance of trademarks in textile marketing.

12. When an informed consumer or design professional sees an ACT certification symbol on contract upholstery, what is understood?

13. Are written warranties mandatory? When are warranties subject to the provisions of the Magnuson-Moss Warranty Act?

14. Identify some differences between full and limited warranties.

15. What is meant by the "lemon" provision?

16. Cite various types of sample labeling. What is the purpose of such labeling?

Notes

1. Copies of the Federal Trade Commission Act are available from the FTC, Distribution Branch, Room 270, Washington, DC 20580.

2. Copies of these acts and their accompanying rules and regulations are available from the FTC.

3. In 1974, the FTC ruled that continuation of the confidentiality of registered numbers was an unfair marketing practice. Consumers may contact the FTC concerning ownership of the assigned numbers.

4. The full text of ASTM standards is available in the *Annual Book of ASTM Standards* Volume 07.01 or Volume 07.02.

5. "Warranties: There Ought to Be a Law," Federal Trade Commission, Washington, D.C., undated.

11

Interior Textile Products and Fire

Consumer Product Safety Commission

Flammable Fabrics Act
   The 1967 Amendment
   New Standards

Combustion Processes and Byproducts
   Combustion Processes
   Byproducts of Combustion

Stages of an Interior Fire
   Stage 1
   Stage 2
   Stage 3

Flammability Testing
   Small-scale Test Methods
   Large-scale Test Methods
   Full-scale Test Methods

Since the late 1960s, consumers, industry members, and local, state, and federal government personnel have given increased attention to the fire-related behavior of interior textile products. This has resulted in the establishment of flammability codes and standards applying to interior products intended for use in certain occupancies; such codes are issued and enforced by various regulatory agencies, several of which were identified in Chapter 1. This attention has also resulted in the establishment of mandatory flammability standards with which specific interior textile products must comply prior to marketing. These standards were established in accordance with provisions of the Flammable Fabrics Act, a congressional act administered by the Consumer Product Safety Commission.

Residential and commercial consumers should be aware of the role interior textiles play in fires. Understanding fire-related terms and processes and the test methods used in fire-safety work will enable them to widen the margin of personal safety, minimize structural damage, and lessen economic losses in the event of fire. It will also prepare the professional to specify products that conform to mandated selection criteria.

Consumer Product Safety Commission

The **Consumer Product Safety Commission (CPSC)** was established as an independent federal agency in late 1972. When the Commission began operation on May 14, 1973, administration and enforcement responsibilities for certain safety-oriented acts, including the **Flammable Fabrics Act (FFA)**, were transferred to it from other federal regulatory agencies. Prior to this transfer, the **FTC** and the **U.S. Department of Commerce (DOC)** administered the FFA.

In carrying out its responsibilities, the CPSC analyzes information and statistics regarding the frequency and severity of injury associated with interior textile and other consumer products. When products are found to pose "an unreasonable risk" to consumers, the Commission has the power to initiate the necessary proceedings that

ultimately may lead to the establishment of a new or revised safety standard. When regulating interior textile products, the CPSC adheres to procedures set forth in the FFA.

Flammable Fabrics Act

The FFA was passed by the U.S. Congress in 1953 and became effective on July 1, 1954. This act prohibits the introduction and movement in interstate commerce of articles of wearing apparel and fabrics so highly flammable as to be dangerous when worn by individuals. Congress amended the act in 1967, expanding its scope to include interior furnishings and permitting the establishment of standards specific to these textile products.

The 1967 Amendment

In addition to expanding the scope of the FFA, the 1967 amendment directed the Secretary of Commerce and the Secretary of Health, Education, and Welfare (now Health and Human Services) to "conduct a continuing study and investigation of the deaths, injuries, and economic losses resulting from accidental burning of products, fabrics, or related materials." Much of the statistical information pertaining to fabric-related burning accidents is provided by the **National Electronic Injury Surveillance System (NEISS)**. The NEISS records personal injury data from scores of hospital emergency rooms throughout the United States and forwards it to the CPSC for analysis.

The 1967 amendment also authorized the Secretary of Commerce to carry out the following four activities:

1. Conduct research into the flammability of products, fabrics, and materials.
2. Conduct feasibility studies on reduction of flammability of products, fabrics, and materials.
3. Develop flammability test methods and testing devices.
4. Offer appropriate training on the use of flammability test methods and testing devices.

The federally funded **National Institute of Standards and Technology (NIST)** carries out much of the investigative work involved in the laboratories of its Center for Fire Research. The NIST does not promulgate standards, but it does provide information to the CPSC and other federal agencies.

When statistical injury data and laboratory test results support the possibility that a new or revised safety standard is needed, it is the responsibility of the CPSC to initiate and carry out the following procedures:

1. Publish the notice of a possible need and the proposed standard in the *Federal Register*. (Prior to April 23, 1976, the notice and proposed standard were published separately.)
2. Invite and consider response from affected and interested persons.
3. Publish the final version of the standard in the *Federal Register*.
4. Allow one year for firms affected by the standard to manufacture products meeting specified performance criteria. (The CPSC may set an earlier or later effective date if it finds good cause.)
5. Prohibit noncomplying products manufactured after the effective date from being introduced into commerce. (The CPSC may allow exceptions.)

New Standards

Five new standards have been promulgated and others proposed as a result of the provisions of the 1967 amendment. Initially, the acronym *DOC* (for Department of Commerce), the letters *FF* (for flammable fabric) or *PFF* (for proposed flammable fabric), and a numerical notation identified each new or proposed standard. The first number indicated the order in which the standards were proposed; the second number indicated the year in which action was last taken on the standard (note that the second number does not indicate the year in which the standard became effective). Frequently, these designations were used and are used in lieu of the title of the standards. In recent years, the standards are usually published with their Code of Federal Regulations (CFR) notation. Professionals and consumers should become familiar with the following standards, four of which apply to interior textile products:

FF 1–70 Large Carpets and Rugs, now 16 CFR 1630
FF 2–70 Small Carpets and Rugs, now 16 CFR 1631
FF 3–71 Children's Sleepwear, Sizes 0–6X, now 16 CFR 1615
FF 4–74 Mattresses and Mattress Pads, now 16 CFR 1632
FF 5–74 Children's Sleepwear, Sizes 7–14, now 16 CFR 1616
PFF 6–81 Upholstered Furniture, now 16 CFR 1633

UFAC Voluntary Action Program

PFF 6–81 *Draft* Proposed Standard for the Flammability (Cigarette Ignition Resistance) of Upholstered Furniture, did not move beyond the proposed stage. Instead, when the original draft proposal (PFF 6–74) was issued, members of the upholstered furniture industry consolidated their efforts concerning more cigarette-resistant upholstering methods. Through this organization, the industry sought to demonstrate that the majority of its member firms would voluntarily participate in a program designed to ensure the production of *safer* products.

Officially launched in April 1979, the **Upholstered Furniture Action Council (UFAC)** Voluntary Action Program was designed to improve the ability of upholstered furniture to resist catching fire from a burning cigarette, the most common source of furniture ignition. The program includes four aspects: fabric classification, which is determined by a prescribed test method; construction criteria, which are paired with six test methods; a labeling plan; and a compliance procedure. The test methods used in the program are described later in this chapter.

By combining the ability of the outer covering to resist catching fire from a burning cigarette with construction method, members of the industry intended to assure the production of *safer* upholstered furniture while avoiding the limitation of a large number of upholstery fabrics traditionally available to consumers.

The labeling plan devised by the UFAC centers on a hangtag that identifies furniture meeting UFAC criteria. Prospective purchasers are informed that the labeled item has been made in accordance with UFAC methods designed to reduce the likelihood of furniture fire from cigarettes (Figure 11.1).

Participation in the UFAC program is strictly voluntary. The UFAC encourages furniture component suppliers and end-product manufacturers to participate and provides technical assistance to promote compliance. An independent laboratory verifies that materials used in

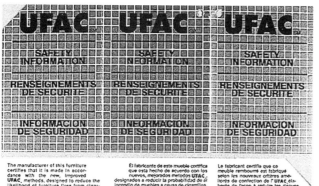

Figure 11.1 UFAC hangtag used on upholstered furniture that complies with UFAC criteria.
Courtesy of the Upholstered Furniture Action Council.

making the items carrying the compliance hangtag meet the performance criteria set forth in the program.

Periodically, the results of the verification tests and the level of industry participation are reported to the CPSC. By such reporting, the UFAC seeks to demonstrate that members of the industry can and will produce safer upholstered furniture items, eliminating the need for a federal flammability mandate.

Combustion Processes and Byproducts

Combustion is a chemical process in which oxidation, the combination of oxygen with elements or compounds, produces heat energy. In some combustion reactions, light and such other byproducts as molten polymer compounds, smoke, and toxic gases are also produced.

Combustion Processes

Flaming combustion processes are initiated by **pyrolysis**, in which heat causes organic compounds to decompose, producing combustible materials. A burning match, a lit cigarette, glowing embers, or an electrical spark may supply heat. While a lighted match, which has a tempera-

ture of approximately 1,000 °F, is a common source of ignition heat for interior textile products, the most common source is a burning cigarette. When the **kindling or ignition temperature** is reached, the combustible materials combine with oxygen, ignite, and produce heat and light in the form of flames. The heat generated by this combustion can promote further decomposition of the textile substance, causing the cyclic process to continue until the structure is consumed.

Spontaneous combustion occurs when a textile substrate is heated to its kindling temperature without the involvement of a flaming ignition source. Although this is not common with fibers, it is a potential hazard with latex foam compounds, especially when they are being tumbled in a heated dryer. Because cellular latex is a good heat insulator, heat builds up, the relatively low ignition temperature of the material is quickly reached, and it bursts into flame.

In addition to flaming combustion, **flameless combustion** can also occur. One type of flameless combustion, **glowing**, is characteristic of cellulosic fibers: after a small area of flame has been extinguished, the fiber continues to be consumed without flames rising. **Smoldering** is another type of flameless combustion, which may occur with fibrous fillings and battings. This suppressed combustion often produces large volumes of dense smoke filled with deadly **toxicants**.

Byproducts of Combustion

Beside the heat energy and light produced during most combustion reactions, burning textiles and other interior materials generate various other products. Among these, toxic gases pose the greatest threat to life.

Molten Polymer Compounds

When thermoplastic fibers are heated to their melting points, the **molten polymer compounds** produced can play conflicting roles in interior fires. When window and wall coverings contain these fibers, for example, the molten polymer may drip and carry the flames downward. This could be a positive event if the burning fabric **self-extinguished** and the flaming droplets fell on a noncombustible flooring material. It would be a negative event if the flaming droplets propagated the fire to a flammable floor covering.

Smoke

The amount and density of smoke generated by items undergoing flaming combustion or smoldering can have a major effect on safe exit procedures because smoke reduces visibility and obscures illuminated exit markers. A test method to evaluate **smoke density** is discussed and illustrated later in this chapter.

Smoke, not heat or flame, is the primary cause of all fire deaths.[1] Smoke is deadly because of the toxicants it contains.

Toxic Gases

Toxicity studies have shown that varied quantities of six specific gases can be detected after the isolated combustion of commonly used fibers. These gases include carbon monoxide (CO), carbon dioxide (CO_2), hydrogen sulfide (HS), hydrogen cyanide (HCN), nitrogen oxide plus nitrogen dioxide (NO + NO_2), and vinyl cyanide (CH_2CHCN).[2] The most toxic of these gases, CO, is present in all fires, whether textiles are involved or not; it causes death by preventing red blood cells from absorbing oxygen.

At the current time, no flammability regulations include specific requirements related to **toxic gases**, although it may be reasonable to expect such mandates in the future. Fire-safety researchers are, in fact, focusing their attentions on the development of a test method to measure the hazards of inhaled toxicants.

Stages of an Interior Fire

The principal concern of industry personnel, educators, government employees, and others engaged in fire-safety work is not for the damage sustained by textile products or other interior items—burned items can be repaired or replaced—but instead for the reduction of the hazard to life. They strive to minimize the likelihood of initial ignition and, in the event of fire, they seek to make the environment safer by preserving the means for quick and efficient **egress** from a burning area or structure.

The critical importance of preserving the possibility of safe egress is confirmed when the three distinct stages through which an interior fire progresses are examined. This examination will also confirm the value of early warning systems and automatic sprinkling systems.

Stage 1

A **Stage 1 fire** is schematized in Figure 11.2. Only the ignited item is burning. The overriding concern is that the

Side Elevation (Room)   Floor Plan (Room)

Figure 11.2 Stage 1 of an interior fire.
I. A. Benjamin and S. Davis, Flammability Testing for Carpet, NBSIR 78-1436, Center for Fire Research, Institute for Applied Technology, National Bureau of Standards, Washington, D. C., April 1978.

Side Elevation (Room)   Floor Plan (Room)

Figure 11.3 Stage 2 of an interior fire.
I. A. Benjamin and S. Davis, Flammability Testing for Carpet, NBSIR 78–1436, Center for Fire Research, Institute for Applied Technology, National Bureau of Standards, Washington, D. C., April 1978.

fire remain localized. If, for example, a burning cigarette is carelessly dropped onto a carpet or an upholstered chair, the item should be designed to resist ignition. If ignition occurs, the item should not propagate or spread the flame throughout the room, making it more challenging to extinguish the fire and more difficult to exit safely.

When a fire is small and isolated, smoke detectors or other alarm systems serve to alert residents. The early warning may enable occupants to contain the fire, preventing its growth to Stage 2.

Stage 2

A **fire in Stage 2** is illustrated in Figure 11.3. Here, the fire has spread from the area of origin, igniting other items in its path. As the fire spreads and grows, more heat is generated and the air in the room becomes hotter and hotter. When sufficient heat has built up, all combustible items in the room burst into flames, producing a situation known as **flashover**.

Automatic sprinkling systems, which are usually heat activated, can halt **flame propagation**, thus minimizing

Side Elevation (Corridor)   Floor Plan (Building)

Figure 11.4 Stage 3 of an interior fire.
I. A. Benjamin and S. Davis, Flammability Testing for Carpet, NBSIR 78–1436, Center for Fire Research, Institute for Applied Technology, National Bureau of Standards, Washington, D. C., April 1978.

heat buildup and preventing flashover. The Federal Management Agency has found that using smoke detectors and automatic sprinkling systems in all buildings and residences could reduce overall injuries, loss of life, and property damage by at least 50 percent.[3]

Stage 3

In **Stage 3 of an interior fire**, shown schematically in Figure 11.4, the flames spread beyond the burning room into the corridor or passageway. In addition to the flames, a significant amount of heat may be radiating into the corridor as the fire "spills" out. If the fire spreads down the corridor, all exits may be blocked.

Fire researchers consider the three stages of fire growth when they design flammability test methods. Members of the Consumer Product Safety Commission and other regulatory agencies consider them when they establish flammability standards for selected interior textile products.

Flammability Testing

Various types of testing are used to measure the fire-related behavior of interior textile products and components. Currently, small-scale, large-scale, and full-scale procedures are used in this work.

Small-scale Test Methods

Small-scale test methods are used in the laboratory to measure specific flammability characteristics. Like other

standard test methods, these are designed to simulate the conditions associated with real-life situations; in some test methods, for example, a lit cigarette is the source of heat for ignition. Small-scale tests enable the producer to make reasonably accurate predictions concerning the behavior of the item being tested in a Stage 1 fire.

Methenamine Tablet (Pill) Test Method

This test method, designated ASTM D 2859, is designed to simulate a situation in which a textile floor covering is exposed to a small source of ignition, such as a burning match, an ignited cigarette, or a glowing ember. Structures that resist ignition and do not propagate the flame could reasonably be expected to contain a fire in Stage 1.

Test Specimens and Procedures   Eight specimens, each one 9 inches square, are dried in an oven so that they will be free of moisture. Then, one at a time, the specimens are placed in a draft-protected burn chamber and covered by a steel flattening frame with an opening 8 inches in diameter. As shown in Figure 11.5, a **methenamine tablet**, which is formulated to burn for two minutes, is placed in the center of the specimen and ignited. Testing is complete when burning of the tablet or the carpet specimen ceases, whichever occurs last.

Analysis of Results   A **char length** measurement is taken on each of the eight specimens. Measurements are made of the shortest distance between the edge of the hole in the ring and the charred area. Smoke and toxic gases are not considered.

Performance Requirements   A specimen meets either standard when the char area does not extend to within 1 inch of the hole in the ring. Seven out of the eight specimens must pass for the floor covering to pass. The provisions of 16 CFR 1631 permit rugs that fail the test to be marketed as long as they carry a label warning: flammable (fails U.S. Consumer Product Safety Commission Standard 16 CFR 1631: should not be used near source of fire).

Adoption of the Method   This test has been adopted as the method to be used in 16 CFR 1630 (FF 1–70) and 16 CFR 1631 (FF 2–70). The **scope of 16 CFR 1630** is limited to large carpets and rugs, those having an area

Figure 11.5 Methenamine tablet test.
Courtesy of Solutia Inc., Fibers Division.

greater than 24 square feet and one dimension greater than 6 feet. Carpet modules, because they are installed to cover large areas, are also subject to the provisions of 16 CFR 1630. The **scope of 16 CFR 1631** includes floor coverings that are not large enough to fall within the scope of 16 CFR 1630. Such structures include scatter rugs, bathroom rugs, and smaller area rugs. These standards became effective in 1971, and virtually all imported and domestic soft floor coverings offered for sale in the United States must conform to the provisions of the applicable standard.

Forty-five-degree Angle Test Method

Although ASTM D 1230 Standard Test Method for Flammability of Apparel Textiles was originally designed for use with apparel textiles, it may be selected to evaluate the flammability of towelings. This small-scale test is also known as the 45-degree angle test.

Test Specimens and Procedure In accordance with ASTM D 1230, exploratory testing is used to determine the direction in which the most rapid rate of flame spread occurs. With pile fabrics, flame spread is most rapid when progressing against the lay of the pile, so the long dimension of the specimens should parallel the lay of the pile. Four specimens are then cut 2 inches by 6 inches, oven dried, and placed in a specimen holder. One at a time, each specimen is placed in the flammability tester at a 45-degree angle. Automated mechanisms are then activated to apply a flame to the lower edge of the specimen for 1 second; timing begins upon application of the flame and ends when burning releases a stop cord.

Analysis of Results The arithmetic mean flame-spread time of the preliminary specimen and the four test specimens is calculated.

Performance Guidelines

Class 1 textiles do not have a raised fiber surface but had an average time of flame spread in the test of 3.5 seconds or more, or they have a **raised fiber surface**, including the pile loops of terry, and an average time of **flame spread** in the test of more than 7 seconds or burn with a surface flash (time of flame spread less than 7 seconds), provided the intensity of the flame is insufficient to ignite, char, or melt the base fabric. Class 2 textiles have a raised fiber surface and had an average time of flame spread in the test of 4 to 7 seconds, inclusive, and the base fabric was ignited, charred, or melted. Class 3 textiles have a raised fiber surface and had an average time of flame spread in the test of less than 4 seconds, and the base fabric was ignited, charred, or melted.

Adoption of Method If purchaser and supplier agree to have the flammability of toweling evaluated, they may use this test (see Chapter 28).

Flooring Radiant Panel Test Method

The National Institute of Standards and Technology maintains corridor-like testing facilities. Using these facilities, fire researchers have confirmed that the amount of heat radiating onto a floor covering directly affects the distance flames spread in a Stage 3 fire.[4] Because such spreading may restrict or prevent safe egress, a small-scale test method including **radiant heat** as a condition is increasingly used to measure the flame spread of floor coverings intended for installation in corridors. The equipment and procedures used in this test are described here.

This test method has been designated as ASTM E 648 and NFPA 253. It accurately simulates real-life floor covering installation practices and the conditions characteristic of a Stage 3 interior fire. This test does assess the critical relationship between heat energy radiating from the ceiling and flame spread along a corridor floor covering. Because it has thus overcome the major shortcoming of the tunnel test, which is described below, the radiant panel test method is in-creasingly used by authorities who have jurisdiction over the selection of interior floor finishes for commercial interiors.

The **panel test apparatus** is much smaller than the other tunnel-shaped furnace devices but, like them, it has a corridor-like design (Figure 11.6). An inclined panel radiates heat energy to the surface of the specimen. Because the level of heat radiating onto a corridor carpet would be highest at the point of **spillover**, the panel is positioned at an angle of 30 degrees to the carpet specimen. The amount of heat energy radiating along the carpet during testing ranges from a maximum of 1.2 watts per square

Figure 11.6 Interior view of the radiant panel flammability test apparatus. *Courtesy of Custom Scientific Instruments, Inc.*

| distance | 100 cm | 75 cm | 50 cm | 25 cm | 0 cm |
| watts/cm2 | 0.10 w | 0.18 w | 0.34 w | 0.80 w | 1.2 w |

centimeter immediately below the panel to a minimum of 0.10 watt per square centimeter at the opposite end of the specimen.

Test Specimens and Procedures A carpet specimen, with or without a separate or attached cushion, is cut 42 inches long and 10 inches wide and placed pile side up on the floor of the chamber. A gas flame is impinged on the surface of the specimen immediately below the preheated panel for 10 minutes. Air is allowed to flow through the chamber bottom and exit via a chimney-like opening. The test continues until the floor covering ceases to burn. Three replicate tests are normally required.

Analysis of Results A numerical value, the **critical radiant flux (CRF)**, is determined by converting the distance of flame spread into watts per square centimeter. The CRF indicates the minimum heat energy that is necessary, or critical, to sustain burning of the floor covering and support flame propagation. The profile in Figure 11.6 shows that a carpet that stopped burning at a distance just short of 20 inches (50 centimeters) down its length would have a CRF of 0.34 watt per square centimeter, whereas a carpet that burned the entire distance would have a CRF of 0.10 watt per square centimeter. Higher CRF values thus indicate safer systems. The CRF value reported is the average of the three replicate tests. No analysis is made of smoke generation.

Performance Requirements The levels of fire performance of soft floor coverings mandated by municipal, state, and federal agencies are frequently based on recommendations set forth in the **NFPA 101® Life Safety Code®**. Table 11.1 summarizes recommendations pertaining to interior finishes, such as carpet installed on walls, and to interior floor finishes. The materials used for interior finishes are classified in accordance with the tunnel test, and those used for interior floor finishes are classified in accordance with the radiant panel test. Because all large floor coverings must conform with 16 CFR 1630 (FF 1–70), the NFPA does not recommend additional testing for floor coverings other than those installed in exit ways and corridors in certain occupancies.

Adoption of the Method Several local, state, and federal regulatory agencies have adopted the panel test in lieu of the tunnel test. Some also have established standards pertaining to smoke development. When these agencies have jurisdiction over an installation, smoke development must be measured in a separate test.

Smoke Chamber Test Method

This test method is assigned the designations ASTM E 662 and NFPA 258. It measures the **smoke generation** of solid materials under flaming and nonflaming (smoldering) conditions. The purpose of such testing is to identify materials that would generate large volumes of dense smoke, which would hinder quick and efficient egress by obscuring exit markers and would also hamper breathing.

Test Specimens and Procedures A specimen, 3 inches square and up to 1 inch thick, is suspended vertically in an enclosed test chamber. Three replicate tests are conducted by exposing the specimen surface to an irradiance level of 2.5 watts per square centimeter; the individual tests are conducted by impinging six flamelets (small flames) across the lower edge of the specimen in combination with the radiant heat. A light beam is passed vertically through the smoke chamber. The test is completed when a minimum **light transmittance value** is reached or 20 minutes have elapsed, whichever occurs first.

Analysis of Results A photometric system measures the continuous decrease in light transmission as smoke accumulates. These measurements are converted into specific **optical density values**.

Performance Requirements Required values vary from a low of 50 to a maximum of 450. In some cases, an agency may specify an average of the flaming and nonflaming tests; in other cases, only the results of the flaming tests may be involved.

Adoption of the Method Various city, state, and federal agencies have adopted this test method for materials installed in facilities they oversee. The General Services Administration, for example, has combined CRF and smoke development limits to establish two classifications, and defined a third through 16 CFR 1630 (FF 1–70). The three classes and the various GSA spaces to which they apply are listed below. These classes must not be con-

Table 11.1 NFPA 101®Life Safety Code® Interior Finish and Interior Floor Finish Recommendations

The following is a compilation of the interior finish requirements of the occupancy chapters of the *Code.*

Occupancy	Exits	Access to Exits	Other Spaces
Places of assembly—new*	A	A or B	A, B, or C
Places of assembly—existing*	A	A or B	A, B, or C
Educational—new	A	A or B	A ,B, or C
Educational—existing	A	A or B	A, B, or C
Open plan and flexible plan*	A	A	A or B
			C on movable partitions not over 5 ft. (1.5 m) high
Child day-care centers—new	A	A or B	A or B
	I or II	I or II	
Child day-care centers—existing	A	A or B	A or B
	I or II	I or II	
Group day-care homes	A or B	A or B	A, B, or C
Family child day-care homes	A or B	A or B	A, B, or C
Health care—new	A	A	A
			B in individual room with capacity not more than four persons
	I	I	
Health care—existing	A or B	A or B	A or B
Detention & correctional—new	A	A	A, B, or C
	I	I	
Detention & correctional—existing	A or B	A or B	A, B, or C
	I or II	I or II	
Residential, hotels—new	A	A or B	A, B, or C
	I or II	I or II	
Residential, hotels—existing	A or B	A or B	A, B, or C
	I or II	I or II	
Residential, apartment buildings—new	A	A or B	A, B or C
	I or II	I or II	
Residential, apartment buildings—existing	A or B	A or B	A, B, or C
	I or II	I or II	
Residential, dormitories—new	A	A or B	A, B, or C
	I or II	I or II	
Residential, dormitories—existing	A or B	A or B	A, B, or C
	I or II	I or II	
Residential, 1- and 2-family, lodging or rooming houses		A, B, or C	
Mercantile—new*	A or B	A or B	A or B
Mercantile—existing Class A or B*	A or B	A or B	ceilings—A or B existing on walls—A ,B, or C
Mercantile—existing class C*	A, B, or C	A, B, or C	A, B, or C
Office—new and existing	A or B	A or B	A, B, or C
Industrial	A or B	A, B, or C	A, B, or C
Storage	A, B, or C	A, B, or C	A, B, or C
Unusual structures*	A or B	A, B,or C	A, B, or C

*Exposed portions of structural members complying with the requirements for heavy timber construction may be permitted.

Notes:

Class A Interior Finish—flame spread 0–25, smoke developed 0–450.

Class B Interior Finish—flame spread 26–75, smoke developed 0–450.

Class C Interior Finish—flame spread 76–200, smoke developed 0–450.

Class I Interior Floor Finish—minimum 0.45 watt per sq. cm.

Class II Interior Floor Finish—minimum 0.22 watt per sq. cm.

Automatic Sprinklers—where a complete standard system of automatic sprinklers is installed, interior finish with spread rating not over Class C may be used in any location where Class B is normally specified and with rating of Class B in any location where Class A is normally specified; similarly, Class II interior floor finish may be used in any location where Class I is normally specified and no critical radiant flux rating is required where Class II is normally specified.

Reprinted with permission from NFPA 101–1985, Life Safety Code, Copyright 1985, National Fire Protection Association, Quincy, MA 02269. This reprinted material is not the complete and official position of the NFPA on the referenced subject, which is represented only by the standard in its entirety.

fused with the A, B, and C classes that categorize the results of tunnel testing.

Class A: a CRF of 0.50 watt per square centimeter or greater and a maximum specific optical density not over 450 flaming. Class A carpet is not needed in office buildings.

Class B: a CRF of 0.25 watt per square centimeter or greater and a maximum specific optical density not over 450 flaming. Class B carpet is required in unsprinklered corridors exposed to office space having a controlled equivalent **fuel load** of 6 pounds per square foot or less.

Class C: the face and back of the carpet and separate cushion pass 16 CFR 1630 (FF 1–70). Class C carpet may be installed in all office areas and in corridors protected with automatic sprinklers.[5]

Motor Vehicle Safety Standard No. 302

The **Motor Vehicle Safety Standard No. 302 (MVSS 302)** became effective on September 1, 1972. This standard is designed to reduce deaths and injuries to motor vehicle occupants caused by vehicle fires, especially those originating in the interior of the vehicle from sources such as matches or cigarettes.[6]

Test Specimens and Procedures Whenever possible, each specimen of material to be tested is a rectangle 4 inches wide by 14 inches long. The specimens are conditioned for 24 hours at a temperature of 70 °F and a relative humidity of 50 percent and each is then clamped in a U-shaped frame, exposing an area that measures 2 inches wide by 13 inches long. A secured specimen is mounted horizontally in a test apparatus, such as that shown in Figure 11.7. A flame is impinged on the bottom edge of the open end of the specimen for 15 seconds.

Timing of the flame spread is begun when the flame from the burning specimen reaches a point 1½ inches from the open end of the specimen. The time elapsed for the flame to progress to a point 1½ inches from the clamped end of the specimen is measured.

Analysis of Results The burn rate for the specimen is calculated by the following formula:

$$B = 60 \times D/T$$

Figure 11.7 Horizontal flammability tester.
Courtesy of United States Testing Co., Inc.

where B = burning rate inches/minute, D = length the flame travels in inches, and T = time in seconds to travel D inches.

Performance Requirements A material is considered to pass the test and be acceptable for use if the burn rate does not exceed 4 inches per minute. If a material stops burning before it has burned for 60 seconds from the start of timing and has not burned more than 2 inches from the point where timing was started, it also meets the requirements.

Adoption of the Method The National Highway Traffic Safety Administration (NHTSA) intends that the rate at which an interior material transmits flame across its surface should not be so rapid as to prevent the driver from stopping the vehicle and all occupants from leaving it before injury occurs as a result of fire. The provisions of MVSS 302 apply to seat cushions, seat backs, seat belts, interior roof lining, front and side panels, floor coverings, and other materials used in occupant compartments of passenger cars, multipurpose passenger vehicles, trucks, and buses.

FAA Paragraph 25.853 (b)

The Federal Aviation Administration (FAA) flammability regulation for textile items used in compartments occupied by the crew or passengers in airplanes is designated

Figure 11.8 Vertical flammability tester.
Courtesy of the United States Testing Co., Inc.

as **Paragraph 25.853 (b)**. Other paragraphs in the standard, which was issued on February 15, 1972, concern such items as landing-gear systems, escape routes, exit markers, and nontextile interior finishing materials. The general focus of the standard is to improve the crashworthiness and emergency evacuation equipment of airliners.[7]

Test Specimens and Procedures The specimens are cut 2¾ by 12½ inches, with the most critical flammability conditions corresponding to the long dimension. The specimens are conditioned for 24 hours at a temperature of 70 °F and a relative humidity of 50 percent; they are then clamped in a U-shaped frame. The secured specimen is vertically suspended in a draft-free test chamber, shown in Figure 11.8. A flame is impinged on the lower edge of the specimen for 12 seconds and then removed.

Analysis of Results Three results are determined for each specimen:

1. The **after flame time** is the time the specimen continues to flame after the burner flame is removed.
2. The **afterglow time** is the time the specimen continues to glow after it stops flaming.
3. The **char length** is measured by inserting the correct weight (determined by the weight of the fabric being tested) on one side of the charred area and gently raising the opposite side of the specimen. The length of the tear is measured and recorded.

Performance Requirements Materials used in compartment interiors must be self-extinguishing. The average char length may not exceed 8 inches and the average after flame time may not exceed 15 seconds.

Adoption of the Method The provisions of Paragraph 25.853 (b) apply to upholstery, draperies, floor coverings, seat cushions, padding, decorative and nondecorative coated fabrics, leather, trays, and galley furnishings. They also apply to such items as acoustical insulation.

NFPA 701 Small-scale Test Method

NFPA 701 Standard Methods of Fire Tests for Flame Resistant Textiles and Films may be used to evaluate the effectiveness of polymer additives and finishing compounds in reducing the flammability of textile window coverings. The small-scale test method can be used to evaluate the flame resistance of fabrics that do not exhibit excessive shrinkage or melting when exposed to a flame.

Test Specimens and Procedures. Ten specimens of the covering are cut 2¾ inches by 10 inches. Five have their long dimension in the direction of the filling and five in the direction of the warp. The specimens are then conditioned in an oven at a temperature of 140 to 145 °F for 1 to 1½ hours, or, if they would melt or distort in the oven, they are conditioned at 60 to 80 °F and 25 to 50 percent relative humidity for a minimum of 24 hours. Each specimen is then placed in an open-ended specimen holder and suspended in a vertical flammability tester, similar to the apparatus in Figure 11.8. The flame from a burner is then applied to the lower edge for 12 seconds.

Flame Resistance Requirements In order for the covering material to pass the small-scale test, the specimens must meet the following three requirements:

1. No specimen shall continue flaming for more than two seconds after the test flame is removed from contact with the specimen.
2. The vertical spread of flame and afterglow (smoldering combustion) on the material, as indicated by the length of char or the measurement from the bottom of the sample above which all material is sound and in original condition, shall not exceed the values listed in Table 11.2.
3. At no time during or after the application of the test flame shall portions or residues of textiles or films that break or drip from any test specimen continue to flame after they reach the floor of the tester.[8]

Table 11.2 Permissible Length of Char or Destroyed Material—NFPA 701 Small-scale Test

Weight of Treated Fabric Being Tested (ounces per square yard)	Maximum Average Length of Char or Destroyed Material for Ten Specimens (inches)	Maximum Length of Char or Destroyed Material for any Specimen (inches)
Over 10	3½	4½
Over 6 and not exceeding 10	4½	5½
Not exceeding 6	5½	6½

Reprinted with permission of NFPA 701-1977, Standard Methods of Fire Texts for Flame Resistant Textiles an Films, Copyright © 1977 National Fire Protection Association, Quincy, MA 02269. This reprinted material is not the complete and official position of the NFPA on the referenced subject, which is represented only by the standard in its entirety.

Adoption of the Method NFPA 701 is intended for use with textiles and films treated with flame-retardant agents or composed of flame-resistant manufactured fibers. Fabrics expected to retain their flame-resistant qualities through dry cleaning, laundering, weathering, or other exposures to water are subjected to accelerated exposure procedures prior to testing. Treated awning fabrics, for example, would be exposed to simulated weathering conditions and then tested.

UFAC Fabric Classification Test Method

The **UFAC Voluntary Action Program**, discussed earlier in this chapter, is designed to improve the ability of upholstered furniture to resist catching fire from a burning cigarette, the most common source of furniture ignition. At the outset, upholstery fabrics are divided into two categories of ignition propensity, based on their ability to resist ignition when exposed to a burning cigarette. The procedures used are outlined in the **UFAC Fabric Classification Test Method—1990**.

Test Specimens and Procedures In this test method, vertical and horizontal panels are upholstered using the cover fabrics to be tested and 2-inch thick polyurethane foam filling materials. As schematized in Figure 11.9, the panels are placed in the test assembly, and a lighted nonfilter cigarette is placed in the crevice of the assembly and covered with a piece of cotton bedsheeting fabric. The cigarette is allowed to burn its entire length unless an obvious ignition occurs. Three replicate tests are required for each fabric.

Test Criteria If ignition occurs on any one of the three specimens, the fabric is Class II. If no ignition occurs, the vertical char length is measured from the crevice to the highest part of the destroyed or degraded cover fabric. If the char length is less than 1¾ inches, the fabric is Class I; if the char length is equal to or greater than 1¾ inches, the fabric is Class II. This classification determines which construction methods must be employed with the cover fabric to comply with UFAC construction criteria.

Adoption of the Method In accordance with the UFAC Voluntary Action Program, Class I fabrics may be used directly over conventional polyurethane in the horizontal seating surfaces of upholstered furniture bearing the UFAC hangtag. Class II fabrics require an approved bar-

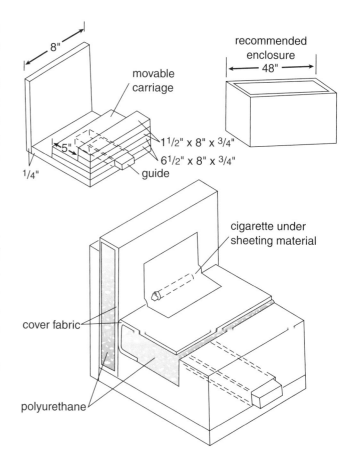

Figure 11.9 The assembly used in the UFAC fabric classification test.
Courtesy of the Upholstered Furniture Action Council Inc.

rier between the cover fabric and conventional polyurethane foam in the horizontal seating surfaces.

UFAC Welt Cord Test Method

This test method is employed to identify welt cording that is suitable for use in seats, backs, and pillows in UFAC-approved constructions. The welt cords must meet the requirement of the **UFAC Welt Cord Test Method—1990**.

Test Specimens and Procedures In this test, welt cording is placed in the center of a piece of UFAC Standard Type II cover fabric that is folded to make an unsewn welt. This cover fabric, a 100 percent bright, regular rayon in basket weave construction, is also used to cover the vertical and horizontal panels. The welt is placed in the crevice formed by the abutment of the horizontal and vertical panels in the test assembly, which is similar to

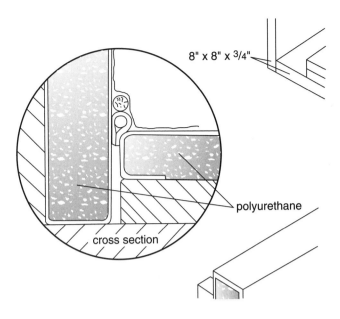

Figure 11.10 Detail of the UFAC welt cord test.
Courtesy of the Upholstered Furniture Action Council Inc.

Figure 11.11 The assembly used in the UFAC decking materials test method.
Courtesy of the Upholstered Furniture Action Council Inc.

that shown in Figure 11.9. As shown in Figure 11.10, a lighted cigarette is placed on the welt and covered with a piece of cotton bedsheeting. Three replicate tests are run.

Test Criteria The welt cording is acceptable if no ignition occurs, or if the maximum height of the vertical char on each of the vertical panels does not equal or exceed 1½ inches. If one specimen has a vertical char equal to or greater than 1½ inches, three additional specimens are tested. If one or more additional specimens have a vertical char equal to or greater than 1½ inches, the test material fails.

Adoption of the Method In accordance with the UFAC Voluntary Action Program, welt cording used with furniture carrying the UFAC hangtag must meet the requirements of this test.

UFAC Decking Materials Test Method

As part of the UFAC Voluntary Action Program, deck padding materials used under loose cushions should resist ignition from smoldering cigarettes. The resistance of polyurethane foam, bonded fiber pads, treated cotton batting, and other padding materials intended for use in decking under loose cushions can be assessed by subjecting them to the **UFAC Decking Materials Test Method—1990.**

Test Specimens and Procedures In preparation for this test, decking material is cut to size and placed on a plywood assembly base, shown schematically in Figure 11.11. The decking material is covered with UFAC Standard Type II fabric and the layered fabrics are held in place by a wooden retainer ring. Three lighted cigarettes are placed on the decking cover fabric and covered with 100 percent cotton sheeting. The cigarettes are allowed to burn their full lengths and the maximum char lengths measured from the cigarettes are recorded.

Test Criteria The decking material is acceptable if it meets the same criteria listed for the Welt Cord Test Method.

Adoption of the Method In accordance with the UFAC Voluntary Action Program, decking material used with furniture carrying the UFAC hangtag must meet the requirements of this test.

UFAC Filling/Padding Component Test Method, Parts A and B

This test method, which has two parts, determines which filling or padding components intended for use in upholstered furniture exhibit sufficient resistance to smoldering cigarette ignition to merit use in items bearing the UFAC hangtag. Part A of this test method is used with slab or garnetted filling/padding components that include, but are not limited to, battings of natural and manmade (manufactured) fibers, foamed or cellular fillings or cushioning materials, and resilient pads of natural or man-made (manufactured) fibers. Part B of this test method is used with fibrous or particulate materials that include, but are not limited to, staple of natural and man-made (manufactured) fibers, shredded foamed or cellular filling materials, and composites of any of these, together with any protective interliners that may be necessary to meet the requirements of the test method.

Test Specimens and Procedures   The filling material to be tested is used in the vertical and horizontal panels of the test assembly shown in Figure 11.9, in place of the polyurethane. It is covered with UFAC Standard Type I mattress ticking, which is composed of 100 percent cotton and has been laundered and tumble-dried once in accordance with prescribed UFAC procedures. One at a time, three ignited cigarettes are placed in the crevice and covered with sheeting fabric.

Test Criteria   In Part A, the filling/padding material is acceptable if no ignition occurs, or if no vertical char equals or exceeds 1½ inches. If one specimen has a vertical char equal to or greater than 1½ inches, three additional specimens are tested. If one or more additional specimens have a vertical char equal to or greater than 1½ inches, the test material fails. Part B has an additional criterion: no specimen can have evolvement of smoke or heat.

Adoption of the Method   In accordance with the UFAC Voluntary Action Program, filling/padding material used with furniture carrying the UFAC hangtag must meet the requirements of this test.

UFAC Interior Fabric Test Method

In order for upholstered furniture items to bear the UFAC hangtag, interior fabrics used in intimate contact with the outer fabrics must exhibit an acceptable level of performance with respect to cigarette ignition resistance. **UFAC Interior Fabric Test Method—1990** can be used to assess this performance.

Test Specimens and Procedures   The assembly used in the required three replicate tests is like that illustrated in Figure 11.9, except that an interior fabric test specimen is placed between the outer covering and the foam filling of the horizontal panels. For this test, the vertical and hori-

zontal panels are covered with UFAC Standard Type I mattress ticking. The three lighted cigarettes are again placed one at a time in the crevice and covered.

Test Criteria.   The test criteria for this test are identical to those for the Welt Cord test.

Adoption of the Method   In accordance with the UFAC Voluntary Action Program, interior fabrics used with furniture carrying the UFAC hangtag must meet the requirements of this test.

UFAC Barrier Test Method

This test method is intended to define the minimum performance level for barrier materials to be placed between Class II fabrics and conventional polyurethane foam in horizontal seating surfaces. This will minimize the likelihood of ignition of the foam in the event a Class II fabric is generating considerable heat as it undergoes decomposition and combustion.

Test Specimens and Procedures   Three tests are run using the assembly illustrated in Figure 11.12. UFAC Standard Type II cover fabric is used as the covering. The barrier material to be tested is placed between the

Figure 11.12 The assembly used in the UFAC barrier test. *Courtesy of the Upholstered Furniture Action Council.*

cover fabric and the polyurethane substrate in both vertical and horizontal panels. A lighted cigarette is placed in the crevice and covered with a piece of sheeting material.

Test Criteria The test criteria for this test are identical to those for the Welt Cord Test Method.

Adoption of the Method In accordance with the UFAC Voluntary Action Program, barrier materials used with furniture covered with Class II fabric and filled with polyurethane foam must meet the requirements of this test if the item is to bear the UFAC hangtag.

The importance of a suitable barrier is underscored by the full-scale fire tests shown in Figures 11.13 and 11.14. When conventional items, including a chair with no flame-resistant barrier, were used, the fire quickly spread, with flashover occurring within two and a half minutes after ignition.

For the test pictured in Figure 11.14, the model room was furnished with bedding, window treatments, and wall-coverings of glass fiber fabrics, and the chair had a flame-resistant barrier of specially coated glass fiber yarns. In this case, the nylon upholstery burned away, the protective barrier charred but did not burn, and the fire was contained in Stage 1.

A closeup photograph of the chairs used in the above tests is shown in Figure 11.15. It is evident that the presence of the protective barrier in the chair on the right prevented ignition of the foam substrate. The charred area is substantial, but it should be noted that the ignition source was a paper-filled grocery bag, not an ignited cigarette.

Figure 11.13 Full-scale fire test in mock hotel room furnished with conventional items, including a chair having no flame-resistant barrier.
Courtesy of Owens-Corning Fiberglas Corporation.

Figure 11.14 Full-scale fire test in a mock hotel room furnished with flame-resistant items, including a chair with a flame-resistant barrier between the outer covering and the foam filling.
Courtesy of Owens-Corning Fiberglas Corporation.

UFAC Standard Test Methods for Decorative Trims, Edging, and Brush Fringes In a continuing effort to make upholstered furniture *safer* when exposed to an ignition source, members of the UFAC developed the UFAC Standard Test Methods for Decorative Trims, Edging, and Brush Fringes—1993.

Test Specimens and Procedures The test apparatus used in this test is similar to that used in the Welt Cord Test Method shown in Figure 11.10. Again, Type II cover fabric, polyurethane foam, and cotton sheeting are used. A lighted cigarette is placed on top of the trim, edging, or brush fringe being tested and covered with sheeting.

Test Criteria If all test specimens have no ignition, or if the vertical char of each is less than 1½ inches upward from the crevice, the test material passes. If one test specimen has a vertical char equal to or greater than 1½ inches, three additional specimens are tested. If all three additional specimens have a vertical char of less than 1½ inches, the test material passes. If one additional specimen has a vertical char equal to or greater than 1½ inches, the material fails. If two or more original test specimens have a vertical char of ½ inches or more, the material fails.

Adoption of the Method Trims meeting the above criteria will be classified as UFAC Type I decorative trim, edging, or brush fringe; providing the remainder of the

Figure 11.15 Close-up view of upholstered chairs used in full-scale tests. The chair on the right had a flame-resistant fabric of specially coated glass fiber installed as a protective barrier between the outer covering and the foam filling. *Courtesy of Owens-Corning Fiberglas Corporation.*

upholstered furniture meets UFAC requirements, the UFAC hangtag may be used when Type I trim is present.

In the event the trim fails to conform to the above criteria, it should be retested, using a polyester fiber barrier and UFAC Standard Type II covering. If the trim then meets the above requirements, it is labeled UFAC Type II trimming. The furniture would then be eligible to bear the UFAC hangtag, as long as a garnetted polyester fiber barrier is used.

If the decorative trim, edging, or brush fringe fails with both the Type II fabric alone and the Type II fabric

and polyester fiber barrier, the trimming is classified as Type III. UFAC hangtags are not permitted with upholstered furniture using Type III decorative trim, edging, or brush fringe.

Large-scale Test Methods

Large-scale test methods are also laboratory procedures, but they use larger test specimens than do small-scale tests. A large-scale test method is used with textile window coverings, soft floor coverings, and mattresses.

NFPA 701 Large-scale Test Method

The **NFPA 701 large-scale test** may be selected for use with covering materials that show excessive melting or shrinkage when tested by the small-scale test. This method is also useful for evaluating the fire behavior of coverings hung in folds, as is typical in window treatments.

Test Specimens and Procedures   Specimens of the covering material may be tested in single, flat sheets or they may be hung with folds. For flat testing, ten specimens, 5 inches by 7 feet, are cut. For testing with folds, four lengths of the covering, each cut 25 inches by 7 feet, are folded longitudinally to form four folds, each approximately 5 inches wide. In either case, half the specimens have their long dimension in the direction of the warp and half have their long dimension in the direction of the filling. The specimens are conditioned as described for the small-scale test.

The specimens, flat or folded, are suspended in the tester, which is a sheet-iron stack 12 inches square and 7 feet high. The lower edge of the specimen is 4 inches above the burner tip and an 11-inch flame is held under the specimen for 2 minutes.

Flame Resistance Requirements   In order for the covering material to pass the large-scale test, the specimens must meet the following four requirements:

1. No specimen shall continue flaming for more than two seconds after the test flame is removed from contact with the specimen.
2. The vertical spread of burning on the material in single sheets shall not exceed 10 inches above the tip of the test flame. This vertical spread shall be measured as the distance from the tip of the test flame to a horizontal line above which all material is sound and in original condition, except for possible smoke deposits.
3. The vertical spread of burning on the folded specimens shall not exceed 35 inches above the tip of the test flame, but the afterglow may spread in the folds.
4. At no time during or after the application of the test flame shall portions or residues of textiles or films that break or drip from any test specimen

continue to flame after they reach the floor of the tester.[9]

In the event of fire, fabrics meeting the flame resistance requirements included in the small- or large-scale test methods would not be likely to propagate the flames to the floor, wall, and ceiling. This reduces the threat of a Stage 1 fire growing into a Stage 2 fire.

Adoption of the Method   As with the NFPA 701 small-scale test method, the large-scale test method may be used to measure the ignition propensity of fabrics to be installed indoors or outdoors.

Tunnel Test Method

This test method, also known as the **Steiner Tunnel Test Method**, measures the surface burning characteristics of building materials. It has been designated as ASTM E 01, NFPA 255, and UL 723. The testing apparatus (Figure 11.16) is structured to simulate a corridor, and the testing procedures and results are used to assess flame spread and smoke generation. The method is thus intended to evaluate the potential hazard of a textile floor covering in a Stage 3 fire.

Figure 11.16 Tunnel-like flammability test apparatus. *Courtesy of Solutia Inc., Fibers Division.*

Figure 11.17 Gas jets in operation during tunnel testing. *Courtesy of Solutia Inc., Fibers Division.*

Test Specimens and Procedures A floor covering specimen, 25 feet by 1 foot 8 inches, is mounted pile surface down on the ceiling of the tunnel chamber. The sample is then subjected to gas jet flames and heat for 10 minutes (Figure 11.17). Temperatures range from 1,600 to 1,800 °F. Testing is complete when 10 minutes have elapsed or the specimen has burned completely, whichever occurs first.

Analysis of Results Time and flame spread distance values are plotted graphically and compared with those recorded for asbestos-cement board (assigned a flame spread rating of 0) and select-grade red oak flooring (assigned a flame spread rating of 100) to arrive at a flame spread classification. Class A includes flame spread ratings from 0 to 25, Class B from 26 to 75, and Class C from 76 to 200. Smoke density values are determined separately.

Performance Requirements Flammability requirements for selected interior finishes, such as carpet used as wall covering, are classified according to the tunnel test. The NFPA 101® Life Safety Code® includes recommenda-

tions that may be mandated by an agency having jurisdiction over an occupancy and the materials to be installed within the facility (see Table 11.1).

Adoption of the Method In recent years, the use of the tunnel test as a method for evaluating the potential fire hazard of textile structures to be installed as floor coverings has been diminishing. Although the long, tunnel-shaped testing apparatus does indeed resemble a corridor, the method has two major shortcomings when correlated to end use. First, because the specimen is mounted on the ceiling, the test does not realistically portray real-life installations. Second, the method fails to incorporate the critical variable of the heat energy that will be radiating into a corridor in the event an interior fire progresses from Stage 2 to Stage 3. Nonetheless, testing by this method continues to be required for some installations, and is often recommended or required for carpet to be used as an interior finish on walls and ceilings (see Table 11.1).

Mattress and Mattress Pad Test Method

The Standard for the Flammability of Mattresses, **16 CFR (FF 4–72)**, was established to protect the public against unreasonable risk of mattress fires. The most common mode of bedding ignition, a burning cigarette, is used as the source of ignition in the test.

Test Specimens and Procedures In testing, the bare sleeping surface of mattresses, including smooth, tape edge, and quilted or tufted locations, is exposed to as least nine ignited cigarettes that are 85 millimeters long and have no filter tips. These locations are also tested by placing nine additional burning cigarettes between two bed sheets that cover the mattress (Figure 11.18). The muslin or percale sheets used must be 100 percent cotton, have no durable press resins or flame-retardant agents, and be laundered one time prior to testing.

Mattress pads are tested in the same manner before they are laundered or dry cleaned and again after they have been cleaned in accordance with prescribed procedures. Pads treated with a flame-retardant agent must be labeled with precautionary care instructions to help prevent the use of agents or procedures that could impair the effectiveness of the finishing compound.

a) mattress preparation

Bare

Two Sheets

Tape Edge

b) cigarette location

Figure 11.18 Mattress preparation and cigarette locations used in 16 CFR 1632 (FF 4–72).
Federal Register, *Vol. 38, No. 110, June 8, 1973, 15100.*

Analysis of Results   The char length of each test location is measured and reported in inches.

Performance Requirements   Individual cigarette test locations pass the test if the char length of the mattress or mattress pad surface is not more than 2 inches in any direction from the nearest point of the cigarette. All eighteen cigarette locations must pass the test in order for the mattress or pad to be marketed.

Adoption of the Method   The provisions of 16 CFR 1632 apply to domestic and imported mattresses. Included in the definition of mattresses are mattress pads; adult, youth, crib, and portable crib mattresses; bunk bed mattresses; corner group and daybed mattresses; rollaway and convertible sofa bed mattresses; high risers; trundle bed mattresses; and **futons**—flexible mattresses filled with cotton batting. Items specifically excluded from 16 CFR 1632 are sleeping bags, pillows, mattress foundations such as box springs, water bed and air mattresses, and other items such as chaise lounges and sofa beds, which are distinct from convertible sofa beds. A **convertible sofa bed** is an upholstered sofa with a mattress concealed under the cushions; a **sofa bed** is an upholstered sofa with a hinged back that swings down flat with the seating cushions to form the sleeping surface.

Full-scale Test Methods

Full-scale testing facilities may be constructed to replicate a room or a corridor. Room-size facilities make possible observation of the progressive growth of an interior fire, and they are particularly useful in assessing the involvement of each of several items. Corridor-like facilities can be used to determine the effects various conditions have on a Stage 3 fire; results obtained with them underscore the importance of preserving a safe means of egress.

In the Life Safety Laboratory maintained by Owens-Corning Fiberglas Corporation, a replica of a typical hotel room has been constructed. For the test shown in Figure 11.19, the room was furnished with conventional, as opposed to flame resistant, items. Flashover occurred within two and a half minutes after the newspaper-filled brown paper bag on the chair was ignited. For the test

Figure 11.19 Full-scale fire test showing the growth of an interior fire from Stage 1 to Stage 2. The room was furnished with flammable items.

Courtesy of Owens-Corning Fiberglas Corporation.

Figure 11.20 Full-scale test showing minimal flame propagation in a room furnished with some flame-resistant items. *Courtesy of Owens-Corning Fiberglas Corporation.*

shown in Figure 11.20, beddings composed of specially coated Fiberglas® and flame-resistant carpet were used. Here, the fire did not spread beyond the immediate ignition site; the growth of the fire from Stage 1 to Stage 2 was prevented.

These investigations show that occupants of a room furnished with some flame-resistant items would have more time for safe egress. Both tests make apparent the value of early warning systems and automatic sprinklers.

Summary

In an effort to reduce the threat to life and property posed by flammable fabrics, the U.S. Congress passed the Flammable Fabrics Act and directed the Consumer Product Safety Commission to monitor the involvement of textile products in burn accidents. As a result, flammability performance standards have been established for carpet, rugs, and mattresses, and a standard has been proposed for upholstered furniture. The test methods adopted in these standards simulate the conditions of real-life situations, so that researchers and producers can make reliable predictions of in-use performance.

Although a flammability standard was considered for upholstered furniture in the 1970s, a mandatory standard has not followed. Instead, the CPSC monitors the fire-related hazards of upholstered furniture and the work of the UFAC. The UFAC developed a program, including several test methods reviewed in this chapter, to improve the ability of upholstered furniture to resist ignition from a burning cigarette. A hangtag identifies items that comply with the UFAC program. Products so labeled are safer, but they are not fireproof, and consumers must exercise care in using smoking materials.

Several practices can widen the margin of fire safety beyond that provided by law. Residential and commercial consumers can select noncombustible fibers and fibers with inherent or engineered flame resistance. Smoke detectors can be installed to alert residents before a small fire spreads. When a fire extinguisher is readily available, the fire can then be extinguished, further property damage prevented, and personal injury avoided. Automatic sprinkling systems can be in place to halt the spreading of an uncontained fire, thus lessening the generation of smoke and lethal concentrations of toxic gases and preserving the means of egress to a safe area. Corridors leading to exits must be kept clear and the exits themselves clearly illuminated. Finally, of course, most textiles require an external source of heat for ignition. To reduce the frequency of ignition, consumers must handle the most common source of ignition, burning cigarettes, and other smoking materials carefully.

Key Terms

after flame time

afterglow time

char length

CFR

combustion

Consumer Product Safety Commission (CPSC)

convertible sofa bed

critical radiant flux (CRF)

egress

Federal Trade Commission (FTC)

flameless combustion

flame propagation

flame spread

flaming combustion

Flammable Fabrics Act (FFA)

flashover

fuel load

full-scale testing

futons

glowing

kindling or ignition temperature

large-scale test methods

light transmittance value

methenamine tablet

molten polymer compounds

Motor Vehicle Safety Standard No. 302 (MVSS 302)

National Electronic Injury Surveillance System (NEISS)

National Institute of Standards and Technology (NIST)

NFPA 101® Life Safety Code®

NFPA 701

NFPA 701 large-scale test
optical density values
panel test apparatus
paragraph 25.853 (b)
pyrolysis
radiant heat
raised fiber surface
safety standard
scope of 16 CFR 1630
scope of 16 CFR 1631
self-extinguishing
small-scale test methods
smoke density
smoke generation
smoldering
sofa bed

spillover
spontaneous combustion
Stage 1 fire
Stage 2 fire
Stage 3 fire
Standard 16 CFR (FF 4-72)
Steiner Tunnel Test Method
toxicants
toxic gases
UFAC Decking Materials Test Method—1990
UFAC Fabric Classification Test Method—1990
UFAC Interior Fabric Test Method—1990
UFAC Voluntary Action Program
UFAC Welt Cord Test Method—1990
U.S. Department of Commerce (DOC)

Review Questions

1. Discuss the responsibilities of the CPSC in fire safety work.

2. What prompts the CPSC to propose a new flammability standard?

3. Has the 1967 amendment to the FFA had far-reaching effects? Cite some of the developments in fire safety that followed this amendment.

4. Why is a one-year grace period allowed before a new flammability standard goes into effect?

5. Discuss the UFAC Voluntary Action Program. What is the purpose of fabric classification? How are construction methods incorporated into the program?

6. When can upholstered furniture bear the UFAC hangtag?

7. Explain the cyclic combustion process.

8. Distinguish between combustion, spontaneous combustion, glowing, and smoldering.

9. Why do toxic gases pose the greatest threat to life in interior fires?

10. Discuss the influence of smoke density on egress.

11. In the event of fire, why is it critical to preserve the means for quick and efficient egress?

12. Differentiate among a Stage 1, a Stage 2, and a Stage 3 fire. Then, discuss the value of early warning systems and automatic sprinklers in each stage.

13. What is the unique value of small-scale test methods, large-scale test methods, and full-scale test methods to fire researchers?

14. How does the methenamine tablet test simulate real-life situations?

15. At which stage of an interior fire is radiant heat an important variable?

16. Cite two significant reasons the flooring radiant panel test method is replacing the tunnel test method in the evaluation of the flammability hazards of soft floor coverings.

17. Which carpet would be safer in the event of fire, one having a CRF of 0.14 watt per square centimeter or one having a CRF of 0.30 watt per square centimeter?

18. Are the standards set forth in the NFPA 101® Life Safety Code® recommended or mandatory?

19. What is the goal of the NHTSA with respect to rate of flame spread and automobile occupant safety?

20. When would the large-scale test method, rather than the small-scale test method, be used for evaluating the flame resistance of textiles and films?

21. Why are full-scale fire testing facilities especially useful in studying the phenomenon of flashover?

Notes

1. Federal Emergency Management Agency, "An Ounce of Prevention," U.S. Fire Administration, Washington, D.C., 3.

2. Michael J. Koroshys, "Flammability of Textiles," *American Dyestuff Reporter*, Vol. 58, No. 3, March 24, 1969, 20.

3. Federal Emergency Management Agency, "An Ounce of Prevention," U.S. Fire Administration, Washington, D.C., 4.

4. Francis E. W. Fung, Miles R. Suchmoel, and Philip L. Oglesby, *NBS Corridor Fire Tests: Energy and Radiation Models*, *NBS TN-794*, National Bureau of Standards, Washington, D.C., October 1973.

5. *Building Firesafety Criteria*, PBS P 5290.0, General Services Administration, Washington, D.C., October 23, 1980.

6. The full text of MVSS 302, is available from the National Highway Traffic Safety Administration, 400 Seventh St., SW, Washington, DC 20590.

7. The full text of FAA Paragraph 28.853(b) is available from the Federal Aviation Administration, 800 Independence Ave., SW, Washington DC 20591.

8. Reprinted with permission of NFPA 701-1977, Standard methods of fire Tests for Flame Resistant Textiles and films, Copyright© 1977, National Fire Protection Association, Quincy, MA 02269. This reprinted material is not the complete and official position of the NFPA on the referenced subject, which is represented only by the standard in its entirety.

9. Ibid.

UNIT TWO

Upholstered Furniture Coverings and Fillings

Unit Two focuses on upholstery coverings and fillings for commercial and residential furniture products. Chapter 12 discusses methods of applying outercovering to furniture framework and their various features. It also reviews the different materials used to fill furniture, along with their performance characteristics.

In Chapter 13, statistical profiles detail fiber and yarn usage in upholstery fabrics, including those channeled to transportation applications, and several textile upholstery fabrics are described. The production of nontextile upholstery fabrics, including genuine leather, simulated leather and suede, and vinyl, is also reviewed.

Chapter 14 presents several performance standards developed by members of the upholstered furniture industry. These standards, which are voluntary, recommend test methods and levels of performance and are tended to serve as guidelines for evaluating the end-use serviceability of finished upholstery fabrics. Most of the standards apply to physical attributes, but one is directed to cleanability and can help the consumer determine what are appropriate cleaning agents. These agents and the proper procedures to follow in maintaining upholstery fabrics also are discussed in this chapter.

12

Construction Features of Upholstered Furniture

Exterior Construction Features
  Deck Fabrics and Bottom Fabrics
  Patterned Fabric Applications
  Cushion and Pillow Treatments
  Skirt Options
  Slipcovers
  Arm Covers and Head Rests
  Surface Embellishments

Interior Textile Components

Fillings Used in Upholstered Furniture
  Fibrous Battings
  Foam Cushions
  Loose Particulate Materials
  Service-related Properties
  Labeling Upholstery Fillings

Residential and commercial consumers have an almost unlimited variety of upholstered furniture styles from which to choose. All these forms and decorative stylings have some components in common. By definition, an upholstered item has an outercovering that surrounds and conceals a filling or stuffing, and such other structural components as springs, fabric linings, and framework. The various construction techniques for applying outercoverings expand the range of styling features available to consumers.

Filling materials in upholstered furniture serve structural as well as functional purposes. Frequently, the in-use behavior of the filling material is more important than that of other components, including the outercovering.

Exterior Construction Features

In addition to the upholstery fabric used to cover the cushions, backs, arms, and sides of furniture items, other fabrics may be used to cover the deck and bottom areas. Bottom fabrics are rarely seen, but deck fabrics may be exposed if the furniture has loose pillows. Other construction features, including the styling of the skirt and any surface embellishments, also affect the appearance of an upholstered item.

Deck Fabrics and Bottom Fabrics

The **deck** of an upholstered item comprises the platform, springs, and filling structures that support the seat cushions. To conceal these units and to prevent dust and objects from falling into the deck, a fabric covers the uppermost filling layer. When the fabric is the same as the exposed outercovering, it is referred to as a **self-deck treatment**; it looks like the outercovering in the event cushions are separated from the furniture in use. If the outercovering is heavy or highly textured, a smoother, lighter weight, less expensive deck fabric may be used; the color of this fabric coordinates with that of the outercovering. When outercoverings have low porosity, as is true for simulated leather fabrics, a porous deck fabric must be used to permit air movement when the seat cushions are compressed.

Bottom fabrics are used underneath the deck to conceal the interior components and give a finished look to the upholstered item if the bottom should come into view. The fabric must be dimensionally stable to prevent sagging. Today, spunbonded polypropylene olefin fabrics are frequently used for bottom fabrics. These lightweight fabrics resist moisture and mildew, do not ravel, and are dimensionally stable. The spunbonded bottom fabric pictured in Figure 12.1 is available in weights ranging from 1.0 to 2.0 ounces per square yard.

Figure 12.1 Accord® spunbonded polypropylene olefin for bottom fabric applications.
Courtesy of Kimberly-Clark Corporation.

a) railroad

b) up-the-bolt

Figure 12.2 Illustrations of terms describing the directional cutting and placement of patterned upholstery fabric. *Courtesy of Pennsylvania House.*

Patterned Fabric Applications

Unless the fabric has an overall design of no particular orientation (as in Figure 12.5), precise fabric cutting and motif positioning are required for upholstery fabrics with woven-in or printed patterns. Attention must first be given to the directional features of the motifs and repeats. These visual characteristics determine whether a fabric should be cut **up-the-bolt** or **to railroad**; the meanings of these terms are schematically illustrated in Figure 12.2. The importance of pattern direction to subsequent placement can be appreciated by examining the floral motifs in the fabric covering the sofa in Figure 12.3. Assuming the linear path of the flowers paralleled the selvages, the flowers would have appeared to grow sideways if the fabric had been cut to railroad.

When a fabric has a main motif, the motif must be centered on the back pillows, as well as on the seat cushions. For maximum aesthetic appeal, distinct patterns can also be cut and applied in a process known as **completion**. A completed pattern flows uninterrupted down the back pillows, the seat cushions, the seat boxing, the seat

Figure 12.3 Sofa with its main motif centered on back pillow and seat cushion. Except for the skirt treatment, the pattern is completed. *Courtesy of Pennsylvania House.*

front, and the skirt. With the exception of the skirt, the completion method was used to place the patterned fabric on the sofa in Figure 12.3; the motifs in the fabric were also centered.

Cushion and Pillow Treatments

Three constructions of upholstery cushions and pillows are illustrated in Figure 12.4. The use of a plain seam to join the fabric pieces is called a **knife-edge treatment**. Inserting a fabric-covered cord into the seam is known as **welting**. The cords may be covered with the outercovering fabric (see Figures 12.3 and 12.5), or, for greater emphasis, with a contrasting fabric. When welts are planned for items covered with highly textured fabrics, a smooth fabric may be used to cover the cords and increase their abrasion resistance. Wrapping a strip of fabric around the front and sides of cushions is known as **boxing**. This treatment (shown in Figure 12.4c) is generally combined with a zipper closure that enables manufacturers to insert the filling materials easily.

Upholstered cushions and pillows are treated two different ways in the construction of end products. In **tight-**

Figure 12.4 Construction treatments for upholstered furniture cushions and pillows.

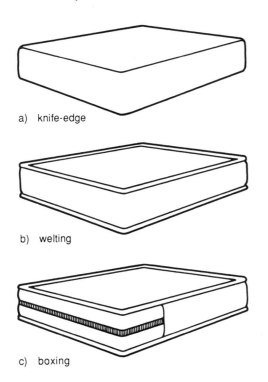

a) knife-edge

b) welting

c) boxing

pillow construction styles, the pillows are securely attached to the framework and cannot be shifted or removed. In **loose-pillow styles** (Figure 12.5), the pillows are not secured. Unless a different fabric has been used to cover the backs of the pillows, they can be frequently reversed to equalize wear patterns and soiling levels.

Skirt Options

Several options are available for the treatment of upholstered furniture skirts. Typical construction styles are illustrated in Figure 12.6. The skirt may be flat with single or double kick pleats; it may be shirred (also see Figures 12.3 and 12.5); it may have box pleats; or it may be shirred only at the corners in a princess style. Buttons may be added as decorative accents (see the skirt on the sofa in Figure 12.8).

When a skirt is designed to hang straight and flat, a firm, bonded-web interfacing is generally employed to control the draping quality and to provide support. Skirts may be lined with a spunbonded fabric in order to reduce bulk and weight.

Slipcovers

Many consumers use **slipcovers** to protect the attached covering from excessive soil accumulation, as well as to change the appearance of the furniture from one season to another (Figure 12.7). Slipcovers are cut, seamed, and fitted over furniture. Some manufacturers offer upholstered furniture **in-the-muslin:** the items are covered in muslin, an undyed, plain-woven fabric composed of carded cotton yarns. Consumers can then order one or more sets of decorative slipcovers.

Arm Covers and Head Rests

Arm covers, also called **arm caps** and **armettes**, protect the arms of upholstered furniture from excessive abrasion and soiling. Frequently, these covers are offered optionally. **Head rests** or **head covers**, sometimes known as **antimacassars**, protect the upholstery fabric from neck and hair oils and hair coloring. They may be cut from the outercoverings, be cut from a highly decorative lace or be richly embroidered, or as is the case in commercial airliners, buses, and trains, they may be cut from disposable fabric.

Figure 12.5 Lounge chair with loose-pillow construction.
Courtesy of Pennsylvania House.

Figure 12.6 Optional skirt treatments.
Courtesy of Pennsylvania House.

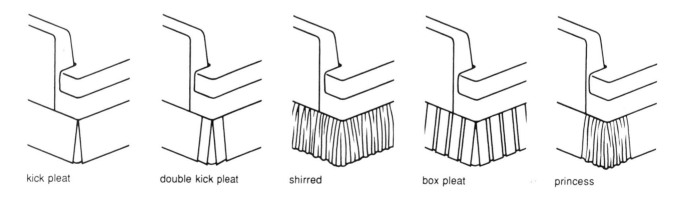

kick pleat   double kick pleat   shirred   box pleat   princess

Figure 12.7 Slipcovers used to protect the permanent covering and to change the seasonal appearance of the furniture. *Courtesy of The Bernhardt Agency.*

Surface Embellishments

The furniture manufacturer can use various treatments to embellish the surface of upholstery fabrics and finished products. These treatments are distinct from others, such as coloring and finishing, which also enrich the surface appearance but are performed on fabric prior to end-product construction.

Quilting is generally offered as an optional fabric treatment. The stitching may be done in parallel rows or on curved and angled lines to create slightly raised design motifs: on pattern fabrics, it may follow the outline of the design motifs (see Figure 9.12d, p. 139). When the surface is **tufted**, buttons secure the outercovering and filling tightly in a deeply indented three-dimensional pattern (Figure 12.8). Extensive buttoning should not be used on delicate fabrics with low levels of tear strength. **Nailhead trimming** may be used to secure heavier coverings, such as genuine leather, to framework (Figure 12.9). The nails are generally aligned to emphasize the lines of the upholstered item.

To select a product that will retain its original appearance and the stability of its exterior construction features longer, residential and commercial consumers should consider its interior components and construction features. Some of these interior components are often textiles.

Interior Textile Components

Within an upholstered furniture item, several textile components, including fabric linings, filling structures, and cords, frequently appear. **Textile cords** are often used to hand tie or hand knot the several spring units together; the network of cords helps to stabilize the configuration of each spring and to minimize lateral shifting. A fabric lining, such as burlap or spunbonded olefin, is generally laid over the springs to prevent them from penetrating the filling materials. Two layers of filling, one for softness and one for firm support, may be used over the fabric linings. In most cases, the inside vertical walls and the extended portions of the frame will be padded with one or more layers of filling.

The framing material used in upholstered furniture may be hardwood, wood veneer, metal, or molded poly-

Figure 12.8 Sofa embellished with button tufting. *Courtesy of Pennsylvania House.*

Figure 12.9 Nailhead trimming used secure genuine leather to the chair framework. *Courtesy of The Bernhardt Agency.*

mer. Although a discussion of these materials is out of place here, consumers are encouraged to ascertain the soundness and stability of the frame prior to purchase. Special attention should be given to the quality and sturdiness of the framing joints. Consumers should also investigate the composition and structural features of the filling materials used. Often, consumers and interior designers can specify the use of a particular filling material.

Fillings Used in Upholstered Furniture

Three types of filling structures—fibrous battings, foam cushions, and loose particulate materials—are available to stuff or cushion upholstered furniture components and pillows. These structures differ in compressibility, loftiness, resiliency, and flammability. The Federal Trade Commission advises manufacturers to disclose the presence of such filling materials as goose down and feathers and requires disclosure of the presence of previously used filling materials.

Fibrous Battings

Battings are three-dimensional textile structures formed directly from fibers, bypassing the yarn stage. Natural or manufactured fibers may be employed.

Cotton Felt

Although batting structures composed of cotton fibers may be referred to as **cotton felt**, the term is descriptive of the felt-like appearance, not of the processing used. Layering thin webs of cotton fibers to form a batt of the desired thickness produces such structures. The natural convolutions of cotton fibers (Figure 3.2b, p. 28) help them to entwine and adhere to another, but for added stability the batt may be impregnated with an adhesive or resin.

The use of cotton, as well as kapok and jute, for upholstery fillings has diminished in recent years. These cellulosic fibers have comparatively low resiliency. Supply and delivery problems also hinder the selection of kapok and jute. Moreover, the results of flammability research have encouraged many manufacturers to restrict voluntarily the use of cotton batting that has not been treated to be flame resistant.

Curled Hair Batting

The use of curled **horsehair**, **cattlehair**, and **hoghair** for upholstered furniture filling has been declining. These three-dimensional hair forms can easily be entwined into **resilient battings**, but they are subject to such moisture- and microbe-related problems as odor and mildew, and, for some people, they can act as allergens. These natural materials, which are byproducts of the leather industry, have generally been replaced by manufactured fiber structures.

Bonded Polyester Batting

Most manufactured fiber batting is composed of staple-length polyester fibers. These fibers are produced by breaking or cutting the crimped filaments in a tow bundle (see Figure 5.3, p. 68).

When used in upholstered furniture, batting must not only provide comfort and superior resiliency, but also firm support, a feature not required of fillings for quilts and comforters. To engineer these features, manufacturers frequently combine two distinctly different layers of polyester fibers into one batt. The upper layer contains fine, low denier fibers that are easily flexed and soft, making for comfort; the lower layer contains coarser, stiffer fibers that provide firm support as they resist flexing and compression. For increased stability and greater re-siliency, resin is sprayed throughout such dual denier batts, bonding the fibers into position.

Foam Cushions

Three-dimensional foam structures, frequently referred to as **slab cushions**, often fill upholstered furniture items to preserve their shape and form. Latex and urethane compounds are used to manufacture these cushions.

Latex Foam Structures

Latex foam may be produced from natural rubber or from synthesized rubber compounds. The compound is foamed, creating tiny, air-filled cells, and formed into a slab of the desired thickness. By controlling the quantity and size of the cells, manufacturers can engineer the **density** of the structure, which in turn determines the degree of firmness or the compression resistance offered by the cushion. Frequently, the latex is **vulcanized** or heated with sulfur to introduce strong chemical cross links that stabilize the shape and add strength. Latex foam cushions are resilient, but they may exhibit gradual aging and deterioration.

Polyurethane Foam Structures

Polyurethane foam is increasingly replacing latex foam in furniture applications. Unlike latex, polyurethane compounds do not exhibit aging, and they are resistant to both microbes and moisture.

During manufacturing, the urethane compound is expanded by heating, increasing the apparent volume and decreasing the density. Structures are produced with lower densities when softness and comfort are the performance features of principal importance, and with higher densities when greater support and resistance to crushing and compression are sought.

As illustrated in Figure 12.10, a latex or polyurethane foam structure may be carefully cut and used alone to fill and impart form to a furniture cushion, or it may form a core unit surrounded by polyester batting. In the latter case, support is provided principally by the foam structure and softness largely by the batting; both components provide resiliency and help the outercovering to maintain its dimensional stability and smoothness.

a) foam cushion filling

b) foam cushion core
surrounded by polyester
batting

Figure 12.10 Foam cushion fillings.
Courtesy of Simmons Company.

Loose Particulate Materials

Masses of loose particles are used to fill some upholstered furniture structures. Today, these particles include shredded or flaked latex or urethane foam, feathers, down, and fiberfill. The use of such materials as straw, sawdust, and newspapers has been discontinued because of cleaning and flammability problems. **Shredded foam particles** are less expensive than slab foam cushions, but they may clump with use. **Down**, the soft undercoat feathers retrieved from waterfowl, is soft, easily compressed, and lightweight, but the labor costs incurred in retrieving the necessary volume of the tiny feathers make the material comparatively expensive. **Feathers** from chickens, turkeys, ducks, and geese are soft and lofty filling materials, but many people are allergic to them. **Fiberfill**, usually composed of crimped polyester fibers, is lofty and resilient. Polyester offers a cost advantage over down, and unlike down and feathers, manufactured fibers are not allergens.

Loose filling materials are frequently enclosed in an inner fabric structure before being inserted into the sewn outercoverings. Today, the inner fabric is often a spunbonded polypropylene olefin fabric.

Service-related Properties

Along with their fire-related behavior, the physical properties exhibited by filling materials greatly influence the serviceability of upholstered furniture items. If, for example, the filling material failed to recover after compression, the cushion would show a deep indentation that would destroy the original design of the item and the smooth appearance of the outercovering.

Compressibility

The ease with which a textile structure can be crushed or reduced in thickness is the measure of its **compressibility**. All filling structures must be somewhat compressible for comfort. An "overstuffed" chair is specifically designed to be easily compressed under the weight of the seated person; unless they are nursing back problems, people generally prefer these chairs over straight-backed, noncompressible wooden ones.

The degree of resistance a filling structure offers to being crushed or compressed can be measured in the laboratory. The test apparatus used in this evaluation is shown in Figure 25.5 (p. 383). Structures that require a heavier load, in pounds per square inch, to produce a given deflection or reduction in thickness provide firmer support than those that reach this deflection with a lighter load.

Loftiness

Loftiness is bulk without heaviness. This feature is especially desirable for fillings used in furniture cushions and pillows. If identical cushion or pillow forms are filled, one with down, and one with sawdust, they would have equal thickness and volume. The sawdust-filled pillow, however, would be significantly heavier, thus failing the loftiness test of bulkiness without undue weight. Down and feather filling materials are prized for their inherent loftiness. Even extremely large upholstered cushions filled with these natural materials are light in weight.

To increase the loftiness of fiberfill without increasing the weight, fiber chemists have engineered polyester fibers with hollow interiors (see Figure 29.4, p. 438). **Hollow fibers** are currently used extensively in bedding products, and their use in upholstered furniture items is increasing.

Compressional Resiliency

Compressional resiliency and **compressional loft** are synonyms that describe the ability of a textile structure to recover from compression deformations. Filling structures must be compressible, but their serviceability depends on their ability to spring back to their original thickness. Without compressional loft or resiliency, fillings would not recover from the force exerted by body weight, and the cushions would develop permanent depressions.

It was noted earlier in this chapter that spraying resin throughout a fibrous batt helps to reduce the compressibility of the structure. This treatment also helps to increase the springiness of a batt, which encourages it to recover after compression.

Flammability

The flammability characteristics of filling materials become very important variables when upholstered furniture catches fire. Because filling materials are always covered by an outercovering, however, their role in upholstery fires must be evaluated in combination with the outercovering and exterior construction features used in a particular item. These fire-related variables are discussed in Chapter 11.

Labeling Upholstery Fillings

The Textile Fiber Products Identification Act and the two FTC guides described below[1] have provisions that apply to the labeling of upholstered fillings. Manufacturers should comply with these provisions to avoid engaging in unfair or deceptive commercial practices.

Textile Fiber Products Identification Act

Although the provisions of the **TFPIA** do not apply to new upholstery stuffings and fillings, manufacturers may voluntarily identify the fiber used by its generic name, and distinguish it with a trade name to make the product more competitive. When the stuffing or filling has been used previously, the product is considered to be misbranded or unfairly and deceptively marketed unless it carries a label or hangtag clearly stating the presence of reused materials. The act does not, however, require the disclosure of the composition of the reused material.

Guides for the Household Furniture Industry

The FTC gives advice in the **Guides for the Household Furniture Industry** concerning the labeling practices manufacturers should use when they elect to provide information about fillings. To summarize these **advisory practices**, the information may not be false (e.g., labeling cotton felt as wool felt), nor may it be deceiving (e.g., labeling shredded or flaked latex or urethane foam merely as latex foam or as urethane foam). Furthermore, foam fillings must be specifically identified as latex or urethane foam, not merely as foam.

Interested readers may review the guides for information regarding the labeling of genuine wood, simulated wood, and wood veneer components of upholstered furniture and of such case goods as tables, cabinets, desks, and chests. Students planning careers as professional furniture designers, interior designers, or retailers should become familiar with the guidelines concerning the use of such terms as "Mediterranean," "French Provincial," and "Danish Modern" to describe furniture manufactured in the United States. Consumers and retailers should also understand the recommended use of such descriptive terms as "new," "used," "floor sample," and "discontinued model" in the marketing of upholstered furniture.

Guides for the Feather and Down Products Industry

The **Guides for the Feather and Down Products Industry** became effective on December 29, 1971. Included in these guides are definitions of the specific terms to be used in labeling feather and down fillings, such as **down**, **feathers**, **waterfowl feathers**, and **nonwaterfowl feathers**. Guidelines are also given for the use of such terms as **all down** and **pure down**. Other guidelines pertain to the use of damaged and crushed feathers and to the cleanliness of the filling materials. Since feather and down filling materials are used more extensively in bedding products than in upholstered furniture, these guides are reviewed in detail in Chapter 29.

We should note that no labeling provisions have been mandated or recommended for other textile components used in the interior of upholstered furniture. Therefore, the composition of textile cords and fabric linings is rarely, if ever, disclosed.

Summary

The fabric that covers the exterior of upholstered furniture may be textile or nontextile. Various construction treatments can be used to apply the outercovering, several of which add decorative features to the item. These treatments range from quilting the fabric surface to gathering the skirt to boxing the cushions and pillows.

Upholstered furniture contains various interior components including springs, framework, fabric linings, and fillings. The fillings may be cotton or bonded polyester batting, latex or urethane foam cushions, or such loose particles as down, feathers, and fiberfill. Manufacturers must disclose the presence of reused filling materials; they should also comply with the labeling practices set forth in guides provided by the Federal Trade Commission.

The end-use serviceability of a piece of upholstered furniture is strongly influenced by the performance characteristics of the filling materials employed. The degree of softness and comfort is primarily determined by the compressibility of the filling; the weight of the cushions is influenced by the loftiness of the filling component; and the long-term retention of the original form and fabric smoothness directly depends on the compressional resiliency of the filling structure.

Key Terms

advisory practices
all down
antimacassars
arm caps
arm covers
armettes
battings
bottom fabrics
bottom skirt accents
boxing
box pleats
cattlehair
completion
compressibility
compressional loft
compressional resiliency
cotton felt
deck
density
feathers
fiberfill
Guides for the Feather and Down Products Industry
Guides for the Household Furniture Industry

head covers
head rests
hoghair
hollow fibers
horsehair
in-the-muslin
knife-edge treatment
latex foam
loftiness
loose-pillow styles
nailhead trimming
nonwaterfowl feathers
polyurethane foam
pure down
quilting
resilient battings
self-deck treatment
shredded foam particles
slab cushions
slipcovers
textile cords
TFPIA
tight-pillow styles

to railroad

tufted trimming

up-the-bolt

vulcanized

waterfowl feathers

welting

Review Questions

1. Discuss the selection and functions of deck fabric.

2. What advantages are offered by spunbonded fabrics when used as bottom fabric?

3. Distinguish between "up-the-bolt" and "to railroad" applications. When is it critical to use the correct positioning of upholstery fabric on the furniture frame?

4. Sketch an example of "completion" as it relates to upholstery fabric application.

5. What is the purpose of zippers in boxed cushions?

6. Do slipcovers have both a functional and a decorative purpose?

7. Why is cotton "felt" a misnomer?

8. Why is the use of curled hair batting diminishing?

9. When two distinctly different layers of polyester fibers are combined into one batt, the structure is referred to as a dual denier batt. Why is this an appropriate descriptive name, and what advantages are offered by the fibers used?

10. What advantages does polyurethane foam offer over latex foam?

11. Distinguish between compressibility and compressional resiliency.

12. Explain the TFPIA requirements pertaining to the labeling of upholstery fabric and furniture fillings.

13. Are the labeling practices included in the Guides for the Household Furniture Industry and the Guides for the Feather and Down Products Industry advisory or mandatory?

Note

1. Copies of these guides are available from the Federal Trade Commission, Washington, DC 20580

13

Upholstery Coverings

Fiber and Yarn Usage
   Fiber Usage in Upholstery Fabrics
   Fiber Usage in Transportation
     Applications
   Dominance of Spun Yarns
   Multifilament Yarn Usage

Flat Upholstery Fabrics
   Plain-woven Fabrics
   Twill-woven Fabrics
   Satin-woven Fabrics
   Dobby-woven Fabrics
   Surface-Figure Woven Fabrics
   Jacquard-woven Fabrics
   Triaxially Woven Fabrics
   Knitted Fabrics

Pile Upholstery Fabrics
   Woven Pile Fabrics

Knitted Pile Fabrics
   Tufted Fabrics

Genuine Leather Upholstery
   Composition and Structure of Raw Hides
   Curing and Cleaning
   Tanning
   Coloring
   Finishing

Vinyl and Simulated Leather and Suede
   Fabrics
   Extruding Film Sheeting
   Expanding Polymer Coatings
   Simulating Genuine Suede
   Labeling Guidelines

Virtually every method of fabrication used to construct apparel fabrics is also used to construct upholstery coverings. Thus, the variety of fabrics available for use on furniture is as extensive as that available for apparel applications. The assortment includes textile fabrics that are essentially two-dimensional and fabrics that are markedly three-dimensional. Nontextile furniture coverings are composed of elements other than textile fibers and yarns. Some of these coverings, including simulated leather fabrics, are produced directly from polymer solutions; others, specifically genuine leather fabrics, are converted from the raw skins and hides of animals.

Some fabrics are composed entirely of simple yarns in simple, compact constructions, making for relatively great durability and little aesthetic interest. Others incorporate complex yarns in simple, loose constructions, providing much visual and tactile interest but less durability. Fabric patterns range in complexity, from small, geometric figures to large and elaborately detailed motifs. Pile upholstery fabrics are available in various construction densities and surface textures. Some pile fabrics are woven, some tufted, and some knitted.

Although virtually every natural and manufactured fiber is used in textile upholstery fabric, current statistical profiles show that cotton and the noncellulosic fibers hold significant portions of the market. Disclosure of the fiber composition is particularly appropriate today, as the use of noncellulosic fibers to simulate natural fibers in upholstery applications increases.

Fiber and Yarn Usage

Currently, the upholstery fabric market is somewhat evenly divided between cotton and the manufactured fibers. At the same time, fabrics used in transportation applications are made principally of manufactured fibers. The dominance of spun yarns in upholstery underscores an apparent preference of consumers and design professionals for more decorative coverings.

Fiber Usage in Upholstery Fabrics

In the four year span shown in Table 13.1, the market share of a single natural fiber, cotton, has increased at the expense of both the manufactured fibers and wool. The quantities of cotton increased from 275.0 million pounds in 1993 (45 percent of the total market) to 369.5 million pounds in 1995 (49 percent of the total market). Concurrently, the market share held by the manufactured fibers declined from approximately 53 percent to 50 percent, while the market share captured by wool fell to slightly more than 1 percent. While the natural beauty, resiliency, and inherent flame and stain resistance of wool fibers are valued characteristics, the relatively high cost of the fiber tends to limit its selection.

Fiber Usage in Transportation Applications

The end-use category of transportation fabrics includes automobile seat upholstery and slipcovers, sidewalls (the

Table 13.1 Fiber Usage in Upholstery Fabric (million pounds)

Year	Total Fiber	Manufactured Fibers*						Cotton	Wool
		Total	Cellulosic		Noncellulosic				
			Yarn	Staple	Yarn	Staple			
1993	613.0	326.8	1.0	36.2	155.2	134.4		275.0	11.2
1997	755.0	377.1		30.4	179.5	167.1		369.5	8.5

*Manufactured fiber end use in 1997 is divided between cellulosic (rayon plus acetate fibers) and noncellulosic (acrylic, nylon, polyester, and olefin; textile glass fiber is excluded for disclosure reasons). Yarn includes monofilaments, and olefin "yarn" also includes film fiber and spunbonded polypropylene. Staple includes tow and fiberfill.
Source: Textiles Economics Bureau, Inc., *Textile Organon*, Vol. 69, No. 10, October 1998, 176.

Table 13.2 Fiber Usage in Transportation Fabrics (million pounds)

Year	Total Fiber	Manufactured Fibers[a]						Cotton	Wool
			Cellulosic		Noncellulosic				
		Total	Yarn	Staple	Yarn	Staple			
1966	83.7	18.7	1.1	7.4	9.4	0.8		65.0	[b]
1985	85.6	74.3	[c]	0.8	54.0	19.5		11.3	[c]
1997	138.9	133.9	[c]	0.0	100.5	33.4		5.1	[c]

[a]Manufactured fiber end use is divided between cellulosic (rayon plus acetate fibers) and noncellulosic (nylon, polyester, acrylic, olefin). Yarn includes monofilaments, and olefin "yarn" also includes film fiber and spunbonded polypropylene. Staple includes tow and fiberfill.

[b]Nominal amounts used (less than 50,000 pounds).

[c]Little or none of the fiber is used.

Sources: Textile Economics Bureau, Inc., *Textile Organon*, Vol. 43, No. 11, November 1972, 170; Vol. 57, No. 9, September 1986, 212; and Vol. 69, No. 10, October 1998, 178.

vertical portion of car seats), interior roof linings, and sheeting. The cotton quantities include the knit and woven fabric used as the backing for vinyl sheeting. The category also includes convertible automobile tops and replacement tops, as well as upholstery used in other modes of transportation, such as airplanes, railroad and subway cars, and buses. It does not include such things as seat padding, window channeling, and carpet and rugs.

The marked shift from cotton to the noncellulosic fibers in transportation fabrics (Table 13.2) can primarily be attributed to the advances made in manufactured fiber processing. Such properties as soil repellency, high resiliency, and flame resistance can be directly engineered into manufactured fibers, whereas finishing agents and treatments must be used to develop such features with cotton. Again, the relatively high cost of wool precludes its widespread selection, but its inherent flame resistance and resiliency make it an attractive choice when the budget is adequate.

The lack of a more marked increase from 1966 to 1997 in the total number of pounds of fiber used in the transportation market should not be interpreted as indicating a similar lack of growth in yardage production. The effect of fiber density must be considered. Noncellulosic fibers, which accounted for some 96 percent of the 1997 market, are not as dense as cotton fibers (see Table 4.2, p. 49). Thus, a greater amount of yardage can be produced from one pound of noncellulosic fibers than from one pound of cotton. Another factor responsible for this modest growth in fiber usage is the smaller size of many of today's automobiles.

Disclosure of Fiber Composition

Upholstery and transportation fabrics offered to consumers and professionals in piece good form must be labeled in accordance with the provisions of the **Textile Fiber Products Identification Act (TFPIA)**. As noted in Chapter 10, the **Wool Products Labeling Act (WPLA) of 1939** specifically exempts all upholsteries, and the TFPIA specifically exempts permanently incorporated outercovering fabrics.

The scope of the TFPIA also includes **slipcovers**, **antimacassars** (fabric covers used to protect upholstery from hair oil), **tidies** (decorative covers placed on the backs and arms of furniture), swatches, and samples. The required information may be listed on the end of a bolt of yardgoods and on a label or hangtag attached to a slipcover. With swatches less than two square inches in size, the information may appear in accompanying promotional matter. Other swatches and samples may be labeled with the required information or keyed to a catalog, indicating to prospective purchasers where the information can be obtained.

Dominance of Spun Yarns

The dominance of spun yarns in upholstery is evident from the data presented in Table 13.1. Together, natural and manufactured staple-length fibers accounted for more than 76 percent of the 1997 upholstery fabric market. More pronounced textural effects and design features, which consumers and designers apparently consider relatively important in selection, can be produced more readily by spinning and plying processes than by throwing operations.

Noncellulosic staple-length fibers are used more extensively than are manufactured cellulosic staple-length fibers and wool. To a large extent, this is the result of the increased use of spun yarns of polyester in lieu of spun yarns of rayon and the increasing use of spun yarns of acrylic or polypropylene olefin fibers to replace more expensive woolen yarns.

While the loops, nubs, and other textural features characteristic of complex spun yarns add aesthetic interest to upholstered furniture, prospective purchasers and specifiers should consider the possible effects of end use abrasion on the raised areas. Consumers and interior designers should also evaluate the hand of the fabric to confirm that novelty yarn features are not too harsh or rough for their comfort or that of their clients.

Multifilament Yarn Usage

Today, filament-length fibers account for more than a fifth of the upholstery fabrics market. In order to produce a softer and warmer hand, increase covering power, and minimize the development of unsightly fuzz and pills, throwsters often introduce a three-dimensional form to the filaments by using one of the texturing processes illustrated in Figure 5.2 (p. 67). For economy, ease of care, and strength, multifilament yarns composed of nylon are increasingly replacing acetate as a substitute for expensive silk filaments.

When stretch characteristics are needed in a woven upholstery fabric, manufacturers may incorporate a few yarns whose spandex filament cores are covered by fibers identical in color to the other yarns in the fabric. As noted in Table 4.3 (p. 51), spandex fibers have 500 to 700 percent elongation at break and 98 percent recovery after 200 percent strain. The requisite fabric elasticity can often be obtained when the highly elastic fiber accounts for as little as 3 percent of the total fabric weight.

Multifilament yarns are especially important in the transportation market. Whereas filament fibers accounted for approximately 12 percent of this market in 1966, they captured some 72 percent of the 1997 market. This increase may reflect the expanded use of textile fabrics in commercial transportation vehicles, installations that are subjected to a high level of use. The increase may also reflect the expanding use of textile upholstery in automobile interiors.

Flat Upholstery Fabrics

Greige goods producers, dyers, printers, stylists, and converters work together to manufacture an expansive variety of flat and pile structures. Several of these are identified by specific fabric names. Traditionally, fiber composition was an important variable in the descriptions of these fabrics. Today, however, the increased use of the noncellulosic fibers has made fiber content less valuable as a distinguishing characteristic, and more useful descriptions are based on structural and appearance features. This section describes and illustrates flat or nonpile upholstery fabrics.

Several relatively simple upholstery fabrics are produced with basic weaving patterns or a variation of these patterns, and a few are produced with a simple knitting operation. Several complex coverings are produced with a decorative dobby, surface-figure, or Jacquard interlacing pattern. These constructions are discussed and illustrated in Chapters 6 and 7.

Plain-woven Fabrics

Homespun, tweed, and hopsacking are plain-woven upholstery fabrics. **Homespun**, shown in Figure 13.1a, is made of heavy, coarse yarns that resemble hand-spun yarns. The use of complex **speck yarns**, shown in Figure 5.7c (p. 72), adds distinctive color styling to **tweed** upholstery fabrics. **Hopsacking** (hopsack), shown in Figure 13.1b, may be made with a plain or a basket weave. This fabric's name is derived from its coarse, irregular yarns, which resemble the rough jute yarns of the gunny sacks use to store hops.

Consumers and interior designers should carefully inspect **backcoated upholstery fabrics** to determine whether the compound is visible on the face of the fabric. This problem generally occurs only when the coating has been used to compensate for low-quality fabric construction. The coating on the fabric shown in Figure 13.2 is color coordinated with the face yarns to make it as incon-

a) homespun

b) hopsacking

Figure 13.1 Plain-woven upholstery fabrics.

spicuous as possible. Because coatings cost less than fibers and yarns, coated fabrics are relatively inexpensive, but may not be durable in use.

Glazed chintz, shown in Figure 17.2 (p. 281), is produced for upholstery applications in somewhat heavier weights than those produced for window treatments. Chintz typically has a floral or geometric pattern printed in bright colors, as well as high surface luster produced by the use of a glazing finishing process. The fabric is often used in removable, fitted slipcovers.

Basket-woven Fabrics

A 4 × 4 basket pattern is often used to weave rope composed of sisal or other natural materials into chair seats and backs. Basket-woven upholstery fabrics often have warp and filling yarns of different colors. This styling is extensively used with upholstery designed and woven in Scandinavian countries.

Filling-rib Woven Fabrics

Upholstery fabrics produced with a filling-rib weave, including rep (repp), faille, bengaline, and ottoman, are shown in Figure 13.3. Fine, crammed warp yarns generally cover the crosswise ribs in these structures. **Rep** has fine ribs, slightly larger than those characterizing taffeta. The ribs in **faille** are slightly larger and flatter still, numbering approximately 36 per inch. **Bengaline** has equally sized and spaced ribs, numbering about 24 per inch, and **ottoman** has large ribs that may be equally sized and spaced or varied in size and spacing.

Twill-woven Fabrics

Different colors or sizes of warp and filling yarns are often used to accentuate the visual diagonal of twill-woven upholstery fabrics. This kind of effect is evident in the **plaid** fabric in Figure 13.4. Some of the blocks have **houndstooth checks**, jagged or broken check motifs said to resemble the tooth of a hound. Similar fabrics are frequently selected for use on contemporary furniture, especially on items designed for casual residential interiors.

Because the yarn interlacings in twill weaves occur less frequently than they do in plain weaves, higher fabric

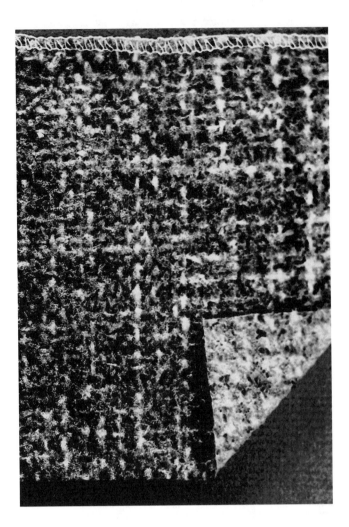

Figure 13.2 Adhesive backcoating on an upholstery fabric with low fabric count.

counts can be used to produce strong, compactly constructed twill upholstery fabrics. Such fabrics are serviceable in high-use residential and commercial applications, including transportation installations; various color stylings can add visual interest.

A draft of a twill interlacing pattern used for weaving rope chair seats is shown in Figure 13.5. Although the distance over which the filling yarns float is twice that of the warp yarns, the use of the warp yarns in paired units results in an even twill.

Herringbone-woven Fabrics

The reversed diagonals of **herringbone** twills make for a visual interest that may be enhanced by using different colors or sizes of warp and filling yarns. The effect may be augmented by weaving in narrow bands of warp yarns that are various shades of the same hue in an uneven, warp-faced interlacing pattern, as in the fabric in Figure 13.6. The term **strié** identifies this kind of coloration.

Satin-woven Fabrics

Frequently, fine, bright acetate or nylon filaments are thrown into low-twist, multifilament yarns for the production of elegant **satin** upholstery fabrics. While such fabrics may have silk-like beauty, the low-twist yarns are relatively weak and the floating yarns may be easily snagged. Therefore, the application of these fabrics as furniture coverings should be limited to items that will not be subjected to high levels of use and abrasion. In most cases, upholstery fabric stylists use satin interlacings in combination with other, more durable interlacings, especially in elaborately patterned Jacquard fabrics.

Sateen-woven Fabrics

A unique upholstery fabric is shown in Figure 13.7. The interlacing pattern used is **sateen**, so the warp yarns appear infrequently on the face. The floating filling yarns are chenille and produce a velvet-like appearance and texture.

Dobby-woven Fabrics

Some dobby-woven upholstery fabrics use a single color and two distinctly different interlacing patterns, one for the designs and another for the background. The slight difference in height between the designs and the ground highlights the motifs, as does the difference in the quantity of light that the yarns in the two interlacings reflect. Other dobby fabrics have yarns of two colors, one appearing in the background and one appearing in the designs. Some dobby fabrics have several colors for added visual interest.

The **goose-eye twill** shown in Figure 13.8c illustrates how a basic weave can be altered to produce a woven-in design. The motifs were formed by selectively reversing the direction of the visual diagonal, creating small diamond shapes said to resemble the eyes of a goose.

a) rep

b) faille

c) bengaline

d) ottoman

Figure 13.3 Filling-rib woven upholstery fabrics.

e) ottoman

Figure 13.4 Plaid houndstooth upholstery fabric.

a) face

Figure 13.5 Pattern-draft for a rope chair seat.

Figure 13.6 Herringbone upholstery fabric with a strié color effect.

b) back

Figure 13.7 Chenille "velvet" upholstery fabric.

Surface-Figure Woven Fabrics

One type of surface-figure weave, the **dot or spot weave** illustrated in Figure 6.12a (p. 88), is used to produce decorative upholstery fabrics. In this weave, extra yarns are interlaced to create small, geometric motifs. The visual impact of the motifs is augmented by the use of contrastingly colored base yarns. For stability and weight, the

a) dobby bows

b) dobby squares

Figure 13.9 Unclipped spot upholstery fabrics.

c) goose-eye twill

Figure 13.8 Dobby-woven upholstery fabrics.

lengths of the extra yarns floating across the back between the motif interlacings are left unclipped, as shown in Figure 13.9.

Jacquard-woven Fabrics

Several distinctive Jacquard-woven fabrics are manufactured for use as furniture coverings. They may be produced with two, three, or four sets of yarns, but all have relatively elaborate motifs and multiple interlacing patterns.

Damask is woven from one set of warp yarns and one set of filling yarns. Removal of individual yarns would destroy the details of the motifs, as well as the fabric integrity. Damask fabrics are essentially two-dimensional and generally incorporate one or two colors. When a single color is used, the design motifs are highlighted be-

a) chenille damask

b) strié damask

Figure 13.10 Damask upholstery fabrics distinguished by the use of simple and complex yarns.

Figure 13.11 Damask upholstery fabric and close-up of motif.

cause their interlacing pattern differs from that of the ground. They may be further accentuated by the use of yarns differing in brightness, level of twist, and degree of complexity from the yarns in the ground. The damask fabrics in Figure 13.10 contain both simple and complex yarns.

Frequently, the motifs in damask have a plain, filling-rib, or sateen weave while the ground has a satin, twill, or filling-rib weave. The visual interest of the ground areas in the damask fabrics in Figures 13.10b and 13.11 are enhanced by strié color styling.

Armure fabrics are distinguished by small motifs in which the warp yarns float on the face of the fabrics and the filling yarns float on the back, producing a pebbly surface. As in damask, two sets of yarns are used.

Liseré fabrics are woven from two sets of warp yarns and one set of filling yarns. One set of warp yarns is generally identical in color to the filling yarns; together,

| **Figure 13.12** Liseré upholstery fabric.

| **Figure 13.13** Brocade upholstery fabric.

these form the ground. The second set of warp yarns is composed of a variety of single-colored yarns. In accordance with the planned pattern, different colors of these yarns are wound in bands of various widths on a separate loom beam. During weaving, the Jacquard mechanism raises these yarns and controls their interlacing to produce detailed motifs in lengthwise bands. In many liseré fabrics, the patterned bands are interspersed with satin-woven stripes (Figure 13.12).

Brocade is woven from more than one set of filling or weft yarns; the number of sets is governed by the number of colors that are to appear in the motifs. The extra yarns are generally woven in a filling-faced twill or sateen interlacing pattern, giving the design motifs a slightly raised effect (Figure 13.13). The ground is compactly constructed in a plain, twill, satin, or filling-rib weave.

Brocatelle is often made from one set of fine warp yarns, one set of heavy warp yarns, and two sets of filling yarns. The design motifs are formed by weaving the heavy warp yarns in a satin pattern, producing a more pronounced relief effect than seen in brocade, while the ground is twill (Figure 13.14). The motifs may also be padded by floating extra yarns behind them.

Jacquard-woven tapestry should not be confused with hand-woven tapestry. The two differ not only in their modes of production, but also in the manner in

| **Figure 13.14** Brocatelle upholstery fabric.

a) face

b) back

 Figure 13.15 Jacquard-woven tapestry upholstery fabric.

which the filling or weft yarns are handled. In machine-woven tapestry, these yarns are carried from one selvage to the other, interlacing into the face when needed. In hand-woven tapestry, they are interlaced within the perimeter of a design motif and then cut, leaving a short length of yarn handling fringe-like on the back. Machine-woven tapestry may also be made of many sets of yarns.

Like hand-woven tapestries, Jacquard-woven tapestries often have picture-like motifs. Yarns not used in the face of these fabrics are floated across the back, producing a mirror-image pattern of opposite colors (Figure 13.15). The fabric is not reversible, however, because the lengthy floats would be snagged and ruptured in use.

Because the motifs and pattern repeats of some machine-woven tapestries resemble those of hand-stitched needlepoint accents (see Figure 9.5, p. 137), they are commonly referred to as **needlepoint weave** fabrics. Although the designs of these fabrics are simple and geometric, as shown in Figures 13.16 and 13.17a, they cannot be woven on a dobby loom; a Jacquard mechanism is required to control the placement of the various colors and the interlacing of the many sets of yarns.

A distinguishing characteristic of Jacquard-woven tapestries is that the various colors are introduced in crosswise or lengthwise bands. When the colors in a band are not used in the face designs, they are interlaced in the back, creating colored bands or stripes on the back side of the fabric (Figure 13.17b).

Fabrics woven of three or more sets of yarns, including liseré, brocade, brocatelle, and tapestry, may be classified as **doublecloth** fabrics. Other Jacquard-woven fabrics, including some tapestries, are also doublecloths, but they are further distinguished by the formation of enclosed **pockets**, areas where there is no interlacing be-

tween two distinct fabric structures that face one another. As shown schematically in Figure 13.18, the face of the pocket is composed of one set of warp yarns and one set of filling yarns, and the back of a second set of warp yarns and a second set of filling yarns. These pockets may show up in the motifs or in the ground; closure occurs where the positions of the face yarns and the back yarns are shifted at the juncture of the motifs and the ground.

In **matelassé**, the pockets are formed in the motifs. The mutual interlacing of the multiple sets of yarns is planned to produce the appearance of quilting stitches. When a third set of filling yarns is floated in the pockets, the designs stand out in relief, puffing the fabric and enhancing the quilt-like appearance (Figure 13.19).

Cloque is another doublecloth fabric in which interlacings of the four sets of yarns are planned to simulate the appearance of quilting stitches. As shown in Figure 13.20a, the mutual interlacings, strategically positioned, create a pattern on the solid-colored surface. Unlike matelassé, cloque is an essentially flat fabric, since the pockets are not padded.

Because Jacquard-woven upholstery fabrics have high production and materials costs, they may be comparatively expensive. Nevertheless, their richly patterned surfaces prompt many designers and consumers to give them priority in the furnishings budget.

Figure 13.16 "Needlepoint weave" tapestry.

Figure 13.17 Tapestry showing characteristic color bands on fabric back.

a) face

b) back

Figure 13.18 Formation of "pockets" in doublecloth Jacquard fabrics.
Courtesy of Brickel Associates Inc.

Figure 13.19 Matelassé upholstery fabrics.

a) face

b) back

Figure 13.20 Cloque upholstery fabric.

Triaxially Woven Fabrics

Triaxially woven fabrics (Figure 6.20, p. 93) display uniform stretch in all directions and high strength in relation to their weight.[1] Because they easily conform to curves and resist tearing, they are used to cover molded furniture frames and automobile seats.

Knitted Fabrics

Virtually all knitted upholstered furniture coverings are flat structures produced by interlooping simple yarns with an interlock stitch (Figure 7.7, p. 101). This stitch helps ensure that the fabrics will be serviceable in end use. These fabrics cannot be varied by incorporating complex yarns or by altering structural features, but textile stylists, often with the assistance of a computer, can provide variety by specifying the use of two colors of yarns, Jacquard patterns, printed patterns, heather colorations, or cross-dyed effects.

The elasticity and flexibility of knitted fabrics make them particularly suitable for use as coverings on curved furniture frames. The loops of the fabric open slightly under stress, allowing the fabric to fit smoothly over the filling and frame. Upholstery knits are generally composed of nylon fibers, which can be heat set to impart dimensional stability and resiliency. Moreover, unlike other weft knitting stitches, the interlock stitch is resistant to running and snagging.

Figure 13.21   Corduroy upholstery fabric.

Pile Upholstery Fabrics

The assortment of pile fabrics available for use as upholstered furniture coverings includes several whose pile yarns are uniformly distributed over the fabric surface, as well as several whose pile yarns are strategically placed to create a patterned layer. The techniques used to produce woven pile fabrics were described and illustrated in Chapter 6, and those used to produce knitted pile and tufted fabrics were discussed in Chapter 7.

Woven Pile Fabrics

Two filling pile fabrics, **corduroy** and **velveteen**, are used as furniture coverings. Both have a cut-pile surface texture and are normally composed of cotton. The surface of most corduroy upholstery fabric is uniformly covered with relatively wide and densely constructed wales (Figure 13.21).

Among the upholstery fabrics produced by interlacing extra warp yarns with base yarns are velvet, velour, friezé, and grospoint. With the exception of grospoint

and some friezé fabrics, these coverings have cut-pile textures.

Velvet is normally woven to have a uniform pile surface. Omitting selected pile yarns and thus exposing some portions of the base fabric produces a variation in velvet upholstery. These fabrics, called **voided velvets**, may have even greater aesthetic interest when a Jacquard mechanism has been employed to control the strategic placement of various colors of pile yarns. In the fabric pictured in Figure 13.22, the voided areas define the shapes of the design motifs forming the pile layer, while Jacquard patterning creates the colored details appearing within each motif. Jacquard patterning may also be used with level-surfaced velvet.

In most velvet upholstery fabrics, only a slight nap is introduced. In **panné velvet**, however, a pronounced nap augments the luster contributed by bright fibers, which are often rayon. The effects of pile yarn orientation on surface reflection are readily seen in the **crushed velvet** in Figure 13.23.

Velour, which is generally produced by the over-the-wire construction technique, has a slightly deeper pile and a more pronounced nap than velvet. Most velour is

Figure 13.22 Jacquard-patterned voided velvet upholstery fabric.

Figure 13.23 Crushed velvet upholstery fabric.

composed of cotton fibers, which give the fabric a soft, warm hand.

Friezé (frisé) upholstery fabrics normally have a level, uncut-pile surface made of multifilament yarns composed of stiff, strong nylon fibers. For variety, manufacturers may incorporate more than one color of pile yarns, expose areas of the base fabric (Figure 13.24a), or selec-

Figure 13.24 Friezé upholstery fabrics.

a) areas of base fabric exposed

b) cut and uncut surface

a) uniform surface

b) areas of base fabric exposed

Figure 13.25   Grospoint upholstery fabrics.

c) patterned surface

tively shear some pile loops to vary the level of surface luster (Figure 13.24b).

Grospoint, pictured in Figure 13.25, has a level surface with pronounced loops larger than those characteristic of friezé. Multifilament nylon yarns are often used in the loops to augment their durability. Surface patterns may be introduced by exposing areas of the base fabric and by combining two or more colors of pile yarns.

Grospoint fabrics are frequently used for covering office chairs and the bottom and back cushions installed in transportation vehicles.

Knitted Pile Fabrics

A limited number of knitted upholstery fabrics have a pile layer. Generally, these structures are used more frequently as bedcoverings than as furniture coverings (see Chapter 29).

Tufted Fabrics

Over the past twenty years, a number of textile firms have succeeded in engineering tufting machines that can produce the pile construction density required in tufted upholstery fabrics. High density is necessary to prevent exposure of the base fabric, especially on curved areas of furniture. Today, some machines can insert some 400 pile yarns per square inch of base fabric. Together with the high rate of production characteristic of **tufting**, these developments may result in increased use of the technique for upholstery fabric production.

Genuine Leather Upholstery

The basic structures used in manufacturing genuine leather coverings—raw skins and hides—are "fabricated" by various animals in assorted sizes, shapes, and thicknesses. **Skins**, retrieved from such small animals as lambs, goats, and calves, are thinner than hides and have an average size that does not normally exceed approximately 9 square feet. **Hides**, retrieved from such large animals as deer, horses, and cattle, on average reach a maximum size of about 25 square feet. Because heavier and larger pieces of leather are required for upholstery applications, hides are usually selected, and they are processed whole.

Composition and Structure of Raw Hides

The processes used in producing leather upholstery can be better understood if the composition and structural features of raw hide are first examined. As shown schematically in Figure 13.26, raw hide has three distinct sections: the epidermis, the corium, and the flesh layer.

The indentations in the top layer, the **epidermis**, are the hair follicles or pores. After the hair is removed, the exposed pores are seen as the **grain markings**, a surface feature found naturally only in coverings produced from the topmost layer of the hide. The central portion of the hide, the **corium**, is a network of interlaced bundles of tiny fibers composed of a protein called **collagen**. Gelatinous matter surrounds the fibrous bundles. The bottommost portion of the hide is **flesh tissue**. It should

Figure 13.26 Schematic illustration of the cross section of raw hide.

be noted that while leather is composed of a network of tiny fibers, these fibers are not classified as textile fibers.

The processing of raw skins and hides is an involved procedure that may be divided into four major operations: curing and cleaning, tanning, coloring, and finishing. A single firm in a vertical manufacturing operation usually carries out these operations.

Curing and Cleaning

Processing begins with **curing**—salting the raw hides. Curing retards bacterial action, helping prevent putrefaction or decomposition, and it also removes the gelatinous matter from the corium. The hides must be thoroughly cleaned, defleshed, and dehaired before further processing. If the hides are thick enough to be split into multiple layers, the splitting will also be done at this stage, prior to tanning.

Tanning

In earlier times, **tanning** solutions were often made from tannins extracted from such sources as tree bark. Because these vegetable tanning agents are slow-acting, they are rarely used in commercial tanning operations. Today, tanning solutions are composed of mineral substances, such as chromium-based salts, and oils. The cured and cleaned hides are immersed in the solution, where the tanning agents react with the collagen, rendering the fibers insoluble. The agents and oils fill the spaces that were formerly filled by the gelatinous materials. The hides are now soft, water- and mildew-resistant, pliable leathers.

Coloring

Coloring may be called for to camouflage an uneven natural color or to introduce currently popular fashion colors. The color may be applied by a piece-dyeing or a surface-dyeing operation.

In piece dyeing, referred to in the leather industry as **drum dyeing**, the tanned leather is rotated in large vessels filled with dye liquor. Piece-dyed coverings may be described in marketing as having an **aniline finish**, a phrase that refers to the use of aniline dyestuffs, not finishing agents. In **surface dyeing**, pigments are mixed with binding agents and spread or brushed over the surface of the leather; this technique is actually a type of staining and colors the surface portion only.

Finishing

Finishing operations may involve the application of lubricants and softening agents to increase the suppleness of the leather. Imperfect areas of grain may be corrected by gently abrading the surface or by shaving a thin film off the surface. If the natural grain is very imperfect, mechanical embossing operations may be employed to impart attractive markings. Resins, waxes, and lacquer-based compounds may be applied and polished for a glazed finish. The high gloss characteristic of **glazed leather** is shown in Figure 13.27a. Compounds used in glazing also increase the moisture resistance of the leather.

Finished leather fabrics are labeled with such terms as full-grain leather, top-grain leather, and split leather.

Figure 13.27 Genuine leather upholstery.

a) glazed leather   b) top-grain leather

The natural grain markings in **full-grain leather** have not been corrected or altered in any way. **Top-grain leather** (Figure 13.27b) has undergone minor corrections to its natural grain markings.

Split leather is produced from a central portion of the hide; since the top layer of the hide is not present in split leather coverings, no natural grain markings appear. Split leather may not be as durable as full- and top-grain leathers.

Genuine suede—leather fabric produced with the flesh side of the hide exposed—is rarely used in upholstery because of its habit of **crocking** or rubbing off color. Laboratory procedures to evaluate crocking are reviewed in the following chapter.

Vinyl and Simulated Leather and Suede Fabrics

Along with the relatively high cost of skins and hides, the lengthy and expensive processing required to convert them into finished coverings puts genuine leather upholstery beyond the financial reach of many residential and commercial consumers. Recognizing this, producers have developed some apparently successful techniques for manufacturing simulated leather coverings. When furniture manufacturers use these coverings, they should follow specific labeling guidelines.

Vinyl and simulated leather fabrics are produced by extruding or expanding polymer solutions. Simulated suede fabrics are produced with selected finishing operations.

Extruding Film Sheeting

The compounds used most often to create **vinyl** and **simulated leather** fabrics include polyvinylchloride and polyurethane. Solutions of these compounds are extruded as film sheeting, using the process described in Chapter 7. To provide the dimensional stability required for upholstery applications, the sheeting is bonded to a supporting fabric, generally a conventional knitted, woven, bonded-web, or spunlaced fabric.

Embossing Grain Markings

The grain markings that distinguish full- and top-grain leathers are introduced to simulated leathers by **emboss-**

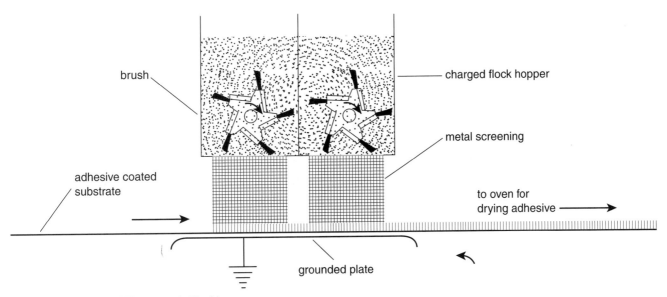

Schematic Diagram of Electrostatic Flocking

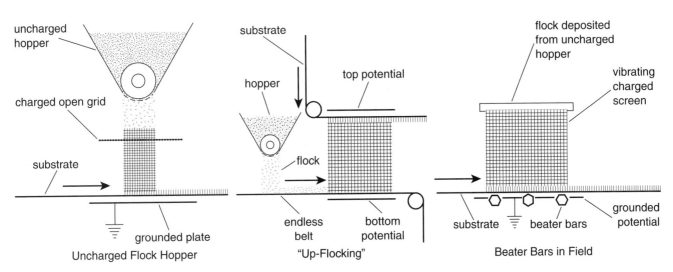

Schematic Diagrams of Various Electrostatic Flocking Arrangements

Figure 13.28 Various electrostatic flocking arrangements.
Courtesy of Solutia Inc., Fibers Division.

ing. This is accomplished by pressing a metal-coated die that has been prepared with the desired markings into the surface of the film.

Expanding Polymer Coatings

Incorporating air into the compounds will **expand polymer solutions**. The effect of this expansion is similar to that produced by whipping cream or egg whites: the apparent, but not the actual, volume is increased. The expanded polymer solution is then applied to a base fabric as a coating. Again, embossing can be used to impart grain markings.

Polymer films and coatings have little or no porosity. Because of this lack of breathability, many people find these fabrics uncomfortable, especially in hot or humid weather.

Simulating Genuine Suede

Many upholstery coverings that appear to be genuine suede are actually simulated structures. Two operations, flocking and sueding, are used to produce these fabrics.

Flocking

An **electrostatic flocking** operation is generally used to produce **simulated suede**. One of the arrangements illustrated in Figure 13.28 is used. Deposition of the flock is followed by sueding or emerizing.

Sueding

In **sueding** or **emerizing** operations, sandpaper-covered disks revolve against the flocked surface. Unlike brushing and smoothing finishes, which raise and orient pile yarns in one direction, and unlike napping finishes, which raise fiber ends, sueding roughens the surface, generally orienting the flock in every direction. However, in Ultrasuede®, a simulated suede marketed by the Skinner Division of Springs Industries, Inc., the flock is given a directional lay or nap.

The durability of a flocked and sueded surface is determined by the cohesiveness of the substrate, resin, and flock. The surface must resist abrasive forces and the resin must be stable to cleaning agents.

Simulated leather and suede fabrics are used extensively to cover dining chairs and the seats, backs, and armrests in automobiles. Apart from any damage caused by cutting or puncturing, heavier vinyl and urethane fabrics can withstand the high levels of use in mass transit vehicles.

Labeling Guidelines

As noted in Chapter 10, labeling guides are advisory in nature and are issued to help members of an industry segment avoid unfair and deceptive marketing practices. Included in the **FTC Guides for the Household Furniture Industry**, which became effective on March 21, 1974, are provisions specifically applying to the labeling of nonleather upholstery coverings that resemble genuine leather. They are intended to ensure that the prospective purchaser is not misled by the appearance of the covering.

In marketing, industry members should conspicuously disclose facts concerning the composition of nonleather upholstery coverings. This may be done by disclosing the true composition of the structure, for example, vinyl or fabric-backed vinyl, or by stating that the material is not what it appears to be, that is, it is simulated leather, imitation leather, or not leather. Trade names denoting nonleather coverings may not include the words "hide," "skin," or "leather." **Homophones** of these words, such as "hyde," may be used as long as facts concerning the composition of the fabric are disclosed as described.

Summary

Both upholstery and transportation fabrics are predominantly composed of manufactured fibers, although a significant amount of upholstery fabric is made of cotton. The widespread use of noncellulosic fibers is largely the result of fiber engineering that enables manufacturers to introduce desirable properties during synthesis and production.

The extensive use of cotton and the growing use of staple-length noncellulosic fibers underscore the importance of complex spun yarns in upholstered furniture coverings. Such yarns contribute decorative interest, but may be ruptured and abraded more readily than simple, smooth yarns. Many flat and pile upholstery fabrics are produced by combining yarns in weaving, knitting, and tufting operations. The balance of the upholstery fabric assortment is produced by converting polymer solutions or raw animal skins into nontextile coverings.

Various techniques are used to convert raw hides and polymer solutions into furniture coverings. Hides undergo lengthy processing, including curing and cleaning, tanning, coloring, and finishing. Polymer solutions may be converted into film sheetings or expanded coatings. To simulate the surface appearance of full- and top-grain leathers, manufacturers emboss films and coatings with grain markings.

Producers have apparently been successful in simulating the appearance of natural leather coverings. The FTC has issued guidelines advising the disclosure of material facts on nonleather structures to ensure that consumers are not misled by the appearance of the simulated fabrics.

Key Terms

aniline finish
antimacassars
armure
backcoated upholstery fabrics
bengaline
brocade
brocatelle
cloque
collagen
corduroy
corium
crocking
crushed velvet
curing
damask
dot or spot weave
doublecloth
drum dyeing
electrostatic flocking
embossing
emerizing
epidermis
expanded polymer solutions
faille
flesh tissue
friezé
FTC Guides for the Household Furniture Industry
full-grain leather
genuine suede
glazed chintz
glazed leather
goose-eye twill
grain markings
grospoint
herringbone
hides

homespun
homophones
hopsacking
houndstooth checks
Jacquard-woven tapestry
liseré
matelassé
needlepoint weave
ottoman
panné velvet
plaid
pockets
rep (repp)
sateen
satin
simulated leather
simulated suede
skins
speck yarns
split leather
strié
sueding
surface dyeing
tanning
Textile Fiber Products Identification Act (TFPIA)
tidies
top-grain leather
triaxially woven fabric
tufting
tweed
velour
velvet
velveteen
vinyl
voided velvets
Wool Products Labeling Act (WPLA) of 1939

Review Questions

1. Noncellulosic fibers hold a significant portion of the upholstery market. What accounts for their growth, and why does their increased use underscore the importance of fiber content labeling?

2. Identify factors that have led to the shifting from cotton to the noncellulosic fibers for transportation applications.

3. Explain why spun yarns dominant the upholstery market.

4. What should the consumer and interior designer consider when selecting upholstery fabric having complex yarns?

5. Identify positive and potentially negative features of backcoated upholstery fabric.

6. Cite reasons why satin and sateen upholstery fabrics may have limited serviceability in end-use.

7. Distinguish between hand-woven and machine-woven tapestry.

8. Why are "needlepoint weave" fabrics so named?

9. Knitted fabric has limited use as upholstered furniture covering. What are the advantages and the limitations of these structures?

10. Grospoint fabrics have frequently been used for commercial upholstery applications. What supports their use in this market?

11. Differentiate among full-grain leather, top-grain leather, and split leather.

12. How are natural grain markings simulated?

13. Review the FTC Guides for the Household Furniture Industry. What is the intent of these guidelines? In order to comply with the recommendations, how must simulated leather and suede upholstery fabrics be labeled?

Note

1. Wayne C. Trost, "Triaxial Weaving," *Modern Textiles Magazine,* June 1973, 60.

14

Evaluation and Maintenance of Finished Upholstery Fabric

Standards for Structural Qualities
  Flaws and Defects
  Yarn Alignment

Evaluations of Physical Performance Properties
  Tear Strength
  Elongation and Tensile Strength
  Dimensional Stability
  Resistance to Yarn Slippage
  Abrasion Resistance
  Resistance to Pilling

Examination of Color Consistency and Retention
  Inconsistencies in Actual and Apparent Color
  Variations in Pattern Repeats
  Fastness Standards

Maintenance of Upholstery Fabrics
  Preventive Maintenance
  Routine Care
  Emergency Action
  Restorative Maintenance
  Salvage Maintenance

The characteristics of the components used and the quality of the manufacturing processes employed influence the appearance and serviceability of finished upholstery fabrics. Although quality finishing can improve the performance and enhance the visual features of fabrics, it cannot compensate for the use of inferior fibers and yarns, unstable colorants, poor pattern registration, or shoddy fabrication. Similarly, the use of high-quality components and fabrication techniques cannot make up for poor fabric conversion. This interdependence encouraged representatives from all segments of the industry to cooperate in establishing standards for finished upholstery fabrics. Much of their work is included in ASTM standards; other results are published as a collection in "Woven Upholstery Fabric Standards," with each standard given a UFS designation.

ASTM D 3597 Standard Specification for Woven Upholstery Fabrics—Plain, Tufted, or Flocked includes specification requirements for such properties as breaking strength, colorfastness, and dimensional stability. UFS standards address these properties, as well as such structural qualities as bow and skewness and such appearance features as uniformity of color and shading due to pile distortion.[1]

The cleanability standard for upholstery fabric is based on the stability of applied colorants when they are exposed to water and to solvent according to prescribed testing procedures. Manufacturers may use the results of such tests to help determine what agents should be used in the overall maintenance of a fabric. The need for overall cleaning can be delayed, however, if routine care and immediate stain removal are consistently used to maintain an outer covering.

Members of the Association for Contract Textiles established performance guidelines for upholstery fabric intended for contract applications. The ACT symbols (Figure 10.4, p. 158) placed on fabrics provide assurance to specifiers that the fabrics have performed to contract standards and pass all applicable testing. The performance properties included in the ACT program are included in this chapter.

Use of the industry standards is strictly voluntary; minimum or maximum levels of performance are recommended, not required. These standards do, however, identify properties that should be considered when selecting woven upholstery fabrics, and they provide a basis for evaluating quality and predicting end-use serviceability.

Standards for Structural Qualities

Two standards concern the structural qualities of finished upholstery. One pertains to flaws and defects and the other to yarn alignment. The ACT standards do not include guidelines for these properties.

Flaws and Defects

Converters should carefully examine finished upholstery fabrics for the presence of unsightly **flaws and defects**. According to UFS guidelines, flat-woven fabrics, such as lightweight printed cotton fabrics, should have no more than an average of one flaw or defect every 7 linear yards with no more than 7 flaws or defects in any 50-yard length. Woven-pile, tufted, and flocked fabrics should have no more than an average of 1 flaw or defect every 5 linear yards with no more than 10 flaws or defects in any 50-yard length.

Yarn Alignment

Problems caused by the use of **off-grain fabrics** are illustrated in Figure 14.1. Furniture items appear to be sagging when covered with a fabric exhibiting **bow** and crooked when covered with a fabric exhibiting **skewness**. These problems are emphasized when colored yarns have been used to create such woven-in linear patterns as stripes and plaids.

In accordance with ASTM D 3882 Standard Test Method for Bow and Skewness in Woven and Knitted Fabrics, measurements of bow are taken at the maximum point of distortion in three widely spaced places along the length of fabric (Figure 14.2). The measurements of maximum distortion produced by skewness are taken parallel to and along a selvage, as shown in Figure 14.3. For each measurement, the maximum bow or skewness is calculated as a percentage of fabric width. Together, the purchaser and supplier reach agreement on the acceptable level of

a) bowed   b) skewed

Figure 14.1 Effects of filling bow and skewness on the appearance of upholstered furniture items.

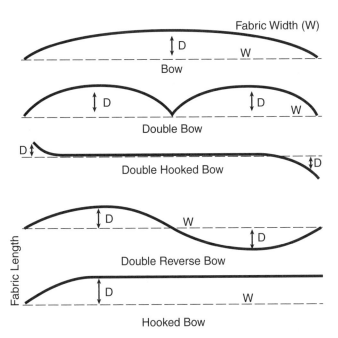

Figure 14.2 Typical bow conditions.
Courtesy of ASTM.

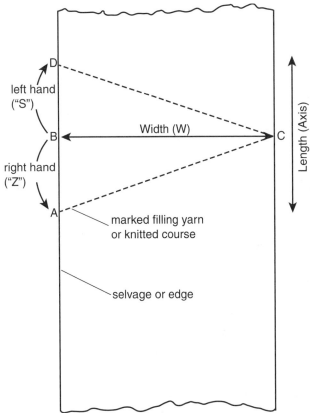

Figure 14.3 Typical skewness conditions.
Courtesy of ASTM.

yarn misalignment. UFS guidelines recommend that the average of the three bow measurements (not percentages) not exceed 0.5 inch, and the average of the three skewness measurements (not percentages) not exceed 1.0 inch.

Evaluations of Physical Performance Properties

Table 14.1 includes selected physical properties, the test methods used to measure these properties, and recommended performance levels noted in ASTM D 3597 or in "Woven Upholstery Fabric Standards." Mutual agreement between purchaser and supplier determines which requirements must be met. In making these decisions, consideration must be given to any fashion or aesthetic preferences currently important to the ultimate consumer. Such variables may take precedence over performance requirements.

Table 14.1 Woven Upholstery Fabric Standards for Physical Properties

Property	Test Methods	Standard
Tear Strength	ASTM D 2262	Category I: 6.0 lbs., min. Category II: 4.5 lbs., min. Category III: 4.0 lbs., min.
Elongation	ASTM D 5034	Category I: 2% min., 5% max. Category II: 1% min., 5% max. Category III: 1% min., 5% max.
Dimensional Stability	ASTM D 3597	Warpwise or fillwise 5% shrinkage, max. 2% gain, max.
Tensile Strength	ASTM D 5034 breaking load-grab method	50 lbs., min.
Abrasion	ASTM D 1175 oscillatory cylinder method	light duty: 3,000 cycles, min. Medium-duty: 9,000 cycles, min. Heavy duty: 15,000 cycles, min.
Resistance to Yarn Slippage	ASTM D 4033 dynamic seam fatigue method ASTM D434 (using 7 stitches per inch)	7,000 cycles, min. 25 lbs., min. (ASTM D 3597) 50 lbs., min. (UFS)
Pilling	ASTM D 3511	3, min. (ACT)

Category I: flat, woven fabrics except lightweight, printed cotton fabrics (less than 8 oz./sq.yd.).

Category II: woven pile fabrics, tufted fabrics, and flocked fabrics.

Category III: lightweight, printed cotton fabrics (less than 8 oz./sq.yd.).

"Light," "medium," and "heavy duty" are explained in Table 14.3.

Source: Joint Industry Fabric Standards Committee, *Woven Upholstery Fabric Standards*, 1980, 6–7.

Tear Strength

ASTM D 2262 Standard Test Method for Tearing Strength of Woven Fabrics by the Tongue (Single Rip) Method (Constant-Rate-of-Traverse Tensile Testing Machine) may be used to evaluate the force required to continue or propagate a tear in a fabric under specified conditions. The test results can predict the likelihood that a small cut or puncture would become a large tear with continued use of the upholstered item.

Test Specimens and Procedures

Test specimens are cut to a size of 3 by 8 inches, with the short dimension corresponding to the direction to be tested. A 3-inch cut is made at the center of and perpendicular to the short side of each specimen, forming two "tongues" or "tails."

After conditioning the specimens for a minimum of 24 hours in a controlled atmosphere of 70 ± 2 °F and 65 ± 2 percent relative humidity, each is successively placed in paired clamps on a **constant-rate-of-traverse (CRT)** testing machine. One tongue is secured in the jaws of the upper clamp and one tongue is secured in the jaws of the lower clamp; thus, opposite sides of the specimen are exposed to the operator. As the machine operates, the lower clamp moves downward at a constant rate for a distance of 3 inches. The loads required to tear each specimen are automatically recorded.

Analysis of Results

The five peak loads recorded during tearing of a specimen are averaged. The **tear strength** values for all replicate specimens are then averaged and reported.

Performance Guidelines

ASTM D 3597 specifies a minimum of 6 pounds of force to propagate the tear. UFS guidelines include three levels of performance. The levels are based on differences in the construction and weight of upholstery fabrics. Category III fabrics, lightweight printed cotton structures, are generally rated "delicate"; therefore, these fabrics should not be buttoned excessively nor should furniture covered with these fabrics be placed where it will receive heavy use.

Elongation and Tensile Strength

The **apparent elongation** and **tensile strength** of upholstery fabrics can be determined in one testing procedure, ASTM D 5034 Standard Test Method for Breaking Strength and Elongation of Textile Fabrics (Grab Test).

Test Specimens and Procedures

In the breaking force-grab method, only a part of the specimen is gripped in the clamps. Each specimen is 4 inches wide and 6 inches long, and is held in the center by 1-inch wide clamps, as shown in Figure 14.4. (Using a larger back clamp is permissible and tends to reduce slippage.) To ensure accurate alignment when securing the specimen in the clamps, a line is drawn 1.5 inches from the long edge of the specimen. A **constant-rate-of-extension (CRE)** or a CRT testing machine may be used.

Analysis of Results

The **breaking force** in pounds is recorded for each replicate specimen tested, and the average of these values is calculated and reported. The apparent elongation is expressed as the percentage increase in length based on the distance between the clamps, which is normally 3 inches (% elongation at rupture = [length stretched/original length] × 100).

Performance Guidelines

As detailed in Table 14.1, the UFS guidelines for elongation differ for different categories of fabrics. Both ASTM and UFS specify a minimum breaking force of 50 pounds for all fabrics, regardless of construction and weight.

ACT standards for contract upholstery breaking force are the same as the ASTM and UFS guidelines. A minimum of 50 pounds of breaking load is required in both the warp and filling or weft directions.

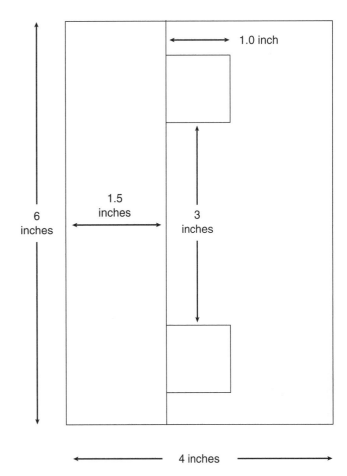

Figure 14.4 Preparation and placement of a specimen for measuring the breaking force and apparent elongation of fabrics by the grab method.

Dimensional Stability

Upholstery fabrics must maintain their original dimensions, within reasonable limitations. With permanently attached, as well as removable, furniture coverings, there should be no prolonged bagging and sagging of the fabric after a person rises from the item; nor should there be excessive **growth** of the fabric in cleaning. Excessive **shrinkage** of the fabric in use or cleaning would cause the fabric to become smaller than the filling, distorting the three-dimensional form of the cushions. It would also place stress on the fabric seams and zipper closures, causing them to ripple or split.

Industry representatives recommend that procedures set out in ASTM D 3597 be followed in measuring the **dimensional stability** of upholstery fabrics. Measurements of the relaxation shrinkage or growth of the specimens are made after exposing them to water.

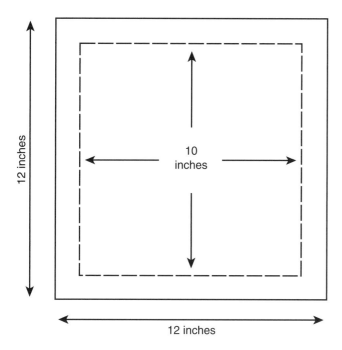

Figure 14.5 Specimen marked for measuring dimensional stability.

Test Specimens and Procedures

In preparation for testing, fabric specimens are cut 12 inches square and marked with sets of three 10-inch-gauge distances in both the warp direction and the filling directions, as illustrated in Figure 14.5. The marked specimens are submerged in distilled water for 10 ± 1 minutes. They are then placed on horizontal screens and allowed to dry for 24 hours.

Analysis of Results

The distance between the gauge marks is measured in each direction. Separate averages are then determined for the warp and the filling. The percentage of change is calculated as directed in the following equations:

$$\% \text{ shrinkage} = [(A - B)/A] \times 100$$
$$\% \text{ gain} = [(B - A)/A] \times 100$$

where A = distance between gauge marks before wetout, and B = distance between gauge marks after wetout and drying.

Performance Guidelines

Upholstery fabrics should not exhibit more than 5 percent shrinkage in either fabric direction. The guidelines also suggest a maximum gain of 2 percent in either direction. The reason for this differential is that upholstery fabric is usually under tension; therefore, shrinkage up to 5 percent is generally less objectionable than fabric gain, which produces bagging.

Resistance to Yarn Slippage

ASTM D 3597 specifies the use of ASTM D 434 Standard Test Method for Resistance to Slippage of Yarns in Woven Fabrics Using a Standard Seam for the evaluation of **resistance to yarn slippage**. The test method is used as an indicator of the tendency of yarns to slip at the seam. Although ASTM D 434 includes a statement that the method is not intended for upholstery fabrics, it can be used with modifications. Rather than the specified 14 stitches per inch, 7 stitches per inch are used to sew the seam. A CRE testing machine is recommended, and the force is exerted until the seam breaks or until the fabric yarns break or tear. ASTM and ACT minimums are 25 pounds of force.

In "Woven Upholstery Fabric Standards," the recommended test method for evaluating yarn slippage is ASTM D 4033 Standard Test Method for Resistance to Yarn Slippage at the Sewn Seam in Upholstery Fabrics (Dynamic Fatigue Method). In this procedure, the seam is stressed by repeatedly dropping a rubber-faced wheel onto the fabric, parallel to and 1 inch from the seam. As shown in Figure 14.6, the specimen is mounted over a piece of resilient polyurethane foam that forms a simulated seat cushion. The seam and specimen are inspected for failure or slippage every 500 cycles.

Testing is complete when the specimen has undergone 7,000 cycles (impacts), or when visual evaluation of the seam reveals yarn slippage, yarn breakage, or sewing thread breakage. In the event seam failure occurs before 7,000 cycles have been completed, the UFS suggests that the seams be reinforced and applications be restricted as set out in Table 14.2. Inserting an extra layer of fabric in the seamline stitching can reinforce seams.

Abrasion Resistance

The extensive use of complex yarns and decorative interlacings in upholstery fabric requires that consumers, inte-

Figure 14.6 The apparatus used in the dynamic seam fatigue test method.
Joint Industry Fabric Standards Committee, Woven Upholstery Fabric Standards, *1980, 31.*

rior designers, and architects consider the level of **abrasion** to which the covering will be subjected in end use. This will assist in the selection of a fabric that will be serviceable for a reasonable length of time, minimizing the potential need for premature replacement or recovering of the item.

For the evaluation of the abrasion resistance of upholstery fabrics, ASTM D 3597 specifies the use of ASTM D 1175. This method, however, has been discontinued and replaced with ASTM D 4157 Standard Test Method for Abrasion Resistance of Textile Fabrics (**Oscillatory Cylinder Method**). This procedure, frequently referred to as the **Wyzenbeek test method**, was selected because it has traditionally been employed in the industry. The Oscillatory Cylinder Abrasive Machine (Figure 14.7) used is described in the following section.

Test Specimens and Procedures

Test specimens are cut 1⅞ inches by 9 inches. The long dimensions are cut parallel to the warp yarns to test warpwise abrasion resistance and parallel to the filling yarns to test fillingwise abrasion resistance. The specimens are secured in the clamps of the apparatus after conditioning. The specimen supports are then lowered over the curved cylinder, which is covered with No. 0 emery paper as the abradant. The cylinder oscillates at the rate of 90 cycles (**double rubs**) per minute, effecting unidirectional rubbing action on the specimens.

Analysis of Results

At the end of 3,000 cycles (double rubs), the specimens are examined for loose threads and wear; slight discoloration from the abradant on light-colored fabrics is disregarded. If no noticeable change is apparent, the test is continued for another 6,000 cycles and the specimens are again examined. If no noticeable change is apparent, the test is continued for another 6,000 cycles for a total of 15,000 cycles.

Performance Guidelines

As noted in Table 14.1, different levels of abrasion resistance are recommended for light duty, medium duty, and heavy duty applications, 3,000 cycles, 9,000 cycles, and 15,000 cycles, respectively. As detailed in Table 14.3, these in-use applications are defined in terms of frequency of use.

Table 14.2 UFS Suggested Uses for Seams Exhibiting Various Degrees of Failure

Degree of Failure	Suggested Use
1,000 cycles or less	Do not use in upholstered furniture.
1,001–2,000 cycles	Use only with reinforced seams and then only in "light" in-use, household applications (as described in Table 14.3).
2,001–4,000 cycles	Use only with reinforced seams and then only in "moderate" in-use, household applications (as described in Table 14.3).
4,001–6,000 cycles	Use only with reinforced seams and then only in "medium duty" household applications (as described in Table 14.3).
6,001–6,500 cycles	At the 6,000- to 6,500-cycle term, it is advisable to reinforce the structural seams.
Above 6,500 cycles	Seam reinforcement is not needed and the fabric can be used for normal household applications (as described in Table 14.3).

Source: Joint Industry Fabric Standards Committee, *Woven Upholstery Fabric Standards*, 1980, 26.

Figure 14.7 Oscillatory cylinder abrasive machine used to evaluate abrasion resistance.
Courtesy of ASTM. Reprinted with permission.

ACT Standards   The ACT guidelines require that general contract upholstery fabric tested by the Wyzenbeek method withstand 15,000 cycles. Heavy duty upholstery should withstand 30,000 cycles.

The ACT guidelines also include abrasion resistance standards for fabric tested by ASTM D 4966 Standard Test Method for Abrasion Resistance of Textile Fabrics (**Martindale Abrasion Test Method**). In this testing, the fabric is mounted flat and abraded in a figure-eight fashion by a worsted wool fabric. General contract upholstery should withstand 20,000 rubs and heavy duty upholstery should withstand 40,000 rubs before showing an objectionable change in appearance.

Resistance to Pilling

Small balls or pills on the surface of fabrics are unsightly, especially when fibers of contrasting colors are present. To assess the extent of **pilling**, ACT recommends that contract fabrics be subjected to the procedures in ASTM D 3511 Standard Test Method for Pilling Resistance and Other Related Surface Changes of Textile Fabrics: Brush Pilling Tester. The fabric specimens are first brushed with nylon bristles to free fiber ends that form fuzz on the surface of the fabric. Subsequently, the face sides of two specimens are rubbed together in a circular motion to roll the fiber ends into pills.

Contract upholstery fabrics that meet or exceed the recommended performance levels in pilling resistance,

Table 14.3 Descriptions of UFS in-use Application Terms

Application	Description
"Light," in-use, household applications	Applications where the upholstered furniture is used mainly for decorative rather than functional purposes; for example, several times a month.
"Moderate" in-use, household applications	Applications where the upholstered furniture is used infrequently, such as, for example, once or twice a week in a "formal" living or dining room.
"Medium duty," in-use, household applications	Applications where the upholstered furniture is used occasionally, every day, for example, for 1 or 2 hours daily.
"Normal," in-use, household applications	Applications where the upholstered furniture is used constantly for several hours or more daily, such as a chair or sofa.

Note: No household furniture fabrics are designed or intended for abusive applications.
Source: Joint Industry Fabric Standards Committee, *Woven Upholstery Fabric Standards*, 1980, 26.

breaking strength, and yarn slippage at seams may be marketed with an ACT symbol. This symbol, a stylized star, is shown in Figure 10.4 (p. 158).

Examination of Color Consistency and Retention

Colorfastness refers to the ability of colorants to retain their original properties when they are exposed to various environmental conditions, cleaning agents, and end-use activities. Residential consumers, contract designers, and architects should be aware of sources of potential harm to colorants and avoid them, if possible. Manufacturers should ascertain the stability of colorants applied to upholstery fabrics and discontinue the use of those failing to exhibit acceptable levels of fastness.

As part of their quality-control work, dyers and printers should examine the uniformity of color characteristics and look for any variability in pattern repeats. End-product producers and consumers may reject upholstery fabrics exhibiting inconsistent color or pattern placements.

Inconsistencies in Actual and Apparent Color

Sophisticated electronic color meters can be used to detect differences in the color characteristics of fabrics. Colors of a fabric should not vary within any single piece or roll, and streaks are unacceptable.

Because changes in the texture of pile fabrics may produce changes in the **apparent brightness** of the fabric, members of the industry recommend that packaging, storing, and handling of these fabrics be controlled to avoid distortion of the original pile yarn orientation. Care during processing and shipping can minimize the development of apparent shading problems.

Variations in Pattern Repeats

The variation of **pattern repeats** should be measured from center point to center point of any contiguous repeats, and a minimum of four measurements should be taken in a continuous length of 50 yards. When pattern repeats are 13 inches or more in length, the variation should not exceed 0.5 inch; when pattern repeats are less than 13 inches in length, the variation should not exceed 0.25 inch.

Fastness Standards

Changes in **color characteristics** may be described in relative terms—"barely perceptible," "quite noticeable," and so on—but the degree of change can be measured and rated in numerical terms by using standard test methods. Manufacturers of upholstery fabrics may elect to compare the results of such tests with the levels of fastness recommended by representatives of the industry. These standards are listed in Table 14.4.

Table 14.4 Woven Upholstery Fabric Standards for Color Retention

Property	Test Methods	Standard
Colorfastness to crocking	AATCC 8 for solids ASTM D 3597 AATCC 116 for prints	Dry: Class 4, min. Wet: Class 3, min.
Colorfastness to light	AATCC 16 ASTM D 3597	Class 4, min. (40 hrs.)
Colorfastness to ozone	AATCC 129	Class 4, min. (1 cycle)
Colorfastness to burnt gas fumes	AATCC 23 ASTM D 3597	Class 4, min. (2 cycles)
Cleanability: Colorfastness to water	AATCC 107 ASTM D 3597	Class 4, min.: color change
Colorfastness to solvents	AATCC 107 ASTM D 3597	Class 4, min.: color change Class 3, min.: staining

Figure 14.8 The Crockmeter testing apparatus.
Courtesy of the American Association of Textile Chemists and Colorists.

Colorfastness to Crocking

Rubbing may cause unstable colorants to exhibit a problem known as **crocking**, the transfer of color from one surface to another area of the same fabric or from one material to another. The loss or transfer can occur under dry or wet conditions. Crocking may occur in upholstery fabric when, for example, apparel fabric rubs against the colored seat of a chair.

The **Crockmeter**, shown in Figure 14.8, is the instrument used in AAATC 8 Colorfastness to Crocking (Rubbing): AATCC Crockmeter Method. During testing, the upholstery fabric is cyclically rubbed by a rod covered with white fabric. Transfer of color from the upholstery surface to the white fabric is evidence of crocking.

The degree of transference is evaluated visually, and a numerical fastness value is determined by comparing the white fabric that covered the rod during testing with pairs of chips on the **International Geometric Gray Scale for Evaluating Staining**.[2] As shown in Figure 14.9, there is no difference between the members of the first pair of chips, and the rating is 5; a perceptible difference appears in the second pair, a combination of the white reference chip and a slightly grayed chip, and the rating is 4.5. The last pair includes a white reference chip and the strongest gray chip: a marked contrast appears, representing a significant level of color transfer.

If no color was transferred from the upholstery fabric surface to the white test fabric, a rating of 5 would be recorded. If transfer occurred, the degree of contrast observed between the unstained and stained areas on the test fabric would be compared with that observed between the paired chips on the scale, and the appropriate number would be assigned. Thus, the higher the reported value, the more stable the colorant and the better the resistance to crocking.

The **AATCC Chromatic Transference Scale**, shown in Figure 18.6 (p. 307), is specified for evaluation

Figure 14.9 International Geometric Gray Scale for Evaluating Staining.
Courtesy of the American Association of Textile Chemists and Colorists.

ified in each test procedure. Because lightfastness is especially critical for draperies, curtains, and awnings, these test methods are explained in Unit Three, Chapter 18.

After completion of the selected lightfastness testing procedure, producers visually evaluate and rate the level of color retention in essentially the same manner as crocking evaluations are made. In this case, however, the **International Geometric Gray Scale for Color Change** is used. As shown in Figure 14.10, the reference chip is a saturated gray color, and it is successively paired with lighter gray chips.

Numerical ratings are determined by comparing the difference observed between an original and an exposed fabric specimen with that observed between the members

Figure 14.10 International Geometric Gray Scale for Color Change.
Courtesy of the American Association of Textile Chemists and Colorists.

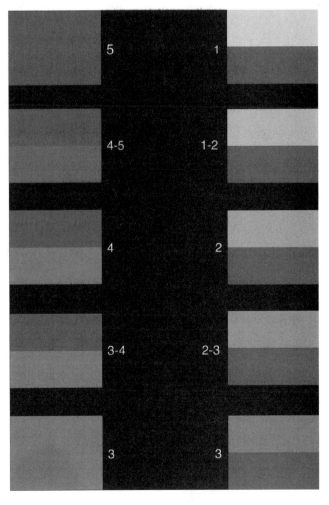

of both dry and wet crocking in ASTM 3597. The numerical ratings are equivalent to the Gray Scale ratings.

The ACT standard requires a Class 4 minimum for dry crocking, and a Class 3 minimum for wet crocking. Contract fabrics meeting or exceeding these minimums may be marked with the ACT symbol, an artist's palette (Figure 10.4, p. 158), to denote compliance.

Colorfastness to Light

AATCC 16 Colorfastness to Light sets out several procedures that can be used to evaluate the **lightfastness** of colored fabrics. There are procedures for accelerated laboratory testing and for extended outdoor exposure testing. Various light sources and testing conditions are spec-

Figure 14.11 Interior view of a gas exposure cabinet.
Courtesy of Atlas Electric Devices Company.

of a pair of chips on the scale. Again, the higher the reported value, the more stable the colorant. A rating of Class 4 or higher after 40 hours of exposure to light is required to meet the standard. Class 5 indicates no fading, while Class 1 indicates a high degree of fading.

Colorfastness to Burnt Gas Fumes

Atmospheric contaminant fading, ozone or O-fading, fume fading, and **gas fading** are terms describing the destructive effects of various gases on colored textiles. Gases that commonly cause problems include oxides of sulfur, oxides of nitrogen, and ozone. Exposing colored textiles to various concentrations of these gases may result in weakening or fading of the original color or an actual change in hue. Either type of change in the color characteristics of interior textile products is a twofold disaster: the harmony among several items in an interior setting is destroyed, and the cost of replacement must be paid.

Greater numbers of fume fading incidents occur in industrial centers, geographic regions where coal and fuel oil are major heating sources, and densely populated areas where personal automobiles are widely relied on. Automobile exhaust can contain as much as fifty thousand times more nitric oxide than a normal atmosphere. While emission control devices on automobiles and clean air standards are reducing the concentrations of some atmospheric pollutants, the increasing use of fireplaces and wood-burning stoves for home heating is generating greater concentrations of others.

Fume fading is a particular problem in acetate fibers dyed with disperse dyestuffs. After prolonged exposure to oxides of nitrogen or sulfur, certain colors gradually and permanently change hue. Blues turn pink, greens turn brownish yellow, and browns turn red. Solution dyeing is necessary to avoid such changes, and trade names may be used to distinguish the solution-dyed fibers.

AATCC 23 Colorfastness to Burnt Gas Fumes can be used for analyzing the negative effects of various gases, but it is generally used to determine the effects of nitrogen dioxide. The test is conducted in an enclosed chamber, such as the one in Figure 14.11, with controlled concentrations of the gas. After completion of two cycles of testing, the level of color change is determined in the same manner as lightfastness ratings are determined,

using the Gray Scale for Color Change. AATCC 129 Colorfastness to Ozone is used to measure the deleterious effects of ozone on colored textiles.

Colorfastness to Cleaning Agents

The fastness of the colorants determines the cleanability of upholstery fabrics when they are exposed to water and to solvents, the agents that are typically used to clean upholstery. Manufacturers are specifically concerned with the potential for color bleeding and migration (movement of the dyestuff through the fabric components). **Bleeding**, either to the interior of the covering or onto cleaning cloths, would weaken the surface color. **Migration** would create various levels of intensity over the surface and could transfer color from one area to another area of a different color.

Colorfastness to Water AATCC 107 Colorfastness to Water is recommended for evaluating the fastness of colored upholstery fabric to water. In preparation for testing, a multifiber fabric, a structure that has narrow bands of six different fibers, backs the fabric specimen. The paired fabrics are immersed in distilled water and then removed, pressed between glass plates, and heated in an oven at 100 ± 2 °F for 18 hours. After air drying, the fabric specimen is visually evaluated and rated for color change using the Gray Scale for Color Change. The multifiber fabric backing is visually evaluated for staining using the Gray Scale for Staining.

Colorfastness to Solvent AATCC 107 is also used to evaluate the fastness of colored upholstery fabrics to solvents. In this procedure, however, the paired fabrics are immersed in a solvent, perchloroethylene, instead of in water. The exposed fabrics are again evaluated for color change and staining.

It should be noted that these colorfastness test methods give reliable information on the stability of colorants to water and to solvent only. They do not take into account the rubbing or blotting action usually involved in a cleaning process. Therefore, fastness to water or solvent does not necessarily guarantee a satisfactory outcome to actual soil and stain removal efforts.

Upholstery fabrics meeting or exceeding the standards recommended for the several properties discussed in this chapter should perform well in end use. However, proper maintenance is required to ensure that the original appearance features are retained at an acceptable level for an extended period of time.

Maintenance of Upholstery Fabrics

Residential and commercial consumers do not expect an upholstery fabric to retain its new, fresh, clean appearance forever. On the other hand, they do not anticipate that soil accumulation will be so rapid that an unreasonable maintenance program will be required. Consumers also expect that the removal of stains will not be an impossible challenge.

Preventive Maintenance

As a preventive maintenance measure, contract designers and other specifiers may request that the surface of upholstery fabrics be laminated with clear or translucent vinyl film sheeting. Although **vinylized fabrics** can be washed with mild detergent and warm water, they are not waterproof; they are not intended for installation outdoors. Because this treatment produces some variation in color and luster, converters suggest that the client examine a treated sample of the fabric before the vinyl application is ordered.

With routine care and immediate stain removal, residential and commercial consumers can assist in the long-term retention of the original appearance of upholstery fabrics. As long as the appearance is satisfactory to the consumer, the need for an overall or restorative cleaning procedure is postponed.

Routine Care

Upholstered furniture products should be frequently and thoroughly vacuumed to remove airborne dust and lint. If possible, loose cushions should be turned and rotated to equalize wear and soiling levels. Protective arm covers and head rests should be cleaned to minimize differences between the appearance of these items and that of other exposed areas.

Simulated leather fabrics with a polyvinylchloride or polyurethane surface may be washed with warm water and a mild soap (not a detergent), and then rinsed with a dampened cloth and dried. As a protective measure, a hard wax can be applied to the surface. However, waxes, oils, and furniture polishes must not be applied to genuine leather coverings as they may damage the finish.

Emergency Action

Prompt action must be taken in the event of spillage or deposition of other foreign matter. Fluids must be immediately absorbed from the surface to confine the area of spillage and to prevent them from penetrating into the fibers and fabric backing. Solid materials, such as candle wax and crayon, should be broken up, scraped, and vacuumed to remove as much of the substance as possible before stain removal agents are used.

When stain removal agents are required, they should first be applied as directed to an inconspicuous area of the outer covering. After the agent has been removed and the fabric has dried, the area should be examined for evidence of change in the original color characteristics. If necessary, different agents should be tried until one causing no change in color can be identified.

In order to avoid spreading the stain and overwetting the fabric, stain removal compounds should be applied in small amounts from the outside edges toward the center of the stain. To avoid distortion of the surface texture, the agent should be blotted on, not rubbed into, the foreign matter and fabric. After the stain has been completely removed, the cleaning agent residue must also be removed by rinsing the fabric and blotting it dry.

Waterborne stains can be removed from most textile upholstery fabrics with a mild detergent diluted with warm water, using one teaspoon of detergent per cup of water. **Oilborne stains** can be removed with a solvent-type dry cleaning fluid, such as K2r®, produced by Texize.

Table 14.5 lists the stain removal agents and procedures recommended for use with wool. Additional stain removal agents and procedures are listed in Tables 27.2, 27.3, and 27.4 (pp. 409, 410, and 411 respectively). Although these are specifically applicable to soft floor coverings, they may also be used with upholstery fabrics. In all cases, however, a pretest should be performed

Table 14.5 Removal of Spots and Stains From Wool Upholstery

Stain	Detergent or Vinegar	Cleaning Fluid	Other
Acids			Detergent
Alcoholic beverages	•	•	
Ammonia or alkali	•		
Beer	•		
Bleach	•		
Blood	•		
Butter		•	
Candy	•		Scrape and vacuum
Chewing gum	•	•	
Chocolate	•	•	
Coffee	•		
Cosmetics	•		
Crayon	•	•	Scrape and vacuum
Egg	•		
Excrement	•		
Fruit and juices	•		
Furniture polish	•	•	
Glue			Alcohol
Grease		•	Scrape and vacuum
Household cement	•	•	
Ice cream	•	•	
Iodine	•		Alcohol
Lipstick	•	•	
Metal polish	•	•	
Milk	•	•	
Mud	•		
Mustard	•		
Nail Polish			Polish remover
Oils		•	
Paint	•	•	
Perfume	•	•	
Salad dressing	•	•	
Sauces	•	•	
Shoe polish	•	•	Scrape and vacuum
Soft drinks	•		
Tar		•	
Tea	•		
Urine	•		
Vomit	•	•	
Washable ink	•		
Wax		•	Scrape and vacuum

Courtesy of The Wool Bureau, Inc.

to confirm that the agent would not alter the color of the fabric or the integrity of the fabric structure.

If warm, soapy water does not remove soil from simulated leather coverings, the surface can be cleaned with a cloth dampened with kerosene or naphtha. These compounds are flammable and should be used with cau-tion in a well-ventilated area to avoid inhalation of the fumes. Ballpoint ink can usually be removed by spraying the stain with hair spray and immediately wiping the surface.

Procedures used to remove stains will also remove accumulated soil. This may result in a localized clean area that can readily be distinguished from adjacent soiled areas. When such differences are apparent, or when large areas are soiled, the entire surface should be cleaned.

Restorative Maintenance

The original appearance of upholstery fabrics can usually be restored by carefully cleaning the fabric surface. Consumers may elect to do the restoration themselves, to send the item to a professional cleaner, or to have a professional cleaner restore the item on-site.

Frequently, upholstery manufacturers voluntarily label their products with a **cleaning code**. The code to be used is determined by measuring the level of color migration and bleeding caused by water and by solvent, using the standard test methods described earlier in this chapter. Industry representatives recommend that all upholstered furniture be identified as to its cleanability code, using the letter codes defined as follows:

W—use water base upholstery cleaner only.
S—use solvent base upholstery cleaner only.
WS—can use water base or solvent base cleaners.
X—do not clean with water base or solvent base cleaners; use vacuuming or light brushing only.

Water-based cleaning agents are commonly labeled upholstery shampoo. These agents are commercially available as foams, concentrated liquids, and dry compounds.

It should be emphasized that these cleaning codes apply to the outer covering fabric only; it is imperative that overwetting of the fabric be avoided to prevent contact with the filling materials. It must also be noted that zippered covers should not be removed for cleaning or excessive shrinkage may occur and the backing compound may be damaged. Zippers are used to facilitate filling the cushions, not to facilitate cleaning.

Genuine leather coverings may be cleaned with cheesecloth soaked in a solution of warm water and any mild soap. The surface should then be wiped with a slightly damp cloth and dried with a soft cloth.

Salvage Maintenance

In the event that an upholstered furniture covering no longer has an acceptable appearance, even after overall cleaning, consumers may elect to have the item reupholstered. Because such projects involve materials costs, skilled labor charges, and, often, transportation expenses, they may be relatively expensive. For this reason, reupholstering is often restricted to well-constructed items and antique pieces.

Summary

Fiber, yarn, and fabric manufacturers, colorists, converters, and end-product producers have established standards for various physical and color-related properties of finished upholstery fabrics. These standards include suggested methods for testing the fabrics in the laboratory and recommended levels of performance. The test methods were chosen because they provide a reasonable simulation of end-use conditions; fabrics meeting the standards based on these methods should therefore display an acceptable level of in-use serviceability.

The original appearance of upholstery coverings can be retained for a longer period of time if vacuuming is routine and removal of stains is prompt. For overall cleaning, informed consumers can interpret the cleaning code that is frequently, albeit voluntarily, listed on upholstered furniture labels or hangtags. Manufacturers whose fabric has been examined for color migration and bleeding after being exposed to water and to solvent use these letter codes.

Key Terms

AATCC Chromatic Transference Scale
abrasion
apparent brightness
apparent elongation
atmospheric contaminant fading
bleeding
bow
breaking force
cleaning code
color characteristics
colorfastness
constant-rate-of-extension (CRE)
constant-rate-of-traverse (CRT)
crocking
Crockmeter
dimensional stability
double rubs
flaws and defects
fume fading
gas fading
growth

International Geometric Gray Scale for Color Change
International Geometric Gray Scale for Evaluating Staining
lightfastness
Martindale abrasion test method
migration
off-grain fabrics
oilborne stains
Oscillatory Cylinder Method
ozone or O-fading
pattern repeats
pilling
resistance to yarn slippage
shrinkage
skewness
tear strength
tensile strength
vinylized fabric
waterborne stains
Wyzenbeek test method

Review Questions

1. Are the recommended levels of flaws and defects in upholstery fabrics reasonable?

2. Distinguish between filling bow and filling skewness. What causes these yarn alignment problems, and how do they affect the appearance of such things as upholstered furniture and window coverings?

3. Explain the differences in operations of a CRE and a CRT testing machine.

4. How would fabric shrinkage affect the appearance of upholstered furniture? Would fabric growth present problems with an upholstered item?

5. Describe the problems caused with yarn slippage at seamlines.

6. How is seam failure measured? Explain the relationship between the various levels of seam failure and use of the seams in end-use items.

7. Why is frequency of use a reasonable measure to use in defining in-use applications terms for upholstered furniture (i.e., light duty, medium duty, and heavy duty)?

8. Explain the membership and work of ACT. What symbols are used by this group, and what connotations are associated with each symbol?

9. Differentiate between brightness and apparent brightness. What causes changes in the apparent brightness of fabrics, especially pile fabrics?

10. Explain how the Gray Scales and the AATCC Chromatic Transference Scale are used in fabric evaluations.

11. Identify the problems that atmospheric contaminants cause with colored textiles.

12. Identify the cleanability codes voluntarily used with upholstery fabric. What does each indicate? How do manufacturers determine which code to include on a label?

Notes

1. The full text of ASTM standards pertaining to textiles may be reviewed in the *Annual Book of ASTM Standards*, Vol. 07.01 and Vol. 07.02.

2. The AATCC Chromatic Transference Scale (Figure 18.6, p. 307) could also be used. The numerical ratings are equivalent to the Gray Scale ratings.

UNIT TWO CASESTUDY

Designer Name: Lisa Cini/Belinda Binford
Dan Binford & Associates

Project Location: Karrington Communities
Columbus, OH

Statement of the Project:

Karrington Communities, based in Columbus, Ohio, is one of the assisted living chains in the United States. They want to achieve a high-end residential look that is appealing to current residents and people looking to reside in these types of communities.

Statement of the Problem:

Assisted living communities need a durable, easily maintained, cost-effective upholstery creating a high-end residential appearance. In dealing with incontinence and soiling, the upholstery also needs to be antibacterial, anti-fungal, antimicrobial and maintain its original appearance qualities. The aesthetics and maintenance were more important to the client than cost.

Selection Criteria:

The upholstery was chosen because of its proven performance and aesthetic value. Crypton® is a chemically treated upholstery covered with the appearance of a fabric yet the durability of a vinyl. It upholsters very well, giving the lounge and dining pieces a very tailored look. From approximately 15 feet away, a chair upholstered in Crypton® looks like a chair upholstered in fabric. Karrington did not want to use vinyl because they felt that it looked low end. Vinylized fabrics, on the other hand, tend to delaminate and turn yellow, which also does not make them good solutions for maintaining the desired appearance. In the 20+ facilities that we have done with Karrington, the Crypton® has performed mairaculously in both durability and aesthetics.

Product Specifications:

Crypton®

- Resists staining of blood, urine, and betadine
- Passes the Tensile Strength test of 284 lbs.
- Passes the Tongue Tear Strength test of 15.4 lbs.
- Resists yard slippage of 100 lbs.
- Resists the Wyzenbeek test of 100,000 double rubs
- Classified in UFAC Class 1
- Passes the State of California Bulletin 117, Section E
- Is antibacterial, antifungal, and antimicrobial

Maintenance and Cost:

In laboratory settings, all stains were easily removed with mild soap and water. Solvent based cleaners are not used to clean Crypton®. Although Crypton® is more expensive than vinylized fabrics and vinyl, the durability of Crypton® makes it a very viable solution. Lower long-term cost is achieved because of its durability over time. Standard maintenance products and simple maintenance procedures also reduce long-term cost.

Discussion Questions:

1. Identify two of the client's requirements for the design project.

2. Identify an aesthetic feature of the product which meets the client's requirements.

3. Distinguish functional features of the product which meet the client's requirements.

4. Discuss the implications of the tactile qualities versus the visual qualities.

5. List the performance advantaged of Crypton®.

6. Compare and contrast long-term appearance retention of Crypton® with vinylized fabrics.

7. Research another product that is appropriate for this application. Next compare and contrast the cost effectiveness, availability, durability, and maintenance of the new product with the one used in the casestudy.

8. If cost was a factor, what other fabrics would be appropriate for the Karrington Communities applications?

Window and Wall Coverings

Unit Three focuses on textiles produced for use in window treatments and as wall coverings. Chapter 15 discusses the influence of appearance features, functional values, cost variables, and performance requirements on the selection of window treatment styles and coverings. Styles of curtain and drapery treatments, blinds and shades, and shutters and awnings are described and illustrated in Chapter 16. The chapter covers measurements and calculations for determining rod length and placement and the amount of yardage required for constructing lined, two-way draw panels. The fibers, yarns, and nontextile elements used in window coverings are identified in Chapter 17. Also described in this chapter are the curtain, drapery, and lining fabrics produced with these components.

Along with the performance guidelines recommended by members of the industry, test methods for measuring various service-related properties of textile window covering fabrics are summarized in Chapter 18. This chapter also reviews procedures for proper maintenance of finished curtain, drapery, and lining fabrics.

Because several fabrics produced for use in window treatments may also be applied to vertical surfaces, the last chapter in this unit, Chapter 19, focuses on textile wall and panel coverings. Attention is given to the selection and installation of these coverings, and to their effectiveness in reducing noise and energy consumption.

15

Selection Criteria for Window Treatments

Appearance Factors
  Aesthetic Preferences
  Structural Factors
  Color-related Variables

Functional Values
  Reduction of Glare
  Restriction on Inward Vision
  Modification of Outward Vision
  Reduction of Interior Noise

Conservation of Energy
Protection of Other Interior Furnishings

Cost Factors
  Initial Costs
  Replacement Costs
  Maintenance Costs

Performance Standards

The selection of window treatments and window coverings is influenced by several variables. At the outset, the **fenestration**—the design, arrangement, and proportioning of the windows and doors in an interior—may limit the range of styles that can be considered. Designers need to consider what the window treatment will look like from the outside, window by window, and in relationship to the entire façade. Structural defects needing to be camouflaged impose additional limitations, and so do desires for such functional properties as privacy enhancement and noise or glare reduction. The range of colored covering choices may be narrowed by such conditions as the source and quantity of light and the presence of atmospheric contaminants. Legal standards or codes may also apply to the covering choices made for certain commercial interiors. In all cases, the selections must be affordable; it must be considered whether multiple fabric components, elaborate hardware fixtures, or extensive trimming will escalate the cost beyond the limit of the furnishings budget. For some treatments, however, future savings in energy could help to compensate for the initial cost.

Fiber, yarn, and fabric features have a great impact on the appearance and serviceability of window treatments. Professionals and consumers should consider these characteristics, as well as those of nontextile materials, when they are specifying or selecting window coverings. As for all product choices, the final selection of window treatment style and materials should also be based on considerations involving more than aesthetics.

Appearance Factors

Window treatment styles and coverings cannot always be selected on the basis of personal preference alone. The fenestration and any structural defects must be considered first if the setting is to appear attractive. The effects of various factors on color must be examined to assure the realization and retention of the planned appearance. Attention must also be paid to the visual and textural features of the yarns and fabrics being considered.

Aesthetic Preferences

At least initially, consumers' personal preferences limit the range of window treatment styles and coverings they will consider. Interior designers typically use design elements and principles to create a treatment that dominates the interior setting or one that attracts little attention and serves as a backdrop for distinctive upholstered items and soft floor coverings. Other solutions may include symmetrically versus asymmetrically balanced designs or informal versus formal treatments. Whatever the design, it should offer the most appropriate solution for the client's need.

For coverings planned to have minimal textural interest, manufacturers use simple yarns in the fabrication operation. Fine monofilament or multifilament yarns are used, for example, to produce the smooth surfaces characterizing ninon, a plain-woven fabric shown in Figure 15.1, and marquisette, a leno-woven fabric shown in Figure 17.13 (p. 286).

Complex yarns are frequently employed to add visual and textural interest to curtain and drapery fabrics. Seed yarns, for example, appear in the novelty marquisette cur-

Figure 15.1 Ninon curtain fabric produced with fine, simple multifilament yarns.

a) marquisette having seed yarns

b) drapery fabric having bouclé yarns

| **Figure 15.2** Complex yarns add visual and textural interest to curtain and drapery fabrics.

tain fabric shown in Figure 15.2a, and bouclé yarns in the drapery fabric in Figure 15.2b.

Relatively coarse and irregular yarns can be made to simulate the appearance of hand-spun yarns. This is typically seen in such curtain and drapery fabrics as osnaburg and monk's cloth (Figures 17.4 and 17.5, pp. 281–282).

All window coverings intended to be used as free-hanging panels must be drapable, but those fabrics intended for such overhead and side treatments as swags, jabots, and cascades must be exceptionally so. The importance of drapability in these applications is readily apparent in the treatment in Figure 16.8 (p. 268). Fabric manufacturers generally use fine, low-twist, multifilament yarns in a satin weave to produce good drapability.

Fabrics produced for curtains, especially ruffled curtains, often are made from fine, high-twist yarns that introduce a crisp hand and provide the body needed to support the folds of the ruffles and the tie-back panels. Fine, soft yarns are selected for fabrics intended to be used in such window treatments as sash curtains and Austrian shades; these yarns produce soft, rounded folds that enhance the shirred effect while preserving the preferred level of transparency. Fabrics intended for awnings or other exterior treatments are often composed of relatively large, high-twist yarns strong enough to resist rupturing when the fabric is stretched over the framework and when it is repeatedly stressed by wind gusts.

Woven wood coverings may be constructed with simple ply or cord yarns contrasting with or matching the color of the wooden slats. They may also be constructed with a variety of highly decorative, complex yarns that are variously colored to coordinate with other interior furnishings. In these coverings, the yarns are often incorporated in lengthwise bands to create stripes that augment the visual and textural interest of the shade.

Structural Factors

Within an interior space, the fenestration may require that two windows be covered with a single treatment, that treatments on neighboring windows be mounted to equalize differences in height, or that the coverings draw one way or not at all. A small, isolated window may require a large-scale treatment with fabric identical to that used for other windows in the interior to make it appear larger and integrated. Certain types of windows preclude the use of certain treatment styles. Bow windows, for example, cannot be covered with Roman shades or with accordion-pleated shades. Windows that open inward cannot be covered with stationary panels unless the panels and rods are attached to the window sashes.

The large expanses of glass that typify contemporary homes and office buildings may require coverings to control light and heat transmission during the day and to provide privacy and avoid a "black wall" effect at night. Walls in need of repair and windows in need of replacement can be camouflaged by covering them with stationary treatments.

Color-related Variables

Various factors that may affect the **apparent color** of textile structures were discussed in Chapter 8. These factors, and those affecting **actual color**, should be considered so that the colors chosen appear the same in the interior and will go on appearing so for a reasonable period of time. Careful consideration will also help assure that the coordination planned between the window treatments and other interior furnishings and wall coverings is realized.

Factors Affecting Apparent Color

It is critically important to confirm the acceptability of any changes in the apparent color of a window covering produced by the lighting conditions in an interior. Professionals and consumers are advised to hang sample lengths of their possible covering choices at their windows, along with any planned shades or linings. If the quantity of incident natural light is judged too high, the consumer may consider adding sheers or exterior awnings.

Because window coverings are normally not subject to the great amounts of abrasion often inflicted on upholstery fabrics and soft floor coverings, changes in texture, and therefore in luster, may be minimal. Because of this, fabrics having prominent relief effects, like those provided by complex yarns, are often appropriate for window treatments. The rate and level of soiling may also be lower with window coverings than with other interior textile applications. However, repeatedly opening and closing panels by pulling on their side hems or headings may lead to rapid soil accumulation; and, especially in stationary treatments, airborne dust, smoke, and oily cooking fumes may settle on the fabrics and gradually alter the apparent colors.

Factors Affecting Actual Color

When window covering fabrics are to be installed indoors, concerns arise for lightfastness, gasfastness, and fastness to cleaning agents. When coverings are to be installed outdoors, concern arises as well for the stability of the colorants to weather elements and changing ambient temperature. The accelerated and long-term testing procedures used to ascertain the colorfastness of interior and exterior window coverings exposed to these conditions and substances are discussed in Chapter 18.

Window coverings are continually subjected to solar rays. Sun-related alterations in the structure of dyes produce concomitant changes in the structure of the fibers. To help minimize the degradation of the colorants and the fibers used in decorative panels, the use of permanently attached or separately hung lining materials, and possibly exterior awnings, is advisable.

Functional Values

Consumers, interior designers, and architects may elect to restrict their style and covering choices to those that can provide specific functional benefits, such as light control, privacy, insulation, and noise reduction. A fabric feature known as "openness" has a major influence on these functional values. Manufacturers often consult with interior designers and architects to identify the functional properties needed or desired by their clients and then determine the appropriate degree of openness for a particular fabric.

Reduction of Glare

The degree of brightness control that window coverings should provide depends on the solar exposure conditions, the type of glass in the window, and the preferences and needs of the people who use the interior space. Windows with a northern exposure are subject to less direct sunlight than those with a southern exposure. Windows with an eastern exposure receive more direct light in the morning, and those with a western exposure more in the afternoon hours. Installing bronze-tinted or reflective-coated vision glass in lieu of clear glass will reduce the level of light transmission, but this reduction may or may not be adequate.

When the degree of transmission fails to coincide with the preferences and needs of the people using the interior, it can be balanced by interior and exterior window treatments. Often, the treatment should be designed to provide varied levels of control throughout the day, ranging from full transmission to total blackout.

The brightness control provided by window treatments is influenced by the color characteristics of the

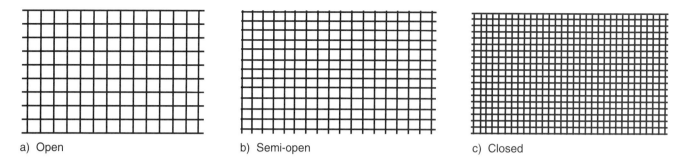

a) Open   b) Semi-open   c) Closed

Figure 15.3 Levels of fabric openness.
Courtesy of PPG Industries, Inc., 1978.

coverings, the number of layers used, the fullness of the panels, the addition of fiber delusterants and fabric coatings, and the fabric openness. **Fabric openness** is the ratio of the open areas between the yarns to the total area of the fabric. It is apparent from Figure 15.3 that an open fabric would permit more light to pass through than would a semi-open or semi-closed fabric. Openness is not, however, the only variable of fabric composition that affects light transmission. As illustrated in Figure 4.1a (p. 45), a portion of the light waves striking a fiber are reflected, another portion absorbed, and the remaining portion transmitted. Light-colored fibers, especially those containing no delusterants, permit more light waves to be transmitted to the interior. Increasing the fullness of the panels reduces this transmission, since more fibers reflect and absorb more waves.

In all textile coverings except those composed of glass fiber, balancing the size of the yarns and the compactness of construction used can readily produce the requisite openness. Because glass fiber has a high specific gravity, increasing the size of the yarns or the compactness of construction would result in a comparatively large increase in fabric weight; increasing the diameter of the yarns would also increase the likelihood of fibrillation. To avoid these problems, manufacturers of glass fiber window coverings often use loop or curl yarns (Figure 5.11d, p. 73) to engineer the desired degree of fabric openness. The airy projections of these complex yarns effectively cover the surface area and increase the opacity (Figure 15.4).

Because the quantity of direct and reflected light varies with the exposure and the hour of the day, consumers may elect to use multiple layers of window cov-

Figure 15.4 Loop yarns reduce openness but add little weight to leno-woven casement composed of glass fiber.

erings to widen the range of brightness control options. For maximum flexibility, various combinations of shades, curtains, draperies, and awnings may be used. For total blackout in such interiors as motel rooms, shades or fabrics with opaque coatings may be installed; examples of such fabrics are given in Figure 17.31 (p. 295).

Controlling the level of brightness may be desirable for aesthetic purposes, but it may be critical to reduce the glare when persons with impaired vision reside or work in the interior. It may also be necessary to reduce the glare for the visual comfort of employees stationed near windows.

Restriction of Inward Vision

Providing privacy has long been a basic function of window coverings. For windows placed so that inward vision must be continually restricted, full, stationary curtains may be selected. Most coverings will reduce the view inward during daylight hours, but a lining or separate curtains may be needed to ensure privacy at night when artificial illuminants brighten the interior. Moreover, when a window faces a private outdoor area, some covering may be considered to relieve any sense of being open to observation.

Modification of Outward Vision

A covering with the appropriate degree of openness can modify an exterior view. As the size of the yarns and the compactness of construction increase, outward vision is decreased. In some settings, complete blockage of an unsightly view may be required; this can be accomplished by combining relatively heavy closed fabrics with opaque linings in stationary mountings.

Reduction of Interior Noise

Three types of sounds may be heard within interiors. **Airborne sounds** radiate directly into the air from people talking and typing, photocopiers and printers producing copies, telephones ringing, video machines, radios, and the like. **Surface sounds** are produced as people traverse across the floor or push and pull items along it. **Impact or structurally borne sounds** result from impacts on a structural surface that cause it to vibrate, for instance, walking, jumping, dancing, bouncing balls, knocking on doors, and hammering nails. Of course, several activities, such as walking and vacuuming, create more than one type of sound. Also, most sounds can be transmitted to areas well beyond their origin. From the exterior come sounds from lawn mowers, cars, trucks, buses, airplanes, and the neighbor's dog.

Sounds that we want to hear can be entertaining and enlightening; but if we don't want to hear the sounds, they become noise, which can be annoying and disruptive. Thus, residential and commercial consumers often seek ways to control sounds and prevent them from becoming unwanted noise.

Figure 15.5 illustrates how interior sound can be prolonged and magnified as it is reflected from the floor to the ceiling and from a bare wall to a bare window. Ceiling materials and soft floor coverings will absorb sound that is traveling vertically; window and wall coverings can be installed to absorb sound that is traveling horizontally. (The sound absorption qualities of wall coverings are discussed in Chapter 19.)

The graph in Figure 15.6 shows that the sound absorption quality of drapery fabric decreases as fabric openness increases. The fabrics were tested with 100 per-

Figure 15.5 Interior sound travel.
Courtesy of PPG Industries, Inc., 1978.

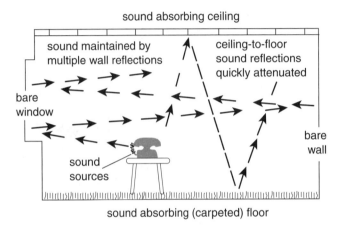

Figure 15.6 Graph of noise reduction coefficient versus fabric openness factor.
Courtesy of PPG Industries, Inc., 1978.

cent fullness. The absorption results are reported numerically in terms of **noise reduction coefficients (NRC)**, with higher values indicating greater absorption.

In multibed hospital rooms, fabric partitions are hung primarily to provide privacy; in large, open interiors they are used principally for decoration and to divide space. However, these interior partitions will also lessen horizontally reflected sound if they are constructed of closed, compactly constructed fabrics.

Conservation of Energy

Along with concern for the depletion of energy sources, especially the limited supply of fossil fuels, the pressures of rising heating and cooling costs have impelled consumers and manufacturers to search for ways to reduce energy consumption. Recently, consumer interest and research projects have focused on the role window treatments and other interior textile products can play in this conservation effort. Producers of window coverings and components, research personnel employed by government agencies and universities, and members of trade associations have sought to identify the styles of window treatments and the fabric-related variables that can contribute to the efficient maintenance of interior temperatures.

The thermal performance criteria for window treatments change as the seasons change. In winter, insulation is necessary to reduce heat loss, and in summer rejection of radiant energy is necessary to reduce heat gain. Reviewing the mechanisms by which heat is lost and gained is good preparation for making the appropriate selections of window treatments and components.

Air movement, including wind and forced circulation, causes heat transfer by **convection**. As wind circulates against exterior surfaces, it will convect heat away; the loss will be more pronounced with higher air speeds and greater differences between inside and outside temperatures. (Convection is the mechanism that causes a bridge surface to freeze before the rest of the road's surface does.) In an interior, warm air may be drawn between the window coverings and the window glass, where it is cooled, becomes heavier, and flows under the lower edges of free-hanging coverings and back into the room. Air movement is also responsible for drafts, the infiltration of cold air through structural openings such as cracks between window and wall frames and wall joints.

Conduction is the movement of thermal energy through solids, liquids, and gases. Insulation resists thermal transfer and stems conduction. In residential and commercial structures, heat energy will be conducted through the walls, doors, floors, and roof areas as well as the windows. However, from 25 to 50 percent of the heat generated in residences may be lost through the windows alone.[1]

The extent to which windows and window treatments retard heat loss in the winter, and heat gain in the summer, can be measured and the results reported numerically in terms of U-values. **U-values** indicate how much heat actually does pass outward in winter and inward in summer. To become familiar with U-values, we can examine the values for various types of windows; these values are approximate and vary with construction, thickness of the glass, and the presence of tints or coatings. Single-pane window glass has a U-value of 1.13, double panes with ¼ inch of insulating air space between them have a U-value of 0.41, and triple panes with a total of ⅜ inch of insulating air space have a U-value of 0.35. A U-value of 1.13 BTU/ft²-hr-°F means that 1.13 British thermal units of heat pass through each square foot of window configuration every hour for each Fahrenheit degree of difference between inside and outside temperatures.

Because air is a poor heat conductor and a good heat insulator, window coverings should be installed to provide a tight enclosure that will entrap dead air between the fabric and the glass, similar to the enclosure between the panes in double- and triple-pane windows. The dead air will retard conduction, and the sealed covering also helps to prevent warm air from being drawn against the window. The installation of a free-hanging, traversing drapery treatment has been found to be minimally effective; it only reduced the winter U-value of a single-pane window from 1.13 to 1.06.[2] By contrast, the use of a tight-fitting closed drapery may reduce the value to 0.88.[3] Similarly, the use of a tight-fitting lining, sealed around the perimeter of the window, has been found to be more effective than a free-hanging lining. Furthermore, the thermal performance of drapery fabrics with different degrees of openness was found to be essentially equal when combined with the same sealed lining.[4]

Multilayered roller shades, many of which are not unlike the familiar mattress pad, can be used for their insulative value, especially in passive solar homes. Dead air is trapped between the layers; again, thermal efficiency improves when the edges of the shade are sealed to restrict air flow.[5]

With Roman shades constructed of woven wood, an increase in the quantity of complex yarns was found to increase the insulative quality.[6] Conventional venetian blinds and vertical blinds, especially those made of metal, are comparatively ineffective in reducing winter heat loss, because of the small gaps remaining between the closed louvers and the high conductivity of the metal components. On the other hand, their louvers can easily be angled to let in sunlight and increase heat gain during daylight hours in winter.

Interior shutters without louvers can contribute significantly to energy conservation, provided they fit tightly and are used consistently. Similarly, covering a window with an insulating panel of such material as expanded polystyrene, expanded polyurethane, cork, or plywood will effectively reduce winter heat loss. A 1-inch-thick panel of expanded polyurethane over a single pane of glass was found to produce a U-value of 0.14.[7]

To minimize air infiltration, weather stripping and caulking compounds should be used to seal any cracks around structural joints. For added protection, consumers and designers may use drapery panels of extra length and width. In these treatments, the draperies extend over the wall joints on each side of the windows, and the panels stack on the floor, acting as infiltration barriers.

Radiation is the transfer of heat in the form of waves or rays. Waves radiating against the exterior surfaces of windows include those emanating directly from the sun, as well as those reflected from the sky and such other surfaces as the façades of neighboring buildings, paved parking areas, streets, and sidewalks. As schematized in Figure 15.7, some of the incident waves are rejected, some absorbed, and some transmitted. Of the rays transmitted through the outdoor glass, various portions will be rejected, absorbed, and transmitted by the indoor glass. Finally, various portions of the rays transmitted through the indoor glass will be rejected, absorbed, and transmitted by the draperies.

Clearly, window treatments that can be opened and closed provide the flexibility needed to control seasonal solar heat gain. On sunny winter days, the coverings can be opened to increase the level of heat transmission; on sunny summer days, they can be closed to increase the level of heat rejection. Solar heat gain in the summer, of course, warms the interior and increases the air conditioning load.

Figure 15.7 Typical heat rejection pattern. *Courtesy of PPG Industries, Inc., 1978.*

The effectiveness of windows and window coverings in reducing the level of radiant energy transmitted into the interior can be measured and the results reported numerically in terms of the **shading coefficient (S/C)**. To calculate the S/C, the total amount of heat transmitted by a window and covering combination is divided by the total amount of heat transmitted by a single pane of clear ⅛-inch-thick glass. S/C values indicate how well a window and covering reduce heat gain, with lower values indicating more effective control; the actual amount of heat gain is reported in terms of the U-value.

A single pane of clear ¼-inch-thick glass has an S/C of 0.93; adding a tint reduces the value to 0.67, and using double panes and a reflective finish further lowers the value, to 0.30 (Table 15.1). While drapery treatments produce insignificant reductions in the S/C value of insulated reflective glass, they produce significant decreases in the values of clear and tinted vision glass. Closed, light-colored draperies produce the most significant reductions in these cases.

Conventional venetian blinds and vertical blinds are relatively ineffective in retarding winter heat loss, but they are quite effective in reducing summer heat gain. When combined with a single pane of clear glass, light-colored venetian blinds reduce the S/C to 0.55 and white vertical blinds reduce the value to 0.29.[8] Various types and colors of roller shades are also highly effective in reducing heat gain. As shown in Table 15.2, a white opaque shade reflects up to 80 percent of the incident solar energy. In contrast, a dark opaque shade absorbs some 88

Table 15.1 Shading Coefficients for Glass with Draperies

Type of Glass (shading coefficient glass only)	ᴵD	ᴵM	ᴵL	ᴵᴵD	ᴵᴵM	ᴵᴵL	ᴵᴵᴵD	ᴵᴵᴵM	ᴵᴵᴵL
¼" clear (0.93)	0.72	0.68	0.65	0.68	0.61	0.56	0.64	0.54	0.46
¼" tinted (0.67)	0.53	0.50	0.49	0.51	0.47	0.44	0.48	0.44	0.39
Insulating glass (0.54) ¼" clear + ¼" tinted	0.43	0.42	0.41	0.42	0.39	0.36	0.40	0.35	0.33
Insulating glass, Reflective coated (0.30)	0.28	0.27	0.27	0.27	0.26	0.26	0.27	0.26	0.25

Classification of Fabrics: I—open weave; II—semi-open weave; III—closed weave; D—dark color; M—medium color, and L—light color.

Courtesy of PPG Industries, Inc., 1978.

Table 15.2 Percentage Light Transmission, Reflection, and Absorption by Various Roller Shades

Shade Characteristics	Light Transmitted	Light Reflected	Light Absorbed
Light color, translucent	25	60	15
White opaque	0	80	20
Dark opaque	0	12	88

Source: S. Robert Hastings and Richard W. Crenshaw, "Window Design Strategies to Conserve Energy," *National Bureau of Standards Building Science Series 104*, U.S. Department of Commerce, June 1977, 403.

percent of the energy. In turn, this absorbed heat will be transferred into the room, a negative effect in the summer but a positive effect in the winter.

Exterior shutters and awnings can be highly effective in reducing solar heat gain. Light colors should be used for both types of coverings for high reflection and low absorption of radiant energy. Heat absorbed by these coverings can be transferred through the windows to the interior; for maximum effectiveness, awnings must be correctly angled over the windows to reflect all direct rays.

Protection of Other Interior Furnishings

The radiant energy of the sun not only warms and brightens interior space; it also weakens textile fibers and, as discussed earlier in this chapter, changes their apparent and actual color characteristics. To protect other textile and nontextile furnishings, window coverings can be drawn to minimize light transmission. This will, of course, subject the window coverings themselves to higher levels of radiant energy. The replacement cost of the window treatments, however, is normally less than that of other furnishings, and relatively inexpensive curtains and linings can be used to protect more expensive overdraperies.

Cost Factors

Various cost-related factors must be considered prior to final selection of window treatments. Together with the initial costs of the materials, labor, and accessories required, residential and commercial consumers should consider financial variables related to replacement and maintenance.

Initial Costs

The initial cost of a window treatment is not limited to the cost of the outercovering; it also includes the cost of any linings, curtains, shades, and shutters to be used. The choice of a relatively narrow fabric with a comparatively high price per yard, elaborate styling, and fuller panels will escalate the materials cost. The cost is higher still when solution-dyed fibers and such treatments as flame-resistant finishes and reflective coatings are specified. Custom projects involve separate charges for consultations with the designer and for measuring, cutting, sewing, trimming, and installing. Whether consumers choose readymade coverings, elect to have a custom-designed treatment, or plan to construct the treatment themselves, added costs include those for the rods and any tie-backs, hold-backs, or overhead treatments.

Residential and commercial consumers should ascertain whether their new treatment qualifies for an energy tax credit. This credit is offered by Congress as an incentive to consumers to reduce their energy consumption voluntarily by selecting materials known to be effective insulators. They may also balance the initial cost of the treatment against any energy savings that will be realized during the use-life of the treatment. Regardless of potential savings, however, the total cost and terms of payment—whether due in full on delivery or made in installments with interest charges—must coincide with the ability of the purchaser to pay. Financial institutions may permit the cost of some window treatment projects to be included in long-term mortgage obligations.

Replacement Costs

When selecting window treatment styles and coverings, consumers should consider the initial cost in relationship to the expected use-life. Fiber and fabric variables, styling features, exposure conditions, and care affect the use-life of textile coverings; the average use-life generally ranges from three to five years. Because linings can extend the service-life of drapery fabrics for a year or more, consumers may determine that linings are especially cost-effective. Solution dyeing, although a comparatively expensive color application technique, should be used whenever coverings composed of acetate are installed in areas having high concentrations of atmospheric pollutants. This will avoid the expense and disruption associated with the premature replacement of a covering that has changed hue.

Unless new hardware is required, replacement costs are normally limited to the cost of the new materials and the labor costs incurred for construction and installation. In some cases, charges may also be assessed for removing the existing treatments.

Maintenance Costs

Several variables related to fabric composition, such as the type of fiber used, the dimensional stability of the fabric, the use of durable press resins, the stability of the colorants, and the structural characteristics of the coverings, are the main determinants of what cleaning method should be used to maintain a window treatment. By considering these variables, consumers can determine whether laundering or dry cleaning is required; if the more expensive dry cleaning is called for, consumers may elect to reconsider their covering options.

Elaborate styling and multiple components, such as shades, curtains, draperies, and swags, will increase maintenance cost, since charges are incurred for the commercial laundering or dry cleaning of each covering and component. Wide, long panels are also more expensive to clean than are narrow, short panels. Separate charges may be assessed for removing and transporting the coverings to the cleaning plant, for ironing and reforming the folds, and for returning and rehanging the treatment. Of course, the anticipated frequency of cleaning—determined to a large extent by the appearance required by the owner—must be considered when estimating long-term maintenance costs.

Performance Standards

Interior designers, architects, and specifiers must ascertain whether an authority with jurisdiction over materials used in a particular facility has established any codes or mandates governing the performance characteristics of window coverings installed there. Today, various city, state, and federal agencies have established flame resistance requirements for the coverings to be installed in several types of commercial interiors. In many cases, the coverings must be tested in accordance with the procedures outlined in NFPA 701 and comply with the flame resistance requirements listed in the standard. The test methods and performance criteria in NFPA 701 are explained in Chapter 11.

Draperies installed in commercial airliners must comply with FAA Paragraph 25.853 (b). The scope, test specimens and procedures, and performance requirements of this standard were explained in Chapter 11. Currently, no federal flammability mandates exist for textile and non-textile window coverings intended for installation in residential interiors.

Summary

To ensure reliable judgments and sound decisions in selecting window treatment styles and coverings, residential and commercial consumers should consider several factors, some of which may limit their choices. They should examine the fenestration to determine which styles can be considered and which would be unworkable. They should consider the immediate and long-term effects of various color-related variables to verify that the planned appearance will be realized and retained. They should determine the need for such functional qualities as glare reduction, energy conservation, privacy enhancement, and view modification. They should also investigate the properties of the fibers and yarns used, the characteristics of the fabric structure, and the effects of the various finishing agents and processes employed. Then they should limit their choices to styles and coverings that are capable of providing the necessary or desirable characteristics.

Professionals must ascertain whether the coverings they select for a commercial interior have to comply with any performance standards and/or codes. All consumers must have sufficient funds to cover the cost of the project; for some projects, the initial cost may be partially offset by energy tax credits and energy savings.

Key Terms

actual color
airborne sounds
apparent color
conduction
convection
fabric openness
fenestration

impact or structurally borne sounds
noise reduction coefficient (NRC)
radiation
shading coefficient (S/C)
surface sounds
U-values

Review Questions

1. Identify complex yarns that give maximum visual and textural interest to window coverings. Why can these yarns be used in window coverings but not in upholstery fabric?

2. Cite examples of how a window treatment can be effectively used in meeting challenges presented by the fenestration in an interior.

3. Identify window styles that severely limit treatment choices.

4. Differentiate between apparent and actual color.

5. Why is it critically important to examine colored textiles in the end-use setting?

6. Discuss the factors that affect the level of light transmission.

7. Explain the roles of yarn size and compactness of construction in determining fabric openness.

8. Discuss factors affecting the apparent color and those that affect the actual color.

9. Explain how the level of fabric openness can be used to help control brightness. Are there other factors to consider?

10. Identify all variables affecting the cost of window treatments.

Notes

1. G. Cukierski and Dr. D. R. Buchanan, "Effectiveness of Conventional, Modified, and New Interior Window Treatments in Reducing Heat Transfer Losses," *Proceedings of the Fourth National Passive Solar Conference*, American Section of the International Solar Energy Society, University of Delaware, Newark, DE, 402–406.

2. Rollin C. Dix and Lawan Zalman, "Window Shades and Energy Conservation," Mechanics, Mechanical and Aerospace Engineering Department, Illinois Institute of Technology, Chicago, Illinois, December 1974, 13; quoted in S. R. Hastings and R. W. Crenshaw, "Window Design Strategies to Conserve Energy," *NBS Building Science Series 104*, Washington, DC, June 1977, 5–7.

3. ASHRAE, *ASHRAE Handbook of Fundamentals*, American Society of Heating, Refrigeration, and Air Conditioning Engineers, New York, 1974, 395.

4. Cukierski, op. cit., 404.

5. Ibid.

6. Ibid., 403.

7. ASHRAE, op cit., 361.

8. Ibid., 402.

16

Window Treatment Styles

Curtain and Drapery Treatments
  Curtain Treatments
  Drapery Treatments
  Headings
  Trimmings
  Overhead and Side Treatments
  Hardware
  Calculating Yardage Required

Blinds and Shades
  Austrian Shades
  Balloon Shades

Accordion-pleated Shades
Honeycomb Cellular Shades
Cascade Loop Shades
Roman Shades
Roller Shades
Venetian Blinds
Vertical Blinds

Awnings and Shutters
  Awnings
  Shutters

Window treatments include curtains, draperies, blinds, shades, shutters, and awnings, used alone or in combinations. These treatments are decorated with such items as rods, cornices, hold-backs, tie-backs, and valances. The styling features of window treatments call for special consideration by consumers and professionals. Some need a highly drapable textile fabric; some require a stiffened fabric; and some, especially those having multiple layers, may demand an unaffordable amount of yardage. Attention should also be given to whether there is a need for hand drawing, the type and number of rods a particular treatment requires, and the like.

Window treatment styles do not change, but their popularity does. For example, priscilla curtains, illustrated in Figure 16.1e, are always distinguished by ruffles and criss-crossed panels, but they may not be fashionable at all times. With each subsequent adoption, however, designers and consumers select from a wide variety of contemporary fabrics, colors, motifs, and components to execute it; thus, identical styles may have dramatically different appearances.

Curtain and Drapery Treatments

In general, **curtains** describes relatively sheer, lightweight coverings that are hung without linings, while **draperies** describes heavy, often opaque, and highly patterned coverings usually hung with linings. The term **casement** may be assigned to numerous fabrics of medium weight and some degree of transparency.

Figure 16.1 Typical curtain styles.

a) stationary casement panels

b) two-way draw curtains

c) sash curtain

d) ruffled, tie-backs

e) priscilla curtains

f) single-tier café curtains

g) multi-tier café curtains

h) cottage or Cape Cod curtains

Casement fabrics may be hung as unlined curtains or as lined draperies. Curtains and draperies are normally textile fabrics, but some novel treatments involve such components as strands of glass and polymer film fabrics.

The coverings in some curtain and drapery treatments are hung as stationary, nontraversing panels. Other coverings are hung as traversing panels that can be opened and closed as desired. Additional styling features may be added with the judicious use of decorative headings and side treatments, trimmings, and hardware fixtures.

Curtain Treatments

Figure 16.1 shows some typical styles of curtain treatments. **Stationary casement panels** (Figure 16.1a) are approximately two and one-half times wider than the window. The panels are supported by a conventional, nontraversing curtain rod inserted through a **casing** sewn into the upper edge of the fabric. The casing may be plain or constructed with a **heading** (see Figures 16.5a and b, respectively).

Some contemporary treatments have fabric panels with limited fullness to accentuate the window and highlight the rod. Frequently, the panel headings have tabs that are formed into two- or three-inch-long loops (Figure 16.5d), knots, or bows for great visual interest. The top may have deep scallops, resulting in a drooping but dramatic effect (Figure 16.2), or it may have large buttonholes for a more tailored look. While the rods are nontraversing, a yard-long wooden rod, known as a **curtain tender**, may be used to open and close the panels.

A traditional panel treatment involves the use of tambour-embroidered curtain panels. The rich embroidery on such transparent fabrics as organdy (Figure 17.18, p. 289), bobbinet (Figure 17.28, p. 293), and voile is shown best by having limited fullness.

A heading, such as pinched pleats, and a traversing rod convert stationary panels into **draw curtains** (Figure 16.1b). Panels anchored at their upper and lower edges are known as **sash curtains**, and are typically used on French doors (Figure 16.1c). As the width of the fabric is increased with respect to the width of the window, the shirred effect becomes more pronounced, increasing privacy and reducing the degree of light transmission.

Whereas the panels in **ruffled, tie-back curtains** (Figure 16.1d) do not cross at their upper edges, the panels in **priscilla treatments** overlap; priscilla treatments

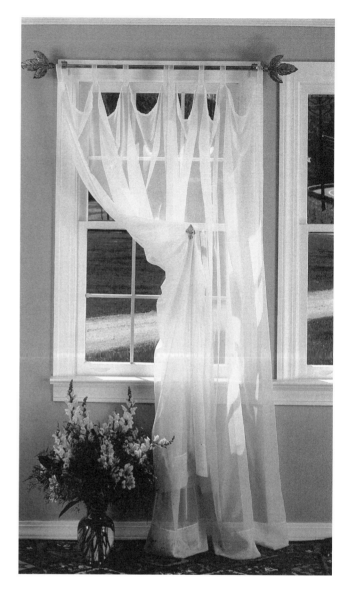

Figure 16.2 Tab-top fabric panels with deep scallops create a dramatic, droopy appearance.
Courtesy of Country Curtains, Country Lion Agency.

always involve ruffled tie-backs, as well (Figure 16.1e). Ruffled curtain treatments must be carefully chosen to avoid an overdressed appearance. The use of such crisp, transparent fabrics as organdy, voile, and dotted swiss (described in Chapter 17) can help to minimize the visual weight of these treatments, as well as provide the body required for attractive ruffles.

Café curtains (Figure 16.1f and g) may be used alone or in combination with draperies. They are frequently constructed with scalloped headings and hung by rings looped over a rod. **Multi-tier café curtains**, with each tier normally overlapping the lower tier by about three inches, may be hung by rings or by rods run through fabric casings. When **single-tier café curtains** are combined with ruffled, tied-back panels, the treatment is labeled a **cottage or Cape Cod curtain** style (Figure 16.1h).

Drapery Treatments

Typical drapery treatments are illustrated in Figure 16.3. **One-way draw draperies** are drawn in one direction, stacking on one side of the window; **two-way draperies** are drawn to stack on both sides.

Cords, chains, medallions, and the like secure the panels in **tied-back** and **held-back** styles, but the panels may be released, if desired. **Pinned-up** styles are held by two-piece, stylized magnets or by decorative pins that function like large tie-tacks. These allow the designer or consumer to be more creative with such things as asymmetrical draping as the pins or magnets are not anchored to the wall or window frame (Figure 16.4). **Pouf or bishop's sleeve treatments** (Figure 16.3e) have tiers of bouffant or billowed-out areas created by periodically gathering the fabric panels.

When draperies are combined with sheer curtains, they are called **overdraperies**, and the curtains are called **sheers** or **glass curtains**. Here, the term "glass" indicates that the curtains hang next to the window glass; it is not describing the use of glass fiber. Combining draperies and curtains increases the cost of a window treatment, but it may also improve interior insulation and acoustics.

Figure 16.3 Typical drapery styles.

a) one-way draw

b) two-way draw

c) held-back

d) tied-back

e) pouf treatment

Figure 16.4 Pin-ups used to create asymmetrical draping. *Courtesy of Country Curtains, Country Lion Agency.*

Headings

Headings appear at the top of curtain and drapery panels. These treatments finish the upper edge and distribute fullness evenly across the finished width. Figure 16.5 illustrates various styles of headings. Headings may be hand measured and sewn or produced with commercial tape. Pleats produced with tape are slightly rounded instead of sharply creased, but the hooks can be removed for cleaning.

Sewn headings, in contrast to those formed with tape, should be interfaced with a fabric such as buckram or crinoline. These plain-woven fabrics are stiffened with sizing, starch, or resin and can provide support for the heading treatment. The stability of the stiffening agent to cleaning agents should be ascertained prior to use.

Trimmings

Curtain and drapery treatments may be enriched by the use of ornamental **trimmings**, such as cord, tasseled or looped fringe, gimp, piping, rickrack, lace, galloons (narrow lengths of braid, embroidered fabric, or lace), or ribbon. Some trimmings may be sewn directly to the covering fabric, while others may be used as tie-backs.

Overhead and Side Treatments

Overhead treatments cover and conceal panel headings and hardware and enrich window treatments. Valances and swags are overhead treatments executed in fabric and are generally used in combination with such side treatments as cascades and jabots; other overhead treatments employ wood or metal.

In effect, **valances** are short draperies and may have any of the headings shown in Figure 16.5. Relatively simple valances may have lower edges that are pointed, curved, or crescent shaped, or finished with trimming or a simple, straight hem. Those in sheer fabric may have the added feature of a French tuck hem. More elaborate valance treatments include Austrian, tapered, puffed, balloon, or festoon styling, some of which are illustrated in Figure 16.6.

Unlike the structured styling of valances, **swags** are softly draping lengths of fabrics. As shown in Figure 16.7a, a swag on a continental rod is used to frame the window in an inverted V-shape. A scarf with fringe on one edge falls in a "fishtail" swag on either side of the window in Figure 16.7b. The fishtail effect occurs when the vertically draping folds are deep and reverse, exposing the inside of the fabric; thus, the appearance of the "wrong" side of the fabric or of the swag lining must be considered.

Cascades are side treatments that are gathered and designed to fall in folds of graduated length; they are used with or without a valance. **Jabots** are pleated side treatments. Their lower edges may be level, or they may be angled as in Figure 16.8. Swags are normally designed to hang behind any valance or festoon, while jabots may be hung in front of or behind the ends of an overhead treatment. However they are hung, the length of the side treatments should be at least one-third that of the window treatment.

Cornices, cantonnières, and lambrequins are rigid overhead treatments constructed of wood or metal. They can be covered with the panel fabric or coordinating fabric, or painted, stained, or left as natural wood. A **cornice** (Figure 16.9a) is mounted to cover the drapery heading

a) plain casing

b) casing with heading

c) scalloped

d) looped

e) clipped

f) shirred

g) sewn pinch pleats

h) pleater tape pinch pleats

i) French pleats

j) box pleats

k) barrel or cartridge pleats

Figure 16.5 Various styles of curtain and drapery headings. *Courtesy of Reader's Digest Association, Inc.*

and hardware. Typically, cornices project 4 to 6 inches from the wall and cover one-seventh of the treatment length. Adding straight sides and shaped front panels to a cornice board converts it into a **lambrequin** (Figure 16.9b). A **cantonnière** fits flush to the wall and has a shaped overhead panel and sides that extend to the floor. While the last-named treatment is frequently fabric covered, a contemporary flair is to have it stenciled to coordinate with the fabric panels, blinds, or shades used (Figure 16.9c).

Hardware

The assortment of hardware used with curtains and draperies includes rods, mounting screws and bolts, batons, curtain tenders, and fabric weights. **Batons** and curtain tenders are used manually to open and close the pan-

els; **fabric weights**, placed in the lower hem area, improve the draping quality of the fabric. The assortment also includes such decorative accessories as café rings and clips, chains, medallions, pin-ups, and two-piece magnets. Medallions are permanently attached to the window frame for use as hold-backs, as shown in Figure 16.3c, while pin-ups and magnets are used selectively to hold the panels in distinctive folds or configurations (see Figure 16.2).

Conventional Rods

A variety of conventional, nondecorative curtain and drapery rods is available today. Conventional rods are comparatively inexpensive, but consumers and interior designers should consider the aesthetic impact of these rods when not covered by the headings. Conventional traversing rods are usually equipped with a system of cords to control opening and closing. A note of safety

a) Valence on a continental rod.

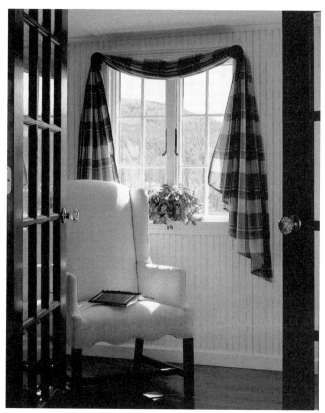

b) festoon

Figure 16.6   Elaborate valance treatments.
Courtesy of Country Curtains, Country Lion Agency.

should be added. When small children or companion animals are in the home, window coverings with closed cord systems should be avoided, or a cord cleat should be mounted on the wall. Winding the cords on these holders keeps them safely out of reach.

A relatively new style of conventional rods has a height of 2½ inches or 4½ inches. The added depth creates the look of a valence when casings, with or without headings (Figures 16.7a), are shirred over the rod.

Decorative Rods

Decorative curtain and drapery rods are made of wood, metal, or plastic finished to resemble, for example, brass, pewter, gold, or natural wood. Coordinating rings secure the panels. In many cases, matching tieback chains, hold-back medallions, and various styles of finials (the decorative pieces attached to the ends of rods) are available. Decorative traversing rods may be controlled electrically, by a system of cords, or by batons.

Nontraversing decorative rods are especially useful for supporting stationary panels. These panels are hung from wooden or metallic rings or fabric tabs looped over the rod. If the panels are to be opened and closed, they should be shifted by a baton or curtain tender and not by pulling on the side hems, which could deform the edge and lead to excessive soiling and wear.

Calculating Yardage Required

The successful execution of a window treatment depends on the accuracy of the measurements taken when determining the amount of fabric required for the project. As is true for any project involving colored textiles, the amount of fabric initially ordered must be sufficient to complete the treatment. As noted in Chapter 8, separate orders generally result in the delivery of fabrics with slightly differing color characteristics; even slight differences may prove to be unacceptable.

a) Austrian

b) fringed scarf fishtail swag

Figure 16.7 Swag overhead treatments.
Courtesy of Country Curtains, Country Lion Agency.

The following sections summarize the variables that generally should be considered when measuring for curtains and draperies. Other publications, readily available from Cooperative Extension Services, product manufacturers, and interior furnishings retailers, may be reviewed for instructions pertinent to specific styles and various overhead treatments. Usually, these materials also include detailed sewing and hanging instructions.

Determining Rod Length and Placement

A yardstick or steel tape should be used for taking all measurements, beginning with those needed to deter-

mine the rod length and placement. Before determining the length of the rod, a decision must be made concerning the extent of the outward view desired when the panels are open. For maximum outward vision, it should be possible to stack the panels back beyond the window glass. The values listed in Table 16.1 will help to determine the length of the rod needed when full clearance of the glass is preferred. The distances can be adjusted when the panels must camouflage a structural defect and when a portion of the glass is to be used for **stackback space**.

Rods should be mounted so that the drapery headings will not be visible to the outside. Headings are normally 4

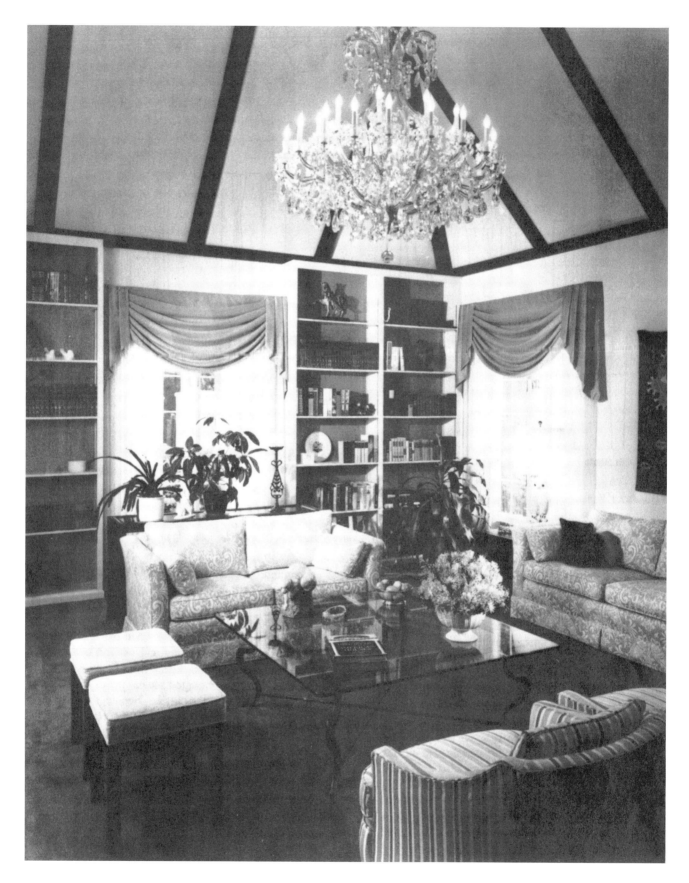

Figure 16.8 Jabot side treatment with festoon.
Courtesy of Kirsch, a division of Cooper Industries, Inc.

a) fabric-covered cornice

b) lambrequin

c) fabric-covered cantonnière

Figure 16.9 Rigid overhead and side treatments.

Table 16.1 Rod Lengths Needed for Various Widths of Windows and Stackback Spaces

If the Glass is	The stackback* should be	Your rod length and drapery coverage should be (add for overlaps and returns)
38″	26″	64″
44″	28″	72″
50″	30″	80″
56″	32″	88″
62″	34″	96″
68″	36″	104″
75″	37″	112″
81″	39″	120″
87″	41″	128″
94″	42″	136″
100″	44″	144″
106″	46″	152″
112″	48″	160″
119″	49″	168″
125″	51″	176″
131″	53″	184″
137″	55″	192″
144″	56″	200″
150″	58″	208″
156″	60″	216″
162″	62″	224″
169″	63″	232″
175″	65″	240″
181″	67″	248″
187″	69″	256″

Figures are based on average pleating and medium weight fabric. For extra bulky fabrics, add to stackback to compensate for the additional space they require.

*For one-way draws, deduct 7″ from stackback.

Courtesy of Kirsch, Division of Cooper Industries, Inc.

inches in height; thus, the rod should normally be located 4 inches above the top edge of the window glass. Again, if structural defects, such as unequal frame heights, must be camouflaged, the location of the rod can be adjusted. The rod should be installed prior to taking the measurements needed for determining the yardage required.

Determining Panel Length

Lengthwise measurements are taken from the top of conventional rods and from the bottom of the rings on decorative rods. The panels may extend to the window sill, to the apron (the horizontal board below the sill), or to the floor. One inch should be subtracted from the measurement taken to the floor to allow for clearance, especially when soft floor coverings are in place. For distinctive styling and reduced air infiltration, consumers and designers may elect to have the panels stack or mound on the floor, in which case extra yardage must be allowed. For the purpose of this discussion, assume the finished panel will be 85 inches in length.

If patterned fabrics are chosen, extra yardage must be added for matching repeats. The lengthwise measurement must be evenly divisible by the length of the repeat. Thus, assuming the length of the repeat is 18 inches, 5 inches must be added to the measured 85 inches so that it will be divisible by 18. Normally, a full repeat is placed at the lower hem of sill- and apron-length panels, and at the top hem of floor-length panels.

Yardage must now be added for the hem allowances. For unlined panels, a doubled, 4-inch top hem is planned, and for lined panels, 0.5 inch is allowed for top turnover. The lower hem allowance is generally 4 inches, but as a precaution against potential relaxation and residual shrinkage, this figure should be doubled. In the event that in-use shrinkage shortens the panels, the fabric needed for lengthening is readily available. The hem allowance must always be doubled when such fabrics as taffeta, faille, and bengaline are to be used. The numerous fibers in the crosswise ribs of these fabrics, especially if they are cotton or rayon, may swell during cleaning; this increase in the diameter of the ribs would draw up the warp yarns, causing lengthwise shrinkage. Whatever its fiber content, any fabric may exhibit from 1 to 3 percent residual shrinkage, even if it was preshrunk to encourage relaxation shrinkage.

The total cut length of the panel fabric may now be calculated as follows:

finished length of panel	85	inches
+ allowance for pattern matching	5	inches
+ allowance for top hem	0.5	inch
+ allowance for bottom hem	8	inches
= total cut length of panel	93.5	inches

For the lining fabric, no yardage is needed for pattern matching; the bottom hem is generally single and 2 inches deep, and the lower edge is 1 inch above the lower edge of the drapery panel. Again, an allowance may be made for potential in-use shrinkage. The total cut length of the lining fabric may now be calculated as follows:

finished length of panel	85	inches
− lining shorter than panel	1	inch
+ allowance for top hem	0.5	inch
+ allowance for bottom hem	2	inches
= total cut length of lining	86.5	inches

Determining Panel Width

Fabric panel is not synonymous with **fabric width**. A fabric panel (Figure 16.10) is formed by seaming a number of fabric widths and, if necessary, a partial width together. "Pleated panel coverage," "pleat coverage," and "coverage" are synonyms that refer to the horizontal distance covered by the pleated area of the panel. Coverage does not include the portion of the panel that covers the overlap at the center, or the portion that covers the return, the bracket extending perpendicularly from the wall at each end of the rod.

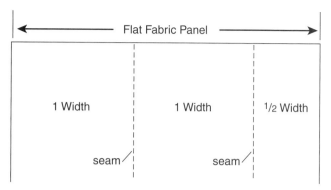

"Flat fabric" refers to the seamed panel before the pleats are put in.

Figure 16.10 Illustrations of terms that describe the measurements taken to determine panel width.
Courtesy of Kirsch, a division of Cooper Industries, Inc.

For the purposes of discussion, we will assume that the length of the installed rod is 56 inches. For a one-way draw treatment, the panel coverage would be 56 inches, with no allowance required for overlap. For a two-way draw treatment, the coverage for each panel would be 28 inches, and the allowance for overlap is normally 3.5 inches. Yardage must now be added for **fullness**, a requirement that generally doubles the yardage but may triple it when sheer fabrics are used. The allowance for the return is equal to the bracket projection distance, typically 3.5 inches. Each of the two side hems requires an allowance of 2 inches. Of this, 0.5 inch will be used as an allowance when seaming the lining, and 1.5 inches will be turned to show at the side of the lining. The total width of one flat, unhemmed panel for a two-way draw treatment may now be calculated as follows:

coverage	28	inches
+ allowance for fullness	28	inches
+ allowance for overlap	3.5	inches
+ allowance for return	3.5	inches
+ allowance for side hems	4	inches
= total width of one flat panel	67	inches

The values listed in Table 16.2 were calculated in this manner and can be used after coverage is determined. The table also contains guidelines for spacing pleats to control the fullness.

One inch must be allowed for seaming the sides of the lining to the drapery panel. The flat, unhemmed lining is thus cut 3 inches narrower than the flat, unhemmed drapery panel that will be turned 1.5 inches inward on each side.

Determining Yardage Total

If, for example, the width of the covering fabric is 45 inches, one full fabric width and one partial width would be seamed to produce the 67-inch-wide panel. Since a second panel is needed for the two-way draw treatment, we may at first assume four fabric widths are

Table 16.2 Fabric Panel Widths and Pleating Guidelines

Desired Pleated Panel Coverage	Flat Fabric Without Hems	Hemmed Flat Fabric	Number of 4″ Flat Spaces Between Pleats	Number of Pleats	Width of Fabric in Each Pleat
16″	43″	39″	4	5	3⅛″
20″	51″	47″	5	6	3¼″
24″	59″	55″	6	7	3⅜″
28″	67″	63″	7	8	3½″
32″	75″	71″	8	9	3½″
36″	83″	79″	9	10	3⁹⁄₁₆″
40″	91″	87″	10	11	3⅝″
44″	99″	95″	11	12	3⅝″
48″	107″	103″	12	13	3⅝″
52″	115″	111″	13	14	3⅝″
56″	123″	119″	14	15	3¾″
60″	131″	127″	15	16	3¾″
64″	139″	135″	16	17	3¾″
68″	147″	143″	17	18	3¾″
72″	155″	151″	18	19	3¾″
76″	163″	159″	19	20	3¾″
80″	171″	167″	20	21	3¾″
84″	179″	175″	21	22	3¾″
88″	187″	183″	22	23	3¾″
92″	195″	191″	23	24	3¾″
96″	203″	199″	24	25	3¾″
100″	211″	207″	25	26	3¾″
104″	219″	215″	26	27	3¾″
108″	227″	223″	27	28	3¾″
112″	235″	231″	28	29	3¾″
116″	243″	239″	29	30	3¾″
120″	251″	247″	30	31	3⅞″
124″	259″	254″	31	32	3⅞″
128″	267″	263″	32	33	3⅞″

Courtesy of Kirsch, Division of Cooper Industries, Inc.

required. In this particular case, half the divided fabric width could be used for each of the two panels and thus, only three fabric widths are required. Such an economical use of fabric is not always possible, especially when allowances must be made for matching crosswise repeats and for seam allowances, but we should be alert to the possibility. For some projects, especially those involving expensive fabric, it may even be desirable to slightly reduce the width of the fabric included in each pleat.

The total amount of fabric to be ordered can be determined by multiplying the total length of the un-hemmed panel by the number of fabric widths needed. The amount of lining fabric is calculated in the same manner.

Blinds and Shades

In contrast to curtains and draperies, which are drawn horizontally, almost all blinds and shades are drawn vertically. Some styles of blinds and shades are executed with textile fabric, others with metal or wood, and still others employ textile and nontextile components.

Austrian Shades

Austrian shades (Figure 16.11) are constructed of textile fabric that is vertically shirred to create lengthwise bands of horizontally draping folds. The level of transparency is determined by the compactness of construction of the fabric and the amount of fabric taken up in the gathering.

Figure 16.11 Austrian shade.

Balloon Shades

Balloon shades, like Austrian shades, are composed of textile fabric and are vertically drawn. Their name derives from the balloon-like puffs they form when raised. The fullness of the panels may be distributed by shirring the top casing over a rod or by using inverted pleats. In inverted-pleat styling (Figure 16.12), the panels are essentially flat until raised, a feature that makes possible full visual appreciation of the fabric.

Accordion-pleated Shades

Accordion-pleated shades are constructed of woven or knitted fabric that has been stiffened and set in a three-dimensional, folded configuration (Figure 16.13). As the shades are raised and lowered, the folds open and close, the same way the folds in an accordion's bellows open and close when the instrument is played. A 24-inch-long

Figure 16.12 Balloon shade.
Courtesy of Kosa House.

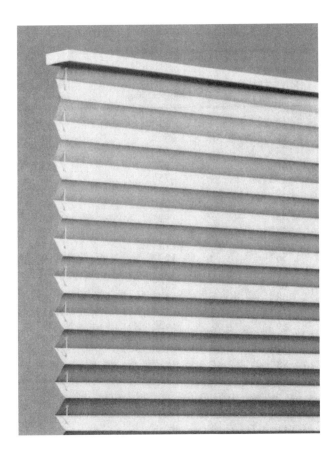

Figure 16.13 Accordion-pleated shade.
Courtesy of Kirsch, Cooper Industries, Inc.

shade takes up only 2¼ inches stackup space when raised, measuring from the top of the headrail to the bottom of the bottom rail; a 96-inch-long shade takes up 3¾ inches. The textural characteristics of these shades vary readily with the style of yarn used; the compactness of construction and the selective application of back coatings control their transparency. Metallic coatings may be used for insulation, and also for static reduction, which reduces the attraction for dust. These window coverings are frequently used in commercial interiors, generally in combination with drapery panels.

Honeycomb Cellular Shades

A relatively new type of accordion-pleated shade is the **honeycomb or cellular shade** (Figure 16.14a). In these coverings, spunbonded polyester fabrics are permanently pleated and paired to create a single or double-cell structure (Figure 16.14b) with an insulating layer of air that significantly reduces heat transfer. The fabric facing outward is always white to provide high heat reflection and

a) Duette™ honeycomb-pleated shade.

b) Single and double-cell structures.

Figure 16.14 Honeycomb cellular shades.
(16.14a) Courtesy of Kirsch, a division of Cooper Industries, Inc. Duette™ is a trademark of Hunter-Douglas.
(16.14b) Courtesy of Country Curtains, Country Lion Agency.

present a uniform exterior appearance. Because the pleats are smaller than those in conventional accordion-pleated shades, a 24-inch-long honeycomb shade requires only 2 inches of stackup space; a 96-inch-long shade requires only 3⅛ inches. With these shades, hardware may be chosen to facilitate lowering the shade from the top or raising it from the bottom; the shades can also be positioned anywhere within the window opening.

Cascade Loop Shades

A **cascade loop shade** is shown in Figure 16.15. Horizontal tucks in the fabric panel add visual interest; soft loops, often called architectural folds, form when the shade is raised.

Roman Shades

Roman shades hang flat at the window until raised; then, horizontal pleats form. These window coverings may be made exclusively of textile fabric, but frequently they are constructed of woven wood, a combination of wooden slats and textile yarns. The yarns used may vary in color, luster, size, and complexity. To permit the necessary folding, the wooden slats always lie across the covering. Fabric linings or coatings are generally necessary for full privacy, especially at night.

Some Roman shades are hand woven, from grasses, cane, or wheat straws crosswise and textile yarns length-

wise. These shades are relatively transparent, but they nonetheless diminish the view into the interior and provide a natural look heightened by the irregularity of the materials and the hand weaving.

A variation of the conventional Roman shade styling is the use of two shades, normally constructed from textile fabric or cellular fabric. In these coverings, known as **athey shades**, one shade is lowered and one shade is raised for full closure.

Roller Shades

A **roller shade** may be plain or patterned, constructed of a textile fabric or a sheet of polymer film. It may mount at the bottom of the window and unroll upward or mount at the top of the window and unroll downward. Decorative hems and pulls, including rings, carved wood, molded plastic, and tassels, augment the visual interest of contemporary blinds.

Venetian Blinds

Venetian blinds are made up of horizontal slats or louvers laced together with textile cords. Traditionally, the slats have nearly always been of aluminum coated with cream-colored enamel. Today, wooden louvers, molded polymer slats, and fashion-colored aluminum slats, ranging in width from ⅝ inch to 1 inch to 2 inches, are also available. In recent years, residential and commercial consumers have increasingly shown a preference for the most narrow slats, known as "micro" or "mini" blinds. Increasingly, designers and consumers are customizing the blinds with a mixture of colors or with colored or striped cloth twill tapes.

A textile cord system or a wand facilitates tilting of the slats to produce the desired level and angle of light and the preferred extent of view inward and outward. The entire covering may also be stacked up at the upper portion of the window.

Vertical Blinds

In **vertical blinds**, which may also be referred to as vertical Venetian blinds, the louvers or vanes are suspended vertically from traversing or nontraversing rods. They may be rotated 180 degrees to balance privacy and inward light transmission. Traversing styles may have a one- or two-way draw.

Figure 16.15 Cascade loop shade.

The louvers or vanes used in vertical blinds may be as narrow as 2 inches or as wide as 6 inches. They may be constructed of vinyl, stable fabric, metal, wood, or woven wood. Fabric vanes may be inserted into ivory or white vinyl backings to give greater light blockage and present a uniform streetside appearance. The compactness of construction of woven and knotted structures has a direct effect on the degree of light transmitted when the blinds are closed.

Initially, vertical blinds were almost exclusively used in commercial interior applications. Today, they can also be found in residential interiors, especially in settings having a contemporary design concept.

Awnings and Shutters

Awnings and shutters may be constructed from rigid materials only or from a combination of rigid materials and drapable textile fabrics. These structures can be used as interior and exterior window treatments.

Awnings

Awnings are basically rigid structures that may be composed of metal or molded polymer sheeting or of textile fabric stretched and held over a rigid frame. Awnings are occasionally used for novel interior applications, but primarily as exterior window treatments. Outside windows, they reduce solar heat transmission and provide protection from weather elements.

Textile awning fabric may be used in outdoor applications other than window treatments, for instance, as screens for privacy, windbreaks, and canopies over patios, gazebos, and carports. For all outdoor applications, fabrics must be composed of fibers resistant to sunlight, mildew, insects, water, wind, and atmospheric contaminants. Acrylic, saran, and olefin fibers are often employed, generally solution dyed for superior colorfastness.

Shutters

Decorative, stationary **shutters** have long framed windows on the exterior of homes and other structures. These panels cannot be unfolded to cover the window glass. Today, folding shutters are increasingly being mounted to unfold over the glass, reducing solar heat gain in the summer and interior heat loss in the winter. This current application of shutters is a revival of the practice of using folding shutters on colonial homes for protection from the elements.

Shutters are usually constructed of pine or oak, which is stained or painted the desired color. Stiles are shifted vertically to open and close the crosswise louvers in each rectangular section, and hinges permit the units to be folded and unfolded to control inward and outward vision, the level of light transmission, and heat gain and loss.

Textile fabrics are sometimes used to soften the appearance of wooden shutters. Shirred fabric may be inserted in some sections, or used in lieu of the wooden louvers.

Summary

Window treatment styles range from the relatively simple, with a single component, to the extremely complex, involving multiple layers, an overhead treatment, and decorative accessories. Some treatments are executed with textiles, some with nontextiles, and some with a combination of components.

The style of window treatment and the components needed to execute it should be chosen with the priority aesthetic, functional, and cost selection variables in mind. When consumers examine these variables before committing themselves—making a purchase or signing a contractual agreement—they will make more informed decisions and be better able to select treatments and components that provide the appearance and functional features they need at a price they can afford.

Key Terms

accordion-pleated shade

athey shade

Austrian shade

awnings

balloon shade

batons

café curtains

cantonnière

cascade loop shade

cascades

casement

casing

cornice

cottage or Cape Cod curtains

curtain tender

curtains

draperies

draw curtains

fabric panel

fabric weights

fabric width

fullness

glass curtains

headings

held-back panels

honeycomb or cellular shade

jabots

lambrequin

multi-tier café curtains

one-way draw draperies

overdraperies

pinned-up panels

pouf or bishop's sleeve treatment

priscilla curtains

roller shade

Roman shade

ruffled, tie-back curtains

sash curtains

sheers

shutters

single-tier café curtains

stackback space

stationary casement panels

swags

tied-back panels

trimmings

two-way draperies

valances

Venetian blinds

vertical blinds

Review Questions

1. Explain what is meant by this statement: "Window treatment styles do not change, but their popularity does." Could the same be said for clothing styles?

2. What is meant by the terms "visual weight?" Why is this an important consideration when choosing ruffled curtain styles or using such fabrics as velvet in over-draperies?

3. Describe the fishtail effect seen with some swag overhead treatments.

4. Design a window treatment having multiple layers (e.g., overdraperies with separate lining and sheers, decorative rods and tie-backs, valance, etc.) Calculate the yardage required and its cost, together with the cost of the hardware. You may want to vary the styling features and fabrics used in two or three treatments and calculate the total cost of each.

5. What advantages are offered by honeycomb or cellular shades?

17

Window Coverings and Linings

Components Used in Curtains and Draperies
  Statistical Profile of Fiber Usage
  Fiber Labeling Laws
  Dominance of Spun Yarns
  *Nontextile Materials Used in Window
    Coverings*

Woven Curtain and Drapery Fabrics
  Fabrics with Simple Interlacings
  Fabrics with Decorative Interlacings
  Fabrics with Pile Interlacings
  Fabrics with Surface Embellishments
  Fabrics Distinguished by Color Styling

Knitted Window Covering Fabrics
  Raschel-Stitched Fabrics
  Fabrics Produced by Weft Insertion
  Stitch-knitted Casements

Knotted and Twisted Window Coverings

Coverings Formed from Fibrous Webs

Drapery Lining Materials
  Permanently Attached Lining Materials
  Separately Hung Lining Materials

With the increased use of such nontextile materials as wood, and with the expanded color styling of metal components, the variety of window covering structures offered to today's residential and commercial consumers has been greatly expanded. The major portion of the assortment, however, continues to be composed of textile fibers and yarns. Cotton and the noncellulosic fibers split the major portion of the market almost equally, with modest amounts of rayon and acetate also used. Both spun and filament yarns are available, ranging from fine, simple, single structures to coarse, complex, multi-unit structures.

Several techniques used to fabricate upholstery coverings are also used to fabricate textile window coverings. Because window coverings are normally subjected to less abrasion than upholstery coverings, however, additional techniques are available for fabricating a greater variety of window coverings. Some of these methods enable manufacturers to incorporate decorative surface features more economically; others facilitate the production of fabrics with maximum openness as well as high-dimensional stability; still others expedite production and thus reduce product cost.

Working together, fabric manufacturers and converters produce drapery fabrics with permanently attached linings. They also produce a vast amount of textile fabric for use in separately hung lining panels. Both types of material help to protect the decorative drapery panels from sunlight and degradation; some materials also help to reduce noise, heat transfer, and light transmission.

Components Used in Curtains and Draperies

Although their importance varies greatly, virtually all of the major groups of fibers are used in textile window coverings. Fortunately, mandatory rules require that information pertaining to fiber composition be available to prospective purchasers. These disclosures enable informed consumers and professionals to assess the properties of the fiber or fibers and select the fiber or blend that offers the best balance of features for their interior or exterior window treatments.

Statistical Profile of Fiber Usage

The data presented in Table 17.1 reveal the growing use of the noncellulosic fibers, as well as the extensive use of cotton fiber, in curtain and drapery fabrics. The cotton poundage listed in the table also includes the cotton fiber used in the production of drapery linings.

With 46 percent of the contemporary curtain and drapery market, cotton continues to hold the dominant position. At the same time, the usage of noncellulosic fibers in curtains and draperies rose from 104.2 million pounds (31 percent of the total market) in 1993 to 181 million pounds (45 percent of the total market) in 1997. Technological advances in fiber engineering and yarn processing and the increased use of polyester fibers to

Table 17.1 Fiber Usage in Curtains and Draperies (million pounds)

Year	Total Fiber	Manufactured Fibers[a]						Cotton	Wool
		Total	Cellulosic		Noncellulosic			
			Yarn	Staple	Yarn	Staple		
1993	341.6	154.0	14.0	35.8	32.5	71.7	187.6	b
1997	399.4	214.5	5.9	27.6	85.6	95.4	184.9	b

[a]Manufactured fiber end use is divided between cellulosic (rayon plus acetate fibers) and noncellulosic (nylon, polyester, acrylic, olefin, saran, spandex, and textile glass fiber). Yarn includes monofilaments, and olefin "yarn" also includes film fiber and spunbonded polypropylene. Staple includes tow and fiberfill.
[b]Little or none of the fiber is used.
Sources: Textile Economics Bureau, Inc., *Textile Organon*, Vol. 69, No. 10, October 1998, 176.

compensate for the poor resiliency of cellulosic fibers are largely responsible for the continued growth in usage of synthesized fibers.

Although the quantity of wool used in curtain and drapery fabrics is not sufficient to warrant listing in statistical reports, its use should be noted. Currently, a limited number of casement fabrics composed of wool are designed and produced for commercial applications, principally in order to capitalize on the inherent flame resistance of the fiber.

The quantity of glass fiber used in curtains and draperies has steadily declined, and usage data is no longer reported. Although glass fiber is noncombustible, it may cause skin irritation. It also has extremely low flex abrasion resistance and relatively high density.

Fiber Labeling Laws

Currently, two labeling laws include provisions that apply to textile fibers used in window covering fabrics. One mandate pertains to fiber composition; the other concerns the potential skin irritation that may result from glass fiber fibrillations.

Disclosure of Fiber Composition

The provisions of the **Textile Fiber Products Identification Act** apply to all curtain, casement, and drapery fabrics and the products made from them. All curtains, casements, and draperies, or any portions of these items that would otherwise be subject to the act, made principally of slats, rods, or strips composed of wood, metal, plastic, or leather, are excluded. Thus, the fiber composition of certain textile components, such as the yarns used in woven wood shades, is not required to be disclosed.

Cautionary Labeling with Glass Fiber Products

Recognizing the problem of **fibrillation** with higher denier glass fibers, the FTC issued a trade regulation rule that requires the use of special labeling with glass fiber window coverings. The provisions of the rule, which became effective on January 2, 1968, apply to glass fiber curtains, draperies, and fabrics. These products must carry a tag or label cautioning purchasers that skin irritation may result: (1) to the exposed skin of persons handling such glass fiber products; and (2) from body contact with clothing or other articles, such as bed sheets, which

have been washed (a) with such glass fiber products, or (b) in a container previously used for washing such glass fiber products unless the glass particles have been removed from such container by cleaning.

Dominance of Spun Yarns

The yarns used in curtains, draperies, and other window coverings are as varied as those used in upholstery fabric. Spun yarns dominate the market, but a number of filament structures are used in curtain fabrics.

The data listed in Table 17.1 reveal that some 77 percent of the fibers used in curtain and drapery fabrics have been spun into yarns. (Relatively few of the staple-length fibers included in the data are used directly in the production of stitch-bonded and spunlaced curtain fabrics.) Filaments are used most often in curtain fabrics as a result of the demand for sheer, yet strong and stable, panels.

Nontextile Materials Used in Window Coverings

The assortment of nontextile window coverings in earlier years was basically limited to structures composed of wood or metal. More recently, the assortment has been expanded to include structures composed of molded polymer compounds and natural grasses.

Metals and Polymer Materials

Formerly, only cream-colored, enamel-coated aluminum slats were used for Venetian blinds. The aluminum slats now come in a wide variety of fashion colors, which makes these blinds more appealing to designers and consumers. A contemporary flair has also been introduced to some of these blinds by constructing them of slats composed of molded polymer compounds.

Metal, glass, and plastic beads are occasionally strung into chains and hung vertically as stationary, panel-like treatments. Metals, generally aluminum, are also frequently used for exterior shutters, awnings, and canopies.

Polymer compounds, such as polyvinylchloride, are extruded as film sheeting for use in manufacturing conventional roller shades. In a contemporary application, the polymer films are pressed onto window panes to simulate frosted/etched glass and to increase privacy. Increasingly, these "window wall papers" and roller shades are printed to coordinate with textile window and wall coverings.

Woods

The slats of Roman shades, Venetian and vertical blinds, and shutters are frequently made of pine, but more expensive structures may be constructed of oak. The wood is first kiln dried to minimize the potential for cracking and splitting; it is then sanded and stained, or painted a fashion color.

Grasses

Although grasses are not used extensively in window coverings, they are hand woven into Roman shades. The variations in thickness and surface texture that grasses exhibit make for a contemporary covering with a natural look.

Woven Curtain and Drapery Fabrics

The aesthetic features of some textile window covering fabrics take precedence over their functional attributes; the converse is also sometimes true. In the production of most fabrics, however, manufacturers seek to strike a balance between appearance and function while also producing a stable structure. A wide variety of interlacing patterns is necessarily used in the production of curtain and drapery fabrics. Various surface embellishment techniques further expand the assortment.

Fabrics with Simple Interlacings

The basic interlacing patterns and their variations were explained in Chapter 6. This section describes and illustrates the several curtain and drapery fabrics constructed using these weaves. These fabrics are defined by such characteristics as yarn structure, interlacing pattern, color styling, finish, and hand. Shifts in fiber usage have diminished the value of fiber composition as a distinguishing characteristic for curtain and drapery fabrics, as is also true for upholstery fabrics.

Plain-woven Fabrics

The plain weave is used to produce several curtain and drapery fabrics that have distinct differences in their appearance features, tactile characteristics, and performance attributes. These variations derive from yarns that differ in size, design features, level of twist, or color styling; from different fabric counts; and from coloring methods and finishing procedures.

When composed of fine, combed cotton yarns, **batiste** has a soft hand, is translucent, and is normally solid colored. Resins and preshrinking treatments may be employed to introduce resiliency and dimensional stability to fabrics made of these natural fibers. Batiste that is woven of yarns composed of polyester has a crisp hand, is transparent, and is often white in color. Heat setting may be used to impart dimensional stability and resiliency to these fabrics. Batiste fabrics are effectively used in all styles of curtain treatments (Figure 16.1, p. 261) and in Austrian shades (Figure 16.11, p. 272). Polyester batiste is increasingly replacing cotton batiste in the production of tambour-embroidered curtain panels (Figure 17.18).

Calico, formerly made exclusively from cotton fiber, is now generally composed of cotton and polyester for improved resiliency and dimensional stability. The fabric has a balanced fabric count (approximately 78 × 78) and small, colorful, printed design motifs on a solid-colored ground (Figure 17.1). Calico is particularly appropriate for multi-tier café curtains, because the short panels require short pattern repeats and the extensive gathering would camouflage large design motifs.

Figure 17.1 Calico curtain fabric.

Figure 17.2 Chintz fabric with a glazed surface.

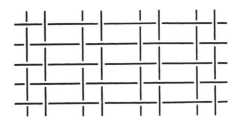

Figure 17.3 Yarn spacing in ninon curtain fabric.

Figure 17.4 Osnaburg window covering fabric.

Chintz (Figure 17.2) is glazed to add body and high surface luster. Most chintz fabrics have colorful, printed designs, but some are solid colored. The fabric, which has relatively low drapability, is frequently used in single- and multi-tier café curtains.

Cretonne, a drapery fabric infrequently used in recent years, is produced from coarse yarns. Large, printed motifs, relatively high stiffness, and a dull surface characterize it.

Gauze or theatrical gauze has a slightly higher fabric count than cheesecloth; stiffening agents are used to impart body. Originally produced for use in stage settings, the transparent fabric may be dyed and used for stationary or traversing curtain panels in residential and commercial interiors.

Ninon (Figure 15.1, p. 249) is used for sheer draw or stationary curtains, generally in combination with overdraperies. Close examination of the fabric shows that every third warp yarn has been omitted to increase the transparency of the fabric. The interlacing pattern in ninon is 1 × 1, not 2 × 1, which the paired spacing of the warp yarns may first suggest (Figure 17.3).

Transparency and a parchment-like hand characterize **organdy**, produced when an all-cotton fabric is exposed to a weak solution of sulfuric acid. In order to partially offset the weakening effect of the acid, the fabric is first mercerized to increase the strength of the fibers.

Organdy is now also made of monofilament nylon, which requires no acid treatment. The sheer cotton or nylon fabrics are effective in most styles of curtain treatments.

Osnaburg is composed of coarse, carded cotton yarns. These are bleached only a little, if at all, to preserve the natural off-white color of the yarns, which are interspersed with bits of dark-colored fibers. Osnaburg was originally produced for use as grain and cement sack fabric; its unrefined look is apparent in Figure 17.4.

Voile is a transparent fabric woven of highly twisted yarns composed of cotton or a blend of cotton and polyester fibers. The fabric has a crisp hand and is generally white in ruffled curtains and printed in other styles. Voile may be flocked with small dots that convert the fabric into **dotted swiss** (Figure 17.17).

Basket-woven Fabrics. Two basket-woven fabrics, namely monk's cloth and duck, are commonly used for window treatments. **Monk's cloth** (Figure 17.5) is usually produced in a 4 × 4 interlacing pattern, but a 2 × 2 pattern may be used. The yarns are spun to simulate those found in the fabric traditionally used for monk's robes. For use in window coverings, the fabric is generally bleached and occasionally dyed to create a refined, contemporary appearance.

Duck, also known as **canvas**, may be constructed in a 2 × 1 basket interlacing or in a plain weave. The fabric is often made from strong, two-ply yarns for use in exterior awning treatments. To make duck and other textile awning fabrics waterproof, converters coat them with vinyl solutions, rubber-based materials, or other synthesized compounds. These agents fill the yarn and fabric interstices, making the structures nonporous.

Filling-Rib Woven Fabrics. Taffeta, faille, and bengaline are produced for use in window treatments. **Faille** and **bengaline** (described and pictured in Chapter 13) have slightly larger ribs than those in **taffeta.** Taffeta's smooth yarns are usually composed of bright acetate fibers; often a wood-grain or water-marked surface pattern is introduced by moiréing. A moiré taffeta fabric is used for the balloon shade shown in Figure 16.12 (p. 272), and as the wall covering pictured in Figure 19.7 (p. 318).

Warp-Rib Woven Fabrics In **dimity**, a sheer fabric used for curtains, a lengthwise rib effect may be produced by periodically placing one large warp among fine yarns, or, as shown in Figures 6.9 (p. 86), and 17.6, by periodically placing a group of warp yarns among fine yarns. Fine, combed cotton yarns produce a smooth surface; they are generally mercerized to increase luster and fiber strength. The degree of fabric openness is similar to that of organdy and voile. The dimity in Figure 17.6 exhibits slight filling bow.

The roller shade fabric shown in Figure 17.7 has a lengthwise rib effect produced by combining fine and coarse yarns. Called **ribcord**, the fabric may be coated on the back with a vinyl compound to increase its opacity.

Other curtain fabrics, such as piqué and Bedford cord, also have lengthwise ribs, but their interlacing patterns are too complicated to be executed on a two-harness loom. To make these fabrics, a dobby loom with multiple harnesses for increased shedding variations is a necessity.

Twill-woven Fabrics

Twill interlacing patterns are rarely used alone in the construction of curtain and drapery fabrics. Instead, they

Figure 17.5 Monk's cloth, a basket weave window covering fabric.

Figure 17.6 Dimity, a warp-rib weave fabric.

are generally combined with other interlacing patterns in decorative weaving procedures, including dobby and Jacquard operations.

Satin- and Sateen-woven Fabrics

Multifilament yarns composed of bright acetate fibers are often woven in a satin interlacing to produce highly dra-pable, lustrous drapery fabrics. Such fabrics are especially suitable for swags, jabots, and cascades (see Figures 16.7 and 16.8, pp. 267 and 268).

Antique satin (Figure 17.8) has simple warp yarns and complex single-slub filling yarns. The slub yarns float over the face of the fabric in a sateen interlacing. When high luster is desired, the fabric is composed of bright ac-etate, and, for low luster, cotton is used. Antique satin en-joys great popularity among contemporary designers and consumers.

Simple interlacing patterns are also used in the pro-duction of woven wood and woven grass window cover-ings. These structures simply employ wood slats or grass strands, rather than textile yarns, as their crosswise ele-ments.

Fabrics with Decorative Interlacings

Several decorative interlacing patterns, including the dobby, dot or spot, and Jacquard weaves, produce fab-rics suitable for use in window treatments as well as in upholstery applications. Additional complex interlacing patterns, including the leno, swivel, and lappet weaves, are used in curtain and drapery fabrics; the relatively low abrasion resistance or low covering power charac-terizing these weaves precludes their use in upholstery coverings.

Figure 17.7 Ribcord, a warp-rib weave fabric used in roller shades.

Figure 17.8 Antique satin drapery fabrics.

Dobby-woven Fabrics

The multiple harnesses and control mechanisms on a dobby loom facilitate the production of novelty curtain fabrics with geometric features woven into the base fabric. Fine lengthwise ribs are found in **plain or pinwale piqué**; larger ribs are found in **Bedford cord**; small, diamond-shaped patterns are characteristic of **birdseye piqué**; and the grid of a waffle iron is replicated in **waffle piqué**. Examples of the piqué fabrics are given in Figure 17.9.

As shown in the cross-sectional sketch of pinwale piqué presented in Figure 17.10, extra warp yarns, called **stuffer yarns**, can be used to support the tunnel-like ribs or **wales**. Stuffer warp yarns may also appear in Bedford cord, and stuffer filling yarns in birdseye piqué.

The low drapability of these fabrics makes them more

a) plain or pinwale piqué

b) birdseye piqué

Figure 17.9 Dobby-woven curtain fabrics.

c) waffle piqué

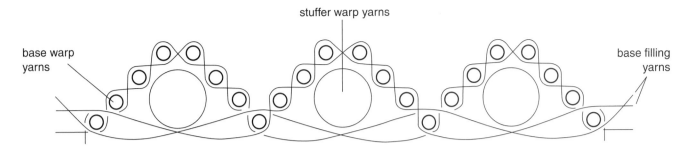

| **Figure 17.10** Cross-sectional view of pinwale piqué with stuffer warp yarns.

suitable for tailored curtain panels than for ruffled and shirred styles. Scalloped headings are especially effective with these fabrics.

Surface-figure Woven Fabrics

Special attachments can be added to dobby looms to facilitate surface-figure weaving. As schematized in Figure 6.12 (p. 88), surface-figure woven fabrics have raised figures or motifs produced by incorporating extra yarns in various ways.

Dot- or Spot-woven Fabrics.   In dot or spot weaving, extra yarns are periodically interlaced with the base yarns to create a small dot or figured spot. Between the decorative figures or dots, the extra yarns are floated on the back of the fabric. When the floating yarns are left in place, the fabric is known as an **unclipped dot or spot** fabric; when the floating yarns are cut away, the fabric is known as a **clipped dot or spot** fabric. When the base fabric is sheer, the floats should be clipped to avoid linear shadows, especially when the fabric is intended for use as a window covering. Either side of a clipped dot or spot fabric can be used as the face side (Figure 17.11). The floating yarns should be left unclipped in opaque fabrics to minimize the possibility that the dots or spots will be removed by in-use abrasion and cleaning.

| **Figure 17.11** Clipped dot curtain fabric.

Swivel-woven Fabrics   In **swivel weaving**, extra yarns periodically swivel around or encircle the base yarns to create small, secure dots (see Figure 6.12b, p. 88). Some imported dotted swiss is produced with this interlacing technique, but the relatively slow rate of production precludes its widespread use.

Lappet-woven Fabrics   In **lappet weaving**, hundreds of needles are used to interlace extra warp yarns. The needles are shifted laterally to create a zigzag surface pattern that resembles hand embroidery (Figure 17.12). Lappet fabrics, like swivel fabrics, are woven at comparatively slow rates.

Figure 17.12 Lappet-woven curtain fabrics.

Figure 17.13 Marquisette, a leno-weave curtain fabric.

Figure 17.14 Leno-woven casement fabric.

Leno-woven Fabrics

Because the crossed warp yarns effectively lock the filling yarns into position and minimize yarn slippage, the leno weave is particularly useful for interlacing fine, smooth yarns into stable window covering fabrics. **Marquisette** (Figure 17.13) is a transparent leno-woven fabric composed of fine monofilament yarns; the lightweight fabric is used extensively in stationary or traversing curtain panels. **Mosquito netting** is also transparent but compactly constructed; it is used as a curtain-like bed canopy in tropical climates, forming a barrier against mosquitoes.

The stability and novel appearance of leno interlacing enables manufacturers to produce a wide variety of highly decorative, leno-woven fabrics. The visual interest of the casement shown in Figure 17.14 is enhanced by the use of slub yarns, and that of the casement

shown in Figure 15.2a (p. 250) is enriched by the use of seed yarns.

Jacquard-woven Fabrics

Such Jacquard-woven fabrics as **damask, brocade,** and **tapestry** (Figures 13.11, 13.13, and 13.15, pp. 213, 214, and 215) are produced for use in drapery treatments as well as in upholstery. The damask drapery fabric in Figure 17.15 has linear motifs that are complemented by the strié color styling of the ground.

Another distinctive Jacquard-woven drapery and upholstery fabric is called **lampas.** The fabric is characterized by elaborate woven-in designs typical of the seventeenth and eighteenth centuries. The detailed motifs are created by combining satin and sateen interlacings (Figure 17.16). In many lampases, two sets of identically colored warp yarns are combined with one or more sets of variously colored filling yarns.

Fabrics with Pile Interlacings

Such pile-woven fabrics as **corduroy, velveteen,** and **velvet,** which were described in Chapter 13, may be used for

| **Figure 17.16** "Venice Art" lampas, multicolor motifs on lacquer red ground. Made in Italy of 81 percent rayon, l5 percent silk, and 4 percent nylon.
Courtesy of Scalamandre.

interior window treatments. Corduroy works well in single-tier café curtains and casual draperies, and velveteen and velvet are effective in formal drapery treatments. When considering these fabrics for use in any style of treatment, designers and consumers should make good use of design elements and principles when assessing whether the three-dimensional texture will be appropriate or too imposing. They should also determine whether extra-strong rods and additional brackets would be required to support the panels constructed from these comparatively heavy fabrics.

Fabrics with Surface Embellishments

Converters can embellish the surfaces of already-woven fabrics to produce distinctive coverings for curtain treatments. They may use a flocking or an embroidering operation.

Flocked Fabrics

Flocked dotted swiss fabric (Figure 17.17) is less expensive than that produced by spot or swivel weaving. Frequently, the base fabric is voile.

Figure 17.17 Flocked dotted swiss.

Embroidered Fabrics

Tambour-embroidered curtain fabric is distinguished by chain-stitched, lace-like designs. The stitching (shown in detail in Figure 17.28) resembles that created by artisans. Frequently, mirror-image panels with finished edges (Figure 17.18) are produced from such fabrics as batiste and organdy.

Eyelet is produced with an embroidery machine used to stitch around holes created in the greige goods (Figure 17.19a). Formerly, destroying cotton fibers with sulfuric acid produced these holes; today, knives are used. The eyelet shown in Figure 17.19b has a scalloped edge, a decorative feature often selected for single-tier café curtain treatments.

Fabrics Distinguished by Color Styling

Many textile window covering fabrics are distinguished by the decorative features of their yarns or the structural features introduced during fabrication; others are distinguished by their color styling. Among the latter group of fabrics are blotch prints, warp prints, toile de Jouy prints, pigment prints, and burnt-out prints.

Roller printing has traditionally been employed to create a color style known as a **blotch print**, in which the ground of the fabric is printed; the motifs may be left as undyed, white designs or they may also be printed. In contrast to discharge prints, blotch prints do not exhibit the same level of color intensity on both sides of the fabric; this difference is evident in Figure 17.20.

A **warp print** color style is produced by first screen printing a web of warp yarns; the colors are applied in precise, well-defined motifs and pattern repeats. The subsequent interlacing of the printed warp yarns with neutral-colored filling yarns will develop a striated appearance (Figure 17.21) similar to that seen in ikat prints (see Figure 8.14, page 119).

Toile de Jouy (*twal duh jzoo-wee´*) **prints** have monochromatic color styling. The motifs have a picture-like quality, and designers must be cognizant of the unidirectional orientation of the motifs (Figure 17.22).

Thick pigment mixtures, typically white or gold, are used to produce **pigment print** curtain fabrics (Figure 17.23). These opaque compounds add visual interest and

Figure 17.18 Tambour-embroidered curtain panels.
Courtesy of Henry Cassen.

a) prior to embroidering

b) after embroidering

| **Figure 17.19** Eyelet curtain fabrics, before and after embroidering.

| **Figure 17.20** Blotch and discharge prints.

| **Figure 17.21** Warp print drapery fabric.

Figure 17.22 Toile de Jouy prints with monochromatic color styling and picture-like motifs.

Figure 17.23 Pigment print ninon curtain fabric.

Figure 17.24 Burnt-out print curtain fabric.

Figure 17.25 Raschel-stitched casement fabric.

Figure 17.26 Casement fabric produced by weft insertion.

quently, rayon), only the acid-resistant fiber (often nylon) remains in the highly transparent areas of the fabric (Figure 17.24).

Knitted Window Covering Fabrics

Knitting is a relatively fast and economical method of combining yarns into fabric structures that is increasingly employed in the fabrication of window coverings. Balancing the gauge and type of yarns used can produce specific levels of fabric openness. Raschel stitching provides high-dimensional stability, non-run performance, and design flexibility; many curtain and casement fabrics are produced with this interlooping technique. Two variations of conventional knitting procedures, weft insertion and stitch-knitting, are also used.

Raschel-stitched Fabrics

The multiple guide bars and latch needles (Figure 7.3, p. 98) on the **raschel** machine facilitate the production of a variety of window covering fabrics, ranging from delicate, lacy curtain structures to heavy, elaborately interlooped casements. A raschel-stitched fabric is shown in Figure 17.25.

Fabrics Produced by Weft Insertion

Because the size and character of the weft or filling yarns effectively control the transparency and covering power of a fabric, manufacturers are increasingly using **weft insertion** to produce window coverings. In the casement fabric shown in Figure 17.26, the manufacturer has inserted various lengths of weft yarns to develop an integral pattern with different levels of fabric openness. Opaque pigments are frequently printed on the surface of such fabrics to reduce their transparency and enhance visual interest.

Stitch-knitted Casements

In Chapter 7, the use of knitting stitches to anchor webs of yarns in **stitch-knitting** operations was explained.

reduce fabric openness. Opaque pigments were also used to print the fabric in Figure 17.26.

Different levels of transparency in the same fabric distinguish **etched-out or burnt-out prints**. After acid has been used to burn away the acid-degradable fibers (fre-

Figure 17.27 Stitch-knitted casement fabrics.

Examples of casement fabrics produced this way are shown in Figure 17.27.

Because the stability and integrity of stitch-knitted fabrics can be lost when loops of the chain-stitching are ruptured, they should not be selected for panels that will be subject to abrasion. Panels of these fabrics must not be opened and closed by hand, and they must be cleaned with care.

Knotted and Twisted Window Coverings

Lace and net window coverings are fabricated with knotting and twisting operations. Designers and consumers desiring an airy, delicate, and highly ornamental **lace fabric** for a window treatment must be aware that the panels are likely to sag. Their stability can be improved when the fabric is made from thermoplastic fibers and properly heat set.

Appliqués may increase the visual interest of **net curtain fabrics**. The fabric pictured in Figure 17.28 has had its surface interest further augmented by the Tambour embroidering that secures the appliqué.

Figure 17.28 Tambour-embroidered appliqué on bobbinet curtain fabric.
Courtesy of Henry Cassen.

Coverings Formed from Fibrous Webs

The stitch-bonding and spunlacing techniques explained in Chapter 7 enable manufacturers to produce window coverings directly from fibers. Because these techniques

Figure 17.29 Stitch-bonded window covering.

ric. These multicomponent fabrics, known as self-lined drapery fabrics, often display specific functional attributes. Other types of linings, virtually all of which are textile fabrics, are hung separately, behind the drapery panels.

Permanently Attached Lining Materials

The application of foamed acrylic compounds to the back of drapery fabric to increase its **insulative value** was introduced in Chapter 9. An example of this is given in Figure 17.30. The air-filled cells of these coatings retard heat loss by convection as the compound restricts the flow of air through the yarn and fabric interstices. The insulative value of window treatments using these fabrics largely depends, however, on how tightly the panels are mounted (see Chapter 15). Acrylic polymers, which have high resistance to sunlight, provide the added benefit of slowing the rate at which the radiant energy of the sun degrades the fibers and colorants in treated fabric.

The amount of light transmitted through a window covering fabric is inversely related to its **opacity** or **level of openness**: increasing the opacity of the structure decreases the **level of light transmission**. In certain interiors, such as hospitals and similar facilities, coverings may

Figure 17.30 Drapery fabric having an aerocellular acrylic backcoating for increased acoustical and insulative values.

bypass spinning operations, such coverings may be less expensive than those fabricated from yarns.

A **stitch-bonded** window covering fabric is presented in Figure 17.29. The surface of this fabric has been printed; for this reason, it may require close examination to confirm that it is not a conventional textile structure.

Manufacturers can produce **spunlaced** curtain fabrics with open, airy constructions by manipulating the positions of the fibers. Such fabrics may be treated as disposable, especially in care-type facilities where maintenance expenses are higher than replacement costs.

Drapery Lining Materials

Two types of lining materials, coatings and film sheetings, may be permanently attached to the back of drapery fab-

a) vinyl coating laminated to base fabric

b) vinyl film sheeting bonded to base fabric

Figure 17.31 Opaque window coverings providing total blackout.

need to be highly opaque to block most of the incident rays and provide **partial blackout**. In other interiors, such as rooms used for viewing films, the coverings must be fully closed or fully opaque, blocking all incident rays and providing **total blackout**.

Converters can increase the opacity of greige drapery fabrics with coatings and film sheetings. For total blackout, a vinyl coating may be spread over the surface (Figure 17.31a) or vinyl film sheeting may be bonded to a base fabric (Figure 17.31b). The vinyl component is frequently fashionably colored for greater aesthetic appeal. In many motel and hotel rooms, especially those operated by national chains, these multicomponent structures are the only window covering, functioning as both covering and lining and providing the necessary privacy and blackout.

Separately Hung Lining Fabrics

Linings designed to be installed as separately hung panels are generally textile fabrics. Virtually all of these fabrics have a plain- or sateen-interlacing pattern, but a variety of surface appearance features and service-related properties are introduced by the use of finishing agents and processes.

Plain-woven Lining Fabrics

A great deal of lining fabric is produced from simple, single yarns of cotton combined in a plain-weave interlacing pattern. The greige goods are then finished in various operations, the first of which is bleaching. Silicone compounds may be applied for water-repellent performance. The silicone slows the rate of moisture absorption, minimizing the wetting of the fabric from moisture condensed on panes and frames and from rain that blows in when windows are inadvertently left open. It may also help to minimize the staining and streaking that can occur when moisture combines with smoke and oily cooking residues that have settled on the fabric; more effective protection against soiling and staining can be provided, however, by fluorocarbon compounds. Compressive shrinkage treatments may be employed to encourage relaxation shrinkage; chemical cross-linking resins may be used to improve appearance retention. Greige lining fabrics finished with some or all of these conversion processes are often marketed with a registered trade name: an example is Roc-lon®, owned by the Roc-lon Corporation, Inc.

Challis (*challie*) is a soft, drapable lining fabric produced from spun yarns of rayon or acetate fibers. During conversion, chemical cross-linking resins may be applied for improved resiliency, and fluorocarbon compounds may be added for water and soil repellency. Frequently, the manufactured cellulosic fibers are engineered to be flame resistant; acetate is often engineered to be sunlight resistant, as well.

Sateen-woven Lining Fabric

Much of the fabric in separately hung drapery lining panels has been produced with the sateen weave. These **sateen linings** are composed of fine, combed cotton yarns, bleached to whiteness or piece dyed. Friction calendering or schreinering (see Chapter 9) may augment the soft luster produced by the floating yarns. At first glance, schreinered sateen lining may appear to have a fine twill interlacing: the "hills" suggest a visual diagonal. Close inspection, however, confirms the presence of floating filling yarns and proves the apparent diagonals to be three-dimensional protrusions of the fabric.

The luster that the floating filling yarns contribute to sateen will last until the yarns are ruptured. Cleaning processes, however, will eventually alter the reflective characteristics introduced by calendering and schreinering operations.

Metallic-coated Lining Fabrics

One side of plain- or sateen-woven lining fabrics may be sprayed with a mixture of metallic or metallic-colored

Figure 17.32 Metallic-coated, reflective textile lining fabric.

particles and resin binders. The silver-colored particles that coat the lining in Figure 17.32 not only increase opacity for a **dimout** (partial blackout) effect, they also increase the level of solar heat rejection. These reflective coverings may be particularly beneficial in large windows with southern exposures.

Summary

Although cotton fiber dominates the textile window coverings market, an almost equal quantity of manufactured fiber is also used. The fiber composition of curtains, draperies, and fabrics must be disclosed. This disclosure enables informed consumers and professionals to consider fiber properties in relationship to the planned end-use. Besides textile yarns, such nontextile materials as wood, natural grasses, and plastic expand the assortment of window coverings available to today's residential and commercial consumer.

Primarily because window coverings do not have to withstand the same high level of abrasion as upholstered furniture coverings, window covering fabrics are manufactured using a more extensive variety of fabrication techniques. Some fabrics, especially those produced in stitch-knitting, stitch-bonding, weft insertion, and spunlacing operations, are relatively inexpensive, and their transparency and covering power is readily controlled.

Other curtain and drapery fabrics, including those produced by knotting, twisting, and surface-figure weaving, display distinctive design features. Still other fabrics, such as those made in leno-weaving and raschel-stitching operations, exhibit a high degree of openness and dimensional stability and virtually no yarn slippage.

Drapery lining materials, whether permanently attached or separately hung, present a uniform appearance to outside viewers and reduce the negative effects of radiant energy on the fibers and colorants used in the decorative panels. They can also provide such functional benefits as insulation, noise reduction, and greater control of light transmission.

Key Terms

antique satin
batiste
Bedford cord
bengaline
birdseye piqué
blotch print
brocade
calico
canvas
challis
chintz
clipped dot or spot
corduroy
cretonne
damask
dimity
dimout
dotted swiss
duck
etched-out or burnt-out print
eyelet
faille
fibrillation
gauze or theatrical gauze
insulative value
lace fabric
lampas
lappet weave
level of light transmission
level of openness
marquisette
monk's cloth

mosquito netting
net fabric
ninon
opacity
organdy
osnaburg
partial blackout
pigment print
plain or pinwale piqué
raschel stitching
ribcord
sateen linings
spunlacing
stitch-bonding
stitch-knitting
stuffer yarns
swivel weave
taffeta
tambour-embroidered fabric
tapestry
Textile Fiber Products Identification Act (TFPIA)
toile de Jouy prints
total blackout
unclipped dot or spot
velvet
velveteen
voile
waffle piqué
wales
warp print
weft insertion

Review Questions

1. What properties support the growing dominance of the noncellulosic fibers in the curtain and drapery markets?

2. Why has the use of glass fiber in curtains and draperies virtually ceased?

3. Explain the problems associated with the fibrillation of glass fibers.

4. What is "window wall paper"? Why is it used?

5. Why has the fiber content of such fabrics as batiste been shifted from 100 percent cotton to a blend of cotton and polyester?

6. Distinguish between voile and dotted swiss.

7. Examine examples of pinwale piqué, birdseye piqué, and waffle piqué. What are their similarities? Which one is reversible?

8. When should the floats be cut in dot or spot fabrics? When should they be left uncut?

9. Name three ways to manufacture dotted swiss. Which one is the least expensive technique? Which one is the most expensive?

10. Describe the features associated with lampases. Why would these fabrics be relatively expensive?

11. What is meant by "visual weight"? Why should it be considered with corduroy, velveteen, and velvet window coverings?

12. Distinguish between a blotch print and a discharge print.

13. What advantages does raschel stitching offer?

14. Explain the role of the filling or weft yarns in fabrics produced with weft insertion.

15. Differentiate between stitch-knitting and stitch-bonding.

16. Identify the advantages of foamed acrylic compounds applied to the back of drapery fabric.

17. Differentiate among total blackout, partial blackout, and dimout.

18. Identify finishes commonly used with textile linings.

18

Evaluation and Maintenance of Finished Window Covering Fabrics

Standards for Physical Performance Properties
  Dimensional Stability
  Distortion of Yarn
  Fabric Strength
  Durability of Back Coatings
  Appearance Retention

Evaluations of Colorfastness
  Colorfastness to Light
  Colorfastness to Atmospheric Gases

Colorfastness to Crocking
Colorfastness to Laundering and Dry Cleaning

Evaluations of Flame Resistance

Maintenance of Window Covering Structures
  Preventive Maintenance Measures
  Routine Care Practices
  Restorative Maintenance Procedures

Laboratory tests conducted on greige goods help to evaluate the potential quality of textile curtain, drapery, and lining fabrics. Reliable assessments of actual quality, however, must be based on tests conducted on the finished fabrics themselves. Results of these tests reflect the effects of the agents and processes used to transform the surface appearance of greige goods, improve performance, and minimize care requirements. Even though producers can make textile window coverings easier to care for, it is up to residential and commercial consumers to use a three-part maintenance program that will prolong the use-life of the fabric.

Manufacturers and converters evaluating the flame resistance of finished window covering fabrics often employ test methods developed by members of the National Fire Protection Association. When evaluating other performance characteristics, they often use the test methods and performance guidelines recommended by representatives of all segments of the window covering industry, as contained in ASTM D 3691 Standard Performance Specifications for Woven, Lace, and Knit Household Curtain and Drapery Fabrics.[1] (See Table 18.1).

Standards for Physical Performance Properties

Because the satisfactory end-use performance of textile window covering fabrics depends on their physical performance, members of the industry set out performance guidelines for such characteristics as dimensional stability, distortion of yarn, and fabric strength in their recommended standard. Guidelines also concern the level of appearance retention that durable press curtain and drapery fabrics should exhibit.

Dimensional Stability

Dimensional stability is a critical performance property for textile window covering fabrics. Sagging and shrinking must be minimized to preserve the appearance and the usefulness of the treatments they compose. In swagged valences and such treatment styles as priscilla curtains and Austrian shades, sagging would destroy the balance of the laterally draping folds. In straight, free-hanging panels, sagging could cause the lower part of the fabric to stack on the floor. Sagging is more likely to occur in fabrics composed of conventional rayon (see Chapter 4), and in fabrics of loose construction, especially when low-twist, spun yarns are involved or the yarns are variously angled, as in lace fabrics.

Shrinkage of the overdraperies in treatments having multiple layers could expose the lower edge of the curtains to the interior, and shrinkage of the lining panels could expose a portion of the overdraperies to the exterior. If the panels shrank, fabric transparency would be reduced and the tight closure that maintains an insulating layer of dead air between the covering and the glass might be destroyed.

Converters can use **compressive shrinkage processes** and **heat setting** operations to stabilize curtain and drapery greige goods. Laboratory tests can be used to evaluate the effectiveness of these treatments. Specimens of the stabilized fabric are prepared as illustrated in Figure 14.5 (p. 232), except they are larger and the inner markings are 18 inches apart. The specimens are laundered in accordance with AATCC 135 Dimensional Changes in Automatic Home Laundering of Durable Press Woven or Knit Fabric, or they are dry cleaned in accordance with ASTM D 2724 Test Methods for Bonded, Fused, and Laminated Apparel Fabrics. As shown in Table 18.1, the performance guideline in ASTM D 3691 states that the fabrics should not change more than 3 percent in their lengthwise and crosswise dimensions after being laundered five times or dry cleaned three times.

Distortion of Yarn

Evaluating the propensity of yarns to shift or distort in such open curtain fabrics as voile, ninon, and marquisette is important. **Distortion of yarn** should also be examined in satin-woven fabrics with smooth yarns. The shifting or slipping of one set of yarns over the other produces areas having different levels of transparency (Figure 9.14, p. 140); in patterned coverings, a stain-like appearance may develop. ASTM D 1336 Test Method for Distortion of Yarn in

Table 18.1 Performance Requirements for Woven, Lace, and Knit Household Curtain and Drapery Fabrics

Characteristics	Knit and Lace	Sheer (woven)	Foam Back, Stitch Bonded, and Conventional Weights (woven)
Breaking strength (load), CRT method, in both directions[e]	. . .	67 N (15 lbf), min	89 N (20 lbf), min
Bursting strength (ball burst)[e]	138 kPa (20 ibf/in.²), min	. . .	. . .
Tear strength (tongue tear), in both directions[e]	. . .	4.4 N (1 ibf), min	6.7 N (1.5 ibf), min
Dimensional change:			
After 5 launderings in both directions	3.0% max	3.0% max	3.0% max
After 3 dry cleanings in both directions	3.0% max	3.0% max	3.0% max
Distortion of yarn:			
1-lbf load	. . .	2.54 mm (0.1 in.), max	. . .
2-lbf load	. . .	. . .	2.54 mm(0.1 in.), max
Colorfastness to laundering:[a]			
Alteration in shade	Class 4[b] min	Class 4[b] min	Class 4[b] min
Staining	Class 3[c] min	Class 3[c] min	Class 3[c] min
Colorfastness to dry cleaning:			
Alteration in shade	Class 4[b] min	Class 4[b] min	Class 4[b] min
Burnt gas fumes, 2 cycles:			
Alteration in shade	Class 4[b] min	Class 4[b] min	Class 4[b] min
After 1 refurbishing	Class 4[b] min	Class 4[b] min	Class 4[b] min
Crocking:			
Dry	Class 4[d] min	Class 4[d] min	Class 4[d] min
Wet	Class 3[d] min	Class 3[d] min	Class 3[d] min
Light (60 AATCC FU), xexon[e]	Step 4[b] min	Step 4[b] min	Step 4[b] min
Ozone, 1 cycle	Class 4[b] min	Class 4[b] min	Class 4[b] min
Fabric appearance	DP 3.5[f] min	DP 3.0 min	DP 3.5 min
Retention of hand, character, and appearance	pass	pass	pass
Durability of back coating	pass	pass	pass
Flammability	pass	pass	pass

[a] Class in colorfastness and DP rating is based on a numerical scale of 5.0 for negligible color change, color transfer, or wrinkling to 1.0 for very severe color change, color transfer, or wrinkling. The numerical rating in Table 18.1 or higher is acceptable.

[b] AATCC Gray Scale for Color Change.

[c] AATCC Gray Scale for Staining.

[d] AATCC Chromatic Transference Scale.

[e] There is more than one standard test method that can be used to measure breaking strength, bursting strength, tear strength, and lightfastness. These test methods cannot be used interchangeably since there may be no overall correlation between them.

[f] For durable-press fabrics only.

(Courtesy of ASTM.)

Woven Fabrics measures the extent to which this unsightly characteristic occurs in woven curtain and drapery fabrics.

Test Specimens and Procedures

As directed in ASTM D 1336, five specimens are cut slightly larger than 4 inches by 8 inches, with their longer dimension parallel to the set of yarns having the greater resistance to shifting. The operator determines this direction by exerting a shearing motion on the fabric with the thumb and forefinger. After conditioning, a specimen is clamped into a rectangular carriage frame and placed between two frictional drums on the testing device (Figure 18.1). The weight of the upper drum is adjusted to provide a total force of one pound when sheer curtain fabrics are being tested and a total force of two pounds when conventional-weight woven fabrics are being tested. The carriage is then shifted so that the drums produce a shearing action on the specimen.

Analysis of Results

After the specimen has been removed from the carriage and allowed to relax for 15 minutes, the widest opening

Figure 18.1 Fabric shift tester.
Reprinted, with permission, copyright American Society for Testing and Materials.

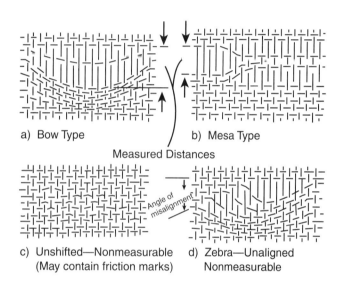

a) Bow Type   b) Mesa Type

Measured Distances

c) Unshifted—Nonmeasurable   d) Zebra—Unaligned
(May contain friction marks)   Nonmeasurable

Figure 18.2 Measurable and nonmeasurable shift openings.
Reprinted, with permission, copyright American Society for Testing and Materials.

of each **shift mark**, or distorted yarn group, is measured as shown in Figures 18.2a and 18.2b, Nonmeasurable openings, illustrated in Figures 18.2c and 18.2d, are described and reported. The average of the five measurements is calculated and reported.

Performance Guidelines

According to the performance specifications included in ASTM D 3691, sheer woven window coverings should exhibit a maximum distortion of 0.1 inch under a one-pound load, and conventional-weight woven coverings should exhibit the same maximum distortion, but under a two-pound load.

Fabric Strength

Performance guidelines for three types of fabric strength measurements are included in ASTM D 3691. Breaking strength and tear strength measurements are made with woven curtain and drapery fabrics; bursting strength measurements are made with knitted and knotted and twisted fabrics.

Breaking Strength

The **breaking strength (load)** of woven curtain and drapery fabrics may be evaluated in accordance with the procedures outlines in ASTM D 1682 Test Methods for Breaking Force and Elongation of Textile Fabrics (Grab Test). This test method was described in Chapter 14. Sheer fabrics, such as batiste, dimity, ninon, and voile, should withstand a minimum load of 15 pounds before rupturing, and conventional-weight woven coverings should withstand a minimum load of 20 pounds.

Tear Strength

The **tear strength** of woven curtain and drapery fabrics may be evaluated as directed in ASTM D 2262 Test Method for Tearing Strength of Woven Fabrics by the Tongue (Single Rip) Method (Constant-Rate-of-Traverse Tensile Testing Machine). This procedure measures the force required to continue a tear in the specimens. (See Chapter 14.) Sheer curtain fabrics should require a force of at least 1 pound to propagate the tear, and conventional-weight woven fabrics should require at least 1.5 pounds.

Bursting Strength

Bursting strength measurements are made only on knitted fabrics. ASTM D 231 Methods of Testing Tolerance for Knit Goods is the specified test method.[2]

In this test, a conditional specimen is secured under an O-shaped plate, one having an opening in the center. A force is exerted against the specimen by a polished, hard steel ball. The test is completed when the ball bursts through the specimen. The maximum force required to burst each specimen is recorded. The average of all replicate tests is then calculated and reported. Knit fabrics should resist a minimum force of 20 pounds per square inch.

Durability of Back Coatings

A performance requirement for back coatings (see Figure 17.30, p. 294) used on drapery fabrics in included in ASTM D 3691. The coating should exhibit no evidence of cracking or peeling when the fabric is subjected to prescribed laundering and dry cleaning tests.

Appearance Retention

Textile window coverings are repeatedly folded and bent as panels are opened and closed. They also are folded, bent, twisted, and crushed during cleaning. To help curtain and drapery fabrics composed of cotton, linen, or rayon to recover from such treatment, converters apply chemical cross-linking or **durable press resins**. As long as treated fabrics retain their smooth appearance in use and care, ironing can be avoided.

Members of the industry have established recommended levels of performance for fabrics with a durable press finish. After specimens of the fabric have been laundered five times as directed in Test II B of AATCC 124 Appearance of Durable Press Fabric After Repeated Home Laundering, their appearance is compared with that of three-dimensional plastic replicas (Figure 18.3). Smoothness progressively increases from the first to the fifth replica; each specimen is assigned the number of the

Figure 18.3 Three-dimensional plastic fabric replicas used to evaluate the appearance retention of durable press fabrics. *Courtesy of the American Association of Textile Chemists and Colorists.*

replica it most closely resembles. Knit, lace, foam back, stitch bonded, and conventional-weight woven curtain and drapery fabrics should have an average minimum rating of 3.5, and woven sheer fabrics should have an average minimum rating of 3.0.

Evaluations of Colorfastness

Manufacturers and textile colorists use various testing procedures to ensure that colored interior and exterior window covering fabrics exhibit acceptable levels of fastness when exposed to potentially destructive conditions and substances. The test methods in ASTM D 3691 are used with textile coverings intended for use in residential interiors. The fastness guidelines set forth in the performance standard apply to household fabrics, but contract designers, architects, and other specifiers may refer to the recommended performance values when making decisions about fastness requirements in their commercial projects. Test methods other than those in ASTM D 3691 may be employed on textile fabrics for outdoor applications. Colorists should always discontinue the use of **fugitive colorants**, those found to exhibit an unacceptable level of fastness.

Colorfastness to Light

Although the **radiant energy** of all spectral rays—visible and invisible—can have a negative effect on textile colorants, ultraviolet waves have been shown to be particularly destructive. Because natural light has a higher quantity of these short waves than do artificial illuminants, concern for color retention is generally focused on the stability of textile colorants to sunlight. Such stability is critical in colorants used in curtains and draperies, and in all textiles installed outdoors, in passive solar residences, and in commercial buildings with large expanses of glass. It is especially important in colorants for textile products installed in a southern exposure.

When solar rays strike a colored textile surface, the heat energy excites the dye molecules and gradually changes their chemical structure. Continued alteration of the molecular structure reduces the ability of the dyestuff to produce its original color characteristics. The textile develops a faded appearance: strong, bright, and pure hues become weak, dull, and grayed.

Several test methods have been developed for evaluating the effects of radiant energy, alone or in combination with moisture and heat, on the colorants used in textile products. Some methods are accelerated laboratory procedures; others are long-term outdoor tests.

Lightfastness of Interior Fabrics

Accelerated testing for **lightfastness** can be performed with the **Fade-Ometer®** (Figure 18.4), using one of two different lamps. A glass-enclosed carbon-arc lamp produces light energy throughout the visible spectrum, and is the light source specified in AATCC 16A Colorfastness to Light: Carbon-Arc Continuous Light. Because this lamp is somewhat deficient in ultraviolet rays below 350 nm, its use is diminishing, and it is not recommended for use in evaluating textiles to be installed outdoors. A xenon-arc lamp more closely simulates natural light and gives a more accurate evaluation when correlating to end-use performance. This lamp is specified in AATCC 16E Colorfastness to Light: Water-cooled Xenon-Arc Lamp, Continuous Light, the method increasingly used for determining the lightfastness of window coverings intended for interior installation.

For testing with either light source, fabric specimens are mounted in holders, which are suspended in the apparatus and rotated for several hours. The number of hours of exposure (calculated as the **standard fading hours** [**SFH**], or **standard fading units** [**SFU** or **FU**]) recommended for window coverings is 60.

After completion of an accelerated test, the color retention of the specimens is visually evaluated and numerically rated. The number is determined by comparing the difference observed between an original and exposed specimen with that observed between a pair of standard gray chips on the AATCC Gray Scale for Color Change, pictured in Figure 14.10 (p. 237). A minimum lightfastness rating of Step 4 is recommended for dyed and printed curtain and drapery fabrics produced for installation in residential interiors.

Lightfastness of Exterior Fabrics

A **Weather-Ometer®**, manufactured by Atlas Electric Devices Company, is used for the accelerated laboratory testing of textile fabrics to be installed outdoors. This unit effectively simulates the natural outdoor environ-

Figure 18.4 Interior view of the Fade-Ometer®.
Courtesy of Atlas Electric Devices Company.

Figure 18.5 Outdoor testing facility used to evaluate the effects of natural light on textile colorants. *Courtesy of South Florida Test Service, Inc., a subsidiary of Atlas Electric Devices Company.*

ment, since it facilitates temperature and humidity changes.

For extended outdoor testing, specimens may be fully exposed, or they may be mounted behind glass (Figure 18.5). Depending on the conditions anticipated in the end-use setting, the fabrics may be exposed continuously for 24 hours a day, placed in an enclosed cabinet to permit testing at elevated temperatures, or tested near the ocean for an analysis of the effects of salt atmosphere on the colorants.

The level of color retention exhibited by exterior fabrics tested in the laboratory or outdoors may be rated on the basis of the AATCC Gray Scale for Color Change. Because the exposure conditions may have degraded the fibers as well as the colorants, measurements are also often made to determine changes in such properties as strength and dimensional stability.

Colorfastness to Atmospheric Gases

The fastness of colored window coverings to controlled concentrations of gases, such as nitrogen dioxide (NO_2) and sulfur dioxide (SO_2), can be evaluated by following the procedures in AATCC 23 Colorfastness to Burnt Gas Fumes. This test method was described in Chapter 14; the apparatus used to expose the specimens is shown in Figure 14.11 (p. 238). Curtain and drapery specimens are exposed to **burnt gas fumes** and evaluated before and after one laundering or dry cleaning. The AATCC Gray Scale for Color Change is used to evaluate the amount of fading or color change, and a minimum Class 4 rating is recommended for acceptable performance.

The negative effects of ozone (O_3), a strong oxidizing agent, on colored window fabrics can be assessed through the procedures outlined in AATCC 129 Colorfastness to

Ozone in the Atmosphere Under High Humidities. After one cycle of exposure, the specimens should have a minimum Class 4 rating when compared to the paired chips on the AATCC Gray Scale for Color Change.[3]

Colorfastness to Crocking

Although **crocking**—the transfer of color from one material to another—is a more serious problem in upholstery fabrics, certain situations may lead to crocking problems in colored curtain and drapery fabrics. Color transfer may occur when fabrics rub together or are handled during shipping, sewing, hanging, opening, and closing.

The colorfastness of solid colors to dry and wet crocking is evaluated by the AATCC 8 Colorfastness to Crocking (Rubbing): AATCC Crockmeter Method. This method was described in Chapter 14; the apparatus used to rub the specimens is shown in Figure 14.8 (p. 236). For printed fabrics, the procedures in AATCC 116 Colorfastness to Crocking (Rubbing): Rotary Vertical Crockmeter Method should be followed.

After the test is completed, the **AATCC Chromatic Transference Scale** (Figure 18.6) is used to evaluate the

Figure 18.6 AATCC Chromatic Transference Scale. *Courtesy of the American Association of Textile Chemists and Colorists.*

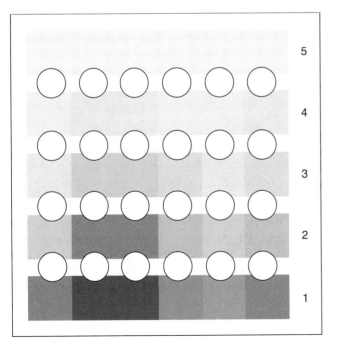

amount of color transferred. The scale is a card with six colors (neutral gray, red, yellow, green, blue, and purple) mounted in each of four horizontal rows. In each of six vertical rows, the chroma or intensity of each hue is varied, beginning with an extremely light tint and ending with a moderately deep shade. The vertically aligned chips are separated by holes in the card.

For evaluation, the stained fabric is placed behind the card and visually examined through the holes. The observer shifts the card until the chroma or intensity of the stain is judged to be similar to that of a color chip, and the number of the row in which this chip is located is assigned to the fabric. Dry tests should yield a minimum rating of Class 4, wet tests a minimum rating of Class 3.

Colorfastness to Laundering and Dry Cleaning

When dyed and printed curtain and drapery fabrics are laundered or dry cleaned, the colorants should not exhibit unacceptable levels of **fading**, **bleeding**, or **migration**. A faded appearance may result when bleaching agents oxidize the colorants or when the dyestuff bleeds from the fabric. Excessive bleeding of the dyestuff into the cleaning solution may stain (in effect, dye) other articles in the load. A stained appearance may also result when the dyestuff migrates or moves through the fabric. Product manufacturers and textile colorists use laboratory test methods to evaluate the potential for excessive fading and staining and to determine what type of cleaning agents should be used.

Accelerated testing for colorfastness to laundry and dry cleaning agents can be conducted with a **Launder-Ometer**® (Figure 18.7). This apparatus contains stainless steel jars to hold the specimens and the specified cleaning solution. During testing, the jars are rotated to simulate agitation. **Washfastness** evaluations are made following the procedures described in Test II A of AATCC 61 Colorfastness to Washing, Domestic, and Laundering, Commercial: Accelerated. In this testing, multifiber test fabric is paired with some specimens to facilitate evaluation of staining.

The effect of repeated dry cleaning is assessed by following the testing procedures outlined in AATCC 132 Colorfastness to Dry Cleaning. Unless otherwise noted on the label, launderable fabrics are assumed to be dry cleanable; thus, staining is not evaluated because migration and bleeding are not expected.

Figure 18.7 Interior view of the Launder-Ometer®.
Courtesy of Atlas Electric Devices Company.

After completion of either testing procedure, the fabrics are evaluated for color change using the AATCC Gray Scale for Color Change; a rating of Class 4 is recommended for acceptable performance in end use. The multifiber test fabrics are evaluated for staining using the AATCC Gray Scale for Staining, which is shown in Figure 14.9 (p. 237). A minimum rating of Class 3 is recommended.

Evaluations of Flame Resistance

Industry representatives included flammability guidelines in ASTM D 3691, but the Consumer Product Safety

Commission has not established a flammability standard with which curtains and draperies must comply prior to their introduction into commerce. However, various regulatory agencies have set forth mandatory flammability standards for window coverings selected for use in certain commercial interiors. In many cases, these mandates are based on recommendations included in the NPFA 101® Life Safety Code®.[4]

NFPA 701 Standard Methods of Fire Tests for Flame Resistant Textiles and Films may be used to evaluate the effectiveness of polymer additives and finishing compounds in reducing the flammability of textile window coverings. Two test methods, both of which may be used to measure the ignition propensity of fabrics to be installed indoors or outdoors, are set out. These test methods, a small-scale and a large-scale procedure, are explained in detail in Chapter 11.

Maintenance of Window Covering Structures

By planning and following an appropriate maintenance program that includes **preventive**, **routine**, and **restorative** practices, residential and commercial consumers can effectively prolong the use-life of window treatments, especially those containing textile components. Manufacturers are not required to provide care instructions, but several voluntarily include them on their product labels. Such instructions are often based on the results of the colorfastness to laundering and dry cleaning tests described earlier in this chapter.

Preventive Maintenance Measures

Preventive maintenance techniques not only preserve the original appearance of window coverings, but may also reduce the weakening suffered by the fibers. Care should be taken to avoid allowing rainwater to blow in on linings and other fabric layers and to prevent panels from hanging in contact with framework on which water condenses. Water, including vapor-phase moisture, may combine with soil present on the fibers and cause staining of the fabric. Water may also combine with pollutants and oily cooking fumes to form weak acids that attack and weaken the fibers (see Chapter 4). When gases and cooking fumes are present, especially in high concentrations, the coverings should be frequently cleaned to prevent accumulation of these acids.

An effort should be made to keep the level of relative humidity around coverings composed of conventional rayon fibers as constant as possible. This will avoid or minimize the development of the elevator effect, the sagging and shrinking problem described in Chapter 4.

Neither textile nor nontextile panels should be allowed to flap in the wind. This could result in tearing and abrading of textile fabrics, splitting and cracking of wood components, and bending of aluminum louvers.

Routine Care Practices

Textile fabric panels, especially those that are stationary or laterally draped, should be vacuumed or tumbled in an automatic dryer, using low heat or none at all, to remove airborne soil. This is especially important for coverings composed of hydrophobic fibers, whose tendency to build up electrical charges increases the fibers' attraction for airborne soil. The louvers and vanes in blinds and shutters and the surfaces of roller shades should be routinely vacuumed to remove accumulated dust.

Restorative Maintenance Procedures

Curtains and draperies are not included in the scope of the FTC trade regulation rule related to care labeling, but many producers elect to provide a cleaning code. Usually, the cleaning code letters for upholstery fabrics are used for curtains and draperies as well. These letters and their meanings were described in Chapter 14.

Unless specifically stated on the label or in literature accompanying glass fiber curtains, draperies, and fabrics, those products must not be dry cleaned or laundered in an automatic washer because the agitation promotes fibrillation. Because soil is held only on fiber surfaces and in yarn and fabric interstices, it may be removed by immersing the coverings in a bathtub or in a commercial cleaning tank filled with a detergent solution. After rinsing, the nearly dry panels should be rehung to dry.

Fabrics with a durable press finish may be laundered in an automatic washer. Strong oxidizing bleaches, such as chlorine compounds, should not be used. In high concentrations, these agents may be retained by the fibers, turning the fabric yellow and further weakening the cellulosic components. The laundered panels should be tumbled with low heat in an automatic dryer until dry, followed by a cool-down cycle and prompt removal.

Excessively high heat should not be used on any fiber. Recommended ironing temperatures are listed in Table 4.8 (p. 56). Unfortunately, consumers often find that iron dials are divided by fiber type or by finish, not by specific temperatures. Moreover, the same setting on different irons may produce quite different temperatures. Consumers and professional cleaners should be alert for signs of fiber and fabric damage. For fabrics composed of thermoplastic fibers, the slightest amount of fabric shrinkage and the slightest resistance of the soleplate to gliding are indications that the ironing temperature is too high.

Commercial and residential consumers may consider having their textile window coverings cleaned by a professional cleaner. This is advisable when long, heavy panels with multiple folds require large cleaning tanks and special pressing equipment. Frequently, laundry and dry cleaning firms offer removal and rehanging as optional services. Consumers can determine for themselves whether the value of these services overrides the burden of the additional charges.

Summary

As part of their quality-control work, producers and converters may subject curtain and drapery fabrics to prescribed laboratory test methods, measuring such properties as bursting strength, flame resistance, and appearance retention. The results of these tests can be compared with the performance guidelines established by members of the industry or the performance mandates of a regulatory agency. Different standards of performance have been set for fabrics with different construction features. If necessary, manufacturers may alter their choice of components or construction methods to improve the quality of their products.

Textile colorists may elect to evaluate the fastness of colorants used in interior and exterior window covering fabrics, following the procedures outlined in an accelerated or a long-term test method. Tests expose the colored fabrics to such conditions and substances as artificial light, natural light, atmospheric contaminants, and cleaning agents. The use of dyes and pigments that exhibit unacceptable levels of color retention in appropriate tests should be discontinued.

The original appearance and condition of curtain and drapery fabrics and other window covering structures can be well maintained by following a planned program. The program should include preventive measures, routine practices, and the use of appropriate procedures when restorative cleaning is needed. Frequently, producers voluntarily provide care instructions with textile window coverings.

Key Terms

AATCC Chromatic Transference Scale
bleeding
breaking strength (load)
burnt gas fumes
bursting strength
compressive shrinkage process
crocking
dimensional stability
distortion of yarn
durable press resins
Fade-Ometer®
fading
fugitive colorants
heat setting

Launder-Ometer®
lightfastness
migration
NFPA 701
preventive maintenance
radiant energy
restorative maintenance
routine maintenance
shift mark
standard fading hours (SFH)
standard fading units (SFU)
tear strength
washfastness
Weather-Ometer®

Review Questions

1. Identify dimensional stability problems that may occur with textile window coverings. Which conversion operations can minimize or prevent them?

2. Why should back coatings on textile fabrics be durable?

3. Identify conditions and substances that are harmful to colored textiles. Explain the changes that may occur in the color characteristics of the dyes or pigments.

4. Why has the use of carbon-arc lamps in lightfastness testing declined in recent years?

Notes

1. The full text of ASTM D 3691 may be reviewed in the *Annual Book of ASTM Standards*, Vol. 07.02.

2. ASTM D 231 has been discontinued. It may be reviewed in *1979 Annual Book of ASTM Standards*, Part 32.

3. The reliability of AATCC 129 as a test for predicting in-service fading due to ozone was investigated and confirmed in a three-year study. See Melvin R. Nipe, "Atmospheric Contaminant Fading," *Textile Chemist and Colorist*, Vol. 13, No. 6, June 1981, 18–28.

4. Life Safety Code® and 101® are registered trademarks of the National Fire Protection Association, Inc., Quincy, Mass.

19

Textile and Nontextile Coverings for Walls and Panels

Selection and Serviceability
    Interior Enrichment
    Functional Values
    Flammability Requirements

Components and Constructions
    Fibers and Yarns
    Construction Techniques
    Backings and Finishes

Installation Techniques
    Shirring
    Stapling
    Using an Adhesive
    Using Premounted Supports

The walls of any interior provide a large surface for interior designers to apply design elements and principles that are essential for successful completion of a design solution. Textiles and nontextiles are used in interiors to cover walls and panels to provide visual and tactile interest. In large, open interiors, textile fabrics often cover panels or partitions to absorb sound and define work areas. In rare cases, wall coverings are installed to increase insulation.

A variety of textile structures is produced exclusively for use on vertical surfaces. Many fabrics produced for use as window and upholstered furniture coverings, and several pile structures produced for use as soft floor coverings, can also be used as wall and panel coverings. Frequently, contract designers and consumers elect to coordinate similar fabrics to cover the walls, windows, and upholstered furniture in an interior.

Selection and Serviceability

Textile wall coverings often serve primarily aesthetic or primarily functional purposes in an interior, but both purposes may be furthered if attention is given to certain selection and serviceability factors. In certain interiors, attention to the fire performance of the covering is regulated by codes. In other interiors, levels of sound transmission are suggested by standards to increase productivity.

Interior Enrichment

The coverings pictured in this chapter show how widely textile wall coverings can differ in color styling, textural features, tactile characteristics, construction, and weight. This wide assortment permits consumers and designers to select a covering that provides the ambiance and decorative impact they seek.

Because dyestuffs applied to different types of substrates inevitably show differences in color characteristics, a precise color match between fabric and paper is normally impossible to obtain. Consumers and designers can avoid a mismatch by having their upholstery or window

fabric backed for application as a wall covering, rather than installing coordinated wallpaper.

Functional Values

Textile wall coverings may be selected to fulfill specific functional needs. They may, for example, provide some measure of acoustical control or of insulation.

Noise Reduction

Bare walls can reflect sound waves and prolong duration of noise (Figure 15.5 p. 253). Textile-covered interior panels or partitions placed throughout open areas interrupt the horizontal travel of sound waves; some of the sound generated within each enclosure can be contained this way. Textile coverings on permanent walls help reduce the amount of waves reflected back into the interior, as well as the amount transferred through the walls to adjoining rooms.

The acoustical benefits of textile structures used on vertical surfaces should be analyzed with testing equipment that can simulate the construction characteristics of the wall or partition and the technique for installing the covering. In one series of tests sponsored by the Carpet and Rug Institute, for example, various carpet specimens were mounted on standard wall constructions. One mounting system (Figure 19.1) places the face of the carpet approximately 2 inches from the structural wall, and accommodates approximately 1¼ inches of filler. The effectiveness of the coverings in reducing noise is numer-

Figure 19.1 A wall sound absorption test.
Courtesy of the Carpet and Rug Institute.

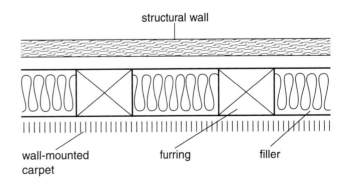

ically reported in terms of a **noise reduction coefficient (NRC)**; higher values indicate greater sound absorption.

When a loop pile carpet with a pile weight of 23 ounces per square yard and no backcoating was tested in this mounting, an NRC of 0.90 was recorded; when a cut-pile carpet having a pile weight of 44 ounces per square yard and having a backcoating was tested, an NRC of 0.70 was recorded. These results show that the structural features of textile coverings directly influence their acoustical properties. Thus, residential and commercial consumers should request actual test results from product manufacturers when selecting wall and panel coverings primarily for noise control.

Energy Conservation

Increasingly, residential and commercial consumers control heat transfer and reduce air infiltration by installing textile structures as interior wall finishes. As is true for acoustical evaluations, assessments of the insulative value of textile coverings must be conducted using a mounting that simulates the construction features of the structural walls and the techniques used to install the covering.

One technique that increases the insulative value of textile wall covering installations is the application of a padding behind the fabric. The cost of the materials and labor incurred in installing these "upholstered walls" may be balanced against potential savings in energy charges.

Interior designers, architects, and specifiers must consult with representatives of the agency that has jurisdiction over a facility to ascertain whether the materials selected for the interior must meet noise or insulation criteria. They must also determine whether the materials are covered by flammability regulations.

Flammability Requirements

City, state, and federal agencies require that materials used inside certain occupancies conform to the requirements of the NFPA 101® Life Safety Code®. As detailed in Table 11.1 (p. 172), material installed as an interior finish (in contrast to an interior floor finish) on building surfaces must exhibit a Class A, B, or C rating, depending upon the type of occupancy and area of installation. The ratings are determined by testing the coverings in accordance with the procedures outlined in ASTM E-84, which is equivalent to NFPA 255. This test method is described and illustrated in Chapter 11.

Components and Constructions

Residential and light commercial textile wall coverings are primarily expected to provide visual and tactile interest, and are subjected to few stresses in use. Thus, distinctive components and construction techniques are appropriate for them. Virtually all fabrics chosen for wall and panel coverings, however, carry some backing applied to impart dimensional stability and facilitate installation. Because wall coverings in contract interiors are exposed to increased levels of abrasion, they are expected to be more durable and serviceable.

Fibers and Yarns

Natural fibers, including wool, silk, linen, jute, and cotton, are extensively and effectively used in wall and panel fabrics. Often, the inherent color variations of these fibers help stylists to design yarns and coverings with a warm and rich appearance. Stylists also capitalize on the natural surface irregularities of these fibers to produce distinctive textural characteristics. Such color and textural variations appear in the linen blend covering in Figure 19.2.

Figure 19.2 Laminated wall covering enriched by the natural color and texture of linen fibers.
Courtesy Sommer® Coverings, division of Allibert, Inc.

Figure 19.3 The use of variously colored complex yarns in single layers increases the visual and textural interest of these wall coverings.
Courtesy Sommer® Coverings, division of Allibert, Inc.

The high stiffness and low elasticity of linen limit its use in certain textile furnishings, but these properties contribute high dimensional stability to wall coverings, helping to minimize sagging. When flame resistance is required by codes for contract interiors or desired in residential spaces, designers and architects can specify the application of flame-retardant compounds to fabrics composed of linen, cotton, or rayon, or they may elect to use wool or glass fibers.

To reduce the cost of coverings composed of some natural fibers, producers frequently blend them with viscose rayon. Although viscose rayon has poor dimensional stability, the use of a backing or coating can overcome the problem, and some coverings are composed entirely of this relatively inexpensive cellulose-based fiber.

Of the noncellulosic fibers, polypropylene olefin fibers have an extremely low specific gravity. They may be used to produce lightweight coverings resembling those composed of wool (Figure 19.5).

Simple and complex yarns are used alone or in combination. Placing the yarns individually in a parallel arrangement on a backing fabric often emphasizes the decorative effects of complex yarns. This technique highlights the varied features of the yarns (see the coverings in Figure 19.3).

Eye-catching reflections appear in wall coverings when they incorporate bright manufactured fibers, silk, metal filaments, and metallic yarns. In some coverings, spiral yarns containing metallic strands are plied with simple yarns strategically positioned to create reflective highlights as viewers pass the wall.

Construction Techniques

Because wall and panel coverings are not subjected to significant levels of abrasion or repeated flexing, a great variety of coverings is available. The assortment of coverings offered to contemporary consumers includes a number of distinctively constructed fabrics, as well as fabrics produced by conventional weaving and knitting procedures. Wall coverings for contract interiors are constructed to provide the increased durability and serviceability that are essential in high-use areas. Typically, vinyl coverings are chosen for contract interiors.

Weaving

Flat-woven wall covering fabrics range from those produced with a simple biaxial interlacing pattern to those produced with a decorative dobby or Jacquard weave.

Figure 19.4 Open woven jute covering permits view of the printed pattern on the backing.
Courtesy Sommer® Coverings, division of Allibert, Inc.

Figure 19.5 Needlepunched wall covering with a three-dimensional, pile-like surface.

The visual and tactile interest of these fabrics is often enhanced with flocking or embroidering. Woven pile fabrics, such as corduroy and velvet, and woven or tufted carpet are also available.

Frequently, fabric stylists design woven coverings with relatively low compactness of construction, so that the backings are visible. Figure 19.4 shows a jute covering in which the trellis print on the backing can be viewed through the face fabric, and the visual interest of the surface is augmented.

Knitting

For high-dimensional stability, most knitted wall coverings are produced with a tricot or interlock stitch. Such fabrics readily conform to curved surfaces.

Needlepunching

Webs of fibers may be layered into a batt and stabilized by needlepunching (Figure 23.13, p. 368). For increased visual and textural interest, the level surface may be punched or embossed to create a three-dimensional, patterned configuration (Figure 19.5). This alteration in fabric form may produce an appearance resembling that of more expensive

woven pile fabrics. Such structural changes may also improve the acoustical value of the coverings, making them especially suitable for covering panels in open office interiors. Measurement of the acoustical benefits of wall and panel coverings was discussed earlier in this chapter.

Laminating

Frequently, a single web or layer of textile yarns is laminated or glued directly to a paper base. In such structures, the parallel yarns may be closely or widely spaced, and the yarns may be fine or coarse, as in the laminated coverings in Figures 19.2 and 19.3.

Extruding

Vinyl wall coverings are manufactured by extrusion. In many cases, they are subsequently embossed to simulate the textural effects of woven fabrics. There are three classes of vinyl wall coverings. Type I vinyl wall covering has a total face weight of 7 to 13 ounces per square yard and is used in residential or light-commercial interiors. Type II vinyl wall covering has a total face weight of 15 to 22 ounces per square yard and is installed in medium-use contract applications. Type III vinyl wall covering has a total face weight greater than 22 ounces per square yard and is used in high-service applications.

Backings and Finishes

Various backings and finishing agents are used with textile wall and panel fabrics. Some of these serve both functional and aesthetic purposes.

Sueding

Genuine suede could be used to cover walls and panels, but such applications would be expensive. Manufacturers do, however, offer simulated suede coverings (Figure 19.6). Not only is the materials cost of the simulated suede lower, but so is the potential for crocking when people inadvertently rub against the surfaces.

Backings

Acrylic foam, vinyl spray, paper, gypsum, or a spunlaced or spunbonded fabric must be applied to the back of most textile fabric coverings to prevent the application adhesive from striking through and producing a stained appearance and to provide dimensional stability. Spunbonded back-

Figure 19.6 Simulated suede wall covering. *Courtesy Sommer® Coverings, division of Allibert, Inc.*

ings, normally composed of polypropylene olefin fibers, are designed to be strippable, a feature attractive to residents anticipating a change in coverings.

Gypsum, a high-density, uncrystallized plaster, may be used to coat the back of open-weave burlap wall covering. When applied, the compound is soft, permitting the coverings to be rolled for shipment. After contact with the special adhesive that secures the fabric to the wall, the coating crystallizes and sets into a hard backing. The compound, available in numerous colors, fills fabric interstices and hides any surface defects.

Backings for vinyl wall coverings are necessary for dimensional stability. The three backings used with vinyl wall coverings are **scrim**, **osnaburg**, and **drill**. Scrim backings weigh an average of 1.2 ounces per square yard and are used with Type I wall coverings. Osnaburg backings, which weigh an average of 2.0 ounces per square yard, are used with Type II wall coverings. Drill fabrics weigh an average of 3.6 ounces per square yard and are used with Type III vinyl wall coverings.

Functional Finishes

For increased safety in the event of fire, textile wall and panel coverings may be treated with a flame-retardant compound. The design professional is advised that these treatments may change such physical properties of the fabric as colorfastness, strength, dimensional stability, and hand. Additionally, the fabric may give off noxious fumes. To reduce the rate of soil accumulation and to protect the coverings from unsightly staining, fluorocarbon compounds may be applied. For maximum protection against soil accumulation, fingerprints, atmospheric contaminants, and general abuse, and to make the surface washable, textile wall coverings may be laminated with a clear or translucent vinyl film. Over time, laminated fabrics may tend to yellow. This treatment, also used on upholstery fabric, was described in Chapter 14.

Installation Techniques

Textile coverings are generally installed over structural wall surfaces with one of four techniques: shirring, stapling, adhesives, or premounted supports. Proper preparation of the substrate is important for the installation of both textile and nontextile wall coverings to eliminate surface flaws from being seen.

Shirring

Shirring is a simple and inexpensive technique for covering walls with nonbacked textile fabrics. After yardage has been allowed for fullness and pattern matching, if necessary, the fabric widths are seamed and the top and bottom edges are finished with a casing. The casing may be plain or constructed with a heading (Figure 16.5, p. 265). Conventional curtain rods are then inserted through the casings and positioned on the walls to support the shirred fabric.

Stapling

When the wall surface is smooth, the edges of textile fabric coverings may be stapled directly to the structural material. Seaming can be avoided by covering the joins with decorative tape or braid or with rigid molding (Figure 19.7). When the wall is rough and damaged, lath strips must be nailed first to the top, bottom, and sides of the wall and next to the framework of the doors and windows. After the fabric is stapled to the laths, decorative tape or braid may be glued over the edges to conceal the staples. Because the lath strips support the fabric a small distance from the wall surface, surface irregularities are concealed.

Using an Adhesive

Textile structures having a paper or foam backing may be handled in essentially the same manner as wallpaper is handled in the hanging procedure. With paper-backed textile structures, the adhesive is generally applied to the paper; with foam-backed structures, the adhesive is generally applied to the wall. With vinyl wall coverings, the adhesive is generally applied to the vinyl prior to installation.

Figure 19.7 Joins of moiré wall covering concealed by rigid molding.
Courtesy of Celanese Corporation.

Using Premounted Supports

As the use of textile structures on walls has increased, specialized mechanisms have been developed to add tension and support to the coverings. In one such system, the fabric is held in wall-mounted channels by locking clips. Another features loop and hook fasteners. The covering is backed with a soft fabric with tiny loops over its surface; the mounting strips have tiny hooks on their surfaces. Contact between the loops and hooks secures the fabric to the wall, and the raw edges are tucked into channels in the strips. Sewn seams are avoided by tucking the fabric edges into parallel panels built into double strips.

Summary

Webs of textile yarns and textile fabrics may be used as interior wall finishes for decorative purposes, noise reduction, and energy conservation. Professionals must confirm the acoustical and insulation values of the textiles prior to installation. Some coverings are composed of natural fibers with their inherent color characteristics; some are composed of manufactured fibers; and some contain metal filaments and metallic yarns. Most textile coverings for use on walls and panels are woven, knitted, needlepunched, or laminated. Paper or foam backings are applied to prevent strikethrough of an application adhesive and to provide dimensional stability. Vinyl structures are chosen for wall applications when durability and serviceability are of paramount importance.

A consumer may successfully execute some wall covering installations, such as shirring and stapling. Other installations, however, should generally be left to a skilled professional.

Key Terms

drill

gypsum

noise reduction coefficient (NRC)

osnaburg

scrim

shirring

Review Questions

1. Discuss design elements and principles that are achieved with the use of textile wall coverings.

2. List two functional characteristics of textile wall coverings.

3. List the advantages of natural fibers for use in wall coverings.

4. What is the purpose of backings for fabrics to be used as wall coverings?

5. How is a three-dimensional patterned configuration achieved in needlepunching?

6. What are three types of vinyl wall covering?

7. What are the disadvantages of applying a flame-retardant finish to fabrics?

8. Over time, what tends to happen to fabrics that are laminated?

9. Discuss the three backings used on vinyl wall coverings.

10. List four methods of installing textile wall coverings.

UNIT THREE CASESTUDY

Designer Name: Diana L. Frucci, ASID
                        Interior Design International

Project Location: Private Residence
                        Atlanta, GA

Statement of the Project:

The newly constructed "garden house" needed textile accessories to complete the "romantic garden feel" that the client wanted. In order to soften the exposed wood of the house, textile window treatments and patio furniture with upholstered seat cushions were suggested.

The garden house is constructed like a gazebo; it has a roof that will provide some shelter from the elements. There are no walls, only a trellis panel to suggest a wall on one side, and three open sides. The house will be used for outside dinner parties, and for larger entertainments it may house a band or buffet table. The house that it complements is Tudor in design, probably constructed in the 1920s. The garden includes a reflecting pool with Japanese goldfish, and many types of English foliage, complete with a creek running through it. The new garden house needed to blend with the garden and be as comfortable as possible for the clients.

Statement of the Problem:

The fabric needed to withstand the elements year round, and be colorfast and mildew resistant. The furnishings also needed to maintain their original appearance for at least five years. Other considerations were the type of thread used to sew the hem in the drapery panels. The thread needed to be colorfast and not support mildew, like the fabric. The hem also had to be approximately 3″ above finished floor (a.f.f.) in order to allow for possible flooding during the spring months. The drapery panels needed to be mounted on boards with stainless steel screws in order to prevent rusting.

Selection Criteria:

The recommendation was to use tailored drapery panels in each of the four corners of the space that would be tied back with a decorative tassel. The fabric recommended was an acrylic solid in a neutral shade of taupe. Chair cushions and settee cushions were recommended to complement the window treatments in a subtle print of taupe on créme. The cushions would then be snapped and tied to the chair seats. The style of chair was also chosen to replicate the trellis motif forming the back "wall."

Product Specifications:

SUNBRELLA®

- #8300 (solid taupe) and SUNBRELLA® #9305-01 (print)

- 100% solution-dyed acrylic fabric

- Width—54″

- Guarantee against mildew and fading

- Warranted for 5 years

Maintenance and Cost:

To reduce maintenance and accommodate the exterior application, the textile needed to resist mildew and fading. The manufacturer's recommended maintenance guidelines include spot washing with a sponge and warm, soapy water. Washing is to be followed by a thorough rinsing with clean water until soap is removed. After the fabric is rinsed, it should be air dried. Fabric spot remover is recommended for stubborn stains. While solution-dyed acrylic does not promote the growth of mildew, mildew may grow on other substances that are attached to the fabric. A solution of one cup bleach plus two capsfull of soap per gallon of water can be used to clean mildew. This solution should be sprayed on the entire area and allowed to penetrate. The fabric should be rinsed thoroughly and allowed to air dry. SUNBRELLA® is a midrange, affordable fabric with a five-year warranty that ensures a lower long-term cost for the product. With proper maintenance and use the life-cycle of the fabric could extend to ten or fifteen years.

Discussion Questions:

1. Identify two of the client's requirements for the design project.

2. Describe one of the aesthetic features that the client requires.

3. Distinguish one of the functional features of the product that meet the client's requirments.

4. Discuss specific features used to accommodate seasonal weather changes.

5. Discuss the importance of the solution-dyed fiber.

6. Research another product that is appropriate for this application. Next compare and contrast the cost effectiveness, availability, durability, and maintenance of the new product with the one used in the casestudy.

7. Assume you have found another fabric that is guaranteed for three years but is one-fifth the cost of the SUNBRELLA® fabric. Which one is more economical?

Soft Floor Coverings
and Cushions

Unit Four focuses on soft floor coverings and cushions. Chapter 20 offers a review of several variables affecting the selection of carpet, rugs, and cushions for residential and commercial interiors. In Chapter 21, statistical profiles detail fiber usage in today's soft floor coverings, and several fiber and yarn properties influencing floor performance are discussed. Chapter 22 explains tufting, the dominant carpet construction technique. Weaving and other machine techniques are examined in Chapter 23, and hand techniques are reviewed in Chapter 24.

The composition, construction, and performance properties of carpet and rug cushions are considered in Chapter 25. Chapter 26 summarizes procedures to measure functional characteristics and performance properties of carpet and carpet and cushion assemblies; it also identifies items included in carpet specification lists. Finally, the installation and maintenance of soft floor coverings is reviewed in Chapter 27.

20

Selection Criteria for Soft Floor Coverings

Appearance Features
   Sizes and Shapes
   Surface Texture
   Surface Coloration

Serviceability Expectations
   Functional Properties
   Use-life Characteristics

Design and Performance Regulations

Cost Factors
   Initial Purchase Price
   Installation Charges
   Maintenance Expenses
   Life-cycle Costing

Several of the selection criteria discussed in Chapter 2 apply to the selection of soft floor coverings. Personal preference, professional recommendation, and anticipated in-use conditions and activities determine the nature and importance of these qualities. In some cases, certain design and performance characteristics are prescribed by regulatory agencies.

Soft floor coverings cannot be selected on the basis of appearance features alone. The built environment should be attractive, but it also must be safe and functional. Because the features of the combined carpet and cushion assembly influence the functional and safety characteristics of floor coverings, attention must be given to the structure and properties of both layers. Special attention should be given to the selection and installation of floor covering assemblies in locations frequented by people with physical or visual limitations. Interior floor finishes should not be hazardous barriers; they should help, not hinder, mobility.

As is true for any other consumer purchase, the total cost of a planned floor covering project must be affordable. The initial materials costs, the installation charges, and the long-term maintenance expenses must all be considered. In many cases, use-cost analyses, which reflect these financial variables, may show carpet and cushion assemblies to be more economical than other flooring materials.

Appearance Features

Residential and commercial consumers have widely varying and constantly changing tastes in the size, shape, color, and texture of soft floor coverings. The visual impact and tactile interest of these features are primary concerns, but consideration must also be given to variables such as end-use lighting and yarn size if the planned appearance is to be realized, and to soiling if the appearance is to be retained. Anticipated traffic levels and safety concerns may preclude the choice of certain appearance features.

Sizes and Shapes

Some soft floor covering products, including rollgoods and modules, are designed to cover all of the floor space within an interior. Other products are designed to define a limited area, such as an entrance foyer or the space under a furniture grouping. The particular style chosen determines the method of installation. Generally speaking, a securely fastened or anchored floor covering is referred to as **carpet**, and a loosely laid structure is called a **rug**. The term **broadloom** is frequently used to identify rollgoods that are more than 54 inches wide. The term does not describe the method of construction, and it carries no implication about quality.

Wall-to-Wall Carpet

Wall-to-wall carpet covers the entire floor space, baseboard to baseboard (Figure 20.1). As is true for other consumer purchases, certain compromises are inevitable when one style of floor covering is selected over another.

A wall-to-wall installation has some negative features:

- The initial cost is higher as more square yardage is required.
- Costs are incurred for installation.
- It must be cleaned in place.
- Repair of large damaged areas is difficult.
- It cannot be shifted to equalize traffic patterns and soiling.
- Extra yardage may be required for matching patterns.
- It is difficult to remove for relocation.

On the other hand, a wall-to-wall installation has these positive features:

+ It is securely anchored to prevent shifting.
+ There are no loose edges to cause tripping.
+ There is no "curb" effect for wheelchairs if low level pile is used.
+ Potential for energy conservation is maximized.
+ The room may appear larger.
+ It can camouflage slightly worn or uneven floors.
+ No special preparation of the floor is usually required.
+ It may improve the resale value of a building.

Figure 20.1 Wall-to-wall installation of rollgoods.
Courtesy of The Wool Bureau, Inc.

Some manufacturers offer broadloom rollgoods with rug-like designs strategically placed. Such goods provide the appearance of a loose-laid rug, but can be securely attached to the floor, an advantage in high-traffic areas in commercial interiors.

Carpet Modules

Carpet modules are also known as squares or tiles, and are generally 18 or 36 inches square. Their use has been increasing, especially in commercial installations. Some are designed to be glued directly to the floor with a permanent or a releasable adhesive; others are manufactured to be extra heavy and stiff so that when they are free-laid, gravity holds them in place. When correctly installed, the surface has many of the same features as wall-to-wall carpet since the squares are laid across the entire floor space.

The installation in Figure 20.2 illustrates the design flexibility offered by carpet modules.

Carpet modules have some limiting characteristics:

– Initial materials costs are high.
– Edge curl can occur with low-quality tiles.
– Butted joints can separate with improper installation.

They also offer some distinct advantages, especially when releasable or no adhesive is used:

+ Loss of materials during installation is minimal.
+ They are easily rotated to equalize traffic and soiling patterns.
+ They may be replaced if damaged.
+ They may be lifted for access to underfloor service trenches.

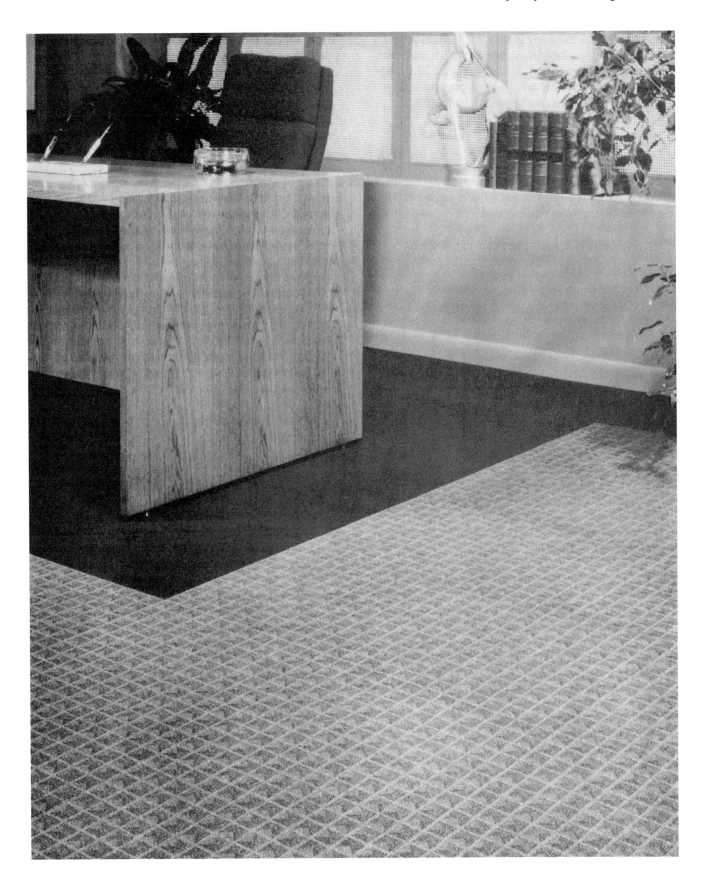

Figure 20.2 Carpet module installation.

Courtesy of Milliken and Company.

Room-Size Rugs

Room-size rugs are intended to be loose-laid, coming within 12 inches of each wall. **Room-fit rugs** are designed or cut to come to or within one or two inches of the walls. Either of these rugs can be cut to follow the contours of a room, with their raw edges finished by serging (machine overcasting), fringing, binding with twill-woven tape, or with a seam-sealing cement. Because these floor coverings can easily be rolled up for moving, they are especially attractive to people who rent and to those who anticipate frequent relocation.

Room-size rugs are often available in such standard sizes as 9 feet by 12 feet and 12 feet by 15 feet. Rugs have some negative features:

- They may have to be cut to fit an unconventional perimeter.
- Cut edges require finishing.
- Unsecured edges may cause tripping.
- A "curb" effect may be presented to wheelchair drivers.

They also have some positive features:

+ They are available in standard room sizes.
+ No installation is required if standard size fits room contour.
+ They are easily moved to a new location.
+ They are highly decorative.

Runners

A **runner** is a long, narrow form of a room-fit rug installed in hallways and on stairs. Runners are normally 27 inches wide, cut to any length, and serged or fringed on the cut ends. On stairs, runners can be held in place with brass rods securely anchored at the back of the treads (Figure 27.6, p. 401).

A special form of runner is the **walk-off mat** used in entrance areas subjected to high traffic levels. These mats are intended to capture tracked-in dirt and grit, protecting the carpet from abrasion and apparent changes in color caused by such materials. For safety, walk-off mats should be heavy and stiff enough to prevent edge curl, which could cause tripping.

Area Rugs

The extensive range of sizes and shapes available on today's market can partly explain the rising popularity of **area rugs**. Whatever the spatial need, an area rug can be chosen to fill it (Figure 20.3). These floor coverings are available in such sizes as 27 inches by 54 inches, 4 feet by 6 feet, and 6 feet by 9 feet. There are square, round, oval, rectangular, octagonal, and free-form shapes; the rug may or may not have fringe. Coupled with the wide variety of constructions, fiber contents, textures, and colorations, these features can make for much design appeal. Some consumers and designers lay area rugs directly on smooth floors, especially on fine hardwood; others lay them over wall-to-wall carpet to define a furniture grouping or accentuate a living area; and still others hang them as decorative wall accents.

The selection of an area rug involves considering their drawbacks:

- They are hazardous to persons having limited vision or mobility.
- They may shift or slide on smooth floors.
- They tend to "walk" off thick cushions and move on carpet.

However, area rugs are attractive:

+ They come in an extensive variety of sizes, shapes, designs, and textures.
+ No installation is required.
+ They are easily moved.

Scatter Rugs

Scatter rugs are small rugs, often 2 feet by 3 feet or smaller. They are used in the home where traffic and soiling are concentrated, such as inside the entrance area and in front of sinks. Novelty scatter rugs serve as decorative accents and are available in imaginative shapes ranging from a dog's paw print to an orange slice. These floor coverings are also relatively inexpensive. However, they are easily tripped over and they slide on smooth surfaces. Their use should be limited, especially when persons with visual or physical limitations use the interior.

Surface Texture

Besides their length and width, most textile floor coverings have a noticeable third dimension, that of depth, produced by a pile or wear layer. Variations in the visual and tactile characteristics of pile layers depend on differences in pile sweep, pile height, pile thickness, pile construction density, and yarn twist, as well as whether the pile tufts have been cut.

Figure 20.3 Area rug used to define a furniture grouping.
Courtesy of Hickory Hill Furniture Corporation.

Pile Sweep

Pile sweep is shown schematically in Figure 9.4 (p. 135). The greater the slant of the pile yarns, the more prominent the nap or lay of the pile layer. This feature determines the quantity of light a floor covering reflects, which increases as the angle decreases. Therefore, when pile floor coverings are installed, care must be taken that the nap goes in the same direction (see Chapter 27).

Pile Height

Pile height is the length of the pile tufts above the backing; the length of that part of the pile yarn incorporated in the backing is excluded. Pile height is normally reported in decimal form, and is routinely supplied to contract designers, architects, and others specifying floor covering variables. Pile heights typically range from 0.187 to 1.250 inches.

Pile Thickness

Pile thickness is the average thickness of the pile material above the backing. Because thickness measurements are made on finished floor coverings, they reflect any pile sweep introduced during conversion operations.

Pile Construction Density

Pile construction density is determined by the closeness of the pile tufts in the wear layer. A dense construction has closely spaced tufts; a sparse construction has widely spaced tufts (Figure 20.4). Density has a major influence on the surface appearance, texture retention, and wear-life of pile structures.

Consumers and professionals can make an eyeball evaluation of construction density by flexing a carpet or rug and judging how much backing is exposed, that is, how much the structure "grins" (Figure 20.5); lower den-

a) Uncut Tufts

b) Cut Tufts

Figure 20.4 High and low pile construction densities.
Courtesy of Allied Fibers.

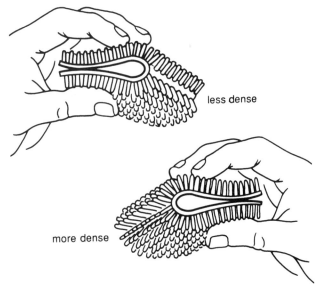

less dense

more dense

Figure 20.5 "Eyeball" evaluation of pile construction density.

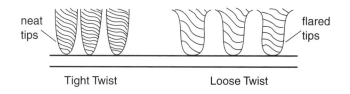

neat tips   Tight Twist   Loose Twist   flared tips

Figure 20.6 Effect of twist level on the appearance of pile yarns.
Courtesy of Allied Fibers.

sities produce broader smiles. Pile construction density and potential exposure of the backing are especially critical factors to examine when selecting carpet for installation on stairs.

Cut and Uncut Pile

The yarn loops in some soft floor coverings are cut, producing independent tufts. In other coverings, the loops are left uncut (see Figure 20.4).

Yarn Twist

The level of twist used in pile yarns has a major influence on the appearance of soft floor coverings. Higher levels create well-defined yarn ends, and lower levels create flared tips (Figure 20.6). Differences in twist level are largely responsible for the appearance differences observed among one level cut pile surface textures (Figures 20.7a through f).

A brief outline will help to sort out the wide variety of textures available in pile floor coverings today. Differences among these surfaces are a result of variations in the textural characteristics described above.

   I. One Level Cut Pile Styles
      A. Velour
      B. Plush
      C. Saxony
      D. Friezé
      E. Shag
      F. Splush
      G. Tip Shear
  II. One Level Loop Pile Styles
 III. Multilevel Loop Pile Styles
 IV. Multilevel Cut and Loop Pile Styles
      A. Sculptured
      B. High-low
      C. Random Shear

One Level Cut Pile Styles

Several cut pile styles have a uniform level across their surfaces. These styles differ among themselves in pile height, pile density, and yarn construction, however.

Velour surfaces are fine, short, dense constructions that are relatively new textures for soft floor coverings

a) velour   b) plush   c) saxony

d) friezé   e) shag   f) tip shear

g) one level, loop   h) multilevel, loop   i) multilevel, cut and loop

Figure 20.7 Surface textures of contemporary pile floor coverings.

(Figure 20.7a). Their production has been made possible by the development of machinery and fabrication processes that can yield high pile construction densities, for example, fusion bonding. High density allows pile height to be decreased without diminishing the important variable of pile yarn weight (see Chapter 22). Velour surfaces normally have a pile height of 0.25 inch.

The pile yarns in **plush**, also called **velvet** and **velvet plush**, surfaces (Figure 20.7b) range in height from 0.625 to 0.750 inch. The pile yarns have relatively low levels of twist: the cut yarn ends blend together for a luxurious, velvet-like look and feel. In use, these textures exhibit shading effects when the orientation of the pile yarns is physically changed. When occasional foot traffic or vacuum cleaning alters the direction of the pile yarns, the effect is normally temporary; the yarns gradually recover their original positions. In areas where directional traffic patterns cross or where pivoting action is common, the pile layer will be repeatedly crushed in opposing directions, and the effect may be permanent. In such areas, a darker area may appear as an irregularly shaped circle, somewhat like a large stain: the pile yarns are oriented in

one direction inside and outside of the circle, and in the reverse direction along the outline. This appearance problem is variously described as **pile reversal, watermarking, shading,** and **pooling.**

Saxony textures (Figure 20.7c) have approximately the same pile height and density as that seen in plush. However, saxony yarns have a higher twist level that is heat-stabilized to reduce the amount of flaring at the tips of the cut yarns. Rather than blending together in a continuous surface, each yarn end is well defined, and the set twist minimizes splaying and improves thickness retention. Apparently, the improved yarn stability and resiliency exhibited by saxony textures have increased their popularity.

Friezé textures, also known as twist textures, are constructed of yarns having maximum twist for high stability and wear-life. Each yarn is clearly visible, since the high twist defines each yarn and encourages it to seek its own direction of orientation in the lower density pile (Figure 20.7d).

The height of pile yarns in **shag** surface (Figure 20.7e) goes up to approximately 1.250 inches. The pile density is lower than that in plush and saxony textures; the longer pile yarns are responsible for covering the backing.

Splash textures have a pile height and a pile construction density between those typically used for plush and shag surfaces. The production of splash has diminished in recent years, largely as a result of an increased preference for saxony textures.

Tip shear surfaces are produced by selectively shearing the uppermost portion of some yarn loops (Figure 20.7f). Subtle differences in luster appear because more light is reflected from the smooth loops than from the sheared fibers. Frequently, low pile, densely constructed floor coverings are sheared to camouflage future soil accumulation.

One Level Loop Pile Styles

In the past, carpet with a short, level loop pile (Figure 20.7g) was normally seen only in such commercial settings as restaurants, airport terminals, and hospitals. Many professionals and consumers thought this surface had an "institutional" appearance. Today, improved color styling and yarn texturing have helped to make the uniform surface more appealing (see Figure 21.1, p. 344), and residential use of this durable, wear-resistant surface has increased.

Multilevel Loop Pile Styles

Multilevel loop pile styles show noticeable differences in the height of their pile yarns (Figure 20.7h). The variations may be random or planned to create a pattern. These surfaces are quite durable if density is reasonably high.

Multilevel Cut and Loop Pile Styles

Combining cut loops, uncut loops, and multiple pile heights (Figure 20.7i) produces various surface constructions. These include sculptured, high-low, and random shear textures.

Sculptured pile surfaces have a definite three-dimensional appearance. In most cases, the higher loops are all cut and the lower loops all uncut for an embossed effect. Normally, the cut pile areas are dominant, and the visual impact is strong and formal. The exquisite texture of some custom floor coverings is produced by hand sculpturing dense, cut pile surfaces.

High-low is the name given to some multilevel cut and loop styles with an informal appearance. Sometimes, the higher tufts have the appearance of shag textures.

Random shear textures differ from tip shear textures because they contain multiple levels of pile yarns instead of a single level. They differ from sculptured surfaces in that the uppermost portions of some of the higher yarn tufts are sheared, not all of them as in sculptured coverings.

Surface Coloration

Soft floor coverings may or may not dominate the aesthetics of an interior. A carpet or rug may have a subdued, solid-colored surface and serve as a backdrop for other more distinctive furnishings; or it may have detailed designs or bold graphic colorations whose strong visual impact attracts attention. Residential consumers are generally free to choose color stylings that please them; contract designers and architects may be limited by the preferences of their clients, but they are able to use their professional training to recommend colorations. Whoever chooses the color styling, the possible effects of end-use conditions and activities on the color must be anticipated.

Color Styling

The color styling of soft floor coverings ranges from solid-colored surfaces in dark, deep hues to finely detailed designs in light, intense hues. Preferences for various color characteristics and styles in carpet and rugs fluctuate in the same cycles that hold for other fashion merchandise, such as apparel and cars. Avocado green surfaces, for example, were treasured in the 1950s; today, they enjoy about the same favor as the doubleknit leisure suits that were prized in the 1970s.

Solid-colored surfaces can be produced in any combination of color characteristics preferred by the professional or consumer. Distinctive multicolored stylings are produced with heather, Berber, space-dyed, and moresque yarns. Authentic **Berber yarns**, a type of speck yarn hand spun by peoples of northern Africa, contain the deep, rich browns and grays of the wool retrieved from the sheep. Simulated Berber yarns (Figure 20.8) are produced by blending dyed, staple-length acrylic, olefin, and/or nylon fibers.

Figure 20.9 Shag carpet with space-dyed color styling.

Figure 20.8 Simulated Berber yarn composed of staple-length, fiber-dyed acrylic fibers.

A carpet of space-dyed pile yarns is shown in Figure 20.9. The varied coloration adds visual interest; its potential effectiveness for masking the appearance of soil and stains is apparent. Other multicolored effects can be produced with operations such as TAK and gum printing, described in Chapter 8.

Patterned floor coverings may have designs created with colored fibers and yarns during construction or printed on the greige rollgoods. The almost infinite variety of patterns and colors available in stock lines can be expanded by custom design and color work. Some commercial carpet producers, in fact, maintain an inventory of floor coverings in a range of neutral colors, so that contract designers and architects can order the addition of distinctive motifs in specific colors.

Factors Affecting Apparent Color

The various conditions and activities that may affect the surface color should affect the choice of a soft floor covering. (Factors affecting apparent color were discussed in Chapter 8; those affecting actual color are identified in Chapter 26.) Special attention should be given to the potential effects of soiling on the apparent surface color. For interiors where there will be low traffic and minimal spillage, such as formal living rooms and executive conference rooms, relatively light, solid colored carpet may be serviceable. For locations where the covering will undergo much spillage and tracked-in dirt, a darker, multicolored surface may be called for to mask the appearance of soil. Tweeds, space-dyed yarns, and small, repetitive motifs may be effective. In some locations, it may even be advisable to coordinate the carpet color with the color of the soil in the area.

When heavy traffic is anticipated, consumers and professionals should select floor coverings whose components and construction features will encourage pile retention and provide abrasion resistance. This can help to minimize the development of a patchy surface luster in use.

Serviceability Expectations

Service-related considerations influence the selection of soft floor coverings. Some of these concern the functional benefits carpet and rugs can contribute, and others, their use-life characteristics.

Functional Properties

Many residential and commercial consumers seek to camouflage structural defects, reduce noise, or conserve energy with soft floor coverings. They may also be looking for improved safety and mobility for people with visual or physical limitations.

Camouflage Worn and Uneven Floors

An increase in building materials costs, and, at times, mortgage interest rates, has encouraged many people to renovate and refurbish older structures. Such structures may be sound but have worn or uneven floors. Installing a carpet and cushion assembly can help to fill uneven spaces and hide damaged floor areas. This approach may be particularly effective when a multilevel loop surface texture is chosen. This property of soft floor coverings is both functional and aesthetic.

Add Comfort and Reduce Fatigue

The comfort provided by soft floor coverings might also be deemed an aesthetic and functional quality. The tactile pleasure of stepping onto a deep pile, cushioned surface is clear in contrast to the lack of give characteristic of such smooth, hard, nonresilient surfaces as slate and quarry tiles.

The compressibility of textile floor coverings enables them to absorb and cushion the impact forces of walking. For people who spend the major portion of the working day on their feet—homemakers, nurses, production managers and technicians, waiters and waitresses, bank tellers, and sales personnel—-the cushioning effect of carpet can be critically important. It may lessen orthopedic problems, reduce fatigue, and increase productivity.

Increase Safety

The compressibility of soft floor coverings contributes comfort; it also is responsible for increasing the margin of safety. When falls are cushioned, the severity of injury can be reduced. This criterion is especially important to the selection of carpet and rugs for use in interiors where older persons work or reside.

Textile floor coverings may reduce the frequency of falling. They provide a slip-resistant surface for better footing, and they do not have the "slippery when wet" problem characteristic of some hard, polished floorings.

Improve Interiors for People with Disabilities

Textile floor coverings can be useful for people with mobility and sight impairments while enriching the interior space with their warmth and beauty of color and texture. Careful attention must be given to their selection and installation, however, to ensure that they do not become barriers. The Veterans' Administration has made recommendations for the design of residences for use by veterans with physical disabilities: "Low pile, high density carpet may be installed in any appropriate location. In addition to its aesthetic qualities, carpet greatly reduces sound transmission and serves to cushion accidental falls."[1]

Soft floor coverings can provide a slip-resistant surface for persons using canes and crutches. Slip resistance is especially critical for swing-through movement, when body weight is transferred to the crutches. All carpet and rug edges must be securely attached to the floor to prevent tripping and to minimize the movement of the carpet surface under force.

Wheelchair users need soft floor coverings with a low pile so that no curb effect is created. Pile should be dense and minimally compressible, allowing for easy movement of the chair over the surface. Shaggy, loose constructions tend to entrap the wheels and restrict forward movement. Cushions may be separate and thin, permanently attached to the carpet back, or not used. Shearing, the movement of the carpet and cushion in opposite directions, can occur when the chair is driven over the surface. Shearing can be avoided, and warping or rippling can be minimized, by gluing the carpet directly to the floor.

Figure 20.10 shows a comparison of the usefulness of several interior floor coverings for people of limited vision or mobility. Depressed grouting in some coverings can hinder mobility. Surfaces that become slippery when wet should be only selectively used.

For people who are blind or have limited sight, certain carpet and rug features can provide cues for increased orientation and mobility. Orientation skills and cues help persons with diminished sight to identify their location within an environment; mobility skills and cues enable them to travel through the space. Total or partial loss of vision does not result in a more acute sense of smell or touch, or more sensitive hearing; but persons with impaired vision become more aware of their other senses and more perceptive with them. Patterns of vari-

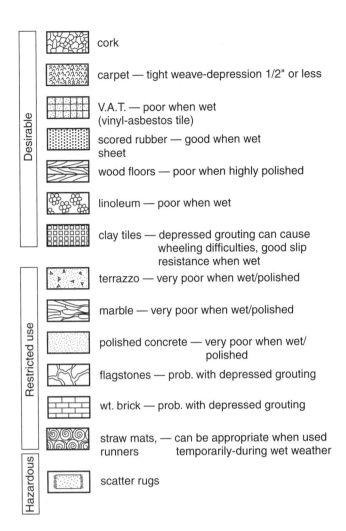

Figure 20.10 Paving suggestions for interior floor space to be accessible to persons of limited mobility.
Design Criteria: New Public Building Accessibility, PBS (PCD): DG5, General Services Administration, Washington, D.C., December 1977, 103.

ance in the texture underfoot may aid in orientation, helping the person to feel where he or she is within the interior. The surfaces must have marked textural differences if they are to be detected; an example would be carpet alternated with a smooth flooring such as tile or linoleum. Different surfaces can also provide auditory cues. The edges of carpet and rugs can serve as a "shoreline," guiding a cane traveler.[2]

Carpet and rug surfaces lack any capacity for the glare and bright reflections characteristic of highly polished smooth surfaces, which are troublesome to persons with a visual limitation. For accent and demarcation, such as at

the nosing of stairs, red-yellow, as opposed to blue-green, colors are more effective.[3] Some persons with limited vision may see differences in value or intensity better than they see differences in hue.[4]

Before modifying any environment for use by people of limited sight or mobility, their advice and counsel should be sought. Help can also be obtained from professional organizations, several of which are listed in Appendix C.

Reduce Noise

Noise abatement is often one of the more important functions of floor coverings and cushions. This is especially useful in such interiors as classrooms and conference rooms, music recording studios, open offices, and healthcare facilities. Along with the tests used to measure the acoustical values of carpet, alone and in combination with cushions, various factors influencing this property are identified in Chapter 26.

Conserve Energy

Extensive research has shown that certain structural features of carpet and cushions increase thermal resistance (see Chapter 26). Research has also shown that certain appearance features can increase light reflectance, decreasing the quantity of light needed from artificial illuminants. Studies have also shown than people may "feel" warmer in a room having carpet than in one without, thus enabling the temperature to be lowered without affecting comfort.

Use-life Characteristics

When selecting one of today's textile floor coverings, consumers and professionals should focus their attention on the variables that govern appearance or newness retention, retention of the original color and texture. Fortunately, minimal attention can be given to questions of wear caused by abrasion: the loss of significant amounts of fiber as a result of abrasive wear has largely been overcome by the use of nylon and improved processing.

If rapid changes in appearance are to be avoided or minimized, the fiber properties, yarn characteristics, and construction features of soft floor coverings must be chosen in light of anticipated end-use conditions. Traffic conditions, for example, vary for different interior loca-

Table 20.1 Traffic Ratings for Selected Interior Spaces

L-M denotes light-medium traffic; H denotes heavy traffic.

Area (by Major Category)	Traffic Rating	Area (by Major Category)	Traffic Rating
Educational		**Commercial**	
Schools and colleges		*Banks*	
administration	L-M	executive	L-M
classroom	H	lobby	H
dormitory	H	teller windows	H
corridor	H*	corridors	H*
cafeteria	H	*Retail establishments*	
libraries	L-M	aisle	H*
Museums and art galleries		check-out	H
display room	H	sales counter	H
executive	L-M	smaller boutiques, etc.	H
lobby	H	window and display area	L-M
		Office buildings	
		executive	L-M
Medical		clerical	H
Health care		corridor	H*
executive	L-M	cafeteria	H
patient's room	H	*Supermarkets*	H
lounge	H	*Food services*	H
nurses station	H		
corridor	H*	**Recreational**	
lobby	H	*Recreational areas*	
		clubhouse	H
Multiresidential		locker room	H
Apartments, hotels and motels		swimming pool	H
lobby/public areas	H*	recreational vehicles	H
corridors	H	boats	H
rooms	L-M	*Theaters and stadiums*	H
		(indoors)	H
Religious		*Convention Centers*	
Churches/temples		auditorium	H
worship	L-M	corridor	H*
meeting room	H	lobby	H
lobby	H		

*If objects are to be rolled over an area of carpet, the carpet should be of maximum density to provide minimum resistance to rollers. For safety, select only level loop or low, level dense cut pile. (Courtesy of Fibers Division, Monsanto Chemical Co.)

tions. High levels of traffic are normally expected in such areas as corridors and lobbies, and low levels in such spaces as executive offices and rooms within apartments (Table 20.1).

In most cases, a soft covering intended for use in areas of little traffic would not be serviceable where traffic is heavy. Early replacement, accompanied by annoying dislocation, interruption of normal activities, and a second outlay of money and time, would be necessary. Conversely, selecting a carpet engineered for use in a commercial corridor for installation in a residential interior may entail a higher initial investment than necessary.

It may also require postponement of the inevitable redecorating desired when tastes and styling preferences change. Quality control and performance evaluations, a routine part of the production efforts of industry firms, provide assistance in making suitability decisions. Testing enables producers to label their products with specific performance data and recommendations pertaining to installations, for instance, whether the products are suitable for low-traffic, residential interiors or for high traffic, commercial interiors (see Chapter 26).

Multicolored surfaces may camouflage accumulated soil. But if large amounts of soil are anticipated, consideration should also be given to the selection of fibers engineered to hide, repel, or shed soil (see Chapter 4) and finishes designed to repel soil and minimize staining (see Chapter 9).

Design and Performance Regulations

Various local, state, and federal regulatory agencies have established regulations pertaining to the design and performance of textile floor coverings selected for use in certain commercial interiors (see Chapter 2). Laws pertain to such structural characteristics as pile height and pile construction density and such functional properties as noise reduction, as well as to flammability.

Specific regulations must be followed when selecting and installing carpet and rugs in interiors mandated by congressional action to be accessible and usable by persons with disabilities. The Architectural Barriers Act of 1968 requires certain federally owned, leased, or funded buildings and facilities to be accessible to people of limited mobility. Coming under the scope of the act are such structures as U.S. post offices, federally assisted housing units, several military facilities, and federal government buildings. Enforcement of the standards set forth in the act is under the jurisdiction of the Architectural and Transportation Barriers Compliance Board (ATBCB). This board was created under section 502 of the Rehabilitation Act of 1973; subsequent amendments expanded its work to include responsibility for establishing minimum guidelines and requirements for accessible designs. The Department of Defense, the Department of Housing and Urban Development, the U.S. Postal Service, and the General Services Administration must establish guidelines consistent with those prescribed by the ATBCB.

A revised edition of the ATBCB Minimum Guidelines for Accessible Design, which became effective on September 3, 1982, includes specific provisions governing the selection and installation of carpet and carpet tiles. Several of these provisions are based on the specifications developed by the American National Standards Institute. Among other things, ATBCB requires that carpet tile used on an accessible ground or floor surface have a maximum combined thickness of pile, cushion, and backing height of 0.5 inch. If carpet is used, then it should also meet this requirement, but in no case shall the pile height

exceed 0.5 inch.[5] (Recall that pile sweep can reduce the thickness of a pile layer without affecting pile height.)

Cost Factors

Three basic elements of cost must be considered when selecting and specifying soft floor covering assemblies: the initial purchase price, installation charges, and maintenance expenses. For the purpose of comparing various types of carpet, cushions, and hard-surfaced floorings, the total use-cost or life-cycle cost of each should be amortized according to its life expectancy. In this way, the important impact of maintenance expenses and the length of the product's use-life are taken into account.

Initial Purchase Price

The purchase price of carpet and cushion materials is normally given in dollars per square yard. Residential and commercial consumers must confirm whether the quoted price is for the carpet only, the cushion only, or for the assembly. Of course, the dollar figure must be multiplied by the number of square yards required, including any extra amount that may be needed for matching pattern repeats and for fitting and trimming (see Chapter 27).

Installation Charges

A number of cost variables are involved in installation. The cost of site preparation should be detailed: there may be per-square-yard charges assessed for removing the existing floor covering, for filling cracks and smoothing rough areas, and for reducing the amount of moisture and alkaline concentration, if necessary. Charges for installing the new carpet may be separate from those for installing the new cushion.

Maintenance Expenses

The cost of maintaining a flooring material at an attractive level of appearance is a critical factor in commercial installations. The major cleaning expense is generally the cost of labor; thus, the more time required for maintaining a flooring material, the greater will be maintenance costs. Other maintenance expenses include the purchase and repair of equipment and the continual replacement costs of expendable cleaning supplies.

The results of an investigative project sponsored by the Carpet and Rug Institute showed that the annual amortized cost (initial cost per square foot of the material divided by years of life expectancy) of purchasing and installing reinforced vinyl tile is significantly less than that of carpet, sheet vinyl, and terrazzo. When maintenance expenses were considered, however, the annual amortized life cycle or use-cost of carpet was significantly less than that of other flooring materials.[6]

Life-cycle Costing

Several producers of commercial carpet have established **life-cycle costing** programs. A life-cycle cost analysis compiles materials, installation, and maintenance costs. Such figures are prepared for each flooring material being considered by the designer or architect, and then form the basis for making use-cost comparisons.

Lending institutions may permit the cost of the soft floor covering assembly in certain new constructions to become part of the mortgage obligation. In such cases, the tax savings on the portion of interest attributable to the carpet and cushion may be considered in the life-cycle analysis. Depreciation and capital investment credits may be additional factors to analyze in the costing of a project. Similar tax-related assessments can be made when replacement installations involve interest charges.

Summary

Several variables affect the selection of soft floor coverings. Decisions must be made about appearance features such as size, shape, surface coloration, and surface texture. Consideration must be given to various factors influencing apparent color of the surface. Prospective purchasers may seek floor covering assemblies providing such functional benefits as noise control, insulation, and usefulness to persons with limited mobility or impaired sight. Professionals must confirm that their selections conform with any applicable design and performance mandates. Ultimately, residential and commercial consumers must be sure that initial costs and long-term maintenance expenses do not outstrip their budgets.

Today, the satisfactory in-use performance of textile floor coverings depends on the level of appearance or newness retention exhibited by the surface; fiber and floor coverings producers have successfully engineered abrasion resistance. Consumers and professionals should therefore investigate composition and construction qualities that will maintain an acceptable appearance and texture, and they should select those best suited to end-use conditions.

Key Terms

area rugs
Berber yarns
broadloom
carpet
carpet modules
friezé
high-low
life-cycle costing
pile construction density
pile height
pile reversal
pile sweep

pile thickness
plush
pooling
random shear
room-fit rugs
room-size rugs
rug
runner
saxony
scatter rugs
sculptured
shading

shag

splush

tip shear

velour

velvet

velvet plush

walk-off mat

watermarking

Review Questions

1. Identify some advantages that carpet modules offer over wall-to-wall installations.

2. Distinguish between room-size and room-fit rugs.

3. Consider some of the aesthetic values offered by area rugs.

4. Why is pile sweep a critical consideration when soft floor coverings are installed?

5. Why is pile height likely to be greater than pile thickness?

6. Why is a "sad" pile floor covering a better choice than a "happy" one?

7. What causes watermarking to occur with soft floor coverings?

8. Identify surface textures and colorations that help to camouflage soil.

9. Describe the color styling seen with Berber yarns.

10. Identify factors to be considered when selecting and installing soft floor coverings in an interior used by a person with mobility limitations. Which of these variables are positive?

11. How can soft floor coverings be chosen to help blind and partially sighted persons?

12. What is the purpose of life-cycle costing?

Notes

1. Department of Veterans' Benefits, Veterans' Administration, *Handbook for Design: Specially Adapted Housing, VA Pamphlet 26–13*, Washington, D.C., April 1978, 28.

2. John Templer, and Craig Zimring, "Accessibility for Persons with Visual Impairments," Access Information Bulletin, National Center for a Barrier Free Environment, Washington, D.C., 1981.

3. Ibid.

4. John Duncan, et al., compilers, "Environmental Modifications for the Visually Impaired: A Handbook," *Journal of Visual Impairment and Blindness*, Vol. 71, No. 10, December 1977, 442–455 (reprint).

5. The full text of the ATBCB Minimum Guidelines for Accessible Design may be reviewed in the *Federal Register*, Vol. 47, Wednesday, August 4, 1982, 33873–33875.

6. A description of this investigative project is available from the Carpet and Rug Institute.

21

Fibers, Yarns, and Constructions Used in Textile Floor Coverings

Fibers Used in Carpet and Rugs
   Fiber Usage in Face Yarns
   Fiber Usage in Backing Structures
   Disclosure of Fiber Composition

Fiber Properties Affecting Floor Performance

Yarn Features Affecting Serviceability
   Structural Characteristics
   Pile Yarn Integrity

Constructions Used in Soft Floor Coverings
   Dominance of Tufting

Current statistical profiles show that noncellulosic fibers have captured the major portion of the soft floor coverings market. The growing consumption of these fibers began in the early 1950s when producers began shifting from weaving with wool to tufting with nylon. The more economical production operation and the less expensive fiber made textile floor coverings more affordable, enabling increased numbers of homeowners, builders, and commercial firms to choose them in lieu of linoleum, tile, and oak flooring. While tufting has become the dominant construction method today, weaving, knitting, and such other techniques as fusion bonding and needlepunching remain important.

The performance of a textile floor covering will not be totally determined by a single feature, but certain performance properties are strongly influenced by one component. A fiber characteristic or a yarn feature has the primary influence on some service-related properties. The development of fuzz on the surface of pile floor coverings, for example, depends on the ability of the yarns to maintain their original level of twist. This chapter discusses this and other yarn properties having a strong effect on floor covering serviceability.

Fibers Used in Carpet and Rugs

Carpet and rug producers used more than 4 billion pounds of textile fibers in 1997.[1] Of this large amount of fiber, approximately 85 percent was incorporated into face or pile yarns, and the balance was used in the backings. The fiber composition of face yarns and backing structures is markedly different.

Fiber Usage in Face Yarns

The relative importance of cotton, wool, and manufactured fibers in **face yarns** is shown in Table 21.1. The changing patterns of fiber consumption in recent decades are apparent from these data.

The rate of growth exhibited by the noncellulosic fibers has been phenomenal. In 1966, noncellulosic fibers controlled roughly 65 percent of the domestic carpet and rug face yarn market, leaving approximately 16 percent to the manufactured cellulosic fibers, 15 percent to wool, and 4 percent to cotton. Today, noncellulosic fibers account for 98.6 percent of the market; wool and cotton share the remaining 1.4 percent.

Importance of BCF Nylon and BCF Olefin

BCF nylon dominates the assortment of fibers used in face yarns, with some 1.240 million pounds used in 1997, up 23.5 percent from that used in 1990. These values should be compared with those for BCF olefin, however, as these fibers have shown impressive growth. Over 926 million pounds of BCF olefin were used in 1997, up more than 61 percent from the 360 million pounds used in 1990.[2] Fiber engineering continues to ensure the serviceability of these manufactured fibers in soft floor coverings.

Wool Usage in Carpet and Rugs

Long considered to be the finest and most luxurious of the face fibers, wool dominated the floor coverings market for centuries. In recent decades, however, the domestic mill consumption of wool has steadily declined. In 1960, 210 million pounds of carpet wool were consumed in the United States.[3] Thirty-seven years later, in 1997, only 26.1 million pounds were consumed (see Table 21.1). This decline has been accompanied by an increase in the price of foreign carpet wool: all wool fiber used in carpet and rugs is imported because domestic wool is too fine for these products. It also reflects a continuing decline in worldwide sheep population.

The decrease in the use of wool has not come about because of any serious deficiencies in the properties or processing of the fiber. The initial challenge was on the basis of cost; the continuing challenge is from the lower cost and improved quality of manufactured fibers. If cost is no consideration, many people believe that the beauty, inherent soil and flame resistance, and excellent resiliency of wool support its choice. In fact, many domestic consumers are purchasing increasing numbers of imported

Table 21.1 Fiber Usage in Face Yarns
(million pounds)

| | | Manufactured Fibers[a] | | | | | | |
| | | Cellulosic | | | Noncellulosic | | | |
Year	Total Fiber	Total	Yarn	Staple	Yarn	Staple	Cotton	Wool
1996	766.9	622.0	1.5	118.5	211.3	290.7	28.9	116.0
1970	1,122.1	1,026.0	0.5	76.7	355.5	593.3	16.0	80.1
1985	2,149.5	2,125.9	[b]	1.3	1,057.5	1,067.1	11.7	11.9
1997	4,062.8	4,006.0	[b]	0.0	2,771.8	1,234.2	30.7	26.1

[a]Manufactured end use is divided between cellulosic (rayon plus acetate fibers) and noncellulosic (nylon, polyester, acrylic, and olefin fibers). Yarn includes monofilaments, multifilaments, and spunbonded. Olefin "yarn" also includes film fiber and spunbonded polypropylene. Staple includes tow and fiberfill.

[b]Little or none of this fiber is used.

Sources: Textile Economics Bureau, Inc., *Textile Organon*, Vol. 43, No. 11, November 1972, 166; Vol. 57, No. 9, September 1986, 211; and Vol. 69, No. 10, October 1998, 177.

wool carpets and rugs, resulting in a net import balance of nearly 49 million pounds.[4]

Fiber Usage in Backing Structures

Most of the fiber produced for carpet and rug backing structures is directed to fabrics for backing tufted goods. A smaller amount of fiber is used for the yarns in the backing layers of other constructions.

In 1985, some 432.5 million pounds of fiber (426 million pounds of manufactured fibers and 6.5 million pounds of cotton) were used in backing structures. Polypropylene olefin was dominant, but minor amounts of nylon and polyester were also used.[5] Some cotton yarn appears in the back of woven constructions and in fabrics used to back small, tufted rugs and mats, but none is used for tufted rollgoods. Other backing materials include foam rubber, kraftcord, vinyl, latex, and jute. Fabrics of jute are dimensionally stable unless they are overwetted during cleaning or flooding. Because they retain moisture and may rot and mildew, they should not be used with floor coverings installed below-grade where ground moisture can move through the floor to the carpet back. Because jute is imported from tropical areas, supply and delivery problems have often plagued producers using jute.

By 1997, this market had grown to 590.8 million pounds of fiber used, 98 percent of which was primarily olefin with small quantities of nylon and polyester filaments also included. The remaining 2 percent (12.6 million pounds) was cotton used in woven constructions. Any quantity of jute used today is minor and not included.[6]

Disclosure of Fiber Composition

The fiber composition of the pile layer of soft floor covering must be disclosed in accordance with the provisions of the Textile Fiber Products Identification Act. Backing fibers and yarns are exempt (see Chapter 10).

Fiber Properties Affecting Floor Performance

The selection of carpet and rug fibers should be based on an evaluation of both engineered and inherent properties. Virtually every inherent property can be engineered or altered for improved performance. Unless a particular feature is required by law, residential and commercial consumers may weigh appearance and performance benefits against any added cost. Such features as abrasion resistance, optical characteristics, static propensity, and soil-related properties are discussed in Chapter 4. Other properties such as microbe resistance and moth resistance are discussed in Chapter 9.

Yarn Features Affecting Serviceability

The appearance and floor performance of carpet and rugs relate to several yarn features, including some structural characteristics and the stability of the yarn twist. Often, spinners and throwsters can produce the desired appearance and expected service-related properties by manipulating these features.

Structural Characteristics

Virtually all carpet and rug yarns are constructed as simple, relatively coarse structures. Spun yarns were dominant until the late 1980s when they peaked at a 40 percent market share. Today, bulked continuous filament (BCF) yarns have captured approximately 66 percent of the market.[7]

Design Features

Complex yarns, except for speck yarns, are not used in floor coverings because loops, curls, and other irregular textural effects would readily be abraded and snagged. Decorative appeal, however, can be introduced by other variables, including color styling, pile height, and yarn twist.

Form

As noted above, spun yarns account for approximately 34 percent of the face yarn market. For good floor performance, two- or three-ply spun yarns are produced from staple fibers 4, 6, or 8 inches long. Longer lengths help to reduce the number of protruding fiber ends and to increase yarn strength, and thus to minimize the problems of shedding, fuzzing, and pilling induced by abrasion during use.

Most multifilament carpet yarns are textured, using the false-twist coiling or knit-de-knit crinkling techniques. Again, as noted above, there has been shifting from spun to BCF yarns. Because most of the filament ends are buried in the yarn bundle, BCF yarns, like longer staple spun yarns, exhibit less pill formation. In combination with heather color styling, BCF yarns often have a wool-like appearance (Figure 21.1).

Size and Weight

The average **denier** of filament carpet yarns composed of nylon, the dominant carpet fiber, has been decreasing over the past several years. The reduction in diameter has largely resulted from changes in fashion styling preferences—most notably a shift toward the finer velour surface texture—but rising raw material costs have had a major impact as well.

Although the average denier of filament nylon yarns has been decreasing, some carpet yarns and some carpet fibers are being manufactured with extra high denier counts. These extra large yarns, which have denier counts as high as 7,000, are used in floor coverings intended for installation in commercial interiors that undergo heavy traffic.

Pile Yarn Integrity

Pile yarn integrity refers to the ability of the face yarns to maintain their stability and resist the effects of abrasion. Loop pile yarns should not rupture, and cut pile yarns should not splay or untwist. Such abrasion-induced changes would be accompanied by changes in the apparent luster, wrongly suggestive of colorant failure. Concomitant changes would be observed in the original textural characteristics: for example, fuzziness would replace smoothness.

When cut pile yarns fail to maintain their original level of twist, they are said to **splay**, flare, or "blossom," as shown in Figure 21.2. Because incident light waves are reflected from the small tips of the multiple, disoriented fibers, areas of splayed yarns appear duller than surrounding areas. Surface luster will also vary when fibers that are part of loop pile yarns are snagged and ruptured.

Pile yarn integrity can be improved with the use of abrasion-resistant fibers, BCF yarns, and more highly twisted and heat-stabilized yarns. Higher pile construction densities also exert a positive influence on the integrity of the yarns in a covering over time.

Constructions Used in Soft Floor Coverings

The division of body construction techniques on the basis of usage and economic importance is useful and meaningful. This separates the dominant technique, **tufting**, from other industrial techniques and from hand operations.

Dominance of Tufting

As shown in Table 21.2, nearly 1.7 billion square yards of carpet and rugs are shipped annually. This is a significant increase from the early 1980s when 1 billion square yards were produced annually. To a great extent, this growth

Figure 21.1 Level loop carpet of Marquesa® Lana polypropylene olefin BCF yarn having a wool-like appearance. *Courtesy of Amoco Fabrics and Fibers Company.*

reflects a general strong economy, a high demand for automobiles, and a robust housing market.

Tufting accounts for more than 90 percent of the floor coverings market. This is largely the result of the economic advantages offered by high-speed, wide-width tufting machines, and by the use of nylon instead of non-resilient cotton and expensive wool fibers. It has also re-

Figure 21.2 Yarn splaying.

Table 21.2 Carpet and Rug Shipments by Construction Method

(Million square yards)

Year	Total	Woven	Tufted	Other	Exports
1988	1,328	21	1,241	66	NA
1997	1,696	27	1,534	136	146

Source: U.S. Department of Commerce, "MA22Q."

sulted from improvements made in the quality of tufted carpet that have enabled designers and architects increasingly to specify tufted floor coverings for commercial interiors, including areas of heavy traffic.

Together with woven constructions and hand techniques, tufting is discussed in detail in the following chapters.

Summary

Today's soft floor coverings market is dominated by tufted constructions having either nylon BCF or olefin BCF face yarns. Olefin has also captured the greatest portion of the carpet and rug backings market. The increasing popularity of these noncellulosic fibers has been accompanied by a concomitant decrease in the use of wool. Like fibers, yarns can have specific structural features chosen for appearance and performance. Yarns can be textured, for example, to reduce pilling, and heat set to minimize splaying and increase appearance retention.

The choice of inherent and engineered fiber and yarn properties should be made in anticipation of traffic conditions and in the light of budgetary limits. It should also entail consideration of construction variables that affect floor performance; these variables are discussed in the following chapters.

Key Terms

denier

face yarns

pile yarn integrity

tufting

yarn splay

Review Questions

1. Identify two fibers that dominate the soft floor coverings face yarn market. What accounts for their prominence?

2. Review the usage of wool in soft floor coverings. What variables have influenced the significant shift in the consumption of this natural fiber for textile floor coverings? In what type of floor coverings does wool usage remain strong?

3. Identify the dominant fiber in the carpet and rug backings market. Why has the usage of jute declined?

4. Discuss the relative importance of spun yarns and BCF yarns in the face or wear layer of soft floor coverings. What advantages are offered by BCF yarns?

5. Explain the shift in the average denier of nylon carpet filament in the past two decades. How has this shift influenced surface texture design?

6. When did tufting begin to enjoy widespread usage as a construction technique? What advantages does it offer over weaving techniques?

Notes

1. Textile Economics Bureau, Inc., *Textile Organon*, Vol. 69, No. 10, October 1998, 177.

2. Ibid., Vol. 69, No. 10, September 1998, 156.

3. Ibid., Vol. 43, No. 12, December 1972, 188.

4. Ibid., Vol. 69, No. 12, December 1998, 215.

5. Ibid., Vol. 57, No. 9, September 1985, 216.

6. Ibid., Vol. 69, No. 10, October 1998, 177.

7. Ibid., Vol. 69, No. 9, September 1998, 156.

22

Construction of Floor Coverings: Tufting

Basic Components of Tufted Floor Coverings
   Pile or Face Yarns
   Primary Backing Fabrics
   Secondary Backing Fabrics
   Adhesives

Tufting Operations
   Forming the Pile Layer
   Creating Multilevel Surface Textures
   Applying an Adhesive and Scrim

Structural Qualities of Tufted Constructions
   Bundle Penetration
   Delamination Strength
   Tuft Bind
   Tufts per Square Inch
   Weight-related Factors

Body construction techniques employed with textile floor coverings may be divided into two broad categories: those that create pile structures and those that create nonpile structures. Nonpile structures are produced by such methods as braiding, weaving, and needlepunching. Weaving produces pile structures, as well. Other pile structures are produced by such methods as tufting, knitting, and fusion bonding. For pile structures, surface textures or constructions do not go hand in hand with body constructions; identical textures can be produced by any of several techniques.

Because tufted floor coverings are used so extensively, residential consumers, interior designers, and architects should understand their structural qualities. This will prepare them to make informed decisions and reliable judgments concerning the suitability of tufted structures for various installations. It will also enable the professional to interpret structural data supplied by producers.

Basic Components of Tufted Floor Coverings

Whether a carpet or rug is machine tufted or hand tufted, the principal components are the same. Tufted constructions include **pile or face yarns**, a **primary backing**, a layer of adhesive, and a **secondary backing** (Figure 22.1).

Figure 22.1 Components in tufted constructions.

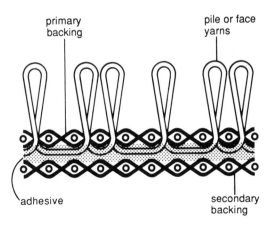

Pile or Face Yarns

The composition and structural characteristics of face yarns used in pile floor coverings were discussed in Chapter 21. BCF yarns of nylon and olefin fibers dominate.

Primary Backing Fabrics

Typical primary backing fabrics are shown in Figure 22.2. Although jute formerly dominated the market, it has largely been replaced by olefin.

Plain-woven fabrics of yarn-like tapes or ribbons of olefin (Figure 22.2b) have high stability unless heated above 338 °F. These fabrics are impervious to moisture; they resist mildew and the development of odors. To minimize raveling, a thin butyl coating is frequently applied to bond the warp and filling strands.

When low pile construction densities are planned, producers can use a plain-woven olefin backing with a "nylon cap," produced by needlepunching a thin nylon batt into the backing (Figure 22.3). Because nylon fibers accept dye more readily than olefin fibers, the needlepunched fibers can be colored to coordinate with the face yarns. In the event the backing is exposed in use, any difference in color between the face fibers and the backing is masked.

Spunbonded olefin fabric (Figure 22.2c) exhibits no fraying or raveling and is not susceptible to problems from moisture. During tufting, the filaments are pushed aside; thus, the needle is only minimally deflected, which helps ensure uniform pile height and tuft placement.

Secondary Backing Fabrics

Secondary backing fabrics, also referred to as **scrims**, must adhere well and provide high dimensional stability. Fabrics composed of jute are naturally rough and adhere well; spunbonded fabrics are smooth and have poor adhesion.

A leno-woven fabric composed of olefin fibers is specifically manufactured for use as a secondary backing. The leno interlacing minimizes yarn raveling at the fabric edges, and the spun filling yarns provide the necessary roughness for adhesion of the fabric (Figure 22.4).

a) plain woven jute

b) plain woven olefin

Figure 22.2 Typical primary backing fabrics.

c) spunbonded olefin

Figure 22.3 Plain-woven olefin backing with a needlepunched "nylon cap" to minimize color differences between pile yarns and backing.

Figure 22.4 ActionBac®, a leno-woven olefin secondary backing, with spun filling yarns for improved adhesion. *Courtesy of Amoco Fabrics and Fibers Company.*

Some manufacturers use a glass fiber scrim to reinforce a vinyl secondary backing. This combination has high dimensional stability and virtually no moisture-related problems.

Permanently attached foam rubber cushions may be used as secondary backings, eliminating the need for a separate cushion. Secondary backings may or may not be used with commercially produced, hand-tufted carpet and rugs.

Adhesives

The most frequently used adhesive is synthetic latex; approximately 12 ounces per square yard are applied to most tufted floor coverings.[1] Some carpet producers are replacing latex adhesives with molten thermoplastic compounds.

To control electrical charge buildup, tufted carpet producers may incorporate a conductive compound into the adhesive used to secure the secondary backing, or they may sandwich an antistatic coating between the primary backing and the adhesive. Some carpet producers combine a conductive compound in the adhesive or backing fabric with an antistatic component in the pile layer. Tufted carpet producers may also incorporate a flame-retardant compound into the adhesive. To be effective, the coating must penetrate the primary backing.

Tufting Operations

Unlike most weaving operations, tufting is a relatively simple and uncomplicated process. Pile yarns are inserted into an already-formed primary backing fabric, and surface textures and construction densities can easily be varied.

Forming the Pile Layer

Pile yarns are supplied from cones mounted on a creel frame erected in back of the tufting machine. So that they will not tangle, the yarns are fed through thin plastic tubes, visible in the upper portion of the photograph in Figure 22.5, to tension control devices and the tufting needles. The tension controls determine the quantity of

Figure 22.5 Commercial tufting machine.
Courtesy of the Hoover Company.

yarn supplied to the needles, helping to ensure the production of the planned pile height.

Many needles are aligned crosswise on the machine. The number of needles required depends on the width and the planned crosswise density or gage. **Gage** is the fractional distance between adjacent needles; it can be converted to a **needle count**, which is the number of needles per crosswise inch on the machine. A gauge of ⅛ inch is equivalent to a needle count of eight; a gauge of ⅒ inch is equivalent to a needle count of ten. To prepare a tufting machine to produce carpet 12 feet wide, with a gauge of ⅒ inch, 1,440 needles must be aligned and threaded with pile yarns (12 feet × 12 inches = 144 inches; 144 inches × 10 needles = 1,440 needles).

The sequence used to form loop pile floor coverings is schematized in Figure 7.8a (p. 101). Threaded with pile yarns, the needles descend through the back of the primary fabric. Working in a timed relationship with the descending needles, loop pile hooks rock forward, catching and holding the yarn loops while the needles ascend. The pile layer is then formed on the face of the primary fabric. One crosswise row of tufts is produced in each tufting cycle.

When a cut pile surface is planned, a knife blade is attached to the pile hook, which cuts the loops, forming one U-shaped tuft from each loop (Figure 7.8b, p. 101). For either loop or cut pile coverings, the descend and ascend tufting cycle is followed by the advancement of the primary backing a predetermined distance and the repetition of the cycle.

The number of tufts or stitches per inch determines the distance the primary backing is advanced after each tufting cycle, and thus governs the lengthwise density. Typically, the number of stitches per inch ranges from 4 to 11. If, for example, a stitch of 8 is selected, the crosswise bank of needles would punch into the fabric 8 times in each lengthwise inch, and there would be ⅛ inch between each crosswise row of tufts.

Modern tufting machines are capable of completing more than 500 tufting cycles per minute. Depending upon width, density, and surface texture, this capability can translate into the production of more than 1,000 square yards of cut pile carpet in 8 hours, and about twice that amount of loop pile carpet.[2]

In comparison to machine tufting, hand tufting is an extremely slow and expensive process. It is used only for custom orders requiring a relatively small amount of yardage. Hand tufting is done with a hand-held, electrically powered tufting gun (Figure 22.6).

Creating Multilevel Surface Textures

Various attachments are available for tufting multilevel surfaces in random and patterned shapes. Differences in pile height are achieved by controlling the quantity of yarn supplied to the needles prior to their descent. The needles and loop hooks continue to operate in the conventional manner.

In some systems, the amount of yarn feeding to the needles is constant, and a level surface will be produced. When the speed is slowed, the amount of yarn feeding to the needles is reduced; then, as the hooks hold the loops while the needles ascend, the "missing" quantity of yarn is robbed mechanically by tension from the previously formed loops. In other systems, photoelectric cells control the amount of yarn fed to each needle. In yet a third technique, pile yarns are fed over slats having notched and uncut areas. When a pile yarn encounters a notched area, it is subjected to less tension and will form higher loops; when a pile yarn encounters an uncut area, its flow is restricted, and it will form a shorter loop. In recent years, the use of these techniques has diminished as manufacturers have adopted computerized programming to control pile height variations.

When tufting of the pile yarns is completed, several operations are required to convert the greige carpet into finished carpet. Among these, tip shearing, random shearing, and hand carving create even more variety in surface texture.

Applying an Adhesive and Scrim

Unless the tufted pile yarns are permanently anchored in the primary backing, they could easily be pulled out when snagged. In cut pile styles, this would show up as an empty space the size of the space once occupied by the removed tufts. In loop pile styles, pulling the continuous

Figure 22.6 Custom tufting with a hand-held, single needle gun.
Courtesy of Cabin Craft Products.

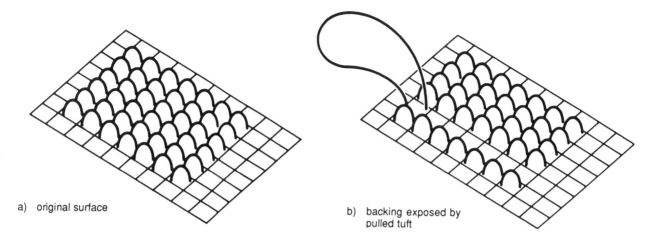

a) original surface

b) backing exposed by pulled tuft

| **Figure 22.7** Potential problem with poorly anchored pile yarns.

length of yarn would expose a lengthwise line of backing void of tufts, as illustrated in Figure 22.7.

In preparation for application of the adhesive, the back of the primary fabric is beaten to drive the pile yarn segments tightly against the fabric base. The coating is then applied uniformly across the back, securely binding the yarns into their positions. The secondary backing is then rolled onto the adhesive coating.

Most tufted broadloom carpet is manufactured in 12-foot widths, although some manufacturers are offering wider widths to meet special needs. The yardage may be in **rollgoods** form or cut into small rugs and mats. The products are converted and then subjected to quality testing.

Structural Qualities of Tufted Constructions

As part of their quality-control programs, tufted carpet producers evaluate such structural features as the strength of the bond between the primary and secondary backings and the pile construction density. Several also measure various weight-related characteristics, for use in selection guidelines that coordinate minimum weight values with anticipated traffic levels.

Bundle Penetration

Visual examination enables carpet producers to estimate how thoroughly the adhesive penetrates the pile yarn

bundle. A high degree of **bundle penetration** helps to prevent individual staple or filament fibers from being pulled out of the yarns and rubbed into fuzz and pills on the carpet surface.

Delamination Strength

Another crucial function of the adhesive coating is to develop a strong bond with the secondary backing. Good adhesion is especially important to prevent **delamination** or separation of the backings when they are subjected to heavy stress forces. The movement of heavy equipment or the flow of much traffic across a carpet surface can have a "snowplow" effect, crushing and pushing the structure, which in turn can cause shearing, the movement of the primary and secondary backings in opposite directions. Unless the bond between the two fabrics is strong, shearing can cause delamination. Delamination could result in bubbling, rippling, and straining at the seams.

The strength of the bond between the backings may be measured in accordance with the procedures outlined in ASTM D 3936 Standard Test Method for Delamination Strength of Secondary Backing of Pile Floor Coverings. In Figure 22.8, stress is exerted on the specimen clamped in the jaws of the test apparatus. The force required to separate the components is measured for each of three specimens; the average is then reported in pounds per inch of specimen width. Values frequently range from 2.5 to 8.33 pounds per inch.

Figure 22.8 Measuring secondary backing adhesion strength.
Courtesy of BASF Corporation Fibers Division.

Tuft Bind

Tuft bind testing may be carried out in accordance with the procedures outlined in ASTM D 1335 Standard Test Method for Tuft Bind of Pile Floor Coverings. The force required to pull one loop of pile tuft from a floor covering is measured by first anchoring the structure in clamps, as shown in Figure 22.9. A hook is inserted into the test loop, and the loops on either side of the test loop are cut. Raising the hook then exerts force. Three replicate tests are run, and the average force required to remove the tufts is reported in pounds-force. Values typi-

Figure 22.9 Measuring tuft bind strength. *Courtesy of Lees Commercial Carpet Company.*

Figure 22.10 Equal pile construction densities having different sizes of yarns.

cally range from 4.5 to 20 pounds. This procedure can also be used on cut pile structures: a tweezer-like device is clamped onto one side or leg of a cut loop.

Tufts per Square Inch

Although the "eyeball" method illustrated in Figure 20.5 (p. 330) can be used to roughly evaluate pile construction density, a more reliable technique is to determine the actual number of **tufts per square inch**. Producers measure and report the necessary lengthwise and crosswise values separately on data and specification sheets.

Gauge, needle count, and number of tufts or stitches per inch were explained earlier in this chapter. Typical

gauge and needle count conversions are listed in Table 23.1 (p. 366). The number of tufts per square inch may be calculated by multiplying the needle count by the number of stitches per inch. If other construction features are equal, carpet and rugs with higher construction density values should exhibit better durability and texture retention.

The important influence of construction density on thickness retention can be appreciated by reviewing a simple principle of physics. When a stress load is distributed over a large, rather than a small, number of supports, the force or load each must bear is minimized. The same idea is behind the "magic" we see when a performer lies on a bed of nails without injury to the skin: each one of many nails supports an extremely small portion of the body weight, so the skin is not punctured. To pursue the analogy, each tuft in a pile floor covering may be considered equivalent to one nail; as the number of tufts is increased, the load each must support is reduced. Denser construction also helps to reduce yarn flexing within the pile because adjacent tufts support one another.

Pile construction density values are important, but they should not be used alone to predict thickness retention. For example, each square in Figure 22.10 has the same number of pile tufts, but the size and thus the weight of the yarns in each is significantly different. Evidently, accurate predictions of serviceability must also include weight factors.

Weight-related Factors

In general, as the weight of a textile floor covering increases, so do its quality, its potential texture retention, and its wear-life. For this reason, producers of tufted carpet and other soft floor coverings generally report various weight-related measurements. These include pile yarn weight, effective face weight, total weight, density factor, weight density, and HUD/FHA density. The challenge to students and practicing professionals is to understand the differences among these measurements. Professionals must also be aware that minimum weight values are often part of design standards established for certain commercial interiors.

Pile Yarn Weight

Pile yarn weight is the weight of the yarns used in the wear layer and those portions of the pile yarn that extend into the backing layer. Pile yarn weight values are expressed in ounces per square yard or in grams per square meter.

Several construction variables are reflected in pile weight values, including fiber density, yarn weight, pile height, and pile construction density. Pile yarn weight values are among the better references for judging the potential serviceability of similarly constructed floor coverings. To compare floor coverings of different constructions, however, consideration should be given to the proportional distribution of the pile yarns between the wear layer and the backing layer.

Effective Face Yarn Weight

The **effective face yarn weight** is a way to express the weight of the pile yarns in the wear layer, excluding those in the backing. Because fusion-bonded structures (discussed in Chapter 23) contain a relatively small amount of their pile yarns in the backing layer, producers of these carpets often report the effective face yarn weight.

Total Weight

The **total weight** of a floor covering includes the weight of the pile yarns as well as the weight of the backing yarns, backing fabrics, and backcoatings. Table 22.1 illustrates how weight measurements and other construction variables should be coordinated with traffic conditions for good performance. (Traffic classifications for various areas within several commercial interiors are listed in Table 20.1, p. 336) Since the weight values listed are minimums, increasing them should provide increased floor performance; but such increases should always be balanced against concomitant increases in cost.

Density Factor

The **density factor** or **density index** is a calculation that reflects both pile construction density and yarn size (denier). The following formula is used to calculate this factor:

$$\text{Density factor} = \text{yarn size} \times \text{needle count} \times \text{stitches per inch}$$

Increasing the density factor will increase floor performance, up to a point: the relationship is shown in Figure 22.11.

The usefulness of pile yarn weight, effective face yarn weight, and total weight measurements is limited in that they do not reflect the true pile density (mass or amount of matter per unit of volume). Consider, for example, two carpets that have the same pile yarn and identical pile construction densities, but different pile heights. The carpet with the higher pile would weigh more, but would

Table 22.1 Recommended Construction Standards for Carpets of Herculon® Olefin

	Light Traffic	**Medium Traffic**	**Heavy Traffic**
Gauge (pitch)	⅛ (216)	⅛, ⅒ (216, 270)	⅛, ⅒, 5⁄64 (216, 270, 346)
Rows or stitches	7	8	8 or above
Pile height	¼ in. or below	¼ in. or below	¼ in. to ⅜ in.
Pile yarn weight	16.0 oz./sq. yd. min.	18.0 oz./sq. yd. min.	28.0 oz./sq. yd. min.
Total weight	55 oz./sq. yd. min.	57 oz./sq. yd. min.	65 oz./sq. yd. min.

Courtesy of Hercules Inc.

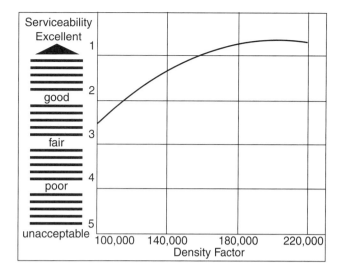

Figure 22.11 Relationship of density factor to floor performance.
Courtesy of Allied Fibers.

have lower true density. On the other hand, if two carpets differed only in their yarn size, the carpet containing the heavier yarns would not only weigh more but would also have a higher true density. The density factor also does not reflect true density because it does not consider pile height. It would seem that structures with equal construction densities and yarn sizes, but different pile heights, will have identical density factors; but increasing the pile height will in fact reduce the true density.

Therefore, measurements that reflect the true density are often reported.

Average Density and Weight Density

Average density and **weight density** measurements take pile height (finished thickness) into consideration and thus can indicate the true density of floor covering structures. Minimum density values may be recommended or required in some settings. Required minimum values are set out, for example, in the HUD/FHA Use of Materials Bulletin 44d (see Chapter 2). Commercial specifiers must select a floor covering that has been certified to meet or exceed the minimum requirements in effect at the time of the project work. Certification must be carried out by an independent laboratory administrator approved by HUD/FHA. The bulletin offers these formulas for calculating average density and weight density:

$$(D) = \text{average density} = \frac{36\,(W)}{(t)}, \text{ where}$$

$(W) = \text{average pile weight in ounces per square yard,}$

$\text{and } (t) = \text{average pile thickness in inches.}$

$$(WD) = \text{weight density} = W(D)$$

Weight-related features not only affect texture retention, but also such functional values as noise control and insulation. Test methods for evaluating these and other service-related properties are discussed in Chapter 26.

Summary

Constructing pile floor coverings through tufting operations is relatively fast and economical. The economic advantages of machine tufting, of course, may be overridden by the selection of more expensive fibers, yarns, and finishes and by the use of higher pile construction densities. Costs can also escalate when production runs are small and specialized, as is generally the case with custom work made to order. The costs will also be higher for small, unique orders that must be hand tufted, a comparatively slow, labor-intensive process.

In their quality-control programs, tufting firms generally measure and evaluate such structural qualities as the strength of the bond between the primary and secondary backing fabrics, the pile construction density, and the weight and density of the pile layer. Tufting firms use the results of these evaluations to help secure the widespread selection of their floor coverings.

Key Terms

average density

bundle penetration

delamination

density factor

density index

effective face yarn weight

gauge

needle count

pile or face yarns

pile yarn weight

primary backing

rollgoods

scrims

secondary backing

total weight

tuft bind

tufts per square inch

weight density

Review Questions

1. Draw and label a cross-sectional illustration of a tufted floor covering.

2. Identify the advantages and limitations of the three types of primary backings.

3. How is a "nylon cap" produced and what positive features does it offer in use?

4. Distinguish between gauge and needle count.

5. Discuss the problems that could occur when pile yarn is not securely anchored in the primary backing.

6. Explain the importance of having the adhesive penetrate the pile yarn bundles.

7. Explain the meaning of "snowplow" effect and shearing.

8. Differentiate between pile yarn weight and effective face yarn weight.

Notes

1. Cecil Davis, "Fine Gauge Tufting," *Modern Textiles*, June 1973, 60.

2. Singer Company, Cobble Division, *Handbook of General Information on Yardage Tufting Machines and Their Use*, Tenn., n.d., 6.

23

Construction of Floor Coverings: Weaving and Other Machine Techniques

Weaving Pile Floor Coverings
  Basic Components
  Axminster Weaving
  Wilton Weaving
  Velvet Carpet Weaving
  Chenille Carpet Production
  Pile Construction Density

Other Machine Operations
  Fusion Bonding Operations
  Braiding
  Flocking
  Needlepunching

Commercial weaving of textile floor coverings began in the United States in the late 1700s. The principal product was a flat, yarn-dyed, reversible structure called **ingrain**. Gradually, this rug began to replace the braided and hand-woven rugs made in the home. Pile carpet was imported until the mid-1800s, when the power loom was adapted for the domestic production of a patterned, loop pile carpet known as Brussels. Over the years, other techniques and looms augmented the production capabilities of domestic manufacturers. In addition to ingrain and Brussels carpet, cut pile constructions, such as Wilton, Axminster, velvet, and chenille, also became available. Together, woven floor coverings dominated markets until the mid-1950s, when large-scale tufting operations were widely adopted.

In addition to tufting and weaving operations, other machine techniques, including fusion bonding, flocking, and needlepunching, are used to produce contemporary carpet and rugs. Although machine techniques other than tufting produce only a relatively small portion of today's residential and commercial floor coverings, even small percentages translate into millions of square yards (see Table 21.2, p. 345).

Weaving Pile Floor Coverings

Several methods of weaving are employed in the manufacture of pile floor coverings. Among these, major differences exist in the structure and operation of the looms, the nature of the surface patterns formed, and the degree of interlacing complexity involved. Some yarn components are, however, common to all forms of woven pile structures.

Basic Components

Most woven pile floor coverings contain chain warp yarns, stuffer yarns, filling shots, and pile yarns. These yarns are illustrated schematically in Figure 23.1.

Filling or weft shots are crosswise yarns used to anchor the **pile warp yarns**. The shots are generally of polypropylene olefin, jute, or cotton, and the pile yarns

may be spun or multifilament yarns of any fiber. For added body and weight, extra warp yarns, called **stuffer yarns**, are inserted in a plane in the back layer. Stuffers are normally kraftcord or stiff jute yarns. **Chain warp yarns** pass over and under the shots, securing all components of the structure tightly together. The zigzag configuration of these yarns in most woven floor coverings makes them easy to recognize. Today, chains are generally composed of polyester, not cotton.

Unlike tufting, in which the pile layer is added to an already-formed base fabric, weaving operations form the pile and backing layers simultaneously. Some methods, such as velvet weaving, are relatively simple procedures that have only limited design capabilities; others, including Axminster and Wilton, are quite complicated and virtually unlimited in the range of designs they can produce. Weaving operations are comparatively slow and labor-intensive, however, so they are used less frequently than tufting by domestic producers.

Axminster Weaving

Two schematic illustrations of Axminster carpet are shown in Figure 23.2. A distinctive feature is the use of paired filling shots, with either two pairs used per tuft row, as shown in the left sketch, or three pairs per tuft

Figure 23.1 Basic components of woven pile carpet and rugs.

U-shaped Pile Tufts

Figure 23.2 Cross-sectional sketches of Axminster carpet with paired filling shots. *Courtesy of Mohawk Carpet.*

row, as shown in the right sketch. This makes the crosswise direction of the carpet somewhat rigid and inflexible, a distinguishing characteristic of Axminster floor coverings.

Preparation for Axminster weaving is lengthy and involved; the more intricate and complex the design and pattern repeat to be woven, the more complicated preparation becomes. First, a colored **print design** displaying the full length and width of one pattern repeat is prepared. A portion of the design prepared for weaving an intricate Oriental pattern is shown in Figure 23.3. Each small block represents one pile tuft. Clearly, the colored tufts must be woven precisely in their planned positions, or the motifs will be irregular and flawed.

When the print design is ready, skilled technicians assemble cones of yarns colored according to its specifications. They then wind the various colors of yarns onto 3-foot-long **spools**, following the sequence printed on one crosswise row of the point design. For a repeat 18 inches in width, the sequence would be used twice on each spool. Spools are linked end to end to form a **bracket**. If the carpet is to be woven 12 feet wide, four spools are used, and the sequence would be repeated eight times across the bracket.

The pitch determines the number of yarns wound on each spool. **Pitch** is the number of pile units (loops or cut, U-shaped tufts) per 27 inches of width; it commonly ranges from 162 to 216. The pitch method of reporting crosswise density in woven carpet has persisted

from earlier times when looms were narrower; carpet was woven in 27-inch widths and seamed as often as necessary. If a carpet is to be 12 feet wide and have a pitch of 189, a total of 1,008 tufts will form each crosswise row. This is calculated as follows: 12 feet × 12 inches = 144 inches; 144 inches divided by 27 inches = 5.33; that is, there are five and a third of the 27-inch segments in the carpet width; and 5⅓ × 189 tufts = 1,008 total tufts. Each bracket thus carries 1,008 yarns, and each 3-foot-long spool carries one-third of the total, or 336 yarns.

After the first bracket is completed, spools are wound with yarns according to the sequence shown in the second row of squares on the print design. The process continues until one bracket has been prepared for each crosswise row in the pattern repeat. The length of the repeat and the planned lengthwise density governs the number of brackets required.

The number of **rows per inch**—the number of crosswise rows of tufts per lengthwise inch—in an Axminster carpet is commonly within the range of seven to ten. If, for example, a count of eight rows per inch is selected, eight brackets would be prepared for weaving one lengthwise inch of carpet. A repeat 25 inches long would then require 200 brackets.

In preparation for weaving, the multiple brackets are positioned in proper order on the loom (Figure 23.4). The brackets are in the central portion of the photographs in Figure 23.4a. Yarn from the first bracket is

LATTICE ORIENTAL, pattern #10   18" wide repeat   set match

POSITION 1   POSITION 2   POSITION 3   POSITION 4   POSITION 5   POSITION 6   POSITION 7   POSITION 8   POSITION 9

Figure 23.3 Print design for a portion of an Axminster pattern repeat.
Courtesy of Mohawk Carpet.

rolled off, lowered into position, and the stuffers, chain warp yarns, and pairs of weft shots are integrated with the pile yarns, locking them into the structure. The amount of yarn reeled off is determined by the planned pile height. The pile yarn is cut, the bracket is moved away, and the second bracket is lowered. A complete cycle of all the brackets would produce the length of one repeat; a second cycle would produce another length, and so on.

Wilton Weaving

Formerly, loop pile carpet woven on a Jacquard loom was called **Brussels**, and cut pile carpet was called **Wilton**. Today, all pile floor covering woven on a Jacquard loom is called Wilton.

The number of colors of pile yarns used in the pattern is denoted by the number of **frames**; for instance, a three-frame Wilton has three colors, a six-frame Wilton has six colors, and so on. When the variously colored yarns are not required to form part of the surface design, they are carried in a plane in the backing layer (Figure 23.5). The presence of such **dead and buried yarns** distinguishes Wilton constructions. Although the hidden lengths contribute weight, cushioning, and resiliency, they also add to the materials cost.

An enlarged section of a print design for a three-frame Wilton carpet is shown in Figure 23.6. The shed for weaving the first crosswise row would be formed by raising a red, a blue, and a green yarn. A blue and a green yarn would be lowered below the red yarn; a green yarn and a red yarn would be lowered below the blue yarn; and a red and a blue yarn would be lowered below the green yarn. The shed for weaving the second crosswise row would be formed by raising a blue, a green, and a red yarn. A red and a green yarn would be lowered behind the blue yarn, and so on. One cone of yarn must be supplied for each color appearing in each lengthwise row of pile tufts. Weaving the three rows of carpet represented in the draft would require nine cones of yarn, one of each color for each row.

The total number of cones of yarn required for Wilton weaving is determined by the carpet width, the pitch, and the number of colors planned. If, for example, a three-frame Wilton is to be woven 12 feet wide with a pitch of 189, a total of 3,024 cones would be required, assuming each color is used in each lengthwise row. Since there are 1,008 pile units in each crosswise row, the total is calculated by multiplying 1,008 by 3, which equals 3,024.

To reduce yarn costs, a system of **planting** colored pile yarns may be employed: an added color of yarn is periodically substituted ("planted") for one of the basic pile colors. Planting can cause a three-frame Wilton carpet to appear to be a four-frame structure; an investigation of the backing, however, would uncover only two buried pile yarns behind each tuft.

Jacquard carpet weaving is similar to other Jacquard weaving operations (see Chapter 6 and Figure 6.14, p. 90). In carpet weaving, however, the Jacquard attachment controls the pile yarns, not the base yarns; additional harnesses are used to control the chain warp yarns; and additional loom beams are used to hold the chain and stuffer yarns. As shown schematically in Figure 23.7, wires are inserted

a)

Figure 23.4 Weaving action on an Axminster loom. *Courtesy of Mohawk Carpet.*

b)

c)

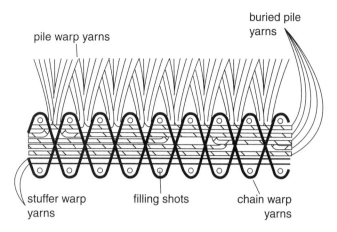

Figure 23.5 Cross-sectional sketch of a Wilton carpet. *Courtesy of Mohawk Carpet.*

green	red	blue
blue	green	red
red	blue	green

Figure 23.6 Enlarged portion of a print design for a Wilton carpet.

into the shed formed by the pile yarns, and weft shots are inserted into the separate shed formed by the chain warp yarns. The reed moves forward, pushing the wire and shot against the already-woven carpet. The heddle-like cords holding the raised pile yarns then descend, lowering the pile yarn over the wires. A weft shot is carried across the carpet, above the pile yarns and below the chain warp yarns. Then, a new pile yarn shed is formed, the harnesses reverse their positions, and the sequence is repeated.

The pile loops are formed over wires whose height determines the pile height. If a cut pile is planned, the wires are equipped with knives on one end; as the wires are withdrawn, they cut the loops. If a looped pile texture is planned, the wires will have rounded ends.

Since one wire is used for each crosswise row of pile tufts, the lengthwise density of Wilton carpet is reported as the number of **wires per inch**. Typically, this number is within the range of seven to ten. The crosswise density commonly ranges from a pitch of 189 to 252, but it may be as high as 270 or 346.

Velvet Carpet Weaving

Velvet carpet weaving is an over-the-wire construction technique (Figure 6.19, p. 93) used to produce velvet carpet. This use of "velvet" must not be confused with its

Figure 23.7 Diagram of Jacquard carpet weaving. *Courtesy of the Hoover Company.*

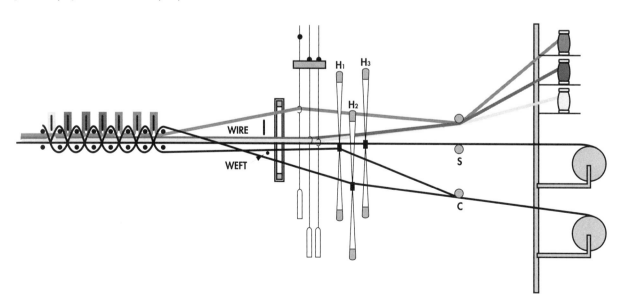

use to name a surface texture nor with its use as a name for an upholstery fabric.

Velvet weaving is one of the least complicated methods of producing pile carpet. As in Wilton construction, the wire height determines the pile height. Again, the wires may or may not have knives on their ends (use of the term *tapestry* to distinguish loop pile velvet carpet has been discontinued). Unlike Wilton weaving, however, no Jacquard attachment is used, so intricate details and elaborate patterns are not possible. Appearance variations may be created by combining cut and loop textures, by incorporating different colors of pile yarns in bands of various widths, or by employing pile yarns with distinctive color styling.

The cross sections in Figure 23.8 show two structural forms of velvet carpet. In Figure 23.8a, the pile yarns are anchored by the upper filling shots only. In Figure 23.8b, they are held by both the upper and lower filling shots: the carpet constructed this way would be described as a **woven-through-the-back** velvet. If other construction variables are the same, a woven-through-the-back velvet is more serviceable because the pile tufts are more securely bound and the total weight is greater. The carpet back in either type of velvet weave may be coated with latex or a thermoplastic compound for greater stability.

The pitch of velvet carpet ranges from 165 to 270. The number of wires per inch ranges from a low of seven to a high of ten.

Chenille Carpet Production

Two completely separate weaving operations are required to manufacture **chenille carpet**. The producer must first manufacture chenille "yarns," using the leno-weaving and fabric-cutting processes described in Chapter 5. The chenille strips are folded for use as pile yarns; the leno-entwined warp yarns form a base and the extended filling yarns form a V shape.

Figure 23.9 details the structural components of a chenille carpet. In addition to the stuffer, chain warp, and filling shots normally found in woven pile carpet, chenille carpet also has catcher or binder warp yarns to secure the chenille pile yarns to the base components.

Chenille carpet is comparatively expensive: the production sequence is involved and time-consuming, and an additional yarn component is required. Because of its cost, this construction technique is rarely used today, and not at all by domestic producers.

Pile Construction Density

The number of tufts per square inch in woven floor coverings can easily be calculated by first dividing the pitch value by 27. The resulting figure, the number of pile units per crosswise inch, is equivalent to the needle count with tufted constructions. Conversions of several commonly used pitch and needle counts are listed in Table 23.1.

After pitch has been converted, the resulting value is multiplied by the number of rows or wires per inch. Direct comparisons can then be made with tufted constructions.

Figure 23.8 Cross-sectional sketches of velvet carpets.

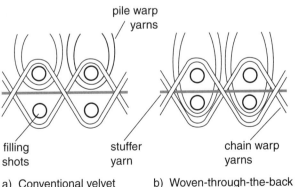

a) Conventional velvet construction

b) Woven-through-the-back construction

Figure 23.9 A chenille carpet.

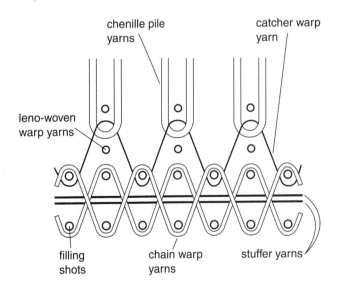

Table 23.1 Pitch and Needle Count Conversions

Pitch	108	143.9	172.8	180	189	216	243	252	256	270	346
Needles	4	5.3	6.4	6.6	7	8	9	9.3	9.5	10	12.8
Gauge	¼	³⁄₁₆	⁵⁄₃₂		⁹⁄₆₄	⅛	⅑			¹⁄₁₀	⁵⁄₆₄

Note: Unless gauge conversions are whole-number fractions, they are omitted.
Courtesy of Fibers Division, Monsanto Chemical Co.

Other Machine Operations

Machine operations other than tufting and weaving are also used to produce soft floor coverings. Among these are fusion bonding, braiding, flocking, and needlepunching.

Fusion Bonding Operations

A significant portion of the recent research efforts of some commercial carpet producers has been channeled to the improvement of **fusion bonding** operations. Some operations are used for the production of rollgoods, which will be installed wall-to-wall; others are used for the production of carpet, which will subsequently be die-cut into modules.

Basic Components

Fusion-bonded structures have a minimum of three components: pile yarns, adhesive, and a primary backing (Figure 23.10). The adhesive, which is generally a vinyl compound such as polyvinylchloride (PVC), is placed on the face of the backing, which may be woven jute or a nonwoven glass fiber fabric. The pile yarns are embedded or implanted into the vinyl; they are not woven or tufted through the primary backing.

Fusion-bonded carpet has approximately 5 to 8 percent of the total pile yarn weight embedded in the adhesive; tufted structures may have 15 to 30 percent of the pile yarn weight enclosed in the primary backing; and woven constructions may have 20 to 50 percent of the total pile yarn weight interlaced in the backing layers. Thus, fusion-bonded carpet and modules can have more of the yarn available to the wearing face. Together with denser gauge fusing capabilities, this feature helps producers to engineer fusion-bonded floor coverings, even those having fine velour textures, to withstand the high levels of traffic encountered in commercial installations. The processing is slower than tufting, however, and

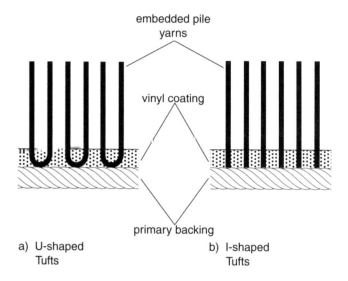

Figure 23.10 Fusion-bonded floor coverings.

the vinyl compound is more expensive than tufting substrates.

A special use of fusion bonding is the production of entrance mats made of coir fibers. Figure 23.11 provides a close-up view of the implantation of the ends of the fibers in PVC. The superior stiffness of these fibers helps them function like hundreds of miniature brushes, efficiently cleaning shoe soles and protecting the interior carpet from excessive amounts of tracked-in dirt. Coir mats generally range in total thickness from 0.68 to 1.2 inches. Some producers offer coir rollgoods and carpet modules, as well as mats.

Braiding

Braided rugs are constructed of braided components; the rugs themselves are not braided. The braids in the rug in Figure 23.12a were formed by interlacing three groups of plied simple yarns; the braids in the rug in Figure 23.12b were formed by interlacing three chenille yarns. In both

Figure 23.11 Close-up view of coir fibers implanted into a liquid plastisol (PVC) layer and then heat fused to form an entrance mat material.
Courtesy of USCOA International Corporation.

rugs, core yarns composed of waste fibers were incorporated for weight, body, and cushioning. It is also possible to enclose yarn-like strands of sponge rubber for these purposes.

Braided strands are assembled side by side in a round or oval shape; machine zigzag stitching links adjacent braids. In a few rugs, flat braids are handled as conventional yarns and interlaced in a plain-weave pattern.

Flocking

Fibers with relatively high denier counts, ranging from 30 to 60, are used for flocked floor coverings. The fibers must be straight and nontextured so that they may be embedded in the adhesive coating in very large quantities. In preparation for the **flocking** operation, the fibers are cut into uniform lengths, ranging from 0.08 to 0.25 inch, and placed in a charged hopper. As shown in Figure 13.28 (p. 223), the flock is drawn into the adhesive coating on a substrate as it passes over a grounded plate. Often, the substrate is heavy-gauge vinyl sheeting.

Because electrostatic flocking draws the fibers vertically into the adhesive, the quantity of fibers per square inch can be greater than that in mechanical flocking. This high density provides better abrasion resistance and durability, performance features that are especially important when the structures are to be used as walk-off mats and automotive floor coverings. The accelerated laboratory tests used to assess the abrasion resistance of floor coverings are detailed in Chapter 26.

Needlepunching

Needlepunched floor coverings are often referred to as indoor-outdoor carpet. These structures are manufactured in the following sequence. Various colors of 3- to 4-inch fibers are blended to achieve uniform distribution of the colors. Long webs, as wide as the needle loom and

Figure 23.12 Braided rugs.

a) braids of simple plied yarns

b) braids of chenille yarns

Figure 23.13 Needle board on a needle loom.
Courtesy of Fibers Division, Monsanto Chemical Co.

weighing approximately 0.5 to 1.0 ounce per square yard, are formed by laying the fibers flat. Layering the webs at 45- or 90-degree angles to one another forms a thick batt of the desired weight, which typically ranges from 16 to 32 ounces per square yard. For strength and dimensional stability, an adhesive-coated jute or nylon scrim may be centered in the batt or placed behind it. The batt is then tacked or prepunched to reduce its thickness and fed into a needle loom (Figure 23.13). Here, hundreds of barbed needles punch into the batt some 800 to 1,200 times per square inch, creating a mechanical chain-stitch among the fibers and locking them into the scrim and adhesive.

The barbed needles used in the punching operation produce flat carpet with a felt-like appearance (Figure 23.14a). Carpet having loop-like protrusions (Figure 23.14b) can be produced by using needles with crescent-shaped points for the final punches.

When needlepunched structures are to be installed outdoors, on patios and golf greens and around pools, their composition is chosen to withstand the ravages of sunlight, rain, and insects. They are permeable, so they can be hosed to flush away dirt. If these structures are installed wall-to-wall indoors, their permeability presents obvious problems when liquids are spilled on them.

Figure 23.14 Needlepunched floor coverings.

a) nonpile texture

b) simulated loop pile textures

Summary

Machine techniques other than tufting used to produce soft floor coverings include weaving, fusion bonding, braiding, flocking, and needlepunching. Axminster, Wilton, and chenille weaving operations are relatively slow and expensive, but Axminster and Wilton weaving can produce patterns of intricate detail and many colors. Fusion bonding is increasingly used to produce rollgoods and carpet modules with fine, velour surface textures.

Key Terms

bracket

braiding

Brussels

chain warp yarns

chenille carpet

dead and buried yarns

filling or weft shots

flocking

frames

fusion bonding

ingrain

needlepunching

pile warp yarns

pitch

planting

print design

rows per inch

spools

stuffer yarns

velvet carpet weaving

Wilton

wires per inch

woven-through-the-back

Review Questions

1. Draw and label a cross-sectional sketch of a woven carpet.

2. What is the purpose of stuffer yarns?

3. How can one identify chain warps?

4. What construction feature tends to make the crosswise direction of Axminster floor coverings inflexible?

5. Explain the use of print designs, spools, and brackets in the preparation of Axminster weaving.

6. Identify the positive and negative features of having "dead and buried" pile yarns in Wilton carpet.

7. How does the Jacquard loom used for weaving floor coverings differ from that used for weaving apparel fabric?

8. Why is the lengthwise density of Wilton carpet reported as wires per inch?

9. Why is chenille carpet construction comparatively expensive?

10. How does one use pitch and needle count to compare the crosswise densities of a woven carpet and a tufted carpet?

11. Fusion-bonded floor coverings are said to have more effective face weight; that is, they have more of the yarn available to the wearing face. How does this help such floor coverings to withstand high levels of traffic?

12. What, in fact, is braided in braided floor coverings?

24

Construction of Floor Coverings: Hand Techniques

Hand-woven Pile Rugs
  Oriental Rugs
  Rya Rugs
  Flokati Rugs

Hand-constructed Flat Rugs
  Khilim Rugs
  Rugs Woven by Native Americans
  Dhurrie Rugs
  Floor Mats
  Other Rugs and Mats

Hand operations produce rugs, not rollgoods. Some of these operations are carried out by highly organized, commercial organizations. In such cases, the quality of the products is carefully controlled and the marketing strategies that promote them are sophisticated. This is typical of the production and promotion of authentic Oriental rugs and rugs woven by Native Americans.

The distinctive styling of many hand-constructed rugs leads many people to use them as ornamental wall accents, perhaps as often as they use them as floor coverings. Whether placed on the floor or on the wall, most of these rugs are produced by weaving, but some are constructed in braiding, hooking, and felting operations. Hand weaving and hand knotting are generally combined to produce pile structures, and plain- or tapestry-interlacing patterns are used to produce many flat structures.

Hand-woven Pile Rugs

Two types of hand-woven rugs, Oriental rugs and rya rugs, contain hand-knotted pile yarns. Another type, the Flokati rug, has a hand-pulled pile layer.

Oriental Rugs

Intricate motifs and many colors are found in the pile layers of **Oriental rugs**. Typical are geometric shapes, stylized dragons, rosettes, medallions, trees, flowers, vines, and many styles of borders. Historically, weavers executed only their own ancestral designs or those first produced in their geographic regions; the designs reflected the cultural heritage and life of the weavers. The origin of these rugs could be identified by their pattern, and they were known by such names as Persian, Turkoman, Chinese, Caucasian, and Indian. Today, weavers throughout the world have adapted most of the traditional patterns, and it is no longer possible accurately to identify the origin of a rug by its design.

Savonnerie rugs, which were first produced in France, present an example of pattern dispersion. The name derives from *savon*, French for "soap," because these rugs were first woven in a factory that earlier had been used for the production of soap. Today, the classic designs and soft pastel colors characteristic of these rugs, and of the fine, loop pile French **Aubusson rugs**, have been liberally copied by rug weavers in other countries. A Savonnerie rug woven in India is pictured in Figure 24.1. The design of Aubusson and Savonnerie rugs is often emphasized by hand carving.

The distinguishing feature of all authentic Oriental rugs is that each pile tuft is hand knotted. The **Sehna (Senna)** or **Persian knot** (Figure 24.2a) or the **Ghiordes** or **Turkish knot** (Figure 24.2b) is used. The Sehna knot can be tied to slant to the left or right, but must be tied the same way throughout a project. The Sehna knot completely encircles one warp yarn and passes under the adjacent warp yarn; as a result, one pile tuft projects from every space between the warp yarns. When the Ghiordes knot is tied, both ends of the pile yarn extend from the

Figure 24.1 Savonnerie rug.
Courtesy of Peerless Imported Rugs.

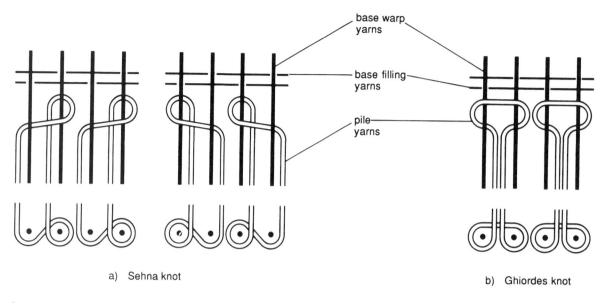

a) Sehna knot

b) Ghiordes knot

| **Figure 24.2** Knots used to form the pile layers in authentic Oriental rugs.

same space; no pile tufts fill the alternate spaces. If other construction features are identical, a Sehna-knotted rug is finer than a Ghiordes-knotted rug, and the pattern is more sharply defined.

During the hand-weaving operation, several weavers may work simultaneously on the same project, knotting the pile yarns in horizontal rows. Normally, one or two filling or weft yarns are used in plain-weave interlacing between each crosswise row of pile knots. Increasing the number of filling yarns decreases the pile construction density.

The quality of Oriental rugs depends on the number of knots per square inch. Whereas the number of warp yarns per inch and the frequency of knot placement determine the crosswise density, the skill of the weavers, the size of the pile yarns, and the number of filling yarns per tuft row determine the lengthwise density. **Antique Oriental rugs**, those produced prior to the mid-1800s, often had as many as 500 knots per square inch. The famous Ardebil Mosque Carpet, produced in 1539–1540 and now housed in London, England, was woven with some 380 knots per square inch. Old or **semi-antique rugs**, those woven during the latter part of the nineteenth century, and **modern rugs**, those produced during this century, generally have 100 to 225 knots per square inch, but some have as many as 324 knots per square inch.

Other important quality-related factors are pile height, fiber content, and level of luster. The use of natural dyestuffs for antique Oriental rugs resulted in a subdued, mellow luster. Synthetic dyestuffs developed in the mid-1850s simplified dyeing operations and were adopted by weavers. Because these colorants produce brighter colors than the natural dyestuffs, many of today's Oriental rugs are treated with chlorine or acetic acid and glycerin to simulate the prized sheen and soft luster of the older rugs: this processing is variously described as **chemical washing**, **culturing**, and **luster washing**. This treatment may weaken the fibers, but many producers and consumers consider the beauty of the rug more important than its wear-life.

Economic considerations have largely been responsible for the diminished use of silk in Oriental rug pile yarns. Today, most of these rugs have pile yarns composed of wool and base yarns of cotton.

The labor-intensive, tedious, and slow production of hand-knotted Oriental rugs makes them relatively expensive, beyond the reach of many consumers. To lower the cost, manufacturers have increasingly produced rugs with traditional Oriental patterns on power looms, principally on Axminster looms. Machine-woven rugs, known as **Oriental design rugs**, generally have a sewn-on fringe, which may differ from the base warp yarns; in hand-knotted rugs, the base warp yarns extending from the ends of the rug form the fringe. Recently, computerized printing systems have been employed to increase the availability and affordability of these prized designs.

Rya Rugs

Rya rugs originated in Scandinavian countries where weavers hand knotted long pile yarns. Today, authentic rya rugs are still hand knotted, but machine-made rya rugs are also available; both are prized worldwide for their decorative value. Typically, yarns in related colors form the pile layer, and the designs are gently flowing and curved (Figure 24.3).

In rya rug construction, the pile yarns are knotted with the Ghiordes knot (Figure 24.2b) as in Oriental rugs. Rya rugs differ from Oriental rugs, however, in two principal ways. First, the pile height in rya rugs is considerably longer, ranging from 1 to 3 inches. As the pile height increases, the spacing between the pile rows can also increase, since the longer pile yarns will readily cover the base fabric. Second, more filling or weft yarns are used between each crosswise row of

Figure 24.3 Rya rug with long pile yarns in related colors. *Courtesy of Peerless Imported Rugs.*

knotted pile yarns in rya constructions. These are interlaced with the base warp yarns in a plain- or tapestry-weave pattern.

So that the pile loops will be uniform in height, the yarn is continuously looped over a **rya** or **flossa stick**. The depth of the stick determines the pile height in the same way the wire height determines the pile height in Wilton and velvet carpet constructions. The stick is grooved to facilitate cutting the loops after a row has been knotted on it.

Pile yarns in authentic rya rugs are normally composed of wool. Along with the large amount of yarn used, the relatively high cost of the fiber makes the rugs comparatively expensive.

Flokati Rugs

Flokati (Flocati) rugs (Figure 24.4) are long pile wool structures woven in Greece. The weaver who pulls a wooden rod inserted under the yarns controls the pile yarn length. The loops are then cut by hand. After weaving, every authentic Flokati rug is immersed in a deep vat in a pool beyond a natural waterfall. Here, the swirling water causes the wool fibers to felt, converting the yarns into pointed strands. Like authentic rya rugs, these rugs use large amounts of wool and labor-intensive processing, making them comparatively expensive.

Hand-constructed Flat Rugs

Most hand-constructed flat rugs are woven in a plain or tapestry-based interlacing pattern. The motifs of these floor coverings, like those of Oriental rugs, often reflect the cultural heritage of the weavers.

Khilim Rugs

Khilim (Kelim, Kilim) rugs are woven in eastern European countries. These colorful floor coverings have graceful, stylized designs depicting flowers, animals, and other natural things (Figure 24.5).

The construction of Khilim rugs is similar to tapestry weaving: the filling yarns are woven in sections according to color. Unlike those in tapestry structures, how-

Figure 24.4 Flokati rug, hand woven in Greece of long pile wool yarns. *Courtesy of The Wool Bureau, Inc.*

ever, the ends of all filling yarns in Khilim rugs are woven in, so the structure is reversible. In some cases, the weaving may produce slits or openings where the colors change in the design motif. These openings are finished and will not ravel (Figure 24.6). The slits may be retained as part of the design or they may be sewn together by hand.

Rugs Woven by Native Americans

Rugs produced by Native Americans, primarily the Navajo, Cheyenne, and Hopi peoples, are hand woven with a tapestry-related interlacing. Because the end of each filling yarn is woven in at the juncture of color changes, these rugs, like Khilims, are reversible. In con-

trast to the Khilim rug technique, however, the filling yarns are woven to avoid slits, with a dovetailing or interlocking technique (Figure 24.7).

The designs used in these rugs are bold graphic symbols (Figure 24.8) or detailed patterns representing tribal life and culture. Weavers throughout the world frequently adapt them. Today, these rugs are often chosen to act as wall accents.

According to the rules and regulations issued by the FTC pursuant to the Textile Fiber Products Identification Act, all hand-woven rugs made by Navajo Indians that carry the "Certificate of Genuineness" supplied by the Indian Arts and Crafts Board of the U.S. Department of Interior are exempt from the provisions of the TFPIA. Here, the term "Navajo Indian" means any

Figure 24.5 Khilim rug.
Courtesy of Peerless Imported Rugs.

Figure 24.6 Slits found in Khilim rugs.

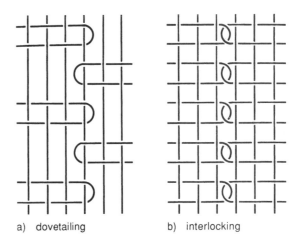

a) dovetailing   b) interlocking

Figure 24.7 Techniques used to avoid the formation of slits in tapestry.

Figure 24.8 Area rug with strong graphic designs characteristic of Cheyenne hand-woven rugs.
Courtesy of Peerless Imported Rugs.

Figure 24.9 Dhurrie rug.
Courtesy of Peerless Imported Rugs.

Indian listed on the register of the Navajo Indian tribe or eligible for listing thereon.

Dhurrie Rugs

Dhurrie (durrie, durry) rugs are flat, hand-woven rugs made in India. They have a plain, twill, or tapestry interlacing. These rugs may display crosswise striations, produced by interspersing various colors of heavy, hand-spun cotton filling yarns, or stylized designs executed with wool filling yarns (Figure 24.9).

Floor Mats

Floor mats composed of various grasses, coir, sisal, linen, hemp, or jute fibers are available in an extensive variety of sizes, shapes, and interlacings. Frequently, twill interlacing is used to create diamond, herringbone, and other geometric patterns over the surface. For larger floor coverings, several small mats can be sewn together.

Other Rugs and Mats

Rag rugs are hand woven in plain-weave interlacing. The filling component is formed by rolling and twisting new or previously used fabric into yarn-like structures. Braiding and felting operations produce other small rugs and mats. Some felted rugs are embellished with surface embroidery.

Summary

Among the pile floor coverings produced by hand techniques are Oriental rugs, rya rugs, and Flokati rugs. Khilim, Navajo, and dhurrie rugs are examples of hand-woven, flat rugs. While Flokati and rya rugs are distinguished by the use of relatively long pile yarns, traditional motifs and colorations generally distinguish other hand-constructed rugs. Color styling is important to selection of these as well as machine-constructed floor coverings.

Key Terms

antique Oriental rugs

Aubusson rugs

chemical washing

culturing

dhurrie (durrie, durry) rugs

Flokati (Flocati) rugs

flossa stick

Ghiordes knot

Khilim (Kelim, Kilim) rugs

luster washing

modern rugs

Oriental design rugs

Oriental rugs

Persian knot

rya rugs

rya stick

Savonnerie rugs

Sehna (Senna) knot

semi-antique rugs

Turkish knot

Review Questions

1. Why is it difficult today to identify the origin of Oriental rugs by their motifs?

2. What is the derivation of the name "Savonnerie" for rugs?

3. Identify differences between the Sehna and Ghiordes knots.

4. Differentiate among the following: antique Oriental rugs, old or semi-antique Oriental rugs, and modern Oriental rugs.

5. Identify differences in the construction of the pile portion of Oriental and rya rugs.

6. How is the pile height controlled in rya rugs and Flokati rugs?

7. Discuss similarities and differences between Khilim rugs and rugs woven by Native Americans.

25

Carpet and Rug Cushions

Fibrous Cushion Structures

Cellular Rubber Cushions
   Sponge Rubber Structures
   Foam Rubber Structures

Urethane Foam Cushions
   Prime Urethane Foam Structures
   Densified Prime Urethane Foam Structures
   Bonded Urethane Foam Structures

Listing Specification Data for Carpet Cushions

Evaluating the Performance of Cushions
   Accelerated Aging
   Compressibility
   Compression Set
   Tensile Strength
   Elongation

Many names—cushion, pad, padding, lining, foundation, underlayment—identify the structure placed between a carpet or rug and the floor. Today, members of the industry prefer to use the term cushion or carpet cushion, although many continue to use the term padding. Carpet cushions vary in chemical composition, thickness, compressibility, resiliency, resistance to moisture and microbes, and cost. They also differ in acoustical value, insulative benefit, and the contributions they make toward extending the wear-life of the soft floor covering. Some cushions can only be used separately; others can be separate or permanently attached to the carpet back. Cushion-related variables should be considered in light of the carpet or rug selected, the kind of "feel" preferred underfoot, the environmental and traffic conditions anticipated in end use, and the floor covering budget.

Professionals must understand the evaluation of carpet cushions, so that they can interpret the data provided by producers and understand requirements set forth by an authority with jurisdiction over certain installations. Professionals must be able to supply accurate data for custom projects. The information required depends on the type of cushion selected. The cushions available on today's market fall into three major categories: fibrous cushions, cellular rubber cushions, and urethane foam cushions.

Fibrous Cushion Structures

Fibrous cushions are produced by needlepunching hair or jute fibers into felt-like structures. Four types of fibrous cushions are on the market: all hair, all jute, blends of hair and jute, and hair or jute fibers or both bonded between sheets of latex.

All-hair structures are normally made of cleaned, stiff cattle hair (Figure 25.1a). Like all-jute cushions, all-hair cushions are relatively inexpensive, but both types tend to shift, bunch, and clump under heavy traffic conditions. For added stability, a loosely woven jute scrim may be centered in the batt prior to needlepunching. Antimicrobial agents are recommended to retard the growth of

a) all hair

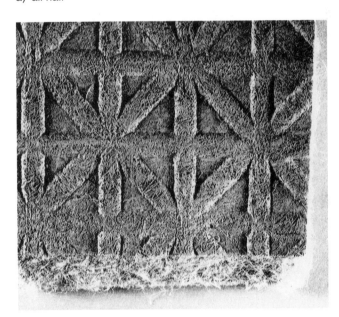

b) jute fibers bonded between latex sheets

Figure 25.1 Fibrous cushions.

mildew and fungi and the odor and deterioration they cause. These cushions tend to exhibit aging; they can crumble and disintegrate after prolonged use. Because these fibers are subject to moisture damage, the use of latex sheets as protective barriers is recommended when below-grade installation is planned. For skid resistance, as well as to compensate for the somewhat low compressibility and resiliency, the surfaces of the fibrous batts and latex sheets are generally embossed (Figure 25.1b).

Fibrous cushions are available in rolls up to 12 feet wide. Their weights range from 32 to 86 ounces per square yard.

Cellular Rubber Cushions

Cellular rubber cushions can be either foam rubber or sponge rubber. Both types can be made from natural or synthesized rubber compounds. For some people, these rubber or latex compounds may be allergens.

Sponge Rubber Structures

Sponge rubber cushions frequently contain chemicals, oils, and fillers that were added to the rubber compound for weight. The mixture is pulverized and then expanded into continuous flat sheets or into three dimensional forms. The three-dimensional cushions are variously referred to as waffle, ripple, or bubble sponge cushions; a typical profile is in Figure 25.2. The flat form is available in uniform thicknesses that range from 0.125 to 0.3125 inch.

Sponge rubber has larger cells and thicker cell walls than foam rubber; sponge structures are therefore more porous and less likely to retain odors. The cellular qualities also contribute buoyancy and softness, characteristics further enhanced when the cushion is three-dimensional. Sponge cushions are highly compressible and produce the plushness often sought in residential interiors and executive offices. Under heavy commercial traffic, however, the waffle forms do not provide uniform support: repeated deformation and flexing of the carpet backing can produce uneven surfaces. Moreover, the clay or ash fillers may grind against other components and crumbling may occur. Flat sponge rubber cushions can provide more uniform support for carpet used in areas of medium and heavy traffic, and better skid resistance for area rugs.

Sponge rubber cushions are available in rolls up to 12 feet wide. Their weights range from 41 to 120 ounces per square yard.

Figure 25.2 Bubble sponge rubber cushion.

Foam Rubber Structures

Foam rubber cushions are manufactured by converting liquid latex and fillers into flat, continuous sheets. The sheets may be as thin as 0.125 inch or as thick as 0.625 inch. A spunbonded fabric is normally applied to the top of sponge and foam rubber cushions. The fabric facilitates handling during installation since it permits the carpet back to slide over the fabric without stretching and distorting the cushion. The spunbonded fabric that covers the cushion in Figure 25.3 has been reinforced with a woven scrim.

Because foam rubber has smaller cells than sponge rubber, foam cushions provide firmer, more uniform support, but they may exhibit more odor retention. Foam rubber cushions are available in rolls up to 12 feet wide, and in weights ranging from 28 to 65 ounces per square yard.

Figure 25.4 Permanently attached foam rubber cushion.

Figure 25.3 Foam rubber cushion covered with a scrim-reinforced spunbonded fabric.

In thinner forms, foam rubber cushions can be permanently bonded to the back of carpet structures (Figure 25.4). The assembly can then be laid on the floor without installing a separate cushion; for maximum stability, it can be glued to the floor.

Minimum standards have been established for attached foam cushions in an effort to promote consistent quality. These standards are listed in Table 25.1. In this table, **density** refers to the amount of rubber per unit of volume; increasing the density would increase the weight of the cushion and the level of support provided. *Compression loss*, also known as *compression set*, is the extent to which the structure fails to recover its original thickness after being compressed 50 percent under a static load.

Compression deflection is the extent (reported as psi or pounds per square inch) to which the structure resists compression force. **Delamination strength** is the force per inch of width required to separate the cushion from the carpet; it is measured as described in Chapter

Table 25.1 Recommended Minimum Specifications for Attached Latex Foam Cushions	
Weight	38 oz./sq. yd.
Thickness	⅛ in.
Density	17 lb./cu. ft.
Compression loss	Maximum of 15% loss
Compression deflection	Not less than 5 psi
Delamination strength	2 lb./in.
Accelerated aging	(a) Heat aging: 24 hrs at 275 °F; after flexing, should remain flexible and serviceable.
	(b) Fade-Ometer® aging: 20 hrs. exposure; sample should show only slight crazing.
Ash content	Maximum of 50%

Courtesy of the Carpet and Rug Institue.

22, using the test apparatus clamps shown in Figure 22.9 (p. 354). Procedures for measuring other properties are discussed later in this chapter.

Several of the recommended specifications for attached foam cushions have been adopted as required standards by a number of federal agencies, including the Office of Housing and Urban Development, the General

Services Administration, and the Veterans' Administration. These authorities have also set forth additional requirements pertaining to fire performance. The test methods used to evaluate flammability are explained in Chapter 11.

Urethane Foam Cushions

Three types of urethane foam cushions are generally available for residential and commercial use: prime or conventional foam, densified prime foam, and bonded or rebond foam. The chemical composition of these cushions is basically the same, but they are manufactured by different processes, and their cellular structures differ.

Prime Urethane Foam Structures

Prime urethane foam cushions are manufactured by foaming the urethane polymer units into a continuous sheet, generally 6 feet wide. "Prime" distinguishes this kind of cushion from the bonded or rebond type.

Prime urethane foam has comparatively large cells shaped somewhat like ellipses, and the foam struts or columns among the cells are vertically oriented. This cellular form provides various degrees of compressibility, depending on density. Under load, these structures may "bottom out": the cushion suddenly flattens under force. Prime foams may contain powdered fillers for weight and polymer additives for increased stability.

Densified Prime Urethane Foam Structures

Densified foam cushions have a higher density than prime foam. The higher density is produced from a finer, elongated cellular structure and somewhat horizontal struts. No fillers are used. These cushions are said to be odorless, resilient, mildew-resistant, and resistant to bottoming out.

Bonded Urethane Foam Structures

Bonded urethane foam cushions are made by bonding and compressing together granulated pieces of prime urethane trim; the term "rebond" is sometimes used to identify these cushions. The strength of these structures largely depends on the strength of the prime urethane foam material used in the trim pieces.

All three types of urethane foam cushions are manufactured in several thicknesses, generally ranging from 0.375 to 0.750 inch, and all generally have a spunbonded facing to facilitate installation. In their thinner forms, these cushions can provide skid resistance to area rugs and runners. As do other types of cushions used for this purpose, the thin form minimizes the problem known as "rug walking" or "rug crawling," the tendency for rugs to shift or move off cushions under the stress of traffic.

The density of urethane cushions is usually within the range of 2.4 to 5.0 pounds per cubic foot. Cushions with higher densities have higher compression deflection values; they provide firmer support underfoot.

Listing Specification Data for Carpet Cushions

Specification listings detail the composition, construction, and performance features of a textile structure. Specification data may be prepared by the producer, or by the trained and experienced professional. The data reported by the producer include values obtained from the accelerated laboratory testing of their products. Professionals list the characteristics and properties they or their clients prefer, or those mandated for textile products used in a particular project. For certain installations, the professional must specify test methods and levels of performance to ensure that the structure conforms to standards established by the authority that has jurisdiction.

Specification listings for cushions are less extensive than those prepared for carpet and rugs (see Table 26.1, p. 388). The data required will depend on the type of cushion selected, the anticipated traffic conditions, the carpet selected, and any mandated features. The recommended minimum specifications for attached foam cushions are listed in Table 25.1; Table 25.2 exemplifies the various features that may be specified for a densified prime urethane foam cushion.

The first item in Table 25.2 states the composition of the cushion; the second item states that a spunbonded fabric is to be applied to the top side of the structure; the next two items describe structural characteristics; and the remaining items detail performance features and levels. The values used are for illustrative purposes only.

Table 25.2 Sample Cushion Specification/Data List

Cushion compound: densified prime, unfilled polyurethane foam; clean and free of defects
Coating: spunbonded polypropylene olefin
Density: 5.0 lb./cu. ft.
Thickness: 0.265 in.
Compressive load deflection:
   25% deflection   1.5 psi minimum
   65% deflection   6.5 psi minimum
   75% deflection   11.0 psi minimum
Compression set: maximum of 15% at 50% deflection
Tensile strength: 25 psi minimum
Elongation: 50% minimum
Flammability: (a) CFR 1630 (FF 1-70/tablet test): passes
           (b) Flooring radiant panel test: greater
               than 0.25 watt/sq. cm.

Laboratory testing confirms that a cushion exhibits specified characteristics.

Evaluating the Performance of Cushions

Some performance features, including compression loss and compression set, are important to all cushion materials. One performance variable, aging, is important only in cellular rubber cushions, and, as noted earlier in this chapter, delamination strength is a concern only with permanently attached cushions.

Accelerated Aging

In prolonged use, rubber cushion compounds may be affected by heat and exhibit aging in the form of cracking, crumbling, and sticking. To assure that the cushion will not show rapid aging, the structure can be evaluated in accelerated laboratory testing. In one procedure, latex cushion material may be exposed for 24 hours to a temperature of 275 °F in a circulating air oven prior to evaluation. In a second accelerated procedure, a specimen may be placed in a Fade-Ometer® (Figure 18.4, p. 305) for 20 hours in accordance with Federal Test Method Standard 191A, Method 5660. As stated in Table 25.1, foam latex samples should withstand these exposures with no more than slight discoloration or surface degradation. Upon flexing, a slight cracking or crazing is acceptable.

Compressibility

Compressibility evaluations measure the degree of resistance a cushion offers to being crushed or deflected under a static load. The measurements are made by following the procedures outlined in ASTM D 1564 and D 3574. In preparation for evaluating this performance quality, cushion specimens are cut into small squares (often 2 inches square) and layered to a thickness of 1 inch. The plied structure is then placed on the platform of a testing unit (Figure 25.5). The support platform has perforations to allow for rapid escape of air during the test. A flat, circular foot is used to indent or deflect the layered specimens.

The force required to deflect or compress the specimen assembly a given percentage of its original thickness is measured for each of two replicate tests. Together with the percentage of deflection used, the average number of pounds per square inch required to compress the cushion

Figure 25.5 Compression deflection testing apparatus. *Courtesy of Custom Scientific Instruments, Inc.*

material is reported to the nearest pound. Several federal agencies have mandated specific levels of **compression load deflection (CLD)**; these vary with the type of cushion and the interior facility.

The compressibility of a cushion correlates with the degree of softness felt underfoot. Cushions having low CLD values are soft and easily compressed; cushions having high values are firmer, less compressible structures. Firmer cushions should be selected for interior floor space subjected to rolling equipment or wheelchairs.

Compression Set

Compression set is synonymous with **compression loss**. It describes the extent to which a structure fails to recover its original thickness after static compression. In most evaluation procedures, cushion specimens are layered to a thickness of 1 inch and deflected 50 percent. The compressed structure is then placed in an oven at 158 °F for 22 hours. At the end of this period, the load is removed and the thickness is measured after a 30-minute recovery period. The compression set is calculated with the following formula: compression set = [(original thickness − thickness after compression)/original thickness] × 100. The average of two replicate tests is reported.

A high recovery of cushion thickness is desirable, and a minimum recovery level of 85 percent (maximum loss of 15 percent) is frequently recommended or mandated. As a cushion recovers from compression, it exerts an upward pressure that encourages the carpet also to recover.

The actual level of recovery depends upon the particular combination of carpet and cushion.

Tensile Strength

The tensile strength of cushion structures is measured in the laboratory according to prescribed test methods, such as FTMS 191A, Method 5100. The value reported is the average of five replicate tests and is the force per unit of cross-sectional area necessary to cause rupture. Required minimum tensile strength values may range from 8 to 20 psi.

Elongation

Elongation values describe how far a cushion structure extends before rupturing. The performance is evaluated as part of the procedure for evaluating tensile strength. The value reported is the average of five readings, each calculated by the following formula: % elongation at break = (length stretched/original length) × 100.

Because cushions are always used in combination with a carpet or rug, some performance evaluations are more meaningful when they are made on the floor covering assembly. This is especially true when such functional values as noise reduction and insulation benefits are being considered. In some cases the functional benefits of an assembly will be more strongly influenced by the cushion than by the carpet; in many cases, carpet and cushion both contribute to a functional value. Evaluations of floor covering assemblies are described in the following chapter.

Summary

Most of the cushions available today can be classified in one of three major categories: fibrous felt cushions, cellular rubber cushions, and urethane cushions. Numerous variations exist within each category, in thickness; weight; density; compressibility; resiliency; resistance to moisture, heat, and microbes; and cost. The choice of a cushion involves an assessment of these features, as well as an analysis of the traffic levels and activities anticipated in the interior area to be carpeted. In light-traffic areas, a thick, low-density structure could be selected for greater buoyancy and softness underfoot. In areas where traffic is heavy, a thin, high-density structure should be used. The cost of installing a separate cushion will normally be higher than using an attached cushion or no cushion, but certain performance benefits may partially offset the additional materials and installation charges. In all installations, the quality of the cushion should be consistent with that of the carpet: a high-quality cushion cannot compensate for a low-quality carpet, and a skimpy cushion cannot support a heavy, high-quality carpet or rug.

Key Terms

compressibility

compression deflection

compression load deflection (CLD)

compression loss

compression set

delamination strength

density

Review Questions

1. Identify the types of fibrous cushions produced and cite the positive and negative features of each.

2. Distinguish between sponge rubber and foam rubber cushions.

3. Why is one form of urethane foam cushions less susceptible to "bottoming out?"

4. How can the consumer minimize "rug walking" or "rug crawling?"

5. What is the purpose of using a spunbonded facing fabric with rubber and urethane cushions?

6. What are the advantages of having minimum compression loss?

26

Evaluations and Specifications for Soft Floor Coverings

Listing Specification Data for Carpet

Evaluating Functional Features
    Acoustical Ratings
    Insulative Value
    Light Reflectance Factor

Evaluating Performance Properties
    Colorfastness
    Flammability
    Static Generation
    Wear Resistance

For suppliers, producers, colorists, and converters of textile floor coverings and components, standard test methods and performance specifications are an important part of manufacturing and marketing efforts. Data gathered from this quality-control work help industry members identify the need for changes in the composition, manufacturing, or conversion of their products. The data also provide the basis for claims about performance made in promotional materials, whether targeted at the trade or at the consumer.

Interior designers, architects, commercial specifiers, and retailers must understand the test methods used to measure structural and performance qualities of carpet and cushions and the implications of the reported data. Such an understanding makes it possible for professionals to interpret data supplied by producers and determine the suitability of a carpet or an assembly for relevant traffic and other end-use conditions. The informed professional also can prepare specification listings that cover specific features and levels of performance required by end-use conditions or a regulatory agency.

Listing Specification Data for Carpet

Because tufting is the dominant floor covering construction technique, the sample **specification listing** presented in Table 26.1 is written for a tufted structure. Several of the items would, however, also be listed for woven and fusion-bonded carpet. Virtually all of the test methods listed in the table and discussed in this chapter apply to all textile floor coverings, regardless of their construction. The specific values listed in the table are for illustrative purposes only.

The first several items listed in Table 26.1 describe the appearance, composition, and construction features of the carpet. The following standard test methods and practices may be used to determine the data reported for these features:

ASTM D 418 Standard Test Methods for Testing Pile Yarn Floor Covering Construction
ASTM D 629 Standard Test Methods for Quantitative Analysis of Textiles

ASTM D 861 Standard Practice for Use of the Tex System to Designate Linear Density of Fibers, Yarn Intermediates, and Yarns
ASTM D 1244 Standard Practice for Designation of Yarn Construction
ASTM D 2260 Standard Tables of Conversion Factors and Equivalent Yarn Numbers Measured in Various Numbering Systems
ASTM D 2646 Standard Test Methods for Backing Fabric Characteristics of Pile Yarn Floor Coverings
ASTM D 5684 Standard Terminology Relating to Pile Floor Coverings
ASTM D 5793 Standard Test Method for Binding Sites per Unit Length or Width of Pile Yarn Floor Coverings
ASTM D 5823 Standard Test Method for Tuft Height of Pile Floor Coverings

As discussed in Chapter 10, trade names frequently distinguish fibers, especially those engineered to exhibit special properties. When a trade name is used to advertise a carpet, the fiber composition of the pile layer must be disclosed in accordance with the provisions of the Textile Fiber Products Identification Act.

Pile construction density, pile height, weight-related factors, and structural variables are specified to ensure that a floor covering will withstand the traffic conditions in the end-use location, and will conform to design codes if these apply. These construction features were reviewed in Chapter 22.

The remaining data in Table 26.1 detail the functional benefits and performance properties of a carpet. Test methods for determining the values reported for these characteristics are frequently identified in specification lists.

Evaluating Functional Features

Carpet and cushion assemblies may be designed and selected to provide such functional benefits as noise control and insulation. Carpet may also be selected to reduce energy consumption by contributing to the efficient man-

Table 26.1 Sample Carpet Specification/Data List

Style: Kamiakin
Surface texture: one level loop
Coloration: jet printed
Face fiber: 99% Super® XYZ nylon; 1% Stat-Redux®
 stainless steel for static control
Face fiber size: 20 dpf
Yarn size: 2.00/2cc (equivalent denier 5315)
Body construction: tufted
 gauge: ⅒
 stitches per inch: 8
 primary backing: 100% woven polypropylene olefin
 secondary backing: 100% woven jute
Pile height: 0.250 in.
Pile yarn weight: 40.0 oz/sq. yd.
Total weight: 65 oz./sq. yd.
Density factor: 425,200
Average density: 4383
Weight density: 122,713
Structural stability:
 bundle penetration: 80%
 delamination strength: 2.5 lbs./in.
 tuft bind: 6.25 lbs.
Acoustical ratings:
 NRC .45 over 40 oz. hair pad; IIC 73 over 40 oz. hair
 pad (INR +22)
Insulative value: R-2 over concrete slab
Light reflectance factor: 15
Colorfastness
 crocking: 4.0 (AATCC 8)
 gas fade: 4.0 (AATCC 23)
 ozone fade: 3.0 (AATCC 129): 4.0 (AATCC 109)
 shampoo: 4.0 (AATCC 138)
 lightfastness: Class 4 (AATCC 16E)
Flammability
 tablet test (ASTM D 2859, 16CFR 1630/FF 1–70): passes
 tunnel test (ASTM E 84): Class A
 flooring radiant panel test (NBSIR 75-950): CRF greater
 than 0.25 watts/sq. cm.
Static generation: 2,500 static volts at 70 °F and 20% RH
 (AATCC 134)
Wear resistance
 textural change: min. 30,000 foot traffic units
 pilling: 3.0
 abrasion (Taber): not worn through to backing after
 10,000 cycles

agement of interior light and by helping to lower the rate of heat exchange.

Acoustical Ratings

One of the more important functional benefits of floor covering assemblies is their **acoustical value**, the extent to which they prevent sound from becoming unwanted noise. The noise reduction benefits of carpet installed on walls and panels were discussed in Chapter 19; those of carpet and carpet and cushion assemblies are discussed here.

Sound Absorption

Residential interiors are often filled with many electrical appliances and pieces of entertainment equipment, each one of which generates sound. Contemporary office designs frequently call for large open areas that will permit maximum flexibility in space utilization: such areas can contain numerous people, telephones, computers, and printers, all of which, again, generate sound. Commercial structures are often built to serve several firms and many employees and executives; places where people assemble, such as theaters, often house thousands; schools accommodate hundreds of students. In these interiors, the constant movement of equipment and people, continual verbal exchange, and the like create sound. Lowering the level of **airborne and surface sounds** in these environments is highly desirable; in some cases it is mandatory.

Table 26.2 presents the results of controlled testing for the sound absorption of various carpets with and without an all-hair cushion. The results are reported numerically as the **noise reduction coefficient (NRC)**. Higher NRC values indicate greater sound absorption. The values reported in Table 26.2 reveal the effects of various structural features. Cut pile textures are somewhat more efficient in absorbing sound than loop pile textures. Increasing the weight of the pile layer or the height of the pile yarns in cut pile structures will increase the sound absorption capabilities. In loop textures, pile height apparently has a greater positive influence than does pile weight. The Carpet and Rug Institute has reported that such structural variations produce similar effects when the carpet is glued directly to the floor. Regardless of the method of installation, the fiber content of the pile yarns has virtually no effect on sound absorption.

From the results listed in Table 26.2, a **permeability principle** can be established: the more permeable the structure, the more efficiently it will absorb sound. For example, the uncoated carpet having a pile weight of 44 ounces per square yard had an NRC of .60; when a latex coating was added and the permeability was reduced, an NRC value of .40 was recorded.

Table 26.2 Sound Absorption of Carpet

Carpet no.*	Backing	Pile wt.	Pile ht.	Surface	Pad	NRC
#1	67 oz. sponge rubber attached	44 oz	.25″	Loop	None	.30
#2	Coated	44 oz.	.25″	Loop	40 oz. hair	.40
#3	Uncoated	44 oz.	.25″	Loop	40 oz. hair	.60
Backing		**Pile wt.**	**Pile ht.**	**Surface**	**Pad**	**NRC**
Coated		44 oz.	.25″	Loop	40 oz. hair	.40
Uncoated		44 oz.	.25″	Loop	40 oz. hair	.60
Coated		40 oz.	.40″–20″	Loop	40 oz. hair	.65
Coated		15 oz.	.25″	Loop	40 oz. hair	.65
Coated		43 oz.	.25″	Loop	40 oz. hair	.50
Coated		40 oz.	.39″	Loop	40 oz. hair	.60
Coated		32 oz.	.56″	Cut	40 oz. hair	.70
Coated		43 oz.	.50″	Cut	40 oz. hair	.70

*See carpet fabric key, Table 26.4.

Courtesy of the Carpet and Rug Institute.

Table 26.3 Sound Absorption of Cushions
Cushions were tested under carpet having a pile weight of 40 oz./sq. yd.

Pad Wt.	Pad Material	NRC
—	None	.35
32 oz.	Hair	.50
40 oz.	Hair	.55
54 oz.	Hair	.55
86 oz.	Hair	.60
32 oz.	Hair jute	.55
40 oz.	Hair jute	.60
86 oz.	Hair jute	.65
31 oz.	³/₈″ foam rubber	.60
40 oz.	Hair jute* foam rubber	.50
42 oz.	Hair jute ¹/₈″* Foam rubber latex	.60
44 oz.	Sponge rubber	.45
86 oz.	Sponge rubber ³/₈″	.50

*Tested foam side down.

Courtesy of the Carpet and Rug Institute.

The same principle holds for cushion materials. As shown in Table 26.3, the more permeable hair and hair-jute cushions were more effective acoustically than the less permeable sponge rubber cushions of similar weight. The less dense, lower weight foam rubber cushion was also more effective than the higher density, higher weight sponge rubber cushion of the same thickness. Further, a comparison of the appropriate values in Tables 26.2 and 26.3 confirms the negative effect of permanently attaching cushions to the back of the carpet. Attaching the cushion reduces the permeability and thus the level of sound absorption.

Within an interior, surface noise is created by the routine activities of walking, running, and shuffling, and by the shifting of furniture and equipment. Experimental testing has indicated that carpet is significantly more effective in reducing **surface noise radiation** than is vinyl tile.[1]

Noise Transmission

Controlling **impact and structurally borne sounds** is especially important in multilevel structures, where impact sounds can be transmitted as noise to the interior spaces below. Evaluations of the acoustical role of carpet and cushions in such a situation are made in a chamber with 100 square feet of either concrete or wood joist flooring. The ISO R 140 Tapping Machine is used to impact the surface, and the noise transmitted to the room-like chamber below is picked up by a microphone (Figure 26.1).

The ability of a floor, carpet, or cushion to minimize **noise transmission** is evaluated and reported numerically as an **impact noise rating (INR)** or as an **impact insulation class (IIC)**. Higher values indicate greater noise control, that is, a reduced level of transmission. IIC values are roughly equal to the INR value plus 51.

The values reported in Table 26.4 show the effectiveness of various carpet and cushion features in reducing the level of noise transmission. In this series of tests, a concrete floor was used in the test facility. Concrete floors are generally used in commercial structures, and they are less effective in controlling impact sounds than

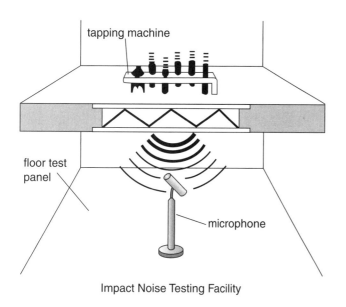

Figure 26.1 Impact noise testing facility.
Courtesy of the Carpet and Rug Institute.

the wood joist floors commonly used in residential construction. When tested without floor coverings, a 5-inch-thick concrete slab had an INR of −17 and a wood joist floor had an INR of −9.

The ratings in Table 26.4 show that increases in the weight of the pile layers of the test carpets improved their performance. All of the carpet and cushion assemblies tested were more effective than any of the test carpets alone. The rubber cushion specimens were more effective when used separately under the carpet than when permanently attached. Here, increased permeability had a negative influence, permitting more sound to be transmitted.

Insulative Value

Heat conductivity and **heat resistivity** are reciprocal terms referring to the rate at which a material conducts

Table 26.4 Impact Noise Ratings of Various Carpets and Cushions on a Concrete Slab
Rating improves as pile weight increases.

Fabric no.	Pad Description	Impact Noise Rating (INR)	Impact Insulation Class (IIC)
No carpet or pad		−17	34
1	None	+2	53
2	None	+4	55
3	None	+6	57
5	None	+9	65
6	None	+14	68
8	3/16″ sponge rubber attached	+17	69
6	40 oz. hair & jute	+22	73
6	Urethane foam pad	+24	76
6	44 oz. sponge rubber	+25	79
6	31 oz. 3/8″ foam rubber	+28	79
6	80 oz. sponge	+29	80

Carpet Fabric Key

Carpet	Pile wt.	Pile ht.
1	20 oz.	.3.35–15″
2	27 oz.	.20″
3	32 oz.	.56″
4	40 oz.	.25″
5	44 oz.	.25″
6	60 oz.	.25″
7	44 oz. with attached 3/16″ sponge rubber pad	.25″

Courtesy of the Carpet and Rug Institute.

or transfers heat. The rate of heat transmittance is given numerically as the **K-value or K-factor**. Materials such as copper conduct heat rapidly and have relatively high K-values. Materials, including textile fibers, that have low K-values are poor heat conductors and can contribute insulative value.

R-values or R-factors numerically describe how effectively structures resist heat flow, that is, how effectively they insulate and prevent heat exchange. The following formula determines R-value: R-value = thickness/K-value. From the formula, it is apparent that resistance to heat flow is determined not only by the rate of conduction, the K-value, but also by the thickness of the structure. Increasing the thickness of a material does not increase its K-value, but does increase its R-factor, making it a more effective insulator.

Several trade associations jointly sponsored a research project to assess the effectiveness of carpet and cushions in reducing heat flow and subsequent heat loss by convection, the transmission of heat energy by air movement. Various carpet construction variables and types of cushions were tested over uninsulated wood floors over a vented crawl space and over a 6-inch-thick concrete slab. Heat was radiated downward from a hot plate to the surface of the carpet; the heat that flowed through the carpet or cushion or both was measured by a cold plate behind the assembly. Computer simulation was used to analyze the energy savings in residential and commercial structures of various sizes and shapes and located in different geographic areas.[2] As a result of this work, the Carpet and Rug Institute published the following findings:

1. The carpet samples tested, typical of those available during the time of the study, had R-values ranging from .55 to 2.46.
2. The contribution of any component of the carpet or cushion test specimens to the total R-value depended more on the thickness of the component than on the fiber or yarn type.
3. R-values varied in direct proportion to thickness and pile density.
4. R-values were additive (R-value of carpet + R-value of cushion = R-value of assembly) for any combination of carpet and cushion.

5. Carpet installed on an uninsulated concrete slab provided greater savings than carpet installed on an insulated wood floor of the same area.
6. Energy savings varied substantially, depending on the R-value of the carpet and cushion assembly. For example, an assembly with an R-value of 4.0 provided estimated energy savings greater than two times the savings estimated for carpet with an R-value of 1.0. Dollar savings varied according to local fuel charges and length of heating and cooling periods.

Light Reflectance Factor

Because light-colored textiles tend to reflect high quantities of incident light waves, light-colored carpet can reduce the energy consumed by artificial luminaires (light fixtures). The reflectance value of soft floor coverings can be measured and reported in terms of a **light reflectance factor (LRF)**, the percentage of incident light that is reflected. The complement of the LRF indicates the amount of light absorbed. Thus, an LRF of 10 indicates that 10 percent of the incident light was reflected and 90 percent was absorbed.

Mohawk Carpet, a division of Mohasco Corporation, has suggested that carpet with an LRF greater than 10 will reduce both the number of luminaires and the wattage required to light an interior space. Table 26.5 details the relationship between various LRF values and interior illumination savings.

Because tracked-in dirt will reduce the light reflectance of carpet, anticipated soil accumulation must be considered when consumers wish to select more reflective carpet. Mohawk Carpet recommends an LRF of 15 as a practical upper limit for carpet to be installed in areas undergoing heavy traffic and soiling.

Evaluating Performance Properties

Besides the functional properties discussed in the preceding section, other properties, including colorfastness, flammability, static generation, and wear resistance, also help to determine the in-use performance of textile floor

Table 26.5 Effect of Carpet Reflectance Factors on Interior Illumination

	Carpet Light Reflectance Factor				
	30%	20%	15%	10%	0%
Theoretical number of luminaires required to light a:					
Small office (140 sq. ft.)	2	2	2	3	3
Large office (6,000 sq. ft.)	65	70	71	76	80
Total wattage required to light a:					
Small office	272	272	272	408	408
Large office	8,840	9,520	9,656	10,336	10,880
Watts per sq. ft. required to light a:					
Small office	1.9	1.9	1.9	2.9	2.9
Large office	1.5	1.6	1.6	1.7	1.8

Courtesy of Mohawk Carpet.

coverings. Such properties should be evaluated prior to selection; again, professionals may be required to specify or select floor coverings exhibiting a mandated level of performance.

Colorfastness

Standard laboratory test methods are available to evaluate the stability of the colorants in most colored floor coverings. Generally, fastness to crocking, atmospheric gases, light, and cleaning agents are measured.

Fastness to Crocking, Gases, and Light

The standard test methods used to measure crocking, the transfer of dye from one surface to another, and gasfastness were discussed and illustrated in Chapter 14; standard test methods used to measure lightfastness were discussed in Chapter 18. The designations of these test methods may be listed with the appropriate fastness ratings, as in Table 26.1.

Fastness to Shampoo and Water

Textile floor coverings are frequently tested for their fastness to water and to shampoo using the methods in AATCC 107 Colorfastness to Water and AATCC 138 Shampooing: Washing of Textile Floor Coverings. Either test method allows for analysis of the test results in terms of bleeding and staining, as well as in terms of

color change. Test specimens are compared with the appropriate Gray Scale (Figures 14.9 and 14.10, p. 237), and the numerical values recorded.

Flammability

As is true of other laboratory testing procedures, test methods that assess the potential flammability of soft floor coverings have been designed to simulate real-life conditions. Prior to marketing most carpet and large rugs, producers must subject them to the methenamine tablet test to confirm that they conform to the performance standards enforced by the Consumer Product Safety Commission. For use in some commercial interiors, carpet and rugs may be required to conform to additional flammability codes. In such cases, the floor coverings are often tested in accordance with the procedures outlined in the flooring radiant panel test. These and other flammability tests are described and illustrated in Chapter 11, and fire performance recommendations are presented in Table 11.1 (p. 172).

Static Generation

The test method generally accepted in the industry for evaluating the static propensity of floor covering assemblies is AATCC 134 Electrostatic Propensity of Carpets. The test procedure, designed to closely simulate actual end-use conditions, is conducted in an atmosphere having 20 percent relative humidity and a temperature of 70 °F. During the testing, a person wearing clean, neolite-soled shoes walks across a carpet while linked to an electrometer. This device measures the voltage building up on the body, and the recorded level is then reported in static volts. (The mechanisms of static voltage buildup and the threshold of human sensitivity to static discharge were explained in Chapter 4.)

Frequently, regulations and/or specifications state that the control of static generation must be durable. In such cases, the agency having jurisdiction may require that floor coverings be cleaned in accordance with the procedures outlined in AATCC 138 Shampooing: Washing of Textile Floor Coverings prior to testing with AATCC 134.

Wear Resistance

The extent to which a carpet or rug exhibits satisfactory in-service performance with respect to appearance retention and durability is determined by several factors. The abrasion resistance of the floor covering will affect the extent to which fuzzing, pilling, and fiber loss occur. The resiliency of the structure will affect the degree to which the original thickness and luster are retained when the assembly is subjected to the static pressure of furniture legs, repeated loads of foot traffic, and the rolling stresses of moving equipment. If the original texture is lost, the consumer may regard the structure as "worn out," even though fiber loss may be negligible. Therefore, service performance analyses related to wear cannot be limited to abrasion-related performance; they must also include evaluations of textural changes.

Textural Changes

ASTM D 6119 Standard Practice for Creating Surface Appearance Changes in Pile Yarn Floor Covering from Foot Traffic may be used in evaluations of textural changes. The practice is directed to appearance changes, such as matting, flattening, or the loss of tuft definition, that do not necessarily involve fiber loss by abrasion or the development of a threadbare appearance. It does not simulate surface appearance changes resulting from soiling, pivoting, or rolling traffic. Carpet specimens are securely placed in a floor layout

having an odd number of traffic lanes that require walkers to automatically reverse their direction with each pass through the course. Counting devices accurately count **foot traffic units**, the number of passes by human walkers (not the number of times each specimen is stepped on). A traffic level high enough to cause noticeable change is used. The cumulative change in surface appearance is analyzed by comparing unexposed and exposed specimens. Purchasers and suppliers may mutually agree on the minimum number of foot traffic units a floor covering should withstand before the textural change is unacceptable.

ASTM D 5251 Standard Practice for the Operation of the Tetrapod Walker Drum Tester may be used to produce changes in texture on the surface of pile floor covering caused by mechanical action. Test carpet is installed as the lining of a rotatable cylindrical chamber with the pile surface exposed. During testing, the plastic-tipped "feet" of the **tetrapod walker** tumble against the carpet surface as the drum revolves, simulating foot traffic. The change in texture may be assessed visually and by measuring the change in pile thickness. The resistance to abrasion may be assessed by measuring the loss in pile weight.

Abrasion Resistance

ASTM D 3884 Standard Test Method for Abrasion Resistance of Textile Fabrics (Rotary Platform, Double Head Method) is used in the carpet and rug industry for the accelerated laboratory testing of the abrasion resistance of floor coverings. The apparatus used in the test has two flat platforms, or turntables, each supporting and rotating one specimen under two abradant wheels (Figure 26.2). The pressure of the wheels on the specimens can be controlled during the testing operation, and a vacuum unit may be employed to remove abraded particles continually. During testing, the abradant wheels rotate in opposite directions (Figure 26.3). This results in abrasion marks that form a pattern of crossed, slightly curved, herringbone-like arcs over an area of approximately 4.5 inches. Some producers evaluate the results in terms of the number of cycles (revolutions of the turntable carrying the specimen) required to cause exposure of the backing. Other producers measure the percent of pile weight loss or the percent loss of breaking load. The value reported is the average of five replicate tests.

Figure 26.2 Taber Abraser with double heads.
Courtesy of Taber Industries.

Figure 26.3 Directions of rotation of the abradant wheels
and support platform during abrasion resistance testing.
Courtesy of Taber Industries.

As noted in Chapter 22, manufacturers of tufted carpet seek to reduce the number of individual fibers that are teased to the surface and rolled into pills through the proper application of adhesive coatings. Part of their quality-control effort involves ascertaining how thoroughly the adhesive has penetrated the pile yarn bundle, to lock the fibers side by side.

Some manufacturers have adapted a floor tread test for use in evaluating the service performance of carpet in-stalled on stairs. Commonly referred to as the **stair tread test**, the method is directed to assessing the extent to which the carpet withstands abrasion, especially at the nosing of stairs. This is a long-term, service exposure test: carpet specimens are installed without a cushion on heavily trafficked stairs. Producers may evaluate the level of abrasion resistance visually; they may measure the pile weight loss; or they may record the traffic count required to expose the backing and create a threadbare appearance.

Summary

Soft floor covering manufacturers use prescribed test methods, as well as some adapted procedures, to evaluate the quality of their products and to predict their in-service performance. In turn, they frequently use the results of these tests to promote the selection of their carpet and rugs.

For commercial interiors, selection prerequisites include not only an assessment of the traffic conditions and activities anticipated in the end-use setting, but also an investigation of performance codes and structural requirements. Special requirements may exist regarding, for example, static generation, flammability, weight-related factors, and colorfastness. The interior designer and architect can use the test data provided by the producer to determine whether a stock product meets or exceeds requirements. When working on a custom project, the professional can specify the composition, construction features, and levels of performance desired or required.

Key Terms

acoustical value

airborne and surface sounds

foot traffic units

heat conductivity

heat resistivity

impact and structurally borne sounds

impact insulation class (IIC)

impact noise rating (INR)

K-values or K-factors

light reflectance factor (LRF)

permeability principle

noise reduction coefficient (NRC)

noise transmission

R-values or R-factors

specification listing

stair tread test

surface noise radiation

tetrapod walker

Review Questions

1. Discuss the value standard test methods and performance specifications have for members of the industry.

2. Explain the usefulness of product performance data for the design professional.

3. Discuss the influence pile construction density, pile height, and pile weight have on the end-use of carpet and rugs.

4. Identify the textural characteristics and weight factors of soft floor coverings that aid in sound absorption.

5. Does any fiber have significantly greater value in absorbing sound?

6. Explain the "permeability principle" as it relates to noise reduction within an interior by carpet and cushions. How does this principle relate to noise transmission?

7. Are textile fibers relatively good heat conductors or relatively good heat insulators?

8. If one wants to improve the insulative value of a carpet and cushion assembly, which is changed, the R-value or the K-value?

9. Explain the relationship between the color of the carpet and the number of luminaires required within an interior. Is soil accumulation a factor to be considered?

10. Does a soft floor covering have to have measurable fiber loss to be perceived as "worn out?"

Notes

1. *Acoustical Benefits: Sound Conditioning with Carpet,* Carpet and Rug Institute, Dalton, Ga., n.d.

2. *Advantages of Carpet and Rugs in Energy Conservation,* Carpet and Rug Institute, Dalton, Ga., 1976.

27

Installation and Maintenance of Floor Covering Assemblies

Installing Soft Floor Coverings and Cushions
  Wall-to-Wall Installation Methods
  Loose-laid Rug Installations
  Factors Affecting Choice of Installation Method
  Determining Yardage Required

Maintaining Textile Floor Coverings
  Initial Care
  Preventive Maintenance
  Interim Maintenance
  Restorative Maintenance
  Salvage Maintenance

To ensure long-term serviceability in their textile floor coverings and cushions, residential and commercial consumers should consider installation and maintenance factors as thoroughly as they do appearance and performance variables. Unless the floor covering assembly is carefully installed by qualified persons, ripples, bubbles, prominent seams, and mismatched patterns may appear. An insecure installation could be hazardous, as well as result in undue stress on the structure itself.

Cleaning and stain removal procedures, if part of a planned maintenance program, should not cause marked changes in texture, nor should they alter the original color of a product. The installation to be used and the maintenance program to be followed should be investigated prior to the final selection of the floor covering assembly.

Installing Soft Floor Coverings and Cushions

Residential consumers, contract designers, and architects should be familiar with the basic procedures used in wall-to-wall installations. This will prepare them for an accurate analysis of whatever factors will influence their choice of method of installation. They should be familiar also with such features as pile lay and types of pattern repeats and with the principles governing seam placement and floor space measurements. Such familiarity is the foundation for correctly planning the carpet layout, determining the yardage required, and estimating the cost of the project.

Wall-to-Wall Installation Methods

Three methods may be considered for the **wall-to-wall installation** of textile floor coverings. These include stretch-in, glue-down, and free-lay techniques. Before proceeding with any installation, the site must be properly prepared. Often, skilled persons fully experienced in the procedures should do this preliminary work and installation.

Site Preparation

An important part of site preparation is the removal of the previously installed floor covering assembly. Old carpet, if left in place, would prevent the new cushion from sliding smoothly into place during installation, causing it to become distorted and thus preventing the proper stretching and smooth installation of the replacement carpet. Moreover, loading of a multilayered installation that included the old floor covering would result in severe and repeated flexing of the new assembly, promoting deterioration of the backing and the development of an uneven wear layer. For glue-down installations, sheet vinyl and linoleum must be removed for the new structure to adhere well.

Although the subfloor should be dry for all installations, dryness is especially critical for glue-down installations. New concrete floors, which may require up to four months to dry, should be checked carefully for dryness; so should subfloors that are close to or in contact with the ground, either on-grade (ground level) or below-grade. Ground moisture may be transported upward through the slab, facilitating the migration of alkaline compounds at the same time. The moisture can prevent good adhesion of the floor covering and foster microbe-related problems. The alkaline substance may react with the adhesive compounds that stabilize the carpet and with those that secure it to the floor, causing degradation and loosening of the carpet. In order to avoid such problems, the moisture condition must be resolved and the alkaline must be neutralized prior to installation.

The interior floor space to be covered should be smooth and free of cracks, crevices, and holes, for a more pleasing appearance and uniform support for the assembly. Rough areas should be sanded, and openings should be filled. Finally, the floor should be free of dust, lint, and grit.

Stretch-in Installations

Stretch-in installations involve stretching rollgoods and fastening them over pin-holding strips that have been secured to the perimeter of the floor space. These plywood strips, also known as **tackless strips**, are approximately 1.5 inches wide, and have rows of rust-resistant metal pins protruding upward at an angle of 60 degrees (Figure 27.1). The strips are up to 0.375 inch thick; the thickness of the strip is coordinated with the thickness of the cushion to be installed. When carpet lengths greater than 30 feet are being installed or when heavy traffic loads are anticipated, three rows of pins should be used; for residential installations and smaller commercial installations, two rows of pins should be sufficient.

The strips are nailed or glued to the floor, with the pins angled toward the wall. A gully or space slightly narrower than the thickness of the carpet is left between the wall and the strip. If a separate cushion is used, it is laid within the perimeter of the strips and stapled or glued to the floor.

When seams and pattern matching are required, the parallel edges of the floor covering must be carefully aligned and trimmed to fit tightly. Butting of factory edges is not recommended since they may be slightly irregular; there may be a slight excess of printed pattern repeats provided for trimming to an accurate match. After the rollgoods are cut, a thin bead of an adhesive should be applied to prevent edge raveling and fraying during subsequent handling, seaming, and use.

Seams may be formed by hand sewing or by applying various types of tape. Crosswise seams are often sewn.

Figure 27.1 Pin-holding strip used in stretch-in tackless installation projects.

Figure 27.2 Tools used to install rollgoods in stretch-in tackless projects. *Courtesy of Roberts Consolidated Industries.*

a) telescoping power stretcher

b) knee kicker

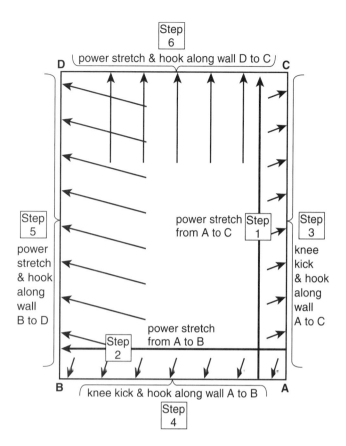

Figure 27.3 Stretching tufted structures.
Courtesy of the Carpet and Rug Institute.

Hot melt tape is often used for lengthwise seams. This tape has a thermoplastic coating that becomes tacky when heated with a special iron. The carpet edges are sealed together by the adhesive when it cools. In lieu of hot melt tape, a strip of pressure-sensitive or adhesive tape may be placed behind the parallel carpet edges and a latex bead applied along the seam line to secure the join.

After the seaming is completed, the carpet is stretched, generally 1 to 1.5 percent in length and width, and anchored over the pins in the wooden strips. A **power stretcher** is used to place uniform stretch over the surface of the carpet, and a **knee-kicker** is used to grip and anchor the edges over the pins (Figure 27.2).

The procedures recommended for stretching tufted carpet are shown in Figure 27.3. The power stretcher is anchored at the base of the walls and telescoped as needed.

Stairway carpet may be installed with a stretch-in technique, using pin-holding strips and a knee-kicker. It may also be glued down.

Glue-down Installations

Glue-down installations involve securing floor covering structures to the floor with an adhesive. When no cushion is used, the procedure may be referred to as direct-glue down; when an attached cushion is involved, the procedure is called glue-down. The same procedures are used in both operations, except that structures without a cushion are rolled onto the adhesive and structures with a cushion are pressed into the adhesive.

When installing rollgoods, the layout and seam placement must be carefully planned, and the floor measurements must be exact. If the carpet is too large, buckles and ripples may develop; if the carpet is too small, separation of the seams may occur. The cut edges of the carpet must be precisely marked, trimmed, and secured with a bead of latex. The selected adhesive is then spread over the floor with a notched trowel and the carpet is bonded to the adhesive.

When working with carpet modules, the installer should locate a starting point that will maximize the cut size of the perimeter modules. From this point, a grid is established and the selected adhesive is spread over the area. Each module is then slid into position, taking care to avoid catching any pile tufts in the joint. Successive tiles should be laid in a pyramid or stairstep manner (Figure 27.4). Perimeter modules can be precisely cut to fit the floor space.

The adhesive used to bond rollgoods and modules may be a nonreleasable (permanent) or a releasable type. Releasable adhesives may permit the floor covering structure to be repeatedly lifted and rebonded into position.

Figure 27.4 Pyramid technique recommended for positioning carpet modules.
Courtesy of Milliken and Company.

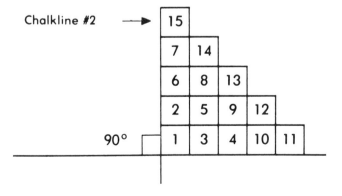

This permits some degree of access to underfloor service trenches or to flatwire cable systems installed directly on the floor. It may also permit the rotation or removal of carpet modules.

Free-lay Installations

Free-lay installations may be considered for carpet modules when consumers wish to maximize the flexibility of the carpet tile, as long as heavy rolling traffic is not expected. Rolling casters on office chairs would have an insignificant effect, but such heavy items as hospital guerneys wheeled down corridors and automobiles driven into showrooms could have a "snowplow" effect, raising the edges of the modules.

Modules must have superior dimensional stability for free-lay use. This feature is often achieved with the application of a heavy secondary backing. Some free-lay tiles alternate layers of heavy-gauge vinyl and glass fiber scrims for the necessary stability (Figure 27.5).

In preparation for installation, a control grid is again planned to maximize the cut size of the perimeter modules. Within this grid, specific crosswise and lengthwise rows of modules should be secured to the floor with adhesive or double-face tape to minimize shifting. Selective glue-down leaves approximately 80 to 90 percent of the

modules in the free-lay mode; tape, which is removed after installation, leaves all of the tiles held by gravity.

Like installations with releasable adhesives, free-lay installations permit easy access to floor and underfloor utility systems. Free-lay also offers maximum convenience in shifting modules.

Loose-laid Rug Installations

Cut edges of rugs and runners must be bound by sewing twill-woven tape over the raw edges or by serging (machine overcasting). Cushions used with loose-laid rugs and runners should be thin and about 1 or 2 inches narrower and shorter than the floor coverings. This allows the rug or runner to lie close to the floor and minimizes the tendency for the soft floor covering to advance off the cushion. On stairs, runners may be securely installed with brass rods (Figure 27.6).

Factors Affecting Choice of Installation Method

Besides the site-related considerations identified in the previous section, other factors may limit the type of installation chosen for soft floor coverings. These include traffic conditions, planned space utilization, and concern for noise reduction and energy conservation.

Traffic Conditions

The traffic conditions in the area to be carpeted include a number of variables. First, the anticipated number of persons who will walk over the floor covering should be esti-

Figure 27.5 Fusion-bonded, free-lay tile with GlasBac™ secondary backing.
Courtesy of Interface Flooring Systems, Inc.

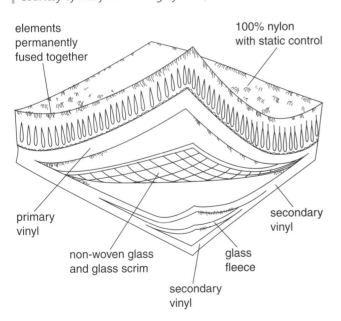

Figure 27.6 Stair runner installed with brass rods.
Courtesy of Peerless Imported Rugs.

mated (see Table 20.1, p. 336). At low and medium levels, 500 to 1,000 traffic counts per day, the carpet may be stretched-in over most types of cushions; at higher levels, the carpet may be stretched-in over a thin, high-density cushion or over no cushion, or it may be glued down.

Second, it is important to consider what type of traffic will be usual. If people with canes, crutches, or limited vision will use the interior, area and room-size rugs and runners should be avoided, or their edges should be securely attached to the floor. When rolling traffic, such as wheelchairs and equipment, will impact the floor covering, strong consideration should be given to gluing the carpet structure directly to the subfloor. This installation technique will help to minimize shearing and seam separation.

A third traffic-related factor to consider is the amount of dirt and grit that will be tracked in. If a rapid rate of accumulation is expected, the specifier may elect to install carpet modules with a releasable adhesive or in a free-lay mode. The modules could then be rotated to minimize apparent and actual differences in appearance and texture throughout the interior. Soiled modules could be removed for off-site cleaning, and damaged modules lifted out and replaced.

Planned Space Utilization

Frequently, modern commercial offices have an open design; movable wall partitions define work stations. As personnel and activities change, the partitions can be moved to define new spaces consistent with current needs. For such interiors, the specifier may investigate the use of carpet modules instead of rollgoods. If rollgoods are installed to the base of each movable wall, shifting the wall would leave a bare strip of subfloor, which would have to be patched with carpet. If wall panels are placed over a carpet, eventual wall shifting may reveal unsightly lines, requiring a large amount of replacement carpet. These problems may be avoided through use of carpet modules.

As shown in Figure 27.7a, a common grid can be planned for the placement of the modules. When a square falls on a wall, it can be cut to fit on either side of the wall (Figure 27.7b). Later, when the wall panels are shifted, the cut modules can be lifted and a row of full-size modules laid in place (Figure 27.7c).

Acoustical and Insulative Control

The need for noise control and insulation may call for the installation of a carpet and cushion assembly, rather than a carpet glued to the floor. As noted in Chapter 26, a sep-

a) common grid for module placement

b) modules cut to fit base of wall panels

c) full size replacement modules

Figure 27.7 Use of carpet modules in interior space with movable walls.
Courtesy of Interface Flooring Systems, Inc.

arate cushion increases the level of sound absorption, and any combination of a carpet and cushion provides greater reduction of impact noise transmission than does the carpet alone. Chapter 26 also discussed the finding that the insulative values of a carpet and cushion are additive, and are higher when the two structures are used separately. If traffic conditions dictate the selection of a glue-down installation, less effective control over noise and energy consumption may be partially offset by increasing the pile yarn weight and pile height of the carpet.

Cost-related Factors

As discussed in Chapter 20, there may be per square yard charges assessed for site preparation, for installation of the new cushion, and for installation of the new carpet. Normally, the cost of installing a separate cushion and carpet will be higher than that of installing a carpet with no cushion or a cushion attached. When selecting a type of installation, however, the consumer may consider acoustical benefits and energy savings that separate structures help realize. If the value of these benefits outweighs the additional installation costs, a separate cushion should be chosen, provided budgetary limitations are not exceeded. Of course, it is advisable to investigate the comparative life-cycle costs of all floor covering options.

Determining Yardage Required

The number of square yards of carpet required for a project must be accurately calculated. If the initial order was insufficient, the additional yardage of a second order inevitably has slightly different color characteristics as a result of being dyed or printed in a separate operation. Of course, if the initial order is excessive, unnecessary materials costs will be incurred.

Careful planning and correct measuring can ensure that the yardage order is accurate. Attention must be given to the direction of pile lay, the placement of seams, and the size and nature of pattern repeats.

Measuring Floor Space

The following lists the important rules to observe when measuring floor space for carpet:

1. Between opposite walls, each of which is uninterrupted, measure the distance from baseboard to baseboard and record the information on a sketch of the floor plan.
2. Between opposite walls, one of which is interrupted by an opening, measure from the baseboard to the

mid-point of an archway or to a point halfway under the bottom edge of the closed door (Figure 27.8). Record the measurement on the floor plan sketch.

3. Measure stairs as illustrated in Figure 27.9. Landings are treated as if they were large steps. From 2 to 4 inches must be added to each of the recorded lengthwise and crosswise measurements. This will provide the yardage required for fitting and trimming.

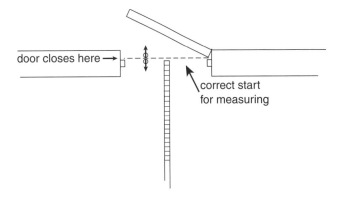

Figure 27.8 Measuring for carpet at a door jamb. *Courtesy of J. P. Stevens.*

Figure 27.9 Measuring stairs and landings for carpet. *Courtesy of J. P. Stevens.*

Positioning the Pile Lay

The directional lay of pile yarns (Figure 9.4, p. 135) must be uniform for all adjoining pieces of carpet. The layout should be planned so that the lay parallels the longest dimension of the largest room to be carpeted, as shown in Figure 27.10a. Unless pattern orientation or a similar feature must be considered, the pile lay direction should be away from the strongest source of light and toward entrance areas.

Figure 27.10 Planning pile lay direction.

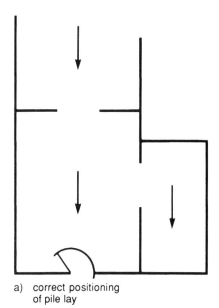

a) correct positioning
    of pile lay

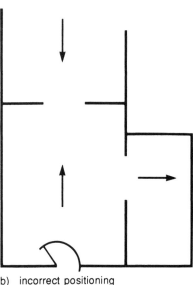

b) incorrect positioning
    of pile lay

Figure 27.10b illustrates an incorrect layout. One length has been reversed and one length has been given a quarter turn. Because the quantity of light reflected by each section would be different, there would be marked differences in their apparent color. The carpet would appear darkest when the viewer is looking at the tips of the pile tufts and lightest when the viewer is looking at the sides of the yarns. Therefore, once the correct positioning of the pile lay direction has been established, all adjoining lengths of carpet of the same color and quality must be laid with their pile lay in the same direction.

Some interior designers and architects may purposely vary the pile direction of adjoining units in order to create marked differences in their apparent brightness. Examples of possible patterns for the placement of carpet modules are shown in Figure 27.11. In each of these four patterns, shading variations would alter the aesthetic characteristics of the installation.

Figure 27.11 Four patterns for installing carpet modules with varied pile lay directions.
Courtesy of Milliken and Company.

a) monolithic—corner to corner
b) monolithic—ashlar
c) random—corner to corner or ashlar
d) parquet

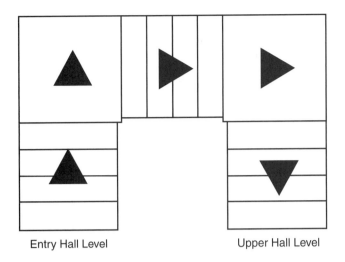

Entry Hall Level   Upper Hall Level

Figure 27.12 Direction of pile lay on angled stairs.
Courtesy of J. P. Stevens.

a) incorrect seam placement   b) correct seam placement

Figure 27.13 Planning carpet seam placement.
Courtesy of J. P. Stevens.

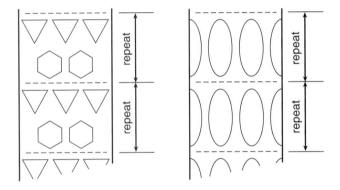

Figure 27.14 Set-match patterns.

When pile carpet is installed on stairs, the width of the carpet must parallel the width of the stairs so that carpet "grin," the exposure of the backing on the nose edges, will be minimized. With angled stairways, this will necessitate installation of the carpet with quarter turns of the pile lay (Figure 27.12). In such cases, the critical importance of avoiding exposure of the backing overrides concern for shade variations.

Planning Seam Placement

Several principles should govern the placement of seams. Whenever possible, seams should run lengthwise, parallel with the pile lay, not crosswise. Crosswise seams interrupt the pile sweep and are highlighted when the quantity of incident light is high. Seams should not run perpendicular to a doorway, although they may run across the opening (Figure 27.13b). A seam condition known as a "saddle," with parallel seams on each side of a doorway, (Figure 27.13a) should be avoided by shifting the carpet and seaming it in a different location. For stability and safety, seams must not be located in traffic pivot areas and on stair treads.

Allowing Yardage for Matching Patterns

Patterned floor coverings have either a set-match or drop-match pattern repeat. The type of match and the lengthwise and crosswise dimensions of the repeat affect the yardage required.

Set-match patterns repeat themselves across the width of the carpet. Depending on the width of the repeat and the width of the carpet, the crosswise repeats may be fully completed or partially completed (Figure 27.14). In the latter case, the pattern is generally scaled so that the complement of the incomplete design is at the opposite edge.

Set-match patterned carpet should be cut at the next highest multiple of the pattern repeat length beyond the amount actually required. Thus, if the repeat is 12 inches long and 17 feet 6 inches are required, the carpet would be cut 18 feet long (18 is the next highest multiple of the 1-foot length); if the repeat is 36 inches long and 21 feet 6 inches are required, the carpet would be cut 24 feet long (24 is the next highest multiple of the 3-foot dimension). This cutting plan would provide the additional yardage

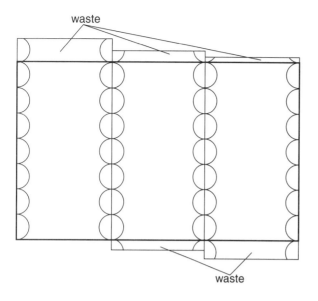

Figure 27.15 Matching set-match patterns.

Figure 27.16 Half-drop-match pattern.
Courtesy of Mohawk Carpet.

needed for side matching. The installer would shift the long edges of the parallel carpet lengths, matching the pattern. The waste would then be cut away, but not necessarily from one end of each length (Figure 27.15).

Drop-match patterns repeat themselves diagonally across the width of the carpet. In half-drop-match patterns, the complementing portion of a design is located at

a point up or down one-half the length of the repeat, as shown in the draft in Figure 27.16.

Two methods may be used to cut carpet having half-drop match patterns. The first method is to cut on multiples of the repeat. If three 9-foot widths of carpet that has a 36-inch-long repeat are being installed in a room that measures 20 feet 6 inches in length, the first and third cuts would be cut on seven multiples or 21 feet. The second strip would then be cut 22 feet 6 inches, minimizing waste.

The second method is to cut on multiples of the repeat plus half a repeat. This method utilizes a half repeat to advantage. For example, a 12-inch pattern can be cut in lengths of 1 foot 6 inches, 2 feet 6 inches, 3 feet 6 inches, and so on. If three widths of carpet with a 36-inch repeat are being installed in a room that measures 22 feet 6 inches in length, all lengths can be cut seven and a half repeats, or 22 feet 6 inches long.

A second type of drop-match pattern is the quarter-drop pattern. This type of repeat is frequently seen in colonial patterns; it has four blocks to a repeat. The figures match one quarter of the repeat on the opposite edge (Figure 27.17). It is apparent that successive pieces of carpet must be shifted and aligned to preserve the diagonal pattern. According to the length required and the length of the repeat, quarter-drop patterns can be cut in

Figure 27.17 Matching quarter-drop-match pattern.

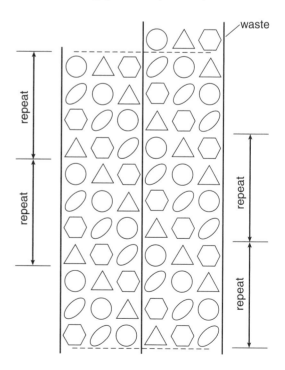

Table 27.1 Conversion of Feet and Inches to Square Yards of 12-Foot-Wide Carpet

Example

74′5″ of 12′ width
74′ = 98.67 sq. yds.
5″ = .55 sq. yd.

Total = 99.22 sq. yds.

Inches

Linear in.	Sq. yds.	Linear ft.	Sq. yds.	Linear ft.	Sq. yds.
1	11	25	33.33	64	85.33
2	22	26	34.67	65	86.67
3	33	27	36.00	66	88.00
4	44	28	37.33	67	89.33
5	55	29	38.67	68	90.67
6	67	30	40.00	69	92.00
7	78	31	41.33	70	93.33
8	89	32	42.67	71	94.67
9	1.00	33	44.00	72	96.00
10	1.11	34	45.33	73	97.33
11	1.22	35	46.67	74	98.67

Feet

Linear ft.	Sq. yds.				
		36	48.00	75	100.00
		37	49.33	76	101.33
		38	50.67	77	102.67
		39	52.00	78	104.00
1	1.33	40	53.33	79	105.33
2	2.67	41	54.67	80	106.67
3	4.00	42	56.00	81	108.00
4	5.33	43	57.33	82	109.33
5	6.67	44	58.67	83	110.67
6	8.00	45	60.00	84	112.00
7	9.33	46	61.33	85	113.33
8	10.67	47	62.67	86	114.67
9	12.00	48	64.00	87	116.00
10	13.33	49	65.33	88	117.33
11	14.67	50	66.67	89	118.67
12	16.00	51	68.00	90	120.00
13	17.33	52	69.33	91	121.33
14	18.67	53	70.67	92	122.67
15	20.00	54	72.00	93	124.00
16	21.33	55	73.00	94	125.33
17	22.67	56	74.67	95	126.67
18	24.00	57	76.00	96	128.00
19	25.33	58	77.33	97	129.33
20	26.67	59	78.67	98	130.67
21	28.00	60	80.00	99	132.00
22	29.33	61	81.33	100	133.33
23	30.67	62	82.67		
24	32.00	63	84.00		

Courtesy of Milliken and Company.

multiples of the repeat plus one, two, or three blocks. Side matching can then be achieved by dropping one, two, or three blocks.

For all planned installations, it is advisable to sketch the layout of the carpet lengths on graph paper, noting the direction of pile lay, the placement of seams, and the orientation of patterns. The floor measurement and the calculations of the extra yardage needed for pattern matching should be rechecked. This plan will help ensure that the tally of the total number of linear feet and inches of carpet required is accurate; later it will serve as the cutting guide.

Linear measurements must be converted into square yards for ordering. Because most carpet is produced 12 feet wide, the conversions presented in Table 27.1 are based on this width. This conversion also facilitates an estimate of materials costs, since these charges are normally quoted on a per-square-yard basis.

When floor covering is received, it should be inspected to confirm that the quantity ordered was delivered and that the structure is free of unacceptable flaws and color variations. Most manufacturers will not assume responsibility for such defects after carpet has been cut.

After the carpet or carpet and cushion assembly has been installed, a planned maintenance program should be initiated. Without proper care, a carpet that has been carefully selected, correctly specified, and skillfully installed may "ugly out" long before it is worn out.

Maintaining Textile Floor Coverings

To ensure that they retain a high level of appearance, textile floor coverings installed in residential and commercial interiors should be maintained through a planned program. Scheduled maintenance can keep the appearance from changing noticeably, in contrast to sporadic maintenance, in which cleaning is undertaken as a last resort after excessive soil has already accumulated and visibly altered the look of the surface.

The primary objective of planned maintenance programs is to prevent soil, ordinarily captured in approximately 20 to 30 percent of the carpet area, from being spread throughout the interior. A second equally important objective is to reduce the amount of grit that becomes embedded in the surface yarns. These objectives are met by strictly adhering to a schedule of regular, frequent vacuuming and cleaning, and, for localized areas that become highly soiled, stain removal. Commercial programs are available, but professionals and consumers may design appropriate plans themselves. However it is arrived at, a planned maintenance program delays or prevents the development of apparent changes in color caused by excessive soil accumulation; it also reduces changes in texture and luster caused when traffic grinds gritty soil against fiber surfaces.

Initially, some corrective measures may be required to mend an occasional flaw or to remove loose fibers. Thereafter, specific preventive, interim, and restorative procedures should be followed, with salvage procedures used as necessary. Each of these activities is scheduled after consideration of the level of appearance preferred by the carpet owner, the anticipated traffic load, and the rate and type of soiling expected.

Initial Care

Inspection of a newly installed carpet may reveal such problems as shedding, sprouting, missing tufts, and small dots of latex. Simple measures can correct these irregularities.

Shedding occurs when short lengths of fibers that have accumulated during manufacturing work to the surface. It is particularly characteristic of cut pile textures and will soon be corrected by regular vacuuming. The fiber loss will not be significant. **Sprouting** refers to the protrusion of a tuft above the surface of the wear layer. This may result from the release of a small fold of pile yarn that was caught during manufacturing. The extended tuft should simply be clipped to the proper pile height; it must never be pulled. The floor covering dealer, in a procedure known as burling, can replace a missing tuft. During manufacturing, a small dot of latex is frequently used to join or splice ends of pile yarns. All visible bits of latex are removed by the factory inspector. If, however, some were hidden and appear in the new carpet, the installer or consumer can simply cut them out, removing any residue with a small amount of dry-cleaning fluid.

Another activity to be carried out after installation of a new carpet is the placement of chair pads under wheeled desk chairs and casters or rests under furniture. These will protect the pile layer from excessive abrasion, shearing, and crushing, prolonging the wear-life and helping to retain the original texture of the carpet.

Preventive Maintenance

Preventive maintenance procedures are protective procedures, employed to capture soil and grit in track-off, funnel, and concentrated traffic areas. If soil and grit particles are continually removed from the sites where they were initially deposited, the amount spread throughout a facility can be significantly reduced. Preventive measures can also help minimize spotting and staining.

Using Protective Mats

Because over 80 percent of carpet soil is tracked-in, preventive maintenance must begin with walk-off mats or runners placed outside and inside of entrance areas. Walk-off mats should also be placed where foot traffic may transfer wax and dust from hard-surfaced floors to carpet surfaces. In areas where commercial traffic is concentrated or channeled, such as lobbies, elevators, in front of vending machines and file cabinets, down corridors, and at doorways, protective mats should be strategically located to capture soil.

In all cases, walk-off mats and runners must be cleaned so they do not themselves become sources of soil and grit. In elevators, removable rugs or carpet modules can facilitate off-site cleaning and rotation.

Vacuuming

In most planned maintenance programs, a thorough vacuuming (five to seven passes of the sweeper over the surface) with an upright, rather than a canister, vacuum is recommended for track-off areas and primary traffic lanes every one or two days. For areas subjected to lower levels of traffic, vacuuming may be light (three passes of the sweeper) and as infrequent as every seven to ten days. Such light maintenance is reasonable for many areas: approximately 70 to 80 percent of all interior floor space is rarely walked on.

An example of a planned maintenance schedule for a commercial interior is presented in Figure 27.18. Vacuuming, stain removal, and interim cleaning activities are listed. Track-off and funnel areas are scheduled for dry cleaning once every twenty days; stain removal and dry cleaning procedures are discussed later in this chapter.

Pretesting Cleaning Products

Pretesting stain removal and carpet cleaning products is an important preventive activity, because it minimizes the chance that products will damage the fibers, cause color

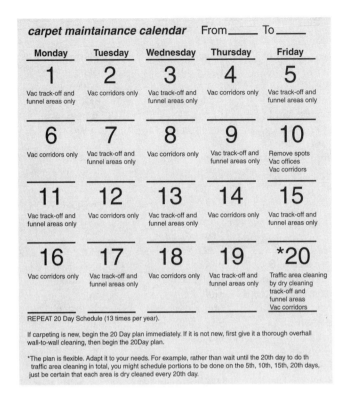

Figure 27.18 Planned carpet maintenance calendar. *Courtesy of Host/Racine Industries, Inc. Copyright 1980, 1981, 1982, 1983, 1984.*

transfer, produce color changes, or leave sticky residues. The Carpet and Rug Institute recommends the use of two types of pretests. In one test, approximately one teaspoon of the prepared product is worked into the fibers in an inconspicuous area of the floor covering. The fibers are then pressed between a clean, white tissue for about ten seconds. The tissue is examined for evidence of bleeding, and the fibers are examined for evidence of damage. The procedure should be repeated until a safe agent is identified.

In the second test, a half cup of the prepared product is poured into a clear glass dish. After the liquid portion of the product has evaporated, the residue is examined. If a dry, powdery residue is found, it would be reasonable to expect that vacuuming could remove such deposits from the carpet. If a sticky or waxy residue is found, it is evident that such deposits would remain in the carpet after cleaning, causing the fibers to adhere to one another and promoting rapid resoiling.

Minimizing and Removing Stains

Another important preventive activity is the prompt and efficient removal of solid and liquid substances deposited or spilled on the carpet. This will help to prevent spot-

ting and staining. A few basic rules should be observed in this practice.

1. Act promptly. Foreign substances are more difficult to remove after they have aged.

2. Vacuum dry substances, scoop up excess thick substances, and absorb as much spilled liquid as possible before proceeding with further removal procedures. To avoid diluting and spreading spilled liquids, do not wet at this time. Immediately place absorbent towels over the spill and apply pressure with the hands or heels to promote transfer of the moisture from the carpet to the towels. Use a blotting action: rubbing could cause distortion of the pile. Continue blotting until no more of the spot shows on the towels. Next, cover the area with a half-inch-thick layer of absorbent tissues topped by a sheet of foil and place a heavy object (for example, a big-city telephone directory) on the foil-covered towels. Wait patiently overnight while the liquid wicks into the towels. If some of the spill remains, proceed with the appropriate removal technique listed in Table 27.3 or Table 27.4.

3. Be prepared. Have a kit of cleaning agents and materials assembled for immediate use. A list of common stain removal supplies is provided in Table 27.2. It does not include carbon tetrachloride, gasoline, or lighter fluid, which are flammable and hazardous to human health. Label the containers and store them in a locked cabinet out of the reach of children.

Table 27.2 Spot and Stain Removal Supplies

Absorbent dry powders—examples include Host® and Capture®
Abundant supply of absorbent white tissues and towels for blotting
Acetic acid or white vinegar solution (⅓ cup of vinegar to 1 cup of water)
Acetone or fingernail polish remover, non-oily type
Aerosol cleaners—commercial type available from floor covering dealers and in grocery stores
Alcohol, denatured or rubbing type
Ammonia solution (1 tablespoon to ¾ cup of water)
Detergent (use 1 teaspoon of mild hand dishwashing type without oily conditioners to 1 cup of warm water or 1 tablespoon of dry powdered laundry type to 1 cup of water)
Dry-cleaning fluid—examples include Carbona®, Renuzit®, and Energine®
POGR (paint, oil, and grease remover)—examples include Pyratex® and Buckeye®
Pre-soak laundry product (enzyme digester)
Squeeze bottles, medicine droppers, wooden scrapers

Table 27.3 Removal of Spots and Stains from Nylon Fibers

Stain/Procedure		Stain/Procedure		Procedure A	Procedure E	Procedure I
Asphalt	A	Lard	A	Apply solvent	Detergent	Denatured
Beer	E	Linseed Oil	A	*POGR	Blot	alcohol
Berries	E	Machine Oil	A	Blot	Ammonia	Blot
Blood	B	Mascara	A	Apply solvent	Blot	Repeat, if
Butter	A	Mayonnaise	B	Detergent	Acetic acid	necessary
Candle Wax	G	Mercurochrome	E	Blot	Blot	Note: pretest
Candy (Sugar)	D	Merthiolate	E	Ammonia	Detergent	as for other
Carbon Black	A	Milk	B	Blot	Blot	solutions
Catsup	B	Mimeo Correction		Detergent	Water	
Charcoal	A	Fluid	C	Blot	Blot	**Procedure J**
Cheese	B	Mixed Drinks	E	Water		Detergemt
Chewing Gum	G	Model Cement	L	Blot	**Procedure F**	Blot
Chocolate	B	Mustard	E		Detergent	Vinegar
Coffee	E	Nail Polish	L	**Procedure B**	Blot	Blot
Cooking Oil	A	Paint—Latex	A	Detergent	Acetic acid	Ammonia
Crayon	A	Paint—Oil	A	Enzyme digestor	Blot	Blot
Crème de Menthe	F	Rubber Cement	A	Soak	Ammonia	Detergent
Dye—Blue, Black,		Rust	D	Ammonia	Blot	Blot
Green	F	Shellac	I	Blot	Water	Water
Dye—Red	E	Shoe Polish	A	Detergent	Blot	Blot
Earth	B	Shortening	A	Blot		
Egg	B	Soft Drinks	E	Water	**Procedure G**	**Procedure K**
Excrement	B	Soy Sauce	B	Blot	Freeze with ice	Blot
Fish Slime	B	Starch	B		cube	Water
Foundation		Tar	A	**Procedure C**	Shatter w/blunt	Blot
Makeup	A	Tea	E	Apply solvent	object	Ammonia
Fruit Juice	E	Tooth Paste	B	*POGR	Vacuum out chips	Blot
Furniture Polish	A	Typewriter Ribbon	A	Blot	Applyt solvent	Detergent
Furniture Polish with		Urine—Dry	J	Apply solvent	Wait several	Blot
Stain	H	Urine—Fresh	K	Blot	minutes	Water
Gravy	A	Varnish	C	Detergent	Blot	Blot
Hair Oil	A	Vaseline	A	Blot	Repeat, if necessary	
Hair Spray	A	Wax—Paste	A	Water		**Procedure L**
Hand Lotion	A	White Glue	B	Blot	**Procedure H**	Polish remover
Ice Cream	B	Wine	E		Apply solvent	(non-oily)
Ink—Ball Point	A			**Procedure D**	Wait several	Blot
Ink—Fountain Pen	F			Detergent	minutes	Repeat
Ink—India	A			Blot	Blot	
Ink—Marking Pen	A			Acetic acid	Detergent	
Ink—Mimeo	A			Blot	Blot	
Lacquer	C			Rust remover	Water	
				Blot	Blot	
				Detergent		
				Blot		
				Water		
				Blot		

Courtesy of Allied Fibers.
*Paint, oil, and grease remover.

Common stains and the procedures recommended for removing them from nylon fibers are listed in Table 27.3. Procedures recommended for removing stains from wool carpet fibers are listed in Table 27.4. Residential and commercial consumers may obtain additional stain removal guides and care instructions from retailers, fiber and carpet producers, and trade associations.

Pretests, described above, should precede the application of any stain removal agent.

Table 27.4 Removal of Spots and Stains from Wool Carpet Fibers

This table includes advice on methods of treating stains and the order in which they should be tried. For instance, if clean water does not remove all traces of a beverage, try a solution of washing powder next. Most of the agents mentioned are easy to obtain; however, if you cannot get a dye stripper or hydrochloric acid, call a professional cleaner instead. A freezing agent is available in aerosol sprays, but you can use ice instead to harden chewing gum in order to remove it. CAUTION: Before proceeding to treat a stain, pretest your treatments on an inconspicuous part of the carpet to check for possible color change. Some recommended treatments may be toxic; therefore all precautions should be taken when handling these products.

Types of treatments
1. Carpet shampoo solution. It is important to use a neutral shampoo on wool carpets, not one that is alkaline. Never use carpet shampoos that smell of ammonia.
2. Evaporating spot remover or dry-cleaning fluid.
3. Warm water.
4. Cold water.
5. Laundry detergent (one teaspoon in one pint warm water).
6. Absorbent paper and hot iron.
7. White vinegar.
8. Rubbing alcohol.
9. Nail polish remover or acetone.
10. Turpentine or white spirits.
11. Vacuum.
12. Starch paste.
13. Scrape lightly with fingers or a coin.
14. Rub gently with coarse sandpaper.
15. Scrape and vacuum.
16. Glycerine.
17. Call a professional cleaner.

Stains

Acids 1, 5, or 7
Alcoholic beverages 1, 2, 5, or 7
Beer 1, 5, or 7
Bleach 1, 5, or 7
Blood 1, 5, 7, or 12
Burn or scorch mark 13 or 14
Butter 1 or 2
Candy 1, 5, 7, or 15
Chewing gum 1, 2, 5, or 7
Chocolate 1, 2, 5, or 7
Coffee 16
Coffee with cream 16 followed by 5
Colas 1 or 4
Cosmetics 1, 2, 5, or 7
Crayon 1, 2, 5, 7, or 15
Cream 1 or 2
Egg 1, 5, or 7
Excrement (human) 1, 5, or 7
    (remove at once—chemicals in excrement
    attack dyestuffs)
Excrement (pet) 17
Fat and oil 6 then 2
    (do not use iron after solvent)
Floor wax 2
Fruit and juices 1, 2, 5, or 7
Furniture polish 1, 2, 5, or 7
Glue 8
Grass 1, 2, 5, or 7
Gravy 1, 2, 5, or 7
Grease 2 or 15
Household cement 1, 2, 5, or 7

Ice cream 1, 2, 5, or 7
Ink (fountain pen) 4 or 5
Ink (ball point pen) 1 or 8
Iodine 8
Jam 3
Lipstick 1, 2, 5, or 7
Medicine 17
Metal polish 1
Mildew 17
Milk 1 or 3
Mud 5 or 7
Mustard 1, 5, or 7
Nail polish 2 or 9
Oils 2 or 1
Paint (emulsion) 4 or 1
Paint (oil) 10, 2, or 1
Perfume 1, 2, 5, or 7
Permanent ink 17
Rust 17
Salad dressing 1, 2, 5, or 7
Sauces 1, 2, 5, or 7
Shoe polish 1, 2, 5, 7, or 15
Soot 11, 1, 2, or 17
Tar 2
Tea 1, 5, or 7
Urine (human) 1, 5, or 7 (remove at once—chemicals
    in urine attack dyestuffs)
Urine (pet) 17
Urine (old stain) 17
Vomit 1, 2, 5, or 7
Wax 2 or 15
Wine 4, 5, 7, or 2

Note: While this advice is offered in good faith, no responsibility is accepted for claims arising from the treatments proposed. If stains fail to respond to treatments listed, call a professional carpet cleaner immediately.

Courtesy of The Wool Bureau, Inc.

When small bits of carpet fibers have been melted or singed, they can be carefully clipped and removed. If the damaged area is large, it must be cut out and replaced with a piece reserved at the time of installation.

Interim Maintenance

Interim maintenance activities are designed primarily to assure a high level of appearance retention for an extended period of time and to delay the need for restorative procedures. Interim maintenance is, specifically, the use of a restorative cleaning procedure in a localized area, such as a track-off area, every twenty or thirty-one days. A planned schedule will prevent soil accumulation in areas of heavy traffic from developing an appearance noticeably different from that of adjacent areas.

Interim cleaning may be done with a dry or a wet cleaning system. Frequently, dry cleaning is recommended so that no drying time is required and the area being cleaned can extend beyond the soiled area to prevent marked differences in appearance between the cleaned site and the adjacent areas. Some examples of dry-cleaning compounds are Capture®, produced by Milliken Chemical, DryCare™, produced by National Labs, Host,® produced by Racine Industries, Inc., and Blue Lustre® Dry, produced by Earl Gressmer Company. 3M Brand Carpet Protector Maintainer/Shampoo, produced for interim wet cleaning, deposits a fluorochemical stain repellent compound on the carpet during the cleaning process.

Other interim maintenance activities should be performed as needed. These may include the removal of pills, fuzz, and snags. Fuzziness may occur with loop pile textures when abrasion causes some fibers to rupture, leaving one end in the base of the yarn and one end protruding. The protruding length should be clipped away; it should not be pulled. Unsightly pills should be clipped away, although this is a tedious job. Snagged tufts are treated in the same manner as sprouting tufts. If rippling or seam separation is evident, the installer should be called to restretch or reglue the structure and to secure the seams. Area and room-size rugs and runners should be reversed and modules rotated to even the level of wear and soiling. Furniture may be shifted a few inches to allow crushed areas to recover: recovery may be assisted by steaming the areas with an iron held approximately 4 inches above the surface. An occasional "rak-

ing" can help to keep the pile tufts in shag floor coverings erect.

Restorative Maintenance

Restorative maintenance involves an overall or wall-to-wall cleaning procedure. The frequency with which such cleaning operations should be undertaken depends on the rate of soil accumulation and the effectiveness of interim maintenance procedures. Of course, the owner's opinion about the acceptability of the surface appearance is usually decisive. Four major restorative maintenance procedures can be considered: dry extraction, dry foam, wet shampoo, and hot water extraction.

Dry Extraction

Dry extraction cleaning is also referred to as absorbent powder or absorbent compound cleaning. The soil-extracting particles are generally composed of water-based cleaning fluids or detergents and a small amount of solvent. Their minute size (they are magnified in Figure 27.19) results in an extremely high surface-area-to-volume ratio that increases their capacity for absorption.

The particles are sprinkled over the carpet structure and vigorously brushed by hand or machine into the pile layer. There, the solvent releases the soil and the porous particles act like tiny sponges, absorbing the soil. Subsequent vacuuming removes the soil-holding particles. Examples of several dry extraction products were listed in the earlier discussion of interim cleaning.

The advantage of dry extraction cleaning is that the fibers are not wetted. This avoids not only the need for drying, but also the problem of overwetting the structure, which could lead to shrinkage and microbe-related problems. When a jute backing is present, overwetting could also cause a problem known as **browning**, staining of the pile as the water wicks from the backing upward. Caution should be exercised when brushing the particles into the pile layer to avoid distortion of cut pile yarns.

Dry Foam

Dry foam cleaning is also called aerosol cleaning. The cleaning agent is generally a water-based shampoo that has been converted into foam. The foam is sprayed onto the carpet surface and worked into the pile layer with a

Figure 27.19 Capture® soil-extracting particles.
Courtesy of Milliken and Company.

Figure 27.20 Dry foam cleaning.
Courtesy of Allied Fibers.

hand-held sponge or with mechanically operated brushes. After the compound dries, the surface must be thoroughly vacuumed or rinsed with a damp sponge to remove the soil-foam residue. Some electrically powered units apply the foam and vacuum the carpet in a one-step operation (Figure 27.20).

Cleaning with dry foam may not be as thorough as other methods, especially if a large amount of soil is deeply embedded in the pile layer. The risk of overwetting the carpet is minimal.

Figure 27.21 Wet shampoo cleaning. *Courtesy of Allied Fibers.*

Figure 27.22 Hot water extraction cleaning. *Courtesy of Allied Fibers.*

Wet Shampooing

The **wet shampoo method** of carpet restoration is commonly referred to as the rotary brush method. The properly diluted detergent solution or foam is driven into the pile with one or two rotating brushes (Figure 27.21). A thorough vacuuming, preferably with a wet vacuum, must follow. Wet vacuums, unlike conventional vacuums, are engineered to suction fluids, as well as dry matter, from surfaces safely and efficiently.

While the mechanical action of the rotating brushes works the detergent solution into the carpet, it may also cause pile distortion, especially of cut surfaces. Care must be taken in applying the solution or foam to avoid overwetting the structure. Vacuuming of the soil-shampoo compound must be thorough, since any residue will accelerate resoiling.

Hot Water Extraction

Hot water or spray extraction cleaning is commonly called steam extraction, although extemely hot water is used, not steam. The properly diluted shampoo is driven into the pile as a spray by high-pressure jets; it is then immediately extracted by the vacuum component of the machine (Figure 27.22).

Because no mechanical brushing is used in this extraction method, pile yarns are minimally distorted. Spots and stains must be removed before the cleaning operation is begun so that the hot water will not set them. As in wet shampooing, the detergent must be thoroughly removed to retard rapid resoiling.

Salvage Maintenance

Salvage maintenance procedures may be required for extremely soiled carpet or for removing built-up residue. When such problems are evident, it may be advisable to use a combination of wet shampooing and hot water extraction. The mechanical action of the rotary brushes will help to loosen the soil, and the extraction will make for better removal.

Summary

Carpet rollgoods may be installed with a stretch-in or glue-down technique. Modules may be glued to the floor, using a permanent or releasable adhesive; some may be free-laid. For all projects, yardage calculations must be accurate. Skilled personnel should generally carry out installation procedures.

Effective procedures and adherence to a planned maintenance schedule can maintain the original appearance of textile floor coverings at a higher level for a longer period of time. Wear-life can also be extended this way, and the need for premature replacement avoided.

Key Terms

browning

drop-match patterns

dry extraction cleaning

dry foam cleaning

free-lay installation

glue-down installation

hot water or spray extraction cleaning

interim maintenance

knee-kicker

power stretcher

preventive maintenance

restorative maintenance

salvage maintenance

set-match patterns

shedding

sprouting

stretch-in installation

tackless strips

wall-to-wall installation

wet shampoo cleaning

Review Questions

1. Identify several tasks that may have to be completed on site before a new floor covering assembly is installed.

2. Explain the techniques used in stretch-in installations. How is the stretching accomplished? How is the carpet secured?

3. Distinguish between glue-down and direct glue-down installations. What advantages are offered by these modes of installation when rolling traffic is anticipated?

4. Identify some advantages of using releasable adhesives with carpet modules.

5. What factors limit the use of free-lay installations with carpet modules? What advantages are offered by this mode of installation?

6. Illustrate and discuss the important influence that the directional lay of pile yarns has on the quantity of light reflected from the carpet surface.

7. Differentiate among set-match, drop-match, half-drop-match, and quarter-drop-match patterns.

8. Cite the objectives of planned maintenance programs.

9. Confirm the importance of pretesting cleaning products.

10. What are the advantages and disadvantages of each of the restorative cleaning procedures?

UNIT FOUR CASESTUDY

Designer Name: Krista Atkins Nutter
Skip Alexander Architects

Project Location: Long Term Care Unit
Berea, KY

Statement of the Project:

The objective was to create a new, updated long-term care unit for the hospital that was comparable to similar units in the region with a goal of providing a truly pleasing environment for the elderly of the community. The textile consideration for this casestudy was the use of carpet down the central corridor.

Statement of the Problem:

The hospital needed a floorcovering that controlled glare and acoustics and established a residential feeling. It was also imperative that it be easily cleaned because of cases of incontinence. The existing vinyl was inadequate in addressing the aesthetics.

Selection Criteria:

Carpet was chosen to replace vinyl for several reasons. Aesthetically, the carpet provided a warmer, softer, more residential and familiar atmosphere for the residents. The residential feeling provides psychological comfort, which is significant to the health and well-being of the user. Extensive research reports and summaries were compiled from such agencies as the Alzheimer's Association and the American Institute of Architects/American Collegiate Schools of Architecture (AIA/ACSA) along with articles from industry publications such as *Facility Care* and *Hospitality Design* to explain the psychological advantages and wellness issues. The carpet was a neutral background with a variety of colored flecks to permit the designer to use more colors on other interior finishes. No pattern is evident to

eliminate confusion for the residents. For safety, the carpet offered more traction, reduced glare, and is slightly softer in case of falls. The carpet was installed using a direct glue-down installation without a carpet pad. A carpet pad would have increased the difficulty for all roller traffic to move across the floor. The carpet also offered an acoustical advantage as the carpet reduces the noise from foot traffic and other every-day hospital occurences. The quiet atmosphere increases the positive psychological affect of the residents, staff, and visitors because it reduces stress and encourages mobility and activity in the residents.

Product Specifications:

Patcraft Carpet

- Pattern: Endeavor #816-038 Progress
- 100% Dupont Antron Lumena® solution dyed
- Continuous filament nylon
- With antimicrobial properties

Maintenance and Cost:

Stains need to be spot cleaned immediately. A list of stains and appropriate cleaning methods for each specific stain was provided by the manufacturer. For moderate traffic (less than 500 walk-ons per day), vacuum 1–2 times per week with a heavy-duty commercial grade vacuum with cylinder brush and bar. Carpet should be cleaned using a dry extraction method (such as Host® or Ban Clene®) twice yearly. If the traffic increased to more than 500 walk-ons per day (heavy traffic), the vacuuming would increase to every 2–3 days and cleaning to quarterly. Over 1,000 walk-ons (extra-heavy traffic) would mean daily vacuuming and monthly cleaning. While the carpet is more expensive than vinyl floorcovering, the psychological advantages justified the additional expense.

Discussion Questions:

1. Identify two of the client's requirements for the design project.

2. Distinguish one aesthetic feature of the product that meets the client's requirements.

3. Distinguish one functional feature of the product that meets the client's requirements.

4. Discuss the psychological impact of the textile on the user of the space.

5. Research another product that is appropriate for this application. Compare and contrast the cost effectiveness, availability, durability, and maintenance of the new product with the one used in the casestudy.

UNIT FIVE

Household and Institutional Textiles

Unit Five focuses on textile products used in household and institutional interiors. Several of these structures fulfill both decorative and functional needs. Chapter 28 examines the composition and construction of textile bath products. It also reviews the federal flammability standard that applies to bath rugs and mats. Chapter 29 covers the wide assortment of textile fabrics manufactured for use in bedding products, as well as the natural and synthesized fillings used in beddings and the flammability regulations with which mattresses and mattress pads must comply prior to marketing. Chapter 30 presents various tabletop accessories, including tablecloths, napkins, table runners, and doilies.

28

Textile Products for the Bath

Towels and Toweling
  Statistical Profile of Fiber Usage
  Manufacturing Toweling
  Constructing Towels
  Evaluating the Physical Performance
    Properties of Towels
  Evaluating Colorfastness
  Evaluating Absorbancy
  Evaluating Flammability
  Caring for Towels

Bath Rugs and Mats
  Constructing and Finishing Bath Rugs
    and Mats
  Evaluating Flammability

Shower Curtains
  Polymer Film Shower Curtains
  Textile Shower Curtains
  Evaluating Physical Performance
    Properties
  Evaluating Colorfastness
  Evaluating Water Resistance
  Evaluating Flammability

Fabric stylists and end-product designers have created many decorative variations of such textile bath products as towels, rugs, mats, and shower curtains, so that these items are often as ornamental as they are functional. While the primary function of towels is absorbency, they nonetheless contribute also to the aesthetics of the near environment. Manufacturers have expanded the size range of towels, increased the types of materials used in shower curtains, and varied the shapes and constructions of small bath rugs and mats. Frequently, contemporary bath products are offered in coordinated ensembles, and sometimes they are part of elaborate collections that include bedding products as well.

Today, bath products are produced and marketed for both household and institutional use. Standard performance specifications, such as those published by ASTM, may be used between purchaser and supplier to establish required structural features and performance levels. With the exception of nontextile shower curtains, these products are subject to the provisions of the Textile Fiber Products Identification Act (see Chapter 10). Small rugs and bath mats are also subject to a federal flammability standard.

Towels and Toweling

Various fabrication techniques, including weaving, stitch-knitting, and bonding webs of fibers, are used to produce toweling. In contrast to many other interior products, which are composed primarily of manufactured fibers, towels and toweling are composed primarily of cotton.

Statistical Profile of Fiber Usage

Fiber usage in towels and toweling is detailed in Table 28.1. The poundage listed includes the fiber used in the production of woven dish towels, but does not include the fiber used to produce bonded-web toweling.

Predominance of Cotton

The towel and towelings market has been and continues to be dominated by cotton. This natural fiber held more than 99 percent of the 1966 market, and although its use has decreased since the late 1960s, it nonetheless holds more than 96 percent of the current market. Cotton is highly absorbent; it is also soft and has relatively high

Table 28.1 Fiber Usage in Towels and Toweling (million pounds)

Year	Total Fiber	Manufactured Fibers[a]					Cotton	Wool
			Cellulosic		Synthetic			
		Total	Yarn	Staple	Yarn	Staple		
1966	282.4	2.5	[b]	2.5	[c]	–	279.9	[c]
1985	351.1	22.3	[c]	0.9	0.2	21.2	328.8	[c]
1997	439.2	15.5	0.1	0.1	5.6	9.8	423.7	[c]

[a]Manufactured fiber end-use is divided between cellulosic (rayon plus acetate fibers) and synthetic (nylon, polyester, acrylic, and olefin). Yarn includes monofilaments, multifilaments, and spunbonded. Olefin "yarn" also includes film fiber and spunbonded polypropylene. Staple includes tow and fiberfill.

[b]Nominal amounts used (less than 50,000 pounds).

[c]Little or none of the fiber is used.

Sources: Textile Economics Bureau, Inc., *Textile Organon*, Vol. 43, No. 11, November 1972, 166; Vol. 57, No. 9, September 1986, 210; and Vol. 69, No. 10, October 1998, 176.

wickability, that is, the ability to move moisture along its surface by capillary action, features that make it an attractive and efficient fiber for toweling. Linen, which has slightly higher moisture absorption and produces less lint than cotton, is also used but in small amounts. The harsh hand and low abrasion resistance characteristic of linen preclude its use in bath towels, and the comparatively high cost of the fiber limits its use in dish towels.

The synthetic staple fibers consumed in towels are generally made into spun yarns that are incorporated in the base of pile toweling for strength and dimensional stability. Although these fibers can be spun into yarns that simulate the appearance and hand of yarns composed of cotton, they do not provide the high absorbency needed for towels. Currently, textile research chemists are investigating ways to make noncellulosic fibers more hydrophilic so that they will exhibit the requisite wickability. When an economically viable technique is perfected, the use of these fibers in flat and pile toweling will no doubt increase.

Manufacturing Toweling

Manufacturers use a variety of fabrication techniques to produce flat or nonpile toweling. They use a warp pile weaving operation to produce pile toweling.

Constructing Pile Toweling

Pile or **terry toweling** is also known as **Turkish toweling**. The components of this toweling are illustrated in Figure 28.1. One set of filling or weft yarns is interlaced with one set of base or ground warp yarns and two sets of pile warp yarns. If loops are planned for only one side of the fabric, only one set of pile warp yarns is used. Fabrics with loops on both sides have more fiber surface area for absorbing moisture, but they are also more expensive if the construction density is not reduced. For visual interest, the pile yarns appearing on each side can be of different colors.

Terry toweling is manufactured by the **slack tension technique** (see Chapter 6). For economical production, terry looms are generally threaded for full-width weaving. When hemmed edges and ends are planned, the dimensions of individual towels are demarcated by the omission of pile yarns in narrow lengthwise and crosswise bands; when fringed ends are planned, the crosswise

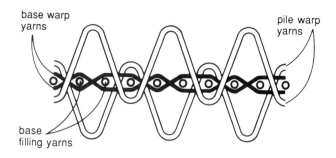

Figure 28.1 Cross-sectional sketch of terry toweling that has three filling picks per crosswise row of pile loops.

bands are also void of filling picks. A dobby mechanism may be used to produce woven-in border designs.

For increased efficiency and economy in both weaving and finishing, textile machinery engineers have developed extra-wide looms capable of simultaneously weaving multiple widths of toweling. Looms of the type shown in Figure 28.2 can weave up to ten widths of toweling during one operation. The several widths of toweling have tucked-in selvages (see Figure 6.2b, p. 81).

Terry velour toweling has a conventional looped pile surface on one side, and a dense, cut pile surface on the other side. The sheared velour surface has a thick and luxurious appearance and hand, but the level of moisture absorption is relatively low since only the small tips of the yarns are exposed.

A small amount of terry is produced by a stitch-knitting operation known by the patent name **Malipol**. In this procedure, an expansion of the stitch-knitting technique described in Chapter 7, pile yarns are incorporated into webs of yarns that are layered and stitched.

Fabricating Flat Toweling

Flat or non-terry toweling is generally produced by weaving yarns in a basic biaxial or dobby interlacing pattern or by bonding webs of fibers. **Crash** is a plain-woven fabric composed of coarse, irregular yarns spun from linen. The fabric is constructed into dish towels intended for the lint-free drying of glassware. Twill-woven toweling, often referred to as **institutional toweling**, is generally produced with brightly colored stripes on each long side and constructed into towels used in restaurants. **Huck toweling (huckaback)** is woven on a dobby loom and has small filling floats. These slightly raised floats, visible in the closeup photo-

Figure 28.2 Loom engineered to weave multiple widths of terry toweling. *Courtesy of Sulzer-Ruti, Inc.*

graph in Figure 28.3, improve the drying efficiency of the towel.

Disposable toweling is produced by bonding webs of fibers with heat or an adhesive. Some items are intended to be used once; others are for repeated use. For increased strength, a scrim of fine yarns may be anchored between the layered webs. The scrim-reinforced toweling in Figure 28.4 is composed of cellulosic fibers.

Constructing Towels

Towels come in a variety of sizes and with a variety of edge and end finishes. Trims and embroidery embellish their surfaces.

Types and Sizes

Several types of towels are included in today's market assortment. The approximate size ranges of the various types are listed in Table 28.2. If the toweling was not preshrunk, the towels may be oversized to compensate for relaxation shrinkage in laundering.

Edge Finishes and Decorative Treatments

Terry toweling is cut along the flat lengthwise and crosswise bands spaced throughout the pile greige goods. Cutting produces unfinished towels of various sizes. The sides may be finished with a small, machine-stitched hem or with machine serging. The ends may be hemmed or left with a yarn fringe. Squares of pile fabric are cut for washcloths, and the four raw edges are serged. For deco-

Figure 28.3 Huck toweling, a dobby-woven fabric with slightly raised filling floats.

Figure 28.4 Kaycel® scrim-reinforced disposable toweling. *Courtesy of Kimberly-Clark Corporation.*

rative interest, bands of embroidered fabric or trim may be sewn across towels and washcloths, or the surface may be embellished with a Schiffli-embroidered monogram or motif.

Coordinated Items

Yarn-dyed, solid-colored, or printed toweling used to construct dish towels may also be used to produce such coordinated items as oven mitts, pot holders, small appliance covers, and aprons. The color styling and decorative treatment of bath towels may be replicated in bedding products; the several bath and bedding products are then offered and promoted as a coordinated ensemble.

Evaluating the Physical Performance Properties of Towels

In order to assure satisfactory performance in use, manufacturers may elect to evaluate the properties of their towels in conjunction with recommendations set forth in ASTM D 5433 Standard Performance Specification for Towel Products for Institutional and Household Use. Specifications for woven terry items, including kitchen towels, dishcloths, bath and hand towels, washcloths, and

Table 28.2 Types and Sizes of Towels

Type	Inches (width × length)
Dish towel	12 × 24 to 16 × 30
Fingertip/guest	9 × 14 to 11 × 20
Washcloth	12 × 12 to 14 × 14
Face/hand towel	15 × 25 to 20 × 36
Bath towel	20 × 40 to 27 × 50
Bath sheet	35 × 66 to 45 × 75

bath sheets, are listed in Table 28.3; those for non-terry fabrics, including dishcloths, huck toweling, and crash, are shown in Table 28.4.

Breaking Force (Load)

The **breaking force (load)** of woven terry and non-terry towelings may be measured in accordance with the grab test procedure of ASTM D 5034 Standard Test Method for Breaking Strength and Elongation of Textile Fabrics (Grab Test). This procedure was discussed in Chapter 14, and the placement of the clamps on the specimen illustrated in Figure 14.4 (p. 231). As shown in Tables 28.3 and 28.4, the minimum force for towelings ranges from 30 to 40 to 50 pounds, depending on the fabric construction and the product.

Table 28.3 Woven or Knitted Specification Requirements for Terry Towel Products for Institutional and Household Use

	Kitchen Towels	Dishclothes	Bath, Hand, Washcloths, Bath Sheets
Breaking force (CRT):			
Length	178 N (40 lbf) min	220 N (50 lbf) min	178 N (40 lbf) min
Width	133 N (30 lbf) min	178 N (40 lbf) min	133 N (30 lbf) min
Bursting force (knits only):			
Diaphragm	222 N (50 lbf) min	222 N (50 lbf) min	222 N (50 lbf) min
Nonfibrous material	3% max	5% max	3% max
Dimensional change:			
Length	10% max	15% max	10% max
Width	6% max	5% max	4% max
Bow and skewness	6% max	6% max	6% max
Colorfastness:[a]			
Laundering			
Shade change	Class 4[b] min	Class 4[b] min	Class 4[b] min
Staining	Class 3[c] min	Class 3[c] min	Class 3[c] min
Crocking:			
Dry	Class 4[d] min	Class 4[d] min	Class 4[d] min
Wet	Class 3[d] min	Class 3[d] min	Class 3[d] min
Light (20 AATCC FU)	Step 4[b] min	Step 4[b] min	Step 4[b] min
Absorbency	Pass	Pass	Pass
Flammability	Class I	Class I	Class I
Laundered appearance	Acceptable	Acceptable	Acceptable

[a]Class for color change and color transfer is based on a numerical scale of 5 for negligible or no color change or color transfer to 1 for severe color change or color transfer. The numerical rating in Table 28.3 or higher is acceptable.
[b]AATCC Gray Scale for Color Change
[c]AATCC Gray Scale for Staining
[d]AATCC Chromatic Transference Scale
Courtesy of ASTM.

Table 28.4 Specification Requirements for Non-Terry Towel Products for Institutional and Household Use

	Huck and Crash Towels	Dishcloths
Breaking force (CRT):		
Length	178 N (40 lbf) min	220 N (50 lbf) min
Width	133 N (30 lbf) min	178 N (40 lbf) min
Bursting force (knits only):		
Diaphragm	222 N (50 lbf) min	222 N (50 lbf) min
Nonfibrous material	5% max	5% max
Dimensional change:		
Length	15% max	15% max
Width	5% max	5% max
Bow and skewness	6% Acceptable	6% Acceptable
Colorfastness:[a]		
Laundering:		
Shade change	Class 4[b] min	Class 4[b] min
Staining	Class 3[c] min	Class 3[c] min
Crocking:		
Dry	Class 4[d] min	Class 4[d] min
Wet	Class 3[d] min	Class 3[d] min
Light (20 AATCC FU)	Step 4[b] min	Step 4[b] min
Absorbency	Pass	Pass
Flammability	Pass	Pass
Laundered appearance	Acceptable	Acceptable

[a]Class for color change and color transfer is based on a numerical scale of 5 for negligible or no color change or color transfer to 1 for severe color change or color transfer. The numerical rating in Table 28.4 or higher is acceptable.
[b]AATCC Gray Scale for Color Change
[c]AATCC Gray Scale for Staining
[d]AATCC Chromatic Transference Scale
Courtesy of ASTM.

Dimensional Change

Because towelings are used for absorption, and they are frequently laundered, it is critical that they exhibit relatively high **dimensional stability**. The fabrics may be tested after five launderings following prescribed care instructions, or in accordance with directions in AATCC Method 135 Dimensional Changes in Automatic Home Laundering of Woven or Knit Fabrics for household use or AATCC Method 96 for institutional use. As shown in Tables 28.3 and 28.4, recommendations range from a maximum of 4 percent shrinkage for bath and hand towels in the crosswise direction to a maximum of 10 or 15 percent shrinkage for the lengthwise direction for both terry and non-terry towelings.

Bow and Skewness

The yarn alignment of towelings may be assessed in accordance with the procedures set forth in ASTM D 3882 Standard Test Method for Bow and Skewness in Woven and Knitted Fabrics. This standard was discussed in Chapter 14, with illustrations of the measurement locations shown schematically in Figures 14.2 and 14.3 (p. 229). While the recommended level of **bow** and **skewness** (bias) is 6 percent, purchaser and supplier may agree upon acceptable performance levels.

Appearance

The appearance of the construction features of towelings (e.g., selvages, hems, seams, and dobby borders) may be evaluated before and after laundering. Purchasers and suppliers should reach mutual appearance requirements.

Evaluating Colorfastness

ASTM D 5433 includes recommendations for the acceptable levels of colorfastness of towelings. These recommendations focus on fastness to laundering, crocking (rubbing), and light.

Colorfastness to Laundering

The colorfastness of towelings to laundering is critical for both household and institutional uses. Because towels are frequently part of coordinated ensembles, marked fading or **shade changes** would be unacceptable. **Bleeding** could lead to **staining** of the body, dishes, swimwear, and so on.

The colorfastness of toweling to laundering may be evaluated in accordance with procedures set forth in Test 4-A in AATCC Method 61 Colorfastness to Washing, Domestic, and Laundering, Accelerated. The general nature of this method is described in Chapter 18, and the apparatus used, the **Launder-Ometer**®, is shown in Figure 18.7 (p. 308). Shade changes are evaluated using the **AATCC Gray Scale for Color Change** (Figure 14.10, p. 237); staining is evaluated using the **AATCC Gray Scale for Staining** (see Figure 14.9, p. 237). The recommended Class ratings are presented in Tables 28.3 and 28.4.

Colorfastness to Crocking (Rubbing)

It is readily apparent that towels exhibiting color transfer when rubbed against the body or other fabrics would be unacceptable. The **crocking** of solid-colored towelings may be assessed by following procedures set forth in AATCC Method 8 Colorfastness to Crocking (Rubbing): AATCC Crockmeter Method; this method was described in Chapter 14; the apparatus used to rub the specimens is presented in Figure 14.8 (p. 236). For printed toweling fabrics, the procedures in AATCC Method 116 Colorfastness to Crocking (Rubbing): Rotary Vertical Crockmeter Method should be followed.

Evaluations are done with the **AATCC Color Transference Scale**, shown in Figure 18.6 (p. 307). Dry tests should yield a minimum rating of Class 4, wet tests a minimum of Class 3.

Colorfastness to Light

With the exception of beach towels, towels and dishcloths are not normally subjected to extended exposure to light. Nonetheless, their lightfastness may be assessed with AATCC Method 16A Colorfastness to Light: Carbon-Arc Continuous Light or AATCC Method 16E Colorfastness to Light: Water-cooled Xenon-Arc Lamp (see Chapter 18). The apparatus used in these tests, the **Fade-Ometer**®, is presented in Figure 18.4 (p. 305).

Both terry and nonterry toweling should exhibit a Class 4 rating on the AATCC Gray Scale for Color Change after 20 hours of AATCC fading units of exposure.

Evaluating Absorbency

How efficiently toweling can absorb liquid water from such surfaces as human skin and dishware is a critical concern for both household and institutional applications. By following the procedures outlined in ASTM D 4772 Standard Test Method for Surface Water Absorption of Terry Fabrics (Water Flow), manufacturers can numerically assess the absorbency of terry toweling.

Test Specimens and Procedures

As directed in ASTM D 4772, three face and three back specimens are secured, one at a time, in an embroidery hoop. The hoop is then mounted at a 60-degree angle to a table surface and a pan is placed below the hoop assembly. Fifty milliliters of distilled water are then allowed to flow onto the surface of the specimen, some being absorbed and some flowing as runoff water into the pan.

Analysis of Results

The difference between the original 50 milliliters of water and the number of milliliters of water in the runoff pan gives the quantity of water absorbed. An average is determined for the three face specimens and for the three back specimens.

Performance Guidelines

The purchaser and the supplier shall agree on an acceptable level of absorbency.

Evaluating Flammability

The purchaser and the supplier shall agree on the flammability requirements of towelings. If flammability is to be tested, ASTM D 1230 Standard Test Method for Flammability of Apparel Textiles may be used. This small-scale test method was described in Chapter 11.

Performance Guidelines

As shown in Table 28.3, a Class 1 rating is recommended for terry fabrics.

Caring for Towels

Although care labeling is voluntary, virtually all towels carry instructions for machine washing using warm water and machine drying. Towels with fancy borders and highly decorative trims may carry extra cautionary care instructions, such as hand wash in cool water and line dry. To avoid excessive fiber damage, white items should be bleached with chlorine compounds only when necessary, not routinely in each successive laundering, and an extra rinse should be used to ensure the complete removal of any residual chlorine. To avoid potential bleeding and staining problems, towels with intense, deep-toned colors should be laundered separately. To avoid excessive deposition of softening agents, which reduces moisture absorption, some liquid fabric softeners should be omitted every third or fourth time the items are laundered.

Bath Rugs and Mats

Soft floor coverings are produced in various sizes and shapes for use in bathroom interiors. **Bath rugs** are larger and normally heavier than **bath mats**, and are used continuously for decoration, softness underfoot, or insulation. Bath mats are used temporarily to protect the floor from moisture and to prevent bathers from slipping. Both floor covering products are subject to a federal flammability mandate.

Constructing and Finishing Bath Rugs and Mats

Bath rugs are generally cut from tufted or knitted carpet that has a lower pile construction density and a greater pile height than carpet produced for other interior applications. For economy and ease of handling in use and care, no secondary backing is applied but an adhesive is used to secure the tufts. For skid resistance, the adhesive compound is normally embossed. End-product producers cut various sizes of round, square, oval, and rectangular shapes from the wide carpet and finish the raw edges by hemming, serging, or binding with firmly woven tape. Frequently, rugs cut from solid-colored greige goods are tufted a second time to introduce a distinctive design to the surface; no additional backcoating is applied to these items to secure the added pile yarns. Other rugs may be embellished with various types of trim, including rhinestone tape, braid, and fringe.

Pile fabric produced for use as a bath rug may also be used to construct such other items as toilet lid and tank covers. Lid covers have an elasticized edge or a drawstring run through a casing to secure them in use and permit their easy removal for laundering.

Bath mats may be woven in narrow widths, with the selvages as the side edges and small hems finishing the ends, or they may be cut from wide fabric and hemmed on all edges. Two different colors of warp pile yarns may be used to produce mats with different colors of loops on each side, or several colors of pile yarns may be used to produce richly patterned, Jacquard-woven mats.

Evaluating Flammability

16 CFR 1631 (FF 2–70) Standard for the Surface Flammability of Small Carpets and Rugs became effective in December 1971. The scope of 16 CFR 1631 includes soft floor covering items that have an area not greater than 24 square feet and no dimension greater than 6 feet; such structures include scatter rugs, bath rugs, bath mats, and smaller area rugs.

Test Method and Acceptance Criteria

Items within the scope of 16 CFR 1631 are tested in accordance with the procedures outlined in the **methenamine tablet test**. This test method is also specified in the flammability standard established for large carpets and rugs, **16 CFR 1630 (FF 1–70)** (see Chapter 11). The acceptance criteria, which are based on **char length**, are the same in both standards.

Labeling Requirement

Small rugs and mats that fail the tablet test may be marketed. They must, however, carry a permanently attached label bearing the following statement: flammable (fails U.S. Consumer Product Safety Commission Standard 16 CFR 1631, should not be used near sources of ignition).

Shower Curtains

Shower curtains may be constructed of textile fabric or polymer film sheeting. Both types are often produced as part of a coordinated bath ensemble.

Polymer Film Shower Curtains

Various types of **polymer film sheeting** are used to produce nontextile shower curtains. The sheetings differ in gauge or thickness, in the level of transparency, and in color styling. Some films are relatively thin, others relatively thick; some are opaque, others transparent; some are solid colored, while others have contemporary designs printed with opaque pigments.

Textile Shower Curtains

With the exception of heavy, stiff structures, virtually any textile fabric may be used for a shower curtain. To protect the fabric from water and soap residue, converters may coat the interior surface with a waterproofing compound, or the consumer may hang a thin film as a separate curtain lining.

Evaluating Physical Performance Properties

ASTM D 5378 Standard Performance Specification for Woven and Knitted Shower Curtains for Institutional and Household Use may be used by purchaser and supplier to establish specification requirements. The physical and structural property evaluations used with towelings are also those used with shower curtains.

Breaking Force (Load)

The grab test procedure in ASTM D 5034, described above with towelings and earlier in Chapter 14, is used to measure the **breaking force (load)** of household and institutional shower curtains. A minimum of 40 pounds of force is recommended for dry fabric strength; a minimum of 20 pounds of force is recommended for wet fabric strength.

Dimensional Change

When measuring the dimensional stability of shower curtains, AATCC Method 135 may be used for household products and AATCC Method 96 may be used for institutional products. A maximum of 3 percent change is recommended.

Bow and Skewness

ASTM D 3882, discussed above and in Chapter 14, is recommended for use in assessing the yarn alignment of shower curtains. ASTM D 5378 includes a recommended maximum of 4 percent skewness (bias).

Appearance Retention

The appearance of the construction features of shower curtains (e.g., hems, ruffles, or other embellishments) may be evaluated before and after laundering. Purchaser and supplier should reach mutual appearance requirements.

Evaluating Colorfastness

ASTM D 5378 specifies the same test methods for evaluating the colorfastness of shower curtains as used with towelings. These include fastness to laundering, to rubbing, and to light.

Colorfastness to Laundering

The colorfastness of household and institutional shower curtains to laundering may be measured in accordance with Test 4-A in AATCC Method 61 (see Chapter 18). As with toweling, shade change of shower curtains is evaluated with the AATCC Gray Scale for Color Change, and bleeding is evaluated with the AATCC Gray Scale for Staining. Recommended minimum performance is Class 4 for shade change and Class 3 for staining.

Colorfastness to Crocking (Rubbing)

AATCC Method 8 may be used to evaluate the fastness to crocking of solid-colored shower curtains, and AATCC Method 116 may be used for printed curtains. These methods were discussed briefly above and in depth in Chapter 14. Evaluations are done with the AATCC Color Transference Scale; recommended minimum performance is Class 4 for both dry and wet tests.

Colorfastness to Light

AATCC Method 16A or AATCC Method 16E (see Chapter 18) may be used to evaluate the fastness of household and institutional shower curtains to light. Evaluations are done with the AATCC Gray Scale for Color Change; recommended minimum performance is Class 4 after 20 AATCC fading units with AATCC Method 16E, which uses a zenon-arc lamp.

Evaluating Water Resistance

The **water resistance** of household and institutional shower curtains can be evaluated as directed in AATCC Method 35 Water Resistance: Rain Test. The performance recommendations listed may be agreed upon between purchaser and seller, or they may be required by an agency having jurisdiction over an interior where shower curtains may be used.

Evaluating Flammability

The purchaser and supplier shall agree on the flammability requirements of shower curtains. Any applicable codes would override such agreements.

Summary

Unlike other interior furnishings, which are primarily composed of manufactured fibers, towels are primarily composed of cotton because it provides softness, wickability, and good moisture absorption. Towels are available in a wide range of sizes and with a variety of decorative features and side and end finishes.

Bath rugs and mats are available in various sizes, shapes, colors, and textures. Like other soft floor coverings, bath rugs and bath mats are subject to a federal flammability mandate.

Shower curtains may be constructed of textile or non-textile fabrics. Along with towels and bath rugs and mats, shower curtains are frequently offered as part of a coordinated group of bath products.

Standard methods of testing, such as tests for fabric strength, colorfastness, skewness (bias), and appearance, may be used to evaluate household and institutional towels and shower curtains. In turn, standard specifications are published to provide recommended levels of performance. In some cases, purchaser and supplier may reach a mutual agreement on the level of performance required.

Key Terms

16 CFR 1630 (FF 1–70)

16 CFR 1631 (FF 2–70)

AATCC Color Transference Scale

AATCC Gray Scale for Color Change

AATCC Gray Scale for Staining

bath mats

bath rugs

bleeding

bow

breaking force (load)

char length

crash

crocking

dimensional stability

disposable toweling

Fade-Ometer®

huck toweling

huckaback

institutional toweling

Launder-Ometer®

Malipol

methenamine tablet test

polymer film sheeting

shade changes

skewness

slack tension technique

staining

terry toweling

terry velour toweling

Turkish toweling

water resistance

wickability

Review Questions

1. Explain the dominance of cotton in the toweling market.

2. Given that linen has higher moisture absorbency than cotton, why hasn't linen captured a larger portion of the towelings market?

3. Describe the slack tension technique used for manufacturing terry toweling.

4. Why is the level of absorbency lower on the cut side of terry velour?

5. Why are stable colorants important to have with textile bath products?

6. Describe the procedures and calculations used in evaluating the absorbency of toweling.

7. Explain the cautionary labeling used with 16 CFR 1631.

29

Textile Bedding Products

Fiber and Yarn Usage in Beddings
    Predominance of Cotton
    Disclosure of Fiber Composition
    Predominance of Spun Yarns

Mattresses, Mattress Foundations, and
    Mattress Protectors
    Mattress Foundations
    Mattresses
    Mattress Covers and Pads
    Flammability Standard

Fillings Used in Bedding Products
    Natural Filling Materials
    Synthesized Filling Materials
    Functions and Properties of Filling
        Materials
    Care of Fillings

Pillows
    Sizes and Forms
    Fillings and Tickings
    Decorative Coverings for Pillows

Sheets and Pillowcases
    Manufacturing Sheeting
    Constructing Sheets and Pillowcases
    Evaluating Sheeting Products

Blankets
    Manufacturing Blanketing
    Constructing Blankets
    Caring for Blankets
    Flammability of Blankets

Bedspreads, Quilts, and Comforters
    Commercial Quilting
    Bedspreads
    Quilts and Comforters
    Evaluating Bedspread Fabrics, Quilts,
        and Comforters

The bedding products industry is an important segment of the interior textile industry: approximately one-third of the total fiber used for home textiles production (excluding soft floor coverings) is channeled to the production of beddings.[1] While the primary function of bedcoverings is to provide warmth and comfort for sleeping, bedding products, like towelings, have high visual impact as well.

The assortment of textile bedding products includes mattresses and box springs, mattress pads and mattress covers, sheets and pillowcases, quilts, throws, comforters, sleeping bags, blankets, bedspreads, and pillows. All of these are produced in different sizes, and some have styling features as distinctive and varied as those typical of fashion apparel. Many of these items are multicomponent structures. Most beddings are composed entirely of textile fibers, but some products, including mattresses, box springs, and sleeping bags, contain some nontextile components.

Fiber and Yarn Usage in Beddings

A statistical profile of the types of fibers used in residential and institutional bedding products is given in Table 29.1. Data cover the use of each item not only in homes, but also in such commercial settings as motels and hotels and in such institutional settings as health care facilities. The poundages listed in the first category, bedspreads and quilts, include the fiber used for producing the outer shells of comforters; the poundages listed in the second category, blankets and blanketing, include the fiber used for producing the bindings applied to the ends of the coverings; and the poundages listed in the last category, sheets and other bedding, include the fiber used to produce the outside cover of quilted pads, mattress pads, mattresses and innersprings, civilian cots, and sleeping bags. None of the poundages tabulated include any quantities of fiber used in fillings.

Since 1966, the total quantity of fiber used in bedding products has increased from 810 million pounds to 925.3 million pounds in 1997. While there has been a reapportionment of the market, cotton remains dominant.

Predominance of Cotton

In 1966, approximately 80 percent of the bedding products market was held by cotton, 13 percent by rayon and acetate, 5 percent by noncellulosic fibers, and the remaining 2 percent by wool. In today's market, little or no rayon or acetate is used, and the noncellulosic (synthetic) fibers and cotton share the market. They do not, however, split it evenly: alone, cotton accounts for some 59 percent of the fiber usage.

Disclosure of Fiber Composition

Most textile bedding products are subject to the labeling mandates set forth in the Textile Fiber Products Identification Act and its accompanying set of rules and regulations. Specifically, the scope of the TFPIA includes all beddings, which, by definition, includes sheets, covers, blankets, comforters, pillows, pillowcases, quilts, bedspreads, pads, and all other textile fiber products used or intended to be used on or about a bed, not including furniture, mattresses, or box springs, or the outer coverings on these items. Fillings incorporated in bedding products primarily for warmth rather than for structural purposes are also included.

As explained in Chapter 10, products within the scope of the TFPIA must carry a label or hangtag that discloses the fiber composition, the name or registered number of the manufacturer, and the country of origin. Products having down or feather fillings should also be labeled in accordance with guidelines specifically established by the FTC for these materials; these guidelines are discussed in the next section.

Predominance of Spun Yarns

Staple fibers are used more extensively than filament fibers in bedding products, accounting for some 94 percent of today's market. All staple-length fibers, natural as well as manufactured, must be spun to produce usable yarn structures; therefore, spun yarns predominate. In comparison with filament yarns, spun yarns are often judged to have a more attractive appearance and a softer,

Table 29.1 Fiber Usage in Bedding Products
(million pounds)

| | | | Manufactured Fibers[a] | | | | | | | |
| | | | | Cellulosic | | Synthetic | | | | |
End-use	Year	Total Fiber	Total	Yarn	Staple	Yarn	Staple	Cotton	Wool
Bedspreads	1966	149.2	42.7	9.9	27.8	4.5	0.5	106.5	b
& quilts	1985	134.6	77.4	c	6.0	17.4	54.0	57.2	b
	1997	182.5	100.8	b	b	32.2	68.7	81.6	b
Blankets &	1966	113.7	70.4	1.9	43.4	3.5	21.6	26.2	17.1
blanketing	1985	73.4	56.4	b	0.2	b	56.2	12.9	4.1
	1997	154.6	63.7	b	b	b	63.7	86.6	4.2
Sheets &	1966	547.1	30.8	1.0	24.5	0.3	5.0	516.3	b
other bedding	1985	452.9	227.0	1.5	12.5	47.9	165.1	225.9	b
	1997	588.2	214.7	b	0.0	22.3	192.4	373.6	b

[a]Manufactured fiber end-use is divided between cellulosic (rayon plus acetate fibers) and synthetic (nylon, polyester, acrylic, and olefin fibers). Yarn includes monofilaments, multifilaments, and spunbonded. Olefin includes polypropylene and polyethylene staple and yarn. Olefin "yarn" also includes film fiber and spunbonded polypropylene. Staple includes tow and fiberfill.

[b]Little or none of the fiber is used.

[c]Nominal amounts used (less than 50,000 pounds).

Sources: Textile Economics Bureau, Inc., *Textile Organon*, Vol. 43, No. 11, November 1972, 166; Vol. 57, No. 9, September 1986, 210; and Vol. 69, No. 10, October 1998, 176.

more comfortable hand, qualities many consumers prefer in their bedding products.

Mattresses, Mattress Foundations, and Mattress Protectors

Beds, and such dual-purpose sleeping equipment as **sofa beds, convertible sofa beds, futons,** and studio couches, have two basic units, a mattress and a mattress foundation. Because mattresses, especially when used with a companion set of box springs, are comparatively expensive, covers and pads are often employed to protect them and prolong their use-life. Unlike other bedding products, mattresses and mattress pads are subject to a federal flammability standard.

Mattress Foundations

With the exception of air-filled mattresses, intended to be placed on the floor or ground, and water-filled mattresses, which are placed within a plastic-lined, boxlike frame, all mattresses are used with a resilient foundation. These foundations may be flat or three-dimensional units.

Flat Bedspring Units

In some flat bedspring units, flexible metal bands are anchored to the ends of the bed frame by tightly coiled springs. Additional springs, placed crosswise, stabilize the parallel bands. In other flat bedspring units, metal bands are interlaced and held to the sides and ends of the frame with spring units. While these nontextile foundations are relatively inexpensive, they do not provide adequate support for everyday use and are normally used only with items intended for occasional use, such as cots and roll-away beds.

Box-spring Units

In box-spring units, hundreds of coiled springs are anchored to wooden slats and framing boards and to each other. Because box springs and mattresses are offered as a coordinated set, the fabric that decorates the mattress also covers the exposed surfaces of the foundation. For

a) double-deck coil

b) platform-top coil

c) convoluted coil

Figure 29.1 Configurations of springs used in box springs and mattresses.

economy, a fine, lightweight fabric such as batiste or spunbonded olefin serves as a dustcover on the back of the springs unit. Various types and amounts of filling are used for top cushioning, and an insulator fabric is placed over the springs to prevent them from penetrating into the filling materials.

While the gauge of the wire used for the support springs in box springs is generally higher than that used for the support springs in mattresses, the configuration of the coils in the units may be identical. In double-deck springs, the tighter coiling of the lower portion is designed to provide firm support and the looser coiling of the upper portion is for resiliency (Figure 29.1a). The flat metal bands anchored over platform-top springs (Figure 29.1b) provide a more uniform surface than that created by open-top springs. The extra coils placed at the top of convoluted springs provide increased support when the foundation is depressed by the weight of the body (Figure 29.1c).

The quality of box springs and innerspring mattresses depends on the gauge of the wires and the level of spring coiling. These features are the main determinants of the use-life of the units; they also help to determine the length of any warranty offered by the manufacturer.

Mattresses

Mattresses are available with different interior components and construction features. They are produced in several sizes and covered with a variety of textile fabrics.

Figure 29.2 Cross-sectional sketch of an innerspring mattress.

Interior Components

Mattresses are available in two constructions: innerspring and foam-core. **Foam-core mattresses** have a single interior component, a slab of rubber or urethane foam. In these units, the level of support varies readily with the density of the foam material. The several components in **innerspring units** are illustrated in Figure 29.2. The spring units may be anchored to one another by coiled wires, metal clips, or flexible metal bands, or each spring may be encased within a fabric pocket and all pockets sewn together to minimize side sway. An insulator fabric like that on box springs prevents the springs from penetrating the upper filling layers. The degree of firmness can be increased by using a high gauge of wire for the spring units and by using resinated batting. Small holes should be built into the sides of mattresses to provide ventilation and preserve the freshness of the interior components.

Exterior Coverings

Ticking is a generic term for any fabric used to cover the exterior of mattresses, box springs, and pillows. Tickings may be plain or highly decorative. To capture the attention of the contemporary consumer, such elaborately patterned fabrics as damask are increasingly used today in place of the familiar twill-woven ticking with its blue or black stripes (Figure 29.3).

For long-term serviceability, tickings should be firmly woven of strong, smooth yarns. Less durable and less expensive coverings generally are made of coarse yarns and contain low fabric counts and excess sizing.

Sizes

Mattresses are produced in a variety of sizes, with each size designated by name, not by dimensions. The names

Figure 29.3 Twill-woven ticking characterized by lengthwise stripes.

Table 29.2 Mattress Sizes and Names	
Name	**Inches (width × length)**
Rollaway bed or cot	30 × 75
Studio couch or daybed	28 × 74
Single bed	33 × 75
Twin bed	39 × 75
Twin bed, extra long	39 × 80
Three-quarter bed	48 × 75
Double bed	54 × 75
Double bed, extra long	54 × 80
Queen-size bed	60 × 80
King-size bed	78 × 80
California bed	72 × 80

and characteristic dimensions of the more common mattresses are listed in Table 29.2.

Larger mattresses should have permanently attached side handles to facilitate the turning of the unit. As a precaution, consumers should measure their mattresses prior to purchasing bed coverings.

Mattress Covers and Pads

Mattress covers protect mattresses from dust, moisture, and abrasion. Mattress pads provide these features and increased cushioning as well.

Covers

Mattress covers may be designed and constructed to completely encase the mattress or to cover only the exposed surfaces. Zippers or elasticized edges ensure a smooth fit. When maximum protection against moisture is needed, a vinyl film sheeting bonded to an acetate or nylon tricot may be used as the covering fabric. For protection against dust, a closely woven fabric composed of cotton or a blend of cotton or polyester may be appropriate.

Pads

Mattress pads are multicomponent structures that cushion and soften while they cover and protect the mattress. Most pads have a batting of polyester quilted between two woven or spunbonded fabrics. Some pads cover the sleeping surface only; others cover the sleeping surface and the vertical sides; and others completely encase the mattress. An example of an encasing style is the Bedsack®, produced by Perfect Fit Industries, Inc. The company also manufactures matching pads for box springs and bed pillows.

Mattress pads of wool have been used in hospitals and health care facilities for some time, but have only recently been promoted for residential use. These structures are produced by locking slivers of lambswool into a knitted base fabric composed of polyester. The fleece-like fabric is placed, pile up, under the bottom sheet, providing softness, warmth, and moisture absorption. The wool used in some of these **underblankets** has been treated with agents that minimize felting shrinkage, permitting the pad to be laundered. The name Superwash® may be used with pads that The Wool Bureau, Inc. has certified to be fully machine washable.

Mattress covers and pads produced for use in hospitals and other health care facilities may be treated with agents that effectively reduce the action of such microbes as bacteria and fungi. Such antimicrobial chemicals can be applied during finishing (see Chapter 9) and are becoming increasingly important as the population ages and incontinence becomes a concern.

Flammability Standard

The Standard for the Flammability of Mattresses, **16 CFR 1632 (FF 4–72)**, was established in an effort to protect the public against unreasonable risk of mattress fires leading to death, personal injury, or significant property damage. The most common mode of bedding ignition, a burning cigarette, is used as the ignition source in the test procedure. This standard and its scope and requirements were discussed in Chapter 11.

Fillings Used in Bedding Products

Filling components in bedding products may be composed of natural or synthesized materials. Some materials are used in loose, lofty masses; others, in stabilized battings; and still others, in well-defined, three-dimensional forms.

Natural Filling Materials

Natural filling materials include down, feathers, wool, cotton, and kapok. Earlier, cotton and kapok were used alone, either loose or in the form of batting. Today, supply and delivery problems have reduced the use of **kapok**, and the low resiliency of cotton has prompted manufacturers to blend it with polyester. Although the use of wool as a filling material is limited, primarily because of its cost, some longer-staple wool fibers are occasionally used to produce lofty, three-dimensional battings for use in comforters.

Down and feathers are virtually always used loose in lofty masses. Bedding products filled with these materials should be labeled in accordance with the provisions of the Guides for the Feather and Down Products Industry.

Guides for the Feather and Down Products Industry

While labeling guides are advisory in nature, manufacturers should adhere to the recommendations included in them in order to avoid engaging in commercial practices that could be considered unfair or deceptive under the provisions of the Federal Trade Commission Act. Included in the **Guides for the Feather and Down Products Industry**, promulgated on October 29, 1971, are definitions of terms and recommended procedures for labeling products filled with these natural materials. Some of these terms and their definitions are listed below:

Down: the undercoating of waterfowl, consisting of clusters of light, fluffy filaments (i.e., barbs) growing from the quill point but without any quill shafts. (The quill is the tube or barrel of a feather.)

Plumules: down waterfowl plumage with underdeveloped soft and flaccid quill with barbs indistinguishable from those of down.

Down fiber: the detached barbs from down and plumules and the detached barbs from the basal end of waterfowl quill shaft, which are indistinguishable from the barbs of down.

Feathers: the plumage or out-growth forming the contour and external covering of fowl, which are whole in structure and which have not been processed in any manner other than by washing, dusting, chemical treatment, and sanitizing.

Waterfowl feathers: feathers derived from ducks and geese.

Nonwaterfowl feathers or **land fowl feathers**: feathers derived from chickens, turkeys, and other land fowl.

Quill feathers: feathers that are over 4 inches in length or that have a quill point exceeding $\frac{5}{16}$ inch in length.

Feather fiber: the detached barbs of feathers that are not joined or attached to each other.

Crushed feathers: feathers that have been processed by a curling, crushing, or chopping machine, which has changed the original form of the feathers without removing the quill. The term also includes the fiber resulting from such processing.

Damaged feathers: feathers that have been damaged by insects, or otherwise materially injured.

Residue: means quill pith, quill fragments, trash, or foreign matter.

According to the provisions of the guides, industry products should be labeled as to the kind or type of filling material used. When the filling material consists of a mixture of more than one kind or type, then the proportion of each should be disclosed in the order of predominance, the largest proportion first. If the term "nonwaterfowl" or "land fowl" is used, it should be accompanied by the name of the fowl from which the products were obtained, for instance, chicken or turkey.

A certain leeway is permitted in the use of the terms down and waterfowl feathers. "Down" may be used to designate any industry product containing the following filling material:

1. Down, plumules, and down fiber
   ....mimimum 80 percent
   Consisting of:
   Down and plumules....................minimum 70 percent
   Down fiber................................maximum 10 percent
2. Remainder ....20 percent
   Consisting of:
   Down fiber, waterfowl feather fiber, and waterfowl feathers, and nonwaterfowl feathers and nonwaterfowl feather fiber ....maximum 2 percent
   Residue ....maximum 2 percent

A product should not be designated "100 percent down," **all down**, **pure down**, or by other terms of similar import unless it in fact contains only down, without regard to the tolerance detailed above.

"Waterfowl feathers" may be used to designate any plumage product containing the following filling material, free of quill and crushed feathers:

Waterfowl feathers....................minimum 80 percent
Nonwaterfowl feathers...............maximum 8 percent
Residue ....maximum 2 percent

The name of a waterfowl species may be included if a minimum of 90 percent of the waterfowl plumage contained in the filling is that of the species.

Synthesized Filling Materials

Synthesized fillings include such materials as noncellulosic fibers, synthetic rubber, and polyurethane. Noncellulosic fibers are virtually always in staple or tow forms for use as filling material. They may be used in loose, lofty masses, known as **fiberfill**, or organized into battings of various thicknesses. Today, fiberfill is almost exclusively composed of noncellulosic fibers.[2] **Batting** structures composed of polyester, as well as those composed of polyester and cotton, may be stabilized by spraying resin throughout the layered fibers. Synthesized rubber and urethane compounds are generally foamed and formed into three-dimensional structures for use in pillows, into thick **slabs** for use in mattresses, and into thin slabs for use in quilts (see Figure 29.10).

Functions and Properties of Filling Materials

In mattresses, fillings provide support for the body; in bed pillows, they cushion the head; in decorative pillows, they impart and maintain a distinctive form. In most other bedding products, fillings are primarily intended for **thermal insulation**. Ideally, filling materials should be lofty or bulky without being heavy. They must be resilient to regain their original **loftiness** after being compressed, and they must be affordable.

To improve the loftiness and insulative value of fiberfill without increasing the weight, textile fiber chemists have engineered fibers with hollow interiors. Examples of fibers with tunnel-like cores are Dacron® Hollofil® polyester (Figure 29.4a) and Dacron® 113 polyester; the latter has four microscopic openings in its interior, as shown in Figure 29.4b. The open interiors of the fibers and the air pockets surrounding them provide a great deal of insulation.

In laboratory testing, the insulative values of goose down, wool, polyester, and olefin were found to be similar.[3] Down and feathers offer the advantage of being inherently lofty and lightweight, but their limited supply in comparison to demand and the labor involved in their retrieval make them comparatively expensive. Wool has

a) Dacron® Single-void T-351

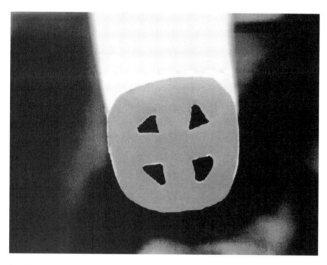

b) Dacron® Four-void T-808

Figure 29.4 Photomicrographs of hollow Dacron® polyester fibers.
Courtesy of E. I. du Pont de Nemours & Co., Inc.

excellent resiliency, but the fibers are comparatively heavy and expensive. Fiberfill is lofty, lightweight, and economical; unlike the natural filling materials, it is also nonallergenic.

Care of Fillings

Bedding products filled with wool batting must be dry cleaned to avoid the agitation that can cause felting shrinkage. Some manufacturers recommend that down, feather, and polyester fillings be dry cleaned to minimize shifting and clumping of the materials. Others recom-

mend that the fillings be laundered and then tumble dried to encourage the materials to regain their original loftiness. In every case, the care procedures performed on the filling must be appropriate for the outer covering and vice versa. To prevent care practices that could cause unnecessary product failure—a problem generally accompanied by the consumer losing confidence in the producer's name—many manufacturers voluntarily label their goods with care instructions.

Pillows

Two categories of pillows, namely bed pillows and decorative pillows, are available on today's bedding products market. The same filling materials and ticking fabrics may be used in both types of pillows, but decorative pillows are produced in a wider variety of sizes and forms and their outer coverings have more elaborate styling features.

Sizes and Forms

Bed pillows are basically rectangular in shape, and most are 20 to 21 inches wide. Their length varies according to the width of the mattress with which they are intended to be paired. **Standard pillows**, intended to be used with a twin or double mattress, are 26 to 27 inches long; **queen-size pillows** are 30 to 31 inches long; and **king-size pillows** are 37 to 38 inches long.

Decorative pillows are available in various sizes and forms. **Neckroll pillows** are cylindrical forms 6 inches by 14 inches or a larger 7 inches by 17 inches; **boudoir pillows**, also called **breakfast pillows**, are 12 inches by 16 inches; **bolster pillows** are cylindrical or lozenge-shaped pillows that may be from 40 to 50 inches in length; **Turkish pillows**, which have gathered corners, are 16 inches square; **European pillows** are 26 inches square; **round pillows** are normally 12 inches in diameter; and a **bedrest pillow** has a back and arms.

Fillings and Tickings

Bed pillows and decorative pillows may be filled with fiberfill, down, feathers, or foam. In many items, the filling material is enclosed in a nonremovable casing that is then protected by a zippered casing. The interior casing

Figure 29.5 Evolution® spunbonded polypropylene olefin pillow ticking.
Courtesy of Kimberly-Clark Corporation.

fabric should have an extremely high fabric count, around 220 when fine down filling materials are used, and the fabrics used for the pillow protectors must be machine washable. Commonly used fabrics include muslin, percale, twill-woven ticking, cotton damask, and more recently, spunbonded ticking composed of polypropylene olefin. The spunbonded ticking pictured in Figure 29.5 weighs 1.5 ounces per square yard; it has been printed for visual interest.

Decorative Coverings for Pillows

For nighttime use, bed pillows are inserted into the familiar pillowcases. These may be plain or have decorative hem treatments. For daytime display, bed pillows may be inserted into a **pillow sham**, a decorative casing, which often has contrasting piping and ruffles. Shams are generally styled to match decorative pillows placed on the bed.

Today, consumers are frequently offered an assortment of decorative pillows covered and trimmed to coordinate with a variety of products included in an ensemble. The pillows are covered with the fabric used in other items in the grouping, and they are finished with identical trimmings. The trimming may include such embellishments as monograms, contrasting piping or fabric banding, Schiffli-embroidered appliqués, ribbons, and ruffles.

Besides decorative pillows, a coordinated ensemble may include a quilt, a bedspread or comforter, sheets, and pillowcases. It may also include round and square tablecloths, towels, curtain and drapery panels, and valences for windows and canopy beds.

Sheets and Pillowcases

The assortment of sheets and pillowcases offered to contemporary consumers includes items ranging from those of minimal aesthetic appeal to those with distinctive color styling and decorative border embellishments. Much of today's sheeting is stabilized and given a resin finish to improve end-use serviceability.

Manufacturing Sheeting

Fabric manufacturers produce the major portion of sheeting fabric for both residential and institutional use in a plain-weave interlacing. For the residential market, however, the assortment has been expanded to include satin, jacquard, and knitted sheetings. Generally, they use spun yarns composed of cotton and polyester.

Fiber and Yarn Usage

As detailed in Table 29.1, 516.3 million pounds of cotton were used in sheets and other beddings in 1966, thus accounting for nearly 95 percent of the market. By 1985, the consumption of cotton in these items fell to 225.9 million pounds, or only about 50 percent of the total. Over the same period, the market share captured by the noncellulosic fibers rose from less than 1 percent to slightly more than 47 percent. The significant increase in the use of noncellulosic fibers at that time was largely the result of the overwhelming acceptance of durable press sheets by consumers. As explained in Chapter 9, durable press resins improve the resiliency of cotton fibers but also weaken them and reduce their abrasion resistance. In order to prolong the use-life of resin-treated sheeting, manufacturers altered the composition of the fabric, increasing the polyester content and decreasing the cotton content.

In recent years, consumers have expressed a preference for **reverse blends** of polyester and cotton (i.e., decreasing the polyester content and increasing the cotton content). Today, cotton accounts for some 63 percent of the sheeting market. Because filament polyester contributes to pilling, spun yarns of polyester and cotton are preferred for blends.

The predominance of spun yarns in all textile bedding products was mentioned earlier. In sheets and other bedding, more than 96 percent of all fibers used, natural and manufactured, are in staple lengths. These fibers are converted into carded or combed yarns by spinning on the cotton system.

Fabricating Sheetings

Most sheeting fabrics have the same simple interlacing pattern, 1×1, but they may have different yarns and different fabric counts. In general, finer yarns and higher fabric counts are characteristic of higher quality sheets. **Muslin** sheeting contains carded yarns and its fabric count may be as low as 112 or as high as 140, although 128 is most common. A large amount of sizing is generally used on muslin that has a very low fabric count. This increases fabric weight but not its durability, and few of these sized or **backfilled** fabrics are produced today. **Percale** sheeting's fabric count may be as low as 168 or as high as 220; 180 is common. Most percale sheeting is woven from fine, combed yarns.

A relatively small amount of woven sheeting is produced with a satin-interlacing pattern. The floating warp yarns produce a smooth, luxurious sleeping surface, but they may be snagged and ruptured, interrupting the pattern of light reflection, producing a stain-like appearance, and shortening the use-life of the sheets. For better durability, manufacturers have decreased their use of warp yarns composed of acetate and increased their use of nylon and polyester. The shift in fiber usage is accompanied by a decrease in moisture absorption and comfort.

Knitted sheets are produced with a jersey (like tee-shirt fabric) or a tricot stitch. The inherent stretchability offered by the interlooped yarns helps to keep the sheets fitting smoothly, but those composed of cotton exhibit relatively low elastic recovery. A broken loop in a jersey-stitched product initiates the development of the unsightly, ladder-like effect known as a "run," and the loops in tricot-stitched sheets may snag and pill.

Coloring and Finishing Sheetings

Rotary screen printing, explained in detail in Chapter 8, is the predominant technique for printing sheeting. Patterns range from those whose tiny motifs cover virtually the entire surface to those whose large motifs combine with sizable areas of white or solid-colored ground. Frequently, producers seek to enhance their position in the market by enlisting the assistance of well-known fashion fabric and apparel designers to create patterns and select the coloration.

A limited quantity of sheeting fabric is made with **duplex printing**. Duplex prints are produced by printing identical or different design motifs on both sides of the fabric. Because more dye paste and two sets of screens are used, duplex prints are relatively expensive; this restricts their widespread production and selection.

Sheeting greige goods may be preshrunk to relax the yarns, minimizing later relaxation shrinkage. Woven goods processed through the compressive shrinkage operation generally exhibit no more than 1 or 2 percent residual shrinkage, unless dried in a dryer. A significant portion of sheeting greige goods is treated with durable press resins to avoid the need for ironing after laundering (durable press processing was explained in Chapter 9).

Converters have responded to the demands of energy-conscious consumers by increased use of napping treatments on sheeting. In use, the raised fibers entrap air and provide thermal insulation. **Flannel** sheets are generally composed of 100 percent cotton, making them relatively expensive but providing the comfort sought by consumers.

Constructing Sheets and Pillowcases

Sheets and pillowcases have few construction details, but are produced in a variety of sizes and types. Decorative trimmings may embellish their hems.

Types and Sizes

Three styles of sheets are produced: flat, semifitted, and fitted. **Flat sheets** are hemmed at both ends and may be used as top or bottom sheets. **Fitted or contour sheets** have four contour corners and can be used only as bottom sheets. The sheeting selvages provide a finished edge on the sides of all sheets; tape binding or elastic banding finishes the lower edges of contour corners.

Table 29.3 Types and Sizes of Sheets and Pillowcases

Type and Name	Inches (width × length)
Flat sheets	
Crib	45 × 68
Twin	66 × 104
Double or full	81 × 104
Queen	90 × 110
King	108 × 110
Fitted sheets	
Crib	29 × 54
Twin	39 × 75
Double or Full	54 × 75
Queen	60 × 80
King	78 × 80
Pillowcases	
Standard	21 × 35
Queen	21 × 39
King	21 × 44

For the construction of cases for bed pillows, sheeting fabric is cut into rectangular shapes of specific dimensions. The fabric is folded lengthwise, right sides together, stitched across one end and the side having raw edges, and then turned. The hem treatment used for the top hem of the coordinating flat sheet is also used to finish the open end of the cases.

Sheets and pillowcases are constructed in various sizes for use with various sizes of mattresses and pillows. Typical dimensions are listed in Table 29.3; actual dimensions vary among producers. It should be noted that the size of flat sheets that producers report is measured prior to hemming.

Hems and Border Embellishments

The hems that finish flat sheets and pillowcases may be simple or highly decorative. A simple hem is normally 1 inch deep at the bottom of sheets and 3 to 4 inches deep at the top of sheets and the end of cases. Decorative hems have such border embellishments as delicate lace, scalloped eyelet trim, and contrasting piping.

Coordinated Items

The sheeting fabric produced and used for a set of sheets and pillowcases frequently also appears in other items offered with the sheets and pillowcases in a coordinated ensemble, such as curtains, draperies, valences, tablecloths,

sheet casings, and dust ruffles. **Dust ruffles**, also known as bedskirts, bed petticoats, and platform skirts, are fabric panels that drape from the top of the foundation to the floor; the panels are normally pleated or gathered. **Sheet casings** are covers that protect comforters and duvets from soil accumulation and abrasion; their releasable closures permit their easy removal for laundering.

Evaluating Sheeting Products

ASTM D 5431 Standard Performance Specification for Woven and Knitted Sheeting Products for Institutional and Household Use may be reviewed for recommended levels of performance. The specifications include requirements for nonflannel sheeting of 100 percent cotton or polyester and cotton blends, for flannel sheeting, and for knitted sheeting.

Blankets

Blankets are primarily used for warmth. Conventional structures provide warmth by reducing the transfer of body heat to the interior; electric blankets provide warmth by generating heat. The blanketing fabrics used to produce these coverings may be produced from yarns or, bypassing the yarn stage, directly from fibers.

Manufacturing Blanketing

Blanketing may be manufactured from yarn structures, using simple and decorative biaxial weaves, knitting, and tufting. It may also be manufactured directly from fibers, through a flocking or needlepunching operation. Like most other bedding products, blankets are composed primarily of cotton fibers but a sizable quantity of staple noncellulosic fibers are also used. Unlike other bedding products, however, some blankets are composed of wool fiber, and a limited number of contemporary blankets are composed of camel hair.

Fibers and Yarns Used

Over the past thirty-year period, the use of the noncellulosic fibers in blanketing has steadily increased; collectively, these fibers now hold about 41 percent of the market. The growth of the noncellulosic fibers in other bedding products has largely been at the expense of cotton; their growth in the blanket market has largely been at the expense of rayon, acetate, and wool. Rayon is relatively weak and is highly flammable; acetate is also relatively weak and used only as edge trimming; and wool is relatively expensive. Moreover, products composed of any of these three fibers generally must be dry cleaned. At the same time, a significant increase in the consumption of cotton in this market has also occurred.

As detailed in Table 29.1, virtually all fibers used in blankets and blanketing are staple length. These fibers are usually processed into yarns on the woolen or cotton spinning systems.

Weaving Blanketing

Plain weaving and **leno weaving** are used to produce a large amount of blanketing. The leno-woven **thermal blanket** in Figure 29.6 is lightweight and lofty for thermal insulation. The filling yarns were spun on the woolen system and the warp yarns on the cotton system.

Weaving one set of warp yarns and two sets of filling yarns together produces **double-faced blanketing**, or **reversible blanketing**, with different colors on each side. One set of filling yarns is carried to the face and one set to the back. The sets of filling yarns may have

Figure 29.6 Leno-woven thermal blanket.

different colors or different fiber compositions. If the fiber compositions differ, a cross-dyeing operation could be used to produce the two colors in one immersion procedure (see Chapter 8). The additional set of yarns adds strength, which compensates for the weakening effect of the heavy napping used on both sides for warmth.

The blanketing in electric blankets is often produced by interlacing four sets of yarns into a doublecloth fabric. The interlacing is planned so that pocket-like channels are created, which will prevent the wires from shifting through the structure.

Knitting Blanketing

Knitted blanketing, which is generally constructed on a **raschel knitting** machine, may have a simple or a complex interlooping pattern. The thermal efficiency of this fabric can be engineered by varying the size of the yarns and the knitting gauge used.

Tufting Blanketing

Tufting, used extensively for the production of soft floor coverings and increasingly for upholstery coverings, has been adapted for the production of a small quantity of blanketing. The pile yarns are punched into the base fabric, using a gauge of $\frac{5}{64}$ or $\frac{5}{32}$ inch and six to fourteen stitches per lengthwise inch. By napping the pile surface, the raised fibers have the effect of increasing the diameter of the pile yarns, helping to secure them in the fabric. The back is napped to soften the surface and further stabilize the pile yarns.

Needlepunching Blanketing

The use of a **needlepunching** operation for the commercial production of blanketing began in the mid-1960s. In the Fiberwoven Process®, developed by Chatham Manufacturing Company, a 5-inch-thick batt is prepared by cross-layering twelve to eighteen webs of staple-length fibers on each side of a web of yarns. The batt is fed into a machine where more than 13,000 pairs of closely spaced, barbed needles punch into the batt, entangling the fibers into a mechanical chain-stitch. The extensive needling, approximately 2,000 punches per square inch, reduces the depth of the batt to about ¼ inch. Subsequent napping raises some surface fibers, softening the appearance and improving the thermal efficiency.

Flocking Blanketing

Lightweight, warm blankets can be produced by **flocking** nylon over the surfaces of a thin slab of polyurethane foam. In Vellux® blankets, manufactured by West Point Pepperell, nylon flock is embedded on both sides of the foam. Together, the flocked fiber and the cellular foam serve to minimize heat transfer by restricting air flow.

Coloring and Finishing Blanketing

Blanketing may be constructed with colored fibers or yarns or the greige fabric may be piece dyed or printed. Whatever fabrication technique is used, virtually all blanketing fabrics are napped.

Constructing Blankets

Most blankets are approximately 84 inches long and they are finished 20 inches wider than the mattress with which they are intended to be used. The side edges may be the fabric selvages or they may be machine overcast, and the ends are enclosed within tightly satin-woven binding (see Figure 29.6). For electric blankets, insulated wires are inserted into the channels before the edges are finished.

Caring for Blankets

Wool blankets must be stored with some type of moth repellent to protect the fibers from attack by moth larvae (see Chapter 9). To avoid **felting shrinkage**, blankets composed of wool fiber should be dry cleaned, unless information on the label directs otherwise. Blankets composed of most other fibers can generally be laundered, unless care instructions voluntarily provided by the producer state otherwise. Electric blankets must always be laundered; dry-cleaning solvents may damage the insulating material covering the heating wires.

Flammability of Blankets

Currently, no federal flammability standard exists for blankets, although a finding of need for such a standard was issued on June 5, 1970. Beginning in 1972, however, members of the blanket industry have voluntarily tested blanketing to identify fabrics that are sufficiently flammable to be unsuitable for use in blankets. The testing equipment, preparation of the test specimens, testing, and eval-uation used are described in ASTM D 4151 Standard Test Method for Flammability of Blankets. The procedures may be used for all types of blanketing, including electric blanketing without the heating wires in place.

Bedspreads, Quilts, and Comforters

It may be helpful to differentiate among bedspreads, comforters, and quilts. ASTM D 4721 Standard Practice for Evaluation of the Performance of Machine Washable and Drycleanable Bedcoverings and Accessories provides useful distinctions. Bedspreads are defined "as a type of bedcovering that is placed over the blankets and sheets for appearance and warmth," a comforter is described as "a bedcovering assembly, consisting of an insulating filler secured between two layers of fabric, used primarily to reduce heat loss," and a quilt is "a bedcovering assembly used primarily for warmth, consisting of an insulating filler secured between two layers of fabric, but generally lighter in weight and thinner than a comforter."

Commercial Quilting

Both of the commercial quilting techniques of **machine stitching** and **pinsonic melding** were discussed in Chapter 9. Typical stitching patterns are illustrated in Figure 9.12 (p. 139), and a pinsonic quilted fabric is shown in Figure 9.11 (p. 139).

In **patterned quilts**, the several pieces are shaped to create a specific pattern repeat; today, skilled quilters often cut and sew selected fabrics to replicate traditional patterns (Figure 29.7). In **crazy quilts**, the pieces are irregularly shaped and they vary in size and color styling. The "patches" in **patchwork quilts** are often square or rectangular. Finishing touches differ from quilt to quilt. The patchwork face fabric in Figure 29.8 has been embellished with embroidery stitches.

Quilting stitches should be uniformly placed to stabilize the layered structure. As shown in Figure 9.12 (p. 139), the stitches may be sewn in parallel rows, in crisscrossing lines, or in undulating waves, or they may follow the outlines of printed motifs or appliqués. Since the stitches create a three-dimensional effect, they may be used to introduce a surface pattern to a solid-colored

Figure 29.7 Hand-stitched quilts with motifs adapted from traditional patterns. *Courtesy of Susan T. Farmer.*

surface or to augment the visual interest of a printed fabric. With hand-quilted coverings, the fineness and evenness of the quilting stitches are indicative of quality.

Two quilting variations used on interior textile products include trapunto quilting and shadow quilting. **Trapunto quilting** is done by placing quilting stitching around a single motif in a pattern repeat. The interior of the quilted shape is then filled by inserting batting material through tiny slits cut in the backing fabric. For long, narrow shapes, a yarn or cord may be drawn between the face and back fabrics. Trapunto quilting is particularly effective when used for decorative pillow coverings with large motifs.

Shadow quilting is done by covering an appliquéd face fabric with a sheer fabric such as organdy or voile. Quilting stitches are then placed around the outlines of the appliqués, joining the layers together. The colored appliqués have a softened or shadowed appearance. This technique is often used for crib quilts.

Bedspreads

Most bedspreads are chosen primarily for their styling and decorative fabric. Others, especially quilted ones, are selected for their insulative value.

Styles

Various styles of **drops** seen with bedspreads, ranging from **tailored** to **ruffled** styles, are illustrated in Figure 29.9 The appearance of any of these drops changes dramatically when executed in different fabrics. The qualities of the fabric must always be appropriate for the styling features of the spread. For example, although a heavy fabric would be suitable for use in a throw style, it would not drape properly in a style with **gathered** or **shirred** sides.

Fabrics

Virtually any fabric may be used for a bedspread. Several fabrics, such as **gingham** and printed percale, are flat, essentially two-dimensional, smooth fabrics; others, including **taffeta** and **ribcord**, show a slightly raised rib effect. Clipped dot or spot fabrics, Schiffli-embroidered **organdy**, and **eyelet**, have slightly raised designs created by extra yarns. Fabrics such as corduroy, velvet, simulated fur fabrics, and tufted fabrics exhibit the conspicuous depth of a pile layer.

Pile bedspread fabrics are produced by weaving, knitting, or tufting. **Corduroy**, a woven filling-pile fabric, is often used for tailored spreads, and **velvet**, a woven warp-pile fabric, is often used for throw spreads. Pile knitting produces the **simulated fur fabrics** often used for throw

Figure 29.8 Closeup of a patchwork quilt face fabric embellished with various embroidery stitches.
Courtesy of Norma Long Mayfield.

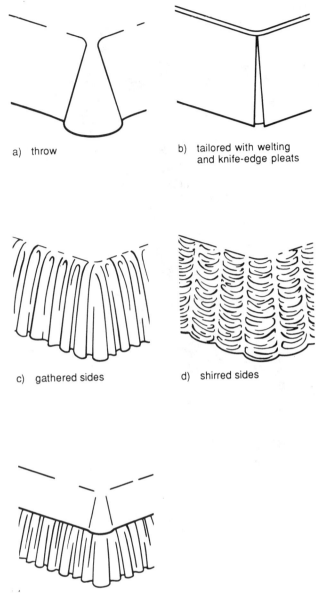

a) throw

b) tailored with welting and knife-edge pleats

c) gathered sides

d) shirred sides

e) short sides with dust ruffle

Figure 29.9 Typical bedspread drops.

style coverings. These three-dimensional coverings are fabricated by incorporating combed fibers into a knitted base fabric.

Tufting is used to produce chenille spreads and candlewick spreads. In **chenille** spreads, the pile tufts are closely spaced and cut, producing the caterpillar-like appearance of chenille yarns; true chenille yarns are not used. After tufting, the level of twist of the pile yarns is reduced, causing them to "bloom" or increase in diameter, and the base fabric is shrunk to effectively lock the pile yarns in position. In **candlewick** spreads, the pile tufts are individually spaced, but, viewed collectively, form a design. The designs resemble those created by a hand-stitching technique in which heavy yarns produced for use as candlewicks are used for the embroidered motifs (see Figures 9.7a and 9.8, p. 137).

Quilts and Comforters

As noted above, quilts and comforters are multicomponent bed coverings. Either structure may be used in lieu of a bedspread.

Quilts

Commercially produced **quilts** usually have a printed face fabric, a fibrous or polyurethane batting, and a coordinating solid-colored or printed back fabric (Figure

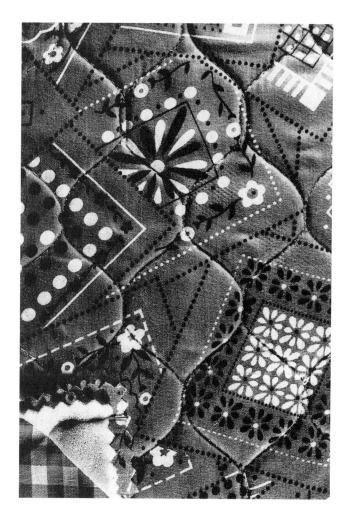

Figure 29.10 Machine-made quilt with a polyurethane batting and pattern quilting.

29.10). Patterned machine stitching is normally used to stabilize the layers. Today, lofty comforters are increasingly replacing such quilts on the beddings market.

Comforters

Comforters are usually filled with down, feathers, or fiberfill; those filled with down are frequently known as **duvets**. They may also be filled with a loose batting of polyester. The closeup photograph in Figure 29.11 shows the use of a spunbonded interior lining fabric to prevent **fill leakage**, the migration or penetration of the filling material through the outercovering. The same fabric may be used on the face and back, or for greater in-use flexibility, different fabrics, for instance, a solid-colored fabric and a printed fabric, may be used. To minimize the need for cleaning, manufacturers often rec-

ommend that comforters be enclosed in a sheet casing. Sheet casings have releasable closures that permit them to be easily removed for laundering.

Most comforters are channel quilted to minimize shifting and clumping of the filling. Some products also use a system of crosswise baffles. Sleeping bags are often constructed in this manner, making them, in effect, folded comforters with zipper closures.

Evaluating Bedspread Fabrics, Quilts, and Comforters

Established ASTM standards may be used to evaluate the performance of bedspread fabrics, quilts, and comforters. These include ASTM D 4037 Standard Performance Specification for Woven, Knitted, or Flocked Bedspread Fabrics, ASTM D 4721 Standard Practice for Evaluation of the Performance of Machine Washable and Drycleanable Bedcoverings and Accessories, and ASTM D 4769 Standard Specification for Woven and Warp Knitted Comforter Fabrics.

Figure 29.11 Comforter with a spunbonded interior lining to prevent fiber migration and to increase insulation.

Summary

Several bedding products, including mattresses, mattress pads, quilts, and comforters, are multicomponent structures. They are generally filled with polyester fiberfill, but other filling materials, including loose masses of down or feathers, foamed compounds, and battings composed of wool, cotton, or cotton and polyester, are also used.

Bedding products may be purchased singly or in coordinated ensembles. Some products, such as mattresses and bed pillows, serve functional purposes; other products, such as sheets, pillowcases, and comforters, are selected for their functional and decorative attributes; and still other products, such as decorative pillows and dust ruffles, are completely ornamental.

The performance of beddings may be evaluated using standards such as those published by ASTM and AATCC. The performance recommended in these standards may be required by an agency having jurisdiction over the selection and use of the products.

Key Terms

16 CFR 1632 (FF 4–72)

all down

backfilled

batting

bedding

blanket, thermal

blanketing, double-faced

blanketing, reversible

candlewick

chenille

comforters

convertible sofa bed

corduroy

down

down fiber

drops

drops, gathered

drops, ruffled

drops, shirred

drops, tailored

duplex printing

dust ruffles

duvet

eyelet

feather fiber

feathers

feathers, crushed

feathers, damaged

feathers, land fowl

feathers, nonwaterfowl

feathers, quill

feathers, waterfowl

felting shrinkage

fiberfill

fill leakage

flannel

flocking

futons

gingham

Guides for the Feather and Down Products Industry

kapok

leno weave

loftiness

mattress, foam-core

mattress, innerspring

mattress covers

mattress pads

muslin

needlepunching

organdy

percale

pillow, bedrest

pillow sham

pillows, bed

pillows, bolster

pillows, boudoir

pillows, breakfast

pillows, European

pillows, king-size

pillows, neckroll

pillows, queen-size

pillows, round

pillows, standard

pillows, Turkish

plumules

pure down

quilting, machine stitching

quilting, pinsonic melding

quilting, shadow

quilting, trapunto

quilts

quilts, crazy

quilts, patchwork

quilts, patterned

raschel knitting

residue

reverse blends

ribcord

sheet casings

sheets, fitted or contour

sheets, flat

simulated fur fabrics

slabs

sofa bed

taffeta

thermal insulation

ticking

tufting

underblankets

velvet

Review Questions

1. Explain the importance of cotton in the bedding products industry.

2. Why has the usage of rayon and acetate fibers declined in bedding products?

3. Identify bedding products included and excluded from the provisions of the TFPIA.

4. Why are spun yarns more widely used than filament yarns in bedding products?

5. Distinguish between down and feathers.

6. Do products labeled "down" have to have 100 percent down present?

7. Differentiate among down, all down, and pure down.

8. Explain why filling materials must retain their original loftiness in order to be effective.

9. Compare the positive and negative properties of down, wool, and polyester for use as filling materials.

10. Explain the use of wool underblankets in institutional settings.

11. Why are cigarettes used as the source of ignition in 16 CFR 1632?

12. Explain factors accounting for the changing market shares held by cotton and polyester in the sheetings market.

13. Distinguish between muslin and percale.

14. Why have rayon, acetate, and wool been increasingly replaced by cotton and the noncellulosic fibers in the blanketing market?

15. Is flammability testing of blanketing mandatory or voluntary?

16. How is fill leakage minimized in comforters?

Notes

1. Textile Economics Bureau, Inc. *Textile Organon*, Vol. 69, No. 10, October 1998, 176.

2. Ibid., 192.

3. W. C. Kaufman, D. Bothe, and S. D. Meyer, "Thermal Insulating Capabilities of Outdoor Clothing Materials," *Science*, Vol. 215, February 5, 1982, 690–691.

30

Textile Accessories for Tabletops

Producing Tabletop Coverings
  Components
  Manufacturing Table Covering Fabrics
Constructing Tabletop Accessories
Evaluating Fabrics for Tabletop
  Accessories

Labeling Textile Table Accessories
  Textile Fiber Products Identification Act
  Trade Regulation Rule

Because many of today's tabletops have a heat-, chip-, and stain-resistant finish, the use of such coverings as tablecloths and placemats is often optional. Nonetheless, these items frequently enrich the dining experience. They may be selected to add warmth and beauty to the table, to carry out a decorative theme, to set a casual or formal mood, or to complement the table service. The use of textile table coverings in such institutional settings as restaurants, for example, adds to the ambiance and to the diners' expectation to pay more for the meal. Even when table coverings are needed to protect fine wood or to camouflage a damaged surface, the assortment of contemporary products is so varied that consumers may choose the items mostly on the basis of their aesthetic features.

At the outset, two terms, napery and linens, should be distinguished. **Napery** is a general term for tablecloths and napkins. Although the term is no longer widely used in commercial activities, it is used in certain standards and labeling rules. In contemporary usage, the term **linens** described sheets, towels, tablecloths, napkins, and related products that formerly were composed entirely or primarily of linen fiber. While the use of linen fiber in these goods has declined significantly, use of the term continues. Today, most all-linen table coverings are not new—they are heirlooms that have been given special care.

Some tabletop accessories are specifically produced for use on dining room tables in homes and in such institutional settings as restaurants and hotels. Several other items are produced for use on tables and other furniture situated throughout interiors.

Producing Tabletop Coverings

The assortment of products produced for use on tabletops includes such items as tablecloths, napkins, doilies, placemats, and silencers. With the exception of silencers, all of these items are visible in use; therefore, they are designed to be attractive additions to the table surface, and often to complement the interior setting as well. Silencers, which are placed under tablecloths and concealed from view, serve purely functional purposes.

Components

Most tabletop coverings are composed of textile fibers. Some distinctive nonfibrous structures are also available.

Fibers and Yarns

Together with rayon and various noncellulosic fibers, several natural cellulosic fibers, including cotton, linen, ramie, sisal, and raffia, are used in dining table products, doilies, and dresser scarves. **Raffia**, a fiber obtained from the leaves of various species of palm trees, is used in long, narrow, yarn-like bands to make woven placemats. **Sisal**, a relatively stiff fiber obtained from the leaves of the sisal plant, is effectively used to produce woven placements and hot pads, examples of which are presented in Figure 30.1.

When stiff fibers, such as **linen** and **ramie**, are used in large items that are normally folded for storage or use, they may be unable to withstand the repeated flexing, and eventually may split on the crease lines (see Figure 3.4, p. 32). To avoid this problem, fabrics composed of these fibers should be stored flat or rolled, and crease positions should be shifted when possible. The need for such storage, in fact, explains the earlier use of special names and

Figure 30.1 Hand-woven placemat and hot pad composed of sisal.

spaces for the storage of fine linens (e.g., the linen drawer, the linen closet).

Most yarns used for table products are spun. For economy and ease of care, spinners frequently use staple-length rayon and polyester to produce yarns that resemble those spun of linen. For improved dimensional stability and resiliency, polyester is increasingly used alone or blended with cotton in various sizes of yarns.

Nonfibrous Materials

Some contemporary placemats are multicomponent structures, made of a layer of aluminum foil or metallized polymer film faced with a clear fabric, such as Mylar® polyester film produced by DuPont, and backed with a conventional textile fabric; such mats have a mirror-like quality. For the placemat in Figure 30.2, clear and colored film sheetings have been used to encase a simulated batik textile fabric. Batik printing is explained in Chapter 8.

Several nonfibrous placemats are composed of polymer foam that has been expanded into a thin, fabric-like structure. For increased visual interest, these mats are generally printed with colorful design motifs.

Manufacturing Table Covering Fabrics

Table coverings are produced by weaving, stitch-knitting, knotting and twisting, spunbonding, and extrusion. Color may be added before or after fabrication, and finishing agents and processes may be used to alter the appearance and improve serviceability.

Fabricating

Woven table coverings may have a casual, contemporary appearance or a formal, traditional appearance; most styles carry no specific fabric name. For institutional use, simple interlacings are used to produce **momie cloth**, a crêpe-like fabric having an irregular, pebbled surface. Elaborate Jacquard interlacing patterns are used to create the distinctive surfaces of single and double damask. The motifs in **single damask** have a five-shaft satin weave, with each warp yarn floating over four filling yarns; the motifs in **double damask** have an eight-shaft satin weave, with each warp yarn floating over seven filling yarns. The ground in these fabrics is generally woven in a twill- or sateen-interlacing pattern. As explained in Chapter 9, **beetling** may be used to flatten the cross-sections of the fibers and yarns, increasing the level of light reflection to highlight the motifs (see Figure 9.1, p. 134).

Stitch-knitted tablecloths and napkins are produced by chain-stitching across webs of yarns, a technique described in Chapter 7. The technique is fast and economical, but rupturing of the chain-stitches can initiate runs. This is the problem with the napkin pictured in Figure 30.3.

Figure 30.3 Stitch-knitted napkin with a run caused by rupturing of the chain-stitches.

Figure 30.2 Placemat with fabric printed to simulate batik and patchwork quilting encased between film sheetings.

Figure 30.4 Nottingham lace doily.

Figure 30.6 Table napkin enriched with embroidery.

Figure 30.5 Spunbonded table covering.
Courtesy of Kimberly Clark Corporation.

A wide variety of lace fabrics is produced for use as tablecloths, dresser scarves, and **doilies**. Machine-made **Nottingham lace**, originally used only for curtains, is used in the doily shown in Figure 30.4. Frequently, lace fabrics are placed over a solid-covered fabric for a color accent that emphasizes the intricate motifs in the lace.

Extrusion of such polymer compounds as polyvinylchloride produces film fabrics that are then sup-

ported by conventional woven or knitted fabrics and cut for use as tablecloths. Extrusion is also used to produce film structures that are then laminated to produce items like the placemat pictured in Figure 30.2.

Spunbonding is increasingly used for the rapid and economical production of fabrics for table coverings. The spunbonded fabric pictured in Figure 30.5 has been printed with a pattern traditionally woven from dyed yarns.

Coloring and Finishing

Table covering fabrics may be manufactured from colored components or color may be applied by dyeing or printing the greige goods. Visual interest may also be added with embroidery (Figure 30.6).

Greige fabrics intended for use as **silencers** will be napped to raise the ends of the fibers to the surface, converting the flat goods into thick, flannel-like fabrics. The added thickness will help the silencer to absorb the impact force of dishes and silverware, reducing noise and protecting the table surface.

Fabrics composed of natural and manufactured cellulosic fibers may have small amounts of chemical cross-linking resin added to them to improve wrinkle recovery and reduce **mussiness**. The use of these agents is critical for fabrics composed of linen since the untreated fabrics have extremely low resiliency and require a great deal of moisture and pressure in ironing. Fabrics composed of cotton and polyester are often treated with a larger amount of resin for durable press or no-iron performance. Fabrics composed of thermoplastic fibers can be heat set to improve their resiliency and dimensional stability.

Soil release compounds may be used with tablecloths and napkins to help the fibers release food stains (see Chapter 9). Because soil release compounds increase the hydrophilic nature of fibers, they are particularly helpful when used with such hydrophobic fibers as polyester and nylon, and with fabrics having a durable press finish. Durable press resins reduce absorbency and thus lessen the efficiency of the detergent in removing soil. Visa® is a trade name that indicates the use of a soil release treatment developed by Deering Milliken for fabrics composed of 100 percent polyester.

Constructing Tabletop Accessories

Tabletop accessories are constructed in assorted sizes and shapes for different uses. Producers employ various techniques to finish the raw edges.

Types and Sizes

Accessories constructed for use on dining tables include tablecloths, runners, placemats, and napkins. These items are available in square, round, oval, and rectangular shapes in various sizes. **Tablecloths** should be selected to cover the tabletop and drop from 5 to 10 inches on all sides. **Runners** are approximately 12 inches wide, and they, too, should drop from 5 to 10 inches. **Placemats** are generally rectangular, but many are round or oval. Rectangular placemats are typically 12 inches by 18 inches. Small **cocktail napkins** are 5 inches square; larger napkins are 12 to 22 inches square.

Accessories constructed for use on cocktail tables, side tables, end tables, dressers, and the like include such items as mats, scarves, coasters, and doilies (Figure 30.4). These products, like dining table accessories, are available in a wide variety of sizes and shapes.

Edge Finishes

The raw edges of fabric used for tabletop items may be finished with a small hem, binding, or fringe, or with machine serging, which may be plain or decorative. When plain overcasting stitches are used on fabrics having relatively large yarns, the stitches often cover only one or two yarns. With continual use and cleaning, the covered yarns and stitching may slide off the edge of the item (Figure 30.7a). The decorative overcasting stitches shown on the napkin in Figure 30.7b extend over several yarns, providing a more secure edge finish.

| **Figure 30.7** Machine serging on edges of tablecloth accessories.

a. plain serging slipping from fabric edge

b. decorative serging secured over fabric edge

The edges of textile placemats are fringed and reinforced with machine zig-zag stitching (see Figure 30.1), serged with plain or decorative stitching, or finished with a small hem. They are also frequently bound with bias-cut fabric.

Evaluating Fabrics for Tabletop Accessories

ASTM D 4111 Standard Performance Specification for Woven Napery and Tablecloth Fabrics: Household and Institutional may be used to evaluate the performance of fabrics intended for use in tablecloths and related items. The specification requirements range from breaking strength (load) to colorfastness to dimensional change.

Labeling Textile Table Accessories

Two federal labeling rules apply to the labeling of textile tabletop accessories. One regulation, the Textile Fiber Products Identification Act, pertains to fiber composition; the other, a trade regulation rule, pertains to representation of product size.

Textile Fiber Products Identification Act

The provisions of the TFPIA apply to tablecloths, napkins, doilies, and dresser and other furniture scarves. Specifically exempted are table placemats made principally of plastic. Most textile tabletop accessories therefore must be labeled with the fiber composition and other information required by this act, which was discussed in detail in Chapter 10.

Trade Regulation Rule

The **Trade Regulation Rule Relating to the Deceptive Advertising and Labeling as to Size of Tablecloths and Related Products** became effective on February 1, 1965. In this rule, the Federal Trade Commission requires that any representation of the "cut size" of tablecloths and related products, such as doilies, table mats, dresser scarves, placemats, table runners, napkins, and tea sets, in advertising or labeling must be accompanied by the words "cut size" and the clear and conspicuous disclosure of the dimensions of the finished size.

Summary

Accessories produced for use on tabletops may be composed of textile fibers or nonfibrous materials. Many table covering fabrics are fabricated by weaving, stitch-knitting, knotting and twisting, and, more recently, by spunbonding. Items intended for use on dining tables may have a soil-release finish to help preserve a stain-free appearance. Items produced for use on occasional tables, dressers, and the like are available in a range of sizes and shapes as varied as that of the dining table accessories.

Virtually all textile tabletop products must be labeled in accordance with the provisions of the Textile Fiber Products Identification Act. When producers make a reference to the "cut size" of most textile tabletop accessories in advertising or labeling, they must also provide the dimensions of the finished size.

Key Terms

beetling
damask, double
damask, single
doilies
extrusion
linen

linens
momie cloth
mussiness
napery
napkins, cocktail
Nottingham lace

placemats

raffia

ramie

runners

silencers

sisal

soil release compounds

spunbonding

stitch-knitting

tablecloths

Trade Regulation Rule Relating to the Deceptive Advertising and Labeling as to Size of Tablecloths and Related Products

Review Questions

1. Distinguish between the terms "linen" and "linens."

2. Identify some natural cellulose fibers used in tabletop accessories. Why do some present storage problems?

3. Distinguish between single damask and double damask.

4. What problem may be encountered with stitch-knitted fabrics?

5. What is the function of silencers?

6. Explain the labeling requirements related to the size of tablecloths.

UNIT FIVE CASESTUDY

Designer Name: Alexis M. Behrens, Allied Member, ASID
West Virginia University Hospitals

Project Location: West Virginia University Hospitals
Morgantown, WV

Statement of the Project:

After nine years of washing and drying, wear and tear, the cubicle curtains in this 376-bed facility needed to be replaced. The existing curtains were a plain, well-washed shade of mauve and did not complement the four different color schemes for patient rooms. They were beginning to show staining and were, in general, not exciting.

Statement of the Problem:

The fabric and mesh of the cubicle curtain needed to be Class A fire rated. State fire codes dictated the distance from the ceiling to the top of the curtain and the size of the openings in the mesh at the top of the curtain to allow for sprinkler coverage on a pulled cubicle curtain. Nylon thread had to be used to prevent breakdown and microbacterial growth. Stainless steel grommets were required to prevent rusting. The top hem was triple reinforced to ensure that the grommets would not rip out with repeated pulling and tugging. The curtains also needed to coordinate with all color schemes, be colorfast, and be reasonably priced.

Selection Criteria:

The recommendation was to choose a patterned fabric, subtle enough to suggest a design, but with enough contrast to make a visual distinction. A strong vertical was not used because some patients suffer from dizziness and it was perceived that the stripes would only add to the condition. Instead a muted and graduated vertical stripe with a faint tree-bark-like design woven into the grey filler threads that create a play on light and shadows was chosen. The graduated colors range from teal, to blue, to rose. This diversity in the colors of this fabric makes for a perfect marriage in all patient rooms.

Product Specifications:

Maharam Textiles

- # 501104 (Mikado Pattern)
- 002 Truffle (Color)
- 100% Trevera, inherently flame-resistant Polyester
- Width—72″
- 9³/₄″ vertical repeat, 9″ high
- Nylon mesh
- ¹/₂″ opening on the diagonal
- Fabricated by Standard Textiles, Cincinnati, OH

Maintenance and Cost:

The following maintenance guidelines are dictated by the manufacturer. The fabric can be washed in 160 °F temperature and dried up to 110 °F. Bleach or caustic soap should not be used with this fabric. The fabric should not be exposed to excessive heat, to avoid the loss of the fabric's permanent-press feature. The fabric is a midrange product that when properly maintained has an average life cycle of 5 years.

Discussion Questions:

1. Identify two of the client's requirements for the design project.

2. Identify aesthetic features of the product that meet the client's requirements.

3. Identify functional features of the product that meet requirements for this application.

4. Discuss the psychological impact of the textile on the user of the space.

5. Research another product that is appropriate for this application. Compare and contrast the cost effectiveness, availability, durability, and maintenance of the new product with the one used in the casestudy.

Glossary

The parenthetical numbers following descriptions identify figures in the text that illustrate the term.

AATCC Acronym for American Association of Textile Chemists and Colorists, a voluntary scientific association that develops standard test methods.

AATCC Chromatic Color Transference Scale Scale used in evaluations of staining (18.6).

AATCC Gray Scale for Color Change Scale used in evaluations of shade changes (14.10).

AATCC Gray Scale for Staining Scale used in evaluations of staining (14.9).

AATCC Technical Manual Publication that includes AATCC test methods.

Abaca Bast fiber used for cordage; also called Manila hemp.

Abrasion resistance Ability of a textile structure to resist damage and fiber loss by friction.

Absorption Penetration of gases or fluids into fibers or within yarn and fabric interstices.

Accordion-pleated shade Window treatment constructed of woven or knitted fabric that has been stiffened and set in a three-dimensional, folded configuration (16.13).

Acetate Manufactured cellulose-based fibers in which approximately 50 percent of the hydroxyl groups are acetylated; effective substitute for silk.

Acid print See *burnt-out print.*

Acoustical value The extent to which a structure prevents sound from becoming unwanted noise.

ACT Acronym for Association for Contract Textiles; a trade association created by members of the contract textile industry to address issues concerning contract upholstery fabrics, including performance guidelines and industry education.

Actual color Color characteristics of hue, value, and intensity are unaffected by such things as the light source, accumulated soil, and textural changes.

Additives agents or compounds added to polymer solutions prior to spinning, e.g., antistatic agents, delusterants, flame retardant agents, softeners, dye pigments, ultraviolet absorbers, optical brighteners.

Adsorption Holding of gases, fluids, or solid materials on fiber surfaces.

Advisory practices Labeling practices that are advisory in contrast to being mandatory.

After flame time The time the specimen continues to flame after the burner flame is removed.

Afterglow Smoldering combustion occurring after flames are extinguished.

Airborne sounds Noise radiating directly into the air (e.g., people talking, telephones ringing).

All down Labeling term used when product contains only down; also known as pure down or 100 percent down. See *down, all.*

Alpaca Hair fiber retrieved from Peruvian sheep of the llama species.

Alpha amino acids Monomer units in natural protein fibers.

Amorphous Molecular arrangement in which the polymer chains are not aligned parallel to each other (3.1a).

Angora Hair fiber retrieved from Angora rabbits.

Anhydrous glucose Monomer unit in natural cellulose fibers.

Aniline finish Denotes use of aniline dyestuffs with leather; not a finish.

Annual Book of ASTM Standards Seventy-two volumes, divided among 16 sections, that contain approved ASTM standards, provisional standards, and related material.

ANSI Acronym for American National Standards Institute, a private corporation that undertakes the development of standards only when so commissioned by an industry group or a government agency.

Antimacassars Fabric covers used to protect upholstery from hair oil.

Antimicrobial agents Chemical agents used to kill or retard the growth of such microbes as bacteria and fungi; especially useful with mattress covers, mattress pads, and soft floor coverings used in care-type facilities.

Antique Oriental rugs Oriental rugs woven prior to the mid-1800s.

Antique satin Sateen-woven drapery fabric with simple warp yarns and slub filling yarns (17.8).

Apparent color Color characteristics of hue, value, and intensity are affected by such things as the light source, accumulated soil, and textural changes so they appear different than they actually are.

Apparent volume or bulk Apparent, but not actual, increase in volume or bulk created by texturizing multifilament yarns (5.1).

Apparent whiteness or brightness Apparent, but not actual, increase in whiteness or brightness created by the presence of optical brighteners.

Appliqué Shaped piece of fabric placed over a second fabric; raw edges are turned under and secured with blind stitches or embroidery stitches.

Appliqué, reverse Needlework in which artisans layer fabrics and cut decreasing sizes of shaped areas from each fabric, turning the raw edges under and stitching the folded edge to each subsequent layer until the base fabric is reached; used in the production of Molas (9.9).

Area rugs Soft floor coverings that range in size from 27 inches by 54 inches to 6 feet by 9 feet, and are available in a wide variety of shapes; moveable (20.3).

Arm caps Accessories used to protect the arms of upholstered furniture; also called arm covers and armettes.

Arm covers See *arm caps.*

Armettes See *arm caps.*

Armure Jacquard-weave fabrics distinguished by small motifs in which the warp yarns float on the face of the fabrics and the filling yarns float on the back, producing a pebbly surface; two sets of yarns are used.

Artificial silk Name used initially for manufactured fibers invented as substitutes for silk; name discontinued in the mid-1920s when the name rayon was adopted.

Asbestos Natural mineral fiber; although fireproof, use of the fiber has been discontinued because it is a known carcinogen.

ASTM Acronym for American Society for Testing and Materials; a not-for-profit, voluntary scientific association having 132 committees that develop full-consensus standards for products, materials, or processes.

Astrojets Dye-loaded needles.

Athey shade Variation of the conventional Roman shade in which two shades are used, with one raised and one lowered for full closure.

Atmospheric fading See *fume fading.*

Aubusson rugs French rugs characterized by classic designs, soft pastel colors, and a fine loop pile.

Austrian shade Window covering constructed of textile fabric that is vertically shirred to create lengthwise bands of horizontally draping folds (16.11).

Auxochromes Components of dyestuffs that are responsible for the selective absorption and reflection of light waves; determine the hue.

Average density Average density, D, considers pile height (finished thickness) and average pile weight to indicate the true density of floor covering structures; calculated by multiplying the average pile weight in ounces per square yard by 36 and dividing the product by the average pile thickness in inches.

Awnings Rigid structures that may be composed of metal or molded polymer sheeting or of textile fabric stretched and held over a rigid frame; generally mounted as exterior overhead treatments to provide protection from weather elements.

Backfilled Use of a large amount of sizing on fabrics that generally have lower fabric counts; also known as loading.

Bacteria Extremely simple vegetative plant forms that can react with perspiration to cause odor and can cause infection and slow the healing process; also referred to as a microbe.

Balanced construction Weave structure in which there is an equal number of warp and filling yarns.

Balloon shades Window coverings composed of textile fabric that form balloon-like puffs when they are raised (16.12).

Base yarn Foundation yarn in decorative yarns; determines yarn length (5.8).

Basket weave Interlacing pattern in which two or more warp yarns, side by side, interlace with one or more filling yarns (6.8).

Bast fiber Classifies cellulose fibers retrieved from stem portion of plants (e.g., jute, linen, ramie, and hemp).

Batch dyeing Dyeing relatively small quantities or batches of carpet in a discontinuous-dyeing operations, using a carpet winch, a jet beck, or a horizontal beam-dyeing machine.

Bath mats Relatively small textile floor covering used to absorb moisture when bathers step on it.

Bath rugs Relatively small scatter rugs used in the bathroom.

Batik print Hand print produced by artisans who apply melted wax to fabric areas that are to resist dye penetration (8.12).

Batiste Sheer, plain-woven fabric composed of fine, combed cotton yarns or spun polyester yarns; used for curtain treatments and Tambour-embroidered panels (17.18).

Batons Rods used manually to open and close curtain and drapery panels; also known as curtain tenders.

Battening In weaving, beating the filling picks against those already in place, aligning them parallel.

Batting Three-dimensional fibrous structure that is bonded into a relatively flat nonwoven fabric (7.10); three-dimensional fibrous structure used as filling in quilts and comforters (29.11).

BCF yarn See *bulked continuous filament.*

Beam dyeing Immersing a beam wound with warp yarns or a full width of carpet into a dyebath when the dye liquor is forcibly circulated (8.9).

Bearding Development of long fiber fuzz on loop pile floor coverings; caused by snagging and poor penetration of pile yarn bundle by adhesive.

Beater bar Loom device used in battening; also known as the lay (6.3).

Bedding Includes sheets, covers, blankets, comforters, pillows, pillowcases, quilts, bedspreads, pads, and all other textile fiber products used or intended to be used on or about a bed.

Beetling Finish in which heavy wooden planks hammer the surface of linen fabric to flatten the cross section of the yarns to increase the surface reflection (9.1, 9.2).

Bedford cord Dobby-weave fabric having lengthwise ribs that are slightly larger than those seen in pinwale piqué.

Below-grade Below ground level.

Bengaline Filling-rib woven upholstery fabric having equally sized and spaced ribs that number approximately twenty-four per inch (13.3c).

Berber yarn Speck yarn, hand-spun by peoples of northern Africa, composed of naturally colored wool; simulated by spinning fiber-dyed acrylic (20.8).

Biaxial weaving Interlacing in which the warp and filling yarns cross at right angles (6.1).

Bicomponent fiber Fiber composed of two or more generically similar polymer compounds.

Biconstituent fiber Fiber composed of two or more generically dissimilar polymer compounds.

Binder or tie yarn Yarn used to secure fancy yarn to base yarn in complex, decorative yarns (5.8).

Birdseye piqué Dobby woven curtain fabric with small, diamond-shaped designs (17.9b).

Bishop's sleeve treatment See *pouf window treatment.*

Blanketing, double-faced Blanketing woven with one set of warp yarns and two sets of filling yarns, with one set of filling yarns carried to the face and one set of filling yarns carried to the back; often has different colors on each side.

Blanketing, reversible See *blanketing, double-faced.*

Blanket, thermal Leno-woven blanket that is lightweight and lofty for thermal insulation (29.6).

Bleaching agents Agents and compounds, such as sunlight, hydrogen peroxide and sodium hypochlorite, used to remove unwanted color.

Bleeding Loss or migration of color when dye mixes with fluids.

Blended filaments Yarns formed by combining two generically dissimilar filaments immediately after extrusion.

Block print Hand print produced by artisans who press a hand-carved, dye-covered block (8.10) onto fabric surface (8.11).

Blotch print Color style in which fabric background is printed, leaving undyed design motifs (17.20).

Bobbin Device that holds the filling yarns when it is inserted by the shuttle (6.3).

Bobbinet Transparent net with six-sided openings that appear round; produced by raschel stitching; used as a base for Tambour-embroidered appliques (17.28).

Bobbin lace Lace created by artisans manipulating multiple pairs of bobbins to twist and cross yarns (7.9).

BOCA Acronym for Building Officials and Code Administrators.

Boiling off Washing silk to remove the natural gum called sericin.

Bonded-web fabric Nonwoven fabric produced by applying adhesive or heat to webs of fibers (7.10).

Bottom fabrics Fabrics used underneath the deck of upholstered furniture to conceal the interior components and give a finished look.

Bouclé yarn Complex yarn with pronounced, closed loops that vary in size and spacing (5.11c, 15.2b).

Bow Distorted yarn alignment in woven fabric; filling yarns curve below straight crosswise grain (9.13a, 14.1a, 14.2).

Boxing Wrapping strips of fabric around front and sides of upholstered cushions and throw pillows (12.3, 12.4c).

Bracket Used in Axminster weaving; formed by linking three or four 3-foot spools that carry the pile yarns.

Braiding Diagonal interlacing of three yarns (23.12).

Breaking Process used in retrieving linen fibers from the flax plant; breaks up or crumbles the rotted woody core.

Breaking force (load) Indicates the load required to rupture a fiber, yarn, or fabric.

Breaking tenacity Strength reported as force per unit of linear density, for example, grams per denier (gpd or g/den) or grams per tex (gpt or g/tex).

Broadloom Carpet produced 54 or more inches wide; does not identify a method of construction and carries no implication of quality.

Brocade Jacquard patterned upholstery and drapery fabric; motifs are created with extra filling yarns interlaced in a filling-faced twill or sateen weave; ground is plain, twill, satin, or filling-rib weave (13.13).

Brocatelle Jacquard patterned upholstery and drapery fabric; motifs are created with heavy warp yarns interlaced in a satin weave; ground is twill; extra yarns pad the motifs (13.14).

Browning Staining of pile yarns as water wicks upward from overwetted jute carpet and rug backing yarns.

Brushing Aligning pile surfaces using straight wires; introduces pronounced fabric nap or pile sweep.

Brussels Name used earlier for loop pile carpet woven on a Jacquard loom; now, all carpet woven on a Jacquard loom is called Wilton carpet.

Bulk or apparent volume See *apparent volume or bulk.*

Bulked continuous filament (BCF) Filament-length fiber given a multidimensional configuration to increase the apparent volume (5.1).

Bullion Fringe composed of metallic-colored strands; used as decorative trimming.

Bundle penetration Adhesive penetration of the pile yarns in tufted constructions; helps to prevent individual staple or filament fibers from being pulled out of the yarns and rubbed into fuzz and pills on the carpet surface.

Burlap Coarse, plain-weave fabric composed of jute fibers; used in the interior of upholstered furniture and as a primary or secondary backing with tufted floor coverings (22.2a).

Burling Repair of imperfections in textile floor coverings.

Burnt-out print Print produced with acid instead of dyestuff; weak acid is used to etch out or destroy an acid-degradable fiber in selected fabric areas, leaving a transparent ground composed of an acid-resistant fiber; also know as etched-out print or acid print (17.24).

Burnt gas fumes Such atmospheric gases as nitrogen dioxide and sulfur dioxide; may cause fading or color change with colored textiles.

Bursting strength Force (load) required to rupture or burst a knitted fabric.

Cable yarn Simple yarn formed by plying two or more cords.

CABO Acronym for Council of American Building Officials.

Café curtains Unlined window coverings used alone or in combination with draperies; frequently constructed with scalloped headings and hung by rings looped over a rod (16.1a and b).

Calendering Industrial ironing using heated and highly polished cylinders.

Calico Lightweight, plain-woven fabric characterized by small, colorful, printed motifs and solid-colored ground (17.1).

Candlewicking An embroidery technique in which the design motifs are created by the extensive use of French knots (9.7c); collectively, the knots create a recognizable pattern (9.8).

Candlewick yarn Four-ply yarns composed of unmercerized cotton.

Cane Long, hollow or pithy, bamboo-like grass retrieved from the rattan, a climbing palm; used in handwoven chair seats and Roman shades.

Cantonniére Rigid overhead window treatment mounted flush to the wall, framing the window; has a curved cornice and side panels that extend to the floor (16.9c).

Canvas, coarse Canvas with three to seven meshes per inch.

Canvas, double-mesh Canvas which has closely spaced pairs of warp and filling yarns; also known as penelope canvas.

Canvas, fine Canvas with 18 or more meshes per inch; used for petitpoint work (9.5).

Canvas, single-mesh Canvas which is plain woven.

Canvas embroidering See *needlepoint stitching.*

Cape Cod curtains Window treatment in which single-tier café curtains are combined with ruffled, tied-back panels; also known as cottage curtains (16.1h).

Carbonizing Using weak acid to degrade cellulosic matter (e.g., cockle burrs, twigs, in wool fleece).

Carded yarns Yarns spun of both long and short cotton fibers and having a relatively low degree of fiber alignment.

Carding Combing fibers to align them in the yarn production process.

Carpet Singular as well as plural form of term used to identify textile floor covering securely attached to the floor; carpets and carpeting are incorrect forms (20.1).

Carpet modules Floor coverings, generally 18-inches square, that are laid wall-to-wall; may be installed with no adhesive or with releasable or permanent adhesive (20.2).

Carpet winch Vessel used for dyeing full widths of carpet which is folded or plaited and fed into the dye liquor; a type of batch dyeing (8.7).

Cascade loop shade Window covering having horizontal tucks in the fabric panels; soft folds form when the shade is raised (16.15).

Cascades Nonrigid side window treatments composed of gathered fabric falling in folds of graduated length; normally hung behind ends of swagged valence.

Casement General term for curtain and drapery fabrics that have medium weight and some degree of transparency (17.14, 17.25, 17.26, 17.27).

Cashmere Fine, soft fiber retrieved from Cashmere goats.

Casing Opening formed by hemming the upper edge of window covering fabric and through which a rod is inserted (16.5a and b).

Cattlehair Natural material used earlier as a filling in upholstered furniture cushions and in carpet cushions.

CC system Cotton count system; used to indicate the size or count or number of yarns spun on the cotton yarn spinning system; gives the yarn count based on length per unit of weight; is an indirect yarn numbering system.

CDC Acronym for Centers for Disease Control.

Cellubiose unit The basis repeating unit in natural cellulose fibers.

Certification marks Coined names and stylized logos that may be used on the labels of end products that conform with fiber content specifications or performance specifications established by the owner of the mark.

CFR Acronym for Code of Federal Regulations.

Chain warp yarns Warp yarns used in machine-woven floor coverings (23.1).

Challis *(challie)* Plain-woven drapery lining fabric composed of spun yarns of rayon or acetate; highly drapable.

Char length The distance of fabric damage produced by flame in standard flammability test methods.

Cheeses Yarn packages.

Chemical washing Use of chlorine or acetic acid and glycerin to simulate the prized sheen and soft luster of older Oriental rugs that were dyed with natural rather than synthetic dyestuffs; also known as culturing and luster washing.

Chenille carpet Soft floor covering woven with chenille yarns as the pile yarns (23.9).

Chenille spread Bedspread fabric produced with closely spaced pile tufts inserted by tufting.

Chenille yarn Yarn-like strand cut from leno-woven fabric that has fine warp yarns and coarse filling yarns; fluffy strand is said to resemble a caterpillar (5.12).

Chintz *(glazed chintz)* Plain-woven fabric characterized by brightly colored floral or geometric motifs and high surface luster (17.2).

Chroma See *intensity.*

Chromophores Components of dyestuffs that are responsible for the quantity of waves reflected, influencing the value of the hue.

Circular braids Narrow, often decorative strands created by interlacing yarns or yarn-like strands around a textile cord.

Cleaning code Letter codes used with upholstery fabric to identify the recommended method of cleaning.

Clipped dot or spot See *dot or spot weave.*

Cloque Jacquard-woven, doublecloth upholstery fabric in which the back yarns are strategically interlaced to create the appearance of quilting stitches on the fabric face (13.20).

Cloth beam Cylinder on the loom that holds the woven fabric (6.3).

Coarse canvas See *canvas, coarse.*

Codes Mandatory practices concerned with the safety and well-being of the general population; they are laws enacted by federal, state, and local governments.

Cohesiveness The ability of textile fibers to adhere to one another mechanically.

Coir Fiber retrieved from husk of coconuts; used in pile layer of track-off mats (23.11).

Collagen Protein compound in leather fibers.

Colorants Dyestuffs used to color textiles.

Color characteristics Distinguishing features of colors, including hue, value, and intensity.

Colorfastness Ability of a colorant or dyestuff to retain its original color characteristics.

Color sealed Term used to identify solution-dyed fibers.

COM See *customer's own material.*

Combed yarns Yarns spun of long cotton fibers having a relatively high degree of fiber alignment.

Combing Combing fibers to align them and to separate the shorter staple-length fibers in a yarn production process.

Combustible Material capable of undergoing combustion.

Combustion Chemical process in which combustible material combines with oxygen to produce heat and light (flame).

Combustion, flameless Combustion in which no flames are evident (e.g., glowing, smoldering).

Combustion, flaming Combustion in which flame and heat are being produced.

Comforters Bed covering having a face fabric, lofty filling, and a backing fabric (29.11).

Commercial interiors Includes stores, shopping centers, offices, schools, hospitals, hotels and motels, libraries and public buildings, religious buildings, restaurants, penal institutions, and the like.

Commercial quilting See *quilting, machine stitching.*

Common names Names of natural fibers (e.g., wool, silk, linen, cotton).

Compacted selvage Selvage in which the number of warp yarns is relatively high to increase the compactness of construction (6.2c).

Completion Application of upholstery fabric so the pattern flows uninterrupted down the back pillows, the seat cushions, the seat boxing, the seat front, and the skirt (12.3).

Complex cords Decorative yarns composed of two or more complex ply yarns.

Complex plies Decorative yarns composed of two or more complex single or ply yarns (5.9).

Complex single yarns Decorative yarns composed of one complex yarn (5.7).

Complex yarns Decorative yarns having a base yarn, a fancy yarn, and/or a binder or tie yarn; may be single, ply, or cord (5.8).

Compressibility The ease with which a textile structure can be crushed or reduced in thickness.

Compressional loft Ability of a textile structure to recover from compression and regain its original loft; also known as compressional resiliency.

Compression deflection The extent to which a structure resists compression force (25.5).

Compression load deflection (CLD) The force required to deflect or compress a specimen assembly a given percentage of its original thickness; reported as the average number of pounds per square inch.

Compression loss The extent to which a structure fails to recover its original thickness after being compressed under a static load; also known as compression set.

Compressional resiliency See *compressional loft.*

Compression set See *compression loss.*

Compressive shrinkage treatment Mechanical treatment used to improve the dimensional stability of fabrics composed of cotton.

Conditioning, textile Placing test specimens in a controlled atmosphere of 70 + or − 2 °F and 65 + or − 2 % relative humidity for a minimum of 24 hours prior to measuring a given property.

Conduction Mechanism by which heat energy, electrical charges, and sound waves are transmitted through solids, liquids, and gases.

Conductors Materials, including textile fibers, that keep electrons flowing, minimizing their accumulation.

Consumer The person or corporation who ultimately pays for a product or service.

Continuous dyeing Dyeing operation that includes wetting the carpet, applying the dyestuff, steaming, washing, drying, and rolling up the dyed and dried goods; used for large quantities of greige goods.

Continuous filament See *filament.*

Contract design The design of commercial spaces.

Convection Transmission of heat energy by air movement.

Conventional selvage Selvage formed by the continuous filling yarn being turned at each edge to produce a finished, nonraveling edge (6.2a).

Converters Textile finishers; convert greige goods into finished fabric.

Convertible sofa bed An upholstered sofa with a mattress concealed under the cushions.

Copolymer Fiber composed of two different monomer units (e.g., polyester, nylon 6, 6).

Corduroy Woven or tufted fabric whose cut pile surface has a pronounced nap; used for covering furniture, windows, and walls (6.15, 6.16, 6.18, 13.21).

Cord yarn Simple yarn formed by plying two or more plied yarns (5.6).

Core-spun yarn Yarn formed by spinning staple-length fibers around an elastomeric filament.

Corium The central portion of hides and skins; composed of a network of interlaced bundles of tiny fibers (13.26).

Corkscrew yarn Complex yarn formed by twisting a fine yarn around a heavy yarn; also known as spiral yarn (5.9d).

Cornice Rigid overhead treatment mounted over drapery heading and hardware (16.9a).

Cottage curtains See *Cape Cod curtains*.

Cotton felt Three-dimensional batting structure used as a filling in upholstered furniture.

Cotton spinning system Spinning system used to spin cotton fibers into yarns.

Courses Crosswise rows of loops in a knitted fabric (7.5).

Covered-core yarn Yarn formed by wrapping or braiding filaments around an elastomeric filament.

Covering power The ability of a textile structure to cover or conceal a surface without undue weight.

CPSC Acronym for Consumer Product Safety Commission; federal agency concerned with the safety of most consumer products; governs marketing of consumer products, including flammable textiles.

Crackle effect Striated appearance seen with batik prints; created by cracking the wax to allow the dye liquor to run through the cracks (8.12).

Crash A plain-woven fabric composed of coarse, irregular yarns spun from linen; constructed into dish towels for the lint-free drying of glassware.

CRE Acronym for constant-rate-of-extension.

Crease resistance Misnomer: creases are planned, wrinkles are not.

Creel frame Device used to hold the yarn cheeses as the warp yarns are wound onto the warp or loom beam (6.4).

Cretonne Plain-woven drapery fabric characterized by large, printed motifs and a dull surface.

Crewel yarns Fine, two-ply strands composed of wool; used in hand embroidery.

CRT Acronym for constant-rate-of-traverse.

Critical radiant flux (CRF) Numerical value determined by converting the distance of flame spread to watts per square centimeter after completion of the flooring radiant panel test; indicates the minimum heat energy necessary to sustain burning of a floor covering that leads to flame propagation (11.6).

Crocheting Interlooping yarns with one needle, in contrast to interlooping yarns with two needles as in knitting.

Crocking Transfer of color from one material to another as a result of surface rubbing.

Cross-sectional shape Lateral shape of textile fibers (e.g., round, trilobal) (4.1a, b, and c).

Cross dyeing Variation of piece dyeing in which a fabric composed of two or more different and strategically placed fibers is immersed into a dyebath formulated with dyestuffs that will be selectively accepted and rejected; produces a multicolored fabric from one immersion process; also known as differential dyeing.

Crushed velvet Velvet characterized by varied levels of surface luster (13.23).

Crystalline Parallel arrangement of polymer chains anchored by lateral bonds (4.7).

Culturing See *chemical washing.*

Cuprammonium Conventional rayon fiber.

Curing Salting the raw hides to retard bacterial action; initial process of converting hides and skins into leather.

Curtains General term for textile window covering fabrics hung without linings (16.1).

Curtain tenders See *batons.*

Customer's own material (COM) Textile or non-textile fabric supplied to end-product manufacturers by consumers.

Cystine An amino acid found in wool fibers.

Damask Jacquard-patterned upholstery and drapery fabric; motifs have plain, filling-rib, or sateen interlacings; ground is satin or twill weave (13.10, 13.11).

Damask, double Jacquard-patterned tablecloth woven using eight harnesses.

Damask, single Jacquard-patterned tablecloth woven using five harnesses.

Dead and buried yarns Yarns carried in the back portion of a Wilton carpet; contribute weight and resiliency (23.5).

Deck Portion of furniture frame that supports the seat cushions.

Degree of polymerization The extent to which monomers link to form polymers; the average number of monomer units in the polymer chains of a fiber.

Delamination Separation of attached layers in a textile structure (22.8).

Delamination strength The force required to separate the primary and secondary backings of tufted floor coverings.

Delusterants Titanium dioxide particles added to the polymer solutions of manufactured fibers (4.1f).

Den number Yarn number determined with the denier system; numerically equal to the weight in grams of 9,000 meters of the strand.

Denier Direct yarn numbering system; gives weight per unit of length measurement of a fiber or yarn.

Density Mass or amount of matter per unit of volume of a fiber or other textile structure; reported as pounds per cubic inch or grams per cubic centimeter.

Density factor Product resulting from the multiplication of yarn size, needle count, and stitches per inch used in a pile floor covering (22.11).

Density index See *density factor.*

Dents Openings in the reed through which the warp yarns are threaded; help to keep the warp yarns aligned and ensure grain straightness (6.3).

Dents per inch Number of openings per inch in a reed; determines compactness of the warp yarns.

Design elements Color, texture, pattern, light, form, and shape; provide a way to evaluate aesthetic considerations for an abstract problem.

Design principles Balance, harmony, rhythm, emphasis, contrast, scale, and proportion; provide a way to evaluate aesthetic considerations for an abstract problem.

Dhurrie (durrie, durry) rugs Flat, hand-woven rugs having a plain, twill, or tapestry interlacing (24.9).

Differential dyeing See *cross dyeing*.

Dimensional stability The ability of a textile structure to maintain its size and shape after use and care.

Dimity Sheer, warp-rib woven curtain fabric (6.9, 17.6).

Dimout Partial blackout, i.e., partial reduction of the level of light transmission.

Directional pile lay See *nap*.

Direct yarn numbering system Systems that give the yarn number as weight per unit of length; as yarn number increases, yarn size increases; examples include the denier and tex systems.

Discharge printing Operation in which fabric is piece dyed before the selective application of an agent that will remove the dye, creating undyed motifs and a solid colored ground (17.20).

Discontinuous dyeing Dyeing operation in which the wet carpet must be removed from the dyeing machine and dried elsewhere; also known as batch dyeing.

Discretionary income Income available to spend on the basis of want rather than need.

Disposable income Income available to spend after taxes; also known as real income.

Disposable toweling Toweling produced by bonding webs of fibers; may be reinforced with a scrim (28.4).

Distortion of yarn Yarns shifting, slipping, or sliding over others, producing areas having different levels of transparency (9.14).

Disulfide cross links Linkages (—S—S—) contained in cystine that are attractive to moth and carpet beetle larvae.

Dobby weave Decorative weave requiring many harnesses; distinguished by small, geometric woven-in motifs (17.9).

DOC Acronym for Department of Commerce.

Doctor blade Squeegee-like metal blade used to clean nonengraved portion of metal-covered printing rollers or to transfer dye liquor from a roller to the surface of greige goods (8.15).

Document fabrics Accurate reproduction of historic fabrics using true colors, replicated patterns, and the same fiber composition and fabric construction.

Doilies Small, decorative tabletop accessories; used under artifacts, fruits, cheeses, etc., or for decoration; often lace (30.4).

Dope dyeing See *solution dyeing*.

Dot or spot weave Surface figure weave in which extra yarns interlace with the base yarns to create a small motif; yarns floating between the motifs may be clipped away (unclipped dot or spot weave) or left in place (unclipped dot or spot weave) (13.9, 17.11).

Dotted swiss Voile curtain fabric having small flocked or woven-in dots (17.17).

Doublecloth construction technique Fabrication in which pile yarns are alternately interlaced in an upper fabric and a lower fabric; as the weaving progresses, the pile yarns joining the two fabrics are cut, resulting in two lengths of fabric (6.17).

Doubleknit fabric Interlocked-stitched fabric with relatively large loops; nonrun and stable (7.7).

Double-mesh (penelope) canvas See *canvas, double mesh*.

Double rubs A forward and backward oscillation of the cylinder used in the Wyzenbeek test method; equivalent to one cycle (14.7).

Down The undercoating of waterfowl, consisting of clusters of light, fluffy filaments.

Down, all Labeling term used only when product contains only down.

Down fiber The detached barbs from down and plumules and the detached barbs from the basal end of waterfowl quill shaft, which are indistinguishable from the barbs of down.

Downstream segments Firms and personnel in the latter part of the production pipeline (e.g., end-product producers), in contrast to those in the earlier portion of the pipeline (e.g., fiber manufacturers).

DPF Denier per filament.

Drapability The ability of a fabric to form graceful configurations, such as folds in curtain and drapery panels.

Draperies Lined textile fabric panels hung to drape gracefully at windows (16.3).

Drapes A verb meaning "hangs gracefully"; incorrectly used as a synonym for draperies.

Draw curtains Unlined window treatment panels that are drawn in one direction, stacking on one side of the window, or in two directions, stacking on both sides of the window (16.1b, 16.3a and b).

Drawing Stretching a manufactured filament to improve its interior order, especially to increase the orientation of the polymer chains.

Drawing out In yarn spinning, combining several slivers into one new sliver.

Drop-match patterns Patterns that repeat themselves diagonally across the width of the carpet; may be half-drop (27.16) or quarter-drop (27.17).

Drops The portion of a bedspread that hangs vertically from the bed surface to the floor; may be tailored, ruffled, gathered, or shirred (29.9).

Drop wire Device used on industrial looms to stop the weaving when a warp yarns ruptures.

Drill Relatively heavy twill-weave fabric used as a backing with vinyl wall coverings.

Drum dyeing Rotating leather in dye liquor rotating in large vessels.

Dry extraction cleaning Absorbent powder that contains water-based cleaning fluids or detergents and a small amount of solvent is sprinkled on the carpet, releasing and absorbing the soil, which is subsequently removed by vacuuming (27.19).

Dry foam cleaning Water-based shampoo in foam form is sprayed onto the carpet, mechanically worked in, and the soil-foam residue is subsequently removed by vacuuming (27.20).

Dry spinning A volatile solvent is used to dissolve the polymer compound, then evaporated after extrusion to allow the filaments to solidify.

Duck Plain- or 2 x 1 basket-woven fabric composed of two-ply yarns; used for exterior awnings.

Duplex printing Printing on both sides of a fabric.

Durable press finishing Chemical treatment used to improve the resiliency of fabrics composed of cellulose fibers; creates strong cross-links (9.17).

Dust ruffles Fabric panels dropping from the top of box springs to the floor.

Duvet Comforters filled with down.

Dye beck Pressure cooker-like vessel used in dyeing (8.3).

Dye liquor Combination of dyestuff and relatively large quantities of water; used in immersion dyeing operation.

Dye migration Movement of dye liquor through fabric; necessary for uniform application of the dye; creates uneven level of dye intensity if in-use cleaning agents or procedures promote such movement.

Dye paste Combination of dyestuff and relatively small quantities of water; used in printing operations.

Dye pigments Insoluble dyestuffs that may be added to polymer solutions prior to spinning.

Dyes or dyestuffs Color-producing compounds that are normally soluble in water.

Dyed-in-the-wool Old adage meaning deeply ingrained and staunchly dedicated; arose from the observation that wool fibers dyed prior to spinning had richer and deeper colors than those produced by dyeing yarns or fabrics.

Dyeing ranges Systems used in continuous dyeing operations, includes units for all stages of the dyeing and drying operation.

Edge abrasion Wear caused by friction where the fabric is folded, as is the case at seamlines.

Effective face weight Weight of the pile yarns in the wear layer of a textile floor covering, not in the backing.

Effect yarn Fancy or decorative yarn found in complex decorative yarns (5.8).

Egress The act of leaving an interior in the event of fire; the exit way or means of egress should be free of obstructions.

Egyptian cotton Cotton fiber which originated in the Nile Valley; up to 1½ inches in length.

Elasticity The ability of a textile structure to be extended and to recover from the extension; also known as stretchability.

Elastic modulus Initial resistance to deformation stress exhibited by a fiber or other textile structure.

Elastic recovery The extent to which a fiber, yarn, or fabric recovers from extension.

Electrical conductivity The relative ease with which a fiber conducts the flow of electrons.

Electrical resistivity The relative ease with which a fiber resists the flow of electrons.

Electromagnetic spectrum Range of waves of electromagnetic energy, from extremely short cosmic and gamma rays to relatively long radio waves (8.1).

Electrostatic flocking Using an electrostatic field to induce flock to embed itself into a fabric coating (13.28).

Elevator effect Euphemism for the sagging and shrinking of curtain and drapery panels composed of conventional rayon fibers when the level of relative humidity fluctuates; also known as hiking and yo-yo effect.

Elongation The ability of a fiber, yarn, or other textile structure to extend or elongate; normally measured and reported as percent elongation at the rupture point.

Embossing Mechanical treatment used to introduce convex and concave design forms to two-dimensional fabric.

Embroidering Hand or machine stitching of colored yarns in decorative patterns on a portion of a base fabric (9.7, 9.8, 17.19b, 29.8).

Emerizing See *sueding.*

End One warp yarn.

End-product producers/designers Members of the interior textile industry who design and manufacture textile end products for use in residential or commercial interiors.

EPA Acronym for Environmental Protection Agency; established to protect human health and safeguard the natural environment (air, water, and land), upon which life depends.

Epidermis The top layer of hides and skins (13.26).

Etched-out print See *burnt-out print.*

Even twill Twill fabric in which an equal amount of warp and filling are visible on the face of the fabric (6.10c).

Expanded polymer solutions Polymer solutions having air incorporated to increase the apparent volume.

Extrusion Mechanical spinning of manufactured filaments; polymer solution is extruded or forced through openings in a spinneret (3.5).

Eyelet Curtain fabric with holes surrounded by Schiffli embroidery (17.19b).

FAA Acronym for Federal Aviation Administration; controls the flammability of items used in airplanes.

Fabrication techniques Ways to make fabrics (e.g., weaving, knitting, felting, braiding, needlepunching).

Fabric count Numerical indication of compactness of construction; equal to the number of warp and filling yarns per square inch of greige goods; also known as thread count.

Fabric nap See *nap*.

Fabric openness The ratio of the open areas of a fabric to its total area (15.3).

Fabric panel Portion of a window treatment in which a number of fabric widths, and, if necessary, a partial width are seamed together (16.10a).

Fabric stylists Personnel who identify the aesthetic features preferred by contemporary consumers, interpret and forecast trends, and design fabrics that will meet end-use requirements and expectations.

Fabric weights Weights that are placed in the lower hem areas of fabric panels to improve the draping quality.

Face yarns Yarns in the face or pile portion of a fabric or floor covering (22.1).

Fade-Ometer® Equipment used in accelerated testing for lightfastness (18.4).

Fading Loss of or weakening of the original color characteristics.

Faille Filling-rib upholstery and drapery fabric with somewhat flat ribs that number approximately 36 per inch (13.3b).

False-twist coiling Texturing technique involving continuous twisting, heat setting, and untwisting; introduces apparent volume and bulk but little or no stretch (5.2a).

Feather fiber The detached barbs of feathers that are not joined or attached to each other.

Feathers The plumage or outgrowth forming the contour and external covering of fowl, which are whole in structure and have not been processed in any manner other than by washing, dusting, chemical treatment, and sanitizing.

Feathers, crushed Feathers that have been processed by a curling, crushing, or chopping machine, which has changed the original form of the feathers without removing the quill; the term also includes the fiber resulting from such processing.

Feathers, damaged Feathers that have been damaged by insects, or otherwise materially injured.

Feathers, land fowl Nonwaterfowl feathers derived from chickens, turkeys, and other land fowl.

Feathers, nonwaterfowl See *feathers, land fowl*.

Feathers, quill Feathers that are over 4 inches in length or that have a quill point exceeding ⁹⁄₁₆ inch in length.

Feathers, waterfowl Feathers derived from ducks and geese.

Federal Trade Commission (FTC) U.S. federal governmental agency empowered and directed to prevent "unfair methods of competition in commerce."

Felt Nonwoven fabric produced by felting shrinkage.

Felting shrinkage Intermeshing of the scales covering wool fiber that results in matting and shrinking of the yarns and fabric; caused by heat, agitation, and moisture.

Fenestration Design, arrangement, and proportions of the windows and doors in an interior.

Festoon Ornamental trimming draped over a valence or other overhead window treatment.

FFA Acronym for Flammable Fabrics Act.

FHA Acronym for Federal Housing Administration; has jurisdiction over the materials used in the interiors of such places as elderly and care-type housing, low-rent public housing projects, and structures insured by FHA.

Fiber cohesiveness Ability of fibers to adhere to one another; affected by such inherent features as the twist in cotton and the scales covering wool; may be introduced with texturing (5.3).

Fiberfill Loose, lofty masses of staple or tow used as filling for pillows; generally polyester.

Fiber dyeing Immersing loose masses of fiber into dye liquor; frequently used with wool fiber; also known as stock dyeing.

Fiber toughness The ability of a fiber to resist abrasion; determined by a combination of strength and elongation.

Fiber variant Manufactured fiber that is chemically related to other fibers in its generic class but distinguished by a structural feature, such as diameter or cross-sectional shape, or by the inclusion of a polymer additive.

Fibrillation Breaking off of minute slivers of glass from high-denier glass filaments as a result of flexing and abrasion.

Fibrils Tightly knit bundles of polymer chains in cotton and linen.

Fibroin Protein found in silk.

Fibrous batts 1. Three-dimensional arrangement of webs of fibers that can be bonded with adhesive or heat into essentially flat structures (e.g., nonwoven interfacing fabric) (7.10). 2. Three-dimensional arrangement of webs of fibers that are stabilized and used as filling or padding in upholstered furniture, quilts, or as carpet cushions (25.1a, 29.11).

Filament An extremely long textile fiber, measured in yards, meters, miles, or kilometers; also known as a continuous filament.

Filling-faced satin weave Interlacing pattern in which the filling yarns float over the warp yarns; also known as sateen weave (6.11b).

Filling knitting Fabrication in which fabric is produced by continuously interlooping one or more yarns from side to side, creating one course after another; also known as weft knitting (7.5).

Filling or weft shots Crosswise yarns in woven carpet; used in pairs in Axminster carpet (23.1, 23.2).

Filling pile fabric Fabric in which the pile layer is created with extra filling yarns (e.g., velveteen and corduroy) (6.15, 6.16).

Filling-rib weave Variation of the plain weave in which larger or grouped filling yarns create a ribbed or ridged effect in the crosswise fabric direction (13.3).

Filling yarns Crosswise yarns in woven fabric; also known as weft yarns and woof yarns (6.1).

Fill leakage The migration or penetration of the filling material through the outercovering; minimized by using a spunbonded interior lining fabric (29.11).

Film sheeting Nontextile fabric produced by forming polymer solutions into a thin film.

Fine canvas See *canvas, fine.*

Finials Decorative pieces attached to the ends of curtain and drapery rods.

Fireproof fiber A fiber that is unaffected by heat (e.g., asbestos).

Flameless combustion See *combustion, flameless.*

Flame propagation Flame spreading (e.g., from original source of ignition to other items within an interior) (11.3).

Flame-resistant fiber Fiber exhibiting relatively high decomposition and ignition temperatures.

Flame retardant Agents added to fibers to increase their relative flame resistance.

Flame spread Distance flame spreads from site of ignition; measured in several flammability test methods.

Flame yarn Complex yarn produced by twisting a simple yarn around a single slub yarn that has large and elongated areas of low twist (5.9b).

Flaming combustion See *combustion, flaming.*

Flammable fiber Fiber that is relatively easy to ignite and sustains combustion until it is consumed.

Flannel Plain- or twill-weave fabric lightly napped on both sides.

Flannelette Plain- or twill weave fabric lightly napped on one side.

Flashover Situation in which all combustible materials burst into flame (11.19).

Flat abrasion Abrasion of a textile while it is fairly flat, such as on the seat cushions of automobiles and interior furniture items.

Flat-bed screen printing Printing the textile surface by forcing dye paste through openings in a screen mounted above the surface; screens have been treated to resist flow through of the paste wherever the fabric is not to be printed (8.18).

Flat braid Narrow, often decorative strand formed by interlacing a minimum of three yarns or yarn-like strands (23.12).

Flaw Defect in finished fabric.

Flesh tissue The bottommost portion of hides and skins (13.26).

Flex abrasion Abrasion of a textile while it is bent or curved, such as on the arms and curved portions of seat and back cushions, as well as with that covering prominent welts.

Flexibility Pliability; improves with fiber fineness; needed for freedom of movement.

Flock Extremely short fibers.

Flocking Embedding extremely short fibers, known as flock, into an adhesive or resin compound (9.10, 13.28).

Flock or flake yarn Complex yarn having enlarged segments created by periodically binding thin bits of roving between plied single yarns.

Flokati (Flocati) rugs Long-pile wool floor coverings woven in Greece; after the pile is formed, the rugs are immersed in a pool of water beyond a waterfall where the swirling waters cause felting of the pile tufts (24.4).

Florocarbon compounds Agents used to lower the critical surface energy of fibers so dirt and lint do not adhere to their surface and fluids bead up rather than pass into the fibers.

Floss yarns Loosely twisted, six-ply strands composed of mercerized cotton; used in hand embroidery.

Flossa stick Stick used in weaving rya rugs; pile is formed over the stick to ensure uniform pile height (24.3).

Fluorescent compounds Agents that absorb invisible ultraviolet light and emit visible blue or violet light; used to neutralize the natural yellow hues of wool or yellowed laundered fabrics; create apparent whiteness and brightness; also known as optical brighteners.

Flying shuttle loom Loom having devices to hammer the canoe-like shuttle in the picking operation to send it "flying" through the shed (6.3).

FPLA Acronym for Fur Products Labeling Act.

Foot traffic units In floor coverings testing, the number of passes by human walkers, not the number of times each specimen is stepped on.

Frames The number of colors in a Wilton carpet is denoted by the number of frames (e.g., 3-frame, 4-frame).

Free-lay installation Installation of carpet modules or squares in which the modules are held in place by gravity, not by adhesive.

Frictional heat energy With floor coverings, for example, the rubbing of the soles on carpet and rug fibers creates frictional heat energy which causes negatively charged electrons to transfer from the fiber surfaces to the body.

Friezé (*frisé*) 1. Upholstery fabric produced by an over-the-wire construction technique; characterized by small loops that may be cut or uncut (13.24). 2. Name assigned to pile floor covering surfaces composed of yarns of maximum twist (20.7d).

Frostiness Absence of dye on yarn tips; planned and executed by gum printing operations.

Frosting Loss of color as a result of abrasion-induced fiber loss.

FTC Guides for the Household Furniture Industry See *Guides for the Household Furniture Industry*.

Fugitive dye Textile colorant exhibiting poor colorfastness.

Full-grain leather Leather having unaltered grain markings.

Fulling Conversion process used to encourage yarns in fabrics composed of wool to relax and shrink, resulting in a more compact fabric.

Fullness Yardage added when calculating the measurement of the fabric panels.

Full-scale testing Flammability testing done in facilities constructed to replicate a room or a corridor.

Full warranty See *warranty, full*.

Fume fading Color change typically seen with acetate dyed blue, brown, or green with disperse dyestuffs and exposed to oxides of nitrogen or sulfur; blues turn pink, browns turn reddish, and greens turn brownish yellow; can be avoided by solution dying the fibers; also known as gas fading and atmospheric fading.

Fungi Extremely simple vegetative plant forms, such as molds and mildew; they feed on cellulosic fibers and sizing, producing stains and odors and weakening and rotting fibers; also referred to as microbes.

Fused selvage Selvage in which the ends of the filling yarns, which must be composed of thermoplastic fibers, are heated to fuse them together; often used with water-jet looms.

Fusion bonding Fabrication technique in which pile yarns are embedded into a vinyl compound coating a base fabric (23.10).

Fusion printing Using heat to secure colored acrylic resins to the surface of glass fiber fabrics.

Futons Flexible mattresses typically filled with cotton batting.

Galloon Narrow, tape-like length of trimming; often contains metallic strands.

Gas fading See *fume fading*.

Gasfastness Stability of colorants when exposed to gases.

Gassing-off Period of time that allows the gases and pollutants from new furnishing and finishes to permeate the air while the space is still vacant; ensures less toxicity for the occupants.

Gauge 1. Fractional distance between needles on tufting machines; reported in whole-number fractions. 2. Number of loops per inch of width in knitted constructions. 3. Thickness of polymer film sheeting.

Gauze See *theatrical gauze*.

Gear crimping Texturing process in which intermeshing gears introduce a planar or two-dimensional crimp to filaments; used to improve fiber cohesiveness (5.2d).

Generic class Class or name of manufactured fibers; defined in terms of chemical composition (e.g., nylon, polyester, acetate, acrylic, spandex).

Genuine suede Suede produced by processing the flesh side of hides and skins.

Ghiordes knot Hand-tied knot used in the production of rya rugs and some Oriental rugs; also known as Turkish knot (24.2b).

Gimp yarn Yarn formed by spirally wrapping one yarn around another, or by braiding three or more strands around one central yarn; interior yarn is completely covered and outer yarns are often metallic strands.

Gingham Plain-weave fabric having narrow bands of colored yarns alternating with equal sizes of bands of white yarns in both the warp and filling directions; bands range in width from ⅛ inch to 1 inch (4.11).

Ginning Mechanical process used to separate cotton fibers from the cotton seeds.

Glass curtains Sheer curtains hung next to the window glass; may or may not be composed of glass fiber; also known as sheers.

Glass transition temperature Temperature at which lateral bonds within a fiber are disturbed, allowing the position of the polymer chains to be shifted.

Glazed chintz See *chintz*.

Glazed leather Leather having a high gloss created by the application and polishing of resins, waxes, or lacquer-based compounds.

Glazing Finishing treatment in which glue, shellac, or resin is added to fabric to create a hard, high shine. See also *chintz*.

Glowing See *combustion, flameless*.

Glue-down installation Installation of carpet or carpet modules in which a permanent or releasable adhesive is used; no pad is used; provides greater stability when rolling traffic is present.

Goose-eye twill Dobby-woven upholstery fabric with small, diamond-shaped motifs said to resemble the eyes of a goose (13.8c).

Grain markings The pores that are exposed when the hair is removed from hides and skins.

Grain straight Characteristic of woven fabric in which all warp yarns are parallel and all warp and filling yarns cross at right angles (6.1).

Grams per denier Indicates force per unit of linear density necessary to rupture a fiber, yarn, or thread; also gpd and g/den.

Grams per tex Indicates force per unit of linear density necessary to rupture a fiber, yarn, or thread; also gpt and g/tex.

Grassing Using sunshine to bleach fabrics of linen.

Green standard A guide to environmentally safe products.

Greige goods Unfinished fabrics.

Grin Exposure of the backing in floor covering with low pile construction density (20.5).

Grospoint Upholstery fabric produced by an over-the-wire construction technique; has larger loops than friezé; often used to cover office desk chairs (13.25).

Growth Unrecovered elongation.

GSA Acronym for General Services Administration; oversees the selection of materials for federal facilities.

Guide bars Devices used in warp knitting to position the yarns around the hooks of the needles; as the number of guide bars is increased, the complexity of the interlooping can be increased.

Guides Collection of labeling provisions issued by the FTC; serve to inform members of a limited portion of the interior textile industry how to avoid engaging in unfair and deceptive labeling practices; advisory in nature.

Guides for the Feather and Down Products Industry Labeling guidelines that include definitions of terms and recommended procedures for labeling products filled with feather and down.

Guides for the Household Furniture Industry Labeling guidelines that include advisory practices regarding disclosure of the composition of furniture.

Gum printing Application of a gum compound to the tips of pile yarns prior to dyeing to prevent dye absorption and migration; develops a frosted appearance.

Gypsum A high-density, uncrystallized plaster used to coat the back of open-weave burlap wall covering.

Hackling Aligning linen fibers prior to spinning.

Hand The tactile qualities of a fabric, perceived by touch; also known as handle; terms relating to the hand of fabrics may be reviewed in ASTM D 123 Standard Terminology Relating to Textiles, Annex A3.

Hand embroidering See *embroidering*.

Harnesses Devices on looms that support the heddles and form the shed (6.3).

Hawser yarn Simple yarn formed by twisting two or more ropes together.

Head covers See *antimacassars*.

Headings Treatments used at the top of curtain and drapery panels to finish the upper edge and distribute fullness evenly across the finished width (16.5).

Head rests See *antimacassars*.

Heat conductivity Rate at which a material conducts heat; reported as K-value; reciprocal of heat resistivity; synonymous with heat transmittance.

Heather Color styling in which two or more colors of fibers are uniformly distributed along the length of a spun yarn or in which two or more colors of filaments have been thrown.

Heat of combustion values Amount of heat energy generated by burning materials that could cause burn injuries as well as maintain the temperature required for further decomposition and combustion; reported as BTUs/lb.

Heat resistivity Rate at which a material resists heat flow, that is, how effectively it insulates and prevents heat exchange; reported as R-value; reciprocal of heat conductivity.

Heat sensitivity See *thermoplasticity*.

Heat setting Use of heat to stabilize thermoplastic fibers, improving their dimensional stability and that of yarns and fabrics composed of them; also improves resiliency.

Heat transfer printing Transfer of dyestuff from printed paper to fabric surface; heat is used to cause the dyestuff to sublime, that is, change from a solid on the paper to a gas to a solid on the fabric (8.23).

Heat transmittance See *heat conductivity*.

Heddles Devices on looms through which the warp yarns are threaded; the threading and shedding patterns determine the interlacing pattern (6.3).

Held-back draperies Window treatment in which the panels are held to the side by such devices as cords, chains, and medallions.

Herringbone 1. Variation of the basic twill weave in which the direction of the visual diagonal is continually reversed (6.10c). 2. Upholstery fabric produced with a herringbone weave (13.6).

Hides Animal hides retrieved from such large animals as deer, horses, and cattle.

High-low Name given to some multilevel cut and loop carpet surface textures; the higher tufts may have the appearance of shag textures (20.7i).

High surface tension   See *surface tension.*

Hiking   See *elevator effect.*

Hoghair   Natural material used earlier as a filling material in upholstered cushions.

Hollow fibers   Manufactured fibers engineered to have hollow interiors for insulation without undue weight (29.4).

Homespun   1. Another name for the plain weave. 2. Plain-woven upholstery and drapery fabric composed of heavy, coarse yarns that resemble hand-spun yarns (13.1a).

Homophones   Polymers composed of one type of monomer (e.g., polyethylene).

Honeycomb cellular shade   Window treatment composed of spunbonded polyester fabric which is permanently pleated and paired to create a single- or double-cell structure with an insulating layer of air (16.14a).

Hopsacking (*hopsack*)   Plain- or basket-woven upholstery fabric composed of irregular yarns and resembling sacks used to gather and store hops (13.1b).

Horsehair   Natural material used earlier as a filling in upholstered cushions.

Hot water extraction cleaning   Properly diluted shampoo is driven into the pile as a spray by high-pressure jets; it is then immediately extracted by the vacuum component of the machine; also called steam extraction (27.22).

Houndstooth check   Broken-check motif said to resemble the tooth of a dog; produced by interlacing different colors of strategically placed yarns in a twill weave (13.4).

Household textiles   Textile products used in residential interiors, including beddings, towelings, and such tabletop accessories as napkins, tablecloths, and runners.

Huck toweling (*buckaback*)   Toweling woven on a dobby loom and having small filling floats that improve the drying efficiency of the towel (28.3).

Hue   Color (e.g., blue, red, green, yellow).

Hydrophilic fiber   Fiber having strong attraction for water; also known as water-loving fiber.

Hydrophobic fiber   Fiber having low attraction for water; also known as water-hating fiber.

IAQ   Acronym for indoor air quality.

ICBO   Acronym for International Conference of Building Officials; publishes the Uniform Building Code.

ICC   Acronym for International Codes Council; seeks to establish a single coordinated set of national codes.

IFI   Acronym for International Fabricare Institute; provides education, research, legislative representation, and industry-specific information for its members.

Ignition temperature   Temperature at which a combustible material combines with oxygen, igniting to produce heat and such other combustion by-products as light and smoke; also known as kindling temperature.

Ikat print   Hand print produced by artisans who tie off selected areas of bundled warp yarns and dye them prior to weaving (8.14).

Impact and structurally borne sounds   Sounds generated by impacts, such as walking, jumping, dropping items on the floor, etc.; concern is for their transmission as noise to interior spaces below.

Impact insulation class (*IIC*)   Numerical value used to indicate the effectiveness of a floor, carpet, cushion, or combination in reducing noise transmission; IIC values are roughly equal to the INR values plus 51.

Impact noise rating (*INR*)   Numerical value used to indicate the effectiveness of a floor, carpet, cushion, or combination in reducing noise transmission; INR values are roughly equal to IIC values minus 51.

Implied warranty   See *warranty, implied.*

Indirect yarn numbering systems   Systems in which the yarn number is determined as the length per unit of weight; as yarn number increases, size decreases; examples include the cc system, ll system, wc system, and wr system.

Inflation Demand exceeds supply and prices rise.

Inherent color Natural color of fibers; may be retained for their natural beauty or removed to avoid interference with fashion colors.

Initial cost Includes such variables as product price, accessories prices, fees for design professional, delivery charges, and installation charges.

Institutional textiles Products such as beddings, towelings, and tabletop accessories designed and selected for use in such hospitality settings as motels, hotels, and restaurants; in such care-type facilities as hospitals; and in such commercial settings as penal institutions and dormitories.

Institutional toweling Twill-woven toweling produced with brightly colored stripes on each long side and constructed into towels used in restaurants.

Insulation See *R-value.*

Insulators Materials, including textile fibers, that offer resistance to the flow of electrons, allowing them to "pool" on their surfaces, readily available for transfer.

Intensity Terms used to describe the purity or strength of a color (e.g., strong, weak); also known as chroma.

Interim maintenance Maintenance activities designed to assure a high level of appearance retention for an extended period of time and to delay the need for restorative procedures.

Interior acid rain Formed when vapor-phase moisture reacts with such gases as sulfur oxide and nitrogen oxide and forms weak sulfuric acid and weak nitric acid; may attack chemical bonds within fibers, rupturing the polymer chains and weakening the fibers.

Interlock stitch Interlooping yarns to create the appearance of two interknitted fabrics (7.7).

International Geometric Gray Scale for Color Change See *AATCC Gray Scale for Color Change.*

International Geometric Gray Scale for Evaluating Staining See *AATCC Gray Scale for Staining.*

In-the-muslin Furniture offered covered in muslin so it subsequently can be covered with a variety of decorative slipcovers.

In-use performance Level of serviceability of a textile product while being used by the customer or client.

ISO Acronym for International Organization for Standardization; engages in the development of standards to help foster international textile trade.

Jabots Nonrigid side window treatments composed of pleated fabric; lower end may be level or angled; normally hung in front of ends of swagged valance (16.8).

Jacquard weave Decorative weave in which independent control of each warp yarns provides for an infinite variety of sheds, and, thus, extremely complex interlacing patterns (6.14, 13.10–13.20, 17.15, 17.16).

Jaspé Descriptive of color style in which space-dyed yarns are woven in narrow, lengthwise bands to produce the effect of irregularly placed stripes; similar to strié.

Jersey stitch Filling knitting stitch distinguished by herringbone-like wales on the fabric face and crescents or half-moon courses on the fabric back; subject to running.

Jet beck Vessel used in the discontinuous dyeing of carpet in rope form; dye is introduced by jets (8.8).

Jet printing Using jets precisely to deliver dye liquor to create detailed designs and pattern repeats.

Jet spraying Using pressurized dye jets to spray dye liquor onto skeins of yarns.

Kapok A cellulosic fiber obtained from the seed pods of the kapok tree; use as a filling material has diminished.

Keratin Protein found in wool fibers; composed of 18 alpha amino acids.

Khilim (Kelim, Kilim) rugs Rugs woven in eastern European countries; may have stylized designs depicting flowers, animals, and other natural things; may have slits; reversible (24.5).

Kindling temperature See *ignition temperature.*

Knap yarn See *nub yarn.*

Knee-kicker Device used to grip and anchor the edges of carpet over the pins in tackless strips (27.1, 27.2b).

Knife-edge treatment Use of a plain seam to join the fabric pieces of upholstery cushions (12.4a).

Knit-de-knit crinkling Texturing technique in which multifilament yarns are first knitted into a fabric that is then heat set and, subsequently, de-knitted or unraveled; introduces a wavy configuration (5.2c).

Knit-de-knit space dyeing Combining jet spraying with knit-de-knit crinkling to produce a texturized, space dyed (variegated) yarn.

Knitting Interlooping yarns to create a fabric (7.1, 7.5).

Knop or knot yarn Complex yarns in which bits of tightly compacted and contrastingly colored fibers are incorporated into nubs.

Kraftcord Heavy, cord-like strands used in the back layers of woven floor coverings.

K-value Numerical value that reports the rate at which a material conducts heat.

Lambrequin Rigid overhead window treatment with a straight cornice and side panels that protrude some distance from the wall and extend some distance down the sides of the window (16.9b).

Lampas Jacquard-woven drapery fabric with detailed motifs created by combining satin and sateen interlacing patterns; often composed of two sets of identically colored warp yarns and one or more sets of variously colored filling or weft yarns; patterns are typical of those seen in the seventeenth and eighteenth centuries (17.16).

Lappet weave Surface-figure weave in which extra warp yarns are shifted laterally to create a zigzag surface pattern that resembles hand embroidery (6.12c).

Large-scale test methods Laboratory procedures which require large test specimens, in contrast to small-scale testing which requires small test specimens.

Latex foam Natural rubber or synthesized rubber having tiny, air-filled cells; used as an upholstered cushion filling material and as a carpet cushion material.

Launder-Ometer® Equipment used in accelerated testing for colorfastness to laundry and dry-cleaning agents (18.7).

Lay See *beater bar.*

Leaf Classifies cellulose fibers retrieved from the leaf portion of plants (e.g., abaca, banana, sisal).

Left-hand twill Twill interlacing in which the visual diagonal ascends from left to right (6.10b).

Leno-reinforced selvage Selvage in which a leno weave is used in the selvage areas (6.2d).

Leno weave Decorative weave in which paired warp yarns cross as they encircle and secure the filling yarns (6.13).

Level of openness Relative opacity of fabric; see also *fabric openness.*

Licensing programs Voluntary programs in which companies sell the right to use their company-owned processes.

Life-cycle cost (*LCC*) The total cost of a product during its expected use-life; includes initial purchase costs, installation charges, and long-term maintenance expenses; the total LCC values of several products may be amortized according to their respective life expectancies to show the annual use-cost of each.

Lightfastness Colorfastness to light.

Light reflectance factor (*LRF*) Numerical value indicating the percentage of incident light being reflected by a carpet surface; complement of the LRF indicates the percentage of incident light being absorbed.

Light transmittance value Numerical value indicating the amount of light passing through smoke generated during flaming and nonflaming conditions; values are converted into specific optical density values.

Limited warranty See *warranty, limited.*

Limiting oxygen index (*LOI*) Numerical value identifying the amount of oxygen required to support the combustion of a textile fiber.

Line Extremely long linen fibers, ranging from 12 inches to more than 24 inches.

Linear density Weight or mass per unit of length; denier and tex indicate linear density.

Linen Natural cellulose fiber retrieved from the flax plant (5.4).

Linens In earlier years, used as a collective term for sheets, towels, table cloths, napkins, and related products composed entirely or primarily of linen fibers; although the use of linen fiber in these goods has declined significantly, the term continues to be used.

Liquor ratio Ratio of pounds of dye liquor to pounds of greige goods.

Lisere Jacquard-patterned upholstery and drapery fabric; an extra set of warp yarns is used to produce detailed motifs in lengthwise bands, which are interspersed with satin-woven stripes (13.12).

Llama Hair fiber retrieved from the South American llama.

LL system Linen lea yarn numbering system; used to determine number of yarns produced on the linen spinning system; the ll number is equal to the number of 300-yard hanks of yarn produced from one pound of fiber.

Lofty Quality of bulk without weight.

Loom beam Cylindrical device used on the loom to hold the supply of warp yarns (6.3).

Longitudinal configuration Lengthwise shape and form of textile fibers (3.2).

Loop or curl yarn Complex yarns with open, airy loops (5.11d).

Loose-pillow styles Style of upholstered furniture having pillows that can be shifted or removed (12.5).

Lumen Hollow core of cotton fibers that becomes smaller as the fiber grows and matures (3.2b, 4.1d).

Luminosity See *value.*

Luster The brightness of a fiber, yarn, or fabric; affected by cross-sectional shape, surface texture, presence or absence of delusterants, finishing agents, directional pile lay, etc.

Luster washing See *chemical washing.*

Lyocell Manufactured cellulose-based fibers composed of cellulose derived from the eucalyptus tree; solvent-spun; generic name established in 1996.

Machine embroidering See *embroidering.*

Machine stitching See *quilting, machine stitching.*

Macramé Relatively heavy fabric constructed by knitting and twisting textile cords.

Magnuson-Moss Warranty Act U.S. Congressional law governing product warranties.

Malipol Mali technique in which pile yarns are incorporated into the chain-stitched layers of base yarns.

Manufactured fiber producers Members of the industry who manufacture usable fiber forms using monomers extracted or synthesized from natural compounds.

Marled Descriptive of the color styling produced by spinning together two differently colored rovings (8.2).

Marquisette Transparent, lightweight leno-woven curtain fabric composed of fine, monofilament yarns (17.13).

Martindale abrasion test method Method used to evaluate the flat abrasion resistance of fabric.

Matelassé Jacquard-woven upholstery fabric in which mutual interlacings between back and face yarns produce the appearance of quilting stitches; a third set of filling or weft yarns pads the motifs and emphasizes the quilt-like form (13.19).

Mattress covers Beddings designed to completely encase the mattress or to cover only the exposed surfaces; may have vinyl film sheeting to protect against moisture.

Mattress, foam-core Mattresses filled with a slab of rubber or urethane foam; support determined by the foam density.

Mattress, innerspring Mattress filled with metal springs that are anchored to one another with metal clips or encased in fabric and sewn together (29.1).

Mattress pads Beddings designed to provide extra cushioning and to protect the mattress; generally a multicomponent quilted structure.

Mechanical flocking Sifting flock through a screen to embed itself in a coated surface (9.10).

Medium canvas See *canvas, medium.*

Melt spinning Heat is used to dissolve the polymer compound; cold causes the filaments to solidify following extrusion.

Members of the trade Interior designers, architects, and other industry members who serve clients and consumers; have access to showrooms that are not open to the ultimate consumer.

Mercerization Treatment of cotton or linen fibers, yarns, or fabrics with NaOH and tension to improve the strength, absorption, or luster.

Meshes per inch Refers to one intersection of yarns used in canvas; number of meshes per inch indicates the compactness of construction.

Metallic yarns Yarns made of colored particles or colored foil encased in clear sheeting that is then slit into thin, yarn-like strands.

Methenamine tablet test Flammability test method in which a methenamine tablet is used as the ignition source, simulating a burning match, an ignited cigarette, or a glowing ember; also known as the pill test; designated ASTM D 2859; adopted in 16 CFR 1631 (11.5).

Microbes See *bacteria* and *fungi.*

Microscopic voids Minute tunnels or conduits that are lengthwise within fibers; deflect incident light waves, obscuring the appearance of soil (4.3c and d).

Migration Movement of dye through fabric; results in varied levels of intensity.

Mildew Growth caused by spore-forming fungi; may result in discoloration, odor, and fiber tendering.

Modern rugs Oriental rugs produced during the twentieth Century.

Mohair Hair fiber retrieved from Angora goat; often used in loop or curl yarns.

Moiré Finish characterized by a wood-grain or water-marked effect (9.3).

Moisture absorbency Ability of textiles to absorb moisture; affects dyeability, static buildup, cleanability.

Moisture regain values Calculations of the ability of fibers to absorb vapor-phase moisture; % moisture regain is determined by subtracting the dry weight of a specimen from its conditioned weight, dividing the result by the dry weight, and multiplying by 100.

Molas Textile accents created with a reverse appliqué technique (9.9).

Momie cloth A crepe-like fabric having an irregular, pebbled surface; used as tablecloths in commercial and institutional settings.

Monk's cloth Basket-woven fabric composed of coarse, irregular yarns; used for curtain and drapery treatments (17.5).

Monofilament yarn Simple yarn composed of a single filament; used in sheer curtain fabrics and as transparent sewing thread.

Monomer Basic building block of textile fibers; several monomers are linked end-to-end to form polymers.

Mordant Compound, usually metallic salt, used to increase the attraction between fibers and dyestuffs.

Moresque Descriptive term used to identify color effect of ply yarn formed by twisting different colors of single yarns.

Mosquito netting Transparent leno-weave fabric used as a curtain-like bed canopy in tropical climates, forming a barrier against mosquitoes.

Moth resistance Ability of wool fibers to resist attack by moth larvae; may be permanently incorporated by introducing a methane group between the sulfur atoms.

Multifilament yarn Simple yarn composed of several filaments.

Multi-tier café curtains Window treatment style in which tiers of café curtains overlap one another (16.1g).

Muslin Sheeting containing carded yarns and having a fabric count as low as 112 or as high as 140, although 128 is most common; may be backfilled with a large amount of sizing.

Mussiness Wrinkling of fabric; minimized with resins or heat setting.

MVSS 302 Acronym for Motor Vehicle Safety Standard No. 302; designed to reduce deaths and injuries to motor vehicle occupants caused by vehicle fires, especially those originating in the interior of the vehicle from sources such as matches or cigarettes.

Nailhead trimming Using nails to secure heavier upholstery coverings, such as genuine leather to framework (12.9).

NAILM Acronym for National Association of Institutional Linen Management; focuses on the efficient, proper, and economical maintenance of institutional linens.

Nap Directional orientation of yarns in pile layers; also known as pile sweep, pile lay, and directional pile lay (9.4).

Napery General term for tablecloths and napkins.

Naphthalene Agents used to make wool moth resistant.

Napkins, cocktail Small napkins, generally five inches square.

Napping Conversion operation in which fiber ends are teased to the surface, making it fuzzy, soft, and warmer.

Natural fiber suppliers Members of the industry who retrieve fibers from such natural sources as sheep, cotton and flax plants, and cocoons.

Natural rush Strands produced by twisting two or three flat cattail leaves together.

Needle count Number of needles per crosswise inch on tufting machines.

Needlepoint stitching Embroidering on canvas (9.5, 9.6).

Needlepoint weave Misnomer; used for Jacquard-woven tapestry having the appearance of hand-stitched needlepoint (13.16).

Needlepunching Fabrication techniques in which barbed needles are used to introduce a mechanical chain-stitch in a fibrous batting (23.13).

NEISS Acronym for National Electronic Injury Surveillance System.

Net Textile fabric having a relatively high level of fabric openness; constructed by raschel knitting or knotting and twisting (17.28).

New wool See *wool, new.*

NFPA Acronym for National Fire Protection Association; voluntary scientific association concerned with fire safety.

NFPA 101® Life Safety Code Publication of the NFPA; includes recommendations to reduce the extent of injury, loss of life, and destruction of property from fire; includes the design of egress facilities permitting the prompt escape of occupants from burning buildings or into safe areas within the buildings.

NFPA 701 Standard methods of fire tests for flame-resistant textiles and films; includes small-scale and large-scale test methods.

NHTSA Acronym for National Highway Traffic Safety Administration; oversees the flammability of items used in motor vehicles.

Ninon Sheer, plain-woven curtain fabric with every third warp yarn omitted (15.1, 17.3).

NIST Acronym for the National Institute for Standards and Technology.

Noil Relatively short cotton staples; separated and removed when producing combed cotton yarns.

Noise Unwanted sound.

Noise reduction coefficient (*NRC*) Numerical value that indicates the effectiveness of textile floor and wall coverings at absorbing sound.

Noise transmission Transmission of unwanted sound to other interior areas; especially important in multilevel structures, where impact sounds can be transmitted to the interior spaces below.

Noncellulosic fibers Fibers manufactured from compounds other than cellulose; includes such fibers as nylon, polyester, acrylic, and spandex.

Noncombustible fiber Fiber that does not burn or contribute significant amounts of smoke; may undergo pyrolysis.

Nonwaterfowl feathers Feathers derived from chickens, turkeys, and other land fowl.

Nonwoven fabric Fabric produced by stabilizing fibrous batts (7.10).

Nottingham lace Flat lace or net with warp and filling yarns; machine-made (30.4).

Nub yarn Complex yarn with tightly compacted projections created at irregular intervals along its length; also known as spot or knap yarns (5.10a).

Nylon cap Web of nylon fibers needlepunched into face of primary backing; color coordinated with pile yarn (22.3).

Off-grain Yarn alignment that exhibits filling bow (9.13a) or filling skew (9.13b).

Oil-borne stain Stain carried by an oily compound.

Oleophobic Oil-hating; resistant to oily soil.

Ombré Descriptive of the color styling produced by a gradual change in the level of intensity of a single hue.

Opacity Level of fabric openness in which light is not permitted to pass through fabric.

Opening and cleaning Initial operation in yarn spinning process; opening the bale of cotton and cleaning the fibers.

Optical brighteners See *fluorescent compounds.*

Optical properties Fiber characteristics such as color, luster, apparent whiteness and brightness, and soil hiding.

Organdy Sheer, plain-woven fabric having a parchment-like hand; produced by degrading cotton fibers with weak sulfuric acid; used in curtain treatments.

Organically grown Fibers cultivated on land that has been chemical free for a minimum of three years, and without the use of chemicals.

Oriental design rugs Machine-made rugs having traditional Oriental patterns; generally woven on an Axminster loom.

Oriental rugs Hand-woven rugs having hand-knotted pile tufts; see **Ghiordes knot** and **Sehna knot.**

Oriented Polymer arrangement in which the polymer chains are aligned in the direction of the long axis of the fiber (3.1b).

Oscillatory Cylinder Method Test method used to measure the abrasion resistance of textile fabrics; also known as ASTM D 4157 and the Wyzenbeek test method (14.7).

OSHA Acronym for Occupational Safety and Health Administration; has goal of saving lives and preventing and controlling disease, injury, and disability.

Osnaburg Plain-woven drapery fabric made of coarse, irregular yarns; originally produced in Osnaburg, Germany, for use in grain and cement sacks (17.4).

Ottoman Filling-rib woven upholstery fabric; has large, flat ribs of equal size and spacing or of unequal size and spacing (13.3d and e).

Outline quilting See *quilting, outline.*

Overdraperies Draperies that are hung in combination with sheers.

Overprinting Printing dye paste or pigments over an initial color application.

Over-the-counter fabric Refers to lengths of piece goods or fabric sold by retail distributors; also called OTC fabric.

Over-the-wire construction technique Fabrication in which the pile yarns are supported by wires during weaving; knives have smooth or sharp ends to leave the pile in loops or cut tufts as they are removed (6.19).

Ozone fading Color loss as a result of exposure to ozone.

Package dyeing Immersing yarns wound on perforated cylinders, that is, packages, into dye liquor held in a dye beck (8.3).

Package-injection technique Using astrojets to repeatedly "inject" packages of yarn with dye liquor.

Panné velvet Velvet with a pronounced nap, high surface luster, and a smooth hand; used for dining chair seats and upholstered furniture.

Pattern quilting See *quilting, pattern.*

Paragraph 25.853 Federal Aviation Administration standard intended to improve the crashworthiness and emergency evacuation equipment of airliners.

Partial blackout Reduction of the level of light transmission in which most of the incident rays are blocked.

Passementerié French term for trimmings, edgings, and the like.

Pattern drafts Graphic representations of interlacing patterns; also known as point designs and print designs (6.5, 6.8, 6.9b, 6.10. 6.11, 23.3).

Pattern repeat In patterned goods, a repetition of the full pattern of motifs and ground.

Pearl yarns Fine cords formed by plying three two-ply yarns composed of mercerized cotton; used in hand embroidering.

Percale Sheeting composed of combed yarns and having a fabric count as low as 168 or as high as 220; 180 is common.

Permanent press See *durable press.*

Permeability principle With respect to the acoustic value of carpet, cushions, and carpet/cushion assemblies, the more permeable the structures, the more efficiently they will absorb sound, lessening the level of noise within an interior; at the same time, the more permeable the structures, the more likely they will allow noise to be transmitted to interior spaces below.

Permethrin Compound used to modify the disulfide linkages in wool, making the fibers mothproof.

Persian knot Knot used in authentic Oriental rugs; can be tied to slant to the left or to the right; also known as the Sehna knot (24.2a).

Persian yarns Loosely twisted three-ply strands composed of wool; used in needlepoint stitching.

Pick One filling or weft yarn.

Picking The second step in weaving in which the filling yarn or pick is inserted through the shed.

Piece dyeing Immersing piece goods into dye liquor.

Pigment print Color styling in which opaque pigments are applied (17.23).

Pigments Insoluble dyestuffs.

Pile construction density Value indicating number of pile tufts per square inch; with tufted constructions, calculate by multiplying the needle count by the stitches per inch; with woven constructions, calculate by multiplying the pitch divided by 27 by the number of rows or wires per inch.

Pile height The length of the pile tufts above the backing.

Pile lay See *nap.*

Pile reversal Pile yarns crushed to lay in opposing directions; area appears as a large stain; also known as watermarking, shading, and pooling.

Pile sweep See *nap.*

Pile thickness Average thickness of the pile material above the backing.

Pile warp yarns Warp yarns used to form pile layer; used with velvet and most woven floor coverings; also known as face yarns.

Pile yarn integrity Ability of pile yarns to retain their original level of twist.

Pile yarn weight The weight of the yarns used in the wear layer and those portions of the pile yarns that extend into the backing layer; expressed in ounces per square yard.

Pile yarns See *face yarns.*

Pilling The formation of pills on the surface of textile fabrics.

Pillow, bedrest Pillow rest having back and arms.

Pillows, bed Pillows used for sleeping; generally 20 to 21 inches wide and varying in length.

Pillows, bolster Cylindrical or lozenge-shaped pillows that may be from 40 to 50 inches in length.

Pillows, boudoir Rectangular pillows, 12 inches by 16 inches; also known as breakfast pillows.

Pillows, breakfast See *pillows, boudoir.*

Pillows, European Pillows that are 12-inches square.

Pillows, king-size Bed pillows constructed for use with king-size mattresses; 37 to 38 inches long.

Pillows, neckroll Cylindrical pillows that range from 6 inches by 14 inches to 7 inches by 17 inches.

Pillows, queen-size Bed pillows constructed for use with queen-size mattresses; 30 to 31 inches long.

Pillow sham Decorative casing used for bed pillows for daytime display.

Pillows, round Decorative pillows that are normally 12 inches in diameter.

Pillows, standard Bed pillows that are constructed for use with twin- or double-size mattresses; 26 to 27 inches long.

Pillows, Turkish Decorative pillows which have gathered corners and are 16-inches square.

Pills Unsightly bunches or balls of fiber formed on fabric surfaces.

Pima cotton Cotton grown in the American southwest; fine and up to 1⅜ inches in length.

Pinned-up panels Window treatment style in which the fabric panels are held by two-piece, stylized magnets or by decorative pins that function like large tie-backs (16.4).

Pinsonic melding See *quilting, pinsonic melding.*

Pinwale piqué Dobby-woven curtain fabric with fine, lengthwise wales or ridges; also known as plain pique (17.9a).

Pitch Number of pile tufts per 27 inches of width in a woven floor covering.

Plain piqué See *pinwale piqué.*

Plain weave Simple interlacing in which warp and filling yarns alternately cross one another; also known as tabby weave and homespun weave (6.5).

Planting Periodically substituting a colored pile yarn for a basic pile yarn in Wilton carpet weaving; reduces quantity of buried yarns and, thus, yarn costs.

Plied slub yarn Complex ply yarns have a decorative slub yarn plied with a simple ply yarn or with a second slub yarn (5.9a).

Plumules Down waterfowl plumage with underdeveloped soft and flaccid quill with barbs indistinguishable from those of down.

Plush One level, cut pile surface texture; pile height ranges from 0.625 inch to 0.750 inch; also known as velvet and velvet plush (20.7b).

Ply yarn Yarn formed by twisting two or more single yarns (5.6, 5.9).

Pockets Areas in Jacquard-woven, doublecloth fabrics in which the face yarns and back yarns are not mutually interlaced (13.18).

Point designs See *pattern drafts.*

Pollutant gases Atmospheric gases such as oxides of nitrogen and oxides of sulfur that react with vapor-phase moisture to form weak acids; cause shade changes and fiber tendering.

Polymer Compound composed of extremely long, chain-like molecules.

Polymer additives Compounds added to polymer solutions to engineer specific properties (e.g., reduced luster, reduced static propensity, colorfastness). See also *additives.*

Polymer ribbons or tape Yarn-like structures produced by slitting film sheeting into long strands of the desired width (5.13).

Polyurethane foam Synthesized compound used as a filling for upholstered furniture and as a carpet cushion.

Pooling Collecting of electrons on fiber surfaces, making them readily available for transfer to shoe soles or other surfaces.

Pouf window treatment Drapery treatment in which tiers of bouffant or billowed-out areas are created by periodically gathering the fabric panels; also known as bishop's sleeve treatment (16.3e).

Power stretcher Device used to place uniform stretch over carpet in wall-to-wall installations (27.2a).

Preventive maintenance Protective cleaning procedures intended to capture soil and grit in track-off, funnel, and concentrated traffic areas.

Priscilla curtains Window treatment in which ruffled panels overlap at their upper edges and are held-back by ruffled tie-backs (16.1d).

Primary backing Base fabric into which pile yarns are tufted (22.1, 22.2).

Print design Graphic representation of color positions in textile structures (23.3).

Producer colored Term used to identify a solution-dyed fiber.

Product showroom Showroom where end-product manufacturers display their merchandise for members of the trade.

Project bid Detailed price listing of all products specified for a particular project.

Project specification A listing of multiple performance criteria that should lead to a single product specification.

Pure down See *all down*.

Pyrolysis Process in which high temperature causes the decomposition of textile fibers and other organic materials.

Quality control work Work undertaken by members of the industry to ensure the quality of their products; often use standard methods of testing and performance specifications.

Quill Device used to hold the filling yarns during weaving; also known as a bobbin (6.3).

Quilting, channel See *quilting, machine stitching.*

Quilting, machine stitching Commercial quilting using many needles to join separate components and to impart a surface pattern (9.12, 29.10).

Quilting, outline See *quilting, machine stitching.*

Quilting, pattern See *quilting, machine stitching.*

Quilting, pinsonic melding Commercial quilting using heat and sound waves to meld separate components at specific points; meld points simulate the appearance of sewn quilting stitches (9.11).

Quilting, shadow Hand quilting stitches are used to secure a sheer fabric over an applique(to join the layers and give a softened or shadowed appearance.

Quilting, trapunto Hand technique in which quilting stitches are placed around a single motif in a pattern repeat; subsequently, batting material is inserted into the quilted shape.

Quilts Multicomponent bed coverings usually having a face fabric, a fibrous or polyurethane batting, and a back fabric; layers are secured with hand or machine quilting stitches (29.10).

Quilts, crazy Quilts in which the fabric pieces are irregularly shaped and vary in size and color styling.

Quilts, patchwork Quilts in which the fabric pieces or patches are often square or rectangular (29.8).

Quilts, patterned Quilts in which several fabric pieces are shaped and sewn together to create a specific pattern repeat (29.7).

Radiant heat Heat that is transferred in the form of waves or rays.

Radiation Mechanism by which heat is transferred in the form of waves or rays.

Raffia A fiber obtained from the leaves of various species of palm trees; used in long, narrow, yarn-like bands to make woven placemats.

Railroad See *to railroad.*

Raised fiber surfaces Fabric surfaces that have been napped or brushed to raise fibers from yarns to give a soft, fuzzy hand; examples are flannelette and flannel.

Ramie Cellulosic fiber retrieved from stem portion of plants.

Random shear Multilevel, cut and loop pile in which the uppermost portions of some of the higher yarn tufts are sheared (20.7i).

Rapier Device used in picking to carry the filling yarn to the center of the shed where it is picked up by a second rapier and carried to the opposite selvage (6.6).

Raschel knitting Warp knitting operation using up to 30 guide bars; used for knitting fabrics ranging from hairnets to power net to rugs.

Ratiné yarn Complex yarn with small, uniformly spaced loops of equal size (5.11a and b).

Raw silk Silk from which the natural gum, sericin, has not been removed.

Reclined diagonal Visual diagonal in a twill weave fabric that falls at an angle less than 45 degrees to the fabric grain.

Recycled wool See *wool, recycled.*

Reed Comb-like device held by the beater bar; has openings through which the warp yarns are threaded (6.3).

Reeling Silk process in which the natural gum, sericin, is softened and skilled technicians collect the filaments and unwind the cocoons.

Regular diagonal Visual diagonal in a twill weave fabric that falls at an angle of 45° to the fabric grain (6.10a and c).

Regulatory agencies Municipal, state, or federal agencies that have jurisdiction to oversee and power to regulate product selection and/or marketing.

Relative humidity The proportion of vapor-phase moisture present in air to the maximum possible at a given temperature; expressed as a percentage.

Relaxation shrinkage Shrinkage of yarns; occurs when yarns recover or relax from strains imposed by manufacturing stresses.

Rep (*repp*) Filling-rib woven upholstery fabric with fine ribs, slightly larger than those seen in taffeta (13.3a).

Reprocessed wool See *wool, reprocessed.*

Residential interiors Interiors in private residences (e.g., mobile homes, apartments, condominiums, town homes, free-standing homes).

Residual shrinkage Shrinkage of fibers; fibers become progressively shorter during use and care.

Resiliency Ability of a textile structure to recover from deformations other than elongation; recovery from folding and bending is commonly referred to as wrinkle recovery and recovery from compression is commonly referred to as crush recovery; see also *compressional loft.*

Resin compounds Compounds used to improve the resiliency and dimensional stability of fabrics composed of cellulosic fibers.

Resist printing Immersing a fabric that has been selectively printed with an agent that will resist penetration of the dye liquor.

Restorative maintenance Maintenance involving overall or wall-to-wall cleaning.

Retting Process in which moisture and bacteria or chemicals are used to dissolve the binding agents, known as pectins, in the bark-like covering of flax stalks.

Reused or indirect light Light being reflected from light-colored walls, ceilings, doors, and furnishings.

Reused wool See *wool, reused.*

Reverse blends Fabrics that earlier had been composed of 65 percent polyester and 35 percent cotton are now composed of 65 percent cotton and 35 percent polyester; consumer demand brought about the shift.

Ribcord A warp-rib weave fabric used in roller shades (17.7).

Right-hand twill Twill interlacing in which the visual diagonal ascends from right to left (6.10a).

Rippling Process in which flax stalks are pulled through a coarse metal comb to remove the seeds, which will be processed to retrieve linseed oil.

Roller printing Using engraved copper-covered rollers to transfer dye paste to the surface of fabrics (8.15).

Rollgoods Soft floor coverings available in widths of 9, 12, and 15 feet and long lengths.

Roman shades Window coverings that hang flat at the window until pleats form when panels are raised; may be constructed of textile fabric or woven wood.

Room-fit rugs Loose-laid rugs designed or cut to come within one or two inches of the walls.

Room-size rugs Loose-laid rugs that are designed or cut to come within 12 inches of each wall.

Rope yarn Simple yarn formed by plying two or more cable yarns.

Rotary screen printing Printing textile surfaces by forcing dye paste through openings in cylindrical-shaped screens; selected areas of the screens are treated to resist flow through of the dye paste (8.19–8.22).

Routine maintenance Practices such as regular vacuuming to remove accumulated dust.

Rows per inch The number of crosswise rows of pile tufts per lengthwise inch in Axminster and chenille floor coverings.

Ruffled, tie-back curtains Window treatments in which ruffled panels do not cross at their upper edges (16.1d).

Rug Soft floor covering that is loose-laid on floor or over wall-to-wall carpet.

Runner A long, narrow form of a room-fit rug installed in hallways and on stairs (27.6).

R-value (*R-factor*) Numerical value indicating how effectively a structure resists heat flow, that is, how effec-

tively it insulates and prevents heat exchange; R-value equals the thickness of the structure divided by its K-value.

Rya rugs Hand-knotted rugs; originated in Scandinavian countries; pile may be from one to three inches (24.3).

Rya stick See *flossa stick*.

Salvage maintenance Maintenance procedures used for extremely soiled carpet or for removing built-up residue.

Sash curtains Window treatment in which the panels are anchored at their upper and lower edges; typically used on French doors (16.1c).

Sateen 1. Lining fabric produced with a sateen interlacing. 2. Variation of basic satin weave in which filling yarns float, that is, interlace infrequently, on the face (6.11b).

Satin Weave in which the warp yarns float or pass over a minimum of four filling yarns (6.11a).

Savonnerie rugs French Oriental rugs originally made in a factory used earlier for the production of soap; distinguished by classic designs and soft pastel colors (24.1).

Saxony One level, cut pile surface texture; pile height ranges from 0.625 to 0.750 inches; yarn twist is stabilized by heat setting (20.7c).

SBCCI Acronym for Southern Building Code Council International.

Scatter rugs Small rugs, often 2 feet by 3 feet; often decorative accents.

Schreinering Calendering process in which etched rollers impart minute diagonal "hills and valleys" into the fabric surface; gives soft luster.

Screen printing See *flat-bed screen printing* and *rotary screen printing*.

Scrim Flat woven fabric with low fabric count; used as backing in tufted floor coverings and as reinforcing layer in needlepunched carpet, hair cushions, and spunbonded fabrics (22.2a, 25.1a, 25.3).

Sculptured Multilevel cut and loop pile surface texture; in most cases, the higher loops are all cut and the lower loops are all uncut (20.7i).

Scutching Linen processing in which the degraded woody core of the flax plant is removed from the linen fiber bundles.

Sea grass Yarn-like structure produced by twisting plied strands of grass into a cord; also known as Chinese grass and Hong Kong grass.

Sea Island cotton Variety of cotton grown originally off the coast of Georgia; up to 2½ inches in length.

Secondary backing See *scrim.*

Seed fibers Natural fibers retrieved from the seeds of plants (e.g., cotton, kapok, coir).

Seed yarn Complex yarn with tiny nubs (5.10b).

Sehna (*Senna*) knot Hand-tied knot used in the production of some authentic Oriental rugs; also known as Persian knot (24.2a).

Self-deck treatment Use of the exposed outercovering fabric to cover the deck.

Self-extinguishing fiber Fiber that stops burning when the source of ignition heat is removed.

Selvages Narrow band on each side of a woven fabric; see also *compacted selvage, conventional selvage, leno-reinforced selvage,* and *tucked-in selvage* (6.2).

Semi-antique rugs Oriental rugs woven during the latter part of the nineteenth century.

Serging Machine overcasting (30.7).

Sericin Natural gum binding silk filaments into a cocoon.

Set-match patterns Patterns that repeat themselves across the width of carpet or wallpaper; the crosswise repeats may be fully completed or partially completed (27.14, 27.15).

SFU Acronym for standard fading unit.

Shade Color feature produced by adding a compound known to absorb all wavelengths, creating black, to a colorant, decreasing its value and lumninosity.

Shade changes Fading of original hue after exposure to such things as sunlight, laundry, and gases; may be evaluated, for example, with the AATCC Gray Scale for Color Change (14.10).

Shading See *pile reversal.*

Shading coefficient (S/C) Numerical rating that indicates light transmission in relation to temperature flow; calculated by dividing the total amount of heat transmitted by a window and window covering combination by the total amount of heat transmitted by a single pane of clear glass ⅛ inch in thickness.

Shag One level, cut pile surface texture; pile height may be as high as 1.250 inches; pile density is lower than that of plush and saxony textures (20.7e).

Shearing Conversion operation in which raised fiber and pile surfaces are cut to be level.

Shed V-shaped opening of the warp yarns through which the filling pick is inserted (6.3).

Shedding 1. Occurs with new carpet when short lengths of fibers that have accumulated during manufacturing work to the surface; fiber loss is not significant. 2. In weaving operations, using the harnesses to raise some warp yarns and lower others, creating the shed.

Sheers See *glass curtains.*

Sheet casings Covers that protect comforters from soil accumulation and abrasion; their releasable closures permit easy removal for laundering.

Sheets, fitted or contour Sheets constructed with four contour corners to fit the mattress.

Sheets, flat Sheets constructed with hems at both ends; may be used as top or bottom sheets.

Skein dyeing Immersing skeins of yarns into a dyebath.

Shift mark Distorted yarn group (18.2a and b).

Shirring Gathering fabric; seen with Austrian shades (16.11) and bedspread drops (29.9d).

Shots Filling yarns used in machine-woven floor coverings (23.1).

Shrinkage See *relaxation shrinkage*, *residual shrinkage*, and *felting shrinkage*.

Shutters Decorative panels hung at the sides of windows; may be stationary or unfolded to cover the glass to reduce heat exchange.

Shuttle Canoe-shaped device used to carry the filling picks through the shed (6.3).

Shuttleless looms Looms which have devices other than shuttles to carry the filling picks through the shed (e.g., grippers, rapiers, jets of water, jets of air) (6.6, 6.7).

Silencers Felt or heavily napped fabric placed under tablecloths; cushion the impact force of dishes, artifacts, etc.

Silicone compounds Agents used to impart water repellency.

Simple cord yarns Simple yarns formed by twisting or plying together two or more simple ply yarns (5.6).

Simple ply yarns Simple yarns formed by twisting or plying together two or more simple single yarns (5.6).

Simple single yarns Simple yarns formed by spinning staple fibers into a simple yarn (5.6) or by combining several filaments into a simple yarn with or without twist.

Simple yarns Yarns having a smooth appearance and a uniform diameter along their length (5.6).

Simulated fur fabrics Pile fabrics formed by incorporating fibers or yarns among base yarns, creating a three-dimensional structure; fiber composition is often acrylic or modacrylic.

Simulated leather Fabric manufactured by coating a base structure with foam or bonding a base structure with film sheeting; often embossed to impart grain markings.

Simulated suede Fabric manufactured by emerizing a coated fabric to roughen the surface, imparting a suede-like hand and appearance.

Single-mesh canvas See *canvas, single-mesh.*

Sisal A natural cellulosic, relatively stiff fiber retrieved from the leaves of the sisal plant; used for ropes and placemats (30.1).

Skew Distorted yarn alignment in woven fabric; filling yarns slant below straight crosswise grain (9.13b, 14.3).

Skewness Characteristic of having filling skew or filling bias; see *skew.*

Skins Animal skins retrieved from such small animals as lambs, goats, and calves.

Slabs Three-dimensional structure generally composed of synthesized rubber or polyurethane foam; used as filling layer in mattresses and quilts (29.10).

Slack tension technique Weaving technique in which the base warp yarns are held under regular (high) tension and the pile warp yarns are held under slackened tension; used to produce terry toweling.

Slashing Adding starch or sizing to the warp yarns prior to weaving to make them smoother and stronger.

Steep diagonal Visual diagonal in a twill weave fabric that falls at an angle greater than 45 degrees to the fabric grain (6.10b).

Slipcovers Furniture coverings that are cut, seamed, and fitted over the permanently-attached coverings; used for protection and/or decorative purposes (12.7).

Slub yarn Complex single yarn with fine and coarse segments along its length, which are produced by varying the level of twist used in spinning (5.7a).

Smoke density Concentration of smoke passing through light measured numerically as the light transmission value and reported as optical density value.

Smoldering Flameless combustion.

Smoothing Laying pile yarns in one direction after the surface has been brushed.

Sofa bed An upholstered sofa with a hinged back that swings down flat with the seating cushions to form the sleeping surface.

Soil Dirt or other foreign matter that is mechanically held and comparatively easy to remove.

Soil hiding The ability of a fiber or coloration to hide or camouflage dirt; carpet, for example, will look cleaner than it is (4.1b,c, and f, 4.3b and d, 8.6).

Soil magnification Occurs when soil particles reflect incident light waves through round, nondelustered fiber; carpet, for example, will look dirtier than it is (4.3a).

Soil reduction Reduction of the quantity of soil accumulated; achieved by chemical finishing agents or by using an extra large denier per filament.

Soil release Fluorocarbon-based compounds increase the surface energy of the fibers, making them more hydrophilic so the water can more readily carry the detergent molecules into the fiber crevices and emulsify and remove the soil material.

Soil repellency Fluorocarbon compounds make textile compounds more oleophobic or oil-hating, as well as more hydrophobic.

Soil shedding Reduction of the quantity of soil accumulated; achieved by using a trilobal fiber that has a microrough surface.

Solution dyeing Adding dye pigments to the spinning solution of manufactured fibers prior to spinning; also known as dope dyeing and producer colored.

Solvent spinning Manufactured fiber spinning technique in which a solvent is used to dissolve the polymer and the solution is extruded into a solvent that is recovered for continued use; used to produce lyocell fibers.

Space dyeing Dyeing spaces or segments of yarns; produces variegated color styling (8.6).

Specification listing A listing of preferred or required features of a product, including such things as appearance, composition, construction features, functional benefits, and performance properties.

Specific gravity The density of a fiber relative to that of water at 4°C, which is 1.

Speck yarn Complex single yarn having small tufts of differently colored fibers incorporated along its length; used in tweed fabrics (5.7c).

Spike yarns Complex, loop-type yarns composed of yarns having different levels of twist; the more highly twisted yarn is introduced at a faster rate, causing the extra length to form well-defined kinks or loops; also known as snarl yarns.

Spillover Refers to the migration of fire from the room of origination to other rooms and/or corridors (11.4).

Spinneret Shower head-like device used for mechanically spinning manufactured fibers.

Spinners Members of the industry who align and spin staple fibers into spun yarns.

Spinning and twisting Process in yarn spinning in which fibers that are aligned in yarn-like structures are spun and twisted into a yarn; twisting introduces strength.

Spiral yarn Complex yarn formed by twisting a heavy yarn around a fine yarn (5.9c).

Splash yarn Complex yarn having elongated nubs along its length (5.10c).

Split leather Leather fabric produced from an inner layer of hide; lacks natural grain markings.

Splush One level, cut pile surface texture; pile height and pile construction density is between those typically used for plush and shag surfaces.

Spoken warranties See *warranties, spoken.*

Spontaneous combustion Combustion process initiated by heat rather than flame.

Spools Three-foot-long spools that are linked end-to-end to form a bracket; used in Axminster carpet weaving.

Spot yarn See *nub yarns.*

Sprouting The protrusion of a tuft above the surface of the wear layer of carpet.

Spunbonding Fabrication technique in which a web of filaments is stabilized with heat or adhesive binders (22.2c).

Spunlacing Fabrication technique in which webs of fibers are mechanically entangled (7.11).

SSA Acronym for Social Security Administration; administers the Medicare and Medicaid programs.

Stackback space Distance on one or both sides of a window that is allowed for the panels to remain when drawn open.

Stage 1 Fire Characterizes a fire when only the ignited item is burning (11.2).

Stage 2 Fire Characterizes a fire when all combustible items in a room burst into flames, producing a situation known as flashover (11.3).

Stage 3 Fire Characterizes a fire when the flames spread beyond the burning room into the corridor or passageway (11.4).

Stain Dirt or other foreign matter that is chemically bonded to the fiber surfaces and is comparatively difficult to remove.

Stair tread test A long-term, service exposure test; carpet specimens are installed without a cushion on heavily used stairs.

Stalwart roller printing Using large cylinders covered with three-dimensional sponge forms, each cut in the shape of the planned motifs, to print the surface of pile fabric (8.16, 8.17).

Standard performance specification A performance specification established by, for example, a voluntary scientific association; see also *performance specification.*

Standard test method A prescribed procedure for measuring a property; established by, for example, a voluntary scientific association.

Staple A relatively short textile fiber; measured in inches or centimeters.

Static propensity Ease with which materials such as textile fibers accumulate electrons and develop electrostatic charges.

Steiner tunnel test method See *tunnel test.*

Stiffness Degree of flexibility exhibited by fibers; affects fabric draping quality.

Stitch-bonding Fabrication technique in which knitting stitches are used to stabilize webs of fibers (17.29).

Stitch-knitting Fabrication technique in which knitting stitches are used to anchor webs of yarns; also known as knit-sewing (17.27).

Stock dyeing See *fiber dyeing.*

Stretch-in installation Technique used to install roll-goods wall-to-wall (27.3); see also *power stretcher.*

Strié (*striaê*) Descriptive of color style in which yarns of various shades of the same hue are woven in narrow, lengthwise bands to produce the effect of irregularly placed stripes; similar to jaspé (13.6, 13.10b).

Stuffer-box crimping Texturing technique in which yarns are rapidly stuffed into a heated, box-like chamber, backing up on themselves; develops a three-dimensional crimp (5.2b).

Stuffer yarns 1. Extra warp yarns running in a plane and supporting wales or other woven-in dobby designs (17.10). 2. Extra warp yarns running in a plane in the back of woven floor coverings, adding weight, strength, dimensional stability, and thickness (23.1).

S twist A left-handed or counterclockwise direction of yarn twist (5.5).

Sublimation Occurs when heat causes a dyestuff to change from a solid to a gas to a solid; occurs in heat transfer printing.

Sublistatic printing See *heat transfer printing.*

Sueding Revolving sandpaper-covered disks against a flocked surface; also known as emerizing.

Surface dyeing Staining the surface of leather to impart a fashion color.

Surface noise radiation Movement of surface noise created by such activities as walking, running, and shuffling throughout an interior space.

Surface tension Determined by the affinity that molecules in a compound have for one another, in contrast for a second surface (9.16).

Surface texture Visual and textural characteristics of a textile surface (e.g., smooth, rough, short pile, fuzzy, etc).

Susceptibility to heat Characteristic of being affected by heat (e.g., scorches).

Swags Softly draping lengths of fabrics hanging at the sides of windows (16.7).

Swivel weave Surface-figure weave in which extra yarns encircle the base yarns to create a motif (6.12b).

Tabby weave See *plain weave.*

Tablecloths Table coverings produced by weaving, stitch-knitting, knotting and twisting, spunbonding, and extrusion; used for dining and decoration.

Tackless strips Pin-holding strip used in stretch-in tackless installation projects (27.1).

Taffeta Filling-rib weave fabric; often composed of acetate and given a moiré finish (16.12, 19.7).

Taking up and letting off In the weaving operation, taking up woven fabric and letting off warp yarns.

TAK printing Adding droplets of intense color to the already-colored pile surfaces.

Tambour embroidering Machine stitching that resembles hand chain-stitching (17.18, 17.28).

Tanning Leather processing in which selected mineral substances react with the collagen, rendering the fibers insoluble.

Tapestry 1. Jacquard-woven upholstery and drapery fabric in which bands of colored yarns appear selectively on the face and produce stripes on the back (13.15–13.17). 2. Hand-woven fabric in which the filling or weft yarns are interlaced within the perimeter of a motif, clipped, and left hanging fringe-like on the back.

Tapestry weave Plain weave in which the filling or weft yarns are crammed to completely cover the warp yarns.

Tapestry yarns Highly twisted, four-ply yarns, which are used without being separated; used in needlepoint stitching.

Tatting Hand technique in which artisans manipulate one small bobbin to twist fine yarns into open, highly decorative lace.

Tear strength Force required to continue or propagate a tear in a fabric; can be used to predict the likelihood that a small cut or puncture would become a large tear with continued use of the fabric.

Tenacity The force per unit of linear density necessary to rupture a fiber, yarn, or thread; reported as grams per denier (gpd or g/den) or grams per tex (gpt or g/tex).

Tendering Weakening of fibers by, for example, sunlight or chemicals.

Tentering Mechanical treatment used to improve the grain of woven fabrics.

Tensile strength The force per unit of cross-sectional area necessary to rupture a fabric; reported as pounds per square inch (psi) or grams per square centimeter.

Terry toweling Toweling having a loop pile on one or both sides of the fabric; also known as Turkish toweling (28.1).

Terry velour toweling Toweling having a loop pile on one side and a cut pile on the other side of the fabric.

Tetrapod walker Device used in the accelerated testing of carpet for changes in texture and fiber loss; has four, plastic-tipped "feet" that tumble against the carpet surface to simulate foot traffic.

Tex number Weight per unit of length measurement of a fiber of yarn; numerically equal to the weight in grams of 1,000 meters of the strand.

Textile Formerly used only in reference to woven fabrics; now applied to fibers, yarns, and fibrous fabrics manufactured in various ways; not applicable to leather and film fabrics.

Textile colorists Members of the industry who add fashion colors to textiles.

Textile designers Members of the industry who design textile fabrics.

Textile end products Goods that are ready for consumer purchase and use; includes such items as apparel, apparel fabric, upholstery fabric, upholstered furniture, curtains and draperies and curtain and drapery fabrics; soft floor coverings, household and institutional textiles, and wall coverings.

Texturing Introducing multidimensional configurations to otherwise parallel and smooth filaments (5.1, 5.2).

TFPIA Acronym for Textile Fiber Products Identification Act.

Theatrical gauze Plain-woven, stiffened curtain fabric having slightly higher fabric count than cheesecloth; also known as gauze.

Thermal insulation Heat insulation.

Thermoplasticity Property that allows a fiber to be softened and stabilized with controlled heat and that results in melting at higher temperatures, also known as heat sensitivity.

Thick-and-thin yarn Complex single yarn characterized by variations in diameter that are created by varying extrusion pressure (5.7b).

Thread Fine, yarn-like strand used for sewing.

Threshold of human sensitivity The level of static voltage that produces a noticeable shock for most people when it discharges from their bodies; the level is normally 2,500 static volts.

Throwing In yarn production, plying or twisting monofilaments into multifilaments.

Throwsters Members of the industry who work in yarn throwing production.

Ticking 1. A generic term for any fabric used to cover the exterior of mattresses, box spring, and pillows. 2. Twill-woven fabric characterized by lengthwise black or blue strips (29.3).

Tidies Decorative covers placed on the backs and arms of furniture.

Tied-back panels Drapery panels tied back to the sides of the window by such items as cords, chains, and medallions.

Tie-dye print Hand print produced by artisans who tie off selected areas of fabric so that they resist penetration of dye liquor (8.13).

Tight-pillow styles Style of upholstered furniture having pillows that cannot be shifted or removed.

Tint Color feature created by adding a compound known to reflect all wavelengths, creating white, to colorants, increasing its value and luminosity.

Tinting Adding colorants that neutralize the natural color (e.g., violet tints may be used to neutralize the natural yellow hues of wool fiber).

Tip shear One level, cut pile surface texture produced by selectively shearing the uppermost portion of some yarn loops (20.7f).

Tippiness Unwanted concentration of dye on yarn tips; result of poor dye migration.

Titanium dioxide Minute white particles used to deluster manufactured fibers (4.1f).

Toile de Jouy Plain-woven fabric printed with landscapes, floral motifs, or other pictorial designs in various shades of a single hue on a cream-colored background; first produced in Jouy, France; used for draperies (17.22).

Top-grain leather Leather having minor corrections of the natural grain markings.

To railroad Cutting upholstery fabric so that the lengthwise grain aligns crosswise on the cushions, given that the fabric motifs and repeats do not directional features (12.2a).

Total blackout Complete blockage of light transmission.

Total weight The total weight of a floor covering including the weight of the pile yarns as well as the weight of the backing yarns, backing fabrics, and backcoatings.

Tow 1. A rope-like bundle of manufactured filaments having crimp but no twist. 2. Linen fibers approximately 12 inches long.

Toxicants Materials or compounds that are toxic or hazardous, especially when inhaled.

Toxic gases Gases that are hazardous when inhaled; generated in the combustion of such things as fibers.

Trade associations Organizations that represent, protect, and promote the interests of their members who provide financial support for the operation and activities of the associations.

Trademarks Distinctive names, words, phrases, and stylized logos that are used to promote product recognition and selection.

Trade practice rules Collection of labeling provisions issued by the FTC in response to requests by members of a limited segment of the industry; advisory in nature; several trade practice rules have been superseded by guides.

Trade regulation rules Collection of mandatory labeling provisions issued by the FTC.

Transfer printing See *heat transfer printing.*

Triacetate Manufactured cellulose-based fibers where not less than 92 percent of the hydroxyl groups are acetylated; no longer produced in the U. S.

Triaxial weaving Fabrication technique in which two sets of warp yarns and one set of filling yarns are interlaced at 60-degree angles (6.20).

Triboelectric series Series that shows the tendency of fibers to develop their own electrical charges; indicates the relative ease with which fibers allow electrons to be rubbed from their surface atoms, leaving a positive balance (Table 4.10).

Tricot stitch Warp knitting stitch produced with spring needles and one or two guide bars; nonrun and stable; distinguished by herringbone-like wales on the face of the fabric and herringbone-like courses on the back of the fabric.

True bias Fabric position falling at 45 degrees to the lengthwise and crosswise grains of woven fabric; position of highest stretch (6.1).

Tucked-in selvage Fabric edge finish in which the ends of the cut filling picks are turned back into the next shed; creates a finished edge that resembles that of a conventional selvage (6.2b).

Tuft bind Average force required to remove a pile tuft from tufted structures (22.9).

Tufted trimming Using buttons to secure the outer-covering and filling tightly in a deeply indented three-dimensional pattern (12.8).

Tufting Fabrication technique in which pile yarns are inserted into a preformed base fabric (7.8).

Tufts per square inch Indicates pile construction density; calculated by multiplying the needle count by the number of stitches per inch in tufted constructions and by multiplying the number of rows or wires per inch by the pitch divided by 27 in woven constructions.

Tunnel test Flammability test method that measures the surface burning characteristics of building materials; assesses flame spread and smoke generation; also known as the Steiner tunnel test method (11.16, 11.17).

Turkish knot See *Ghiordes knot.*

Turkish toweling See *terry toweling.*

Turns per inch *(tpi)* Numerical indication of the level of yarn twist.

Twill weave Basic weaving pattern in which the warp and filling yarns are interlaced to create a visual diagonal (6.10).

Twisting Used to introduce strength to spun yarns; used to combine monofilaments into multifilaments.

Two-way draperies Window treatment style in which the drapery panels are drawn to stack on both sides of the window (16.3).

UFAC Acronym for Upholstered Furniture Action Council.

Unclipped dot or spot fabric See *dot or spot weave.*

Underblankets Fleece-like mattress pad having a knitted base and pile of lamb's wool; placed under the bottom bed sheet to provide softness, warmth, and moisture absorption.

Uneven filling-faced twill Twill fabric in which more filling yarn than warp yarn shows on the face of the fabric (6.10b).

Uneven warp-faced twill Twill fabric in which more warp yarn than filling yarn shows on the face of the fabric (6.10a).

Union dyeing Variation of piece dyeing in which a fabric composed of two or more different and strategically placed fibers is immersed into a dyebath formulated with dyestuffs that will be selectively accepted and rejected; produces a single, uniform color from one immersion process.

Upland cotton Variety of cotton ground inland, in contrast to on an island; most fibers are a relatively short $^{13}/_{16}$ inch in length.

Upstream segments Firms and personnel in the earlier part of the production pipeline (e.g., fiber manufacturers and suppliers), in contrast to those in the latter part of the pipeline (e.g., end-product producers).

Up-the-bolt Cutting upholstery fabric so that the lengthwise grain runs vertically on the cushions, given that the motifs and repeats have a directional feature (12.2b).

Usable fiber form Relatively long and thin form, in contrast to being relatively short and thick; affects flexibility.

U-values Numerical indications of how much heat actually does pass outward through windows in winter and inward in summer.

Valence Overhead window treatment composed of fabric; may be pleated, scalloped, shirred, or draped as a swag (16.6).

Value Color characteristic referring to the quantity of light being reflected from a textile or other surface; also known as luminosity.

Vapor-phase moisture Water vapor held in the air.

Variegated yarns Space-dyed yarns having a variety of colors along their lengths.

Velour Warp pile fabric having a short, dense pile; used for upholstery.

Velvet Upholstery fabric produced by a doublecloth construction technique; has a cut pile surface created with an extra set of warp yarns (6.15, 6.16, 13.22, 13.23).

Velvet carpet weaving Weaving floor coverings using an over-the-wire-construction technique (6.19); pile may be conventional or woven-through-the-back (23.8).

Velveteen Upholstery fabric produced with an extra set of filling yarns; has dense cut pile surface.

Velvet plush See *plush*.

Venetian blinds Window coverings made up of horizontal slats or louvers laced together with textile cords.

Vertical blinds Window coverings in which the louvers or vanes are suspended vertically and may be rotated 180°.

Vinyl Compound often applied as a coating or bonded as a film sheeting to a base fabric to produce a simulated leather or a vinyl upholstery fabric; also known as polyvinylchloride or PVC.

Vinylized fabric Fabric given a vinyl coating to protect it from such things as soil and spilled fluids.

Virgin wool See *wool, virgin*.

Visible spectrum Portion of the electromagnetic spectrum containing wavelengths that can be interpreted by the eye when reflected (8.1).

Visual diagonal Surface feature created with twill interlacing patterns (6.10).

Voided velvet Velvet characterized by the absence of pile yarns in selected areas (13.22).

Voile Sheer, crisp, plain-woven curtain fabric; often flocked with dots to produce dotted swiss (17.17).

V pattern interlacing Pile interlacing in which the pile yarn is anchored by one base filling yarn (6.18a).

Vulcanizing Heating latex with sulfur to introduce strong chemical cross links that stabilize the shape and add strength.

Waffle piqué Dobby-woven curtain fabric resembling the grid of a waffle iron (17.9c).

Wales Ridge-like features created in filling pile weaving (e.g., pinwale corduroy) (6.15, 6.16) or dobby weaving (e.g., pinwale piqué) (17.10).

Walk-off mat Floor covering used in entrance areas subjected to high traffic levels to capture tracked-in dirt and grit, protecting the carpet from abrasion and apparent changes in color.

Wall-to-wall installation Installation of carpet to cover the entire floor space, baseboard to baseboard (20.1).

Warp knitting Fabrication in which adjacent warp yarns are interlooped (7.1).

Warp pile fabric Fabric in which the pile layer is created with extra warp yarns (e.g., velvet, terry, terry velour, friezé, grospoint) (6.17–6.19).

Warp print Color style produced by printing the warp yarns prior to weaving; distinguished by striated or blurred appearance; used for draperies (17.21).

Warp yarns Lengthwise yarns in a woven fabric; also known as ends (6.1).

Warp-rib weave Variation of the plain weave in which larger or grouped warp yarns create a ribbed or ridged effect in the lengthwise fabric direction (6.9).

Warranty or guarantee programs Program offering some level of protection from defective or faulty merchandise; most warranties are legally binding. See also *warranty, full; warranty, implied; warranty, limited; warranty, spoken;* and *warranty, written.*

Warranty, full Guarantee program designation that indicates what the warrantor agrees to do for the purchaser, as well as what is expected of the purchaser; gives more than a limited warranty.

Warranty, implied Guarantees that come automatically with every sale unless the product is sold "as is"; rights are provided by state law.

Warranty, limited Guarantee program designation that indicates what the warrantor agrees to do for the purchaser, as well as what is expected of the purchaser; gives less than a full warranty.

Warranty, spoken Verbal promise; virtually impossible to enforce.

Warranty, written Legally binding promise that the warrantor is ensuring quality and performance; subject to the provisions of the Magnuson-Moss Warranty Act.

Washfastness Resistance of colored textiles to fading, bleeding, migration, and/or color change when laundered.

Water-borne stain Stain carried by water.

Waterfowl feathers Feathers derived from ducks and geese.

Watermarking See *pile reversal.*

Water resistance Characteristic of repelling water, delaying absorption.

WC system Worsted count (wc) yarn numbering system.

Wear layer The face or pile yarns above the backing in pile floor coverings.

Weather-Ometer® Apparatus used for the accelerated laboratory testing of textile fabrics to be installed outdoors.

Weft insertion Fabrication technique in which weft or filling yarns are inserted through loops of a tricot-stitched fabric (7.4, 17.26).

Weft knitting See *filling knitting.*

Weft yarns Another name for filling yarns; also known as woof (6.1).

Weight density Product of the average pile weight in ounces per square yard and the average density of soft floor coverings.

Welt Fabric-covered cord inserted in seam lines of upholstered furniture coverings (12.3, 12.4b, 12.5).

Wet shampoo cleaning Restorative maintenance procedure in which a diluted detergent solution or foam is driven into the pile with rotating brushes, followed by a thorough vacuuming (27.21).

Wet spinning Manufactured fiber spinning technique in which a basic solvent is used to dissolve the polymer and the solution is extruded into a weak acid bath where filaments coagulate.

Wickability The ability of a fiber to transport moisture along its surface by capillary action.

Wilton Carpet woven on a Jacquard loom; distinguished by having buried pile yarns (23.5).

Wires per inch The number of wires used per lengthwise inch in the construction of Wilton and velvet carpet; also the number of crosswise rows of tufts per lengthwise inch in Wilton and velvet carpet, since one wire is used per row of tufts.

Woof yarns See *weft yarns.*

Wool Labeling term that means the fiber from the fleece of the sheep or lamb, or hair of the Angora or Cashmere goat (and may include the so-called specialty fibers from the hair of the camel, alpaca, llama, and vicuna) that has never been reclaimed from any woven or felted wool product.

Wool, new See *wool, virgin.*

Wool, recycled Labeling term defined in the WPLA of 1939 to identify wool fibers obtained by reducing a previously manufactured product to its original fibrous state and then again subjecting the fibers to the product manufacturing sequence.

Wool, reprocessed Labeling term used to identify the resulting fiber when wool had been woven or felted into a wool product that, without ever having been used in any way by a consumer, subsequently had been returned to a fibrous state; replaced in 1980 by the term "recycled wool."

Wool, reused Labeling term used to identify the resulting fiber when wool or reprocessed wool had been spun, woven, knitted, or felted into a wool product that, after having been used by a consumer, subsequently had been returned to a fibrous state; replaced in 1980 by the term "recycled wool."

Wool, virgin Labeling term that means the constituent fibers have undergone manufacturing only once; they have not been reclaimed from any spun, woven, knitted, felted, braided, bonded, or otherwise manufactured or used product; synonymous with "new wool."

Woolen yarn Yarn spun of both long and short wool fibers and exhibiting a relatively low degree of fiber alignment.

Worsted yarn Yarn spun of long wool fibers and exhibiting a relatively high degree of fiber alignment.

Woven-through-the-back Velvet carpet in which the pile yarns are anchored by both the upper and lower filling shots (23.8b).

W pattern interlacing Pile interlacing in which the pile yarn is anchored by three base filling yarns (6.18b).

WPLA of 1939 Acronym for Wool Products Labeling Act of 1939.

WR system Woolen run (wr); yarn numbering system used to determine yarn number of yarns spun on the woolen spinning system.

Wrinkle recovery Recovery from folding and bending deformations, minimizing fabric mussiness; see *resiliency*.

Written warranty See *warranty, written*.

Wyzenbeek test method See *Oscillatory Cylinder Method*.

Yarn count See *yarn number*.

Yarn dyeing Dyeing in the yarn stage. See also *package dyeing*, *beam dyeing*, *skein dyeing*, and *space dyeing*.

Yarn number Numerical designation of the fineness or size of a yarn; based on length per unit of mass (weight) or mass (weight) per unit of length; also known as yarn count.

Yarn raveling Yarn falling from a raw edge of fabric.

Yarn slippage Moving or "traveling" of warp or filling yarns (9.14).

Yarn splay Untwisting of yarns, resulting in a loss of tuft definition.(21.2).

Yo-yo effect See *elevator effect*.

Zimmer flat-bed screen printing Flat-bed screen printing in which a vacuum system is used to pull the dye paste into the pile yarns (8.18).

Z twist A right-handed or clockwise direction of yarn twist (5.5).

Bibliography

Advantages of Carpet and Rugs in Energy Conservation, Dalton, Ga.: The Carpet and Rug Institute, 1976.

AATCC Technical Manual, Research Triangle Park, N.C.: American Association of Textile Chemists and Colorists, published annually.

Alexander, Patsy R., *Textile Products: Selection, Use, and Care,* Boston: Houghton Mifflin, 1977.

Annual Book of ASTM Standards, Philadelphia: American Society for Testing and Materials, published annually.

Benjamin, I. S. and S. Davis, *Flammability Testing for Carpet,* NBSIR 78-1436, Washington, D.C.: U.S. Department of Commerce, National Bureau of Standards, April 1978.

Beutluck, Tradek, *The Technique of Woven Tapestry,* New York: Watson-Guptill Publications, 1967.

Birrell, Verla, *The Textile Arts,* New York: Harper & Row, 1959.

Cammann, Nora, *Needlepoint Designs from American Indian Art,* New York: Charles Scribner's Sons, 1973.

Carpet and Rugs, 12th ed., North Canton, Ohio: The Hoover Company, 1983.

Carpet Specifier's Handbook, 2nd ed., Dalton, Ga: The Carpet and Rug Institute, 1976.

Cook, J. Gordon, *Handbook of Polyolefin Fibres,* London: Merrow Publishing Company, 1967.

Cook, J. Gordon, *Handbook of Textile Fibres,* Vols. 1 and 2, London: Merrow Publishing Company, 1968.

Corbman, Bernard P., *Textiles: Fiber to Fabric,* 6th ed., New York: McGraw-Hill, 1983.

Diamond, Sidney A., *Trademark Problems and How to Avoid Them,* revised edition, Chicago: Crain Books, 1981.

Frings, Gini Stephens, *Fashion: From Concept to Consumer,* Englewood Cliffs, N.J.: Prentice-Hall, 1982.

The Govmark Book on Flammability Standards and Flammability Test Methods of Textiles, Plastics and Other Materials Used in Home and Contract Furnishings, Bellmore, N.Y.: The Govmark Organization, Inc., 1982.

The Govmark Book of Reprints of Flammability Standards and Flammability Test Methods of Textiles, Plastics and Other Materials Used in Home and Contract Furnishings, Bellmore, N.Y.: The Govmark Organization, Inc., 1982.

Harries, Nancy G., and T. E. Harries, *Textiles: Decision Making for the Consumer,* New York: McGraw-Hill, 1974.

Held, Shirley E., *Weaving: A Handbook for Fiber Craftsman,* New York: Holt, Rinehart and Winston, 1973.

Hilado, Carlos J., ed., *Flammability of Fabrics,* Westport, Conn.: Technomic Publishing Co., Inc., 1970–74.

Hollen, Norma, Jane Saddler, and Anna L. Langford, *Textiles,* 5th ed., New York: Macmillan, 1979.

Joseph, Marjory L., *Essentials of Textiles,* 2nd ed., New York: Holt, Rinehart and Winston, 1980.

Joseph, Marjory L., *Introductory Textile Science,* 5th ed., New York: Holt, Rinehart and Winston, 1986.

Larsen, Jack Lenor, and Jeanne Weeks, *Fabrics for Interiors,* New York: Van Nostrand Reinhold Company, 1975.

Lewin, Menachem, and Jack Preston, eds., *Handbook of Fiber Science and Technology: Volume III, High Technology Fibers: Part A,* New York: Marcel Dekker, 1984.

Lewin, Menachem and Stephen B. Sello, eds., *Handbook of Fiber Science and Technology: Volume I, Fundamentals and Preparation, Part A and Part B, and Volume II, Functional Finishes, Part A and Part B*, New York: Marcel Dekker, 1983–84.

Lewis, Alfred Allan, *The Mountain Artisans Quilting Book*, New York: Macmillan, 1973.

Linton, George E., *The Modern Textile and Apparel Dictionary*, 4th ed., Plainfield, N.J.: Textile Book Service, 1973.

Lyle, Dorothy S., *Modern Textiles*, 2nd ed., New York: John Wiley & Sons, 1982.

Lyle, Dorothy S., *Performance of Textiles*, New York: John Wiley & Sons, 1977.

Moncrieff, R. W., *Man-made Fibers*, 6th ed., New York: John Wiley & Sons, 1975.

NFPA 101® Life Safety Code®, Quincy, Mass.: National Fire Protection Association, Inc., 1981.

Perrone, Lisbeth, *The New World of Needlepoint*, New York: Random House, 1972.

Pizzuto, J. J., *Fabric Science*, revised by Arthur Price and Allen C. Cohen, New York: Fairchild Publications, 1974.

Reznikoff, S. C., *Specifications for Commercial Interiors, Professional Liabilities, Regulations, and Performance Criteria*, New York: Whitney Library of Design/Watson-Guptill Publications, 1979.

Robertson, Seonaid, *Dyes from Plants*, New York: Van Nostrand Reinhold Company, 1973.

Shoshkes, Lila, *Contract Carpeting*, New York: Whitney Library of Design/Watson-Guptill Publications, 1974.

Smith, Betty F., and Ira Block, *Textiles in Perspective*, Englewood Cliffs, N.J.: Prentice-Hall, Inc., 1982.

Souchal, Genevieve, *Masterpieces of Tapestry from the Fourteenth to the Sixteenth Century*, New York: The Metropolitan Museum of Art, 1973.

Specifier's Guide for Contract Carpet Installation, 1st ed., Dalton, Ga: The Carpet and Rug Institute, 1980.

Springer, Jo, *Pleasures of Crewel*, New York: Universal Publishing Company, Inc., 1973.

Standard Practice for Installation of Textile Floorcovering Materials, CRI Standard 104, Dalton, Ga.: The Carpet and Rug Institute, March 1982.

Tortora, Phyllis G. *Understanding Textiles*, 2nd ed., New York: Macmillan, 1982.

Wingate, Isabel, *Dictionary of Textiles*, 6th ed., New York: Fairchild Publications, 1979.

Wingate, Isabel, and June F. Mohler, *Textile Fabrics and Their Selection*, 8th ed., Englewood Cliffs, N.J.: Prentice-Hall, 1984.

Woodhouse, J. Michael, *Science for Textile Designers*, London: Paul Elek (Scientific Books) Ltd., 1976.

Periodicals

American Dyestuff Reporter
630 Third Avenue
New York, NY 10017

American Fabrics and Fashions Magazine
Doric Publishing Company
343 Lexington Avenue
New York, NY 10016

Daily News Record
Fairchild Publications, Inc.
7 East 12th Street
New York, NY 10003

High Performance Textiles
Elsevier International Bulletins
Journal Information Center
52 Vanderbilt Avenue
New York, NY 10017

Home Furnishings Daily
Fairchild Publications, Inc.
7 East 12th Street
New York, NY 10003

Interiors
Billboard Publications, Inc.
1 Astor Plaza
New York, NY 10036

Modern Textile Business (formerly *Modern Textiles*)
Vista Publications Inc.
9600 West Sample Road
Coral Springs, FL 33065

Textile Chemist and Colorist
P.O. Box 12215
Research Triangle Park, NC 27709

Textile Organon
Textile Economics Bureau, Inc.
101 Eisenhower Parkway
Roseland, NJ 07068

Scientific Organizations

American Association of Textile Chemists and Colorists
(AATCC)
P.O. Box 12215
Research Triangle Park, NC 27709

American National Standards Institute, Inc. (ANSI)
1403 Broadway
New York, NY 10018

American Society for Testing and Materials (ASTM)
1916 Race Street
Philadelphia, PA 19103

National Fire Protection Association, Inc. (NFPA)
Batterymarch Park
Quincy, MA 02269

Government Agencies

Architectural and Transportation Barriers
Compliance Board
U.S. Department of Health and Human Services
330 C Street, SW
Washington, DC 20201

Committee on Barrier Free Design
U.S. President's Committee on Employment of the
Handicapped
1111 20th Street, NW
Washington, DC 20210

Consumer Product Safety Commission (CPSC)
Washington, DC 20207

Federal Aviation Administration (FAA)
U.S. Department of Transportation
800 Independence Ave., SW
Washington, DC 20591

Federal Housing Administration
U.S. Department of Housing and Urban Development
Washington, DC 20410

Federal Trade Commission
6th and Pennsylvania Ave., NW
Washington, DC 20580

General Services Administration
7th and D Streets, SW
Washington, DC 20407

National Bureau of Standards
Washington, DC 20234

National Highway Traffic Safety Administration
U.S. Department of Transportation
400 7th St, SW
Washington, DC 20590

National Technical Information Service
U.S. Department of Commerce
5285 Port Royal Road
Springfield, VA 22161

Office of Civil Rights for the Handicapped
U.S. Department of Health and Human Services
330 Independence Ave., SW
Washington, DC 20201

U.S. Government Printing Office
Washington, DC 20402

Trade Associations

American Furniture Manufacturers Association
P.O. Box 2436
High Point NC 27261

American Textile Manufacturers Institute, Inc. (ATMI)
1101 Connecticut Ave., NW, Suite 300
Washington, DC 20036

Association of Interior Decor Specialists, Inc. (AIDS
INTERNATIONAL)
2009 N. 14th Street #203
Arlington, VA 22201

Belgian Linen Association
280 Madison Ave.
New York, NY 10016

California Furniture Manufacturers Association (CFMA)
1933 South Broadway
Los Angeles, CA 90007

Canadian Carpet Institute (CCI)
280 Albert St., Suite 502
Ottawa, Ont. KIP5G8

Carpet Cleaners Institute
1411 W. Olympic Blvd.
Los Angeles, CA 90015

Carpet Cushion Council (CCC)
21780 Partridge Lane
Farmington Hills, MI 48018

Carpet Manufacturers Association of the West (CMAW)
100 N. Citrus St. #235
W. Covina, CA 91791

Carpet Manufacturers Marketing Association, Inc. (CMMA)
1514 West Walnut Avenue
Dalton, GA 20720

Carpet and Rug Institute (CRI)
P.O. Box 2048
Dalton, GA 20720

Cotton Incorporated
1370 Avenue of the Americas
New York, NY 10019

Decorative Fabrics Association (DFA)
950 3rd Avenue
New York, NY 10022

Furniture Manufacturers Association of Grand Rapids
(FMA)
220 Lyon Street NW
Grand Rapids, MI 49502

International Fabricare
12251 Tech Road
Silver Spring, MD 20904

International Home Furnishings Representatives
Association (IHFRA)
666 Lake Shore Drive
Chicago, IL 60611

International Linen Promotion Commission
280 Madison Avenue
New York, NY 10016

Jute Carpet Backing Council
30 Rockefeller Plaza
New York, NY 10020

Jute Manufacturers Development Council
19 W. 44th St., Suite 503
New York, NY 10036

American Fiber Manufactures Association, Inc.
(formerly) Man-Made Fiber Producers Association
(MMFPA)
1157 17th St., NW, Suite 310
Washington, DC 20036

National Association of Decorative Fabrics Distributors
(NADFD)
6022 West Touhy Ave.
Chicago, IL 60648

NAILM
2130 Lexington Road, Suite 1
Richmond, KY 40475

National Association of Floor Covering Distributors
(NAFCE)
13-186 Merchandise Mart
Chicago, IL 60654

National Cotton Batting Institute (NCBI)
1918 North Parkway
Memphis, TN 38112

National Cotton Council of America (NCCA)
1030 15th St., NW, Suite 700
Washington, DC 20036

National Home Fashions League, Inc. (NHFL)
107 World Trade Center
Dallas, TX 75258

National Home Furnishings Association (NHFA)
900 17th St., NW, Suite 514
Washington, DC 20006

Northwest Furniture Manufacturers Association
(NWFMA)
Box 2233
Tacoma, WA 98401

Retail Floor Covering Institute (RFI)
1889 Merchandise Mart
Chicago, IL 60654

The Society of the Plastics Industry (SPI)
355 Lexington Avenue
New York, NY 10017

Southwestern Furniture Manufacturers Association
(SWFMA)
9061 World Trade Center
P.O. Box 58258
Dallas, TX 75258

Synthetic Turf Council
P.O. Box 326
Dalton, GA 30720

Upholstered Furniture Action Council (UFAC)
Box 2436
High Point, NC 27261

The Wool Bureau, Inc.
1360 Lexington Ave.
New York, NY 10017

Appendix A

Selected Fiber Trade Names

Trade name	Generic class	Distinguishing feature	Producer
Acrilan	acrylic		Monsanto Fibers Company
Anso	nylon		AlliedSignal Fibers
Anso IV	nylon	Soil repellent	AlliedSignal Fibers
Anso IV HP	nylon	Soil repellent high dpf	AlliedSignal Fibers
Antron	nylon		DuPont Company
Antrol III	nylon	antistatic	DuPont Company
Antron XL	nylon	High dpf, soil hiding	DuPont Company
Arnel	triacetate		Hoechst Celanese Corporation
Arvil	polyester		Avtes Fibers, Inc.
Arvil	rayon	High wet modulus	Avtes Fibers, Inc.
Bekinox	metallic	Stainless steel, antistatic	Bekaert Steel-wire Corporation
Beta	glass	Low dpf	Owens Corning
Bi-Loft	Acrylic		Monsanto Fibers
Brunsmet	metallic	Stainless steel, antistatic	Brunswick Corporation
Camalon	nylon		Camac Corporation
Caprolan	nylon		AlliedSignal Fibers
Coloray	rayon	Solution dyed	Courtaulds North America, Inc.
Cordura	nylon		DuPont Company
Creslan	acrylic		American Cyanamid Company
Dacron	polyester		DuPont Company
Dacron Hollofil	polyester	Hollow interior	DuPont Company
Fiberglass	glass		Owens Corning
Fibro	rayon		Courtlands North America, Inc
Fi-Lana	acrylic		Monsanto Fibers
Fortrel	polyester		Fiber Industries, Inc.
Kevlar	aramid		DuPont Company
Kynol	novoloid		American Kynol, Inc.
Lycra	spandex		DuPont Company
Marquesa	olefin	Bulked filaments	Amoco Fabrics and Fibers Co.
Marquesa lana	olefin	Bulked, wool-like	Amoco Fabrics and Fibers Co.
Marves	olefin		Phillips Fibers Corporation
Nomex	aramid		DuPone Company
Nypel	nylon		AlliedSignal Fibers
Orlon	acrylic		DuPont Company
Pa-Qel	acrylic		Monosanto Fibers
Patlon	olefin	Fibrillated ribbon	Amoco Fabrics and Fibers Co.
Remember	acrylic		Monsanto Fibers
SEF	modacrylic	self-extinguishing	Monsanto Fibers
Shareen	nylon		Courtlands North America, Inc.
So-Lara	acrylic		Monsanto Fibers
Trevira Pentron	polyester	Pentalabal, soil repellant	Hoechst Celanese Corporation
Ultron	nylon		Solutia, Inc.
Ultron Z	nylon	Soil shedding	Monsanto Fibers
Ultron 3D	nylon	High dpf	Monsanto Fibers
X-Static	nylon	Silver coated, antistatic	Sauquoit Industries
Zeftron ATX	nylon	Pentalobal, hollow voids, soil hiding	BASF Corp.
Sefftron 500 ZX	nylon	Soil hiding, solution dyed	BASF, Corp.

Appendix B

The International System of Units-SI/Metric

The information in this appendix is courtesy of PPG Industries, Inc., 1984.

SI BASE UNITS

Quantity Measured	Unit of Measure	Symbol
Length	meter	m
Mass[a]	kilogram	kg
Time	second	s
Electric current	ampere	A
Thermodynamic temperature[b]	kelvin	K
Amount of substance	mole	mol
Luminous intensity	candela	cd

[a]The kilogram is the unit of mass but not of force. The Newton (N) is the unit of force. (For more detailed explanation of mass and force, refer to ASTM E 380.)

[b]While the kelvin is the correct SI unit of thermodynamic temperature, in practice, degree Celcius (°C) is most commonly used (1K = 1°C).

PREFIXES USED WITH THE SI METRIC SYSTEM

Prefix	Symbol	Multiplying Factor	
tera	T	1000 000 000 000	$= 10^{12}$
giga	G	1 000 000 000	$= 10^{9}$
mega	M	1 000 000	$= 10^{6}$
kilo	k	1 000	$= 10^{3}$
hecto	h	100	$= 10^{2}$
deka	da	10	$= 10^{1}$
deci	d	0.1	$= 10^{-1}$
centi	c	0.01	$= 10^{-2}$
milli	m	0.001	$= 10^{-3}$
micro	μ	0.000 001	$= 10^{-6}$

For additional prefixes, refer to ASTM E 380.

CUSTOMARY INCH-POUND MEASURES AND EQUIVALENT SI UNITS

Inch-Pound Measure and Symbol

inches	in
inches	in
feet	ft
yards	yd
miles	mi
square yards	yd^2
ounces (avdp.)	oz
pounds (advp.)	lb

Equivalent Metric Measure and Symbol

centimeters	cm
millimeters	mm
meters	m
meters	m
kilometers	km
square meters	m^2
grams	g
kilograms	kg

CUSTOMARY UNITS OF MEASURE IN SI UNITS

Length

1 meter (m) = 100 cm	=	1000 mm
1 millimeter (mm)	=	0.001 m
1 centimeter (cm)	=	0.01 m
1 decimeter (dm)	=	0.1 m
1 dekameter (dam)	=	10 m
1 hectometer (hm)	=	100 m
1 kilometer (km)	=	1000 m

Weight

1 gram (g) = 100 cg	=	1000 mg
1 milligram (mg)	=	0.001 g
1 centigram (cg)	=	0.1 g
1 decigram (dg)	=	0.1 g
1 dekagram (dag)	=	10 g
1 hectogram (hg)	=	100 g
1 kilogram (kg)	=	1000 g

Capacity

1 liter (L) = 100 cL	=	1000 mL
1 milliliter (mL)	=	0.001 L
1 centiliter (cL)	=	0.01 L
1 deciliter (dL)	=	0.1 L
1 dekaliter (daL)	=	10 L
1 hectoliter (hL)	=	100 L
1 kiloliter (kL)	=	1000 L

SELECTED INCH-POUNDS/SI METRIC CONVERSION FACTORS AND REFERENCES

Quantity	Inch-Pound Units	SI units	To Convert Inch-Pound units to SI Multiply By:	To Convert SI Units to Inch-pound Multiply By:
Length	inch	mm	25.400	0.03937
	inch	cm	2.5400	0.3937
	foot	m	0.3048	3.2808
	yard	m	0.9144	1.0936
	mile	km	1.6093	0.6214
Mass	ounce (avdp.)	g	28.3495	0.0353
	pound (avdp.)	kg	0.4536	2.2046
	ton (2,000 lbs.)	t	0.9072	1.1023
	ton (2,240 lbs.)	t	1.0161	0.9842
Force	pound	N	4.4482	0.2248
Volume	ounce (fluid	mL	29.5735	0.0338
	Quart (liquid)	L	0.9464	1.0567
	gallon	L	3.7854	0.2642
	quart (dry)	L	1.1012	0.9081
	bushel	L	35.2391	0.0284
	$inch^3$	cm^3	16.3871	0.0610
	$feet^3$	dm^3	28.3168	0.0353
	$yard^3$	m^3	0.7646	1.3079
Area	$inch^2$	cm^2	6.4516	0.1550
	$feet^2$	m^2	0.0929	10.7639
	$yard^2$	m^2	0.8361	1.1960
	acre	hectare	0.4047	2.4710
Temperature	°F	°C	$5/9(°F-32°)$	$9/5°C + 32°$
Density	lb/in^3	g/cm^3	27.6799	0.0361
	lb/ft^3	kg/m^3	16.0185	0.0624
Velocity	ft/sec	m/s	0.3048	3.2808
	yd/min	m/min	0.9144	1.0936
	mi/hr	km/h	1.6093	0.6214
Energy	ft lb	J	1.3558	0.7376
	BTU	kJ	1.0551	0.9478
	kWh	MJ	3.6000	0.2778
Pressure	lb/in^2	kPa	6.8947	0.1450
Textile	oz/yd	g/m	31.0034	0.0323
	oz/yd^2	g/m^2	33.9057	0.0295
	turns/in(tpi)	turns/m(tpm)	39.3700	0.0254
	yds/lb	m/kg	2.0159	0.4961

*Definitions and symbols for the complete international system are given in ASTM E 380.

Index

A

Abrasion resistance
  as fiber property, 47–48
  for soft floor coverings, 393, 396
  for upholestery fabrics, 232–34
Absorbency
  evaluating for towels and toweling,
    426–27
  as fiber property, 57–58, 59–60
Accelerated aging in evaluating cushion
  performance, 383
Accordian-pleated shades, 272–73
Acetate, 35
Acid printing, 126–27
Acordis Cellulosic Fibers, 36
Acoustical value, 388
Acoustics. See also Noise
  and carpet installation, 402–3
  and draperies, 263
  for soft floor coverings, 388–90
  and textile structures, 313–14
Acquisitions, 8
Acrylic fibers, 36
Actual color, 127
  factors affecting, 251
Additives
  fibers with, 60
  in manufactured fibers, 33
Adhesives
  in installing wall coverings, 318
  for tufted floor coverings, 349,
    351–52
Advertising firms, 7
Advisory practices, 201
Aesthetics
  in selecting interior textiles, 15
  in selecting window treatments,
    249–50
After flame time, 175
Afterglow time, 175
Airborne sounds, 253, 388
Allied Fibers, 57, 58, 143, 145
Alpha amino acids, 29
American Association of Textile Chemists
  and Colorists (AATCC), 18
    Chromatic Transference Scale, 237,
      307
    Color Transference Scale, 426
    Gray Scale for Color Change, 306,
      426
    Gray Scale for Staining, 308, 426
    Technical Manual, 17
American Fiber Manufacturers
  Association, 7
American National Standards Institute
  (ANSI), 19

American Society for Testing and
  Materials (ASTM), 18–19
Amino acids, alpha, 29
Amorphous arrangement, 27
Anhydrous glucose, 31
Aniline finish, 222
Annual Book of ASTM Standards, 17, 18
Anso® IV, 58
Anso V Worry Free®, 145
Antimacassars, 195, 206
Antimicrobial agents, 57, 143
Antique Oriental rugs, 372
Antique satin, 283
Apparent brightness, 46, 235
Apparent color, 127
  factors affecting, 251, 333
Apparent volume, 66
Apparent whiteness, 46
Appearance
  retention for window coverings, 303–4
  for soft floor coverings, 325–33
  for towels, 426
Appliqué work, 137
Aramid, 36–37
Architects, 6, 14–15
Architectural and Transportation Barriers
  Compliance Board (ATBCD), 337
Ardebil Mosque Carpet, 372
Area rugs, 328
Arm caps, 195
Arm covers, 195
Armettes, 195
Armstrong World Industries, 58
Armure fabrics, 213
Artificial silk, 35
Asbestos, 32
Association for Contract Textiles (ACT),
  7, 9, 17, 157, 228
Astrojets, 113
Athey shades, 274
Atmospheric contaminant fading, 239
Atmospheric gases, colorfastness to, 306–7,
  392
Aubusson rugs, 371
Austrian shades, 272, 280
Auxochromes, 109
Average density, 356
Awnings, 275
Axminster weaving, 359–62

B

Backcoated upholstery fabrics, 207–8
Back coatings, durability of, 303
Backfilled fabrics, 440
Backings
  fiber usage in, 342
  primary, 347
  secondary, 347, 349
  for textile wall coverings, 317

Bacteria, 143
Balanced construction, 81
Balloon shades, 272
Base yarn, 72
BASF Corporation, 57, 58, 60, 143
  6ix Again program, 10
Basic weaving operation, 83–85
Basket weave, 85, 208, 282
Bast fiber, 31
Batch-dyeing operations, 114
Bath, textile products for, 420–29
  rugs and mats, 427
    constructing and finishing, 427–28
    evaluating flammability, 428
  shower curtains
    colorfastness to light, 429
    flammability of, 429
    physical performance properties of,
      428–29
    polymer film, 428
    textile, 428
    water resistance of, 429
  towels and toweling, 421–27
    absorbency of, 426–27
    caring for, 427
    colorfastness of, 426
    constructing, 423–24
    flammability of, 427
    physical performance properties of,
      424–26
    statistical profile of fiber usage,
      421–22
Batik printing, 117–18
Batiste, 280
Batons, 265
Battening, 84
Battings, 198–99, 437
Beam dyeing, 111–12
Beater bar, 82
Bedding products
  bedspreads and comforters, 443–46
  blankets, 441–43
  fiber and yarn usage in, 432–33
  fillings used in, 436–38
  mattress covers and pads, 435–36
  mattresses, 434–35
  mattress foundations, 433–34
  pillowcases, 440–41
  pillows, 438–39
  quilts, 443–44, 445–46
  sheets, 439–41
Bed pillows, 438
Bedrest pillows, 438
Bedspreads, 444–45
  evaluating fabrics for, 446
Beetling, 133–34
  in table coverings, 451
Beford cord, 284
Bekaert Steelwire Corporation, 60

Bekinox®, 60
Bekitex®, 60
Bengaline, 208, 282
Berber yarns, 332
Biaxial weaving, 80
Bicomponent fibers, 41
Biconstituent fibers, 41
Biking, 50
Binder or tie yarn, 72
BioFresh®, 57, 143
Biological resistance, 143
Birdseye piqué, 284
Bishop's sleeve, 263
Blackout
    partial, 295
    total, 295
Blankets, 441
    caring for, 443
    coloring and finishing, 443
    constructing, 443
    double-faced, 442
    fibers in, 441–42
    flammability of, 443
    flocking, 443
    knitting, 442
    manufacturing, 441–43
    needlepunching, 442
    reversible, 442
    thermal, 442
    tufting, 442
    weaving, 442
    yarns in, 441–42
Bleaching agents, 133
Bleeding, 239, 307, 426
Blended filaments, 41
Blinds
    Venetian, 274, 280
    vertical, 274–75, 280
Block printing, 117
Blossom, 343
Blotch print, 288
Bobbin, 82
Bobbinet, 262
Bobbin lace, 102
Body construction techniques, 347
Boiling off, 30
Bolster pillows, 438
Bonded polyester batting, 199
Bonded urethane foam structures, 382
Bonded-web or nonwoven fabrics, 103
Bonding fibrous batts, 103
Bottom fabrics, 193
Bouclé yarns, 73
Boudoir pillows, 438
Bow
    for shower curtains, 428
    for towels, 426
    for upholstery fabric, 228
Bowed yarn alignment, 140
Bow windows, 250
Boxing, 195
Box pleats, 195
Box-spring units, 433–34
Bracket, 360
Braided rugs, 366–67

Braiding yarns, 103
Breakfast pillows, 438
Breaking, 32
Breaking force (load), 231
    for shower curtains, 428
    for towels, 424
Breaking strength of fabrics, 302
Breaking tenacity, 53
Brighteners, 46
Brightness, 46
    apparent, 235
    increasing apparent, 142
Broadloom, 325
Brocade fabric, 214, 287
Brocatelle, 214
Browning, 412
Brunsmet®, 60
Brunswick Corporation, 60
Brushing, 135
Brussels, 362
Building codes, organizations establishing model, 20–21
Building costs, 8
Building Officials and Code Administrators (BOCA), 20, 21
Bulk, 66
Bulked continuous filament (BCF) nylon, 341
Bulked continuous filament (BCF) olefin, 341
Bulked continuous filament (BCF) yarns, 68, 343
Bundle penetration, 352
Burlap, 31
Burlington Industries, Inc., 57, 143
Burning test, 25
Burnt gas fumes, colorfastness to, 239
Burnt-out print, 126
Bursting strength of fabrics, 303

C
Cable yarns, 71
Café curtains, 262–63
Calendering rollers, 133
Calico, 280
Candlewick bedspreads, 445
Candlewicking, 136
Candlewick yarns, 136
Cane, 76
Cantonnière, 265
Canvas, 282
Canvas embroidering, 136
Cape Cod curtains, 263
Carbonizing, 29
Carded yarns, 69
Carding, 68
Carothers, Wallace, 40
Carpet, 325. See also Soft floor coverings
Carpet and Rug Institute, 7
Carpet beetle larvae, 144
Carpet cushions. See Soft floor coverings
Carpet modules, 326
Carpet winch, 114
Cascade loop shades, 274
Cascades, 264

Casements, 89
    fabrics for, 261–62
    stitch-knitted, 292–93
Casing, 262
Cattlehair, 199
Cellular rubber cushions, 380–82
Celluloise unit, 31
Cellulosic fibers, 31, 35–36
Cellulosic polymers, extracting, 33
Centers for Disease Control and Prevention (CDC), 11
Certification marks, 157–58
Chain-stitching, 99, 101
Chain warp yarns, 359
Challis, 295–96
Channel quilting, 138
Char length, 168, 175, 428
Cheeses, 82
Chemical resistance, as fiber property, 54
Chemical washing, 372
Chenille carpet production, 365
Chenille spreads, 445
Chenille yarns, 75
Chinese grass, 76
Chintz fabrics, 134, 280, 281
    glazed, 208
Chroma, 109
Chromophores, 109
Circular braids, 103
Cleaning agents, colorfastness to, 239, 392
Cleaning code, 242
Cleaning raw hides, 221
Clipped dot fabric, 88, 285
Cloque, 216
Cloth beams, 82
Coarse canvas, 136
Coated filaments, 60
Coatings, applying, 143
Cocktail napkins, 453
Codes
    organizations establishing model building, 20021
    in selecting interior textiles, 18
Coir, 31
Collagen, 221
Color, 45
    actual, 127
        factors affecting, 251
    apparent, 127
        factors affecting, 251, 333
    characteristics of
        hue, 109
        intensity, 109
        value, 109
    consistency and retention of, 235–40
    factors affecting apparent, 127–29
    inherent, 45
        removing, 133
    removing inherent, 133
Colorants, 45, 109–10
    and color perception, 108
        nature of light, 108–9
    fugitive, 304
Coloration, for soft floor coverings, 332–33

Colorburst®, 121
Colorfastness, 235, 392
    to atmospheric gases, 306–7, 392
    to burnt gas fumes, 239
    to cleaning agents, 239, 392
    to crocking, 236–37, 307, 392, 426, 429
    to dry cleaning, 307–8
    to laundering, 307–8, 426, 429
    to light, 237, 239, 304–6, 392, 426, 429
    for shower curtains, 429
    to solvent, 239–40
    testing procedures for, 304
    of towels, 426
    to water, 239, 392
Coloring
    for raw hides, 222
    in yarn stage, 111–13
Colorless acid dyes, 144
Color-sealed, 110
Color styling, 332–33
    fabrics distinguished by, 288, 292
Combing, 69
Combining fibers, 103, 105–6
Combustion. See also Flammability
    byproducts of, 166–67
    defined, 166
    processes of, 166
Comforters, 446
    evaluating fabrics, 446
Commerce, U.S. Department of, 164
Commercial interiors, 5
Commercial quilting, 138
Commercial weaving of textile floor coverings, 359
Common names, 24
Compactness of construction, 81
Completion, 194
Complex plies and cords, 71–72
Complex yarns, 71–73, 83
Composition and structural variables, 129
Compressibility
    in evaluating cushion performance, 383–84
    of textile structure, 200–201
Compression load deflection (CLD), 384
Compression set in evaluating cushion performance, 384
Compressive shrinkage processes, 141, 295, 300
Conduction, 254
Conductive filaments, 61
Conductors, 59
Constant-rate-of-extension (CRE) machines, 51, 231
Constant-rate-of-load (CRL) machines, 51
Constant-rate-of-traverse (CRT) machines, 51, 230
Construction of towels and toweling, 423–24
Consumer Product Safety Commission (CPSC), 20, 164, 166, 168, 308
Consumers, 6–7
    challenges to, 14–15

Contour sheets, 440
Contract design, 6
Convection, 254
Conventional rods, 265–66
Conventional selvages, 80
Converters, 5, 139
Convertible sofa beds, 184, 433
Cooperative Extension Services, 267
Copolymers, 37
Corduroy, 89, 91
    for bedspreads, 444
    for upholstered fabrics, 218
    for window coverings, 287–88
Cord yarns, 71, 75
Core-spun yarn, 73
Corium, 221
Corkscrew yarns, 72–73
Cost factors
    in selecting interior textiles, 16–17
    in soft floor coverings, 337–38
    for window treatments, 256–57
Cottage curtains, 263
Cotton
    in bedding, 432
    in towels, 421–25
    in upholstery fillings, 199
Cotton count (cc) system, 74
Cotton felt, 199
Cotton fibers, 31
Cotton Incorporated, 7, 157
Cotton spinning system, 68–69
Council of American Building Officials (CABO), 20
Courses, 97
Courtalds Fibers, Inc., 36
Covered-core yarn, 73
Covering power, of textile fibers, 49–50
Crackle effect, 118
Crash, 422
Crazy quilts, 443
Creel frame, 82
Cretonne, 281
Crewel yarns, 136
Critical radiant flux (CRF), 171
Crocheting, 99
Crocking, 236, 426
    colorfastness to, 236–37, 307, 392, 426, 429
Crockmeter, 236
Cross dyeing, 116
Cross-sectional shape, 45
Crushed feathers, 437
Crushed velvet, 218
Crushing, 136
Crystalline, 27
Curing, raw hides, 221
Curled hair batting, 199
Curl yarns, 73
Curtains, 261, 262–63
    café, 262–63
    calculating yardage required, 266–67, 269–72
    components used in, 278–80
    cottage or Cape Cod, 263
    draw, 262

    hardware, 265–66
    headings, 264
    overhead, 264
    priscilla, 261
    ruffled, tie-back, 262
    sash, 262
    shower, 428–29
    side, 264
    trimmings, 264
    woven fabrics, 280–92
Curtain tender, 262
Cushions
    slab, 199
    for soft floor coverings (See Soft floor coverings)
    for upholstered furniture, 195, 199
Customer's own material (COM), 18, 24–25
Cut pile, 330
Cystine, 30

D
Damaged feathers, 437
Damask fabrics, 133, 212–13, 287
Dead and buried yarns, 362
Deck, 193
Decorative coverings for pillows, 439
Decorative interlacings, fabrics with, 283–87
Decorative rods, 266
Delamination strength for tufted floor coverings, 352
Delusterants, 45, 61
Denier, 343
Denier (den) system, 74
Denier per filament (dpf), 53
Densified prime urethane foam structures, 382
Density, 49
Density factor, 355–56
Density index, 355–56
Dents, 82
Department stores, 6
Design
    elements of, 15
    as factor for soft floor coverings, 337
    principles of, 15
Design for the Environment program, 10
Design professionals, 6
    challenges to, 14–15
Design Tex, 9
Dhurrie rugs, 376
Differential dyeing, 116
Dimensional change
    for shower curtains, 428
    for towels, 426
Dimensional stability
    for textile shape, 141
    for upholstery fabrics, 231–32
    for window fabric, 300
Dimity, 282
Dimout effect, 296
Directional pile lay, 135
Direct yarn numbering systems, 74

Disabled, textile floor covering for, 334–35
Discharge printing, 127
Discontinuous dyeing, 114–15
Discount stores, 6
Discretionary income, 8
Disposable income, 8
Disposable toweling, 423
Distributors, 6
Disulfide cross links, 144
Dobby-woven fabrics, 87, 209, 284–85
Doctor blade, 119
Document fabrics, 30
Doilies, 102, 452
Dope dyeing, 110
Dotted swiss, 88, 262, 281
Dot weaving, 88, 211–12, 285
Doublecloth fabrics, 92, 216
Double-faced blanketing, 442
Doubleknit fabrics, 99
Double-mesh canvas, 136
Double rubs, 233
Dow Corning, 57, 143
Down products, 200
    for bedding, 436
    labeling, 201
Downstream firms, 7
Downstream segments, 3
Draperies, 263–64
    and acoustics, 263
    calculating yardage required, 266–67,
        269–72
    components used in, 278–80
    hardware, 265–66
    headings, 264
    lining materials, 294–96
    overhead, 264
    side, 264
    trimmings, 264
    woven fabrics, 280–92
Draw curtains, 262
Drawing, 34–35
Drawing out, 69
Drill for textile wall coverings, 317
Drop-match patterns, 406–7
Drop wire, 82
Drum dyeing, 222
Dry cleaning, colorfastness to, 307–8
Dry extraction cleaning for soft floor
    coverings, 412
Dry foam cleaning for soft floor coverings,
    412–13
Dry spinning, 34
Dry weight, 57
Duck, 282
Duplex printing, 440
DuPont, 61, 143, 144, 145
    "Partnership in Carpet Reclamation,"
        10, 57
Duppionisilk filaments, 71
Durability of back coatings, 303
Durable press finishing, 145
Durable press resins, 303
Dust ruffles, 441
Dye beck, 111
Dyed-in-the-wool, 110

Dyeing
    beam, 111–12
    cross, 116
    discontinuous, 114–15
    fiber, 110–11
    in fiber stage, 110–11
    greige goods, 114–15
    package, 111
    piece, 114
    skein, 112
    solution, 110
    space, 112–13
    stock, 110–11
    union, 116
    in yarn stage, 111–13
Dye liquor, 110
Dye paste, 117
Dye pigments, 45
Dyes, 109
Dyestuffs, 109

E
Economic factors, affecting interior textile
    industry, 8–9
Effective face yarn weight, 355
Effect yarn, 72
Egyptian cotton, 31
Elasticity of textile fibers, 50–52
Elastic modulus, 50
Elastic recovery, 52
Electrical conductivity and resistivity, 59
Electromagnetic spectrum, 108
Electrostatic flocking, 138, 224
Elevator effect, 50
Elongation strength, 50–51
    in cushion performance, 384
    in upholstery fabric, 231
Embellishment of fabric surfaces, 136–39
Embossing, 134–35
Embossing grain markings, 222–23
Embroidered fabrics, 288
Embroidering
    hand, 136–38
    machine, 138
Emerizing operations, 224
End, 80
End-product designers, 5
End-product producers, 5, 7
Energy conservation
    floor coverings in, 335
    textile wall coverings in, 314
    window treatments in, 254–56
Energy costs and concerns, 8
Environmental agencies, 10–11
Environmental factors
    affecting interior textile industry, 9–11
    in selecting interior textile, 16
Environmental Protection Agency (EPA),
    9, 10–11
EnviroSense: Partners for the
    Environment, 10
Epidermis, 221
Etched-out or burn-out prints, 126, 292
Ethylene, 39
European pillows, 438

Even twill, 87
Extruding in textile wall coverings, 316–17
Extruding polymer solutions, 105
Extrusion, 452
Eyelet, 288
    in bedspreads, 444

F
Fabrication
    of interior textile products
        braiding, 103
        combing fibers, 103, 105–6
        extruding polymer solutions, 105
        fusion bonding, 102
        knitting, 97–101
        knotting and twisting, 102–3
        tufting, 101–2
        weaving, 80–93
    techniques in, 4
Fabric count, 80–81
Fabric immersion, 127
Fabric lining, 197
Fabric manufacturers, 4
Fabric nap, 135
Fabric openness, 252
Fabric panel, determining width of, 270–71
Fabric producers, 4
Fabrics, 302
    armure, 213
    basket-woven, 208, 282
    bottom, 193
    breaking strength of, 302
    brocade, 214
    brocatelle, 214
    calculating yardage of, for window
        treatments, 266–67, 269–72
    correcting grain, 140
    damask, 212–13
    deck, 193
    with decorative interlacings, 283–87
    distinguished by color styling, 288,
        292
    dobby-woven, 209, 284–85
    dot- or spot-woven, 285
    embellishing surfaces, 136–39, 197,
        288
    embroidered, 288
    filling-rib woven, 208, 282
    flocked, 288
    herringbone-woven, 209
    Jacquard-woven, 212–16, 287
    knitted, 218
    knitted pile, 220–21
    knitted window covering, 292–93
    lappet-woven, 285
    leno-woven, 286–87
    liseré, 213–14
    metallic-coated lining, 296
    with pile interlacings, 287–88
    pile upholstery, 218–21
    plain-woven, 207–8, 280
    plain-woven lining, 295–96
    produced by weft insertion, 292
    raschel-stitched, 292
    sateen-woven lining, 296

satin- and sateen-woven, 283
satin-woven, 209
separately hung lining, 295–96
with simple interlacings, 280–83
stabilizing shape of, 141
strength of, 302–5
surface-figure woven, 211–12, 285
swivel-woven, 285
tear strength of, 302–3
triaxially woven, 217
tufted, 221
twill-woven, 208–9, 282–83
warp-rib woven, 282
weights of, 265
width of, 270
woven pile, 218–20
Fabric stylists, 4
Face yarns, 347
    fiber usage in, 341–42
Factory outlets, 6
Fade-Ometer®, 304, 426
Fading, 307
    atmospheric contaminant, 239
    fume, 239
    gas, 239
    ozone or O-, 239
Faille, 208, 282
False-twist coiling, 68
Feather and Down Products Industry,
    Guides for, 201
Feather fiber, 437
Feather products, 200
    for bedding, 436
    labeling, 201
Federal Aviation Administration (FAA), 20
    flammability regulation, 173, 175
Federal Housing Administration (FHA),
    19–20
Federal Trade Commission (FTC), 24, 35,
    150
    Guides for the Household Furniture
        Industry, 224
    investigative and rulemaking
        procedures, 150–51
    responsibilities and powers, 150
    trade regulation rule of, 454
Felted wool yarns, 76
Felting fibrous batts, 103
Felting shrinkage, 443
Fenestration, 249
Fiber cohesiveness, 68
Fiberfill, 200, 437
Fibers. See also Textile fibers
    acetate, 35
    acrylic, 36
    aramid, 36–37
    in backing structures, 342
    bast, 31
    in bedding, 432
    bicomponent, 41
    biconstituent, 41
    in blankets, 441–42
    cellulosic, 31, 35–36
    coir, 31
    combining, 103, 105–6

composition of
    in bedding, 432
    disclosure of, 206, 279, 342
    cotton, 31
    cross-sectional shape, 28
    dyeing, 110–11
    in face yarns, 341–42
    filament, 4
    flax, 32
    heat-sensitive, 35
    hydrophilic, 57
    hydrophobic, 57
    jute, 31–32
    labeling laws for, 151–54, 279
    length, 28
    line, 32
    linen, 32
    lyocell, 36
    manufactured, 33–41
    mineral, 32
    modacrylic, 37–38
    natural, 29–32
    noncellulosic, 36–40
    nylon, 38–39
    olefin, 39
    polyester, 39–40
    protein, 29–30
    rayon, 36
    reducing flammability of, 142
    saran, 40
    seed, 31
    in sheeting, 439–40
    silk, 30
    spandex, 40
    spunlacing, 105
    staple, 4
    statistical profile of, 278–79
    surface texture, 28
    in tabletop coverings, 450–51
    in textile wall coverings, 314–15
    thermoplastic, 35
    tow, 32
    in transportation applications, 205–6
    in upholstery fabrics, 205
    variants in, 40
Fiber suppliers and producers, 3–4
Fiber trademarks, 156–57
Fibrillation, 52, 279
Fibrils, 31
Fibroin, 30
Fibrous batts, 198–99
    bonding, 103
    felting, 103
    needlepunching, 105
Fibrous cushions, structure of, 379–80
Fibrous webs, window coverings formed
    from, 293–94
Filament fibers, 4
Filaments, extruding and solidifying, 33–34
Filling-faced satin weave, 87
Filling knitting, 99
Filling materials
    for bedding products, 436–38
    care of, 438
    flammability of, 201

functions and properties of, 437–38
    labeling, 201
    for pillows, 438–39
    for upholstered furniture, 197,
        198–201
Filling pile fabrics, 89, 91–92
Filling-rib woven fabrics, 85, 208, 282
Filling shots, 359
Filling yarns, 80
Fill leakage, 446
Film sheeting, 105
Fine canvas, 136
Finishing, raw hides, 222
Fire safety. See also Flame resistance;
    Flammability
    and combustion process, 166–67
    and fiber properties, 54
    and Flammable Fabrics Act, 164–66
    and stages of interior fire, 167–68
Fitted sheets, 440
Flake yarns, 72
Flameless combustion, 166
Flame propagation, 167–68
Flame resistance, 54, 175, 308–9
Flame retardants, 142
Flame spread, 169
Flame yarn, 72
Flaming combustion, 166
Flammability. See also Combustion
    for bath rugs and mats, 428
    for blankets, 443
    for filling materials, 201
    for mattresses, 436
    reducing fiber, 142
    for soft floor coverings, 392
    testing, 168
        full-scale test methods, 184–86
        large-scale test methods, 181–84
        small-scale test methods, 168–81
    for textile wall coverings, 314
    for towels and toweling, 427
Flammable Fabrics Act (1953), 164
    1967 Amendment, 164–65
    new standards, 165–66
Flammable fiber, 54
Flannel, 143
Flannelette, 143
Flannel sheets, 440
Flare, 343
Flashover, 167, 184
Flat-bed screen printing, 122
Flat bedspring units, 433
Flat braids, 103
Flat sheets, 440
Flat toweling, fabricating, 422–23
Flat upholstery fabrics, 207
    dobby-woven, 209
    Jacquard-woven, 212–16
    knitted, 218
    plain-woven, 207–8
    satin-woven, 209
    surface-figure woven, 211–12
    triaxially woven, 217
    twill-woven, 208–9
Flax fiber, 32

Flesh tissue, 221
Flexibility, 52
Flocked fabrics, 288
Flocked floor coverings, 367
Flocking, 138, 224
     in blankets, 443
Flock yarns, 72
Flokati rugs, 373
Floor coverings. See also Pile floor
     coverings; Soft floor coverings; Tufted
     floor coverings
          acoustics in, 402–3
          hand-constructed flat rugs, 373–76
          hand-woven pile rugs, 371–73
Flooring radiant panel test method,
     169–71
Floor mats, 376
Flossa stick, 373
Floss yarns, 136
Fluorescent compounds, 46
Fluorocarbon compounds, 58, 144
Flying shuttle looms, 83
Foam-core mattresses, 434
Foamed acrylic compounds, 294
Foam rubber structures, 380–82
Foot traffic units, 393
Forty five degree angle test method, 169
Frames, 362
Free-lay installations of wall-to-wall
     carpeting, 401
Frictional heat energy, 58
Friction calendering, 133
Frieze, 93, 219–20
Friezé textures, 331
Frosted appearance, 145
Frostiness, 127
Fugitive colorants, 304
Full-grain leather, 222
Fulling, 141
Fullness, 271
Full warranty, 159–60
Fume fading, 35, 239
Functional finishes for textile wall
     coverings, 317
Functional performance, engineering,
     142–45
Fungi, 143
Fur Products Labeling Act (FPLA) (1952),
     153
Fused selvage, 80
Fusion-bonded carpet, 366
Fusion bonding, 102
Fusion printing, 126
Futons, 184, 433

G
Gas fading, 35, 239
Gasfastness, 35
Gassing-off period, 10
Gauge, 97, 350
Gauze, 281
Gear crimping, 68
General Services Administration (GSA), 20
Generic names, 24
Genuine suede, 222

George Institute of Technology, 9
Ghiordes knot rugs, 371–72, 373
Gimp yarns, 73
Gingham in bedspreads, 444
Ginning, 31
Glare, reduction of, 251–52
Glass curtains, 263
Glass fibers, 33
Glass transition temperature, 35
Glazed chintz, 208
Glazed leather, 222
Glazing, 134
Glenn Street Studio, 10
Glowing, 166
Glue-down installations of wall-to-wall
     carpeting, 400–401
Goose-eye twill, 209
Grain markings, 221
Grain-straight, 80
Grams per denier, 53
Grams per tex, 53
Grasses for window coverings, 280
Grassing, 133
"Green" products, 9–10
Green standard, 9
Greige goods, 1, 293, 452
     dyeing, 114–15
     engineering functional performance,
          142–45
     improving quality and serviceability of
          structural features, 139–42
     printing, 116–27
     transforming surface appearance,
          133–39
Grosspoint, 93, 220
Growth of the fabric, 231
Guide bars, 98
Guides for the Feather and Down
     Products Industry, 436
Gum printing, 127
Gypsum for textile wall coverings, 317

H
Hackling, 32
Half-drop-match patterns, 406
HaloFresh®, 57, 143
Hand, 31, 47
Hand-constructed flat rugs, 373–76
     Dhurrie, 376
     Khilim (Kelim, Kilim), 373–74
     woven by Native Americans, 374–76
Hand embroidering, 136–38
Handle, 31, 47
Hand needleworking, 136
Hand printing, 117–19
Hand quilting, 139
Hand-woven pile rugs, 371–73
     Flokati, 373
     Oriental, 371–73
     rya, 373
Hardware for curtains and drapes,
     265–66
Harnesses, 82
Hawser, 71
Head covers, 195

Headings, 262
     for curtains, 264
     for draperies, 264
Head rests, 195
Heat conductivity
     as fiber property, 56
     for soft floor coverings, 390–91
Heat of combustion values, 54
Heat-related properties of fibers, 54–56
Heat resistivity for soft floor coverings,
     390–91
Heat sensitivity of fibers, 3, 55
Heat setting, 35, 141, 145, 300
Heat transfer printing, 125
Heat transmittance, 56
Heddles, 81
Held-back drapes, 263
Herringbone weave, 87, 209
Hides, 221
High-low, 332
High surface tension, 144
High wet modulus (HWM), 36, 50
Hoechst Fibers Industries, 58
Hoghair, 199
Hollow fibers, 200
Homespun weave, 85, 207
Homophones, 224
Honeycomb cellular shades, 273–74
Hong Kong grass, 76
Hopsacking, 207
Horsehair, 199
Hot water or spray extraction cleaning for
     soft floor coverings, 414
Houndstooth checks, 208
Household textiles, 5
Huck toweling (huckback), 422
Hue, 109
Hydrophilic fibers, 57
Hydrophobic fibers, 57, 144

I
Ignition temperature, 166
Ikat printing, 119
Impact insulation class (IIC), 389
Impact noise rating (INR), 389
Impact sounds, 253
Implied warranties, 159
Income-related variables, 8
Indirect light, 128
Indirect yarn numbering systems, 74
Indoor air quality (IAQ), 9, 10
Indoor Radon program, 10
Inferior textiles, evaluating, 17–19
Inflation, 8
Ingrain, 359
Inherent color, 45
     removing, 133
Innerspring units, 434–35
Inorganic compounds, combining, 33
Installation
     of soft floor coverings, 337, 398–407
     for textile wall coverings, 317–18
Installation factors, in selecting interior
     textiles, 16–17
Institutional textiles, 5

Institutional toweling, 422
Insulative value, 294
    andcarpet installation, 402–3
    increasing, 142–43
    for soft floor coverings, 390–91
Insulators, 59
Intensity, 109
Interim maintenance
    for soft floor coverings, 412
    for textile floor coverings, 412
Interior acid rain, 54
Interior designers, 6
Interior enrichment, 313
Interior furnishings, role of window
  coverings in protecting, 256
Interior textile industry
    associate members of, 7–8
    challenges to, 14
    developments in, 9–10
    economic factors affecting, 8–9
    environmental factors affecting,
      9–11
    major segments of, 3–7
Interior textiles
    agencies regulating product selections,
      19–20
    colorants and color perception,
      108–10
    and combustion processes and
      byproducts, 166–67
    converting greige goods, 133–45
    discharge printing, 127
    dying, 110–16
    evaluating, 17–19
    fabricating
      braiding, 103
      combing fibers, 103, 105–6
      extruding polymer solutions, 105
      fusion bonding, 102
      knitting, 97–101
      knotting and twisting, 102–3
      tufting, 101–2
      weaving, 80–93
    factors affecting apparent color,
      127–29
    flammability testing of, 168–86
    and Flammable Fabrics Act, 164–66
    labeling, 150–60
    organizations establishing model
      building codes, 20–21
    printing greige goods, 116–27
    resist printing, 127
    selecting, 14–17
Interlacing patterns
    basic, 85–87
    decorative, 87–89, 283–87
    fabrics with simple, 280–83
Interlock stitch, 99
International Codes Council (ICC), 20
International Conference of Building
  Officials (ICBO), 20, 21
International Fabricare Institute (IFI), 8
International Geometric Gray Scale
  for Color Change, 237
  for Evaluating Staining, 236

International Organization for
  Standardization (ISO), 19, 24, 74
International Residential Code (IRC), 20
In-the-muslin, 195
In-use performance, 14

J
Jabots, 264
Jacquard weave, 89
    for carpet, 362, 364
    in fabrics, 212–16, 287
    for tapestry, 214–16
Jersey stitch, 99
Jet beck, 114–15
Jet Foam Printer®, 121
Jet printing, 121–22
Jet spraying, 113
Jute, 31–32
    in upholstery fillings, 199

K
Kapok, 436
    in upholstery fillings, 199
Keratin, 29
Khilim (Kelim, Kilim) rugs, 373–74
Kick pleats, 195
Kindling temperature, 166
King-sized pillows, 438
Knap yarns, 73
Knee-kicker, 400
Knife-edge treatment, 195
Knit-de-knit crinkling, 68
Knit-de-knit space dyeing, 113
Knitted fabrics, 218
Knitted pile fabrics, 220–21
Knitted sheets, 440
Knitted window covering fabrics, 292–93
Knitting, 97
    filling, 99
    in textile wall coverings, 316
    warp, 97–98
    weft, 99
Knitting blankets, 442
Knop yarn, 73
Knotted and twisting yarns, 102–3
    for window coverings, 293
Knot yarn, 73
Kraftcord, 76
K-value or K-factor, 391

L
Labeling
    fiber, 279
    guidelines for upholstery coverings,
      224
    regulatory and advisory practices,
      151–56
    sample, 160
    textile table accessories, 454
    trade practice rules and guides
      regarding, 156
    trade regulation rules regarding, 154
    upholstery fillings, 201
    voluntary programs for, 156–60
Lace fabric, 293

Lace making, 102–3
Lambrequin, 265
Laminating in textile wall coverings, 316
Lampas, 287
Land fowl feathers, 436
Lappet weave, in fabrics, 285
Latex foam, 199
Laundering, colorfastness to, 307–8, 426,
  429
Launder-Ometer®, 307, 426
Leather
    full-grain, 222
    glazed, 222
    split, 222
    top-grain, 222
Leather upholstery
    genuine, 221–22
    stimulated, 222–24
Left-hand twills, 86
Leno-reinforced selvages, 80
Leno weave, 88–89, 442
Leno-weave, in fabrics, 286–87, 347
Letting off, 84–85
Licensing programs, 158
Life-cycle cost, 16–17
    for floor coverings, 338
Light
    colorfastness to, 237, 239, 304–6, 392,
      426, 429
    nature of, 108–9
    quantity of, 128
Lightfastness, 237, 304
    of exterior fabrics, 304, 306
    of interior fabrics, 304
Light reflectance factor for soft floor
  coverings, 391
Light source, 127–28
Light transmission, 294
Light transmittance value, 171
Limited warranty, 160
Limiting oxygen index (LOI), 54
Linear density, 53
Line fibers, 32
Linen, 450
Linen fiber, 32
Linen in tabletop coverings, 450
Linen Lea (III) system, 74
Linen system, 69
Liseré fabrics, 213–14
Loftiness
    in bedding products, 437
    of textile structure, 200
Longitudinal configuration, 45
Loom beams, 81
Looms, 81
    jacquard, 89
    parts of simple, 81–82
    threading, 82–83
Loop yarns, 73
Loose-laid rug installations of soft floor
  coverings and cushions, 401
Loose-pillow styles, 195
Luminosity, 109
Luster, 45–46
    surface, 133

Luster washing, 372
Lyocell, 36

M
Machine embroidering, 138
Machine operations
    braiding, 366–67
    flocking, 367
    fusion bonding, 366
    needlepunching, 367–68
Machine stitching, 138, 443
Macramé, 102
Magnuson-Moss Warranty Act, 150, 159
Maintenance in selecting interior textiles, 15
Malden Mills, 10
Malimo, 99
Malipol, 422
Manufactured fibers, 33–35
    cellulosic, 35–36
    engineering, 40–41
    noncellulosic, 36–40
    producers of, 4
Marled, 110
Marquisette, 88–89, 286
Martindale Abrasion Tester Method, 234
Matelassé, 216
Mats, bath, 427–28
Mattress and Mattress Pad Test Method, 183–84
Mattress covers, 435
Mattresses, 434–35
Mattress foundations, 433–34
Mattress pads, 435–36
Mechanical flocking, 138
Medium canvas, 136
Melt spinning, 34
Members of the trade, 6
Mercerizing, 143
Mergers, 8
Meshes per inch, 136
Metal fibers, 60
Metallic-coated lining fabrics, 296
Metallic yarns, 76
Metals and polymer materials for window coverings, 279–80
Methenamine tablet test method, 168–69, 428
Microbes
    reducing action of, 143
    resistance to, as fiber property, 56–57
Microfresh®, 57, 143
Microscopic voids, 47
Migration, 116, 239, 307
Milliguard® Carpet Protector, 58
Milliken and Company, 58
Milliken Carpets, 121
Millitron®, 121
Mineral fiber, 32
Modacrylic, 37–38
Model building codes, organizations establishing, 20–21
Modern rugs, 372
Moiréing, 134
Moiré taffeta fabric, 282

Moisture absorption, increasing, 143
Moisture regain values, 57
Moisture-related properties, of fibers, 57–58
Molas, 137–38
Molecular arrangements, 27–28
Molecular units, 27
Molten polymer compounds, 166
Momie cloth in table coverings, 451
Monk's cloth, 282
Monofilament yarn, 66
Monomers, 27
    synthesizing, 33
Monsanto Chemical Company, 61
Mordants, 109
Moresque, 112
Mortgage interest rates, 8
Mosquito netting, 286
Moth resistance as fiber property, 58
Moths, repelling, 144
Motor Vehicle Safety Standard No. 302 (MVSS 302), 173
Multifilament yarn usage, 207
Multilayered roller shades, 254–55
Multilevel cut and loop pile styles, 332
Multilevel loop pile styles, 332
Multilevel surface textures, creating, 351
Multi-tier café curtains, 262–63
Muslin sheeting, 440
Mussiness, 452

N
Nailhead trimming, 197
Nanometers, 108
Napery, 450
Naphthalene compounds, 144
Napping, 143
National Association of Institutional Linen Management (NAILM), 7–8
National Building Code (NBC), 21
National Council for Interior Design Qualification (NCIDQ), 6
National Electronic Injury Surveillance System (NEISS), 164
National Fire Protection Association (NFPA), 19, 300
    101® Life Safety Code®, 171, 183, 308
    701 large-scale test method, 182
    701 small-scale test method, 175–76
    Life Safety Code®, 18
National Highway Traffic Safety Administration (NHTSA), 20, 173
National Institute of Standards and Technology (NIST), 165, 169
Native Americans, rugs woven by, 374–76
Natural fibers
    cellulosic, 31
    engineering, 32
    mineral, 32
    production, 29
    protein, 29–30
    suppliers of, 3–4
Natural filling materials, 436–37
Natural rush, 76
Neckrow pillows, 438

Needle count, 350
Needlepoint stitching, 136
Needlepoint weave fabrics, 215
Needlepunching, 367–68
    in blankets, 442
    in fibrous batts, 105
    in textile wall coverings, 316
Needleworking, hand, 136
Net curtain fabrics, 293
Ninon, 281
Noise. See also Acoustics
    floor coverings for abatement, 335
    reduction of interior, 253–54
    textile wall coverings for reduction of, 313–14
    transmission of, by soft floor coverings, 389–90
Noise reduction coefficients (NRC), 254, 313–14, 388
Noncellulosic fibers, 36–40, 206
Noncombustible fibers, 54
Nonfibrous materials in tabletop coverings, 451
Nontextile materials, used in window coverings, 279–80
Nontraversing decorative rods, 266
Nonwaterfowl feathers, 436
Nottingham lace, 452
Nub yarns, 73
Nylon, 38–39

O
Occupational Safety and Health Administration (OSHA), 9, 11
Off-grain fabrics, 140, 228
Oilborne stains, 240
Olefins, 39, 60
Oleophobic, 144
Ombre, 110–11
One level cut pile styles, 330–31
One level loop pile styles, 332
One-way draw draperies, 263
Opacity, 294
Optical brighteners, 46
Optical density values, 171
Optical properties of textile fibers, 45–47
Organdy
    in bedspreads, 444
    in curtains, 262, 281
Organically grown cotton, 9
Oriental design rugs, 372–73
Oriental rugs, 371–73, 373
Oriented, 27
Oscillatory Cylinder Method, 233
Osnaburg, 281
    for textile wall coverings, 317
Otting, 121
Ottoman, 208
Outline quilting, 139
Overdraperies, 263
    shrinkage of, 300
Overprinting, 126
Over-the-wire construction technique, 92–93
Ozone or O-fading, 239

P

Package dyeing, 111
Package-injection technique, 113
Panel test apparatus, 170–71
Panné velvet, 218
Partial blackout, 295
Patchwork quilts, 443
Patent and Trademark Office, United
    States, 156
Pattern drafts, 83
Patterned fabrics for upholstered furniture,
    194–95
Patterned quilts, 443
Pattern quilting, 138–39
Pattern repeats, variations in, 235
Pearl yarns, 136
Percale sheeting, 440
Performance
    in selecting interior textiles, 15, 17–18
    in soft floor coverings, 337, 391–95
Permeability principle, 388
Permethrin, 144
Persian knot rugs, 371
Persian yarns, 136
Physical performance properties,
    evaluating for towels and toweling,
    424–26
Picking, 68, 80, 83–84
Piece dyeing, 114
Pigment print, 126, 288, 292
Pigments, 109
Pile floor coverings
    construction density, 329–32, 365
    forming layer, 349–51
    hand-woven, 371–73
    height, 329
    reversal, 331
    sweep, 135, 329
    thickness, 329
    weaving, 359–66
Pile interlacings, fabrics with, 287–88
Pile toweling, constructing, 422
Pile upholstery fabrics, 218
    knitted, 220–21
    tufted, 221
    woven, 218–20
Pile warp yarns, 359
Pile weaving, 89–93
Pile yarns, 347
    changing orientation of, 135–36
    directional lay of, 404–5
    integrity of, 343
    weight of, 355
Pilling, 47
    reducing, 142
    resistance to, 234–35
Pillowcases, constructing, 440–41
Pillows
    bed, 438
    bedrest, 438
    bolster, 438
    boudoir, 438
    breakfast, 438
    construction styles for, 195
    decorative coverings for, 439

European, 438
    fillings and tickings, 438–39
    king-sized, 438
    neckrow, 438
    queen-size, 438
    round, 438
    sizes and forms, 438
    standard pillows, 438
    standards, 438
    Turkish, 438
Pillow sham, 439
Pillow treatments, in upholstered
    furniture, 195
Pima cotton, 31
Pinned-up drapes, 263
Pinsonic melding, 138, 443
Pitch, 360
Placemats, 453
Plaid fabric, 208
Plain or pinwale piqué, 284
Plain weave, 85
    in fabrics, 207–8, 280
    in lining fabrics, 295–96
Planned space utilization and carpet
    installation, 402
Planting, 362
Plied slub yarns, 72
Plush, 331
Ply yarns, 71, 74–75
Pockets, 216
Pollutant gases, 54
Polyester, 39–40
Polymer compounds in window coverings,
    279–80
Polymer film shower curtains, 428
Polymerization, 33
Polymers, 27
Polymer solutions
    extruding, 105
    forming, 33
Polymer tapes, 76
Polyurethane foam, 199
Polyvinylchloride in window coverings,
    279–80
Pooling, 331
Pouf sleeves, 263
Power stretcher, 400
Premounted supports in installing textile
    coverings, 318
Preventive maintenance
    for textile floor coverings, 408–12
    for window covering structures, 309
Primary backing fabrics, 347
Prime urethane foam structures, 382
Princess style pleats, 195
Print design, 360
Printing
    acid, 126–27
    batik, 117–18
    block, 117
    discharge, 127
    hand, 117–19
    ikat, 119
    jet, 121–22
    pigment, 126

resist, 127
    roller, 119–20, 288
    screen, 122, 124–25
    TAK, 121
    tie-dye, 118
    transfer, 125–26
    warp, 125
Printing greige goods, 116–27
Priscilla curtains, 261, 262
Processing agent usage, reduction of, 9
Producer-colored, 110
Product selections, agencies regulating,
    19–20
Product showroom, 6
Project bid, 16
Project specification, 16
Propylene, 39
Protective mats, using, for textile floor
    coverings, 408
Protein fibers, 29–30
Publishers, 7
Pyrolysis, 166
Pyrolytic characteristics, 54

Q

Quality, improving, in structural features,
    139–42
Quality-control work, 14
Quarter-drop pattern, 406–7
Queen-size pillows, 438
Quill, 82
Quill feathers, 436
Quilting, 138–39
    channel, 138
    commercial, 138–39, 443–44
    hand, 139
    pattern, 138–39
    shadow, 444
    Trapunto, 444
    for upholstered furniture, 197
Quilts, 445–46
    crazy, 443
    evaluating fabrics, 446
    patchwork, 443
    patterned, 443

R

R9000 Soil Shield®, 58
Radiant heat, 169–70
Radiation, 255
Rag rugs, 376
Railroad, 194
Raised fiber surface, 169
Ramie in tabletop coverings, 450
Random shear textures, 332
Ranges, 116
Raschel stitch, 98, 292
Raschel-stitched fabrics, 292
Ratiné yarns, 73
Raw material consumption, reduction of, 9
Raw silk, 30
Rayon, 35, 36
Reactant compound, 145
Real income, 8
Reclined angle, 86

Recycled PET (polyethylene terephthalate), 10
Recycled wool, 152
Recycling carpet, 10
Reed, 82
Reeling, 30
Regular angle, 86
Regulatory agencies, 19–20
Regulatory and advisory labeling practices, 151–56
Relative flammability, 54
Relative humidity, 60
Relaxation shrinkage, 141
Rep, 208
Reprocessed wool, 152
Residential interiors, 5
Residual shrinkage, 141
Residue, 437
Resiliency, 145
    in battings, 199
    of textile fibers, 52
Resins, 145
    durable press, 303
Resist printing, 127
Restorative maintenance, 242
    for soft floor coverings, 412–14
    for window covering structures, 309–10
Retting, 31, 32
Reused light, 128
Reused wool, 152
Reverse appliqué, 138
Reverse blends, 440
Reversible blanketing, 442
Ribcord
    in bedspreads, 444
    in curtains, 282
Right-hand twills, 86
Rippling, 32
Rods
    decorative, 266
    determining length and placement of, 267, 269
    nontraversing decorative, 266
Roller printing, 119–21, 288
Roller shades, 274, 282
    multilayered, 254–55
Roman shades, 274, 280
Room-fit rugs, 328
Room-size rugs, 328
Rope, 71
Rotary screen printing, 122, 124–25
Round pillows, 438
Routine care of window covering structures, 309
Rows per inch, 360
Ruffled, tie-back curtains, 262
Rug crawling, 382
Rugs, 325. See also Floor coverings; Pile floor coverings; Soft floor coverings; Tufted floor coverings
    antique Oriental, 372
    area, 328
    Aubusson, 371
    bath, 427–28

braided, 366–67
Dhurrie, 376
fibers used in, 341–42
Flokati, 373
Ghiordes knot, 371–72, 373
hand-constructed flat, 373–76
hand-woven pile, 371–73
Khilim (Kelim, Kilim), 373–74
modern, 372
Oriental, 371–73
Persian knot, 371
rag, 376
room-fit, 328
room-size, 328
rya, 373
Savonnerie, 371
scatter, 328
Sehna (Senna) knot, 371
semi-antique, 372
Turkish knot, 371–72
woven by Native Americans, 374–76
Rug walking, 382
Runners, 328, 453
R-values or R-factors, 391
Rya rugs, 373

S
Safety
    in selecting interior textiles, 15
    soft floor coverings in increasing, 334
Salvage maintenance, 242
    for soft floor coverings, 414
Sample labeling, 160
Sanforized®, 158
Sanforized® Company, 158
Sanfor-Knit®, 158
Sanfor-Set®, 158
Saran, 40
Sash curtains, 262
Sateen linings, 296
Sateen weaves, 87, 209, 283
    in lining fabric, 296
Satin weaves, 87, 209, 283
Savonnerie rugs, 371
Saxony textures, 331
Scatter rugs, 328
Schreinering process, 134
*Scotchgard®, 58, 144
Screen printing, 122, 124–25
Scrim
    applying, 351–52
    for textile wall coverings, 317
Sculptured pile surfaces, 332
Scutching, 32
Sea grass, 76
Sea Island cotton, 31
Seam placement, planning for carpet, 405
Secondary backing fabric, 347, 349
Seed fibers, 31
Seed yarns, 73
Sehna (Senna) knot rugs, 371
Self-deck treatment, 193
Self-extinguish, 54, 166
Selvages, 80
Semi-antique rugs, 372

Separately hung lining fabrics, 295–96
Sericin, 30
Serviceability
    improving, in structural features for soft floor coverings, 333–37
    yarn features affecting, 342–43
Service organizations for maintenance, 7–8
Set-match patterns, 405–6
Shade changes, 426
Shades, 109, 110–11
    accordian-pleated, 272–73
    athey, 274
    Austrian, 272, 280
    balloon, 272
    cascade loop, 274
    honeycomb cellular, 273–74
    roller, 274, 282
        multilayered, 254–55
    Roman, 274, 280
Shading, 331
Shading coefficient (S/C), 255
Shadow quilting, 444
Shag surface, 331–32
Shearing, 135
Shed, 83
Shedding, 83, 408
Sheers, 263
Sheet casings, 441
Sheets
    constructing, 440–41
    evaluating, 441
    fiber in, 439–40
    knitted, 440
    manufacturing, 439–40
    Muslin, 440
    percale, 440
    yarn in, 439–40
Shirring in textile wall coverings, 318
Shower curtains, 428
    colorfastness for, 429
    colorfastness to light, 429
    flammability of, 429
    physical performance properties of, 428–29
    polymer film, 428
    textile, 428
    water resistance of, 429
Shredded foam particles, 200
Shrinkage
    of fabric, 231
    of overdraperies, 300
Shutters, 275, 280
Shuttle, 82
Shuttleless looms, 83
Silencers, 452
Silk, artificial, 35
Silk fibers, 30
Simple yarns, 71
Simulated fur fabrics in bedspreads, 444–45
Simulated suede, 224
Singeing, 142
Single damask in table coverings, 451
Single-mesh canvas, 136
Single-tier café curtains, 263

Single yarns, 74
Sisal in tabletop coverings, 450
Site preparation for wall-to-wall
   installation, 398
Skein dyeing, 112
Skewed yarn alignment, 140
Skewness
      for shower curtains, 428
      for towels, 426
      for upholstery fabrics, 228
Skins, 221
Skirt options in upholstered furniture, 195
Slab cushions, 199
Slack tension technique, 93, 422
Slashing, 83
Slipcovers, 195, 206
Slub yarn, 71
Slygard™, 57, 143
Smoke, 166–67
      density of, 167
      generation of, 171
Smoke chamber test method, 171, 173
Smoldering, 166
Smoothing, 135
Smoothness retention, improving, 145
Snarl yarns, 73
Social Security Administration (SSA), 20
Sofa beds, 184, 433
Soft floor coverings, 5
      acoustics for, 388–90
      appearance features, 325
            sizes and shapes, 325–28
            surface texture, 328–32
      braiding, 366–67
      constructions used in, 343–45
      cost factors
            initial purchase price, 337
            installation charges, 337
            life-cycle costing, 338
            maintenance expenses, 337–38
      cushions
            cellular rubber, 380–82
            fibrous, 379–80
            installing, 398–407
            listing specification data for, 382
            in upholstered furniture, 195
                  foam, 199
            urethane foam, 382
      design and performance regulations,
            337
      fibers used in, 341–42
      flocking, 367
      functional features, 387–91
      fusion bonding operations, 366
      installing, 398
            determining yardage required, 403–7
            factors affecting choice of method,
                  401–3
            loose-laid rug, 401
            wall-to-wall methods, 398–401
      listing specification data for carpet,
            387
      maintaining, 407–14
      needlepunching, 367–68
      performance properties, 391–95

serviceability expectations, 333
      functional properties, 334–35
      use-life characteristics, 335–37
      surface coloration, 332–33
Soil accumulation, 128–29
Soil hiding as fiber property, 46–47
Soil magnification as fiber property, 47
Soil reduction as fiber property, 53
Soil release
      compounds for, 453
      as fiber property, 145
Soil repellency as fiber property, 58
Soil resistance, imparting, 144–45
Soil shedding as fiber property, 53
Solution dyeing, 110
Solvent, colorfastness to, 239–40
Solvent spinning, 34
Sound absorption, by soft floor coverings,
      388–89
Southern Building Code Council
      International (SBCCI), 20, 21
Space-dyeing, 112–13
Spandex, 40
Specialty stores, 6
Specification listing for soft floor
      coverings, 387
Specific gravity, 49–50
Speck yarns, 71, 207
Spike yarns, 73
Spillover, 170
Spinneret, 33–34
Spinners, 4, 66
Spinning, 68–69, 69
Spiral yarns, 72–73
Splash yarns, 73
Splay, 343
Split leather, 222
Splush textures, 332
Spoken warranties, 159
Sponge rubber structures, 380
Spontaneous combustion, 166
Spools, 360
Spot fabric, 88
Spot weaving, 88, 211–12, 285
Spot yarns, 73
Sprouting, 408
Spunbonded olefin fabric, 347
Spunbonding, 105, 452
Spunlaced curtain fabrics, 294
Spunlacing fibers, 105
Spun yarns
      dominance of, 206–7, 279
      predominance of, in bedding, 432
Stackback space, 267
Stage I fire, 167
Stage 2 fire, 167–68
Stage 3 fire, 168
Staining, 426
StainMaster®, 145
Stain resistance, imparting, 144–45
Stains, 144
      minimizing and removing, for textile
            floor coverings, 409–12
      oilborne, 240
      waterborne, 240

Stair tread test, 395
Stalwart roller printing, 119, 121
Standard Building Code (SBC), 21
Standard fading hours (SFH), 304
Standard fading units (SFU), 304
Standards pillows, 438
Standard test method, 17
Staple fibers, 4
Stapling in textile wall coverings, 318
Static generation
      fibers used to control, 60–61
      of soft floor coverings, 392–93
Static propensity as fiber property, 58–61
Stationary casement panels, 262
Statistical profiles of fiber usage
      for towels and toweling, 421–22
      for window coverings, 278–79
Steep angle, 86
Steiner Tunnel Test Method, 182–83
Stiffness of textile fibers, 52
Stitch-bonded window covering, 294
Stitch-bonding, 101
Stitches
      in warp knitting, 97–98
      in weft knitting, 99
Stitch-knitted casements, 292–93
Stitch-knitted table coverings, 451
Stitch-knitting, 99
Stock dyeing, 110–11
Strength
      breaking, for fabrics, 302
      bursting, for fabrics, 303
      delamination, in tufted floor
            coverings, 352
      tear, for fabrics, 302–3
      in textile fibers, 53
      in upholstery fabrics
            elongation and tensile, 231
            tear, 230–31
Stretch-in installations, 398–400
Structural features, improving quality and
      serviceability of, 139–42
Structurally borne sounds, 253
Stuffer-box crimping, 68
Stuffer yarns, 284, 359
Sublistatic printing, 125
Suede
      genuine, 222
      simulating genuine, 224
Sueding, 224
      for textile wall coverings, 317
Sunlight resistance, as fiber property,
      61–62
Surface dyeing, 222
Surface embellishments, fabrics with,
      136–39, 197, 288
Surface-figure weave, 87–88, 211–12, 285
Surface luster, 133
Surface noise radiation, 389
Surface sounds, 253, 388
Surface texture, 45
      for greige goods, 133–39
      for soft floor coverings, 328–32
Susceptibility to heat, 55–56
Swags, 264

Swivel weave, 88, 285
Synthesized filling materials, 437
Synthesizing monomers, 33

T
Tabby weave, 85
Tablecloths, 453
 constructing, 453–54
 evaluating fabrics for, 454
 labeling, 454
 manufacturing, 451–53
 producing, 450–54
Tackless strips, 398–99
Tactile characteristics, of textile fibers, 47
Taffeta, 134
 in bedspreads, 444
 in drapes, 282
Taking up, 84–85
TAK printing, 121
Tambour-embroidered curtain fabric, 288
Tanning, raw hides, 221
Tapestry, 287
Tapestry yarns, 136
Tatting, 103
Tear strength, 230–31
 of fabrics, 302–3
Teflon®, 144
Tencel®, 36
Tendered, 61
Tendering, 30
Tensile strength
 in cushion performance, 384
 in upholstery fabric, 231
Tentering, 140
Terry toweling, 422
Testing
 interior textiles, 17
 textile fibers, 25
Tetrapod walker for soft rug coverings, 393
Tex system, 74
Textile Chemist and Colorists (monthly journal), 18
Textile colorists, 4
Textile cords, 197
Textile designers, 4–5
Textile end products, 14
Textile fabrics for wooden shutters, 275
Textile Fiber Products Identification Act (TFPIA), 153–54, 201, 206, 279, 374, 454
Textile fibers, 24–41, 45. See also Fibers
 aesthetic features of, 45–47
 chemical properties of, 54–62
 classification of, 24
 composition and structure, 27–28
 external features of, 28
 identification of, 24–25, 27
 longitudinal configuration, 28
 manufactured, 33–41
 mechanical properties of, 47–53
 natural, 29–32
Textile industry, interior, 3–11
 associate members of, 7–8
 challenges to, 14

 developments in, 9
 economic factors affecting, 8–9
 environmental factors affecting, 9–11
 major segments of, 3–7
Textile machinery engineers, 4
Textile products. See also Interior textiles
 agencies regulating selection of, 19–20
 for the bath, 420–29
 bedding, 432–46
 for floor coverings, 341–45, 407–414359
 recycling of existing, 9–10
 reuse of existing, 9
 for tabletops, 449–54
 for wall coverings, 313–18
Textile shower curtains, 428
Textile structures, and acoustics, 313–14
Textile table accessories, labeling, 454
Texture
 changes in, 128
 improving retention, 141–42
 in soft floor coverings, 393
Texturing, 66–68
Theatrical gauze, 281
Thermal blankets, 442
Thermal insulation, 437
Thermoplasticity, 35, 54–55, 55
Thick-and-thin yarn, 71
Thowsters, 4
3M Brand Carpet Protector, 58
3M Company, 58, 144
Three-dimensional designs, 134–35
Threshold of human sensitivity, 59
Throwing, 30, 66
Throwsters, 66
Ticking
 for mattresses, 435
 for pillows, 438–39
Tidies, 206
Tied-back drapes, 263
Tie-dyeing printing, 118
Tinting, 29
Tippiness, 116
Tip shear surfaces, 332
Titanium dioxide, 46
Toile de Jouy prints, 288
Top-grain leather, 222
Total blackout, 295
Total weight, 355
Toughness, 48
Tow, 68
Towels and toweling, 421
 absorbency of, 426–27
 caring for, 427
 colorfastness of, 426
 constructing, 423–24
 flammability of, 427
 physical performance properties of, 424–26
 statistical profile of fiber usage, 421–22
Tow fibers, 32
Toxic gases, 167
Trade associations, 7

Trademarks, 156
 fiber, 156–57
Trade practice rules and guides, regarding labeling, 156
Trade regulation, rules regarding labeling, 154
Trade Regulation Rule Relating to the Deceptive Advertising and Labeling as to Size of Tablecloths and Related Products, 454
Traffic conditions and carpet installation, 401–2
Transfer printing, 125–26
Transportation applications, fiber usage in, 205–6
Trapunto quilting, 444
Trevira® Pentron™ polyester, 58
Triacetate, 35
Triaxial weaving, 93, 217
Triboelectric series, 59
Tricot stitch, 98
Trimmings
 for curtains, 264
 for draperies, 264
True bias, 80
Tucked-in, compacted selvages, 80
Tuft bind, 353–54
Tufted fabrics, 221
Tufted floor coverings
 applying adhesive and scrim, 351–52
 basic components of, 347–49
 creating multilevel surface texture, 351
 dominance of, 343–44
 fibers used in, 341–42
 forming pile layer, 349–51
 performance of, 341
 structural qualities of, 352–56
 yarn features affecting serviceability, 342–43
Tufting, 101–2, 197
 in blankets, 442
Tufts per square inch, 354
Tunnel test method, 182–83
Turkish knot rugs, 371–72
Turkish pillows, 438
Turkish toweling, 422
Turns per inch, 70
Twill interlacings, even and uneven, 86–87
Twill weaves, 86
 in fabrics fabrics, 208–9, 282–83
Twisted paper, 76
Twisting, 69

U
Ultrasuede®, 224
Ultron®, 61
Unclipped dot or spot fabric, 88, 285
Uncut pile, 330
Underblankets, 436
Uneven filling-faced twill, 87
Uneven warp-faced twill, 87
Uniform Building Code (UBC), 21
Union dyeing, 116
United Recycling, 10

Upholstered furniture
  coverings for, 205–25
    dominance of spun yards, 206–7
    fiber and yarn usage, 205–7
    flat, 207
      dobby-woven, 209
      Jacquard-woven, 212–16
      knitted, 218
      plain-woven, 207–8
      satin-woven, 209
      surface-figure woven, 211–12
      triaxially woven, 217
      twill-woven, 208–9
    genuine leather
      coloring, 222
      composition and structure of raw
        hides, 221
      curing and cleaning, 221
      finishing, 222
      tanning, 221
    pile, 218
      knitted, 220–21
      tufted, 221
      woven, 218–20
    vinyl and simulated leather and
      suede fabrics, 222
      expanding polymer coatings, 223
      extruding film sheeting, 222–23
      labeling guidelines, 224
      simulating genuine suede, 224
  exterior construction features
    arm covers and head rests, 195
    cushion and pillow treatments, 195
    deck fabrics and bottom fabrics, 193
    patterned fabric applications,
      194–95
    skirt options, 195
    slipovers, 195
    surface embellishments, 197
  fabrics for, 228–42
    color consistency and retention, 235
      fastness standards, 235–40
      inconsistencies in actual and
        apparent color, 235
      variations in pattern repeats, 235
    fillings used in, 198
      fibrous battings, 198–99
      foam cushions, 199
      labeling, 201
      loose particulate materials, 200
      service-related properties, 200–201
  flammability, 164–86
  interior textile components, 197–98
  maintenance of
    emergency action, 240–42
    preventive, 240
    restorative, 242
    routine care, 240
    salvage, 242
  market for, 5
  multifilament yarn usage, 207
  physical performance properties, 229
    abrasion resistance, 232–34
    dimensional stability, 231–32
    elongation and tensile strength, 231

    resistance to pilling, 234–35
    resistance to yarn slippage, 232
    tear strength, 230–31
  structural qualities, 228
    flaws and defects, 228
    yarn alignment, 228–29
Upholstered Furniture Action Council
  (UFAC), 7
  Barrier Test Method, 178–81
  Decking Materials Test Method -
    1990, 177
  Fabric Classification Test Method -
    1990, 176–77
  Filling/Paddling Component Method,
    Parts 1 and B, 177–78
  Interior Fabric Test Method - 1990,
    178
  Voluntary Action Program, 165–66,
    176
  Welt Cord Test Method - 1990,
    176–77
Upland cotton, 31
Upstream firms, 7
Upstream segments, 3
Up-the-bolt, 194
Urethane foam cushions, 382
Usable fiber form, 24
U-values, 254

V
Vacuuming for textile floor coverings,
  408
Valances, 264
Values, 109
  light transmittance, 171
  optical density, 171
Vapor-phase moisture, 57
Variegated yarns, 112–13
Velour, 218–19
Velour surfaces, 330–31
Velour toweling, 422
Velveteen, 91–92, 218, 287–88
Velvet plush, 331
Velvets, 218, 287–88, 331
  in bedspreads, 444
  in carpet, 93, 364–65
  crushed, 218
  panné, 218
  voided, 218
Venetian blinds, 274, 280
Vertical blinds, 274–75, 280
Vinyl and simulated leather and suede
  fabrics, 222
    expanding polymer coatings, 223
    extruding film sheeting, 222–23
    labeling guidelines, 224
    simulating genuine suede, 224
Vinylized fabrics, 240
Virgin wool, 152
Visible spectrum, 108–9
Visual diagonal, angle and direction of, 86
Voided velvets, 218
Voile, 262, 281
Voltage buildup, fiber properties affecting,
  59

Voluntary labeling programs, 156–60
V pattern, 92
Vulcanization, 199

W
Waffle piqué, 284
Wales, 97, 284
Walk-off mat, 328
Wall coverings, 5
  backings and finishes, 317
  components and constructions,
    314–15
  construction techniques, 315–17
  for energy conservation, 314
  flammability requirements for, 314
  functional values of, 313
  installation techniques, 317–18
  and interior enrichment, 313
  for noise reductions, 313–14
  selection and serviceability, 313–14
Wall-to-wall carpet, 325–26
  installation of, 398–401
Warp knitting, 97–98
Warp pile fabrics, 92–93
Warp printing, 125, 288
Warp-rib weave, 85, 282
Warp yarns, 80
Warranties, 158–60
  full, 159–60
  implied, 159
  limited, 160
  spoken, 159
  written, 159–60
Washfastness, 307
WasteWi$e program, 10
Water
  colorfastness to, 239, 392
  increasing repellency, 144
Waterborne stains, 240
Waterfowl feathers, 436
Watermarking, 134, 331
Water resistance, evaluating for shower
  curtains, 429
Wear resistance for soft floor coverings,
  393
Weave
  basket, 85
  dobby, 87
  dot, 88
  filling-rib, 85
  herringbone, 87
  jacquard, 89
  lappet, 88
  leno, 88–89
  plain, 85
  sateen, 87
  satin, 87
  spot, 88
  surface-figure, 87–88
  twill, 86–87
  warp-rib, 85
Weaving
  Axminster, 359–62
  biaxial, 80
  blanketing, 442

Weaving (*continued*)
    interlacing patterns
        basic, 85–87
        decorative, 87–89
    leno, 442
    loom and weaving fundamentals, 81–85
    patterns in, 207
    pile, 89–93
    pile floor coverings
        Axminster, 359–62
        basic components, 359
        chenille carpet production, 365
        construction density, 365
        velvet carpet, 364–65
        Wilton, 362, 364
    in textile wall coverings, 315–16
    triaxial, 93
    velvet carpet, 364–65
    Wilton, 362, 364
    yarn components and positions, 80–81
Weft insertion, 98
    fabrics produced by, 292
Weft knitting, 99
Weft shots, 359
Weft yarns, 80
Weight density, 356
Weight-related factors for tufted floor
    coverings, 354–56
Welting, 195
Wet shampoo method of carpet restoration
    for soft floor coverings, 414
Wet spinning, 34
Wheeler-Lea Act (1938), 150
Whiteness, 46
Wickability
    as fiber property, 31, 58
    in towels, 422
Wilton weaving, 362, 364
Window treatments, 5, 249–57
    appearance factors, 249
        aesthetic preferences, 249–50
        color-related variables, 251
        retention, 303–4
        structural factors, 250–51
    awnings, 275
    blinds, 274–75
    blinds and shades, 272–75
    colorfastness, to light, 304–6
    cost factors, 256
        initial, 256–57
        maintenance, 257
        replacement, 257
    curtains, 261–72, 278–80
        calculating yardage required,
            266–67, 269–72
        components used in, 278–80
        hardware, 265–66
        headings, 264

        hedings, 264
        overhead and side treatments,
            264–65
        treatments, 262–63, 263–64
        trimmings, 264
        woven fabrics for, 280–92
    draperies, 261–72, 278–80
        calculating yardage required,
            266–67, 269–72
        hardware, 265–66
        headings, 264
        lining materials, 294–96
        overhead and side treatments,
            264–65
        treatments, 263–64
        trimmings, 264
        woven fabrics for, 280–92
    energy conservation of, 254–56
    fibrous web coverings, 293–94
    flame resistance, 308–9
    functional values, 251
        conservation of energy, 254–56
        modification of outward vision, 253
        protection of other interior
            furnishings, 256
        reduction of glare, 251–52
        reduction of interior noise, 253–54
        restriction of inward vision, 253
    knitted fabrics for, 292–93
    knotted and twisted, 293
    maintenance of structures, 309
        preventive measures, 309
        restorative procedures, 309–10
        routine care practices, 309
    performance standards, 257
    physical performance properties, 300
        appearance retention, 303–4
        dimensional stability, 300
        distortion of yarn, 300–302
        durability of back coatings, 303
        fabric strength, 302–5
    shades, 272–74
    shutters, 275
Wires per inch, 364
Woods for window coverings, 280
Woof yarns, 80
Wool, 29–30, 69, 152
    in carpet and rugs, 341–42
    recycled, 152
    reprocessed, 152
    reused, 152
    virgin, 152
Wool Bureau, Inc., 7, 76, 157
Woolen and worsted systems, 69
Woolen run (wr) system, 74
Woolmark and the Woolblend Mark, 157
Wool Products Labeling Act (WPLA)
    (1939), 29, 152–53, 206

Worsted count (wc) system, 74
Worsted yarns, 69
Woven pile fabrics, 218–20
Woven-through-the-back velvet, 365
W pattern, 92
Written warranty, 159–60
Wyzenbeek test method, 233

Y
Yardage, calculating, for window
    treatments, 266–67, 269–72
Yarn-like structures, formation of, 75–76
Yarn number, 74
Yarns
    alignment of, in fabric, 228–29
    in bedding, 432
    in blanketing, 441–42
    braiding, 103
    chenille, 75
    classification and nomenclature, 70–73
    complex, 71–73
    construction of, 73–75
    cord, 75
    distortion of, 300–302
    dominance of spun, 206–7, 279
    dyeing, 111
    features affecting serviceability,
        342–43
    felted wool, 76
    knotting and twisting, 102–3
    metallic, 76
    multifilament, 207
    pile, changing orientation of, 135–36
    ply, 74–75
    production of, 4, 66–70
        spinning, 68–69
        texturing, 66–68
        throwing, 66
    raveling, 140
    in sheeting, 439–40
    simple, 71
    single, 74
    in tabletop coverings, 450–51
    in textile wall coverings, 314–15
Yarn slippage, 140
    minimizing, 140
    resistance to, 232
Yarn stage, coloring in, 111–13
Yarn twisting, 69–70, 330
Yo-yo effect, 50

Z
Zefstat®, 60
Zeftron® 500™, 57, 58, 143
ZePel®, 144
Zimmer flat-bed screen printing, 122
Z twist, 70
ZX nylon, 57, 58, 143